CSCL 2
Carrying Forward the Conversation

Computers, Cognition, and Work
Gary M. Olson, Judith S. Olson, and Robert Kraut, Series Editors

CSCL 2
Carrying Forward the Conversation

Edited by

Timothy Koschmann
Southern Illinois University

Rogers Hall
University of California, Berkeley

Naomi Miyake
Chukyo University

LEA
2002

LAWRENCE ERLBAUM ASSOCIATES, PUBLISHERS
Mahwah, New Jersey   London

Lawrence Erlbaum Associates, Inc., Publishers
10 Industrial Avenue
Mahwah, NJ 07430

Cover design by Kathryn Houghtaling Lacey

Library of Congress Cataloging-in-Publication Data

CSCL II, carrying forward the conversation / edited by Timothy
Koschmann, Rogers Hall, Naomi Miyake.

   p. cm. (Computers, cognition, and work)
   Sequel to: CSCL, theory and practice of an emerging
   paradigm. c1996.

Includes bibliographical references and index.
   ISBN 0-8058-3500-8 (cloth : alk. paper)
   ISBN 0-8058-3501-6 (pbk.: alk. paper)
1. Educational technology. 2. Computer-assisted instruction. 3.
Group work in education. I. Title: CSCL 2, carrying forward the
conversation. II. Title: CSCL 2, carrying forward the conversa-
tion. III. Koschmann, Timothy D. IV. Hall, Rogers. V. Miyake,
Naomi. VI. CSCL, theory and practice of an emerging paradigm.
VII. Series.
LB1028.3 .C769 2002
371.33—dc21

                                        2001040219
                                              CIP

Books published by Lawrence Erlbaum Associates are printed on
acid-free paper, and their bindings are chosen for strength and durability.

Printed in the United States of America
10 9 8 7 6 5 4 3 2 1

For
Jan Hawkins,
a colleague lost

CONTENTS

II Empirical Studies of Learning in Collaborative Settings

CONTRIBUTORS

Sasha Barab
School of Education
Indiana University

Philip Bell
College of Education
University of Washington

Tammy Bennington
Dept. of Communication
Cornell University

Michael Cole
Dept. of Communication
University of California, San Diego

Vanessa Colella
Media Lab
Massachusetts Institute of Technology

Allan Collins
Boston College and
Northwestern University

Charles Crook
Dept. of Human Sciences
Loughborough University (U.K.)

Frank de Jong
University of Nijmegen and the Police
Education and Knowledge Centre
Landelijk Instituut Selectie en Opleidingen
Politie (Netherlands)

Richard Duschl
School of Education
King's College, London (U.K.)

Mark Felton
College of Education
San Jose State University

Jim Garrison
Teaching and Learning
Virginia Polytechnic Institute
and State University

Geraldine Gay
Dept. of Communication
Cornell University

James Greeno
School of Education
Stanford University

Kai Hakkarainen
Dept. of Psychology & IT
Center for Schools
University of Helsinki (Finland)

Rogers Hall
Graduate School of Education
University of California at Berkeley

David Hammer
Depts. of Physics, Curriculum,
and Instruction
University of Maryland at College Park

Giyoo Hatano
Department of Human Relations
Keio University (Japan)

Jim Hewitt
Ontario Institute for Studies in Education
University of Toronto

Sanna Järvelä
Department of Teacher Education
University of Oulu (Finland)

Victor Kaptelinin
Dept. of Informatics
Umeå University (Sweden)

Hiroshi Kato
Research and Development Dept.
National Institute of Multimedia
Education (Japan)

Timothy Koschmann
School of Medicine
Southern Illinois University

Deanna Kuhn
Teachers College
Columbia University

Hideaki Kuzuoka
Institute of Engineering Mechanics
and Systems
University of Tsukuba (Japan)

Curtis LeBaron
Marriott School of Management
Brisham Young University

James Levin
College of Education
University of Illinois, Urbana–Champaign

Xiaodong Lin
Peabody College
Vanderbilt University

Lasse Lipponen
Dept. of Psychology
University of Helsinki (Finland)

Gaby Lutgens
Maastricht McLuhan Institute
Universiteit Masstricht (Netherlands)

Douglas Macbeth
School of Educational Policy
and Leadership
Ohio State University

Ray McDermott
School of Education
Stanford University

Hiroyuki Miki
Corporate R&D Center
Oki Electric Industry Co., Ltd. (Japan)

Naomi Miyake
School of Computer and
Cognitive Science
Chukyo University (Japan)

Bonnie Nardi
Agilent Technologies
Palo Alto, CA

Ricardo Nemirovsky
TERC
Cambridge, MA

Jun Oshima
Faculty of Education
Shizuoka University (Japan)

Ritsuko Oshima
Faculty of Education
Shizuoka University (Japan)

Robert Rieger
Dept. of Communication
Cornell University

Rebecca Scheckler
Center for Research on Learning
and Teaching
Indiana University

David Williamson Shaffer
Graduate School of Education
Harvard University

Randall Smith
Sun Microsystems
Palo Alto, CA

Gerry Stahl
University of Colorado at Boulder and
The German National Research Center
for Information Technology (GMD-FIT)

Susan Leigh Star
Dept. of Communication
University of California at San Diego

Reed Stevens
Dept. of Educational Psychology
University of Washington

Hideyuki Suzuki
Dept. of Communication Studies
Ibarki University (Japan)

Else Veldhuis-Diermanse
Dept. of Social Science
Wageningen University (Netherlands)

Akiko Yamazaki
Department of Systems Information
Science
Future University Hakodate (Japan)

Keiichi Yamazaki
Faculty of Liberal Arts
Saitama University (Japan)

Earl Woodruff
Ontario Institute for Studies in Education
University of Toronto

SERIES EDITORS' COMMENTS

Computers as educational tools have been in classrooms for more than three decades. Integrating the design and deployment of these tools with educational theory, however, has been more problematic. In the waning years of the 20th Century, educators began to look more systematically at the role of cooperation and collaboration among learners. In the early 1990s, largely under the leadership of Timothy Koschmann, a field that goes under the deliberately ambiguous moniker of CSCL, has emerged that "focuses on the use of technology as a mediational tool within collaborative methods of instruction [Koschmann, 1996, p. 2]." Throughout the past decade, the field of CSCL has emerged as a forum for discussion of the many issues pertaining to this perspective. The emergence of CSCL coincides with a much broader appreciation for the important ways in which cognitive and social activities are intertwined.

We are delighted to include *CSCL 2: Carrying Forward the Conversation* in the Computers, Cognition, and Work series. This is a sequel to the earlier *CSCL: Theory and Practice of an Emerging Paradigm*, published in the series in 1996. The "conversation" metaphor introduced with this volume is well chosen. The editors have used the format of contributed chapters, invited commentaries, and responses to the commentaries to foster these conversations. To this end, they have assembled an impressive roster of chapter authors and commentators. As evidenced by these exchanges, it is clear that the conversational issues for CSCL are both lively and contentious.

But it is through such conversations that advances in both theory and practice should emerge.

—*Gary M. Olson, University of Michigan*
—*Judith S. Olson, University of Michigan*
—*Robert Kraut, Carnegie Mellon University*

REFERENCE

Koschmann, T. (1996). Paradigm shifts and instructional technology: An introduction. In T. Koschmann (Ed.) *CSCL: Theory and practice of an emerging paradigm*. Mahwah, NJ: Lawrence Erlbaum Association.

PREFACE

The subtitle "Carrying Forward the Conversation" highlights two aspects of this collection, one thematic, the other structural. As a follow-up to an earlier collection on CSCL theory and research (Koschmann, 1996), this book serves to 'carry forward the conversation' in the sense that the advancement of work in this field can be viewed metaphorically as an ongoing conversation. Much has happened in the years that have passed since the publication of the earlier CSCL volume in 1996. There have been two additional international conferences on this topic—one at the University of Toronto in 1997 and a second at Stanford in 1999.[1] The first European conference on CSCL (Euro-CSCL 2001) took place in the Netherlands in 2001 and plans are moving forward for the next biennial CSCL meeting to take place at the University of Colorado at Boulder in 2002. Our object here, however, is less to document how the field has grown than to foster a meaningful discussion on how the research program might be advanced in substantive ways.

The volume is also designed, to 'carry forward the conversation' in its structure. Most of the 12 chapters forming the core of the book originated as presentations at CSCL '97. Each was subsequently expanded to a chapter-length treatment. Recognizing the long-standing traditions of CSCL work

---

[1]Proceedings from these conferences (and for CSCL '95) are available from Lawrence Erlbaum Associates. Links to the conference web pages can be found by visiting the CSCL home page (http://www.cscl-home.org).

in Europe (O'Malley, 1995) and Japan (Cole, Miyake, & Newman, 1983), we sought to broaden participation and expand the conversation in this sequel, both geographically and topically. For each chapter, our goal was to not only show how the chapter connects to past and future work in CSCL, but also how it contributes to the interests of other research communities. To do this, we solicited commentaries on each of the chapters from a diverse collection of writers. The commentary authors include prominent scholars in anthropology of education, social studies of science, CSCW, argumentation, Activity Theory, language and social interaction, ecological psychology, and other areas. Their selection was intended to enrich the conversation in two ways: alerting the chapter authors to relevant work going on outside of the CSCL community and, at the same time, introducing the commentary authors to the contributions emerging from research in CSCL. In most cases, responses were provided by the chapter authors.

The chapters are broken into three sections, each with a separate editor. The first section, edited by Naomi Miyake, discusses the issue of technology transfer with regard to a particularly prominent piece of CSCL technology, the CSILE program, by examining four diverse case studies. The second section, edited by Rogers Hall, consists of four empirical studies of learning in collaborative settings. Each study raises important questions about the theories and methods of research in CSCL. Timothy Koschmann edited the third section. These chapters describe novel technologies designed to support collaboration and learning and the theories underlying their design.

ACKNOWLEDGMENTS

We owe a great deal of gratitude to many people who helped to make this project possible. Of special note is Linda Medlock, who cheerfully undertook many grueling hours of work gathering manuscripts and getting them ready for submission, helping to prepare indices, and performing uncounted other tasks essential to the project. Honorable mention should also go to Michie Shaw of TechBooks, who saw the volume through its phases of production, and Lori Hawver of Lawrence Elrlbaum Associates, who helped us bring this whole thing to successful conclusion.

In closing, let us remember Jan Hawkins, whom we have lost since the 1997 conference. Jan was a pivotal member of the CSCL community and a source of inspiration to all. As the conversation moves on, let us not forget her numerous contributions to the field.

Timothy Koschmann
Rogers Hall
Naomi Miyake

REFERENCES

Cole, M., Miyake, N., & Newman, D. (Eds.). (1983). *Proceedings of the Conference on Joint Problem Solving and Microcomputers* (Tech. Rep. No. 1). La Jolla: University of California, San Diego, Laboratory of Comparative Human Cognition. (ERIC #ED238397)

Koschmann, T. (Ed.). (1996). *CSCL: Theory and practice of an emerging paradigm*. Mahwah, NJ: Lawrence Erlbaum Associates.

O'Malley, C. (Ed.). (1995). *Computer supported collaborative learning*. Berlin: Springer-Verlag.

Pea, R. (1996). Seeing what we build together: Distributed multimedia learning environments for transformative communications. In T. Koschmann (Ed.), *CSCL: Theory and practice of an emerging paradigm* (pp. 171–186). Mahwah, NJ: Lawrence Erlbaum Associates.

I

SECTION I: CASE STUDIES OF TECHNOLOGY TRANSFER

Realizations of CSCL Conversations: Technology Transfer and the CSILE Project

Naomi Miyake
Chukyo University

Timothy Koschmann
Southern Illinois University

The notion of a *realization* was introduced in an article on technology, collaboration, and learning by Rubin and Bruce (1990) and later expanded upon in other publications (Bruce & Peyton, 1990, 1993). Bruce and Peyton (1990) describe two views of the implementation of an educational innovation. In the conventional view, the innovation is idealized "as a well-defined plan of action, often accompanied by associated objects, such as teacher guides, student texts, and new technologies" (p. 172). What ultimately happens in the classroom, that is the "innovation-in-use" (p. 172), is expected to be a more or less accurate reproduction of this idealization. Bruce and Peyton contrast this with an alternative view in which what counts as the innovation "is re-created by the teachers and students who actually use it" (p. 171). They state, "our goal is to understand the process whereby realizations of an innovation are generated and to provide insight to practitioners attempting to implement innovative approaches" (p. 171).

In this section we will examine a number of realizations of the oldest and most successful computer-supported collaborative learning (CSCL) applications, the CSILE program (Bereiter & Scardamalia, 1989; Scardamalia & Bereiter, 1996; Scardamalia, Bereiter, McLean, Swallow, & Woodruff, 1989) developed at the Ontario Institute for Studies in Education (OISE). In all its various implementations (e.g., MacCSILE, WebCSILE, and Knowledge Forum), CSILE is essentially a discussion board.[1] What distinguishes it from the plethora of other similar tools now available is the way in which the program embodies a particular theory about how learning should be structured. CSILE was designed to foster "intentional learning" on the part of students (Bereiter & Scardamalia, 1989). It rests upon a *constructivist* view of learning and a *constructionist* theory of instruction.[2] This is consistent with research

---

[1]For a more detailed treatment of the functionality of the program, see Scardamalia et al. (1989) and the Hewitt chapter in this section.

[2]The definition of the latter is usually attributed to Papert (1991) who wrote, "Constructionism—the N word as opposed to the V word—shares constructivism's connotation

in cognitive science that has shown that externalizing cognitive processes and sharing externalized representations are beneficial, possibly even essential to learning (Kirsh & Maglio, 1994; Shirouzu & Miyake, in preparation). An electronic and networked discussion board is the standard, most widely available tool for such externalization and sharing. In theory this enables a distinguished form of conversation to occur, one that will contribute to the development of a "knowledge building community" (Scardamalia & Bereiter, 1996).

The four chapters comprising this section can each be viewed as a case study. Each is concerned in different ways with the issue of technology transfer, that is, the process of moving a designed technology (CSILE in this case) from its development site to the classroom. One might expect a relatively simple form of technology such as a discussion board to fit comfortably into virtually any sort of classroom. Historically, however, the introduction of all forms of instructional technology (computer-based and otherwise) has often proven to be problematic (c.f. Cuban, 1986; Tyack & Cuban, 1995) for a variety of reasons. For one thing, the theories of learning and instruction embedded in the design of the technology may clash with the beliefs about learning and teaching held by teachers, students, and parents. Furthermore, the introduction of any new technology requires changes to existing habits, practices, and institutional arrangements. It is in understanding how these changes are accomplished that the usefulness of Rubin and Bruce's notion of a realization is revealed. It serves to focus our attention directly upon the process of re-creation undertaken in the classroom and provides us with a helpful way of thinking about the four case studies presented here. Employing this notion, our task becomes one of understanding how a certain form of technologically mediated conversation is realized in a diverse collection of learning settings.

The Case Studies

Case Study #1: The Evolution of Teaching Practices in a CSILE Classroom. The first case study was prepared by Jim Hewitt, a researcher at OISE and a member of the CSILE project team. In his chapter, he examines how a teacher changed his teaching practices to create a "Knowledge Building Community" (Scardamalia & Bereiter, 1996) in his classroom. In particular, Hewitt focuses upon the teacher's planning for a CSILE-based curricular unit in his second attempt at using such a unit. The teacher's altered strategies included reorganizing the ways in which postings to the CSILE database

---

of learning as "building knowledge structures' irrespective of the circumstances of the learning. It then adds the idea that this happens especially felicitously in a context where the learner is consciously engaged in constructing a public entity, whether it's a sand castle on the beach or a theory of the universe"(p. 1).

were composed, providing students with templates for note construction, encouraging student conjecture-building, providing students more guidance in the selection of "thinking type tags" (e.g., My Theory, I Need to Understand, What We Have Learned), promoting student comments based on content rather than form, and, finally, stressing the importance of understanding over simple task completion. Rubin and Bruce (1990) stipulated that "it is critical to leave enough time for many realization cycles" (p. 262) when undertaking a study of an innovation-in-use. Hewitt's case study provides us with a narrative account of two such cycles. It makes clear that the process of introducing an innovation into a classroom is not one of passive adaptation, but rather one that calls for continuous improvisation and redesign work on the part of the participants.

In his commentary on this chapter, Allan Collins makes a distinction between "education as research" and "education as apprenticeship." He observes that the classroom activity described in the Hewitt chapter rests upon a metaphor for instruction that encourages students to emulate the practices of scientific investigators. Collins notes, however, that many aspects of authentic research practice are missing from the planned activity. He proposes that education should be modeled after a form of apprenticeship in which a task orientation is balanced with a commitment to developing a basic set of competencies. Hewitt acknowledges the merit of Collins' call for richer environments for student investigation, but he argues that this can and should be achieved within a framework that emphasizes improved understanding.

Case Study #2: Use of CSILE at a Japanese University. The second case study was prepared by Ritsuko and Jun Oshima. Like Hewitt, Jun Oshima had worked as part of the CSILE project team at OISE (e.g., Oshima, Scardamalia, & Bereiter, 1996). The authors describe multiple realizations of CSCL conversations in a series of courses conducted at a Japanese university. Most past research on CSILE usage has been done in North American and European educational settings. Given the cultural differences in Japanese schools, one might anticipate differences in the way that a tool such as CSILE would be used there. The chapter describes three experiences using CSILE, two in graduate seminars and one in an undergraduate course. By examining differences between the graduate seminars and the undergraduate course, the authors hoped to elucidate differences in CSILE usage by "expert" and "novice" learners. One of the graduate seminars was conducted exclusively online; the other seminar and the undergraduate course adopted a mixed-mode structure in which discussion board postings were intermixed with lectures or other face-to-face activities. This led the authors to investigate how students coordinated their interaction between asynchronous (i.e., computer-mediated) and synchronous (i.e., face-to-face) channels of communication.

Jim Levin, in his commentary on this chapter, argues the importance of doing long-term studies of the adoption of learning technologies. His position is consistent with that of Rubin and Bruce (1990) who observed that if you view classroom-based realizations as "teacher's active re-creations of classroom activity" (p. 262), then understanding these realizations is likely to take years of study. Levin also argues the need for additional research on the adoption of new technologies in different cultures. In a second commentary, Xiadong Lin and Giyoo Hatano echo this point. They seek a theoretical middle ground between the *universalist assumption* "that technology progresses in a linear fashion and that the more advanced technology is more effective everywhere than the less advanced one"[3] and the *localist assumption* whereby the value of a built technology is strictly culturally determined. They suggest that cross-cultural adoption of new technologies can have the beneficial side effect of occasioning new forms of self-knowledge on the part of cultural members. It can, they argue, also contribute to changing cultures in productive ways.

As a response to the two commentaries, Oshima and Oshima offer data from a fourth effort to use WebCSILE in a Japanese course. This realization of a CSCL conversation employed synchronous and asynchronous forms of communication in another undergraduate course. Although more extensive forms of support were provided to students, the authors found the argument threads developed by the students in their online discussions to be of lower quality than those seen in the earlier undergraduate course. They offer various theories to account for this finding.

Case Studies #3 & #4: Introducing CSILE in Dutch and Finnish Schools. The chapter by de Jong et al. describes the use of CSILE in a university course and a vocational course at the secondary level, both in the Netherlands. Most of the chapter is given over to the analysis of student participation patterns in the university course, an undergraduate course in educational psychology. In this study, the production of CSILE postings and the reading of notes fell off sharply after the third week of the course. CSILE participation in the Dutch vocational studies program was more uniform, but the total number of notes generated by the secondary students was only 7% of those produced by the university students. They concluded that active coaching by teachers was necessary for a learner-directed form of instruction to succeed. The Hakkarainen et al. chapter describes a comparative study of CSILE use in three primary education classrooms, two in Canada and one in Finland. The authors report findings that suggest that differences seen in the

---

[3]See Miyake (1997) for an illustrative example of this view.

types of questions posed in the CSILE database and the types of information produced across classrooms were connected to the interventions made by teachers and that this was more important than whether the classroom happened to be situated in Toronto or Helsinki. Both chapters, therefore, direct our attention to the importance of the teacher's role in initiating and sustaining knowledge-building activities in the classroom. This highlights a point made by Bruce and Peyton (1990) with regard to the study of realizations of technologically based innovations: "The innovation process doesn't end, but begins with the teacher" (p. 190).

Earl Woodruff, in his commentary on the de Jong et al. and Hakkarainen et al. chapters, points out the importance of building communities in classrooms if innovations such as CSILE are to succeed. He directs our attention to an issue raised by Robbie Case (1996), namely, should communities be construed as bodies constituted by the learners who are its members or does it make more sense to treat learners as products of the communities of practice to which they belong? In his commentary on these two chapters, Gerry Stahl raises a number of methodological issues. He asks, how would we go about demonstrating empirically that participation in collaborative undertakings leads to knowledge building? To do so, he argues, requires adopting a new view of what it means "to know." He postulates, "Knowledge [in CSCL conversations] is not so much the ownership by individuals of mental representations in their heads as it is the ability to engage in appropriate displays within the social world." Such a shift, Stahl argues, will necessitate a rethinking of the methodologies for doing research in CSCL. Unlike the other chapters in the book, which all began as presentations at CSCL '97, the de Jong et al. chapter was added later. Because of the timing of its inclusion, it was not possible to solicit responses from the chapter authors for the Woodruff and Stahl commentaries.

Building Classroom Communities

The recurrent theme throughout this section is that before transferring software from the development site to the classroom, we need to build up some sort of practice (e.g., Greeno & Goldman, 1998) or community (e.g., Brown & Campione, 1994) in the classroom. We must create communities where knowledge sharing is taken as a common ground for knowledge building and where collaborative construction of each individual learner's knowledge is regarded without question as a fundamental source for the intellectual growth of the whole community. This is not yet an established norm in most classrooms today and simply introducing CSILE is not in and of itself likely to change this state of affairs. For CSILE to succeed, it is essential to establish such forms of community first, a point that is made vividly in the four chapters of this section. Establishing such forms of community takes time, however, and the struggles involved in doing so can be seen in each of the chapters.

One change that has occurred during the three years we have been preparing this book is the emergence of research on how to foster the growth of knowledge-building communities. Some trails have been blazed without any overt attempts to do so. The Apollo 13 project at Georgia Tech (Holbrook & Kolodner, 2000) is one such trail. Kids, who view the *Apollo 13* video and engage in small projects highlighting why externalization, comparison, and modification of each group's endeavor is important, show considerable progress in subsequent coursework involving learning by design. The researchers at Georgia Tech have proposed this as a new form of scaffolding. Interestingly enough, what is being scaffolded here is not something learners could achieve during, or even at the end of, the project. The project scaffolds something that comes much later. In this sense, it represents a positive step toward the establishment of a new set of cultural norms in the classroom. Bell and Davis (2000) also report an example of generic, domain-independent guidance that promoted better learning, better in the sense that the students reflect often and produce coherent explanations. This is promising because, if this kind of research can clarify conditions under which generic guidance works, it will provide important clues for how we can begin to build new communities in the classroom.

An associated question is how we should organize the course activities and related learning materials for a sequence of classes, not just for a single, isolated class. One of the authors has been experimenting with a set of technological support materials such as an enhanced note-sharing system and a commentable bulletin board for collaborative learning and has come to realize that for a collaborative community to emerge, learning materials and activities must be structured both within and between classes (Miyake & Masukawa, 2000; Miyake, Masukawa, Nakayama, Shirouzu, & Yuasa, 2000; Miyake, Masukawa & Shirouzu, 2001). An illustrative example would be a university class sequence on CSCL where five big projects, say CSILE, CLP (Linn & Hsi, 1999), Jasper (Cognition and Technology Group at Vanderbilt, 1997), etc., are studied from three different perspectives, such as pedagogy, practice, and technology use. An elaborately structured jigsaw method can be used here so that a certain student could become expert on the pedagogy of CSILE. Because of the tight course structure, he or she could be knowledgeable with respect to the pedagogical aspects of the other projects and, at the same time, with respect to other perspectives of the CSILE project. This can be achieved by participating in a study group on CSILE at one time and on pedagogy in general, at another time. Moreover, this class sequence can be and should be supported by simpler questioning-and-answering and comment-sharing activities as in previous classes with collaborative learning support technology. Such a class sequence could also be subsequently developed into more research-oriented, discussion-based classes with graduate students, other faculty members, and researchers outside of the university. Learning in these classes can aggregate in building-block fashion by providing students with opportunities to reflect upon their own learning experiences from course to course.

Learning must and does occur in a longer time span than we as researchers traditionally tend to frame it in our work. It is not just that discussing something leads us directly to solving a problem at hand. It is, rather, that discussing something with others leads us to forms of reflection and realization and it is through these that the collaborative act is then able to promote deeper understanding and better application of knowledge in the future. Discussion as a form of collaborative action should be introduced into learning situations for just this reason. Technology as simple as a discussion board when employed in a well-structured context can make this happen. In this way, the CSCL conversation is carried forward by changing the ways in which we ourselves do our teaching and conduct ourselves in the classroom. As a result, the opportunities to pursue our own CSCL conversations are available to us all. For those who choose to avail themselves of these opportunities, you will find some helpful warnings and wisdom in the pages that follow.

REFERENCES

Bell, P., & Davis, E. (2000). Designing Midfred: Scaffolding students' reflection and argumentation using a cognitive software guide. In B. Fishman & S. O'Connor-Divelbiss (Eds.), *Proceedings of the Fourth International Conference of the Learning Sciences* (pp. 142–149). Mahwah, NJ: Lawrence Erlbaum.

Bereiter, C., & Scardamalia, M. (1989). Intentional learning as a goal of instruction. In L. B. Resnick (Ed.), *Knowing, learning, and instruction: essays in honor of Robert Glaser* (pp. 361–392). Hillsdale, NJ: Lawrence Erlbaum.

Brown, A., & Campione, J. (1994). Guided discovery in a community of learners. In K. McGilly (Ed.), *Classroom lessons: Integrating cognitive theory and classroom practice* (pp. 229–270). Cambridge, MA: MIT Press.

Bruce, B., & Peyton, J. K. (1990). A new writing environment and an old culture: A situated evaluation of computer networking to teach writing. *Interactive Learning Environments, 1*, 171–191.

Bruce, B., & Peyton, J. K. (1993). A situated evaluation of ENFI. In B. Bruce, J. Peyton, & T. Batson (Eds.), *Networked-based classrooms: Promises and realities* (pp. 33–49). New York: Cambridge University Press.

Case, R. (1996). Changing views of knowledge and their impact on education research and practice. In D. Olson & N. Torrance (Eds.), *The handbook of education and human development* (pp. XXX–XXX). Malden, MA: Blackwell.

Cognition and Technology Group at Vanderbilt (1997). *The Jasper Project: Lessons in curriculum, instruction, assessment, and professional development*. Mahwah, NJ: Lawrence Erlbaum.

Cuban, L. (1986). *Teachers and machines: The classroom use of technology since 1920.* New York: Teachers College Press.

Greeno, J. G., & Goldman, S. V. (Eds.). (1998). *Thinking practices in mathematics and science learning.* Mahwah, NJ: Lawrence Erlbaum.

Holbrook, J., & Kolodner, J. L. (2000). Scaffolding the development of an inquire-based (science) classroom. In B. Fishman & S. O'Connor-Divelbiss (Eds.), *Proceedings of the Fourth International Conference of the Learning Sciences* (pp. 221–227). Mahwah, NJ: Lawrence Erlbaum.

Kirsh, D., & Maglio, P. (1994). On distinguishing epistemic from pragmatic action. *Cognitive Science, 18,* 513–549.

Linn, M. C., & Hsi, S. (1999). *Computers, teachers, peers: Science learning partners.* Mahwah, NJ: Lawrence Erlbaum.

Miyake, N. (1997, December). Contribution to closing panel [digital video]. Presented in E. Woodruff (Chair), *Where do we go from here?* Second International Meeting on Computer Support for Collaborative Learning (CSCL '97), University of Toronto, Ontario, Canada. (Available on T. Koschmann, L. Sadler, M. Lamon, & B. Fishman (Eds.) (2000). *CSCL '97 CD-ROM.* Mahwah, NJ: Lawrence Erlbaum.)

Miyake, N., & Masukawa, H. (2000). Relation-making to sense-making: Supporting college students' constructive understanding with an enriched collaborative note-sharing system. In B. Fishman & S. O'Connor-Divelbiss (Eds.), *Proceedings of the Fourth International Conference of the Learning Sciences* (pp. 41–47). Mahwah, NJ: Lawrence Erlbaum.

Miyake, N., Masukawa, H., Nakayama, T., Shirouzu, H., & Yuasa, K. (2000, November). *Construction of collaborative learning culture in college-level cognitive science classrooms.* Paper presented at the International Workshop on New Technologies for Collaborative Learning, Awajishima, Japan.

Miyake, N., Masukawa, H., & Shirouzu, H. (2001). The complex jigsaw as an enhancer of collaborative knowledge building in undergraduate introductory cognitive science courses, *Proceedings of Euro-CSCL* (pp. 454–461).

Oshima, J., Scardamalia, M., & Bereiter, C. (1996). Collaborative learning processes associated with high and low conceptual progress. *Instructional Science, 24,* 125–155.

Papert, S. (1991). Situating constructionism. In I. Harel & S. Papert (Eds.), *Constructionism* (pp. 1–11). Norwood, NJ: Ablex Publishing.

Rubin, A., & Bruce, B. (1990). Alternate realizations of purpose in computer-supported writing. *Theory into Practice, 29,* 256–263.

Scardamalia, M., & Bereiter, C. (1996). Computer support for knowledge-building communities. In T. Koschmann (Ed.), *CSCL: Theory and practice of an emerging paradigm* (pp. 249–268). Mahwah, NJ: Lawrence Erlbaum.

Scardamalia, M., Bereiter, C., McLean, R. S., Swallow, J., & Woodruff, E. (1989). Computer-supported intentional learning environments. *Journal of Educational Computing Research, 5,* 51–68.

Shirouzu, H., Miyake, N., & Masukawa, H. (in preparation for *Cognitive Science*). "Cognitively active externalization for situated reflection in collaboration".

Tyack, D., & Cuban, L. (1995). *Tinkering towards utopia: A century of public school reform.* Cambridge, MA: Harvard University Press.

1

FROM A FOCUS ON TASKS TO A FOCUS ON UNDERSTANDING: THE CULTURAL TRANSFORMATION OF A TORONTO CLASSROOM

Jim Hewitt
Ontario Institute for Studies in Education of the University of Toronto

INTRODUCTION

For the past ten years, a grade six teacher at Huron Public School in Toronto, Canada has been working with researchers on the Computer-Supported Intentional Learning Environments (CSILE) project to transform the way that students work and learn in his classroom. Over that period, he has gradually abandoned many of the task-centered practices common to Canadian schooling (e.g., project-based work, class assignments) in favor of new practices that focus on understanding. Large portions of each school day are now dedicated to the kind of progressive problem solving that one usually associates with scientific research teams. With minimal teacher guidance, students collaboratively pose problems of understanding, invent and debate theories, engage in research, and generally strive to make intellectual progress in key curricular areas. In short, the teacher has fashioned a culture of classroom practice that is grounded in intentional learning and collaborative inquiry. Scardamalia and Bereiter (1994) refer to this educational model as a *Knowledge Building Community*.

This chapter begins with an examination of the rationale for employing a knowledge-centered pedagogy in place of traditional task-based instruction and continues with an exploration of how the Huron School teacher transformed his classroom over a crucial three-year period. Particular attention is paid to the teacher's early difficulties, the strategies he subsequently devised, and the way in which a technology called CSILE supported the teacher's efforts to foster a Knowledge Building Community.

CONCERNS ABOUT CONTEMPORARY EDUCATIONAL PRACTICES

Proponents of constructivism often criticize contemporary educational practices as being grounded in the "transmission model" (e.g., Pea & Gomez, 1992) of learning. The transmission model suggests that learning is a process of knowledge transfer (Fig. 1.1) in which knowledge originates with the teacher (or some other source of domain expertise) and is then transmitted through the instructor's words and actions to the learner (Reddy, 1979). Given this model, the quality of the teacher's presentation becomes the key determinant of the student's understanding. If ideas are presented clearly then learning is likely to occur. However, if students have difficulty understanding a particular concept, the lesson needs to be improved. Thus, pedagogical success is tightly tied to the teacher's ability to deliver content, while the students' role is to receive the knowledge passed on to them.

Critics of the transmission model suggest that its portrayal of the learning process is overly simplistic and neglects recent findings about the nature of knowledge and the role of the learner. In particular, it fails to acknowledge that understanding develops through an active, constructive process. Therefore, real educational gains may be made if schools abandon their transmission model methods and work to help students become active knowledge creators instead of passive knowledge recipients. However, this argument for instructional reform must be tempered with the recognition that modern day teachers are not unsympathetic or unknowledgeable with regard to constructivist theory. Most educators encourage active learning, problem solving, and peer collaboration. The transmission model should not be viewed as a reflection of contemporary teaching philosophy, but as a collection of historic and cultural beliefs that persist in the form of traditional

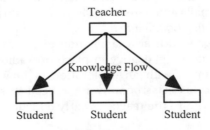

FIG. 1.1. The transmission model of learning.

classroom practices. Unfortunately, these practices are so deeply entrenched in the day-to-day activities of the classroom that they are rarely recognized or questioned, even though they may have adverse effects on learning. Four examples are presented below:

1. Teacher Domination of the Educational Agenda

Generally, it is the teacher, not the student, who organizes the lessons, who asks the questions, and who synthesizes and summarizes. By taking charge of these operations, the teacher preempts the possibility of students planning their own research, developing their own explanations, and identifying their own problems of understanding (Scardamalia & Bereiter, 1991). Instead of actively pursuing personal knowledge advancement, as autonomous learners do, students are, instead, placed in the more passive position of responding to the teacher's directions. This is not to suggest that immature and inexperienced students can immediately take charge of their own learning. However, as Scardamalia and Bereiter (1991a) point out, it may be feasible to develop a curriculum in which students *gradually* take responsibility for high-level operations. Traditional notions that the teacher must control all aspects of the instructional agenda persist to the end of high school, resulting in an unhealthy dependence on instructor guidance and direction. This problem becomes most evident when high school students enter college and find many of these supports missing.

2. Artificial Discourse

One common type of classroom discourse is the three-step IRF sequence. The IRF is a two-person dialogue in which the teacher *initiates* with a question, the student *responds*, and the teacher provides *feedback* (Sinclair & Coulthard, 1975; Mehan, 1979). This three-step procedure is used to focus learners on particular aspects of the curriculum materials, to elicit information as a demonstration of understanding, and to provide immediate feedback. Thus, the IRF engages students, while simultaneously informing the teacher about learner comprehension (Mercer, 1992; Newman, Griffin, & Cole, 1989). The dominant role that the IRF plays in contemporary classrooms demonstrates its ongoing importance as an instructional tool.

Critics of the IRF do not dispute its use as an instrument for engaging students or for uncovering misconceptions, but they question its long-term effect when used as a dominant form of classroom dialogue. One problem with the IRF is that it provides no impetus for students to assess their own comprehension level or to pose questions that will advance their own understanding, because these are the teacher's responsibilities. In this fashion, it reinforces the teacher's control of high-level processes (see #1 above). A second problem is that the IRF misrepresents learning as a simplistic process of producing answers to questions. It fails to convey the progressive, iterative nature of learning and the importance of making connections between ideas.

3. An Orientation Toward Classroom Products

A third line of criticism concerns an excessive orientation toward educational products (Scardamalia & Bereiter, 1997; Brown & Day, 1983). A large part of what students do in school is concerned with completing workbook exercises, writing essays, preparing projects, and so forth. For some learners, task-based learning can be educationally worthwhile. However, researchers have found that some students are remarkably adept at completing classroom assignments while doing a minimal amount of actual learning (Scardamalia & Bereiter, 1997). Studies of student behavior have identified several strategies that are inefficient from an educational standpoint but are effective techniques for rapid task-completion. Two of these strategies are called *Knowledge-Telling and Copy-Delete*:

1. Knowledge-telling is the practice of reiterating what one already knows about a particular topic. It is a convenient strategy to use with project-based work because it does not require planning, organization, or the analysis of new information (Scardamalia & Bereiter, 1991b, 1993).
2. Copy-delete is a pseudo-summarization strategy in which students copy much of the source material, occasionally deleting phrases or rewording them slightly. This gives the appearance of understanding without the accompanying cognitive effort (Brown & Day, 1983).

Strategies such as knowledge-telling and copy-delete emerge because the student's goal (e.g., to hand in a project by a certain date) is different from the teacher's goal (e.g., to encourage learning) (Scardamalia & Bereiter, 1997). Even students who recognize and appreciate the underlying learning objectives are often placed in a situation in which deadlines and other time pressures encourage practices that are educationally suboptimal.

4. An Emphasis on Memorization

A fourth criticism of standard classroom practice is that it inadvertently encourages memorization as a learning strategy. The IRF sequence can have this effect. Studies have shown that the average time taken between the teacher's initiation and the student's response can be as little as one second

(Rowe, 1974). This favors students who have answers already prepared over those who take the time to formulate a solution. Test-taking is another classroom practice that can promote memorization. As Scardamalia and Bereiter (1997) point out, test questions that require the recall of a list of items (e.g., "Name the four steps of the water cycle") promote rote learning over understanding. The importance of rapid recall during oral questioning (e.g., IRF) and examination may lead many students to mistakenly believe that learning and memorization are the same thing.

Perceiving learning as a process of memorization may result in what Whitehead (1929) calls *inert knowledge*. To extend understanding, the learner must establish connections between new information and their own existing understanding of the world (Wittrock, 1974). King (1994) points out that this is consistent with the distinction that Kintsch (1986) makes between *learning about text* and *learning from text*. Associations developed within the context of the new material are less effective for long-term recall than those developed between the new material and one's prior understanding. Students who use memorization as a learning strategy are less likely to make these ties.

Students' tendencies to answer questions without understanding, to use memorization inappropriately, and to engage in knowledge-telling and copy-delete strategies are probably familiar behaviors to most teachers. Experienced instructors may call attention to some of these practices and attempt to deal with them directly. However, some researchers are now suggesting that simply changing student behavior is not enough; what is required is a transformation of the classroom conditions that make inefficient strategies feasible and practical (Scardamalia & Bereiter, 1997). That is, there is a need to move away from artificial discourse, teacher monopolization of high-level operations, and product-orientation. In short, there is a call for new cultures of learning that overcome the deep-rooted and persistent problems in our current school system.

THE KNOWLEDGE BUILDING COMMUNITY MODEL

One alternative to conventional task-based instruction is Scardamalia and Bereiter's (1994) Knowledge Building Community model. A Knowledge Building Community is a group of individuals dedicated to sharing and advancing the knowledge of the collective. Research teams in the scientific disciplines provide a prototypical example, although Knowledge Building Communities can also exist in the form of film societies, literary cliques, industrial firms, and even some families (Scardamalia & Bereiter, 1993). What is unique about a Knowledge Building Community is not formal association (e.g., department, club, company) or physical proximity (although that is

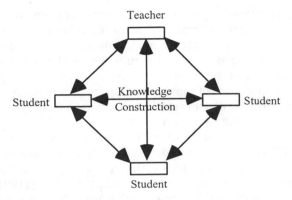

FIG. 1.2. The Knowledge Building Community model.

often important) but, rather, a commitment among its members to invest their resources in the collective construction of knowledge.

Applied to schools, the Knowledge Building Community model is distinctly different from contemporary in-class practices, which appear to oscillate between didactic and child-centered instruction. First, rather than knowledge being viewed as flowing from the teacher (Fig. 1.1), it instead becomes a collaborative construct of many participants (Fig. 1.2). Second, not all students deal with the same subject matter. Instead, different people develop expertise in different areas. This is a significant departure from standard school practice in which everyone in the class learns essentially the same thing. In a Knowledge Building Community, the knowledge of the collective is the focus. This lends a dynamic, adaptive flavor to the learning enterprise because to advance the knowledge of the group, you must first know its boundaries. New contributions by one person will influence subsequent investigations by others. Thus, individual understanding is driven forward by the dual need to be familiar with the knowledge of the collective and the desire to advance that knowledge.

The concept of a Knowledge Building Community is perhaps best understood from a sociocultural perspective. According to sociocultural theory, knowledge is fundamentally situated in cultural activity. By this, socioculturalists mean that what most people consider to be learning (e.g., the acquisition of new ideas, new vocabulary, and new skills) is more accurately viewed as knowing how to participate in different communities of practice (Pea & Gomez, 1992; Eckert, 1989). Cognition is distributed, "stretched over, not divided among—mind, body, activity and culturally organized settings (which include other actors)" (Lave, 1988, p. 1). Therefore, individual learning is not a matter of cognitive self-organization but is a matter of taking a participatory role in established cultural practices (Lave & Wenger, 1991;

Eckert, 1989). From a sociocultural perspective, the establishment of a class-wide Knowledge Building Community is an attempt to acculturate students into a community of practice that is aimed at building knowledge through sustained collaborative investigation. Unlike conventional classroom education, the goal is to turn over more of the high-level operations to the student, encourage authentic peer discourse, and emphasize understanding over memorization.

COMPUTER-SUPPORTED INTENTIONAL LEARNING ENVIRONMENTS

To support teachers in their efforts to foster classroom-based Knowledge Building Communities, Scardamalia, Bereiter, McLean, Swallow, and Woodruff (1989) have developed CSILE, a networked learning environment. Students use CSILE to build and refine a class database of text and graphics notes. Typical notes might include a question, a graphic illustrating a theory, a research plan, and a summary of information found from resource materials. Every note is public and can be examined by any member of the class. Students interact with one another by connecting their notes with links and comments, by coauthoring notes, and by engaging in online discussions. Thus, a CSILE database is best understood as a student-generated, hypermedia-based research environment that is constructed collaboratively and continually evolves (Scardamalia et al., 1992).

This CSILE software package consists of two applications that operate across local-area and wide-area computer networks (Fig. 1.3): the server, which manages the classroom database, and the client, which communicates with the server from other computers on the network. The client application, which is more commonly called CSILE, is the one that students

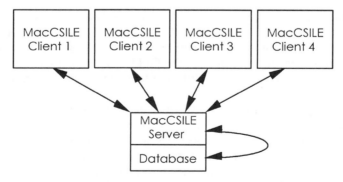

FIG. 1.3. A conceptual representation of CSILE information flow.

use at their desks. At the beginning of the year, the database is empty. Students use the CSILE client to create notes. As they complete their notes, they select Save from a menu, which automatically transmits their notes to the server, which in turn stores them in the class database. When students want to recover their notes at a later date, the server sends the notes to the appropriate client. By this method, students can access the entire contents of the database from any computer in the classroom.

The *ILE* in CSILE signifies an important aspect of CSILE's design philosophy: a focus on intentional learning. Intentional learning is defined by Bereiter and Scardamalia (1989) as, "cognitive processes that have learning as a goal rather than an incidental outcome" (p. 363). Essentially, it concerns student goals and whether or not these goals are oriented toward understanding. Bereiter and Scardamalia (1989) argue that certain activities discourage intentional learning by focusing students on the completion of tasks rather than focusing them on their own thinking. Essay writing and project work often fall into this category. Schoolwork of this sort assumes that understanding will emerge as a natural by-product of student efforts to complete their assignments. However, as discussed earlier, this does not always take place. Scardamalia and Bereiter (1997) suggest that one of the problems with task-based methodologies is that the goals of the teacher are in conflict with the goals of the student. The teacher's goal is to help the student understand the material, while the student's goal is to simply complete an assignment. Inevitably, some individuals develop strategies that are effective for task completion but yield few cognitive benefits. CSILE, as an intentional learning environment, attempts to circumvent this problem by involving students in the purposeful pursuit of understanding. It facilitates this process by providing the following supports for knowledge construction, collaboration, and progressive inquiry.

Supports for Knowledge Construction

Supports for knowledge construction include a framework to record ideas using text and graphics (Fig. 1.4), a flexible note retrieval mechanism, and tools for establishing links between notes. Using these facilities students are able to represent their ideas in the CSILE database, create connections between related notes, and view information from multiple perspectives.

Supports for Collaboration. CSILE can be thought of as a discourse medium because of the many ways in which the program promotes student interaction. The public nature of the database itself is perhaps CSILE's most significant collaborative feature. Because everyone can see everyone else's work, there arise opportunities for collaboration in CSILE that might be missed in regular classroom activities (Scardamalia, Bereiter, Hewitt, &

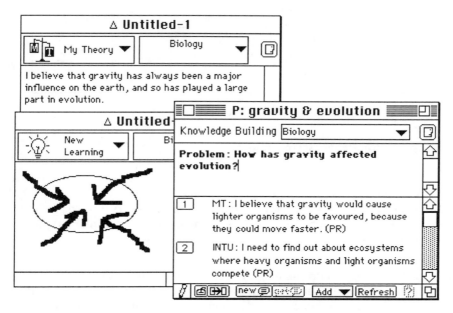

FIG. 1.4. A CSILE text note, graphics note, and discussion.

Webb 1996). In some ways, interaction in CSILE is superior to traditional groupwork because the entire class can review all exchanges. Unlike face-to-face conversation, which is transitory, computer-mediated communication preserves discourse, allowing students to return more easily to their ideas and study them from a variety of perspectives (Levinson, 1990; Mason & Kaye, 1990).

A second support for CSILE collaboration is called *commenting*. Students typically create comments when they want to share an idea or a reaction to someone else's note. A comment is a note that is linked to the note it is commenting on (called the target note). When examining a note in CSILE, students can quickly access all the comments that have been made on it and, if they wish, add one of their own. Because comments are notes themselves, they can also be the subject of other comments, leading to a comment chain (Fig. 1.5). Commenting is somewhat similar to e-mail but such comparisons do not fully capture the level of interaction that CSILE is attempting to promote. E-mail tends to involve a private exchange between two people. On CSILE, two people may (and do) exchange ideas through comments but their exchange becomes part of the public database. Thus, a more accurate portrayal of CSILE would view commenting as occurring not just to benefit the individual participants but also to advance the understanding of the entire class (Scardamalia & Bereiter, 1994).

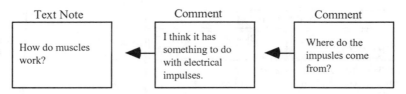

FIG. 1.5. A comment chain.

Supports for Progressive Inquiry

A key principle of CSILE's design is to bias students toward activities that focus them on cognitive goals (Scardamalia et al., 1989). To do this, a set of thinking type tags has been developed that direct learners toward particular cognitive operations. Some of the most commonly used thinking type tags are as follows:

1. *Problem (P)*: A Problem entry is associated with a note that describes a student's learning objectives. Research indicates that even children in grade six can produce and recognize educationally productive questions (Scardamalia & Bereiter, 1991a). Prompting students to identify their own problems of understanding is intended to encourage an active, intentional stance toward learning. The goal is for students to view learning as a process that they control rather than as a teacher-directed, school-specific activity.

2. *My Theory (MT)*: The My Theory thinking type is used by students to describe what they know about a problem and to suggest hypotheses. This serves both to activate their prior knowledge and to engage them as builders of explanations. Initial theories are frequently unrefined and contain misconceptions. However, CSILE teachers tend to be accepting of early, faulty attempts and encourage students to work toward revising their explanations as understanding develops.

3. *I Need To Understand (INTU)*: The phrase I Need to Understand prompts students to take a more active role in identifying problems of understanding. Members of a Knowledge Building Community are always asking more questions and looking for more information. There are no final answers, just progressively deeper explanations. INTU statements are intrinsically motivating because they develop out of the learner's own curiosity about phenomena in the world.

4. *New Information (NI)*: When students discover new information that is relevant to a problem, they record it with a New Information (NI)

thinking type. Books, CD-ROMs, magazines, teachers, parents, and peers are common sources of information. At the grade six level, the teacher provides some guidance in the selection of resource materials. However, the responsibility for extracting the relevant information remains largely with the student.

5. *What We Have Learned (WWHL)*: The thinking type What We Have Learned (WWHL) is used to summarize the advances that a group of students have made on a problem.

In summary, Scardamalia and Bereiter offer the Knowledge Building Community model as an alternative to traditional educational methodologies. In this model, the class becomes a research team that builds knowledge through sustained, collaborative inquiry. A program called CSILE supports class-wide knowledge sharing through a central, public database in which students access each other's ideas, questions, theories, and discoveries. Other CSILE tools, in the form of thinking type prompts, invoke a bias toward a more intentional approach to learning. In theory, CSILE combined with a new classroom emphasis on knowledge building should overcome some of the inefficient practices of modern-day classrooms and give students greater control over their own educational agenda.

REINVENTING THE CLASSROOM

The task-based practices of North American classrooms are difficult to overcome. Traditional school culture is continually reinforced and perpetuated by parents, teachers, curricular guidelines, and the policies of educational administrators. Consequently, reinventing the classroom as a Knowledge Building Community involves changing well-rehearsed, almost instinctive, practices and fighting upstream against the expectations and conventions of the school community.

To better understand the nature of this problem, we explore one teacher's ongoing efforts to rethink pedagogical priorities and restructure classroom routines accordingly. Two grade six Human Biology units serve as "before" and "after" snapshots of classroom activity. In the "before" unit, the teacher makes an initial effort to foster collaborative knowledge building. Although thoroughly familiar with the project's constructivist underpinnings, the teacher runs into a number of problems. By the time the "after" unit takes place (two years after the first unit), the teacher has developed new instructional strategies that bring his class much closer to the Knowledge Building Community ideal. These strategies are described in detail and the rationale for their success is examined.

Human Biology Before Trial

In the first unit, the teacher encouraged his students to work together to collaboratively advance their knowledge of human biology. He impressed upon them the need to develop good questions, help each other with their research, and advance their personal and collective understanding of the subject matter. Students were instructed to organize themselves into 10 groups, each consisting of 3 or 4 members. Every group was asked to identify a subdomain that they wanted to pursue (e.g., the heart). The teacher recommended that each student explore his or her selected area by writing at least one CSILE note for each of the thinking types provided by the software. For instance, an individual studying the heart would create one note that poses a Problem, another that provides New Information, and so on. In this fashion, the student would engage in all the cognitive activities supported by CSILE.

One of the expectations in this particular class was that students should work to publish one or more of their notes over the course of the unit. Publishing is a CSILE feature that allows the teacher to bestow special status on notes that are exemplary, or meet some predefined criteria.

Teacher: I see my role as chiefly one of monitoring students and of assisting those in difficulty. The publishing feature on CSILE is a useful means for meeting with students to discuss their contributions. I insist that all notes, which are to be used for evaluation, must be published. To be granted the status of published, a note must be a significant contribution to the database and it must be grammatically correct. As I meet with students to discuss their notes, I try to guide them to explore more deeply into the problem they are working on. I may also suggest related or alternative approaches that they could take. Every student has individual needs and a unique style, so what is appropriate for one, might be far too difficult for another. CSILE provides an environment where it is possible to address such differences, but I have found that it is helpful to work with students on a one-to-one basis, usually while examining their work on the CSILE screen, to get the best results. (Excerpt from a note submitted to a CSILE database for teachers, 1995)

The unit lasted approximately six weeks. Each student had access to CSILE for thirty-minutes each day. All groups were provided with additional thirty-minute research periods during which they could visit the school library or examine the resource materials that the teacher made available.

Periodically, the teacher would gather the class together to discuss the groups' progress. He encouraged them to create comments on each other's work and to publish their notes as frequently as possible. As part of their grade, students were expected to help each other with their research by writing at least one CSILE comment to another person.

The results were disappointing. Although students followed the teacher's instructions it was felt that the class was still a long way from becoming a Knowledge Building Community. The following issues were identified as problematic:

1. *Lack of collaboration*: To assess the level of collaboration in the database, each note was examined to determine if it implicitly or explicitly referred to one or more other notes written by other authors. Notes that met this criterion were labeled as *collaborative*. Only 15% percent of the Human Biology notes were assigned this rating during the first trial. Of these, approximately two-thirds of the collaborative notes were concerned with superficial and low-level issues such as spelling and grammar. Thus, student interaction was infrequent, and when it occurred, it was rarely aimed at advancing knowledge.

Allan...
I have made this comment on your lung cancer note.
1. You had good English in your note.
2. I learned a lot that will help me in Biology.
3. Decent spelling could be better.
Chris

Low levels of collaboration may have been partially due to a lack of understanding among students regarding the nature and purpose of CSILE. Students seemed to perceive the program as an environment for project-based work in which their main objective was to seek out and replicate information from texts. From that perspective, collaboration would be a secondary, less critical activity, because no one except the teacher was considered a domain expert or a reliable source of information. Indeed, although most children wrote at least one comment to one of their peers, few wrote more than one. Their goal, it appears, was to simply meet the teacher's request to write at least one comment to another student.

Another troublesome observation concerned the failure of students to respond to their peers' comments. Of the 32 comments made over the course of the unit, none of them received replies. Consequently, it is difficult to consider any of the online interaction in the Human Biology unit as genuine discourse. It is possible that low-level concerns of the comments (e.g., spelling, grammar) were partially responsible for their failure to inspire responses. Many of the comments did not warrant a reply because they dealt with surface features or because they failed to provide specific advice. Because there was no evidence of students discussing substantive issues, there was little reason for sustained discourse.

> Gill,
> I think your plan on biology is very good because you put the nurses office and other people didn't even think of that. And where you're going to find your information is excellent but I think you have a few spelling mistakes otherwise it's perfect.
> Nancy.

In summary, a number of problems associated with student interaction were identified at the end of the first Human Biology session. Most of the notes that were rated as collaborative dealt with superficial and low-level issues. This finding, combined with the failure of comments to receive responses, suggests that CSILE was not used as a medium in which knowledge was advanced through collaborative means. It is hypothesized that students engaged in online interaction to satisfy the teacher's requirements and not out of a genuine desire to collaborate.

2. *Lack of conjectures*: Students rarely shared their theories or conjectures with others in the database. In fact, only one conjecture was detected during the entire unit:

> Skin cancer is a disease people say you get from being out in the sun to long. I'm going to find out if that's true or you have it when you are born. Maybe it's a combination of both. I think some people can get it more easily than others.

The scarcity of conjectures was not completely surprising because conjecture-building was not emphasized by the teacher. However, it does suggest that conjecture-building was not something that students engaged in spontaneously. It is possible that the class did not consider CSILE to be an environment in which their opinions and ideas would be of value. Or perhaps the absence of conjectures is indicative of a more systemic failure: a school culture in which student guessing is either frowned upon or discounted. Regardless, the notes in the Human Biology database contained few conjectures, and this was a concern at the end of the unit.

3. *Weak student plans*: The plans that students generated in CSILE tended to be brief and organized around topics rather than problems of understanding. For instance, in the following note, the student seems intent on pursuing topical interests (blood cells, nerve cells, brain cells) rather than specific queries.

My plan
****
I will be working on the blood cells, brain cells and nerve cells. I will do research when ever possible.
Who I will ask
****
I will ask my parents, their friends and my friends.

This pattern was typical of notes with a Plan thinking type. None of the plans presented questions that the students thought were important to address.

Teacher: Looking back, I can see that Plan was simply a listing of topics or items which might be studied and they seemed to be, in many cases, related only in a superficial way to one another. Few plans were concerned with problems or a set of problems which might lead the students to a better understanding of a process. Also, there didn't seem to be a very definite commitment to a particular series of activities such as time spent in the library or speaking to specific people.[1]

4. *Poor Information gathering*: Students tended to examine broad areas of interest (as opposed to a specific problem). As a result, they often accumulated information about their subject area in a rather nondiscriminating fashion. The following note is a typical effort.

Cells
Cells are made up of atoms. Cells are the smallest common unit of life we study. There are about 10 trillion cells in your body right now. The cells in your body might look like something you might find in the sea or ocean. They might have tentacles or hair or even spikes. Cells can't be seen by the bare eye. You would need a really good microscope. When you put cells together you make tissues. All living things are made of cells. Some small things that live in the sea only have one cell. Bacteria is the smallest kind of cell. Nerve cells are the largest kind of cell. Some nerve cells are three feet long. The cell membrane gives food and oxygen for the cell to eat to make energy. Plant cells are bigger than animal cells therefore are easier to see. Plant cells and animal cells differ in many ways such as animal cells need oxygen to live and plant cells need carbon dioxide to live. Most plant cells can make there own sugar substance. It is made of the energy from the light and water and carbon dioxide. This substance is called photosynthesis. Each cell in your body has its own personal job. Cells

---

[1]Unless otherwise indicated, all teacher quotations were taken from an interview conducted in November, 1995.

do not live very long except for brain cells which you should have for life. The jelly like stuff in the cell is called cytoplasm. The nucleus controls the cells reproduction. The blood brings digested food to the cell. Cell is a Latin word that means "a little room." The cell became known after they invented the microscope because you couldn't see the cell with your bare eye. When carbon dioxide gets near the cell, the cell will not let it in. The organelles are like our organs.

Undoubtedly, this student learned some new information about cells during this exercise and she gained experience using the classroom encyclopedia. However, there is also the sense that she has just collected a list of facts, many of which she will not retain. The text does not appear to be directly copied, but a copy-delete strategy was likely employed. There are few indications that she is making an effort to extend her own understanding.

Notes like this one are symptomatic of a task-based perspective. It suggests that students viewed their CSILE work as a collection of loosely related tasks that they had to complete for a grade. There didn't seem to be any appreciation of how these different activities could tie together and build on one another. For example, the writing of a New Information note would be interpreted as fulfilling one of the teacher's unit requirements rather than an opportunity to extend personal understanding.

5. *Too many unanswered questions*: Student questions tended to be grouped together in a single note rather than individually (see some examples below). On average, students listed approximately five questions per note. This phenomenon appears to be a process of question-brainstorming, in which students invented as many questions as they could about a particular subject area.

1. How does lung cancer form?
2. How does cancer kill?
3. Are there any preventions for cancer?
4. Are there more then one type of cancer?
5. If the answer to question 3 is yes, do all cancers kill?
6. Can cancer kill kids?
7. Are there a 100% proven cure for cancer?
8. Can you do anything to stop cancer?

1. How do you get AIDS?
2. What group of people are more in danger of getting AIDS?
3. What causes AIDS?

4. What does the hiv virus do to you?
5. What is the treatment for AIDS?
6. What are the precautions for AIDS?
7. If someone who has AIDS looks different what do they look like?
8. Why is AIDS not a laughing matter?

Notes containing lists of questions were not pivotal ones in the database. Students rarely made direct reference to their questions in the notes that followed. In fact, only once did a student refer back to earlier queries and acknowledge which questions had been addressed and which ones had not. The questions apparently played little or no role in guiding or structuring research.

In summary, there was little evidence in the first unit of online collaboration. There was also an absence of conjectures. Students appeared to view their time on CSILE as a process of fulfilling requirements for the teacher. They developed questions, conducted research, and wrote comments on each other's work, but they treated these activities as individual jobs to perform rather than as a coordinated effort to improve personal understanding. Despite the teacher's efforts to encourage a more collaborative, problem-centered classroom culture, it appeared that students were approaching CSILE from a task-based perspective.

Human Biology After Trial

Two years after the initial Human Biology unit, the teacher taught the unit again. Once again, the teacher allocated six weeks to the unit and provided each student with thirty minutes of CSILE time and thirty minutes of research time per day. However, by now he had developed a number of effective strategies for combating the task-based mentality that caused problems in the first unit. Six of these strategies are discussed here.

Teacher Strategy 1: Place a Greater Focus on Problem-Centered Collaboration. In the first Human Biology unit only 32 comments were written, a disappointingly low number. The teacher felt that collaborative processes needed a greater presence and visibility in the CSILE database. His solution was to instruct students to use CSILE in a different way than in previous years. Instead of recording ideas in separate CSILE notes, students were asked to store ongoing group dialogues in a single, coauthored note called a "discussion." Groups were told to begin their discussions with a problem of understanding (e.g., "How does the heart work?") and then progressively append their individual contributions (Fig. 1.6). Each entry was to begin

Problem: How do we breathe? (TA)

I Need To Understand: To understand some of the lower respiratory conducting tract I must know more about the trachea and bronchi.(SG)

New Information: I know that inside our chest we have something called the bronchial tree. The bronchial tree consists of the trachea, also know as the windpipe, the bronchi which is connected to the trachea, the bronchioles which are connected to the bronchi and the alveoli which are tiny air sacs at the end of the bronchioles.(TA)

I Need To Understand: I know about the positions of the parts of the lungs and bronchial tree but I still need to know about all the functions.(TA)

I Need To Understand: I need to understand what the bronchi is made of.(AG)

Comment: Dear April, while reading about the windpipe I did not find out what it is made of but I found that it is tough and flexible so that you can twist and turn your head.(TA)

New Information: While reading about the lungs and bronchial tree I found that the entire bronchial tree is a series of air tubes. (TA)

New Information: I found out that there is a muscle called the diaphragm. It is like a rubber sheet which stretches out over the bottom of the chest. When we breathe in the diaphragm flattens and makes a larger space in the lungs. Then the space is filled with air. When we breathe out the diaphragm curves upwards and makes the space smaller so the air is pushed out. (TA)

FIG. 1.6. A CSILE discussion.

with a thinking type (e.g., I Need To Understand) and end with the student's initials. A CSILE discussion thus served as a chronologically ordered record of a group's thinking about a Human Biology question.

Discussions were advantageous because they brought together the text of all participants in the same window and focused students on the same problem of understanding. The high visibility of different people's texts, combined with a shared interest in resolving a particular problem, increased the likelihood that individuals would read, and respond to, each other's work. This arrangement also allowed an entire discussion to be accessed in a single database retrieval no matter how large the conversation grew. In contrast, each note in the first Human Biology unit was a separate entity and required a separate database call to be displayed. Group work was less visible and required more time to access.

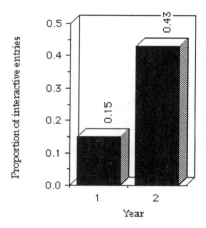

FIG. 1.7. Change in the proportion of collaborative entries.

The invention of CSILE discussions resulted in much more extensive discourse than in the first Human Biology session. The proportion of collaborative entries jumped from 15% to 43% ($p < 0.05$), a significant increase (Fig. 1.7).

Teacher: I remember thinking there was a qualitative difference in what the discussion group was doing. It was so different from the text notes, which read more like an electronic research project. The discussions seemed to engage the students in a higher level of thinking and knowledge building and writing, than I'd ever seen.

Teacher Strategy 2: Guide Students Toward Educationally Productive Queries. Since a CSILE discussion is an attempt to resolve a particular problem of understanding, it is important that students select problems that are educationally worthwhile. For this reason, the teacher often discussed the process of question-asking with students. He explained that the goal was to select a problem that was neither too broad nor too narrow, and preferably one that investigated a process. Phrases such as, "How does x work?" were provided as templates. The teacher suggested that students begin by identifying personal areas of uncertainty or confusion, and then out of that thinking, formulate an effective problem statement.

The teacher also discussed the issue of question follow-up with his class. He explained that once a question was recorded in CSILE, it was important that students make some effort to resolve it. The teacher acknowledged that in many cases the school's resources would not provide sufficient information. Occasionally, students may pose queries that even scientists have been unable to resolve. However, the important thing was to make as much progress as possible. Even after local resources have been exhausted, students should still make conjectures, ask more questions, and critique each other's ideas.

Teacher Strategy 3: Make Student Thinking Focal. Many factors may have contributed to the low number of conjectures in the first Human Biology unit. Some individuals may have felt uncomfortable speculating about unfamiliar issues. Others may not have considered theory building to be an educationally productive activity. At best, their theories would be validated by classroom reference materials that needed to be consulted in any case. At worst, their theories would reveal the depth of their own ignorance. Thus, for some students, posing conjectures may have seemed to be a futile endeavor, and perhaps even risky, because they might invite unwanted criticism.

One case that highlights the risk of conjecture building occurred during a study of prehistory. It began with a student, Lisa, who decided to share her thinking about the process of human evolution:

> I think that first there were monkeys, and they evolved into gorillas, and they evolved into apes, and apes evolved into humans.

This inspired the following response from another student, John:

> For your information, gorillas and monkeys are apes. And they are all still around, if you don't believe me then you can just check your local zoo.

John's first criticism, that gorillas and monkeys are apes, is partially correct. Ape is a generic term referring to primates without tails, such as the gorilla, the chimpanzee, the orangutan, and the gibbon. However, a monkey is not an ape.

John's second criticism concerned the process of evolution. If monkeys evolved into gorillas, then why are there still monkeys around? It was an interesting line of reasoning and an important challenge to Lisa's theory, but it was obscured by the tone of the message. Lisa responded to John's comment, but her response seemed to be written more in anger than as a constructive critique of his ideas:

> How do you know there are still apes around? You can't believe everything you read, you know.

It is evident from even this short exchange that posing a conjecture in a public forum such as CSILE opens students to criticism. It is much safer to reproduce information found in reliable resource materials than to invent explanations that are likely to be incorrect. It is also apparent that some students do not always phrase their comments in a completely constructive manner.

In an attempt to encourage higher levels of conjecture building, the teacher proposed the following guidelines:

1. Students were expected to use the My Theory thinking type in response to the Problem and I Need To Understand thinking types in their CSILE discussions. This guideline was intended to make conjecture building a regular and important part of the students' daily activities.

2. Students were asked to generate theories *before* they consulted any research materials. This guideline was introduced because some students gathered information from an encyclopedia and other classroom texts and misrepresented it as personal conjectures. The teacher assured the class that they would not be penalized for having incorrect information in their My Theory entries. He explained that the purpose of My Theory was to encourage students to think on their own about a problem and to invent reasonable explanations.

3. Students were asked to respond to other people's theories in a constructive manner. The teacher explained that many of the My Theory entries would contain misconceptions and it was important not to criticize others unduly for their initial efforts. Of course, it was also expected that students would work collaboratively to replace their early misconceptions with progressively better explanations.

4. Students who wished to modify a theory were not asked to rewrite it or delete it, but instead they were asked to create a new theory at the bottom of the discussion. In this way students could see how their understanding improved over time.

The teacher's new guidelines made theorizing an important part of classroom activity. The percentage of CSILE notes in the second unit rated as conjectures rose significantly to 37% from the 1% value (Fig. 1.8) of the first Human Biology unit ($p < 0.001$). The teacher felt that the new emphasis on My Theory involved students more deeply in their research:

Teacher: I think [My Theory] is really important for them because it provides a starting point, it gets them thinking in some depth about a problem. In the beginning, their theories are usually fairly brief, but if I can see a way that I can encourage that student to put more detail in that theory, I'll ask them to go

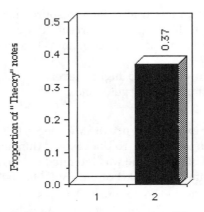

FIG. 1.8. Change in the proportion of student theories.

back and do that. Theories give them something interesting to do the research about, they want to know whether they are right, and they'll often comment that, "In the beginning I thought such-and-such, but after doing the research I found that I was wrong," or "correct" in other cases. Theories give them a mental model to start with so they are less likely to use copy-delete and knowledge-telling methods.

Furthermore, the teacher thought that My Theory provided him with a better awareness of student beliefs and misconceptions.

Teacher: Theories are also useful because it's usually in theories that misconceptions are revealed. This gives me an idea of the direction I need to encourage in the research so that those misconceptions might be overcome. It's also just plain interesting to read and see how startling some of the misconceptions can be. Had I stood up in front in the class and taught a lesson, most times I never would have realized that the students' understanding of the basic principles, which I was taking for granted, was really much less developed, or poorly developed, than I would have thought.

Teacher Strategy 4: Make Evident the Iterative Progression of Learning.
A fourth strategy shared with students during class meetings concerned the progression of CSILE discussions. The teacher suggested that there should be a sense of flow between thinking types and that online interactions should

read like a conversation. To make this idea more tangible, he presented some guidelines for the selection of thinking types. He recommended that My Theory entries be employed in response to a Problem or an I Need To Understand entry. The thinking type I Need To Understand, in turn, should be created in response to My Theory (if the student is attempting to identify what is needed to advance that theory) or in response to New Information (if the student has a question about new findings). Finally, the New Information thinking type should be used to help verify or disprove a theory.

> Teacher: I try to get the students to begin working on their problem with a theory because I think it gives them an opportunity to think in some depth about possible solutions. I then think it's important for them to generate an INTU based on their theory because it sets out a direction, related to the problem, which their research can take. Otherwise, there is a tendency to persist in topic- based fishing trips in the encyclopedia or other resource material. I do spend quite a bit of time with individuals asking them what problem they're working on when they're doing their research. The answer often is, "I'm working on energy," (for example) so I take that opportunity to redirect them to a problem which they are trying to solve. I explain to them how difficult it is to find information related to a specific problem and how they will have to consult many sources before they are likely to be successful. It's another attempt to move them away from the model of source material determining the direction of research, rather than the problem determining the direction of research.

The teacher also pointed out that the research should be iterative in the sense that questions lead to theories, theories lead to new information, and new information leads to even deeper questions. Miyake (1986) notes in her study of people trying to understand the functioning of a sewing machine that the participants learned in an iterative fashion. As they gained understanding at one level, they would identify new conceptual problems at a more detailed level. They would then attempt to develop an understanding of that next level. This was the pattern that the teacher was striving for in CSILE— a progression partially evident in the discussion, "How does a cell function?" The first INTU was an attempt to clarify the first two My Theory statements. Subsequent INTUs were attempts to extend the information reported in the NI. Each subsequent query drove the investigation a little deeper (see Fig. 1.9).

Problem: How does a cell function? (AR)

My Theory: I think a cell functions by oxygen coming into the cell and the cell then can do its work by breathing. (AR)

My Theory: I agree with your theory but when the cell functions I don't think it is breathing, I think that the oxygen you're breathing in is doing it. (JD)

My Theory: I think a cell functions by the "things" inside the cell. (organelles) (AK)

My Theory: I think that the cell functions with the help of the organelles. (MS)

I Need To Understand: How does the oxygen get into the cell, if the cell really does breathe oxygen? (AR)

My Theory: I don't think that cells breathe oxygen, I just think that the cell needs oxygen to do its work. But if the cells do breathe oxygen, I think that there is some kind of a tube in the cell that helps the cell get the oxygen it needs. (AK)

New Information: I found out that the cell takes food and oxygen in through the membrane. This happens regularly. The cell then changes the food and oxygen into energy. It uses the energy to do its work. (AR)

I Need To Understand: How does the food and oxygen get to the cells membrane? (AR)

My Theory: I think there are very small tubes that lead to each cell and the food and oxygen goes down those tubes and into the cell through the cell's membrane. (AR)

My Theory: I disagree with your theory Anna, I think that the oxygen and food goes into the cell automatically as a daily process. (AK)

Comment: April, I do think the food and oxygen goes automatically as a daily process. I just think it goes automatically down very small tubes to each cell. (AR)

I Need To Understand: What the oxygen does when it gets to the cell? Note: Also need to know how the oxygen gets to the cell. (AR)

My Theory: This is what I think the oxygen does when it gets to the cell. I think that the oxygen goes into the cell through the membrane and it then goes to the nucleus where it is turned into energy. Then the cell can do its job with the help of the energy. (AR)

FIG. 1.9. An example of iterative inquiry.

By underscoring the complex, iterative nature of learning, the teacher hoped to move students beyond the simple question–answer epistemologies that tend to be fostered by the IRF discourse patterns of conventional classrooms.

Teacher Strategy 5: Encourage Substantive Collaboration. Although the teacher continually encouraged students to respond to each other's ideas, he discouraged efforts that were overly critical or lacked substance. He explained that collaborative contributions should offer new ideas or new questions that the author of the target note had not previously considered. Examples such as "I think you did a good job" and "I really like your note" fail in this regard. The notion that students should orient themselves toward knowledge advancement was frequently revisited in an ongoing effort to make them more cognizant of their role as learners and the role they should play when collaborating with peers.

Teacher: I used many different techniques to try to get students to understand the difference between low and high-level comments. I've tried to get them to write about the knowledge and/or understanding that is present in the entry that they are commenting on. I've given them cheat-sheets with suggested lead-ins, such as "I want to question your statement that . . . ." I've also spoken to the whole class and to individuals and tried to get them to see the difference between a comment based on form and a comment based on content.

Teacher Strategy 6: Stress Understanding. A common thread underlying all of the teacher's direction to his class was an emphasis on understanding. For example, with regard to the reading of resource materials, the teacher was very concerned that students not mindlessly transfer information from classroom texts into CSILE notes. He shared these concerns with his class and recommended that students not bring library books to the computer. Instead, they were asked to take notes on paper, reflect upon the new information, and then, later, express these findings in their own words in CSILE. In this way, students were less likely to adopt cut-and-paste strategies and were more likely to take an intellectually active role with respect to the new material.

Teacher: I keep reminding them that when they go to do research they should have a problem in their mind that they are trying to solve. I'll say to them, "What problem are you working on?" and I'll say, "What do you need to understand to make some progress in solving this problem?" Then I'll say, "You should read the text, try to understand what it is about. You may have to look in many different places before you can solve this problem. Just read it and think about it, and try to understand it, and if you do, just jot down some point- form notes in your research books to remind you what you learned. You shouldn't be copying out of the book, shouldn't be writing in sentences. The important thing is understanding." So, I'll say something like that, or parts of that, periodically to kids as they're working on their research.

Teacher Reflections

In the following passage, the teacher discusses his own perspectives on the changes that occurred in his classroom:

I introduced CSILE into my classroom nine years ago, and since then I have used it extensively in knowledge building activities in different curriculum areas. I use it primarily for knowledge building in science, but I have also used it for language, social science (particularly history), and mathematics.

When I began using CSILE, I relied much more heavily on direct instruction than I do now, and what the students tended to produce were individual research reports with better illustrations and better organized information, but reports which were otherwise similar to those they had written by hand. It has taken a long time to change students' approach and ideas about learning and it has not been an easy task. Now, the students' study of curriculum units probes deeper using both text and pictorial information and, with the inclusion of the commenting feature, is combined with constructive criticism of one another's ideas.

A few years ago I began using discussion notes, which were designed to encourage students to be more aware that they should be trying to construct knowledge rather than just telling (or copying) information. Discussion notes allow students to contribute to, and follow, the development of knowledge and understanding, both their own and that of their classmates. I have found discussion notes to be a very powerful means of developing students' knowledge building skills because they make it easier to follow the development of the ideas and learning over time.

Students use problems, rather than topics, as the basis of all the work that they do. These problems are usually centered on processes so that students are encouraged to build their understanding of how things actually work rather than just describing the characteristics of areas under study. It is an approach that stresses function more than structure. In my experience, students are usually oriented towards topics and telling knowledge, and often the knowledge is descriptive. Changing their way of thinking to knowledge construction is difficult and time consuming but CSILE can be an effective support in this endeavor. Most of the problems are defined by the students themselves and I have found that with practice and appropriate guidance, they are able to construct problems which can be very profitably explored by themselves and their peers. It does require some time to establish the difference between problem solving and problem-centered learning.

Overall, the major change in my own classroom has been one of approach. The locus of control has shifted from me to the student. The students have taken on much greater responsibility for their own learning. I have tried to stress to students that their goal should be real understanding rather than the production of a report or the achievement of a high test score. The student is responsible for making sound educational decisions; I am responsible for providing an environment that allows this to happen. This has not been an easy task, at least for me. I have found that by the time students are in grades five and six, they have become very skillful at the school game and they are quite adept at completing their tasks with a minimum of really deep thinking about the issues or problems being studied. Insisting that they focus on processes and develop a real understanding of how things work requires constant encouragement and support. It also helps to stress that learning is never over. Students should begin to see that it is possible to probe deeper into virtually any problem, and that the learning from one set of problems can often have applications in a different set.

I try to use this approach in all areas of the curriculum, not just in the work which the students are doing directly on CSILE. In this way I hope that the benefits of such an approach will be realized more quickly than might otherwise be the case. Some students, of course, are not mature enough to handle this kind of responsibility and then it is up to the teacher to intervene. But, in my experience, most students recognize their problems and, if they cannot solve them, they will seek the advice of the teacher or a friend.

To support this process even further, I've recently tried to increase my efforts and activities with the parents of my students, to try to get them to support the type of knowledge building approach that I use in the classroom. For example, instead of asking their child, "What did you do today?," they might ask, "What did you learn today?," "What problems are you working on in science?," "What are the learning goals for today's math assignment?," "How do you think that process works?," and so on.

In my view, training students to become familiar with CSILE should be incidental to the achievement of learning goals. But obviously, when introducing students to the CSILE system, the teacher can choose knowledge building units that emphasize a particular aspect of the program—for example, a study of biological species that requires extensive use of the graphics program.

The methods I use to introduce problem areas vary depending on the students' previous experiences and my own thoughts about students' abilities. I may give specific problems to solve but students also generate their own problems, which is a very important aspect of their work on CSILE. Sometimes my introductions are quite brief and at other times our work on CSILE follows a considerable amount of time spent on classroom activities. Often, by the second term, students anticipate the next area of study and may begin to prepare for it in advance. What I am looking for from the class is knowledge building—not copying out of books but really seeking to understand, collaboration, problem definition, substantive commenting, theory generation, and re-thinking. I adjust my expectations according to the students' abilities and to the time of year. In the fall, when CSILE may be new to many of the students, they require more direction; in the spring, each student should be able to contribute, through comments and collaboration, to the knowledge building of other students.

I'm sure there are many effective approaches to using CSILE. The following four examples are ones which I have found to be useful:

1. To define and examine the principles on which scientific observations are based. A recent example was a unit we did on "How Electricity Works." We carried out several class experiments, and each student wrote a report on CSILE on what was observed combined with an in-depth study (including the use of graphics notes) to come up with a model of what was occurring during the passage of an electric current through a metal or a liquid. Prior to this study I introduced the students to the concept of molecules. Group work required them to generate theories, to define areas of uncertainty needing more research, and to comment on the ideas of other students. Eventually, the class formed a single group whose aim was to arrive at a satisfactory understanding of the processes involved.

2. To explore a problem which is both real and current. A while ago we did a unit on "How Our Environment Is Threatened." The student groups were of varying size depending on the special interest of the members; two students were interested in acid rain, four others in the depletion of the ozone layer, and so forth. Ultimately, the groups pooled their information in CSILE's communal database, and through discussion, monitoring the database, and commenting, the students became aware of the interrelationship between the various issues and arrived at an overview of the environmental threat.

3. To design an experiment, environment, or structure. I have used CSILE to have students design a city or a series of experiments. There is the potential to use the graphics notes more extensively in these situations and then to provide a justification of choices in the linked discussion or text notes. It may be necessary to complete some preliminary research in a design environment on CSILE, but it is also quite appropriate to have students really think about something without referring to external sources.

4. To create a forum for all the knowledge built around a specific problem or group of problems. Two units where CSILE performed this function were "How the Human Body Works" and "How Evolution Works." After the students had generated an overall body of knowledge, groups explored specific problems that interested them—for example, "How is pain transmitted?" or "How are physical features inherited?" The communal database reflected the in-depth thinking of groups and individuals on specific problems and, at the same time, unified them in a common orientation. By reading and commenting on each other's notes, the students gained insight into knowledge in a way that would have been impossible in a traditional classroom.[2]

---

[2]Excerpt from the PCN database, April 1995.

CONCLUSION

Transforming a classroom into a Knowledge Building Community is a difficult endeavor for many teachers because the model conflicts with conventional school practices. In particular, the traditional emphasis on completing tasks encourages a "What do you want me to do?" mentality that focuses students on products rather than on personal understanding. The difficulties in the first Human Biology session were at least partially due to a clash in expectations and values. Although the teacher provided many of the conditions necessary for a Knowledge Building Community to develop, the students were still focused on task completion. Only when the teacher made the emphasis on understanding explicit did activity patterns change.

The second Human Biology unit shows significant gains in student interaction, theory development, and the level of problem-centeredness. On average, students collaborated with more of their peers and their in-group discourse was more sustained. The thinking type My Theory was assigned to 37% of the notes, a significant increase from the 1% posted in the first unit ($p < 0.001$). Also, students pursued more of their own questions and they pursued them in greater depth. On many different levels, the class appeared to be acquiring many of the characteristics of a Knowledge Building Community.

It is proposed that the new class emphasis on discussions and theory building was fundamental in bringing about many of the aforementioned changes. What was crucial about this process was the shift away from the notion of students as knowledge gatherers toward the notion of students as knowledge builders. Using the thinking type My Theory, the teacher legitimized student beliefs, explanations and arguments as important class objects worthy of collaborative analysis. In a similar fashion, the teacher's instructions regarding the New Information thinking type encouraged a more constructivist class perspective. In the first unit, New Information was often used to replicate information found in books. Now the information was used to validate, disprove, and advance student theories. A new Knowledge Building culture was emerging, one more intent on developing explanations and refining them.

In summary, the students' initial use of CSILE was characterized by a task-based mentality in which the goal was to write certain kinds of notes. The strategies employed by the teacher in the later unit seemed more effective at focusing the class on understanding. His instructions concerning question generation, the construction and extension of theories, and the application of an iterative research methodology brought about greater levels of Knowledge Building than in his first attempt. In particular, the teacher's directives concerning the use of discussions and the My Theory thinking type appear to have been an important part of this transformation.

ACKNOWLEDGMENTS

This chapter is one of the products of a four-year research collaboration between myself and Dr. Jim Webb, a grade 5/6 teacher at Huron Public School in Toronto. Dr. Webb is an exceptional teacher who goes to extraordinary lengths to provide his students with rich educational experiences. His ideas and classroom experiments have greatly contributed to the CSILE team's research effort.

I would like to thank Marlene Scardamalia, Carl Bereiter, Robert McLean, Gordon Wells, Clare Brett, Jud Burtis, and Lena Paulo for their comments and suggestions on earlier drafts of this paper. I am also grateful for research support provided by the TeleLearning Network of Centres of Excellence.

REFERENCES

Bereiter, C., & Scardamalia, M. (1989). Intentional learning as a goal of instruction. In L. B. Resnick (Ed.), *Knowing, learning, and instruction: Essays in honor of Robert Glaser* (pp. 361–392). Hillsdale, NJ: Lawrence Erlbaum.

Brown, A., & Day, J. (1983). Macrorules for summarizing texts: The development of expertise. *Journal of Verbal Learning and Verbal Behavior, 22*, 1–14.

Eckert, P. (1989). *Jocks and burnouts.* New York: Teachers College Press.

King, A. (1994). Guiding knowledge construction in the classroom: Effects of teaching children how to question and how to explain. *American Educational Research Journal, 31*(2), 338–368.

Kintsch, W. (1986). Learning from text. *Cognition and Instruction, 3*, 87–108.

Lave, J. (1988). *Cognition in practice: Mind, mathematics and culture in everyday life.* New York: Cambridge University Press.

Lave, J., & Wenger, E. (1991). *Situated learning: Legitimate peripheral participation.* New York: Cambridge University Press.

Levinson, P. (1990). Computer conferencing in the context of the evolution of media. In L. Harasim (Ed.), *Online education: Perspectives on a new environment* (pp. 3–14). New York: Praeger Publishers.

Mason, R., & Kaye, T. (1990). Toward a new paradigm for distance education. In L. Harasim (Ed.), *Online education: Perspectives on a new environment* (pp. 15–38). New York: Praeger Publishers.

Mehan, H. (1979). *Learning lessons.* Cambridge, MA: Harvard University Press.

Mercer, N. (1992). Talk for teaching-and-learning. In K. Norman (Ed.), *Thinking voices: The work of the National Oracy Project* (pp. 215–223). London: Hodder and Stoughton for the National Curriculum Council.

Miyake, N. (1986). Constructive interaction and the iterative process of understanding. *Cognitive Science, 10*, 151–177.

Newman, D., Griffin, P., & Cole, M. (1989). *The construction zone: Working for cognitive change in school.* New York: Cambridge University Press.

Pea, R. D., & Gomez, L. M. (1992). Distributed multimedia learning environments: Why and how? *Interactive Learning Environments, 2*, 73–109.

Reddy, M. J. (1979). The conduit metaphor: A case of frame conflict in our language about language. In A. Ortony (Ed.), *Metaphor and thought* (pp. 284–324). New York: Cambridge University Press.

Rowe, M. B. (1974). Wait-time and rewards as instructional variables, their influence on language, logic, and fate control: Part one: Wait-time. *Journal of Research in Science Teaching, 2*(2), 81–94.

Scardamalia, M., & Bereiter, C. (1991a). Higher levels of agency for children in knowledge building: A challenge for the design of new knowledge media. *Journal of the Learning Sciences, 1*, 38–68.

Scardamalia, M., & Bereiter, C. (1991b). Literate expertise. In K. A. Ericsson & J. Smith (Eds.), *Toward a general theory of expertise: Prospects and limits* (pp. 172–194). New York: Cambridge University Press.

Scardamalia, M., & Bereiter, C. (1993). *Computer support for knowledge building communities.* Draft Document.

Scardamalia, M., & Bereiter, C. (1994). Computer support for knowledge building communities. *Journal of the Learning Sciences, 3*, 265–283.

Scardamalia, M., & Bereiter, C. (1997). Adaptation and understanding: A case for new cultures of schooling. In S. Vosniadou, E. D. Corte, R. Glaser, & H. Mandl (Eds.), *International perspectives on the psychological-foundations of technology-based learning environments* (pp. 149–163). Mahwah, NJ: Lawrence Erlbaum.

Scardamalia, M., Bereiter, C., Brett, C., Burtis, P. J., Calhoun, C., & Smith Lea, N. (1992). Educational applications of a networked communal database. *Interactive Learning Environments, 2*, 45–71.

Scardamalia, M., Bereiter, C., Hewitt, J., & Webb, J. (1996). Constructive learning from texts in biology. In K. M. Fischer & M. Kibby (Eds.), *Knowledge acquisition, organization, and use in biology* (pp. 44–64). Berlin: Springer-Verlag.

Scardamalia, M., Bereiter, C., McLean, R., Swallow, J., & Woodruff, E. (1989). Computer-supported intentional learning environments. *Journal of Educational Computing Research, 5*(1), 51–68.

Sinclair, J., & Coulthard, R. (1975). *Towards an analysis of discourse: The English used by teachers and pupils.* London: Oxford University Press.

Whitehead, A. N. (1929). *The aims of education.* New York: Macmillan.

Wittrock, M. C. (1974). Learning as a generative process. *Educational Psychologist, 11*, 87–95.

THE BALANCE BETWEEN TASK FOCUS AND UNDERSTANDING FOCUS: EDUCATION AS APPRENTICESHIP VERSUS EDUCATION AS RESEARCH

Allan Collins
Northwestern University, Boston College

Jim Hewitt in his paper describing the transformation of one classroom over 10 years shows how the teacher moved from a focus on tasks to a focus on understanding. There is perhaps no better description of how the Computer-Supported Intentional Learning Environment (CSILE) can transform education, so we owe a great debt to Hewitt for describing that transformation so compellingly. But the transformation itself raises questions that I have been wrestling with for the past decade: What should be the balance between a task focus and an understanding focus in schooling and more generally how should we prepare students for the complex world they are entering?

The focus on understanding in CSILE classrooms addresses several problems. As Hewitt points out, if you give students the task of doing a project they usually will try to minimize their work. They have a number of strategies for doing this. One trick is to investigate questions for which there are ready answers in the encyclopedia or other resources they have at hand. There is a tendency for students to use "knowledge-telling" (Scardamalia & Bereiter, 1997) and copy-delete strategies (Brown & Day, 1983) in producing text for their report. The copy-delete strategy is particularly perverse, because it can be carried out with practically no thought by simply copying text and deleting elements that do not seem necessary for the purpose at hand. The goal of the students is to produce a product that looks good but that they do not have to work to produce.

Another motivation for moving away from a task focus to an understanding focus derives from Dweck's work (1986). Dweck has shown how students who adopt performance goals put their energy into looking good and tend to give up when they fail. But those students who adopt learning goals learn more from their mistakes and pursue learning in the face of failure. A major concern is that an emphasis on tasks leads students to adopt performance goals and to focus on production values rather than on meaningful learning.

The response of the teacher that Hewitt describes and that Scardamalia and Bereiter (1994) advocate is to move from the goal of producing products to pursuing learning and understanding. The teacher in Toronto has developed a number of very successful strategies to accomplish this goal. One technique has been to encourage groups of students to carry on threaded discussions where they start with a problem that they want to resolve, they articulate their initial theories, and then they jointly seek out information to answer the questions that they have in order to refine their theories. In this way, instead of producing individual notes that nobody ever responds to, the groups carry on a knowledge building dialogue that results in a much deeper understanding than students in most classrooms ever attain. The teacher Hewitt describes is one of the most gifted teachers working with CSILE and he has been able to create a true learning community (Bielaczyc & Collins, 1999: Brown & Campione, 1996).

There is a question in my mind about how much task focus and product orientation remains among the students in the classroom. The teacher states in one comment about the earlier version of the Human Biology unit, "I insist that all notes, which are to be used for evaluation, must be published. To be granted the status of published, a note must be a significant contribution to the database and it must be grammatically correct." Whether he continued to use publication as the basis for assessment is unclear. In most school settings, students will do what it takes to get a good grade (D'Amico, 1999) and so it is possible to imagine them creating published notes that give the illusion of their thinking and learning, while minimizing their efforts. But I suspect the teacher moved away from basing their grades on publication to basing them on the effort they made to understand the topic and to refine their theories over time. In any case, the assessment strategy the teacher uses is key to moving students away from an emphasis on production values to an emphasis on learning and understanding.

The metaphor underlying this approach is "education as research" (Scardamalia & Bereiter, 1994). Students are carrying out investigations and building theories and then arguing publicly to refine their theories. In the world of research there are a wide variety of activities that practitioners carry out. They generate and investigate questions, they conduct experiments and analyze data, they build theories and models, they write papers and make presentations to colleagues, they listen to their colleagues and debate about ideas and methods, they develop tools and techniques for carrying out investigations, they search for contradictory evidence to shoot down prevailing theories and explanations, etc. Much of this activity is going on in the classroom Hewitt describes, but not all. There is very little experimentation and model building, there are no conferences where ideas are presented and fought over, and no papers are published that lead to counter-arguments and extensions. The world of research is, in fact, as much task oriented as it is understanding oriented.

In contrast to the "education as research" metaphor, I would like to present two cases I have worked with where the underlying metaphor was something like "education as apprenticeship." The first example is "Discover Rochester" that Sharon Carver (Carver, 1990; Collins, Hawkins & Carver, 1991) developed in a middle school in Rochester, New York. In the Discover Rochester Project, "at risk" eighth graders spent one day each week exploring aspects of the Rochester environment from scientific, mathematical, historical, cultural, and literary perspectives. They worked in groups to conduct their own research about topics ranging from weather to industry to theater to employment, using a variety of strategies including library and archival research, telephone and face-to-face interviews, field observation, and experimentation. Based on their research, students developed a Hyper-Card exhibit for the Rochester Museum and Science Center, including text, audio, graphics, maps, and music.

The primary focus of the Discover Rochester curriculum was on explicitly teaching general strategies while students investigated multiple aspects of their own community to design an interactive learning exhibit. Thus, students' learning was situated in an exploration of real world topics for a real world purpose. The particular skills targeted by the Discover Rochester curriculum are strategies for learning and communicating information. Students learned to coordinate five types of skills to complete their exhibit: question posing, data gathering, data interpretation and representation, presentation, and evaluation—an elaborated version of the Bransford, Sherwood, Vye, and Rieser (1986) IDEAL program.

What I want to emphasize is the research focus within a task orientation, where production values were a central part of the learning. The problem of students finding ways to minimize their work was undoubtedly still present, but the overall goal drove most students to try to produce an interesting product. Furthermore, their work was critiqued by their peers since it was going out into the world as a representation of the school. So the project generated motivation beyond looking good to get a good grade, where students were developing the knowledge and skills to produce a good product.

My second example is taken from dissertation work by my student, Diana Joseph (Collins, 1997; Joseph & Collins, 1999). Over the past three years she has been working out the idea of what we call a passion curriculum in a school with inner-city children. She has chosen the making of video documentaries as a context to develop the design for a passion curriculum. Video is intrinsically interesting to the late elementary students she is working with, and so it provides a good context for her design work. She has developed a system of certifications for students in a variety of areas, such as script writing, interviewing, camera operation, etc. based on the Scout merit badge system. At the same time she has been working at systematically "interweaving" into the video curriculum important skills and concepts, such as math skills in the context of budgeting, writing skills in script writing, and planning skills in the development of a documentary. There is also an emphasis on learning content around the topic of each video they develop. For instance, in a video about the weather, there was an emphasis on meteorological and geographical content.

This structure for learning allows for a true cognitive apprenticeship (Collins, Brown, & Newman, 1989; Collins et al. 1991) to be developed, where there is an emphasis on students learning important content and skills in the context of carrying out complex tasks. Joseph has developed a four-stage model for a cognitive apprenticeship in a passion curriculum: (1) Students come in as novices and work on a project of their own with one of the more experienced students mentoring them as they carry out the project. (2) As they gain experience, they begin to work on larger projects with other students, where more advanced students serve as project and subproject leaders. (3) After they have worked on a number of different projects, they are ready to serve as a mentor for a new incoming student. (4) After they have done their mentoring successfully, they are ready to begin serving as a project or subproject leader on larger projects. This is a wholly new way to think about classroom organization.

Again, in this example, the emphasis is on learning content and skills in the context of producing products that students care about. The notion of "interweaving" (Collins, 1994, 1997) is central to the argument I am making. Much of schooling is like learning tennis by being told the rules and practicing the forehand, backhand, and serve without ever playing or seeing a tennis match. If tennis were taught that way, it would be hard to see the point of what you were learning. Students are taught algebra and Shakespeare without being given any idea of how these might be useful in their lives. That is not how a coach would teach you to play tennis. A good coach would have you go back and forth between playing games and working on particular knowledge and skills. The essential idea in teaching is to tightly couple a focus on accomplishing tasks with a focus on the underlying competencies needed to carry out the tasks. What is striking about Discover Rochester and the video passion curriculum is how the knowledge and skills are taught in service of task goals. To maintain a dual focus, it is necessary to go back and forth between teaching the knowledge, skills, and dispositions students need to succeed and executing the jobs necessary to accomplish the larger task.

By pursuing a goal of understanding, the teacher Hewitt describes is dealing with very real problems of students working in a CSILE environment. The metaphor of education as research that is embedded in his classroom seems very viable. But I would argue that there needs to be a richer research environment, where the kinds of tasks that researchers carry out in the world become meaningful to students. In such a research environment, understanding would serve a larger goal of accomplishing meaningful tasks, such as giving talks to a knowledgeable audience and writing papers that defend an explicit thesis.

REFERENCES

Bielaczyc, K., & Collins, A. (1999). Learning communities in classrooms: A reconceptualization of educational practice. In C. M. Reigeluth (Ed.), *Instructional- design theories and models: A new paradigm of instructional theory* (pp. 269–292). Mahwah, NJ: Lawrence Erlbaum Associates.

Bransford, J. D., Sherwood, R., Vye, N., & Rieser, J. (1986). Teaching, thinking and problem solving: Research foundations. *American Psychologist, 14*, 1078–1089.

Brown, A., & Campione, J. (1996). Psychological theory and the design of innovative learning environments: On procedures, principles, and systems. In L. Schauble & R. Glaser (Eds.), *Innovations in learning: New environments for education* (pp. 289–325). Mahwah, NJ: Lawrence Erlbaum Associates.

Brown, A., & Day, J. (1983). Macrorules for summarizing texts: The development of expertise. *Journal of Verbal Learning and Verbal Behavior, 22*, 1–4.

Carver, S. M. (1990, April). *Integrating interactive technologies into classrooms: The Discover Rochester project.* Paper presented at the annual meeting of the American Educational Research Association, Boston, MA.

Collins, A. (1994). Goal-based scenarios and the problem of situated learning: A commentary on Andersen Consulting's design of goal-based scenarios. *Educational Technology, 34*(9), 30–32.

Collins, A. (1997, November). Cognitive apprenticeship and the changing workplace. In *Proceedings of the Fifth Annual International Conference on Post-compulsory Education and Training.* Brisbane, Queensland, Australia: Griffiths University.

Collins, A., Brown, J. S., & Newman, S. E. (1989). Cognitive apprenticeship: Teaching the crafts of reading, writing, and mathematics. In L. B. Resnick (Ed.), *Knowing, learning, and instruction: Essays in honor of Robert Glaser* (pp. 453–494). Hillsdale, NJ: Lawrence Erlbaum Associates.

Collins, A., Hawkins, J., & Carver, S. M. (1991). A cognitive apprenticeship for disadvantaged students. In B. Means, C. Chelemer, & M. S Knapp (Eds.), *Teaching advanced skills to at-risk students* (pp. 216–243). San Francisco: Jossey-Bass.

D'Amico, L. (1999, April). *The implications of project-based pedagogy for the classroom assessment infrastructures of science teachers.* Paper presented at the annual meeting of the Educational Research Association, Montréal, Québec, Canada.

Dweck, C. (1986). Motivational processes affecting learning. *American Psychologist, 41*, 1040–1048.

Joseph, D., & Collins, A. (1999, April). *A design for schools based upon students' passions.* Paper presented at the annual meeting of the Educational Research Association, Montréal, Québec, Canada.

Scardamalia, M., & Bereiter, C. (1994). Computer support for knowledge building communities. *Journal of the Learning Sciences, 3*, 265–283.

Scardamalia, M., & Bereiter, C. (1997). Adaptation and understanding: A case for new cultures of schooling. In S. Vosniadou, E. D. Corte, R. Glaser, & H. Mandl (Eds.), *International perspectives on the psychological-foundations of technology-based learning environments* (pp. 149–163). Mahwah, NJ: Lawrence Erlbaum Associates.

STRIKING A BALANCE BETWEEN A TASK FOCUS AND AN UNDERSTANDING FOCUS

Jim Hewitt
OISE/University of Toronto

In his commentary, Allan Collins suggests that activity in CSILE (Computer-Supported Intentional Learning Environments) be organized around the kinds of tasks that researchers perform, such as giving talks and writing papers. Collins bases these recommendations on his experience with the Cognitive Apprenticeship model of learning (Collins, Brown, & Newman, 1989), an approach that interweaves the teaching of content and skills within a framework of tasks that students find meaningful. Collins provides two compelling examples of research projects that employ this approach. The first project, called Discover Rochester, engages students in the construction of an interactive multimedia computer exhibit for the Rochester Museum and Science Center. To build the exhibit, learners must collaboratively develop an extensive knowledge of Rochester's history and culture. The second project is a passion curriculum organized around the production of video documentaries. Students are responsible for conducting documentary research, script-writing, film production, etc. In both of these projects, authentic tasks are coupled with the careful interweaving of content acquisition and skill development. Collins feels that students in CSILE classrooms would find their online activities more meaningful if their efforts were similarly directed toward an authentic end product. For example, a CSILE investigation might culminate in a class-wide conference or writing papers.

I would like to begin my response to Collins' commentary by considering his CSILE recommendations separately from the larger issue of organizing instruction around task goals or understanding goals. Collins proposes several ways that CSILE activity might be enriched: encourage students to conduct experiments, promote the building of models, and hold conferences in which learners write papers and make presentations. These are all excellent suggestions. In fact, some of these ideas (class conference, paper writing) have been tried, with promising results, by the teacher described in my original chapter. These sorts of activities are not particularly common in CSILE classrooms and Collins is correct to point out that more could be done to further the research team metaphor. However, there is an important issue to be resolved regarding the implementation of these activities. Should reports and conferences be presented as culminating class events that students work toward? Or, should students view such events as serving a larger goal of advancing personal and collective knowledge? More specifically, should the primary goal of students be one of completing a task or one of advancing their own understanding?

The task versus understanding issue is complex. In many respects, CSILE and Discover Rochester share the same ideals. Both offer rich educational experiences in which students take some ownership over their own learning. Both also forge tight bonds between the teaching of content and the teaching of cognitive skills. In the hands of a skilled teacher, these programs can foster an exciting sense of discovery and purpose in the classroom. They differ, however, in terms of student goals. The Scardamalia and Bereiter (1996) model places understanding at the forefront. Tasks (reading, research, and writing) are performed in service of that understanding. In comparison, activity in a cognitive apprenticeship classroom is centered on a meaningful task, and the completion of that task requires attention to cognitive concerns. Thus, although both models value understanding and employ tasks, there are important differences in student focus.

CSILE's philosophy of making understanding the focus is based on intentional learning theory. Work in CSILE is not aimed at completing a particular task but at furthering understanding. One appeal of this approach is its directness. Students identify what they need to learn, and then, in collaboration with their peers, they take steps to achieve that goal. Task-based approaches, in comparison, are indirect. Students are required to complete a task and, in doing so, hopefully become more knowledgeable in a subject area. One advantage of intentional learning is that it aligns student and teacher objectives (Scardamalia & Bereiter, 1996). Both parties work toward the same goal of deepening learner understanding.

Task-based pedagogies use assignments and projects to engage students in a particular body of material. Carefully designed tasks, like the ones described by Collins, can be particularly motivating for students. The knowledge developed during the completion of the task is made more relevant (and possibly more memorable) by virtue of its strong connection to a real-world application. Collins sees these associations as an essential part of teaching and describes a technique called "interweaving" that continually frames knowledge and skills in the context of meaningful tasks. Interweaving is a powerful educational idea. By creating strong ties between knowledge and its application, learners also become better at recognizing those situations in which it is appropriate to apply their knowledge.

What should be the balance between a task focus and an understanding focus in the classroom? One response is to champion a cognitive apprenticeship model, which embeds knowledge and skill development within the context of a task. This approach offers a number of advantages. However, there are other benefits to be gained by making understanding a primary focus of students, as CSILE does. I discuss four of those benefits below:

1. Greater focus on cognitive and metacognitive skill development. CSILE is fundamentally designed to focus students on their own thinking processes. Scaffolds such as "I Need To Understand" and "My Theory" encourage students to reflect on their own understanding and build explanations that fill gaps in their knowledge. Task-centered activities, even when well designed, make these kinds of processes a secondary consideration for students.

2. Appreciation of the aesthetic value of learning. Activity in schools today is overwhelmingly task-centered. Learning tends to be something that students do (sometimes reluctantly) in the service of a particular task. This approach fails to capture the aesthetic value of learning. Individuals who enjoy a rich intellectual life often learn things out of curiosity or a sense of fascination with a particular subject area. For example, I am continually extending my knowledge of cosmology, even though I have yet to apply that knowledge to a task. Other people pursue studies of history or classical literature because of their interest in those disciplines. Similarly, in CSILE, students pose questions about unfamiliar subjects and then look for answers. The answers may not serve a purpose other than satisfying the learner's curiosity but that does not, in my mind, make the process any less valuable. CSILE portrays learning as an activity worth pursuing in its own right. I think this is a positive alternative to task-based approaches in which learning serves utilitarian purposes. Learning is often a means to an end, but sometimes it can be a satisfying end in itself.

3. Improved understanding of the nature of learning. Research conducted in the CSILE teacher's classroom suggests that students' conceptions of learning mature over the course of the academic year. There is evidence that a person's beliefs about learning influences the way he or she approaches and pursues tasks (Dweck, 1989). In an effort to assess student beliefs about learning, a multiple choice "Learning Questionnaire" was administered to the class taught by the teacher described in the preceding paper. An OISE/UT researcher, Jud Burtis, designed the questionnaire to investigate the long-term effect of CSILE on student epistemologies (Lamon, Chan, Scardamalia, Burtis, & Brett, 1993). He hypothesized that CSILE's emphasis on collaborative knowledge building would engender deep conceptions of learning, concerned with thinking and understanding, as opposed to shallow conceptions concerned with paying attention, completing exercises, and memorization. A nine-item, multiple-choice test was given to the CSILE class in the autumn and spring of the school year. Each question contained one deep response (b, in this following example) and two shallow ones.

> The most important thing you can do when you are trying to learn science is
>
> (a) faithfully do the work the teacher tells you to do.
> (b) try to see how the explanations make sense.
> (c) try to remember everything you are supposed to know.

According to paired t-test analyses, the scores of the students in the CSILE teacher's classroom increased significantly ($t(26) = -3.54$, $p = .002$), suggesting that, in this one classroom at least, student conceptions about learning had matured over the course of the year.

4. Preparation for the future. As students progress through the school system they need the skills and self-discipline to drive their own intellectual growth even when faced with poor teachers, unimaginative projects, or unmotivating activities. By focusing on understanding, the CSILE project fosters the kinds of cognitive and metacognitive skills that students require to take charge of their own educational agenda. CSILE-based investigations are intrinsically motivating. Students ask questions about phenomena that puzzle them and then systematically pursue answers. In contrast, task-based approaches rely on the task to motivate students. When students are later faced with less appealing tasks, or an absence of structured tasks altogether, there may be less incentive to learn.

In summary, Collins makes a number of excellent recommendations for CSILE classrooms that fit the research team metaphor. However, I feel that the activities he proposes would be best implemented within an intentional learning framework. Classrooms today are predominantly task-centered and a program such as CSILE provides students with an important opportunity to focus directly on their own learning processes. I feel this conveys a number of benefits including greater opportunities for the development of certain cognitive skills, an improved understanding of the nature of learning, and an increased ability for students to take charge of their own educational agenda. This is not to suggest that all classroom learning should be organized around an understanding focus. Students in CSILE classrooms engage in many of the same sorts of tasks and activities as other elementary school children. Art projects, mathematics quizzes, and story writing are all common components of their school day. By balancing these traditional activities and their CSILE explorations, the students experience the best of both worlds.

REFERENCES

Collins, A. (1994). Goal-based scenarios and the problem of situated learning: A commentary on Andersen Consulting's design of goal-based scenarios. *Educational Technology, 34*(9), 30–32.

Collins, A. (1997, November). Cognitive apprenticeship and the changing workplace. In *Proceedings of the Fifth Annual International Conference on Post-compulsory Education and Training.* Bruisbane, Queensland, Australia: Griffiths University.

Collins, A., Brown, J. S., & Newman, S. E. (1989). Cognitive apprenticeship: Teaching the crafts of reading, writing, and mathematics. In L. B. Resnick (Ed.), *Knowing, learning and instruction: Essays in honor of Robert Glaser* (pp. 453–494). Hillsdale, NJ: Lawrence Erlbaum Associates.

Dweck, C. S. (1989). Motivation. In A. Lesgold & R. Glaser (Eds.), *Foundations for a psychology of education.* Hillsdale, NJ: Lawrence Erlbaum Associates.

Lamon, M., Chan, C., Scardamalia, M., Burtis, P. J., & Brett, C. (1993, April). *Beliefs about learning and constructive processes in reading: Effects of a computer supported intentional learning environment (CSILE).* Paper presented at the annual meeting of the American Educational Research Association, Atlanta, GA.

Scardamalia, M., & Bereiter, C. (1996). Adaptation and understanding: A case for new cultures of schooling. In S. Vosniadou, E. DeCorte, R. Glaser, & H. Mandl (Eds.), *International perspectives on the design of technology-supported learning environments* (pp. 149–163). Mahwah, NJ: Lawrence Erlbaum Associates.

COORDINATION OF ASYNCHRONOUS AND SYNCHRONOUS COMMUNICATION: DIFFERENCES IN QUALITIES OF KNOWLEDGE ADVANCEMENT DISCOURSE BETWEEN EXPERTS AND NOVICES*

Jun Oshima
Ritsuko Oshima
Shizuoka University

INTRODUCTION

A challenge posed by Computer Support for Collaborative Learning is to stimulate the development of communities of learners. Computer-Supported Intentional Learning Environments (CSILE) as proposed by Scardamalia, Bereiter, and their colleagues is an educational philosophy for the design of computer-supported learning environments (Scardamalia & Bereiter, 1991, 1993, 1994, 1996; Scardamalia, Bereiter, Brett, Burtis, Calhoun, & Smith-Lea, 1992; Scardamalia, Bereiter, & Lamon, 1994; Scardamalia, Bereiter, McLean, Swallow, & Woodruff, 1989). CSILE software (i.e., regular CSILE 1.5 and Knowledge Forum) is a communal database system in which learners are allowed to externalize their thoughts mainly in the form of texts and/or graphics

---

*An earlier version of this paper was presented at the annual meeting of the American Educational Research Association, San Diego, CA, USA, April, 1998. The study was financially supported by Telecom Frontier Research Fund in Japan. We would like to thank the people who participated in this study for giving us important insights. We also thank Marlene Scardamalia, Carl Bereiter and CSILE/Knowledge Building Research Team for their help to set up the WebCSILE site in Japan. Finally, we really appreciate Naomi Miyake for her repeated comments and encouragement to complete this chapter.

called "notes" and then engage in collaboratively organizing their knowledge as objects to advance their communal understanding as a whole. This communal database structure has been found to provide learners with opportunities to be involved in knowledge advancement through distribution of their expertise (e.g., Oshima, Bereiter, & Scardamalia, 1995; Oshima, Scardamalia, & Bereiter, 1996) and to eventually facilitate learners' conceptual understanding of complex scientific phenomena in comparison with traditional instructions (e.g., Scardamalia et al., 1992). Thus, empirical studies so far have shown that CSILE is a powerful tool for transforming learning activities into knowledge building.

This study is aimed at exploring whether CSILE has generic effects to improve knowledge building discourse by extending the use of CSILE in a different culture. CSILE has been developed in Western culture and has been used in schools that have Western cultural values. Studies have shown that CSILE has positive effects on learning in the school system. The results may be limited by the cultural background. Students in Western classrooms have opportunities in the curriculum to express themselves and participate in discussion. In contrast, in Japan there is no established curriculum on discussion skills, although such skills are currently being considered as a potentially useful part of a student's education. Based on the differences in discussion skills between the two cultures, we may infer that CSILE would work in cultures where discussion or discourse is regarded as important. However, in cultures where the skills are not developed through educational practices, CSILE might fail in its goal of knowledge advancement. For investigating generic effects of CSILE on learning, we established a CSILE site in Japan to investigate the conditions necessary for its successful use. We first deployed the CSILE-based activity system in expert learners' activities to see how they would use CSILE and recognize it as a tool for knowledge advancement. Then, we went on to set up another CSILE site for novice learners based on results from the study of experts. Finally, through comparisons between the experts and the novices, we attempted to identify crucial factors for the successful use of CSILE and further scaffoldings for novice learners.

For describing and evaluating learners' activities supported by CSILE, we take the "design experiment approach" (e.g., Brown, 1992; Collins, 1990). As Brown (1992) argues, it is not strictly possible for educational researchers to control a variety of variables or factors in educational settings to determine the effects of the individual variables on educational outcomes. Educational practices are dynamic activities in which a variety of critical factors interact with one another. Because effects on educational outcomes come from such interactions among the variables, what we have to consider are not changes in individual variables but interactive relationships among the variables and their consequences. Therefore, strict manipulation of variables in such dynamic activities may often disturb appropriate interactions among the variables; consequently, the outcomes are not necessarily what we would like to investigate. This study, in particular, investigates three different communities in different contexts supported by CSILE. The use of CSILE and its effects totally depended on how CSILE was utilized within the users' schedule or intentions. We are, therefore, concerned with how to improve each practice by designing activities supported by CSILE rather than with the individual factors that affect specific performance measures.

Because we are concerned with the design of learning environments, traditional experimental design and its analysis techniques are inappropriate for our research purpose. For describing dynamic functions of learning, we base our analysis on Activity Theory by Engeström (1987, 1993, 1996). Engeström's framework of human activity consists of six sociocultural components of human activities and gives us some perspectives on how learners as a community engage in their activities supported by various tools. We attempt to evaluate CSILE deployment in three communities by analyzing how learners' recognitions on learning or their activities change through the deployment of CSILE by content analysis of their discourse in CSILE, participatory observation, interviews with learners, and questionnaires.

In this study, we have two research questions. The first is how the asynchronous communication by CSILE with or without face-to-face communication changes learners' activity systems and which format of curriculum is better in facilitating knowledge advancement. Information technologies (ITs) such as CSILE are based on a computer network and would be expected to be used for distance learning. A key component in distance learning is the set of tools for asynchronous communication on the computer network. It is useful for us to discuss whether the asynchronous distance communication can be a substitute for the current synchronous communication in learning activities, and if not, then how asynchronous communication tools could be incorporated into synchronous learning activities for creating more effective distance learning curriculum. Asynchronous communication tools are considered important in conducting intentional learning in the classroom as well (Bereiter & Scardamalia, 1989). Educational practice would become more learner-centered and project-based in the future. Asynchronous communication tools such as CSILE are expected to play crucial roles in conducting such practices by providing support for learners to collaborate beyond physical and temporary limitations in the classroom.

Our second research question involves comparing expert and novice learners in their approach to engaging in more productive discourse on the computer network. For expert learners, CSILE philosophy would be much easier to accept because the expert learners are engaged in knowledge building activities. However, for novice learners, the philosophy is difficult to accept because it is different from the philosophy they have developed through their schooling (Scardamalia & Bereiter, 1994). Even if they can accept the philosophy itself, the novices need to develop strategic knowledge and skills for managing their knowledge building with CSILE. We attempted to identify what strategic knowledge novices need for their knowledge advancement supported by CSILE.

In Study 1, we focus on expert learners. Two graduate school programs are targeted as communities supported by CSILE. In Community A, graduate students use CSILE as a new communication channel in addition to their normal channel (i.e., face-to-face communication). In Community B, graduate students take a course through CSILE only.

A variety of analyses were conducted with participatory observation data, interviews with the students, and contents reported in the database. We found through our observation and interview data that: (1) students in Community A efficiently used CSILE because they had recognized problems with their synchronous communication, (2) students in both communities reported CSILE as a powerful tool for improving their knowledge advancement through self-monitoring and asynchronous collaboration, which they thought had not been possible before using CSILE, and (3) students in Community A intentionally changed the roles of their face-to-face communication so that their CSILE communication could be incorporated into their activity.

With respect to what discourse the two communities engaged in, it was found that Community A produced better inscriptions of their arguments than did Community B. One of the remarkable factors for the better inscription was that discourse on the network by Community A was constructed through coordination of learning in face-to-face discourse.

From the above results, we concluded: (1) that expert learners were able to utilize CSILE for improving their knowledge building activities and (2) that necessary factors for the successful use of CSILE would be users' recognition of necessity of such technologies for resolving their communication problems and effort to coordinate the different communication channels (i.e., synchronous and asynchronous ones).

Based on the results in Study 1, we designed learning activities for novices that combined face-to-face and asynchronous communications in Study 2. Sophomores in an undergraduate course on cognitive science used CSILE as part of their regular curriculum. The students were given four lectures, in between which they had a few weeks for discussing the themes through CSILE communication. Data were collected through questionnaires, participatory observations, and contents reported by the students.

Results based on questionnaires and observations showed that: (1) students who had frequently used CSILE recognized the effects of CSILE on their learning, (2) students who effectively used CSILE had learning goals in the course, and (3) some students in transition from task-oriented to learning goal-oriented had difficulties in reporting their thoughts as notes and managing their learning schedules.

Novices were found to start their collaborative discourse by repeating questioning–answering and then gradually establishing simple structures of arguments as inscriptions such as reference–claim–qualification. These results suggested that (1) a missing skill in novice learners was the ability to work in a culture of learning while inscribing their thoughts as arguments (i.e., they did not have social rules of inscription development through collaboration) and (2) their discourse was mostly devoted to knowledge telling activities (Bereiter & Scardamalia, 1987) and hence they missed the metadiscourse that controls activities of constructing inscriptions.

METHODOLOGICAL ISSUES

Descriptions of Global Views of Educational Settings Targeted in This Study

We use the Activity Theory approach to our design experiments. Figure 2.1 shows Engeström's (1987) triangular model of human activity. Engeström extends a simple triangular structure of tool-mediated activity (Leontiev, 1981) by placing it in a more culturally based structure of activity. In his framework, a human activity mediated by tools is not viewed as independent of other activities but is totally dependent on the activities that are simultaneously being conducted by the members of the community in a

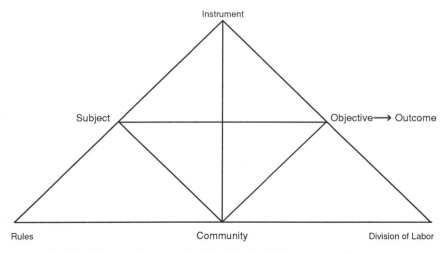

FIG. 2.1. The general framework of the human activity system by Engeström (1987).

more global structure of activity. The framework suggests that every human activity (the relationship among subject, instrument, and object) should be described from the perspectives of: (1) how the human is conducting the activity as a member of a cultural community (i.e., the relationship among subject, community, and rule) and (2) how his/her activity contributes to the accomplishment of the more global activity in the community (the relationship among subject, community, and division of labor). Thus, in applying this triangular model to learning settings, how learners engage in their activities can be described from the perspectives of: (1) how they are working as members of the learning community and (2) how their activities are organized in constructing the learning activity.

From the point of view of learners' activity in CSILE, the following hypothetical framework of activity could be articulated. In CSILE, because every learner is engaged in collaboration through computer communication as well as face-to-face communication, we can constitute as many activity systems as there are learners in a setting. All participants including the target participants can be put in the component of "community" as a team of inquiry. Furthermore, the following constitute the component of "instrument" in the framework: As a typical semiotic tool for thinking, written discourse as well as oral discourse works as a tool for learning. The database allows participants not only to represent their thoughts and knowledge but also to manipulate them in the represented form. It enables participants to organize knowledge and to asynchronously collaborate with others.

Analysis of Discourse as Knowledge Advancement by Using Toulmin's Argument Framework

This study focuses on the structure of discourse in the asynchronous communication as well. In academic disciplines, written discourse, particularly journal publishing, plays a crucial role in knowledge advancement (Bereiter & Scardamalia, 1993). Scientific arguments in written discourse have a specific structure (Eichinger, Anderson, Palincsar, & David, 1991; Toulmin, 1958). Any *claims* in the discourse should be based on *data* (or *references*), *warrants*, and *backups*. Further, the claims should be articulated through *qualification* and *rebuttals*. Scientific discourse is progressive in the sense that scientists are attempting to challenge others' and their own claims to construct higher levels of understandings as social agreements in the communities (Bereiter, 1994). They are engaged in reflective and metacognitive activities to attain such high qualities of scientific knowledge. Thus, knowledge represented in written discourse is structured based on the specific frameworks of arguments and elaborated with metacognitive rules. In this study, we attempt to describe how experts (represented by graduate students) and novices (represented by undergraduates) structured their arguments in psychology and cognitive science courses and then collaboratively articulated their arguments through asynchronous communication.

STUDY 1: DEPLOYMENT OF WEBCSILE WITH OR WITHOUT FACE-TO-FACE COMMUNICATION IN GRADUATE PROGRAMS

Study 1 was aimed at exploring how CSILE would be integrated into our current university courses, particularly at the graduate level. We had the following reasons for implementing CSILE in graduate schools. First, we had some requests from faculty to implement CSILE in their classes. Particular reasons in each class will be described later. Second, we thought it worthwhile to deploy CSILE in a graduate program as a means of exploring how expert learners make use of the new communication tool for improving their activities. Two graduate courses at two different universities were targeted in this study.

Community A

Subjects and Community. This community consisted of 19 graduate students (master and doctoral) and a postdoctoral fellow in a psychology course titled "Human-Environmental Psychology." The instructor had been an associate professor at his university for five years. The students were from a variety of subdisciplines in psychology such as psychiatry, cognitive psychology, educational psychology, and environmental psychology. The course continued through the first semester.

Objectives. The shared objective for them to pursue in the course was to understand recent ideas on "tool-mediated human activities" and "affordance" and then to consider designs of "human friendly" environments.

Instruments. For the purpose of the course, the participants decided to read three books related to their theme. The course took place once a week in a face-to-face classroom. During the two weeks prior to implementing WebCSILE, students had been writing their thoughts on index cards and then submitting the cards to the instructor on a weekly basis. The instructor had organized the cards and made copies to distribute as a means of allowing students to share their thoughts with others in the class. Then, instead of the cards, they began to use WebCSILE for additional discussion following their face-to-face discussion. Although all participants did not have unlimited Internet access, they could use computers at their laboratories when they wanted to access CSILE.

Rules and Division of Labor. The community had a traditional learning style in graduate courses at Japanese universities. Some portion of the reading assignments was assigned to students every week. The responsible students prepared brief summaries for their discussion and then presented their initial arguments. Thus, there was an obligation for each member of the seminar to prepare their assigned portion of the reading assignments and this led to a rigid division of labor, which usually did not change over time.

One of the reasons that the instructor in the course wanted to use CSILE was the challenge he faced in changing students' rules in the class. Through our participatory observation and informal talks with students, we had recognized that knowledge-building activities in the community had not been sufficiently collaborative. Students did not frequently ask questions and did not comment on other participants. One crucial factor leading to this phenomenon might be the discussion style in Japanese culture. However, another factor, we thought, might be the physical and temporary limitations of face-to-face communication. In our informal talks with the students, they reported difficulties in coordinating a variety of ideas on reading assignments and then articulating their own ideas in face-to-face discussions although they recognized that collaborative activities were important to advance their knowledge. Furthermore, in our attempt to have them talk in small group settings in a face-to-face context, they could efficiently manage their collaborative works. We thought that CSILE would provide this community with another layer of communication, which is asynchronous, so that they could go beyond the limitations of face-to-face communication.

Community B

Subjects and Community. This community consisted of five M.A. students and an instructor. The instructor had been a faculty member at the university for one and a half years. The students were from different disciplines in the school of education.

Objectives. This course took place as summer sessions from July through September in 1997. In the first class, the instructor introduced the aim of the course and the reading assignment, a book on computing in education written by a professor well known in the area. The students were required to read the book and then discuss ideas in it to consider and design educational environments supported by information technologies.

Instruments. As an attempt of our design experiment approach, we decided to manage this course only online through the World Wide Web (WWW). The existence of face-to-face communication has been one of the factors frequently discussed in CSCW (Computer Supported Cooperative Work) literature. Some studies showed that an e-mail conference system dramatically reduced discussion time dominated by particular individuals and facilitated more productive discourse (e.g., Dubrovsky, Kiesler, & Sethna, 1991). Other studies focused on unique characteristics of asynchronous communication in comparison with face-to-face communication (e.g., Finholt, Sproull, & Kiesler, 1990; Kraut, Galegher, Fish, & Chalfonte, 1992). They suggested that the two types of communication (synchronous and asynchronous) play different roles in conducting complex cognitive tasks and that coordination of the two is crucial. Through our design experiment, we were concerned with what roles the two types of communication played in knowledge building activities and how learners recognized the types of communication in their activities.

Besides the reason that this was part of our design experiment, we had other reasons to manage the class in this manner. First, we had difficulties in managing regular face-to-face meetings in the summer sessions. The participants, including the instructor, had tight schedules in the summer. Second, the network communication was new to most of the students. The instructor thought that this was a good opportunity for the students to involve themselves in such a communication style to discuss their theme (i.e., educational environment supported by information technologies).

Rules and Division of Labor.   One rule applied by the instructor in this course was that the instructor regularly summarized portions of the book so that the students could see what to discuss. Then, the students built their thoughts on the instructor's summaries. In addition to this, they were allowed to start their own discussion if they wanted to do so. The division of labor in this course was somewhat similar to that in Community A. The students were required to read all the materials assigned by the instructor; their main task was then to report their thoughts in the database.

WebCSILE as an Asynchronous Discourse Engine

We set up a World Wide Web server for WebCSILE at the authors' university site. WebCSILE is a WWW version of CSILE 1.5. The network architecture is shown in Fig. 2.2. Although functionalities in WebCSILE were limited in comparison with those of the regular CSILE 1.5, it could be used more widely across different sites with clients across Windows and Macintosh platforms. Since most of the participants in this study had Windows machines and had to access CSILE through the Internet, we decided to use WebCSILE rather than the regular CSILE 1.5. Another reason for the use of WebCSILE was that it was compatible with the Japanese operating system.

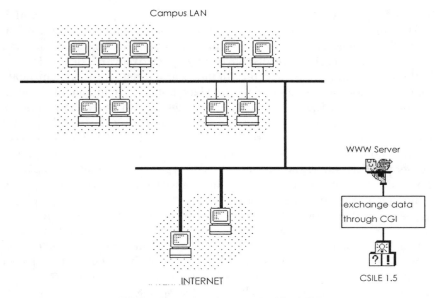

FIG. 2.2. Network architecture for WebCSILE.

Participants in this study could access WebCSILE through the WWW if they had Internet access. Figure 2.3 shows the first page on the Web. The participants were required to type in their username and password and then click on the "Sign On" button. Next, they were given a topic page shown in Fig. 2.4. There were topics for four different communities, as they shared one database. The participants in each community had to choose one topic to contribute to their community. Finally, they could see the title window in which related notes were structured in threads as default. They could change the view among "thread," "author," and "date" options. The "author" view was a list of notes sorted by authors, and the "date" view was a list sorted by dates beginning with the most recent note. Thus, each view provided the participants with different information on the database.

After signing on, the participants could report their thoughts at any window. The left side of the window showed possible options. Participants could type in their thoughts as new notes or comments on others' thoughts. In the text area, they could use Hypertext Markup Language (HTML). If the participants were familiar with HTML, they could visually elaborate their notes. Furthermore, they could put their graphical information in their personal directories so that they could link the graphics in their HTML area of their notes. In addition to its multimedia nature of notes, WebCSILE had another functionality to support participants moving between notes. Figure 2.5 is an example of a WebCSILE note. This WebCSILE note had two different

FIG. 2.3. The window of WebCSILE top page through Netscape.

hyperlinks automatically created by CGI scripts. One type of link was "references." This was a metaphor from journal papers. Participants could jump to the target note on which the note commented. The other type of link was unique in the hypertext structure of the WWW, "notes that refer to this note." This link took participants to notes that referred to the original note. Thus, in WebCSILE, learners' manipulation of asynchronous discourse was supported by its hypertext nature as well as its database functionalities.

CSILE Use With or Without Face-to-Face Communication

Activity Systems in the Two Communities

Here, we describe how each community changed its recognition of learning activities through use of WebCSILE. Based on the Activity Theory

FIG. 2.4. The window of a topic page of WebCSILE through Netscape.

framework (e.g., Bødker, 1996; Engeström, 1993, 1996), we particularly focused our analysis on how rules in their communities were changed, how
their division of labor was changed, and how WebCSILE was deployed within
their ongoing activities.

Community A. Eight students were regularly involved in written discourse on WebCSILE. Through our participatory observation in the course,
the students were found to be "knowledge building goal-oriented" (Ng &
Bereiter, 1991). Although the course theme was not directly related to their
research topics, they all were interested in constructing further arguments
based on the theoretical ideas discussed in the course.

The knowledge building goal-oriented group had been concerned with
learning situations. Their main problem in the lab, some of them reported,

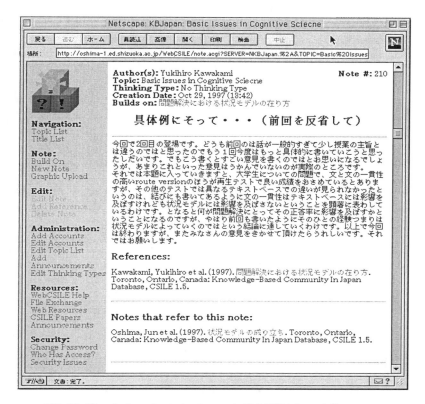

FIG. 2.5. The window of a student's note in WebCSILE through Netscape.

was that they could not efficiently manage ideas through their face-to-face communication. When some good thoughts appeared, they were frequently lost because no one thought to write them down. They needed some collaborative notebooks so that anybody could trace the previous discourse at any time. Another problem they had was that the pattern of turn taking in their face-to-face communication had been mostly centered around the instructor. There had not been many exchanges among students. Division of labor in their face-to-face communication had been distributed between the instructor and the students but not among the students.

Through the deployment of WebCSILE, the knowledge building goal-oriented group engaged in collaborative discourse, which had not been seen in their face-to-face communication. Our interviews revealed that participants in the goal-oriented group recognized WebCSILE as a useful tool for their knowledge advancement. In particular, they valued the following features: (1) the capability for reflecting on their thoughts in written discourse at different times and (2) the fact that they could individually grasp what had been concluded as a group or community.

Knowledge advancement through the use of WebCSILE might stem from a couple of reasons. First, members of the knowledge building goal-oriented group had already recognized their problems in managing their thoughts in the synchronous communication and had been looking for technologies that could support them. Second, the asynchronous communication worked as a channel for the students to exchange their thoughts. The instructor did not often report his thoughts. This fact led the students to communicate more frequently with one another, without the instructor.

Community B. These participants were interested in the design of learning environments supported by computers. Their shared objective was to build their knowledge on learning environments through their collaborative discourse in WebCSILE. Thus, they shared a knowledge building goal.

Because the participants were from a variety of programs at the graduate school of education and most of them had not seen each other before the course, we could not describe rules or division of labor of their activity system before starting the course. Further, they only engaged in the written discourse, without face-to-face communication. Therefore, based on our interviews with them, we describe how they came to realize rules and division of labor through their written discourse communication.

First, the participants recognized the importance and the effectiveness of asynchronous communication. They reported that they could grasp a whole picture of discourse by running through the title view or reading note by note at their convenience. Second, they also reported that they had felt a lack of intensive communication. Although their written discourse could be arranged in the three different views in the database so that the students could reflect on their thoughts in some contexts, they could not be sure how each participant recognized the discourse going on in the database. This "meta" level of discourse is crucial for organizing thoughts, and some studies conclude that such a metadiscourse is usually mediated through oral discourse (e.g., Perkins, 1993). Thus, the solo use of written discourse in the asynchronous communication may not be the best approach to knowledge advancement. Coordination of the two types of discourse should be crucial to sustaining productive discourse.

Discourse Seen in WebCSILE

For describing how progressive discourse in WebCSILE proceeded in each community, we took the case study approach. We chose one example of discourse in each community evaluated as best by two university professors; we then attempted to describe each discourse through the argument framework by Toulmin (1958).

Toulmin's framework of the argument has been applied to collaborative learning research to describe what's going on in students' discourse, or to discern how similar to or far from scientific discourse their discourse is. Eichinger et al. (1991), for instance, investigated how elementary school students managed their ideas through their collaboration in problem solving and then how their discourse appeared based on the argument framework by Toulmin. The results showed that patterns of discourse were critically different from those employed by scientists. Elementary school students attempted to defend their own claims and attack those of others. Scientists, however, did not have clear claims in the initial stage of their discourse. Rather they attempted to qualify their tasks from a variety of points of view and collaboratively considered warrants and backups for each possible claim. Thus, discourse by the experts was found to be socially constructed through distributed expertise, and this aspect was found to be crucial to scientific discourse.

Although the argument framework by Toulmin was a useful tool for us to describe how written discourse was progressing in WebCSILE, we had some difficulties in applying the framework to our data. First, our data were written discourse in university courses and the tasks were ill-structured, unlike the carefully structured task in the Eichinger et al. (1991) study. The students were asked to solve this problem after learning appropriate scientific knowledge on the matter. The task for our participants was to collaboratively advance their knowledge reading assignments. Because of the nature of the task, it was difficult for us to identify alternatives of possible claims. The range of possible claims was very broad and the problem spaces in which the participants were engaged were in a continuous state of flux. For these reasons, we considered the participants' discourse to be based upon the reading assignments and other available resources. Three social scientists (one faculty and two graduate students) read the reading assignments in each community and then evaluated discourse in WebCSILE based on its relevance to the reading assignments.

Second, because the task in which the participants in this study were engaged was not to choose which one of several alternative claims were a correct answer but to create claims, streams of their discourses were multidimensional. Therefore, we described how new claims were related to previous discourse.

Third, since arguments in the discourse were socially constructed through collaboration, the participants sometimes requested others to describe specific components of the argument framework, such as claims ("What do you think of this?"), qualifications ("Is anyone an expert on this?"), and backups ("Does anybody have data or evidence?"). We added these requests as new components of the argument framework to analyze the written discourse.

Discourse in Community A. Appendix A shows the argument framework in a progressive discourse seen in a thread by Community A. This thread consisted of nine notes by six participants created over a period of more than a month. The target argument in reading assignments was focused on concepts of "invariants" and "direct perception" in the affordance theory (e.g., Gibson, 1979). In the first three notes, three different students started three different streams of discourse through their rebuttals, qualifications, and claims. Although the three referred to different aspects of the original argument or discourse in face-to-face context (these are represented as "Ref_1," "Ref_2," and "Ref_3" in Appendix A), students who followed the discourse attempted to construct their understanding through articulation of the three perspectives on the same phenomena (they referred to the instructor's simple demonstration in class).

Discourse in Community B. Appendix B shows the argument framework in the discourse seen in a thread by Community B. This thread consisted of 13 notes created by all the participants in the course during a period of 28 days. The target argument was written on the topic of learner-centered design of learning environments. Besides the characteristics stated in Community A, this discourse had a unique feature. The participants expanded their problem space by approaching the problem from many perspectives rather than by focusing on a few specific aspects with claims and rebuttals. Although the participants actively engaged in their discourse, this discourse was not evaluated by the professors as crucial knowledge advancement.

From our perspective that discourse should be convergent to reach social agreements of participants' understanding, the framework of discourse by Community A might be more ideal than that by Community B. Participants in Community A were more focused on a specific aspect of their reading assignments or face-to-face discourse as their target references. They then approached the discourse from multiple perspectives such as by creating some hypothesis or model and then searching for evidence to support or reject their perspective. Two remarkable characteristics seen in the discourse by Community A in comparison with discourse by Community B were that (1) participants carefully summarized their previous discourse in their face-to-face context (e.g., "what we have reached so far in our class talk was, I guess, . . . "), and then attempted to follow the direction of their face-to-face discourse, and (2) through our interviews with the participants and participatory observation on their face-to-face discourse, we learned that the participants spent time in their face-to-face discourse preparing for discussion in WebCSILE rather than reaching any social agreements.

We found in Study 1 that expert learners tended to coordinate their different communication channels for the purpose of advancing their knowledge. WebCSILE was welcomed as a powerful tool for them to organize different perspectives on their face-to-face discourse. This finding was also supported by the data from Community B, members of which did not engage in face-to-face communication in the course. The students in Community B reported the importance of their face-to-face communication to make their asynchronous communication more progressive or productive. Thus, graduate students as expert learners succeeded in adapting themselves in the IT-supported learning environment through their efforts to collaboratively coordinate their communication channels. Most important is that qualities of their face-to-face communication were changed with the deployment of the new asynchronous communication. The participants missed their meta-layer of discourse, which is very important in intensive decision making.

In summary, results of Study 1 demonstrated the following: First, WebCSILE was useful for expert learners to advance their knowledge in the context of graduate courses. They successfully coordinated the new communication channel with their original activities by changing the roles of their face-to-face discourse to prepare them for the written discourse. Second, as reported by some participants, frequent externalization of their thoughts was quite new even to graduate students. This activity was found to facilitate self-reflection on their previous ideas and collaboration to reach shared understanding through coordination of their various perspectives.

STUDY 2: IMPLEMENTATION OF WebCSILE IN AN UNDERGRADUATE COURSE

In Study 2, we extended target communities to novice learners. We had two study purposes. First, we were concerned with how novice learners made use of CSILE in their course work. Second, we were interested in how novice learners learned in the context where synchronous and asynchronous communication were coordinated by the course instructor. Although this study was not conducted to make direct comparison with the results in Study 1, we thought that we could explore some crucial factors for the successful use of WebCSILE for the improvement of discourse by novice learners.

Community C

Subjects and Community. This community consisted of 30 undergraduate students (sophomores) in a course with an instructor. All students were from the department of computing in education.

Objectives. The main aim of the course was to learn basics in cognitive science, which is particularly related to educational research. The students were required to take part in the instructor's seminar and discuss the topics on WebCSILE.

Instruments. It was difficult for the instructor to have all students actively participate in discussion face-to-face because of the class size. Unlike the instructor's expectation, face-to-face communication in his previous courses had been the traditional "knowledge-transmission" model of learning. Written discourse on the computer network, however, was expected to produce opportunities for the students to communicate in a more flexible way. Students were required to report their thoughts in WebCSILE and then articulate their thoughts for the purpose of being prepared for their final reports. With regard to access to the Internet, they all had their own laptop computers with Local Access Network (LAN) cards so that they could access the network at any time in designated places within their campus.

Rules and Division of Labor. As is usually seen in any class at Japanese universities, undergraduates had a culture based on a "knowledge-transmission" model of learning. The students reported, in a survey conducted during the course, that they perceived themselves as recipients of knowledge from the instructor. They had not yet created a culture of collaboration to attain mutual understanding in the class. Their main activities in courses they had taken before had been organized as individual tasks.

To give students the opportunity to intentionally engage in knowledge building through collaborative articulation of their thoughts, the instructor decided to use WebCSILE as a discourse engine in the course. This course took place in the second semester consisting of 15 weeks. The instructor had four face-to-face meetings in which he presented educational studies in cognitive science and asked the students to report their thoughts in the database between the meetings (usually two or three weeks apart).

What Happened in the Community of Novice Learners

In this section, we first describe the participants' performances in Web-CSILE to clarify how they used WebCSILE as a tool for their knowledge advancement. We next describe their activity systems through use of the technology in their activities.

Statistical Indices of WebCSILE Use

Table 2.1 shows frequencies of reported notes in isolation and threads.[1] In Communities A and B, numbers of single notes were almost equal to numbers of thread notes. In contrast, in Community C, the number of thread notes

---

[1]We define threads here as sequences of commentaries that do not include the first notes if the notes were for summarizing the contents as anchors.

TABLE 2.1
Note Frequencies*

	Thread Notes	Single Notes
Community A	34	19
Community B	25	24
Community C	106	59

*Thread notes versus single notes.

was almost twice the number of single notes. Thus, undergraduate students in Community C were more engaged in turn taking in the written discourse.

An advantage of asynchronous communication is that a stream of talk or turn taking does not have to be temporarily constrained. Figure 2.6 shows such an advantage of the written discourse in the asynchronous communication. The figure is an example of a title view sorted by thread. Each line manifests a note with its title, note number (in order to be reported), and author's name. First, the stream of turn taking is multidimensional. Starting with the first note #140, three comments followed the note (#143, #149, and #156). Further, in the third stream through note #156, two comments followed. Second, asynchronous commenting in each stream should be addressed as well. As we can see in the note numbers, these notes in each stream were not reported continuously. (If the notes were reported continuously, the numbers would be continuous.) Thus, asynchronous communication tools can provide participants with a new communication channel by which they could control multiple threads of discourses.

For the analysis of asynchronous turn taking, we assigned a value of how each note was asynchronously reported using the following calculation:

$$\text{asynchronicity value} = (\text{note number assigned to each comment})$$
$$- (\text{note number assigned to the target note}) - 1.[2]$$

Then, a one-way analysis of variance (ANOVA) on mean values of thread notes among the three communities was conducted. The results showed that a mean value in Community C was significantly higher than those in Community A and B, $F(2, 112) = 5.40$, $p < .05$, (Fig. 2.7).[3]

---

[2]The first notes in threads were not considered as comments.

[3]The analysis was affected by the size of the communities. The more learners that were engaged in asynchronous discourse, the higher the asynchronicity values. One possible way of reducing the effect of community size may be to reduce the asynchronicity value of each thread note by average numbers of single notes. This is based on the assumption that single notes were written at equal pace between thread notes. On the basis of the data we had in this study, this reduction of the asynchronicity value would make the original differences more remarkable.

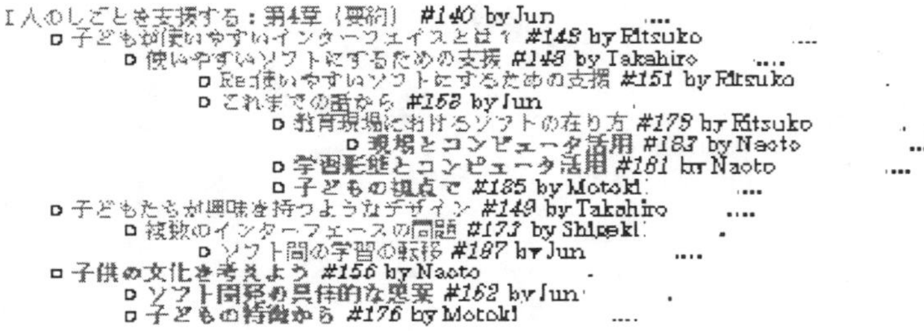

I 人のしごとを支援する：第4章（要約）#140 by Jun   ....
  □ 子どもが使いやすいインターフェイスとは？ #148 by Ritsuko   ....
    □ 使いやすいソフトにするための支援 #143 by Takahiro   ....
      □ Re:使いやすいソフトにするための支援 #151 by Ritsuko   .
        □ これまでの要から、#153 by Jun
          □ 教育現場におけるソフトの在り方 #179 by Ritsuko   .
            □ 現場とコンピュータ活用 #183 by Naoto   ....
          □ 学習形態とコンピュータ活用 #181 by Naoto   ....
            □ 子どもの視点で #185 by Motoki   ....
        □ 子どもたちが興味を持つようなデザイン #149 by Takahiro   ....
          □ 複数のインターフェースの問題 #173 by Shigeki   .
            □ ソフト間の学習の転移 #197 by Jun   ....
      □ 子供の文化を考えよう #156 by Naoto   .
        □ ソフト同志の具体的な思案 #162 by Jun   .
          □ 子どもの特徴から #176 by Motoki   ....

FIG. 2.6. An example of turn taking in a thread.

Activity System in Community C

Community C consisted of 30 undergraduate students who were major-ing in computing in education. Because they usually met in the class but did not talk about the contents in the whole group, patterns of their face-to-face communication were analyzed based on our sociometrics question-naire conducted during the course. Comparison of the synchronous and the asynchronous communications showed that the students engaged in totally different communication patterns through the two channels. In the asyn-chronous communication through WebCSILE, the participants were com-menting on thoughts by others with whom they did not frequently commu-nicate face-to-face.

As learning went on, the students developed three types of goals. One group, which adopted a "learning goal-oriented" (Ng & Bereiter, 1991) approach, was frequently engaged in written discourse to understand the contents of the course. In the questionnaire conducted in the class, they reported their recognition on the importance of the asynchronous communication tool, monitoring their own learning, and problems of their learning activities to effectively use the technology. There was a transitional group that was engaged in the written discourse in some threads. In the questionnaire, the transitional group reported difficulties in using the tech-nology to make their learning more productive and to reflect on their own learning. The final group consisted of participants who rarely participated in the written discourse. In the questionnaire, participants in this final group reported how problematic it was for them to access the homepage for the course, but they did not report any reflections on their own learning.

In Community C, the learning goal-oriented and the transitional groups made use of WebCSILE as a tool for knowledge advancement. Through the new asynchronous communication channel they succeeded in expanding their learning community. They came to recognize that learning through

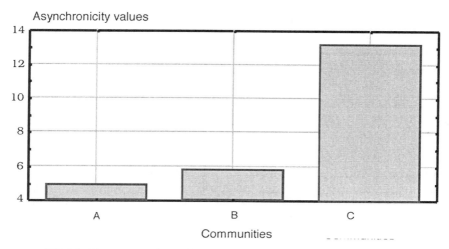

FIG. 2.7. Mean scores of asynchronous turn takings seen in the three communities.

collaboration with others was crucial to knowledge advancement. However, the third "task goal-oriented group" was not aware of learning as knowledge construction. They did not think that communication with others led them to further advancement of knowledge.

Discourse in Community C

From results in Study 2, it was found that undergraduate students had difficulty in managing asynchronous discourse. (We will discuss the reasons for this later). Typical discourses seen in Community C were simple turn-takings such as qualification–request–qualification and claim–request–claim. Someone asked a question and then another answered it in such threads. However, as learning went on, a few important discourses were evaluated as progressive by university professors. Appendix C shows such a discourse framework. The thread consisted of eight notes by four students and the instructor over a period of 18 days. They debated: (1) how we transfer our knowledge and (2) whether there are general strategies for knowledge transfer. They discussed the mechanism of knowledge transfer and then debated ideas of domain-specific principles of knowledge and general problem-solving strategies to reach a shared understanding.

The argument framework in the undergraduates' WebCSILE discourse suggests to us that novice learners had difficulties in engaging in knowledge advancement. However, they could gradually adapt themselves to the new environment by collaboratively articulating their discourse. This result suggests that learners will create their own cultures of learning when they are exposed to a new learning environment. This culture will be more productive if the students have learning or knowledge building goals and if they receive sufficient support both from the system and their instructors.

Discussion

In Study 2, we deployed WebCSILE in an undergraduate course for the purpose of investigating how novice learners could make use of the new asynchronous communication tools to advance their knowledge and how they coordinated their different communication channels to make their discourse more productive or progressive. Even though they did not frequently engage in asynchronous discourse, it was found that even novices could gradually create a culture of learning as they kept on using WebCSILE. Here, through the comparisons of results between Study 1 (experts) and Study 2 (novices), we attempt to speculate on some crucial factors that would make the novices' knowledge advancement more productive.

First, even though the undergraduate students were engaged in both synchronous and asynchronous communication, it was found that the role of their synchronous channel was quite different from the graduates' in its quality. As we discussed in Study 1, the graduates recognized different roles of synchronous and asynchronous communications in their activities. Students in Community A managed synchronous communication to clarify directions of discourse that could be conducted in their asynchronous communication. Students in Community B clearly felt that they had missed such a discourse when they had been engaged in asynchronous communication only. In contrast, the undergraduates in Study 2 did not report the importance of different roles for the two channels. From our participatory class observations, we found them not to be involved in metacognitive or reflective discourse on their written discourse. Further, as stated in our sociometric analysis, their communication maps in synchronous and asynchronous communications were totally different from each other. The results suggest that their synchronous communication was disjointed from their asynchronous communication. Although the synchronous and asynchronous channels were both helpful for them to expand their discourse among more friends, the availability of the two channels did not frequently lead them to more productive discourse.

Second, it was found that novice learners in the study had learning goals or task goals rather than knowledge building goals. The students attempted to "understand" what they had listened to in class, but they did not engage in knowledge building activities. A relatively large number of students in the course claimed that they did not sufficiently understand the purpose of writing their thoughts on the computer network. What they reported in WebCSILE was mainly what they thought, what they felt, and experiences they had related to the topics they had studied. These discourses were useful for them to reach a deeper understanding but not sufficient for them to manipulate their knowledge as objects. This may be because, to function like expert learners, novices may need numerous information resources, strategic knowledge to organize productive inquiry, and the ability to monitor their activities.

Information Resources and Background Knowledge. Compared with the graduate students as expert learners, the undergraduates as novice learners missed background knowledge in the domain that they did learn and discuss. The instructor provided them with four different cognitive studies as information resources and explained the basic concepts needed for the students to understand the studies. However, such information resources were not sufficiently organized and represented as WWW homepages in the system so that the students could reflect on what they had learned and what they had not understood. Thus, the materials provided to the students in synchronous and asynchronous communication were insufficient in their amount and structure.

Skills for Scientific Discourse. As seen in the comparison of discourse frameworks between novices and experts and the data from the questionnaire, the novice learners did miss some important skills for scientific discourse and strategic knowledge for managing their discourse, such as using metadiscourse. With respect to skills for scientific discourse, the novice learners did not recognize how to represent their thoughts through scientific discourse, for instance, based on an argument framework. Their discourse was not found to be progressive because it did not have references, claims, and rebuttals in particular. They seemed to hesitate to articulate thoughts in such a way that others could criticize or share their ideas. In addition, the novices did not take multiple perspectives on their problems. Consideration of problems from multiple perspectives naturally generates rebuttals and multiple claims. Through such multiple perspective taking, the experts further attempted to converge their thoughts through qualification, warrants, and backups.

With regard to strategic knowledge for scientific discourse, one of the most remarkable differences in discourse between the experts and the novices was that the novices did not clearly put metadiscourse (e.g., Crismore, 1990) in their writing. Strategic knowledge for metadiscourse was found to be important for participants in focusing on a specific aspect of an argument from a specific perspective. The graduate students as expert learners in Study 1 were mainly using two strategies of metadiscourse in constructing their discourse on the computer network. The first was a citation strategy, such as paraphrasing or summarizing discourse in their face-to-face or original arguments in their reading assignments. The second was an abstract strategy, such as digesting what they wanted to discuss in their writing. Through these efforts, they succeeded in keeping multiple perspectives on specific problems, which eventually converged into their shared understanding. In contrast, written discourse by the novices did not show these efforts. They did not clearly identify what problems they were discussing or how they would solve them. No one requested such a qualification or specification in their written discourse. We need to consider instructional support for improving novices' knowledge of their scientific discourse.

EDUCATIONAL IMPLICATIONS

Through the two consecutive studies, we have seen how expert or novice learners made use of a new technology (i.e., WebCSILE) in their learning contexts. The results in Study 1 investigating expert learners' activities showed that the expert learners recognized differences in qualities of synchronous and asynchronous communication. In struggling to coordinate the two channels, they employed the synchronous one to organize their thoughts so that they could follow up in the asynchronous channel. The results of the second study with novice learners showed that (1) some novices could gradually engage in their knowledge advancement discourse and recognize the importance of WebCSILE as a tool but that (2) their knowledge resources, such as domain-specific knowledge, skills for scientific discourse, and strategic knowledge for the discourse, were still insufficient for conducting knowledge building activities. In this final section, we discuss some ideas on instructional interventions for improving novices' discourse in the IT-supported learning environment.

Project-Based Learning. For novice learners, activities in a new IT-supported learning environment are not sufficiently organized because they require doing something new but do not specify exactly what to do. Novices need some guidance of what to do for what purpose. One observed difference in activities between experts and novices was that the experts saw their learning as problem solving or as a project to create shared knowledge. The novices, however, saw their learning as a product of their problem solving (Bereiter & Scardamalia, 1989). Unlike a naive definition of "projects," the experts' projects had some conditions. First, the projects they engaged in were generically collaborative. People who took different perspectives were welcome; then efforts were made to converge those multiple perspectives. The group consisted of people who had different expertise in their shared domain at different levels (e.g., Brown, Ash, Rutherford, Nakagawa, Gordon, & Campione, 1993; Brown, & Campione, 1994). Second, projects were directed by knowledge building goals, that is, the expert learners did not see any final goals that ended their discourse. Rather, their problem solving activities were ill-structured or emergent goals-oriented. As they solved any problem, they then found new problems. Thus, their shared goals were to continue to advance their knowledge through their discourse.

To have novice learners conduct project-based learning as experts do, we have to prepare some activity guidance so that they can acquire different knowledge resources and then contribute to their discourse from multiple perspectives. The most typical pitfall in conducting such project-based learning may be that the organized activities are directed by clear, concrete goals such as creating products or finding one answer. If the activities are constrained by such goals, discourse would not be progressive or sustained. As found in the experts' activities in this study, we should focus the activities on knowledge building or creating arguments on their knowledge-based problems. This type of commitment to discourse is thought to be the most crucial factor for discourse in science (e.g., Bereiter, 1994; Popper, 1972). Face-to-face discourse should play a crucial role in managing the organized activities. As a metadiscourse channel, face-to-face communication would be used for monitoring total progress in knowledge advancement by learners and for providing opportunities for learners to exchange emergent problems that direct their progressive discourse in the future. Further, ITs such as CSILE would play the role of providing representations of discourse so that learners in the organized activities could reflect on what they have done and on their emergent goals.

Materials for Learning. We need to provide learners with the resource materials they need to conduct their knowledge advancement. There may be two streams of consideration that we should finally coordinate. The first is that the instructors' side should create such materials for learners. We expect the learners to construct their knowledge based on their learning the prepared materials. What we should keep in mind here is that we should not rigorously control the direction of their learning. All that may be required is to provide the basic materials by which learners can grasp the key ideas in target domains. The second is that learners themselves should search for and create materials for their own learning. For this to happen, we need strong search engines and material databases. WWW resources or any other mobile media are candidates. WWW resources prepared by reliable experts, in particular, may be a good resource of information in specific domains of interest.

Construction of materials would be mediated through face-to-face and asynchronous discourse in learning. Learners can discuss what sorts of materials or resources are needed to conduct further knowledge advancement so that we as instructors provide some hotlinks to get necessary information on a WWW page. Further, in WebCSILE, learners can easily create hyperlinks to WWW resources in their notes. They, as learners, can create their own materials as they conduct knowledge advancement on a computer network.

Scaffolding for Scientific Discourse. From results in the studies, it was found that novice learners need scaffolding both for discourse skills and strategic knowledge. With respect to skills for scientific discourse, novice learners were found not to invoke a framework of discourse as arguments or to share knowledge objects with others. Although an example of rhetorical representation of scientific discourse, Toulmin's framework of arguments would work as a tool for us to create knowledge as an object to share and articulate. It may be effective to have novice learners use a specific framework of discourse such as Toulmin's as shared rules of representing their knowledge (e.g., Streiz, Hanneman, & Thüring, 1989).

Nonetheless, it seems fair to say that discourse for knowledge advancement does not happen only by providing novice learners with specific framework of discourse as rules. The discourse framework itself is just a rhetorical technique of representing our thoughts. The rhetorical representation should be articulated through reflective thinking by learners. For reflective thinking, we should support novice learners in improving their strategic knowledge for scientific discourse (i.e., comprehending, monitoring, and revising their discourse as arguments). In studies of discourse comprehension and written discourse, some strategic knowledge used by expert learners in learning have been articulated (e.g., Bereiter & Bird, 1985; Bereiter & Scardamalia, 1987; van Dijk & Kintsch, 1983). What these studies addressed is reflective manipulation of knowledge between rhetorical and content spaces, that is, metacognitive activities for creating arguments in scientific discourse. We think that the most important scaffolding by instructors is support for the metacognitive manipulation of discourse. We as instructors should consider how we can have novice learners participate in metacognitive manipulation of their discourse in face-to-face or asynchronous communication. In such efforts, knowledge media provided by technologies such as CSILE should work as powerful engines for instruction.

APPENDIX A

An Example Argument Framework of Written Discourse in a Thread by Community A[4]

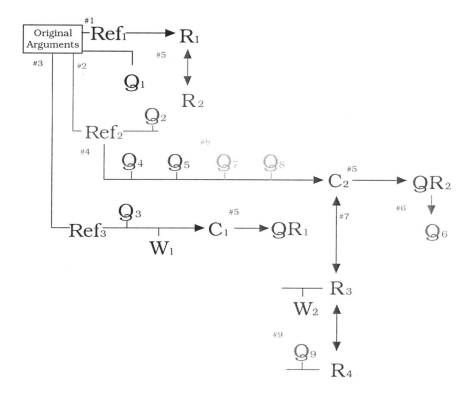

APPENDIX B

An Example of Argument Framework of Written Discourse in a Thread by Community B

Numbers with # show the order of notes to be reported. Ref, C, Q, W, B, R, CoR, QR CR represent Reference, Claim, Qualification, Warrant, Backup, Rebuttal, Confirmation Request, Qualification Request, and Claim Request, respectively.

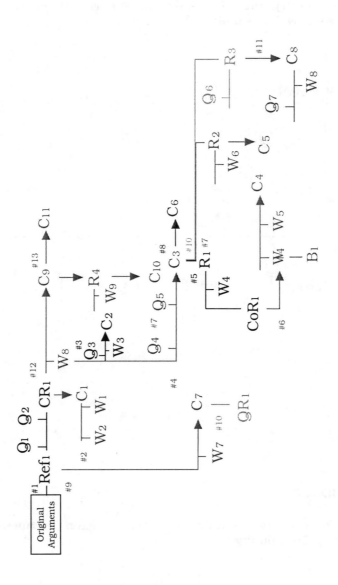

APPENDIX C

An Example of Argument Framework of Written Discourse in a Thread by Community C

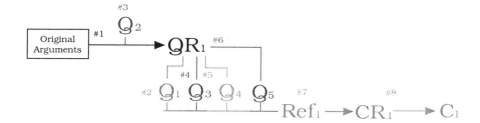

REFERENCES

Bereiter, C. (1994). Implication of postmodernism for science education: A critique. *Educational Psychologist, 29*, 3–12.

Bereiter, C., & Bird, M. (1985). Use of thinking aloud in identification and teaching of reading comprehension strategies. *Cognition and Instruction, 2*, 131–156.

Bereiter, C., & Scardamalia, M. (1987). *The psychology of written composition.* Hillsdale, NJ: Lawrence Erlbaum Associates.

Bereiter, C., & Scardamalia, M. (1989). Intentional learning as a goal of instruction. In L. B. Resnick (Ed.), *Knowing, learning, and instruction: Essays in honor of Robert Glaser* (pp. 361–392). Hillsdale, NJ: Lawrence Erlbaum Associates.

Bereiter, C., & Scardamalia, M. (1993). *Surpassing ourselves: An inquiry into the nature and implications of expertise.* Chicago: Open Court.

Bødker, S. (1996). Applying activity theory to video analysis: How to make sense of video data in human–computer interaction. In B. A. Nardi (Ed.), *Context and consciousness: Activity theory and human–computer interaction* (pp. 147–174). Cambridge, MA: MIT Press.

Brown, A. L. (1992). Design experiments: Theoretical and methodological challenges in evaluating complex interventions in classroom settings. *Journal of the Learning Sciences, 2*, 141–178.

Brown, A. L., Ash, D., Rutherford, M., Nakagawa, K., Gordon, A., & Campione, J. C. (1993). Distributed expertise in the classroom. In G. Salomon (Ed.), *Distributed cognitions: Psychological and educational considerations* (pp. 188–228). New York: Cambridge University Press.

Brown, A. L., & Campione, J. C. (1994). Guided discovery in a community of learners. In K. McGilley (Ed.), *Classroom lessons: Integrating cognitive theory and classroom practice* (pp. 229–270). Cambridge, MA: MIT Press.

Collins, A. (1990). *Toward a design science of education* (Tech. Rep. No. 1). New York: Center for Technology in Education.

Crismore, A. (1990). Metadiscourse and discourse processes: Interactions and issues. *Discourse Processes, 13*, 191–205.

Dubrovsky, V. J., Kiesler, S., & Sethna, B. N. (1991). The equalization phenomenon: Status effects in computer-mediated and face-to-face decision-making groups. *Human–Computer Interaction, 6*, 119–146.

Eichinger, D. C., Anderson, C. W., Palincsar, A. S., & David, Y. M. (1991, April). *An illustration of the roles of content knowledge, scientific argument, and social norms in collaborative problem solving*. Paper presented at the annual meeting of the American Educational Research Association, Chicago.

Engeström, Y. (1987). *Learning by expanding: An activity-theoretical approach to developmental research*. Helsinki: Orienta-Konsultit Oy.

Engeström, Y. (1993). Developmental studies of work as a testbench of activity theory: The case of primary care medical practice. In S. Chaiklin & J. Lave (Eds.), *Understanding practice: Perspectives on activity and context* (pp. 64–103). Cambridge, MA: Cambridge University Press.

Engeström, Y. (1996). Innovative organizational learning in medical and legal settings. In L. M. W. Martin, K. Nelson, & E. Tobach (Eds.), *Sociocultural psychology: Theory and practice of doing and knowing* (pp. 326–356). New York: Cambridge University Press.

Finholt, T., Sproull, L., & Kiesler, S. (1990). Communication and performance in ad hoc task groups. In J. Galegher, R. E. Kraut, & C. Egido (Eds.), *Intellectual teamwork: Social and technological foundations of cooperative work* (pp. 291–325). Hillsdale, NJ: Lawrence Erlbaum Associates.

Gibson, J. J. (1979). *The ecological approach to visual perception*. Boston: Houghton Mifflin.

Kraut, R., Galegher, J., Fish, R., & Chalfonte, B. (1992). Task requirements and media choice in collaborative writing. *Human–Computer Interaction, 7*, 375–407.

Leontiev, A. N. (1981). The problem of activity in psychology. In J. V. Wertsch (Ed.), *The concept of activity in Soviet psychology*. Armonk, NY: Sharpe.

Ng, E., & Bereiter, C. (1991). Three levels of goal orientation in learning. *Journal of the Learning Sciences, 1*, 243–271.

Oshima, J., Bereiter, C., & Scardamalia, M. (1995, October). *Information-access characteristics for high conceptual progress in a computer-networked learning environment*. Paper presented at the Computer Support for Collaborative Learning '95, Bloomington, IN.

Oshima, J., Scardamalia, M., & Bereiter, C. (1996). Collaborative learning processes associated with high and low conceptual progress. *Instructional Science, 24*, 125–155.

Perkins, D. N. (1993). Person-plus: A distributed view of thinking and learning. In G. Salomon (Ed.), *Distributed cognitions: Psychological and educational considerations* (pp. 88–110). Cambridge, MA: Cambridge University Press.

Popper, K. R. (1972). *Objective knowledge: An evolutionary approach*. Oxford: Clarendon Press.

Scardamalia, M., & Bereiter, C. (1991). Higher levels of agency for children in knowledge building: A challenge for the design of new knowledge media. *Journal of the Learning Sciences, 1*, 37–68.

Scardamalia, M., & Bereiter, C. (1993). Technologies for knowledge-building discourse. *Communications for the ACM, 36*(5), 37–41.

Scardamalia, M., & Bereiter, C. (1994). Computer support for knowledge-building communities. *The Journal of the Learning Sciences, 3*, 265–283.

Scardamalia, M., & Bereiter, C. (1996). Student communities for the advancement of knowledge. *Communications of the ACM, 39*(4), 36–37.

Scardamalia, M., Bereiter, C., Brett, C., Burtis, P. J., Calhoun, C., & Smith-Lea, N. (1992). Educational applications of a networked communal database. *Interactive Learning Environments, 2*, 45–71.

Scardamalia, M., Bereiter, C., & Lamon, M. (1994). CSILE: Trying to bring students into world 3. In K. McGilley (Ed.), *Classroom lessons: Integrating cognitive theory and classroom practice* (pp. 201–228). Cambridge, MA: MIT Press.

Scardamalia, M., Bereiter, C., McLean, R. S., Swallow, J., & Woodruff, E. (1989). Computer-supported intentional learning environments. *Journal of Educational Computing Research, 5*, 51–68.

Streiz, N., Hanneman, J., & Thüring, M. (1989). From ideas and arguments to hyperdocuments: Traveling through activity space. *Proceedings of ACM Hypertext* (pp. 343–364). New York: ACM Press.

Toulmin, S. (1958). *The uses of argument*. New York: Cambridge University Press.

van Dijk, T. A., & Kintsch, W. (1983). *Strategies of discourse comprehension*. new York, NY: Academic Press.

TRACKING THE EVOLUTION OF TECHNOLOGY USES

James A. Levin

University of Illinois, Urbana-Champaign

The Oshima and Oshima chapter describes case studies of the uses of a web-enabled collaborative learning environment (WebCSILE) in Japanese university courses. In some of these cases, the desired goal of fostering "progressive discourse" was achieved; in other cases it was not.

One lesson to be learned from this chapter is that the use of any instructional technology does not guarantee the accomplishment of instructional goals—the learning environment contains many elements and the technologies used are only a part of that larger environment. Another lesson is that a given technology has different impacts on different kinds of students. The authors found a difference in the uses of WebCSILE by graduate students and undergraduate students.

One key issue for this line of research is how uses evolve over time—the case studies suggest that during the initial uses studied, there was a developmental sequence as students and faculty learned the technology and discovered its strengths and weaknesses. Presumably this process would continue—students and faculty using WebCSILE for a second course would continue to change. And the developmental process would continue at an organizational level—as such uses become known more widely in a given university or department, the uses even by relative novices would be different than when it is unknown.

Part of the difficulty of conducting research on new technologies is that while these developmental changes are occurring, the technologies themselves change. So while these studies were conducted with interactions based on CSILE 1.5, by the time this book is published, there will be a new version of CSILE, as well as version 1.0 of some newer collaborative learning technology. Oshima and Oshima do a good job of focusing on aspects of the learning that have implications beyond the specifics of this particular technology, lessons that can be applied when most of the details have changed with yet newer and more powerful learning media.

This chapter points to difficulties that learners have in integrating a new technology into their constellation of skills and knowledge about how to learn. One productive line of research suggested by these case studies is further study of this process of learning to use a new learning technology, so that we can better support the metalearning of newer learning technologies in the future.

In the context of other studies of CSILE, this study adds to evidence of the similar impact of that technology on learning across different cultures. Although such findings of universality are valuable, it is also interesting to use the body of studies of such a technology across different cultures as a way to discover the unique uses of the "same" technology in different cultures as well. Something as simple as the use of emoticons in e-mail can vary quite strikingly between cultures (Americans use :-) while Japanese use ^^ for "smiling faces"). The initial content lines of e-mail messages also are quite different between cultures (Americans start out with a salutation phrase— "Dear Taku"; Japanese start with a personal introduction statement— "This is Sugimoto at U. Tokyo") (Sugimoto & Levin, 1999).

Why is it useful to focus on differences in the uses of technologies in different cultures? Knowing about these differences makes it easier to predict which uses will actually work in a given culture. Knowledge about differences also makes it easier to teach someone in a given culture about a particular technology use. But probably more important in the long run is that intercultural activities can be designed that draw upon the differences as a resource rather than a barrier. This point was made in the early 1980s in the InterCultural Learning Network project, which involved students in solving problems common to their own locations in California and Illinois in the United States, in Japan, in Israel, and in Mexico (Cohen, Levin, & Riel, 1985; Levin, Riel, Miyake, & Cohen, 1987; Waugh, Miyake, Levin, & Cohen, 1988).

Whereas different cultures face similar problems, they take different approaches to solving those problems. The differences can be a valuable source of innovative ideas for better solving the problems in each place, and electronic network environments can allow learners to serve as mediators between the experts in the different cultures. For example, each of the places in the InterCultural Learning Network faced the problem of shortage of drinkable water. Because of the cultural and physical differences, different approaches were used at each site (as well as some shared approaches). Once each site reported what was done at their location, each site could use the descriptions of the other sites as a source of plausible solutions, which the learners in each site could then investigate to see which could be used at their own sites. When questioned by local experts on aspects of a proposed novel (for that site) approach, the learners could pass those questions along to the learners at the remote sites who could ask their own local experts.

Drawing upon the diversity provided by new communication media allows it to be used more widely to contextualize and motivate learning since the comparison between what we do and what others do spans the entire spectrum of domains. The use of a web-enabled collaborative learning environment such as the one studied in this chapter may become even more powerful when used to connect distant learners as well as those in the same location if diversity is seen as a resource instead of a barrier and if learning activities are designed to draw upon that resource of diversity.

REFERENCES

Cohen, M., Levin, J. A., & Riel, M. M. (1985). *The world as functional learning environment: An InterCultural Learning Network* (ITL Rep. No. 7). La Jolla, CA: Interactive Technology Laboratory.

Levin, J. A., Riel, M., Miyake, N., & Cohen, M. (1987). Education on the electronic frontier: Teleapprenticeships in globally distributed educational contexts. *Contemporary Educational Psychology, 12,* 254–260.

Sugimoto, T., & Levin, J. A. (1999). Multiple literacies and multimedia: A comparison of Japanese and American uses of the Internet. In C. Self & G. Hawisher (Eds.), *Global literacies and the World-wide Web* (pp. 133–153). London: Routledge.

Waugh, M., Miyake, N., Levin, J. A., & Cohen, M. (1988). *Problem solving interactions on electronic networks.* Paper presented at the annual meeting of the American Educational Research Association, New Orleans.

CROSS-CULTURAL ADAPTATION OF EDUCATIONAL TECHNOLOGY

Xiaodong Lin
Vanderbilt University

Giyoo Hatano
Keio University

Two research questions were addressed by Oshima & Oshima's study of CSILE in Japan: (1) how the asynchronous communication in CSILE, with or without face-to-face communication, changes learners' discourse and knowledge advancement and (2) what scaffolds could support novice learners engaging in productive discourse in the CSILE environment. We noticed the following findings to be quite interesting:

- The expert learners were able to use CSILE to improve their knowledge building activities; they recognized the usefulness of such a technology tool. In addition, they changed their roles assigned for face-to-face discourse in order to better prepare for CSILE communication. They used their CSILE discourse for self-reflection and identifying areas for improvement and adjustment.
- The novice learners, who used CSILE frequently, recognized the usefulness of the tool. Those who effectively used CSILE set learning goals for themselves instead of task performance goals and were able to gradually adapt themselves to the CSILE learning environment by collaboratively articulating their discourse. Their synchronous and asynchronous communication became totally different.
- The novice learners had a difficult time changing to a culture in which knowledge was built on argumentation, instead of knowledge telling. Lack of background domain knowledge may contribute to their difficulties in building arguments and in fully taking advantage of the information provided by the instructor.

We comment on the above findings from the following three perspectives: (1) multiple functionality of educational technology tools, (2) interaction between culture and technology artifacts, and (3) our learning from the Japanese application of CSILE. We conclude our commentary by pointing out some issues that are not adequately dealt with in the chapter by Oshima and Oshima.

MULTIPLE FUNCTIONALITY OF EDUCATIONAL TECHNOLOGY TOOLS

We start with the notion of multiple functionality of tools in general, and of educational technology in particular. Usually a tool or an artifact is designed to be used in a specific way and is expected to be most useful in that way. However, as Suchman (1991) and others have demonstrated, the same tool may actually be used in different ways when it is put in different contexts. That is, tools mediate human actions in multiple ways. Even if a tool is constructed for a particular purpose, it may be used for other purposes as well. By using it in different contexts and different ways, we can learn its potentialities or multiple functionality.

We may go a step further to claim that some tools should be, by design, flexible and adaptable rather than rigid and overly prescriptive, because their users have different expectations and goals for using them. In other words, these tools should allow their users to improvise in response to situational demands.

Educational technology tools are extremely variable in terms of functions, because their use is mediated by teachers and students who have different mental models about and needs for learning. Traditionally, the purpose of designing educational technology tools has been to induce targeted changes in student knowledge and skills. Tools tend to be designed in overly rigid ways since they are aimed at teaching certain skills in a specific environment (Lin et al., 1995), that is, the tools are usually not designed to adapt themselves to students' learning in contexts and emergent cultural needs. However, such rigid design features may not support the adaptation of tools in general, especially generic kinds of tools, such as CSILE and other communication tools.

The importance of adopting flexible designs was shown especially clearly by a case study that examined how a fifth grade Hong Kong mathematics teachers responded to the introduction of a technology artifact from the U.S., called The Adventures of Jasper Woodbury (Lin, 2001a). This technology artifact is a video-based narrative that embodies American ideas about learning math in realistically complex, problem solving contexts (Cognition & Technology Group At Vanderbilt, 1997). The use of Jasper in

Hong Kong looked different from its use in the United States, because the tool is flexible and provides affordances for adapting it to the cultural norms and expectations of that society. The types of adaptations we observed in a Hong Kong classroom would not have been possible, if the Jasper material had relied exclusively on specific lesson plans or scripts of teaching practice developed by the designers. We believe it is important to provide the kind of instructional designs that can help teachers and students flexibly adapt the instruction to their own culture, where "culture" includes differences in the goals, contexts, and other artifacts of the community, school, and classroom within as well as between nations (e.g., Lin & Schwartz, accepted).

Having said that flexible tools make adaptations possible, we point out that very flexible tools with a generic purpose, such as CSILE, also have a few potential problems. A danger of such generic and flexible tools is that learning goals are forgotten when we rely on them, more often than when we use tools that have clear and strong domain-specific learning goals, such as the Jasper mathematics problem solving series. For example, when CSILE is used in the American classrooms, discussions may remain at a very superficial level unless the tool is integrated into the overall curriculum goals and instructional activities (Lamon et al., 1996). Furthermore, teachers have to monitor students' discussions and help the students deepen them (e.g., Scardamalia & Bereiter, 1991). Three kinds of teacher competence are fundamental in this enterprise: (1) teachers' content knowledge, (2) their critical questioning ability, and (3) their ability to provide social support to students throughout the course of discourse learning. In the United States, we know, when teachers lack sufficient content knowledge, their feedback on students' discourse tends to take a general form, such as: "I like your ideas" or "I like what everybody has said here" (Scardamalia, Bereiter, & Lamon, 1998). The quality control of the learning process is weak, and opportunities for conceptual deepening and growth are seldom recognized and exploited. As a result, higher level discussions do not occur often. We wonder how much knowledge and skills the instructors in Oshima and Oshima's studies possessed, what roles they played in the CSILE learning environment, and whether these factors affected Oshima and Oshima's findings about the novices learners. It would also be interesting to investigate how different kinds of teachers' knowledge and skills affect knowledge building and discourse in the CSILE environment.

A related challenge for generic and flexible tools is how to constrain a variety of activities by imposing an overall framework, so that students can see where they are going. How engaging in various learning activities relates to the construction of "big ideas." Using CSILE in developing a group knowledge-building environment is like using a word processing tool to write this paper. Its advantage is that we can write anything we want and move paragraphs around freely with its flexibility; however, we can see only one screen at a time. Without presenting and laying out all the pages we cannot make sense of where we are going, what are our "big ideas," and how our ideas have developed as writing goes on. Only when a framework or the main idea of the paper is provided, will we be able to coherently connect each screen or each section to it, instead of generating isolated thoughts.

Similarly, students may be involved in the act of discussing through CSILE without realizing how the discussion activities fit into the overall goals of learning. The discontinuities between the synchronous and asynchronous discussions found in the Oshima and Oshima studies suggest that some kind of framework may need to be provided so that synchronous and asynchronous discussions are better integrated. Experts usually have a framework that enables them to see the CSILE discussion as problem solving within that framework or in relation to big ideas. Novices, in contrast, usually see learning activities in pieces and bits, instead of in an integrated manner (as shown, for instance, by Chi, Glaser, & Rees, 1982). To help teachers and students develop such a framework, Schwartz and his colleagues have developed a software shell called STAR Legacy (see Schwartz, Lin, Brophy, & Bransford, 1999). This software shell makes explicit the learning cycles for complex content learning and discussion and has modular components that afford the inclusion of various additional technology tools and resources. Such an integration could provide a balance between flexibility and struc-ture for generic technology tools, such as CSILE. Would the potential of CSILE tool be fuller utilized if combined with the Legacy learning environ-ment? We are very interested in learning what are other kinds of tools that Oshima and Oshima suggest to provide a stronger framework for CSILE learning.

INTERACTION BETWEEN CULTURE AND TECHNOLOGY ARTIFACTS

The second part of the commentary discusses issues involved in culture and software interaction effects (e.g., whether educational software can be applied to cultures other than the one in which it is produced, what we can learn from a cross-cultural application of educational software, and so on). We reject both (1) the universalist's assumption that technology progresses in a linear fashion and that the more advanced technology is more effective everywhere than the less advanced one and (2) the localist assumption that we cannot benefit from any cross-cultural application of technology (Serpell & Hatano, 1997). Instead, we propose cross-cultural understanding and collaboration through the application of software. More specifically, we claim as follows.

First, technology *can* be shared across cultures. It is beneficial in principle for both users and designers to share artifacts, because a variety of prior experiences useful for solving problems are embodied in technology artifacts. Often, we hear people say: "The tool is developed in another country and will not work in ours." This should not be taken at its face value, however. Every advanced technology requires a new set of skills for effectively using it (Wertsch, 1995), and there may be some reluctance to adopting it, and the reluctance is often justified by its alien nature. Needless to say, to be effectively applied and developed, tools should be valued by the local culture either for reducing the weakness or reinforcing the strength of the culture. For example, if the mathematical practice embedded in the Jasper artifact had not been valued by the Hong Kong teachers, it would not have been applied at all.

Second, we believe, when applied to a different culture, artifacts must be adapted to that culture to be successful. The adaptation usually takes forms of replacing some components and/or adding auxiliary feature. It is obvious that most educational software, before being exported, must be adjusted to the orthography and the level of literacy skills of students of the target culture. The adaptation may take subtle forms of changing emphases of secondary functions, contexts of applications, target populations, etc. This implies that only flexible artifacts can effectively be applied cross culturally. Moreover, because some of the needed adaptations have to be done on the spot, the users and designers should be open-minded and willing to improvise if necessary. Again, the case of Jasper in Hong Kong nicely illustrates this process of adaptation.

Third, we also argue that through deliberate and careful reflection on one's own action and decision making, sharing technology tools in a cross-cultural setting may make the invisible cultural needs and beliefs more visible so that further scaffolds can be provided for learning. For example, using Jasper in a Hong Kong classroom helped the teachers discover their own strengths and weaknesses as well as their students; these would have had remained invisible in routine practice. These discoveries necessitated scaffolds for teachers and students using Jasper that were quite different from what were provided originally. In this sense, technology artifacts can be used to bridge cultural contacts, and often promote mutual understanding and respect among the original designers, users, and their cultures and practices, as well as learning about content.

Fourth and finally, new tools may even lead to the reorganization of culture as a result of the adaptations made by the local people using new artifacts. As asserted above, it is necessary for artifacts to be adjusted to a given culture, but culture must also be adjusted to a new technology. The introduction of the snowmobile into the Arctic communities, for example, allowed the native culture to become less nomadic because the snow-machine allowed inhabitants to reach their hunting grounds in one-sixth of the time needed before (Pelto & Muller-Wille, 1987).

Although this may be an extreme example, introducing technology artifacts may help the local people become aware of and identify the areas that need improvement. For example, our interviews of Hong Kong teachers who used Jasper showed that they started to question their examination systems and teaching techniques in new ways. They realized that simply testing students' ability to calculate and to use mathematics formulas would not reveal students' strength in presenting and explaining their thoughts and arguments. They also realized the need to control less and provide students with more opportunities to explore and learn.

It is interesting to ponder about the extent the use of CSILE changes the classroom instruction and culture and about what the perceived changes by its users are. We are particularly interested in knowing whether CSILE can change the traditional "knowledge transmission" models of learning, and to what extent its asynchronous discussion changes the structure of participation between males and females, the talkative and the less talkative, etc., in the classroom.

WHAT CAN WE LEARN FROM THE JAPANESE APPLICATION OF CSILE?

In this final section, we return to the chapter by Oshima and Oshima, focussing on whether CSILE would work in non-Western cultures. Its application to the Japanese educational institutions illuminates its multiple functionality, for sharing ideas, building knowledge, argumentation, reflection on one's prior ideas, etc. However, we would like to learn more about interactive effects of CSILE tools. We need to understand the impact of specific features of the technology artifacts on classroom culture and social structures. We also need to explore how the classroom culture (including kinds of tasks, goals, learners, teachers, instructional styles, etc.) affects the uses of CSILE. Although Oshima and Oshima started their chapter with a very interesting question of whether and how CSILE would work in cultures where discussion skills are not regarded highly, they do not seem to offer any elaborate answers to this question. More specifically, how did Japanese educational communities perceive the purpose of CSILE that would promote alien kinds of skills and interactions? Did CSILE create such a culture that encourages students' initiatives, searching, and ability to construct? Did it make, through its use, both teachers and students more flexible and adaptive? To examine these questions, it would seem necessary to investigate in detail students' and teachers' mental models about learning as well as various technology tools.

We conclude our commentary by pointing out some issues that are not adequately dealt with in the chapter or in our commentary. Among others, we raise three issues: (1) What roles did the instructors play in these Japanese CSILE communities? (2) What opportunities for learning were exploited and what were missed? (3) How much metacognitive knowledge did the teachers and students develop about themselves, the tools, and the culture of their communities through the use of the CSILE software?

The role of teacher needs to be further investigated as teachers are the key in mediating the interactions between the tool and the students. It should be noted that Hakkarainen et al. (this volume) emphasize the teacher's strong engagement as a precondition of the effective use of CSILE. Without help from teachers, students cannot effectively use the supports offered by the technology tools and the cultural environment.

Even with teachers' help, there must be many missed learning opportunities in this study as in others that rely on discourse as a major learning forum. We need to scrutinize these missed opportunities and carefully study how to exploit the use of discourse as a learning resource. Teachers' "revoicing" of students' "utterance" (O'Connor & Michaels, 1993) and their invitation of other students to evaluate the "utterance" might be incorporated into the CSILE learning environment (Inagaki, Hatano, & Morita, 1998).

When changes occur, people tend to reflect more and need more reflection to make smart decisions for adaptation, a phenomena called reflective adaptation (see Lin, 2001a). The fact that experts make a fuller use of the potential provided by the tool and they are more metacognitively aware of their uses of tools implies the need to scaffold students' metacognitive thinking. One kind of scaffolding is to help students experience and understand the usefulness and benefits of the tools, as in Ann Brown's (1978) informed training of solution procedures. This is in a sharp contrast with the introduction of tools without discussing why they are useful (e.g., Brown's work on blind training, Brown, 1978). Research has proven that blind training is unsuccessful (Brown, Bransford, Ferrara, & Campione, 1983; Lin, 2001b; Lin & Lehman, 1999). We need to find various ways to support metacognition using technology artifacts in general, and CSILE in particular (Lin, Hmelo, Kinzer, & Secules, 1999). We are also curious about whether a different kind of metacognition, that is, students' identity as learners, is influenced by the use of new artifacts such as CSILE, especially its asynchronous communication, which requires different roles of participants. Special attention should be given to how to support students' role shifting and the subsequent psychological changes when new technology is in use.

Therefore, when studying how technology, local culture, and individuals interact, it is important to consider three factors simultaneously: (a) the affordances of the technology artifact; (b) support and constraints offered by the local culture; and (c) the individual users' reflection and decisions that influence the adaptation of new technologies.

ACKNOWLEDGMENTS

The preparation of this article was made possible by the National Academy of Education/Spencer postdoctoral fellowship, and Small Spencer grant. The opinions expressed in the paper do not necessarily reflect those of the granting agency.

REFERENCES

Brown, A. L. (1978). Knowing when, where, and how to remember: A problem of metacognition. In R. Glaser (Ed.), *Advances in instructional psychology*, Vol. 7 (pp. 55–111). New York: Academic Press.

Brown, A. L., Bransford, J. D., Ferrara, R. A., & Campione, J. C. (1983). Learning, remembering, and understanding. In J. H. Flavell & E. M. Markman (Eds.), *Handbook of child psychology: Vol. 3. Cognitive Development* (4th ed., pp. 77–166). New York: John Wiley and Sons.

Chi, M. T. H., Glaser, R., & Rees, E. (1982). Expertise in problem solving. In R. J. Sternberg (Ed.), *Advances in the psychology of human intelligence*, Vol. 1 (pp. 7–75). Hillsdale, NJ: Erlbaum.

Cognition and Technology Group at Vanderbilt (1997). *The Jasper project: Lessons in curriculum, instruction, assessment, and professional development.* Mahwah, NJ. Lawrence Erlbaum Associates, Inc.

Inagaki, K., Hatano, G., & Morita, E. (1998). Construction of matematical knowledge through whole-class discussion. *Learning and Instruction, 8*, 503–526.

Lamon, M., Secules, T. J., Petrosino, T., Hackett, R., Bransford, J. D., & Goldman, S. R. (1996). Schools for thought: Overview of the international project and lessons learned from one of the sites. In L. Shauble & R. Glaser (Eds.). *Contributions of instructional innovation to understanding learning* (pp. 243–288). Hillsdale, NJ. Erlbaum.

Lin, X. D. (2001a). Reflective adaptation of a technology artifact: A case study of classroom change. *Cognition & Instruction, 19*(4), xx (Fall Volume).

Lin, X. D. (2001b). Designing metacognitive activities. *Educational Technology Research & Development, 49*(2), 23–40.

Lin, X. D., Bransford, J. D., Kantor, R., Hmelo, C., Hickey, D., Secules, T., Goldman, S. R., Petrosino, T., & the Cognition and Technology Group at Vanderbilt (1995). Instructional design and the development of learning communities: An invitation to a dialogue. *Educational Technology, 35*(5), 53–63.

Lin, X. D., Hmelo, C., Kinzer, C., & Secules, T. (1999). Designing technology to support reflection. *Educational Technology Research & Development, 47*(3), 43–62.

Lin, X. D., & Lehman, J. (1999). Supporting learning of variable control in a computer-based biology environment: effects of prompting college students to reflect on their own thinking. *Journal of Research in Science Teaching, 36*(7), 1–22.

Lin, X. D., & Schwartz, D. L. (Accepted). Reflection at the cross roads of cultures. A Special Issue in *Mind, Culture & Activity*.

O'Connor, M. C., & Michaels, S. (1993). Aligning academic task and participation status through revoicing: Analysis of a classroom discourse strategy. *Anthropology and Education Quarterly, 24*, 318–335.

Pelto, P. J., & Muller-Wille, L. (1987). Snowmobiles: Technological revolution in the Arctic. In H. R. Bernard & P. J. Pelto (Eds.), *Technology and social change* (pp. 207–258).

Scardamalia, M., & Bereiter, C. (1991). Higher levels of agency for children in knowledge building: A challenge for the design of new knowledge media. *Journal of the Learning Sciences, 1*, 37–68.

Scardamalia, M., Bereiter, C., & Lamon, M. (1998). CSILE project: Trying to bring students into World 3. In K. McGilley (Ed.). *Classroom lesson: Integrating cognitive theory and classroom practice* (pp. 201–229). Cambridge, MA: M.I.T. Press.

Schwartz, D., Lin, X. D., Brophy, S., & Bransford, J. D. (1999). Toward the development of flexible adaptive instructional designs. In C. M. Reigeluth (Ed.). *Instructional design theories and models* (pp. 183–215). Hillsdale, NJ: Erlbaum.

Serpell, R., & Hatano, G. (1997). Education, schooling and literacy. In J. W. Berry, P. R. Dasen, & T. S. Sarawathi (Eds.). *Handbook of cross-cultural psychology* (Vol. 2), pp. 339–376.

Suchman, L. (1991). *Workplace project* (video). Xerox Parc, Systems Science Laboratory.

Wertsch, J. V. (1995). The need for action in sociocultural research. In J. V. Wertsch, P. del Rio, & A. Alvarez (Eds.), *Sociocultural studies of mind* (pp. 56–74). New York: Cambridge University Press.

NEXT STEP IN DESIGN EXPERIMENTS WITH NETWORKED COLLABORATIVE LEARNING ENVIRONMENTS: INSTRUCTIONAL INTERVENTIONS IN THE CURRICULUM

Jun Oshima
Ritsuko Oshima
Shizuoka University

We appreciate the constructive commentaries by Jim Levin, Xiaodong Lin, and Giyoo Hatano. They raise some interesting issues that we would like to pursue further. In this reply we describe some subsequent work related to the original chapter and then attempt to answer some questions raised in the commentaries.

Jim Levin was concerned that, in our chapter, we did not get into the specifics of target systems, such as WebCSILE, and did not discuss how our findings generalize to other contexts. At the time we started this project, we were keen to take up these issues. We had some reasons, however, to pursue some general questions pertaining to the use of CSCL in learning rather than to focus on the details of WebCSILE functionalities. As Jim pointed out, there is a definite need to analyze findings using a variety of different tools to provide guidelines for curriculum designers who want to use CSCL systems. We were also not in a position to address these issues at the time that we wrote the chapter because we were just starting the CSILE deployment in Japan.

As Jim observed in his commentary, additional work is needed to understand the developmental processes when instructors and learners use technology over an extended period of time. Over time tool users come up with new ideas for how to utilize the tools to improve their activities including learning. We think, and Xiaodong Lin and Giyoo Hatano apparently concur, that activities should be constructed through the interaction of tools and users' perceptions of the tools. We are now in our third year of studying WebCSILE use at the university as described in the chapter. In the following section, we summarize some of our design experiment work since completing the earlier report.

DESIGN EXPERIMENTS AFTER THE ORIGINAL STUDY

We report here the next step of our design experiment for CSILE deployment in Japanese post-secondary institutions. In our original studies, we deployed a WebCSILE system in expert learners' activities (i.e., graduate programs) to see how the learners use WebCSILE and recognize it as a tool for knowledge advancement. Then, we set up another WebCSILE site for novice learners (i.e., undergraduates) based on results from the study of experts. Studies of experts showed that graduate students recognized WebCSILE as a new communication channel and then assigned different roles in synchronous and asynchronous communications. In particular, graduates used their synchronous communication channel (i.e., face-to-face communication) for coordinating their discourse on WebCSILE. They reported in our interviews that they could expand their communication among members in the class by using WebCSILE and that they had been aware of the importance of asynchronous communication for reflecting on their own and others' previous thoughts. The less expert undergraduates, in contrast, had difficulties coordinating their activities in the two different channels and lacked skills for scientific writing in WebCSILE.

Currently, we are further expanding the target learners in our research to novice learners, undergraduates in universities. Here, we report our attempt at deploying WebCSILE in novice learners' activities and discuss factors crucial to successful use of WebCSILE for the purpose of improving knowledge advancement by novice learners. As the next step of design experiments after our original studies, we further considered curriculum design by referring to Collins, Brown, and Newman's (1989) framework for evaluating learning environments.

The Collins et al. framework consists of four major characteristics: (1) content, (2) method, (3) sequencing, and (4) sociology. In the content, various types of knowledge including domain knowledge are targeted. Collins et al. emphasizes that traditional classrooms underestimate heuristics, metacognitive knowledge, and learning strategies. They also argued for necessary changes in instructional methods. In particular, they emphasized the need to model expert performance, scaffold learners' performance, and foster reflection by learners. In the sequencing, it is argued that the increase in complexity and diversity of tasks are crucial. With respect to sociology, they argue that meaningful contexts of authentic learning are crucial and that a culture of expertise should be developed through cooperation.

In this study, we attempted to set undergraduate course curricula for improving students' knowledge advancement. For this purpose, we focused on metacognitive knowledge and learning strategies as targets of our learning environment design. Learning was self-directed in most part of the curricula, and students were encouraged to collaborate through WebCSILE communication. The tasks we gave were global, complex, and sufficiently diverse that learners could approach them in a variety of ways. Further, we emphasized the importance of collaboration for knowledge advancement, particularly collaborative discourse.

STUDY DESIGN

The aim of the studies in our chapter was to figure out what was needed to improve novices' knowledge advancement. In the study reported here, we attempted to invest some instructional intervention and scaffolding for improving novices' progressive discourse.

Participants

Novice participants in the chapters were undergraduate students who took a course "Basic Issues in Cognitive Science" taught by Jun Oshima in the academic year of 1997. In this study, 24 sophomores participated in another course entitled "Computing in Education." Both groups of students were from the same program in the university though the data come from different years. We assumed that their academic levels were comparable.

Learning Contexts

Both courses continued for a semester (about 14 weeks). Because we found in our expert studies that coordination of different communication channels was a key activity for improving knowledge advancement, we scheduled ordinary class meetings once a month for lecture, providing materials, and discussion for WebCSILE communication. In "Basic Issues in Cognitive Science," the task for the students was to comprehend relations between learning theories and education. The instructor introduced one chapter of a seminal book on learning and instruction (Resnick, 1989) in each ordinary class meeting. The students were required to report their understanding and questions on the introduced topics and help each other in advancing their knowledge. The final assignment for them was to write a proposal report in which they should identify problems in the introduced studies and describe how they could be addressed through experimentation.

In "Computing in Education," the task for the students was to synthesize material obtained from the Internet on instructional computing in Japanese

TABLE 2.2
Characteristics of Learning Environments

Characteristics	LE'97	LE'98
Content		
Domain Knowledge	Target domain knowledge	Target domain knowledge
Control Strategies	N/A	Metadiscourse knowledge
Learning Strategies	N/A	Collaboration strategies for knowledge advancement
Method		
Coaching	Instructor's participation in discourse	Instructor's participation in discourse
Scaffolding	N/A	Argument framework
Reflection	Face-to-face discussion	Face-to-face discussion
Exploration	Self-directed learning	Self-directed learning
Sequencing		
Increasing Complexity	Ill-structured problems	Ill-structured problems
Increasing Diversity	Ill-structured problems	Ill-structured problems
Global Before Local Skills	Global problems	Global problems
Sociology		
Culture of Expert Practice	Theory or curriculum construction	Theory or curriculum construction
Exploiting Cooperation	WebCSILE communication	WebCSILE communication

schools and propose new ideas to promote learning. In so doing, the students were to consider learning from various points of views. There were many Japanese web pages on the topic of computing in education. Some described theoretical issues and others reported and discussed practices conducted by teachers at various levels of schooling, such as elementary, junior high, senior high, and university. The students were required to search for materials they thought were valuable and to discuss and report the contents in a specific argument framework so that others could fully understand them. As scaffolding, we prepared a web page with information on how to structure their contributions. Class meetings were conducted once a month, as was done in the second study described in the chapter. Table 2.2 summarizes characteristics of learning environments in the two communities.

RESULTS

Statistical Indices of WebCSILE Use

In the learning environment in 1997 (LE'97), 30 students created 165 notes total. One hundred and six notes (64.24%) appeared in threads. The remaining 59 notes were single notes without commentaries. A chi-square analysis of the differences in thread and single notes showed that students were more likely to produce notes in threads, $\mathcal{X}^2(1) = 13.39$, $p < .05$. As participation indices, we further analyzed numbers of notes read and written by students: 24.9% of single notes and 31.1% of thread notes (excluding their own notes) on the average were read by students; 1.9 single notes and 3.4 thread notes on the average were created by students. The t tests on mean numbers of notes showed that students were more likely to read thread notes, $t(29) = -3.7959$, $p < .01$, but equally likely to create single notes as thread notes.

In the learning environment in 1998 (LE'98), 24 students created 145 notes total. One hundred and nine notes (75.17%) appeared in threads. The remaining 36 notes were single notes that did not have any commentaries. The difference in proportions of thread and single notes created by students was significant in that thread notes were more likely created by students, $\mathcal{X}^2(1) = 36.75$, $p < .05$. As participation indices, we further analyzed numbers of notes read and written by students: 35.9% of single notes and 42.8% of thread notes (excluding their own notes) on the average were read by students; 1.4 single notes and 4.4 thread notes on the average were created by students. t tests on mean numbers of notes showed that students were more likely to read thread notes, $t(23) = -2.386$, $p < .05$, but equally created single and thread notes. On the basis of this analysis, both communities of students utilized WebCSILE in similar ways.

The discourse threads were evaluated by two expert readers. In LE'97, there were 31 threads. The average thread rating was 2.3 (with a maximum of 10) and a range of 0.5 to 5.0). Figure 2.8 shows the distribution of thread ratings for the "Basic Issues in Cognitive Science" course. In LE'98, there were 37 threads. The average score was 1.8 with a range from 1.0 to 4.5. Figure 2.9 shows the distribution of thread ratings for the "Computing in Education"

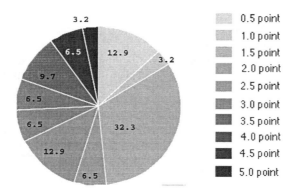

FIG. 2.8. Distribution of thread ratings for progressive discourse in "Basic Issues in Cognitive Science" (LE'97).

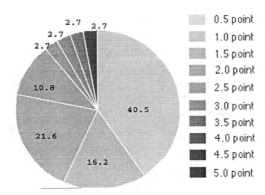

FIG. 2.9. Distribution of thread ratings for progressive discourse in "Computing in Education" (LE'98).

course. Because frequency distributions scores were quite skewed, we did
not conduct any statistical analysis on these ratings. However, it can be seen
that the threads in LE'97 tended to receive higher ratings despite the fact
that no scaffolding was provided in this course.

One possible reason may be that students did not understand our instruction and, therefore, the argument framework did not develop as we
had expected. Another reason may be our assumption that an established
argument framework is crucial to higher qualities of progressive discourse
was not correct. This latter possibility can be tested in the analysis of relationships between qualities of progressive discourse and its framework of
arguments.

Discourse in each note was transformed into its argument framework
by referring to Toulmin (1958) as in the chapter. Table 2.3 shows frequencies of components of the argument framework that appeared in student-
generated notes. (In Table 2.3 Ref, Q, C, R, W, B, QR, CR, and CoR represent
the components Reference, Qualification, Claim, Rebuttal, Warrant, Backup,
Qualification Request, Claim Request, and Confirmation Request, respectively.) A chi-square analysis showed a significant difference in proportions
of components between the communities and suggested that students in

TABLE 2.3
Frequencies of Components of Toulmin's Argument Framework

Ref	Q	C	R	W	B	QR	CR	CoR
Basic Issues in Cognitive Science (LE'97)								
8	24	12	5	6	1	8	6	0
Computing in Education (LE'98)								
37	17	29	8	20	1	7	2	0

LE'98 produced more Reference, Claim, and Warrant components, $\mathcal{X}^2(8) = 54.65, p < .01$.

Furthermore, we conducted multiregression analyses to determine which components of the argument were crucial to higher qualities of discourse. In LE'97, it was found that the components in totality explained a significant amount of variance, $F(8, 22) = 4.5862, p < .01$. A further stepwise analysis revealed that particularly Reference and Qualification Request components were contributing to the explained variance, $ps < .05$. In LE'98, the components accounted for a significant amount of the variance, $F(7, 29) = 3.8033, p < .01$. A further stepwise analysis revealed that Claim and Qualification components made a significant contribution to the observed variance, $ps < .01$.

Student Survey Data

In LE'97, the learning goal-oriented and the transitional groups made use of WebCSILE as a tool for knowledge advancement. Through the new asynchronous communication channel, they succeeded in expanding their learning community. They came to recognize that learning through collaboration with others was crucial to knowledge advancement. However, the third "task goal-oriented group" was not aware of learning as knowledge construction. They did not think that communication with others led them to further advancement of knowledge. Contrary to our expectations, students in LE'98 did not report any recognition on their own learning. Their recognitions were quite similar to those by the task goal-oriented group in LE'98. Although they said that using the computer network was worthwhile for their learning, their reports were quite abstract and superficial.

The second questionnaire had a section that asked students to make a list of persons (up to five) whom they had communicated with face-to-face. Based on the data, we created communication matrices in the face-to-face context (i.e., who communicated with whom). Similarly, we created matrices of communication online (i.e., who commented on whom). By combining the two types of matrices, we created global communication matrices. In LE'97, less than 1% of patterns overlapped in the face-to-face and the online context, whereas, in LE'98, about 42% of communication did overlap.

DISCUSSION

At the level of performance online, undergraduate students did seem to utilize WebCSILE as a tool for their collaborative discourse. They were more likely to read thread notes, which suggests that they were likely to participate in collaboration rather than just expressing themselves. Furthermore, the analysis of communication matrices showed us that their communication patterns online were quite different from those offline. Students had already created some cohorts in the class. The presence of the cohorts is considered to have affected their communications offline. The drastic differences in the patterns between online and offline communication suggested that WebCSILE had successfully expanded the students' communications with others whom they had rarely communicated with offline.

With regard to the argument framework of discourse on WebCSILE, the comparisons of the frameworks between the communities showed that students who used our scaffolding web page created more elaborate argument frameworks in their discourse. Students in LE'98 created basic components of discourse (Reference, Claim, and Warrant) significantly more than students in LE'97. The result suggests to us that the instruction worked.

Then, what about the content of their discourse? Was it progressive? In our chapter, we compared the qualities of discourse by experts and novices. As expected, the discourse by the experts had significantly higher scores than that of the novices. One remarkable point in this study was that novices who did not receive any instruction on argument framework produced more highly rated threads than did those who did. We will next examine this unexpected result.

The comparisons between experts and novices showed that (1) novices do not have appropriate control strategies and learning strategies for knowledge advancement and (2) the novices' motivations for learning were not necessarily oriented by knowledge building goals. Students in LE'97 reported difficulties in managing their own learning and writing their ideas. Therefore, we implemented a schedule for WebCSILE activities and a scaffolding homepage for helping students in writing their ideas in a scientific manner. We expected that the quality of the discourse by students in LE'98 would improve as a result. However, this did not prove to be the case. These results suggest that the argument framework itself is insufficient for knowledge advancement in discourse, although we still believe that the framework is necessary.

Reports in questionnaires suggest some reasons for why the scaffolding did not lead students to higher qualities of discourse for knowledge advancement. The reports rarely described learning or evaluations of knowledge building. Instead, they did seem to simply follow our instruction to complete tasks they recognized during the course (i.e., constructing discourse as scientists do). Furthermore, in reading their notes on WebCSILE, we realized a critical difference in discourse between students in LE'97 and LE'98. That was the presence of metadiscourse in LE'97. In their discourse, students in LE'97 struggled with creating some forms of discourse that could be shared with others. They did not create elaborate frameworks of arguments but discussed the contents at the metacognitive level. They described why they commented on others' thoughts, how they created their forms of discourse, and so on. Surprisingly, such discourse was rarely found in LE'98. We expected that LE'98 students could manipulate their thoughts in such a metacognitive way when they were given specific forms of discourse. This did not work. They did seem to recognize our scaffolding as tasks that had to be completed by specific dates. Our instructional interventions were easily transformed into simple tasks.

Lessons From the Next Step of Design Experiments

The findings from this subsequent study raise two important questions: (1) Does our implementation of the learning environment in undergraduate courses work as we expected? and (2) What we can do to revise our implementation?

Regarding the first question, metacognitive aspects of progressive discourse (i.e., control strategies) were not developed well by students themselves. Unlike our expectation, providing the argument framework in discourse did not lead the students to higher qualities of discourse. Rather, the framework led the students to be task goal-oriented. We need to consider revising our instructional methods to facilitate more metadiscourse either online or offline. Coaching and scaffolding did not seem to be sufficient. The instructor participated in some threads to implicitly direct discourse by giving some requests for qualification and claims. However, he did not sufficiently focus on metacognitive aspects of discourse nor did he request that students attend to this aspect of their own discourse.

In reference to the second question, we are giving consideration to implementing some new features. First, we are planning to implement modeling and articulation methods for facilitating metacognitive discourse. Students in the future LE will be allowed to access thread notes in previous databases that had been highly rated by experts to see how previous students engaged in progressive discourse. Furthermore, the instructor will attempt to collaboratively discuss with students why the previous thread notes were highly evaluated by experts and why this type of discourse is valuable for knowledge advancement. Second, we hope to intrinsically motivate students in the class through a collaborative decision-making process. In our studies so far, although problems were sufficiently complex and diverse and students were allowed to self-direct their learning, materials such as reading assignments were predetermined by instructors. We will discuss with students how to approach these problems and how authentically they can be involved in courses.

CONCLUSIONS

On the basis of this new work, let us attempt now to briefly address two of the questions raised by Xiaodong and Giyoo. First, they asked about the roles of the instructors in constructing the Japanese CSILE communities; what specific competencies did they bring to the task and how did these competencies affect student learning? Second, they asked how much metacognitive knowledge was acquired by the students (and teachers) through their use of the CSILE software.

With regard to the first question, Xiaodong and Giyoo are particularly concerned with the level of knowledge and skills the instructor had in terms of (1) content knowledge, (2) critical questioning ability, and (3) social support for maintaining discourse. Currently, our design experiments are mainly being conducted at a site in which one of the authors is teaching students. The reasons for choosing the Alpha site were related to the concerns raised by Xiaodong and Giyoo. Tools such as CSILE work effectively only if teachers and curriculum designers sufficiently understand their educational philosophy. We chose courses in our university in which we had sufficient content knowledge and could control course schedule. As the instructor for the course, Jun Oshima did not attempt to give his students answers, but rather he provided questions for them to make further inquiries on their original problems. Further, he suggested some notes for students to read or comment on so that they succeeded in maintaining their discourse. As we discussed in our original chapter and this reply, this was helpful for some and not for others.

By referring to Collins et al.'s (1989) framework of learning environments, we exploited some instructional interventions in LE'98. In LE'98, we gave students more specific goals of the course. The big idea pursued in the course was to collaboratively construct the concept of "computing in education." For pursuing the final goal, we instructed the students to search for information on the World Wide Web during the first month and to read and comment on others' notes in the next month. Then, in the final month, students were allowed to do more research and discuss their findings on WebCSILE. We provided a specific rhetorical framework in scientific writing. The lesson we learned from this design experiment is that preparing a framework in rigid ways does not work for improving learning, particularly for adult learners. They like to discuss what and how to pursue their problems and need support for accomplishing the difficult tasks. Curriculum design itself should be negotiated between the instructing side and the learning side. It should be flexible, depending on how learners engage in activities. Generic tools for learning such as CSILE, we believe, would show us their power of transforming learning to knowledge building.

Xiaodong and Giyoo's second question has to do with the extent to which the use of CSILE changes the classroom instruction and culture and how these changes are perceived by users. Because we were, in this case, the instructors, the most remarkable changes appeared in the students. As discussed in this reply, crucial changes in classroom cultures do not always happen. The best scenario for novice learners that we found so far in Japan is the group of students who pursued their learning goals in LE'97. Through the questionnaire and interviews, the learning goal-oriented learners recognized that activities on WebCSILE led them to reflect on their own thoughts and those of others to facilitate their understanding of materials. They also reported how different learning activities with WebCSILE was from their ordinary course work. A cognitive process that they engaged in but others did not is metadiscourse on their discourse. The learning goal-oriented learners, in particular, were concerned with the necessity of rules for their discourse to understand each other. They were involved in a metacognitive activity to evaluate their discourse on WebCSILE depending on their learning goals (i.e., how could they improve their writing to make others easily understand). They gradually produced more data or reference for their claim in their writing. A culture of learning through written discourse in networked learning environments could be seen to emerge. What we can do for learners is to support them to construct their "progressive discourse" by providing cultural tools such as scientific genre and rhetoric at the time they need help. In this way, we can further exploit metadiscourse environments as a means for designers and learners to collaboratively reconstruct their learning environments.

REFERENCES

Collins, A., Brown, J. S., & Newman, S. E. (1989). Cognitive apprenticeship: Teaching the crafts of reading, writing, and mathematics. In L. B. Resnick (Ed.), *Knowing, learning, and instruction: Essays in honor of Robert Glaser* (pp. 453–494). Hillsdale, NJ: Lawrence Erlbaum Associates.
Resnick, L. B. (Ed.) (1989). *Knowing, learning, and instruction: Essays in honor of Robert Glaser.* Hillsdale, NJ: Lawrence Erlbaum Associates.
Toulmin, S. (1958). *The uses of argument.* New York: Cambridge University Press.

3

COMPUTER-SUPPORTED COLLABORATIVE LEARNING IN UNIVERSITY AND VOCATIONAL EDUCATION

Frank P. C. M. de Jong
University of Nijmegen

Else Veldhuis-Diermanse
Wageningen University and Research Centre

Gaby Lutgens
Universiteit Maastricht

Student learning could become more effective and productive if students collaborate by exchanging concepts, comparing individual learning strategies and debating each others' contributions to the learning process (De Corte, Greer, & Verschaffel, 1996). The process of collaboration should stimulate students to explicate and formulate their thoughts more clearly. Moreover, these kinds of interactions should initiate students' reflections on their learning and thinking. Supporting this kind of effective learning and reflection on the metacognitive aspects of learning is becoming extremely important in the context of the paradigm shift by which education is confronted by the changing demands of society. This is because society is becoming more and more knowledge intensive. For instance, a simple tomato that we eat still looks the same as in former days. However, its production has become enormously more knowledge intensive as a consequence of the intensity of the production and the effort to make the product less sensitive to pathogens and less perishable.

The rapid succession of changes in society, in terms of economic and environmental demands and increasing complexity, as well as the emergence of knowledge-intensive problems and modes of production, creates a need for ongoing personal development and learning. Not only do people need access to a great deal of information, they must also be able to use higher-order learning skills, cognitive flexibility, and effective cognitive strategies so as to translate their knowledge into "effective action in the domain of existence" (Maturana & Varela, 1992). This demands active construction of knowledge rather than solitary processing of information (de Jong, 1995). Consequently, education is no longer about rote memory and the reproduction of external knowledge. In education studies and classroom praxis we see the failure of traditional educational methods, sometimes referred to generically as the "Transfer of Knowledge (TOK) paradigm." The TOK paradigm implies an epistemological point of departure with the view that "learning is the (passive) absorption and reception of objective knowledge." As Bruner (1996) described, this arises from three core beliefs in traditional education: (1) Knowledge of the world is approached as the "objective reality" that can be transferred from one person to another. (2) A medium, such as a teacher, the Internet, a book, or an extension agent, is required to transfer the knowledge from the one who knows to the one who does not. (3) Learning is institutionalized.

One of the reasons for the demise of TOK is the lack of evidence for transfer of formal school and scientific knowledge to the use and creation of knowledge in real-life working situations. So education sees itself confronted with changing goals. It is a shift from the TOK paradigm toward a paradigm that Bruner (1996) has described as the Learner-as-Thinker (one could call it the LAT paradigm). The new professional discourse in education emphasizes the subjectivist character of knowledge construction as a result of students' individual knowledge and strategic experiences and their interpretations of the world around them (Duffy & Knuth, 1991; Cunningham, 1992; Spiro & Jehng, 1990). The (re)construction of knowledge is not a goal in itself but an attempt to realize less rigid knowledge acquisition and to maximize the application of learned knowledge in real-life situations.

The shift from the TOK toward the LAT paradigm in education leads, according to Bruner (1996) and others, to different perspectives:

- Education leads to insight and conception instead of only allowing learners to carry out academic and intellectual activities.
- The knowledge that learners acquire is more practicable when it is "discovered," that is to say, constructed by learners' own cognitive activities and effort. Knowledge in that sense is more related to the learners' prior knowledge.
- No matter how complex the subject of education is, it is not fruitful to present the related knowledge in a fragmented format.
- The goal of education is not to cover a whole subject domain but to offer profundity.

- The curriculum is a spiral going from intuitive concept representations of the domain to more formal, general, and abstract representations.
- The teacher is a guide who coaches the learner to deep understanding,
  someone who helps the learner to discover the world and construct
  knowledge by him- or herself while developing toward a self-regulating
  and self-responsible learner.
- Learning not only results from individual thinking but also from
  collaborative/collective thinking.

Although many issues in "the new learning," such as scaffolding, distributed cognition, and co-learning didactics (especially in Internet and ICT
contexts) still need to be studied in more depth, the outcomes of ongoing
projects are promising in terms of delivering alternatives to TOK. For example, Scardamalia and Bereiter (1994) propose that scientific thinking can
be facilitated by organizing a classroom to function as a scientific research
community and guiding students to participate in practices of progressive
scientific discourse. Analogous to scientific discovery and theory formation,
learning is a process of working toward more thorough and complete understanding. It is an engagement in extended processes of question-driven
inquiry. Hakkarainen (1998) discovered that children at the age of 10–11
are, with the aid of computer support for collaborative learning (CSCL) and
appropriate pedagogical and epistemological teacher guidance, already capable of pursuing processes of inquiry that exhibit the principal features of
mature scientific inquiry. In this process of progressive inquiry the following phases are essential: creating context, formulating a principal problem,
constructing a working theory, performing critical evaluation, searching for
new information, formulating a subordinate problem, and constructing a
new working theory. In this context, CSCL supports interaction and sharing
of expertise. This sharing has the format of critical thinking in collaborative
discussion (Duffy, Dueber, & Hawley, 1998) and reflective interaction (Baker
& Lund, 1997).

Another promising approach is that of the "learning-communities." This
approach aims at supporting the growth of individual knowledge by advancing collective knowledge (Scardamalia & Bereiter, 1994; Bielaczyc & Collins,
1998). To this tradition belong notions such as the "Knowledge-Building
Classroom" (Scardamalia & Bereiter, 1996), the "Fostering a Community of
Learners (FCl) model" (Brown & Campione, 1996), and the "Mathematics
Classroom" (Lampert, 1990). These approaches attempt to develop skills
and knowledge adequate for dealing with the challenges of a world that
is becoming increasingly complex. This involves an ability to manage one's
own learning, to work with and listen to others from diverse backgrounds

and views, and to develop ways of dealing with complex issues and problems that require different kinds of expertise.

In summary, the discourse underpinning of education and professional practice has undergone a tremendous upheaval, radically altering its epistemological basis, paradigms, principles, approaches, and theories. But the change is relatively recent. TOK is alive and well in many classrooms: in the assumptions on which educational policies are based, in the societal incentives for teachers and pupils' achievements, in criteria for school evaluation; in the expectations of parents and employers, and in the pragmatic pressure of implementing educational innovations infused by politicians and managers for promoting their own careers instead of for improving the learners' learning. At the same time, education is bursting with new enthusiasm and promise. However, the new ideas must still be elaborated into a new and effective operational praxiology that can meld educational practices, expectations, institutional designs, policies, and so forth into a coherent whole (Röling & De Jong, 1998). The studies reported here, being part of a large-scale project, focus on three main questions: (1) Can computer-supported collaborative learning be introduced in the regular (university) curriculum effectively? (2) Is collaborative knowledge building being promoted when collaborative learning networks are being introduced? (3) What kinds of teacher interventions are needed for collaborative knowledge building?

THE STUDIES

The studies reported here are a part of the European Collaborative Learning Networks Project (CL-NET). The central objective of the CL-NET project is to investigate the cognitive and didactic aspects of computer-supported Collaborative Learning Networks (CLNs). CLNs are learning environments in which educational multimedia and GroupWare are used to create a community of learners who build knowledge together. CLNs are learning contexts in which equipment, information networks, but also teachers, learners, and learning methods are included. The general question of the project is: How can intentional learning or knowledge building in CLNs be supported in European schools, principally in primary and secondary education, but also in post-secondary education as well? Partners in the project are the University of Nijmegen (the Netherlands), University of Leuven (Belgium), University of Turku (Finland), University of Helsinki, (Finland), University of Athens (Greece), University of Amsterdam (the Netherlands), University of Wageningen (the Netherlands), University of Roma (Italy), University of Bari (Italy), and CNS (Italy). The European Community under the Targeted Socio-Economic Research (TSER) program funds the project. The project partners are interested in determining whether different types of software, supporting collaborative learning, can be introduced in a classroom effectively and whether they can be used to promote knowledge building. The focus is on how the use of software affects the teacher–student and student–student interaction that takes place in the classroom. The different CL-NET project partners have different degrees of expertise in the use of software that supports collaborative learning. The Dutch, Finnish, Greek and Belgian partners are using WebCSILE or Knowledge Forum. The Italian partners use *Discover Your Town*, a multimedia prototype for sociohistorical education, and *Our World*. This software creates a learning environment for environmental education. School classes all over the country are invited to contribute to a library of documents (written text, a drawing, or a mixture of both) with the outcomes of their explorations carried out in the environments where they live. Therefore, children's productions address and negotiate with an external audience. A third software product called *Telecomunicando* is used by the Italian partners for the construction of hypermedia and for communication (hypertext, e-mail, Internet, and video-conferencing).

All CL-NET partners attend closely to both individual learning and the social environment that is constructed. However, the Finnish groups focus more on the teacher–student dynamics, the three Italian groups on the extended social interactions that contribute to personal and school learning, and the Dutch, Belgian, and Greek groups on individual achievement and didactics. Most of the projects involve primary school students ranging in age from 9 to 11 years old. The Telecomunicado project also involved some high school students. In the Dutch projects, studies also included university students. The studies reported here present our investigations of CLN using educational sciences undergraduates. Also reported are some of our experiences with CLN in agricultural secondary vocational education.

STUDY 1: UNIVERSITY CONTEXT

The study reported here presents our experience with the use of Knowledge Forum with educational sciences undergraduates in a course entitled "Psychology of the Teaching and Learning Process." The project was undertaken collaboratively by the University of Nijmegen and the University of Wageningen.

Method and Procedure

In this study we investigated the effectiveness of a CLN in the university course Psychology of the Teaching and Learning Process (PSYOLP) of the department of Educational Sciences, University of Nijmegen. Our reasons for using the web-based version of Knowledge Forum in this course arise from the following considerations (de Jong & Biemans, 1998):

- To focus on the student instead of the teacher (student centered focus).
- To start from the students' prior knowledge.
- To focus on learning as a result of students' mental knowledge (re)construction.
- To focus on learning as a collaborative act of coming to understanding and reaching learning goals.
- To focus on learning as a social interaction among multiple perspectives.
- To view the learner as being self-responsible for his or her learning and the learning of his or her colleagues.

There were some practical reasons as well, such as:

- The program is user friendly; students can access it by the Internet with a web browser independent of time and place.
- Students gradually create a communal knowledge database for producing, searching, classifying, and linking a knowledge database by contributing notes. This makes it possible for teachers to follow students' learning activities and to analyze the process during the course.
- Students are stimulated to articulate their own theories and thoughts because the system facilitates the sharing of ideas by providing each student access to all text notes, comments, and charts produced by their fellow students.
- Collaborative learning between students is facilitated through advanced facilities for searching out and commenting on the ideas and suggestions of the other participants.
- Students use Knowledge Forum by writing notes, creating charts, and reading and commenting on each other's productions.
- Knowledge Forum is also designed to facilitate reflection and metacognition because it allows students not only to communicate their ideas but also to make them an object of critical examination.
- Students can work cooperatively to coauthor notes and up- and download documents in a shared directory.

Subjects and Procedure

Twenty-five second- and third-year undergraduate psychology and educational sciences students participated in the study. The learning styles of

Students' average learning styles scores

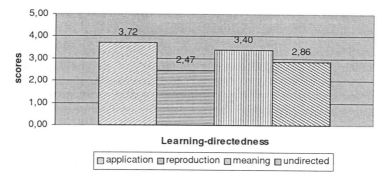

FIG. 3.1. Students' average learning styles.

the students were assessed using the method described by Vermunt (1995). The learning styles are derived from composition scores on cognitive processing strategies (deep, stepwise, and concrete processing), regulation strategies (self-regulation, external regulation, and lack of regulation), student's mental models of learning, and their learning orientations. Their learning styles tended toward "application-directed" and "meaning-directed" styles. However, it must be said that the "undirected" learning style is even a bit more prevalent than the "reproduction-directed" style (Fig. 3.1). The "reproduction-directed" style correlated significantly with the "undirected" style ($r = .62$, $p = .003$).

Because of the rather large group of students, it was decided to let students cooperate according to the "jigsaw-method" (Mattingly, VanSickle, & Ronald, 1991; Slavin, 1983). After making an individual inventory of prior knowledge, students studied specific subjects (recent theories, instructional models, applied active instruction, metacognition, and self-reflection) in "subjects perspective groups." During the last weeks, students worked on the final task in subgroups put together by different persons of each perspective group. During 12 weeks of the course, nine meetings were held to coach the students' learning process. Student progress, problems, and plans were discussed. Students could also ask for more information about a subject. Only twice was a traditional lecture given. A summary of educational, teacher, and student activities is listed in Table 3.1. The following phases can be distinguished in the educational process:

1. *Actualizing*: Individual brainstorming of available foreknowledge and "own" theories; formulating learning goal perspectives; inventorying of own foreknowledge and theories from a learning goal perspective; installing subject perspective groups.

TABLE 3.1
Summary of Educational, Teacher, and Student Activities

Meeting	Educational Activity	Teacher/Student Activity
1	Introduction + short lecture into the domain related to educational principles the way the course should proceed	Teacher: Preparation of the database and short lecture. Selecting literature. Student: Contributing own theories and commenting on other students' notes.
2	Inventory of individual foreknowledge by students	Teacher: Direction of ideas, monitoring of the learning process (reading notes, also the next weeks). Students: In groups reading all notes from a certain perspective. Summarizing.
3	Filtering and categorization of foreknowledge	Teacher: Process monitoring, rearranging views and learning goal perspectives into subjects' perspective groups. Students: Writing a publication note as a summary of the foreknowledge in the database from a particular perspective. Generating questions of own interest and study; setting up an activity plan.
4	Reading of literature	Teacher: Student coaching in "fine-tuning" their questions and making related literature suggestions. Student: Revising the group planning, reading the literature, and making contributions.
5	Lecturing learning styles and independent learning	Teacher: Preparing a lecture. Student: Following the lecture, studying literature and relevant (web)sources.
6	Elaborating literature and other sources	
7	Elaborating literature and other sources Taking part in a science seminar	Teacher: Coaching and supporting students. Students: Studying literature and relevant (web)sources, following a seminar of a scientist. Preparing a second publication note about the sources studied.
8	Final task Visiting a exhibition about teaching technology and material	Teacher: Preparing and authentic task. Students: Studying literature and relevant (web)sources, visiting a exhibition. Preparing a second publication note about the sources studied.
9	Final task	Teacher: Coaching and supporting students. Students: Rewriting submitted proposal by schools for ICT-projects from an educational point of view.
10	Evaluating the final products. Discussing and reflecting on the total learning process in the Knowledge Forum	Teacher: Evaluating and accrediting the final products, learning process, database analysis. Students: Commenting on the teacher evaluation. Making suggestions for further courses.

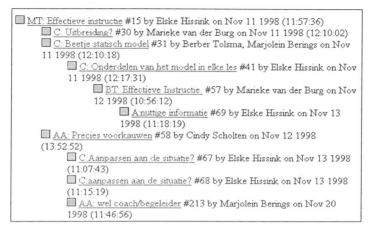

FIG. 3.2. Notes and "build-on" notes in the Knowledge Forum database.

2. *Planning*: Formulating personal learning questions on the basis of individual interests; formulating learning goal perspectives; drafting of a plan of group activities.

3. *Deepening*: Sharing new insights and knowledge gained by studying literature and other sources within and between groups.

4. *Experiencing*: Rearranging the groups by making use of the jigsaw method; in groups, apply acquired insights and knowledge by working on an authentic, real-life problem and producing a final product.

In all phases, the dialogue within in the groups, between groups, and between individuals was consistently a central activity. These dialogues comprised ("new") notes and "build-on" notes (see Fig. 3.2).

For structuring the activities of the students and the database the students were working in "views" (see Fig. 3.3). A "view" is a separate part of the database. The brainstorming during the actualizing phase and personal learning interest took place in a particular view. In the deepening phase, a group of students studied the theme Psychology of the Teaching and Learning Process from a particular scope based on their interests. In these views students studied insights brought forth by "recent educational approaches," "instructional design theories," "theories on independent learning and learning styles," "theories on the role of the teacher as a coach," and "practical instructional settings." Groups reported the result of their study to other groups in (coauthored) notes for publications, which were brought together in the view "publication notes." These published notes refer to and are linked to related notes in other views. Traces of notes spread out over different views could be easily followed by just clicking on the references in a note.

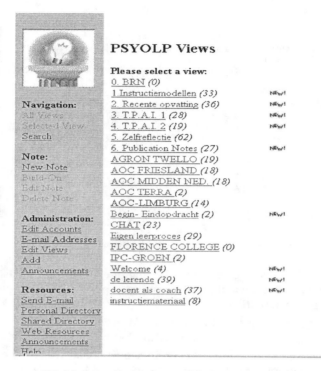

FIG. 3.3. Example of views in a Knowledge Forum database.

Although the study in a particular view was assigned to a group of students the other students could read and create notes in other views as they were assigned. The activities during the experiencing phase were initiated in other views (for instance, AOC Friesland), but the earlier work was still accessible and could be referred to.

To stimulate students' awareness of their own learning processes and of supporting the dialogue thinking types, a form of scaffolding was used. These codes were assigned to a note by putting it in the note's title (Fig. 3.4). This indicates the type of contribution the note makes to both themselves and to others. Thinking type tags include: MT (my theory), C (comment), WA (what is this about?), INU (I need to understand), and P (we need to plan our activities).

Results

Knowledge Forum provides reports on the time students spend reading and writing notes in the database. In the course studied, each of the 25 students spent an average of 11 hours using the database. Figure 3.5 summarizes

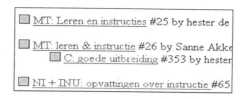

☐ MT: Leren en instructies #25 by hester de

☐ MT: leren & instructie #26 by Sanne Akke
   ☐ C: goede uitbreiding #353 by hester

☐ NI + INU: opvattingen over instructie #65

FIG. 3.4. An example of scaffolding using "Thinking Types."

how this time was utilized. On average, the students read 30% ($SD = 13.5$) of the notes. The percentage is based on the notes in the selected section of the database that the student has opened. This may provide an exaggeration of the number of notes the student has actually read. It is computed as the number of different notes the student has opened, divided by the total number of different notes within the views and dates selected (authored by anyone), and then converted to a percentage. That is, the selection of views and dates is used to pare down the database to just those notes of interest—all the notes in that section of the database, regardless of author, are considered to be available to be read. About 45% ($SD = 14.6$) of the notes are linked with each other. A note has been linked to another note if it is a build-on (it references another note). A note is counted as linked even if the note it is linked to is not within the selected view.

The high number of revised notes is a result of the fact that students coauthored notes. Revisions are the number of times a student has saved a note since the first time it was saved provided it was created during the time period and in the views selected (or the difference between the total number of times a student has saved relevant notes and the number of

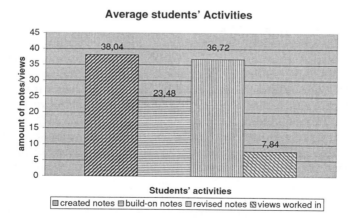

FIG. 3.5. Summary of the student activities while working in Knowledge Forum.

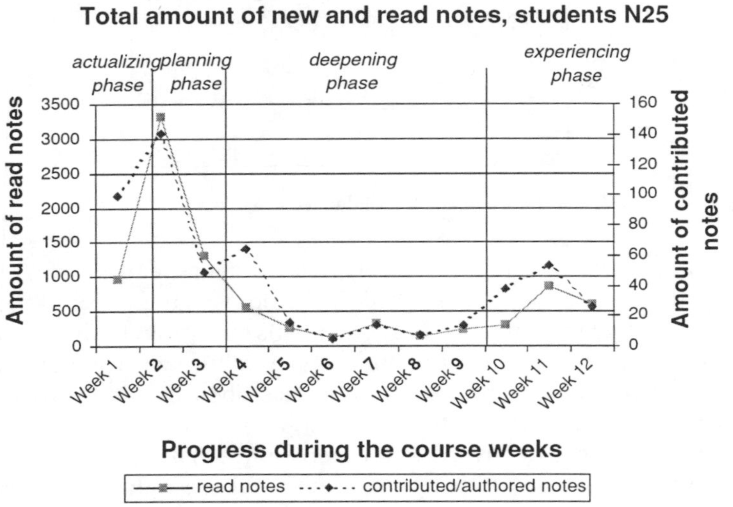

Total amount of new and read notes, students N25

FIG. 3.6. Summary of student activities (contributing and reading notes) over the four phases of the course.

different relevant notes the student has saved). Knowledge Forum records a note as being saved only if the note has been changed, and so opening and closing a note without changing it also does not count. On average, students worked in almost 8 of the 17 views.

The number of views worked in is the number of different views that the student has authored a note in (i.e., the number of different views, 7.8 ($SD = 1.9$)) from the number of views selected ($N = 17$). Accumulating the students' activities over the 12 weeks of the course results in 951 note contributions (consisting of 587 build-on notes and 364 new notes), 918 note revisions, and 9,029 read notes.

A weekly progress picture (see Fig. 3.6) gives a better impression of students' activities. This progress is assigned to the educational phases stated above. What we see is that students are most active in the actualizing, planning, and experiencing phases. Students are less active in the deepening phase during which they are studying literature and other resources. Students tend to read notes but are creating fewer notes.

To investigate the relationship between students' learning style directions and the displayed activities, correlations were calculated between those variables. Concerning the variable learning styles, only the application-directed learning style correlated significantly with the total amount of created notes by students ($r = .56$; $p = .01$; $N = 20$). In a stepwise regression analysis, with the application-directed learning style as independent variable and the created notes as dependent variable, a significant regression

TABLE 3.2
Pearson Correlations Among Knowledge Forum Variables*

Variable	Build-on	Notes Created	% Notes Read	% Linked	Time in Knowledge Forum
Build-on		.82	.70		.53
Notes Created	.82		.60		.52
% Notes Read	.69	.60		.55	.60
% Linked	.78		.55		
Notes Revised	.62	.46	.58	.46	.61
Views Worked	.49	.72	.74		.51

*$N = 25$ students.

turned up ($B = 22.9$; Std error $= 8.2$; $\beta = .56$ ($t = 2.9$; $p = .01$); regression $F = 8.2$; $DF = 1,18$; $p = .01$; $R^2 = .31$).

The knowledge building variables build-on notes, notes created, percentage notes read, percentage linked, and notes revised were significantly correlated with each other (Table 3.2).

The creation of notes primarily consisted of build-on notes, indicating a high level of collaboration in the database. The activity of opening (reading) notes is highly related to the other activities in the database. The correlation with the views worked in indicates that students did not focus only on their own subgroup contributions but also of those of other groups. Because of rearranging groups and learning perspectives within groups, it was expected that views were more related to particular educational phases in the course.

In addition to their work in the database, the students also revised a set of proposals for ICT projects that had been submitted to the ministry of education by various schools. The rewriting of these proposals resulted in high-quality policy notes produced by the students.

STUDY 2: A VOCATIONAL CONTEXT

A second study reported here involved the use of CLNs in agricultural secondary vocational education. The Knowledge Forum software was used to form a community of learners. Of special interest is whether the GroupWare is effective in situations where students engage in practical experience for several weeks in the field (e.g., in agricultural industries (including the food industry)). During this period of out-of-school learning, the students focused on a theme such as "effective management" and used Knowledge Forum to create a knowledge database. On the basis of their school knowledge and their experience outside school, they discussed and exchanged knowledge experiences to achieve more depth and insight in their coursework. Subjects were in the second and third levels of a four-year secondary vocational agricultural education (second level: $N = 11$, mean age of 18.20, SD $= 1.55$, six male, four female; third level: $N = 12$, mean age of 19.73, SD $= 1.42$, five male, seven female). The second-level group is a mixed class combined from two parallel classes. They worked and learned at their practical training positions in the same period and had similar assignments. Only students with Internet connections at home participated in the Knowledge Forum group. The second-level group studied the topic of management. The third-level group studied the topic of producing agricultural products (especially those involving food technology). During the 10-week period students worked at practical training positions.

There were two teachers for each group. In this database the role of the teacher is rather unsystematic. The only assignments given were in the first week and two more in the fourth week. Two of these assignments were content specific and one was focused on the procedure. Also, in Week 8, some teacher contributions were created.

Results

The period began with an assignment by the teacher and after this contribution the students started to write and react as if they had been anxiously waiting for this assignment. In the third week the students' activity dropped (see Fig. 3.7). In response to a note from the teacher in Week 4 students reacted again with writing contributions. Most activity took place in Week 5. Shortly before the end of the period a rise in activity is seen again after a contribution from the teacher. There seems to be a tendency in which students only show activity in the database if they received an explicit assignment from the teacher to contribute.

Number of created notes

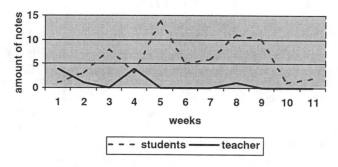

FIG. 3.7. Student and teacher activity in the vocational study.

CONCLUSIONS

This chapter describes two experiences using Knowledge Forum, one at the university level and the other in vocational education. The university study concerned a more systematic didactic approach whereas the study in the vocational setting concerned a more unsystematic coaching of students. In both studies, students were very enthusiastic. The amount of created, read, and linked notes are an indication of this enthusiasm. The university students, in particular, liked to collaborate and deepen their own insights and understanding in the domain. The vocational students consider coaching and stimulating important. Teachers' contributions were needed to get students actively involved in the database. We now return to the three questions raised in the introduction, namely: (1) Can computer-supported collaborative learning be effectively introduced in the regular (university) curriculum? (2) Is collaborative knowledge building being promoted when collaborative learning networks are introduced? (3) What kinds of teacher interventions are needed for collaborative knowledge building?

With regard to the first question, there is no single answer. Results show that students are not accustomed to sharing their knowledge and, in particular, that goal setting and teacher interaction are necessary to stimulate building on each other's notes. Not only do students need to develop their knowledge building attitudes, but teachers also have to use a systematic didactic. They have to learn to use the time normally expended on lecturing to monitor and stimulate the processes of learning. This must be done in such a way that students develop the skills to enable them to assume responsibility for their own learning in the database. Students with prior knowledge of HTML had an impact on the activity of the groups by providing more structure in the database by inserting mark-up language in their notes. In comparison with previous courses in which students were directed through the course by closed tasks, we can conclude that the use of Knowledge Forum resulted in a much more collaborative form of learning. The whole course was much more student-centered. The quality of the final learning products (i.e., a set of educational policy notes in a school context) shows that the approach and use of Knowledge Forum resulted in sufficient transfer of the acquired understanding to work within an authentic problem.

The second question can be addressed by looking at the average and cumulative knowledge building results. The high correlations among the knowledge building variables indicate a level of collaboration that is otherwise difficult to achieve in a more conventional classroom. However, it must be said that most of the activities take place at the beginning of the course during which the teacher involvement is high. The relationship between teacher involvement and student activity applies to university students and students in secondary vocational education. In the university course it means that Knowledge Forum most supported the explication and inventory of students' prior knowledge by students themselves. It enabled students to start from their own theories and formulate their learning questions based on their own interest and their own discovered knowledge deficiencies. During the phase of "deepening," the high rate of note production was brought to a halt. This might be because of the more individualized task of reading literature and describing it in a compact way in the database. The knowledge building in the database went down. It is unclear if this relates to a lower involvement of the teacher or that more discussion was going on outside the database in small groups. From the didactic point of view, more attention has to be paid to this phase to optimize the use of Knowledge Forum to support the exchange of new insights when students studying external resources. As currently used it does enable students to achieve an optimal level of shared understanding. Possibly because of their normal study habits, students insufficiently used Knowledge Forum to make use of their own multiple perspectives and understanding during the phase of deepening by studying literature and other resources.

With regard to the question of teacher didactics, students treat coaching and stimulating by the teachers as very important. The studies show that it is insufficient just to create an open environment of discussion. The openness of working in Knowledge Forum is not related to "undirected" (as opposed to "self-regulated") learning styles. Working in Knowledge Forum does not serve students who have a latent orientation toward "undirected" learning. Students with an "application-directed" learning style probably fit better into the Knowledge Forum approach. The teacher must be aware that an effective use of Knowledge Forum needs a systematic didactic approach and high degree of teacher involvement. The importance of the didactic phase seems to be in actualizing, planning, deepening, and experiencing learning. The phase of deepening needs a greater teacher involvement than was the case in the presented studies. Important steps include articulating prior knowledge and students' theories, relating to students' own interests and questions, making use of the jigsaw-method, and using authentic final tasks to experience the use of knowledge. Also, the production of public notes by students stimulates the sharing of knowledge and understanding. Last, but not least, the face-to-face meetings each week are very important, not for lecturing, but for the coaching of students, that is, discussing student progress and coming to collaborative solutions to facilitate the learning in Knowledge Forum. The teacher also needs to be well acquainted with the knowledge domain to be able to coach students. It can be concluded that using Knowledge Forum not only encourages students to take on more responsibility for their own learning but also enables teachers to be more effective coaches.

REFERENCES

Baker, M., & Lund, K. (1997). Promoting reflective interactions in a CSCL environment. *Journal of Computer Assisted Learning, 13*, 175–193.

Brown, A., & Campione, J. (1996). Psychological theory and the design of innovative learning environments: On procedures, principles, and systems. In L. Schauble & R. Glaser (Eds.), *Innovations in learning: New environments for education* (pp. 289–325). Mahwah, NJ: Lawrence Erlbaum Associates.

Bruner, J. (1996). *The culture of education.* Cambridge, MA: Harvard University Press.

Bielaczyc, K., & Collins, A. (1998). Learning communities in classrooms: A re-conceptualization of educational practice. In C. M. Reigeluth (Ed.), *Instructional design theories and models: Vol. 2. A new paradigm of instructional theory* (pp. 269–292). Hillsdale, NJ: Lawrence Erlbaum Associates.

Cunningham, D. J. (1992). In defense of extremism. In T. M. Duffy & D. H. Jonassen (Eds.), *Constructivism and the technology of instruction* (pp. 157–160). Hillsdale, NJ: Lawrence Erlbaum Associates.

De Corte, E., Greer, B., & Verschaffel, L. (1996), Mathematics learning and teaching. In D. C. Berliner & R. C. Calfee (Eds.), *Handbook of educational psychology* (pp. 491–549). New York: Macmillan.

de Jong, F. P. C. M. (1995). Process-oriented instruction: Some considerations. In F. P. C. M. de Jong & S. Volet (Eds.), Process-oriented instruction: Improving students' learning [special issue]. *European Journal of Psychology of Education, X-4*, 317–323.

de Jong, F. P. C. M., & Biemans, H. (1998). Constructivistisch Onderwijs. In J. Vermunt & L. Verschaffel (Ed.), Onderwijzen van kennis en vaardigheden. *Onderwijskundig Lexicon, editie III* (pp. 67–85). Alphen aan den Rijn: Samson.

Duffy, T. M., Dueber, W., & Hawley, C. L. (1998). Critical thinking in a distributed environment: A pedagogical base for the design of conferencing systems. In C. J. Bonk and K. King (Eds.), *Electronic collaborators: Learner-centred technologies for literacy, apprenticeship and discourse* (pp. 51–78). Mahway, NJ: Lawrence Erlbaum Associates.

Duffy, T. M., & Knuth, R. A. (1991). Hypermedia and instruction: Where is the match? In D. Jonassen and H. Mandl (Eds.), *Designing hypermedia for learning* (pp. 199–225). Heidelberg: Springer-Verlag.

Hakkarainen, K. P. J. (1998). *Epistemology of scientific inquiry and computer supported collaborative learning.* Toronto, Canada: University of Toronto, Department of Human Development and Applied Psychology.

Lampert, M. (1990). When the problem is not the question and the solution is not the answer: Mathematical knowing and teaching. *American Educational Research Journal, 27*(1), 29–63.

Mattingly, R. M., VanSickle, & Ronald, L. (1991). Cooperative Learning and achievement in social studies: Jigsaw II. *Social Education, 55*(6), 392–395.

Maturana, H. R., & Varela, F. J. (1992). *The Tree of Knowledge, the biological roots of human understanding* (Rev. ed). Boston: Shambala Publications.

Röling, N., & de Jong, F. P. C. M. (1998). Learning: Shifting paradigms in education and extension studies. *International Journal of Agricultural Education and Extension, 5*(4), 143–160.

Scardamalia, M., & Bereiter, C. (1994). Computer support for knowledge-building communities. *Journal of the Learning Sciences, 3*, 265–283.

Scardamalia, M., & Bereiter, C. (1996). Engaging students in a knowledge society. *Educational Leadership, 3*, 6–10.

Slavin, R. E. (1983). *Cooperative learning. Research on Teaching Monograph Series.* New York: Longman, Inc.

Spiro, R. J., & Jehng, J. (1990). Cognitive flexibility and hypertext: Theory and technology for the nonlinear and multidimensional traversal of complex subject matter. In D. Nix & R. Spiro (Eds.), *Cognition, education, multimedia. Exploring ideas in high technology* (pp. 163–205). Hillsdale, NJ: Lawrence Erlbaum Associates.

Vermunt, J. D. (1995). Process-oriented instruction in learning and thinking strategies. In F. P. C. M. de Jong & S. Voletb (Eds.), Process-oriented instruction: Improving student learning [special issue]. *European Journal of Psychology of Education, X-4,* 325–350.

EPISTEMOLOGY OF INQUIRY AND COMPUTER-SUPPORTED COLLABORATIVE LEARNING[1]

Kai Hakkarainen
Lasse Lipponen
University of Helsinki

Sanna Järvelä
University of Oulu

INTRODUCTION

The purpose of the present study was to analyze the epistemological nature of elementary school students' process of knowledge-seeking inquiry in the Computer-Supported Intentional Learning Environments (CSILE) (Scardamalia & Bereiter, 1991). The problem addressed in the study was whether school children could achieve certain fundamental aspects of scientific inquiry, such as engaging in a sustained question-driven process of inquiry, invoking explanation-driven processes of understanding, working collaboratively to improve constructed explanations, and participating in progressive discourse. The problem was studied by analyzing the epistemological characteristics of knowledge produced by one Finnish and two Canadian CSILE classes.

Technical infrastructure for the study was provided by the CSILE environment (Scardamalia & Bereiter, 1989, 1993, 1994, 1996). A central part of

[1]The present study is a part of the Schools of Helsinki 2001 project organized by the Helsinki City Education Department. The research part of the overall project is coordinated by the Finnish IT Center for Schools, Vantaa Institution for Continuing Education, University of Helsinki. Finnish research on the CSILE environment is based on a research agreement between the Centre for Applied Cognitive Science, Ontario Institute for Studies in Education and the Department of Psychology, University of Helsinki.

the CSILE environment is a communal database for producing, searching, classifying, and linking knowledge. The system facilitates sharing of cognitive achievements by providing each student access to all text notes, comments, and charts produced by their fellow students. CSILE is designed to foster collaborative learning through its advanced facilities for searching out and commenting on knowledge. Students use CSILE by writing notes, creating charts, and reading and commenting on each other's productions in the context of such domains of knowledge as physics and biology.

CSILE is designed to facilitate elementary school students' participation in higher-level practices of inquiry characteristic of scientific inquiry. An analogy between the history of science and the development of scientific thinking in childhood as well as between scientific thinking and children's thinking has been a very important foundation of cognitive research on educational practices. Several philosophers and historians of science (Kitcher, 1988; Nersessian, 1989, 1992; Thagard, 1992) as well as cognitive researchers (e.g., Carey, 1986; Cobb, Wood, & Yackel, 1991; Duschl, Hamilton, & Grandy, 1992; Hawkins & Pea, 1987; Piaget & Garcia, 1989; Scardamalia & Bereiter, 1994) have argued that there is a close relationship between the process of scientific thinking and learning science as well as between the philosophy of science and science education.

Many past efforts to bring scientific inquiry into schools have, however, suffered from promoting an idealistic model of scientific inquiry that does not correspond to actual practices of scientific inquiry (Scardamalia & Bereiter, 1994). Rather than trying to pursue abstract forms of scientific thinking in education, it would be profitable to start with certain practices of working productively with knowledge that characterize scientific inquiry and rely on extended cognitive resources embedded in a community of inquirers. A promising new approach to facilitating scientific thinking in education is based on the idea that scientific inquiry represents a special kind of cultural practice. Several researchers have proposed that to facilitate higher-level processes of inquiry in education, cultures of schooling should more closely correspond to cultures of scientific inquiry (Cobb et al., 1991; Hawkins & Pea, 1987).

Scardamalia and Bereiter (1994) proposed that scientific thinking could be facilitated in a school by organizing a classroom to function like a scientific research community and guiding students to participate in practices of progressive scientific discourse. They have argued that there are *no* compelling reasons why school education should not have the dynamic character of scientific inquiry. The analogy between school learning and scientific inquiry is based on a close connection between processes of learning and discovery. Inquiry pursued for producing new knowledge and inquiry carried out by learners working for understanding new knowledge are based on the same kinds of cognitive processes (Scardamalia & Bereiter, 1994; see also Nersessian, 1989, 1992). Learning, analogously with scientific discovery and theory formation, is a process of working toward a more thorough and complete understanding. Although students are learning already existing knowledge, they may be engaged in the same kind of extended processes of question-driven inquiry as scientists and scholars.

In the present study, the sustained processes of advancing and building of knowledge characteristic of scientific inquiry are called *knowledge-seeking inquiry* (Hakkarainen, 1998). Several concurrent, cognitive research projects share a common goal of fostering such research-like processes of inquiry in education (Brown & Campione, 1996; Carey & Smith, 1995; Lampert, 1995; Perkins, Crismond, Simmons, & Unger, 1995; Scardamalia & Bereiter, 1994; Xiadong, Bransford, Hmelo, Kantor, Hickey, Secules, Petrosino, Goldman, & The Cognition and Technology Group at Vanderbilt, 1996). Knowledge-seeking inquiry entails that knowledge is not simply assimilated but constructed through solving problems of understanding. By imitating practices of scientific research communities, children can be guided to participate in extended processes of question- and explanation-driven inquiry.

By synthesizing the philosophy of science and cognitive research, a framework can be constructed for analyzing the essential aspects of progressive knowledge-seeking inquiry that characterize scientific research. The process of knowledge-seeking inquiry starts from an agent's *cognitive or epistemic goals* that arise out of his or her dissatisfaction with the state of present knowledge (Hintikka, 1985). Cognitive goals guide and regulate the process of inquiry. Knowledge-seeking inquiry is facilitated by learning that is focused on working toward a more coherent and deeper understanding through the recognition of weaknesses and limitations of one's own knowledge (Scardamalia & Bereiter, 1993, 1996).

Recent approaches to the philosophy of science have strongly emphasized the role of problems, or questions, in scientific inquiry (Laudan, 1977; Hintikka, 1985). From a cognitive point of view, inquiry can be characterized as a *question-driven* process of understanding. Without a research question there cannot be a genuine process of inquiry, although information is frequently produced at school without any guiding questions. A research question activates a learner's background knowledge by facilitating an in-depth search of the learner's memory; simultaneously, it facilitates the making of inferences from one's knowledge and guides one continuously to relate what he or she already knows to the new information (Hintikka, 1982; Macmillan & Garrison, 1988; Sintonen, 1990; Hakkarainen & Sintonen, 1999). From the cognitive viewpoint, particularly important questions arise from problems of understanding and explanation, and, correspondingly, explanation-seeking research questions have a special cognitive value (Bereiter, 1992; Scardamalia & Bereiter, 1992).

The question-driven process of inquiry provides heuristic guidance in the search for *new scientific information*. Considerable advancement of inquiry cannot be made without obtaining new information. Further, large bodies of information cannot be managed without questions that guide and constrain the knowledge-seeking process and help to structure the information obtained. All scientific information does not have equal cognitive value; explanatory or theoretical knowledge has a key role in conceptual understanding and, thus, a special status in the cognitive process of inquiry. An additional characteristic of knowledge building activity is the problematic way in which conflicting information is treated (Bereiter & Scardamalia, 1993; Chan, Burtis, & Bereiter, 1997).

Another important aspect of inquiry is generation of *one's own explanations, hypotheses, or conjectures* (Carey & Smith, 1995; Lampert, 1995; Perkins et al., 1995; Scardamalia & Bereiter, 1989, 1993). To foster dynamic change of conceptions and integration of knowledge structures, a learner has to engage in an intentional process of generating his or her own explanations and theories. If the process of inquiry is carried out as a strong, systematic cognitive effort and relevant new information is obtained, the agent often succeeds in creating increasingly more sophisticated explanations. Knowledge emerges through his or her intentional attempts to explain and understand the problems being investigated; it is usually connected with the learner's other knowledge in a rich web of meaningful connections.

Several important aspects of knowledge-seeking inquiry characteristic of scientific research outlined above are implemented in the structure of the Computer-Supported Intentional Learning Environment and corresponding cognitive practices. CSILE is designed to engage students with an extensive process of setting up research questions, generating and improving their own intuitive explanations, and searching for scientific information. Participation in all aspects of the process of knowledge-seeking inquiry is facilitated by the use of CSILE's Thinking Types. Further, CSILE fosters socially distributed inquiry by providing tools for sharing of cognitive achievements. The CSILE student community is collectively responsible for their knowledge advancement. The system provides the users with advanced tools for communicating with other members of the learning community. Thus, it appears that the CSILE environment has a potential to facilitate participation in higher-level practices of inquiry.

The present study focuses on analyzing CSILE students' practices of knowledge processing. It is important to notice, however, that CSILE provides only a technical infrastructure for knowledge-seeking inquiry; hence, it can also be used as a new means toward traditional ends (see Salomon, in press). In order to have significant pedagogical advantages, CSILE use should be intentionally grounded on practices of knowledge-seeking inquiry. It seems that to effectively facilitate participation in higher-level practices of inquiry in education and exploit new technology-based learning environments at school, constraints and conditions for successful application of computer-supported collaborative learning should be carefully examined. There is not enough research data, for instance, about how this kind of knowledge-seeking inquiry works in different school environments and classroom cultures or how teachers with different pedagogical and domain expertise may use the new cognitive resources provided by CSILE and implement the practices of collaborative knowledge-seeking inquiry (Hakkarainen, Järvelä, Lipponen, & Lehtinen, 1998). Thus, an important aim of our study was to examine how different practices of computer-supported collaborative learning influenced the epistemological nature of the students' inquiry.

The study focused on examining conditions for which computer-supported collaborative learning facilitates higher-level practices of inquiry by comparing three groups of CSILE students. Epistemology of inquiry was examined through analyzing the role of basic elements of inquiry such as question generation, theory formation, and peer interaction in different classroom cultures representing both Canadian and Finnish CSILE groups. This kind of cross-cultural comparison of educational processes is, in some respects, problematic; there are often historical and cultural differences that may easily be overlooked. However, in the present case, the Canadian and Finnish CSILE students were working with the same technology-based learning environment by carrying out the same kinds of study projects. Moreover, the Finnish CSILE experiment was intentionally designed to replicate achievements of the Canadian CSILE groups. As a consequence of working with the same learning environment, both the structure and process of the students' inquiry were relatively homogeneous. Further, the knowledge processed by the CSILE students was analyzed from an epistemological viewpoint with emphasis more on the epistemological nature of inquiry than on the concrete contents of problems solved or projects carried out. So there is a reason to presume that the epistemological level of analysis, in the present case, can be abstracted from potentially culture-specific factors. The study was entirely based on a conceptual as well as a qualitative and quantitative analysis of students' written productions from CSILE's database, and, therefore, it did not give direct information about psychological processes involved in CSILE use.

METHOD

Subjects

The purpose of the study was to examine how practices of knowledge production and peer interaction differed between three groups of CSILE

TABLE 4.1
Study Group and Gender

Group	Male	Female	Total
Canadian A	9	19	28
Canadian B	19	9	28
Finnish	13	13	26
Total	41	41	82

students. These groups did the same sorts of things with CSILE, such as project learning, but followed different pedagogical practices. The Canadian study material represented productions of two parallel grade 5 and 6 classes (Canadian classrooms A and B) over a period of one year at an inner-city public school in Toronto, Canada. In the school studied, a larger than normal proportion of children came from middle-class and upper middle-class homes. However, the student population was ethnically heterogeneous and included a number of students from educationally disadvantaged homes (Scardamalia, Bereiter, Brett, Burtis, Calhoun, & Smith, 1992). Processes of inquiry in these groups were compared with corresponding processes in a Finnish grade 4 CSILE class (10-year-old students) from the city of Helsinki (see Lipponen & Hakkarainen, 1997, for background of the Finnish experiment). Data regarding the composition of groups that participated in the study are presented in Table 4.1. Although assignment the students to these two classes was reported by teachers and principal to be random, gender distribution of the students in the Canadian classrooms was outside of what might be expected with randomized sampling (see Table 4.1). The relative proportion of female students was larger in Canadian classroom A than in classroom B ($\chi^2 = 7.1, df = 1, p < .008$).

There were significant differences between the Canadian and Finnish CSILE groups. The Canadian CSILE students had started their schooling at age 6, having one year more experience of education than the Finnish group who started their schooling at age 7. Moreover, the Canadian groups were mixed grade 5/6 classrooms so that 67.9% ($n = 38$) of the 56 students were at the grade 6 level. It is possible that the older students provided a kind of expert model for the younger students in the Canadian groups and, therefore, affected the general quality of inquiry in the groups. However, as the Finnish students had started to use CSILE at grade 3 they had more experience working with CSILE (three whole terms) than the Canadian subjects; only 44.6% ($n = 25$) of the Canadian students had used CSILE over a two-year period. Presumably, this difference compensated for the higher age level of the Canadian students. The groups shared a common structure and process of inquiry and worked with the same type of independent study projects.

Therefore, the groups can be compared insofar as the differences mentioned above are taken into consideration.

Study Material

The study was based on an analysis of CSILE students' written productions, posted to CSILE's database. The material represented data occurring naturally while the students carried out their study projects working with CSILE. In working with CSILE, the students produced daily, or at least several times a week, computer entries called "notes" in the context of their study projects. The study was carried out by qualitatively and quantitatively analyzing knowledge produced by the students and stored in the CSILE database.

The Canadian CSILE students conducted many different kinds of projects in biology and physics. In the case of the Canadian classroom A, the analysis concerned three different projects (Force, Cosmology, and Electricity) in physics and one project (Human Biology) in biology. The purpose of the Force project was to explain different forms of force, especially gravity. In the Cosmology project the students were asked to explain how the universe changed and how it will be in the future. The Electricity project was focused on explaining what happens inside a wire when electric current passes through it. The Human Biology project focused on examining biological processes in the human body, such as how cells or the circulatory system function. The students in the Canadian classroom B were often working on individual projects; therefore, their topics were more heterogeneous than those of the Canadian classroom A. Biology was the main focus of the Canadian classroom B and the most important projects carried out were Geographical Areas and Protozoa. Further, the classroom conducted the Mammoth (lever) project in physics and the Continental Drift project in geology. In addition, the group used CSILE in working with mathematics, which was not a focus of the two other groups; such work was excluded from the analysis. The Finnish CSILE group used CSILE to carry out study projects in biology and environmental studies (Northern Countries, Natural

TABLE 4.2
Productions of the Two Canadian and the Finnish CSILE Group
Analyzed Qualitatively

Group	Research Questions		Knowledge Ideas		Communicative Ideas		Total	
	f	%	f	%	f	%	f	%
Canadian A	983	30.3	1727	53.2	537	16.5	3247	100.0
Canadian B	569	31.3	721	39.6	530	29.1	1820	100.0
Finnish	150	13.5	341	30.7	619	55.8	1110	100.0

Phenomena, Ecology, and Human). Frequencies of CSILE students' ideas, analyzed qualitatively, are presented in Table 4.2. The CSILE students produced hundreds of research questions, notes presenting their intuitive and scientific knowledge, and written comments.

From Table 4.1 it can be inferred that there were considerable differences in productivity among the Canadian classrooms A and B and the Finnish group. It is particularly evident that the Finnish students did not produce as many research questions as the Canadian students.

Method of Data Analysis

By relying on conceptual tools provided by the philosophy of science and cognitive theory, methods were developed for analyzing the epistemological nature of the students' inquiry. CSILE students' written productions (or "postings" to the database) from CSILE's database were analyzed through qualitative content analysis (see, for example, Chi, 1997). Coding categories used in the qualitative content analysis were derived from the theoretical review concerning knowledge-seeking inquiry in order to increase validity of the study. The analysis was semantic in nature and focused on the basic categories of CSILE students' knowledge-seeking inquiry (i.e., research problems, intuitive explanations, scientific information sought by students, and comments).

To make a reliable qualitative classification of the material possible, CSILE students' notes were first partitioned into *ideas* (regarding segmentation of data for content analysis; see Chi, 1997). An idea as the unit of analysis corresponded to the basic elements of CSILE students' inquiry, such as their research questions, intuitive explanations, pieces of scientific information or explanation sought by them, or comments between the students. The reliability of partitioning was assessed by asking two independent coders to segment 200 notes into ideas. The Pearson correlation between number of ideas identified by the two coders was 93.8.

A basic assumption of the study was that knowledge-seeking inquiry is a question-driven process. The general nature of research questions appeared to determine the epistemic nature of the knowledge-seeking process and what kinds of cognitive operations were available for a student during inquiry. The epistemological nature of the students' research questions was analyzed by classifying each research question according to whether it was fact- or explanation-seeking in nature. *How* and *why* questions are typical explanation-seeking questions and cannot be satisfactorily answered without elaborating an explanation. Moreover, many *what* and indirect questions can be transformed into explanation-seeking *why* or *how* questions. *Who, where, when, how many*, and some *what* questions represented fact-seeking questions that can be answered by providing factual information.

In answering their research questions, CSILE students searched for different kinds of scientific information and generated their own intuitive explanations and theories. Each knowledge idea was classified according to type of knowledge, that is, whether its main content represented (a) new scientific information or (b) the student's own intuitive explanation. "Scientific information" means that a student reviewed or introduced pieces of new scientific facts or theories (i.e., provided information that he or she or the group as a whole was not yet familiar with). "Intuitive explanations" refers to notes in which a student generated his or her own view or an explicit theory about the phenomenon in question.

To analyze the epistemological nature of knowledge produced by the CSILE students, the *mean explanatory level of knowledge* was analyzed across students' productions representing their intuitive conceptions and scientific information researched by them. Each knowledge idea constructed by the students to answer their research questions was classified by using a five-step scale starting from (1) separated pieces of facts to (5) explanation:

Level 1. Isolated Facts. A rating of 1 was assigned to CSILE students' knowledge ideas representing either simple statements of facts or lists of facts with hardly any connecting linkages that would have provided some coherence or integration. Ideas representing isolated, unconnected facts usually represented answers to corresponding fact-seeking questions.

> Some related animals are, Sponges, Venusus Flower basket, Portuges man of war, Sea Anomes, Jelly Fish and Hydra.

Level 2. Partially Organized Facts. A rating of 2 was given to ideas that represented loosely connected pieces of factual information. These ideas can be separated from level 1 ideas because the former represented more organized descriptions about empirical phenomena and certain linkages were provided to connect pieces of facts together. Frequently, however, these ideas were not very coherent or comprehensive; at this level, information was still produced in a list-like fashion.

> I think that there are many different kinds of cells with totally different functions. I only know the names of some cells, the red blood cell, white blood cells, muscle cells and nerve cells.

Level 3. Well-Organized Facts. A rating of 3 was assigned to ideas in which factual information was introduced in a rather well-organized way. These ideas were used to describe different biological and physical phenomena without, however, connecting the description with deeper causal or explanatory relations. Although it was sometimes possible to reconstruct an explanation-seeking question that would be answered by level 3 ideas, no explicit explanation was actually provided.

> The absorptive cell is located around the epithelial cells and small intestines. Its purpose is to eat and/or collect food molecules, salts and water that are in the body. Absorptive cells need to use their entire cell structure to move around.

Level 4. Partial Explanation. A rating of 4 was assigned to ideas that represented some characteristics of explanation but with rather limited or only partially articulated content. Typical for these ideas was an explicit attempt to answer an explanation-seeking question and produce an explanation. However, certain important aspects of the explanation were left open so that the explanation had apparent weaknesses. For example, while answering a question, "Why do sponges and related animals have three ways of reproducing and other animal forms only have one?," a student produced the following explanation:

> I think that the nerves control themselves and that they send messages to the brain so that the brain can control the body. The nerves are just there to tell the brain what is happening because the brain can't be every where at once.

Although the ideas were clearly intended to be explanations, there is an apparent need for further articulation; one or several pieces of explanation remain to be explicated. However, regardless of limitations of the explanatory sketches provided, these productions can be separated from level 3 ideas, which clearly did not go beyond introducing factual or descriptive information.

Level 5. Explanation. A rating of 5 was assigned to ideas in which a relatively well-elaborated explanation was provided. This rating presupposed neither correctness nor coherence of explanation; it was enough that a student clearly constructed and elaborated his or her own intuitive explanation or introduced a scientific explanation.

> I think that cells reproduce because we couldn't live on the two cells that we start out as. Somehow the cells know that they have to reproduce. I think that how they reproduce is the cells start to split and the parts of the cell also start to split and they go to the new cell. It's kind of like there are two cells stacked on top of each other and then the one cell just moves off the other cell and you have two cells. Now you have two cells and both those cells reproduce giving you four cells and so on.

My theory of how the glial cells hold the brain together is that, they might be the bigger cells in the brain, that SH talked about. They might work in twos, one to cradle the neuron cells and the other one to sit on top of it to gently squish it, so it wouldn't move around. The glial cells themselves are stuck to the outer covering of the brain.

CSILE students' peer interaction was analyzed by examining contents of their written communication mediated by the CSILE network. Communicative ideas appeared to reflect how the students themselves conceptualized their knowledge-seeking inquiry.

CSILE students' comments were classified according to type of communicative idea, that is, whether an idea (1) supported the note commented on, expressing agreement, (2) represented neutral exchange of ideas, or (3) was critical in nature, expressing disagreement. Neutral communicative ideas were further divided into two subgroups according to function of the neutral communicative idea: (a) communicative ideas in which a student requested information or an explanation or asked a question and (b) communicative ideas in which he or she provided information or an explanation or answered a question.

The object of cognitive activity determines to a great extent the psychological nature of inquiry. Communicative ideas within a comment were analyzed by specifying, in each case, the *object of inquiry*, that is, whether the communicative idea was about (1) linguistic form (e.g., spelling mistakes), (2) student-generated research questions being pursued, (3) methods of inquiry, (4) quantity or quality of information sought by the students, (5) intuitive explanations generated by the students or scientific information sought by them, (6) other ideas (e.g., technical aspects of CSILE use), or (7) an unspecified aspect. Each communicative idea was considered to represent only one of the above-mentioned categories. CSILE students' peer interaction was analyzed by distinguishing inquiry-related comments from comments that were unspecific or focused on linguistic form, or from technical aspects of CSILE use. Further, the proportion of explanation-related communicative ideas was used to assess the epistemological nature of CSILE students' peer interaction. Explanation-related comments were designed to either assess explanation constructed by the student being commented upon or to provide an explanation generated by the student him- or herself. An explicit reference to explanation was not, however, a necessary prerequisite for categorizing a comment as explanation-related; also, comments that referred to how hard or easy it is to understand the ideas presented in the note commented upon were regarded as explanation-related.

The investigators analyzed how CSILE students explicated referential relations of their communicative ideas. The analysis was carried out by using a three-step scale for assessing explication of referential relations, and the

CSILE students' comments were classified as explicated, partially explicated, and unexplicated. Some of the unexplicated ideas were completely unspecified; in these cases, the main object of the comment could not be specified at all, that is, one could not determine whether a communicative idea was focused on linguistic form or some aspect of the process of inquiry. Typically, in this kind of comment, reasons for disagreement or agreement were left completely open (e.g., "I like your note." or "Your note is not good."). An explicated comment was self-explanatory, that is, it was understandable without any background or contextual knowledge.

To analyze the reliability of the classification, two independent coders classified 200 research questions, 200 knowledge ideas, and 300 communicative ideas representing both Canadian classrooms A and B. The reliability of classifying the Finnish data was assessed in a corresponding way by using two independent raters. Inter-coder reliabilities of the classification were satisfactory and exceeded .70 across practically all variables. Disagreements were discussed after the reliability analysis and those ideas that were classified differently by the two coders were analyzed again and coded according to a mutual agreement.

Because the classification of CSILE students' productions was made at the level of ideas, several observations were obtained for each student. On average, the students produced 74 ($SD = 53$) ideas during the period analyzed. To identify the most important differences between the groups of CSILE users, the relative importance of different contents in individual students' comments and notes was studied proportionately.

An Analysis of Teacher Guidance

We also analyzed how teachers of the three groups guided their students' inquiry by examining the teachers' comments posted to the CSILE's database. The analysis focused on examining teachers' participation in CSILE discourse and whether their comments facilitated deepening their students' inquiry. Data directly concerning teacher practice was not gathered.

RESULTS

Practices of Knowledge Production

CSILE students' knowledge production was examined by analyzing the nature of research questions produced as well as the explanatory level of the scientific and intuitive knowledge processed. A direct discriminant analysis was performed using three variables representing the nature of CSILE students' knowledge production as predictors of membership in a CSILE group.

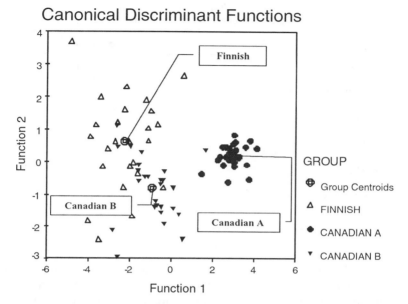

FIG. 4.1. Plots of three group centroids on two discriminant functions derived from three knowledge-production variables: proportion of explanation-seeking research questions, mean explanatory level of scientific information, and mean explanatory level of intuitive knowledge.

The predictors were mean proportion of student-generated explanation-seeking research questions, mean explanatory level of intuitive knowledge, and mean explanatory level of scientific information. CSILE group (Canadian A, Canadian B, Finnish) was used as a grouping variable.

Two discriminant functions were calculated, with a combined $\chi^2(6) = 161.9, p < .0001$. After removal of the first function, strong association remained between groups and predictors, $\chi^2(3) = 22.1, p < .0001$. The two discriminant functions accounted for 93.8% and 6.2% of the between-group variability, respectively. As shown in Fig. 4.1, the first discriminant function maximally separates the Canadian classroom A from the Finnish classroom and Canadian classroom B. The second discriminant function partially discriminates the Canadian classroom B and Finnish classroom from each other.

The loading matrix of correlations between predictors and discriminant function, as seen in Fig. 4.1, suggested that the best predictors for distinguishing between the Canadian classroom A and the two other groups (first function) were mean explanatory level of scientific knowledge and mean explanatory level of intuitive knowledge. The level of scientific information searched by the Canadian A classroom (mean = 4.15) was higher than that of the Finnish classroom (mean = 2.18) or the Canadian classroom B

TABLE 4.3
Results of Discriminant Function Analysis of Knowledge-Production Variables

Predictor Variable	Correlations With the Discriminant Function		
	1	2	Univariate F (2,79)
Mean proportion of explanation-seeking questions	.22	.68	15.8
Mean explanatory level of intuitive knowledge	.61	−.64	77.7
Mean explanatory level of scientific knowledge	.83	.50	137.9
Canonical R	.91	.50	—
Eigenvalue	5.00	.33	—

(mean = 2.35). Moreover, the mean level of intuitive knowledge was higher in the Canadian classroom A's productions (mean = 4.14) than in those of the Finnish classroom (mean = 2.16) or the Canadian classroom B (mean = 3.35).

Two predictors, the proportion of explanation-seeking research questions and mean explanatory level of intuitive knowledge, had a loading in excess of .50 on the second discriminant function, which separates the Finnish classroom from the Canadian classroom B. The Finnish classroom (mean = .69) produced a higher proportion of explanation-seeking research questions than the Canadian classroom B (mean = .53). Simultaneously, however, the mean explanatory level of intuitive knowledge was lower in the Finnish classroom (mean = 2.61) than in Canadian classroom B (mean = 3.32).

An examination of the pooled within-group correlations among the three predictors revealed that one of the three correlations would show statistical significance at the alpha = .05 level if tested individually. There is a positive relationship between mean level of scientific explanation and proportion of explanation-seeking research questions ($r(82) = .34$, $p < .05$), indicating that a higher proportion of explanation-seeking research questions was associated with a high mean explanatory level of scientific information.

With the discriminant classification procedure for the total usable sample of 82 students, 84% were classified correctly, compared to 27 (33%) that would have been correctly classified by chance alone. The 84% classification rate was achieved by using sample proportions as prior probabilities. The likelihood of correctly classifying the Canadian classroom A students (100%, 28) was higher than that of classifying the Finnish (77%, 20) or the Canadian classroom B (75%, 21) students, indicating that practices of inquiry were more heterogeneous in the latter groups.

The analysis revealed that the epistemological nature of knowledge production differed substantially among the groups. An explanation-oriented process of inquiry had a prominent role in the Canadian classroom A's practices of knowledge processing. The Canadian classroom A clearly differed from the two other groups in terms of a higher proportion of explanation-seeking research questions and the mean explanatory level of scientific information and mean explanatory level of intuitive knowledge. It was also noticeable that the Canadian classroom A represented very homogeneous practices of knowledge production; practically all students were carrying out the same kinds of practices of explanation-oriented inquiry. In contrast, inquiries by students in Canadian classroom B and the Finnish classroom focused on processing factual knowledge and making empirical generalizations. Even if the students of the Finnish classroom produced a relatively high proportion of explanation-seeking research questions exceeding, in this sense, the Canadian classroom B, it was not correspondingly engaged with construction of its own explanations or search for explanatory scientific information.

The present results, however, should be taken with caution because an examination concerning homogeneity of variance–covariance matrices revealed a significant divergence from the assumptions of multivariate analysis (Box's $M = 109.9$, $p < .0001$). The varying within-group variances seemed, however, to represent an important aspect of the phenomenon studied. Variance, for example, concerning the mean proportion of explanation-seeking research questions was lower in the Canadian classroom A than in the two other groups because practically all students engaged in producing this kind of question. Thus, unequal variances represented an important educational achievement instead of being just a statistical problem (compare Howell, 1987, p. 181). Taking the robustness of statistical methods used as well as effect sizes of the phenomena measured into consideration, the results may be considered as providing a relatively accurate description of differences among the CSILE groups.

Practices of Peer Interaction

A direct discriminant analysis was performed using four variables representing the nature of CSILE students' peer interaction as predictors of membership in a CSILE group. The predictors were mean proportion of explanation-related comments, mean proportion of critical comments, mean level of explication, and mean proportion of inquiry-related comments. The grouping variable was CSILE group (Canadian A, Canadian B, and Finnish). Of the original 82 cases, only one case representing the Canadian classroom A was dropped from analysis because of missing data (no comments were produced).

Canonical Discriminant Functions

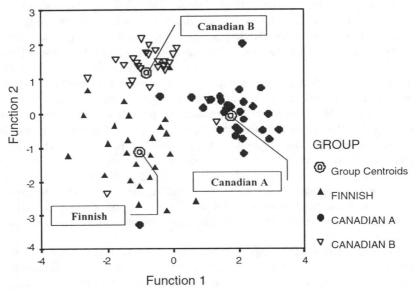

FIG. 4.2. Plots of three group centroids on two discriminant functions derived from four communicational variables: mean level explication and respective proportions for explanation-related comments, critical comments, and inquiry-related comments.

Two discriminant functions were calculated, with a combined $\chi^2(8) = 126.6$, $p < .0001$. After removal of the first function, strong association remained between groups and predictors, $\chi^2(3) = 50.3$, $p < .0001$. The third discriminant function, however, was not significant. The two discriminant functions accounted for 64.7% and 35.3%, respectively, of the between-group variability. As shown in Fig. 4.2, the first discriminant function separates Canadian classroom A from Canadian classroom B and the Finnish classroom. The second discriminant function discriminates the Finnish group from the Canadian classroom B.

The loading matrix of correlations between predictors and discriminant function, as seen in Table 4.4, suggest that the best predictors for distinguishing between Canadian classroom A and the Finnish classroom (first function) were mean proportion of explanation-related comments and mean level of explication. The students of Canadian classroom A (mean = .49) produced a higher mean proportion of explanation-related comments than did the Canadian classroom B (mean = .07) or Finnish (mean = .18) students. Furthermore, a higher mean level of explication of referential relations characterized the Canadian classroom A's (mean = 2.78) inquiry than

TABLE 4.4
Results of Discriminant Function Analysis of Peer-Interaction Variables

Predictor Variable	Correlations With the Discriminant Function		
	1	2	Univariate F (2, 79)
Mean proportion of explanation-related comments	.70	−.34	36.7
Mean proportion of critical comments	.43	.48	20.4
Mean level of explication	.74	−.14	36.8
Mean proportion of inquiry-related comments	.54	.71	38.0
Canonical R	.79	.69	—
Eigenvalue	1.68	.91	—

those of the Finnish classroom (mean = 2.21) or the Canadian classroom B (mean = 2.16).

As seen in Table 4.4, two predictors, mean proportion of inquiry-related comments and mean proportion of critical comments, had a significant loading on the second discriminant function, which separates the Canadian classroom B from the Finnish classroom. A significantly higher proportion of classroom B students' comments (mean = .80) was inquiry-related than those of the Finnish students (mean = .38). Moreover, the mean proportion of critical comments was higher in the Canadian classroom B (mean = .30) than in the Finnish classroom (mean = .10).

An examination of the pooled within-group correlations among the four predictors indicated that two of the four correlations would show statistical significance at the alpha = .05 level if tested individually. There was a positive relationship between mean proportion of explicated comments and mean proportion of inquiry-related comments ($r(82) = .42$, $p < .05$), indicating that inquiry-related comments are more likely to be explicated than other kinds of comments. Further, higher mean proportion of explanation-related comments appeared to be associated with a higher mean proportion of explicated comments ($r(82) = .24$, $p < .05$).

With the discriminant classification procedure for the total usable sample of 82 students, 89% were classified correctly, compared to 27 (33%) that would have been correctly classified by chance alone. The 89% classification rate was achieved by using sample proportions as prior probabilities. The likelihood of correctly classifying the Canadian classroom A students (93%, 26) was higher than that of classifying the Finnish (89%, 23) or the Canadian classroom B (86%, 24) students.

Results of the analysis indicated that only the Canadian classroom A engaged systematically in explanation-oriented discourse interaction; in the other two groups the proportion of explanation-related comments was significantly lower. In addition, explanation-oriented discourse was closely associated with a higher mean level of explicated comments, suggesting that the explanation-related comments tend to be more explicated than other kinds of comments. Further, the proportion of inquiry-related comments was lower in the Finnish group than in the two Canadian groups. The Finnish students were frequently discussing linguistic form and technical aspects of CSILE use (such as the use of Thinking Types and signing of one's notes). It was also characteristic of the Finnish group to engage in a rather neutral discussion, which produced relatively few supportive or critical comments; this appeared to represent their question–answer discourse (see Hakkarainen, Järvelä, Lipponen, & Lehtinen, 1998). Critical comments were frequently produced by the Canadian classroom A in which a very constructive culture of communication was dominant. The present results, however, should be taken with caution because an examination concerning homogeneity of variance–covariance matrices revealed a significant divergence from the assumptions of multivariate analysis (Box's $M = 60.1$, $p < .0001$). The varying within-group variances seemed, however, to represent an important aspect of the phenomenon studied.

Teacher Guidance

The analysis of teacher participation in CSILE discourse revealed that although the Finnish teacher produced only one comment, the teacher of Canadian classroom A (henceforth called "Teacher A") produced 24 comments and the teacher of Canadian classroom B (referred to hereafter as "Teacher B") produced 32 comments. Thus, it appears that the Finnish teacher left his students to work alone in CSILE and perhaps did not even read the students' productions. Teacher B, in contrast, participated actively in CSILE discussion. However, his comments were produced in the context of one project, Continental Drift. Across all projects, Teacher A was equally active and commented on students' productions.

An examination of the contents of the teachers' comments indicated that 75% (24 out of 32) of the comments of Teacher B were supportive in nature ("this is a very reasonable answer to this question"; "your answer makes good sense"), yet the reasons for support were not usually specified so that his remarks provided only general encouragement for the students. Further, only 21% (5 out of 24) of Teacher A's comments were supportive in nature ("this is interesting"; "this is a good problem"). This finding reflected the general nature of classroom A's discourse in which students very constructively pursued their inquiry; members of this learning community apparently did need to emphasize their mutual support in their discourse interaction. The comment produced by the Finnish teacher was also supportive ("your note is good but the arrow representing wind is in a wrong place").

Both Teacher A and Teacher B requested that the students do more research through their comments. However, Teacher A's focus appeared to be on students' understanding whereas Teacher B focused more on factual knowledge. Eighty-eight percent (21 out 24) of Teacher A's comments were explicitly focused on requesting students to explain or clarify their theories with comments such as "Why do you think this is so?" or "Could you explain it?"

Teacher A appeared to guide the students indirectly to deepen their inquiry; he did not give the student information about subject matter but pushed the student themselves to further articulate their theories. The following are typical examples of Teacher A's comments.

> I think this is a very interesting note. I was wondering if you were going to consider how the cells differ in function? For example, do they have any special structures that enable them to communicate with other cells? (Teacher A)

> In your NI [New Information] you wrote that the only nerve cells you get are the ones that you are born with. Does this mean that your brain is its maximum size at birth? Also, how would your nerve cells service the increased volume of your body as you grow? (Teacher A)

> You raise some interesting points in this note. I wonder what antigenic proteins are? Could you explain that? What do you suppose the relationship is between antigens and antibodies? (Teacher A)

Teacher B's comments, in contrast, were only seldom explicitly focused on explanation. Only 22% (7 out of 32) of his posted comments contained an explicit request of explanation. Instead, he asked students to "give some examples," "add more details," or to provide a more exact description of the phenomenon being investigated. Presumably, he tried to guide students toward specification of their own conceptions or toward a right answer.

> I think that your idea is a good one. I would suggest that you go back to the note and make sure that it makes sense. You need to write down exactly what you think happened. In other words; do some more thinking and add details. (Teacher B)

> This is a good beginning comment on the continents but you could give some details as to exactly how the continents are attached. A drawing on Kid Pix attached to your hypothesis would help. (Teacher B)

This is a very logical answer. Perhaps you could be more specific and say or show [Kid-Pix] exactly where you think Hawaii might have fit into North America. Here is another clue: Find out what kind of soil Hawaii has. (Teacher B)

Your answer makes good sense. Perhaps you could do some research and try to find out if what you think is true. (Teacher B)

Teacher B's guidance appeared to be more direct than Teacher A's guidance. Teacher A's comments were frequently questions whereas Teacher B's comments were statements. However, Teacher B's comments did not appear to affect the depth of students' inquiry whereas Teacher A's requests of explanation led, in many cases, to significant deepening of inquiry.

In conclusion, there were substantial differences between the Finnish and Canadian teachers in terms of intensity of commenting; the Canadian teachers participated in CSILE discourse much more actively than did the Finnish teacher. Further, Teacher A's comments were focused on facilitating elaboration of the students' own theories and explanations whereas Teacher B guided the students to work to obtain a more detailed and exact account of the problem being investigated. Also, Teacher A's style of guidance seemed to be more indirect in nature than that of Teacher B.

DISCUSSION

The analysis indicates that there were substantial differences concerning the epistemological nature of inquiry among three groups of CSILE students. Although Canadian classroom A engaged with explanation-oriented process of inquiry, the Finnish classroom and Canadian classroom B dealt with factual and descriptive information. In evaluating the results, one should take into consideration that the groups differed from each other in several ways; therefore, it is not possible to determine a single factor that would explain differences among the groups. Nevertheless, the analysis revealed that there were striking similarities between the present Canadian classroom B and the Finnish classroom in spite of different cultural backgrounds and educational contexts. Moreover, practices of knowledge production of these two groups diverged more from the Canadian classroom A than from each other. Such findings are to be taken as suggestive; further rigorously designed research is necessary to more definitively identify variables implicated in the three groups' performances.

This study indicates that an important explanation for the differences between the CSILE groups may be found in the implicit epistemological assumptions and cognitive design of the CSILE projects conducted in the three classrooms. Typically, of the Finnish classroom and Canadian classroom B took on conceptually unchallenging study projects that focused on the familiar everyday environment. The design of study projects carried out by these groups guided the students in working with factual knowledge rather than in searching for explanatory scientific knowledge. Although the Finnish group and Canadian classroom B produced explanation-seeking research questions, the scientific information processed by the groups was at a substantially lower explanatory level than that of Canadian classroom A. The projects of these groups focused mostly on observable empirical phenomena such as selecting an interesting phenomenon (e.g., species, countries, places) and searching for basic information about it. The most challenging task carried out by the Canadian classroom B or Finnish group seemed to be to examine *differences* and *similarities* between phenomena being investigated. The similarity-based approach (Murphy & Medin, 1985; Keil, 1989), adopted by the Finnish class and Canadian classroom B, seemed to lead to generation of list-type solutions instead of elaboration, articulation, or integration of knowledge.

Although the projects of the Canadian classroom B or Finnish groups would have provided a good opportunity to learn to conceptualize biological taxonomies in a principled way (e.g., warm-blooded versus cold-blooded animals), these taxonomies were frequently used as *labels*, and none of the students used group membership as a tool for inference (cf. Thagard, 1990). Furthermore, the students working in the Finnish classroom and Canadian classroom B did not come to discover deep biological principles, such as reproductive success (see Brown & Campione, 1996), in explaining the adaptation of the species studied. Although the projects carried out by the groups would have provided a good opportunity to acquire conceptual understanding of deep biological or physical principles (see Brown & Campione, 1996), the students were frequently bound to surface-level phenomena. The epistemological nature of Canadian classroom A's projects was different from that of the two other groups. It was characteristic of Canadian classroom A to conduct conceptually challenging study projects that focused on gaining theoretical understanding of the problems being investigated.

Common to Canadian classroom B and the Finnish classroom was that the students' own intuitive theories were not systematically facilitated. In many cases, students were explicitly guided simply to describe experimental procedures used and to form their own qualitative observations but not encouraged to construct their own hypothesis, conjectures, or theories. Lampert (1995) pointed out that engaging students in a genuine process of inquiry is a very challenging task requiring much effort from teachers. It requires building a new culture of learning where such generation of students' own theories has a legitimate role. A necessary prerequisite for the emergence of a constructive, scientific style of inquiry appears to be a culture in which each student is encouraged to articulate his or her intuitive theories, and in which each theory is respected as well as critically evaluated. This kind of culture, of which the Canadian classroom A provided an excellent example, allows each student to participate in articulating explanations without being afraid of unavoidable mistakes. The present analysis of the Canadian classroom A's process of inquiry has revealed that they were ready to take the challenge. White and Gunstone's (1989) analysis has shown how difficult this kind of change may be to achieve.

Results of the present study indicate, further, that there is a very close relationship between the epistemological nature of knowledge produced by an individual student and the learning tasks carried out. Classroom culture and the nature of learning tasks appear to create an economy of inquiry that significantly constrains each student's practices of inquiry. It would have required considerable mental effort from students in the Canadian classroom B and Finnish classroom to transform the given learning tasks into more challenging ones and to go deeper into the topic when the learning tasks in question did not require in-depth conceptual understanding. The nature of knowledge produced was empirical across all students; this seemed to reflect the nature of the learning tasks carried out rather than individual cognitive achievements. This contention was supported by the fact that differences between the collaborative and the two other groups were far more substantial than within-group differences between low- and high-achieving students. It appears that elementary school students do not break the constraints of concurrent pedagogical practices or the boundaries of empiricist epistemology without the teachers' cognitive and epistemological guidance (Hakkarainen, Lipponen, Järvelä, & Niemivirta, 1999; Järvelä, Hakkarainen, Lipponen, Niemivirta, & Lehtinen, 1997; Lipponen & Hakkarainen, 1997; Lipponen, 1999). Without a teacher's guidance or examples of advanced models of cognitive practices, *all* students, regardless of their individual cognitive competencies, might well remain at a more elementary level in their inquiry, as is observed in the case of the Canadian classroom B and Finnish group.

Examination of the material indicated that the Canadian classroom A's extraordinary epistemic achievements presupposed a very strong engagement of the teacher; the conceptually challenging study projects could not have been carried out without the teacher's guidance and active participation in CSILE discourse. The teacher of the Canadian classroom A apparently gave the students a great deal of epistemological support by providing an expert model of higher-level processes of inquiry. Like a facilitator in problem-based learning, the teacher consistently communicated with the students at a metacognitive level by requesting explication of explanatory relations; he guided the students in monitoring the progress of their understanding without directly giving them information (Savery & Duffy, 1996). This orientation turned out to be very effective; the students were often able to detect their misunderstandings, revise their theories correspondingly, and refocus their inquiry on the basis of the teacher's and the other students' requests for explication. With minimal instructional intervention, the teacher was able to guide the students to ask relevant questions, create ingenious intuitive theories, and find explanatory scientific information.

The teacher of the Finnish group did not participate in the students' process of inquiry as actively as the teachers of the two Canadian groups. He provided certain preliminary questions for the students to answer, but he did not systematically comment on the students' productions. Yet, without actively engaging in a CSILE-type discourse the teacher cannot help the students advance in their process of inquiry, nor recognize significant contributions, nor generalize emerging progressive practices of inquiry. To successfully elicit higher-level practices of inquiry, the teacher should not leave the students alone but provide an expert model by his or her own example. The Canadian classroom A, by contrast, appeared to represent a second-order environment in which the teacher and students continuously went beyond their earlier achievements (Bereiter & Scardamalia, 1993).

In assessing the Canadian classroom B's and Finnish classroom's epistemic achievements, it must be emphasized that the present study analyzed the epistemology of inquiry rather than the commonly constructed "educational value" of activities the students undertook. Yet, there is no doubt that participation in CSILE activities, such as more intensive writing and peer interaction, was educationally valuable in all of the CSILE groups. Comparisons of school achievements between the CSILE classes and normal classes have revealed that both of the Canadian groups achieved better results than students working in conventional classrooms (Scardamalia et al., 1992). One may distinguish between first-order and second-order effects of educational technology. The *first-order effects* refer to the learning of skills of using information technology, developing skills of knowledge acquisition, increased motivation, and using extended sources of information. It is also likely to involve changed structures of classroom activities and changed division of cognitive labor between the teacher and the students; students engaged in CSCL are not doing the same kinds of things anymore but are involving themselves in many different kinds of independent research projects. These first-order effects appear to be a normal consequence of engagement with computer-supported collaborative learning but do not, as such, break the boundaries of traditional empiricist educational epistemology. The *second-order effects* involve engaging students in a sustained question- and explanation-driven inquiry and progressive discourse analogous to scientific practice. It means a profound change in the students' conceptions of what learning and knowledge are all about. This kind of epistemological shift cannot be achieved without strong pedagogical support from the teacher.

However, systematic observational or other kinds of process-sensitive data concerning CSILE teachers' classroom practices were not available. Based on our review of published studies (Hakkarainen, 1998; see also Lehtinen, Hakkarainen, Lipponen, Rahikainen, & Muukkonen, 1998), including those of fellow members of the CSILE project, we conclude that the significance of the teacher's contribution has not been sufficiently emphasized in CSCL research until recently; researchers have almost entirely focused on documenting and examining students' activities. In the case of the present study, the full significance of teacher guidance became salient to the researchers only after the data were collected. The present data, although suggestive of the importance of teachers' practice, do not establish in what specific manner these practices are linked to desired collaborative outcomes. Further research is needed to answer questions about the specific causal and facilitative roles of such practice. With respect to method, the results of the present study, however, do indicate that it is crucial to document carefully how successful CSCL teachers function in their classroom so that educators and educational psychologists may be able to promote successful higher-level practices of inquiry through CSCL. We argue that new online research methods (based on videotaped participation observations) are needed for helping to provide an adequate account of the teacher's role in CSCL. Beyond teacher guidance, these online methods would also help us to examine in detail how students' motivational orientation (see Hakkarainen, Lipponen, Järvelä, & Niemivirta, 1999; Järvelä, 1998), learning strategies, or cognitive and regulative practices of inquiry (de Jong et al., this volume) affect their participation in the knowledge building process.

Because learning is not only an individual knowledge-acquisition process but also a process of participating in cultural practices and communities (Sfard, 1998), facilitation of a new kind of participation is the most important goal of computer-supported collaborative learning. The present study, however, discusses collaboration and collaborative learning at a general level; we had not yet begun to conduct detailed and specific analyses concerning how the students were sharing their cognitive achievements. Thus far, we who have been investigating CSCL in a number of environments have relied on quantitative and qualitative analysis of *students'* written productions within the CSCL databases. Similarly, the de Jong et al. chapter (this volume) does not provide specific information about collaboration between the students; rather, it gives general information about how students were reading and building others' notes. As researchers continue to investigate CSCL, it may be profitable to examine not only activities and characteristics of individual students but also relations among students. In this regard, it might be fruitful to apply, for instance, social network analysis to examine participatory structures, relationships, and interaction processes in CSCL environments (Palonen & Hakkarainen, 2000). This method could also be applied to analyze a network environment's log files and, thereby, to take a closer look at relationships among students' ideas (Nurmela, Lehtinen & Palonen, 1999). As we investigate the relationships among participants of networked learning, we come to a better understanding and deeper explanations of the collaborative processes that involve the individual students.

In summary, results of the present study indicate, generally, that students need a great deal of pedagogical and epistemological guidance to participate at a process level of inquiry analogous to scientific inquiry. The students cannot be expected to discover these practices by themselves without guidance and expert modeling. De Jong et al.'s (this volume) design experiment of using Knowledge Forum in university and vocational education indicates, further, that a lecturer's or tutor's external structuring and regulation is vital to secure students' active participation in CSCL. In conclusion, a teacher or a tutor has a very important role in computer-supported collaborative learning from the elementary (Lipponen & Hakkarainen, 1997; Lipponen, 1999) and secondary (de Jong et al., this volume) to university level (de Jong et al., this volume; Muukkonen, Hakkarainen, & Lakkala, 1999) education. The challenge is to provide support and external structure just sufficient to enable productive participation but not to replace the students' own self-regulative efforts.

Furthermore, a special effort should be made to provide epistemological guidance to the students, to make them aware of the cognitive value of different kinds of questions and of the advantages of forming one's own intuitive theories, and to help them to recognize the valuable kinds of explanatory scientific knowledge. However, implementation of higher-level practices of inquiry at school is constrained by the fact that teachers themselves have seldom had personal experience or the opportunity to become acquainted with the epistemology of scientific inquiry. These considerations suggest that more resources should be invested in teacher education, in giving preservice teachers personal experience as well as conceptual understanding of advanced processes of knowledge-seeking inquiry. Preservice teachers could be guided to participate in analyzing school children's processes of inquiry mediated by CSILE or some other piece of groupware in collaboration with researchers. The same methods could be used to facilitate the professional development of practicing teachers.

The present study of Hakkarainen, Lipponen, and Järvelä as well as that of De Jong et al. (this volume) indicate that there are serious challenges— the nature and intensity of teacher facilitation and coaching, the degree of students' participation and engagement in deepening inquiry, and the epistemological nature of knowledge processed—that have to be better understood or overcome to productively scale up practices of CSCL across different levels of education and domains of knowledge. These challenges arise because of our attempt to promote the educational use of the new information/communication technology while simultaneously trying to implement new pedagogical and cognitive practices of learning and instruction (Lipponen, 1999). Our own experiences of CSCL studies indicate that even if the new collaborative technology and knowledge-building pedagogy support each other, the current transformation of education demands the utmost of both teachers and students.

REFERENCES

Bereiter, C. (1992). Problem-centered and referent-centered knowledge: Elements of educational epistemology. *Interchange, 23*, 337–361.

Bereiter, C., & Scardamalia, M. (1993). *Surpassing ourselves: An inquiry into the nature and implications of expertise.* Chicago: Open Court.

Brown, A. L., & Campione, J. C. (1996). Psychological theory and the design of innovative learning environments: On procedures, principles, and systems. In L. Schauble & R. Glaser (Eds.), *Innovations in learning. New environments for education* (pp. 289–325). Mahwah, NJ: Lawrence Erlbaum.

Carey, S. (1986). Cognitive science and science education. *American Psychologist, 41*, 1123–1130.

Carey, S., & Smith, C. (1995). On understanding scientific knowledge. In D. N. Perkins, J. L. Schwartz, M. M. West, & M. S. Wiske (Eds.), *Software goes to school* (pp. 39–55). Oxford, UK: Oxford University Press.

Chan, C., Burtis, J., & Bereiter, C. (1997). Knowledge building as a mediator of conflict in conceptual change. *Cognition and Instruction, 15*, 1–40.

Chi, M. T. H. (1997). Quantifying qualitative analyses of verbal data: A practical guide. *Journal of the Learning Sciences, 6*, 271–315.

Cobb, P., Wood, T., & Yackel, E. (1991). Analogies from philosophy and sociology of science for understanding classroom life. *Science Education, 75*, 23–44.

Duschl, R. A., Hamilton, R. J., & Grandy, R. E. (1992). Psychology and epistemology: Match or mismatch when applied to science education. In R. A. Duschl & R. J. Hamilton (Eds.), *Philosophy of science, cognitive psychology, and educational theory and practice* (pp. 19–48). Albany: State University of New York Press.

Hakkarainen, K. (1998). *Epistemology of scientific inquiry and computer-supported collaborative learning.* Unpublished doctoral dissertation, University of Toronto.

Hakkarainen, K., Järvelä, S., Lipponen, L., & Lehtinen, E. (1998). Culture of collaboration in computer-supported learning: Finnish perspectives. *Journal of Interactive Learning Research, 9*, 271–288.

Hakkarainen, K., Lipponen, L., Järvelä, S., & Niemivirta, M. (1999). The interaction of motivational orientation and knowledge-seeking inquiry in computer-supported collaborative learning. *Journal of Educational Computing Research, 21*, 261–279.

Hakkarainen, K., & Sintonen, M. (1999, September). *Interrogative approach on inquiry and computer-supported collaborative learning.* Paper presented at the Fifth History, Philosophy, and Science Teaching Conference, University of Pavia, Italy.

Hawkins, J., & Pea, R. D. (1987). Tools for bridging the cultures of everyday and scientific thinking. *Journal of Research in Science Teaching, 24*, 291–307.

Hintikka, J. (1982). A dialogical model of teaching. *Synthese, 51*, 39–59.

Hintikka, J. (1985). True and false logic of scientific discovery. In J. Hintikka (Ed.), *Logic of discovery and logic of discourse.* New York: Plenum.

Howell, D. C. (1987). *Statistical methods in psychology.* Boston: Duxbury Press.

Järvelä, S. (1998). Socioemotional aspects of students' learning in cognitive-apprenticeship environment. *Instructional Science, 26,* 439–471.

Järvelä, S, Hakkarainen, K., Lipponen, L., Niemivirta, M., & Lehtinen, E. (1997, August). *The interaction of students' motivational orientation and cognitive processes in CSILE-based learning projects.* Paper presented at the symposium, Computer-Support for Collaborative Learning: Advancements and Challenges. The 7th Conference for Research on Learning and Instruction, August 26–30, 1997, Athens, Greece.

Keil, F. C. (1989). *Concepts, kinds, and cognitive development.* Cambridge, MA: MIT Press.

Kitcher, P. (1988). The child as a parent of the scientist. *Mind and Language, 3,* 217–228.

Lampert, M. (1995). Managing the tension of connecting students' inquiry with learning mathematics in school. In D. N. Perkins, J. L. Schwartz, M. M. West, & M. S. Wiske (Eds.), *Software goes to school* (pp. 213–232). Oxford: Oxford University Press.

Laudan, L. (1977). *Progress and its problems.* Berkeley: University of California Press.

Lehtinen, E., Hakkarainen, K., Lipponen, L., Rahikainen, M., & Muukkonen, H. (1998). *Computer supported collaborative learning: A review of research and development. CL-Net project* (J. H. G. I. Giesbers Rep. on Education No. 10). The Netherlands: University of Nijmegen, Department of Educational Sciences.

Lipponen, L. (1999). The challenges of computer supported collaborative learning in elementary and secondary level: Finnish perspectives. In C. Hoadley (Ed.), *Proceedings of The Third International Conference on Computer Support for Collaborative Learning* (pp. 368–375). Mahwah, NJ: Lawrence Erlbaum.

Lipponen, L., & Hakkarainen, K. (1997). Developing culture of inquiry in computer-supported collaborative learning. In R. Hall, N. Miyake, & N. Enyedy (Eds.), *Proceedings of the CSCL97 conference, University of Toronto,* December 10–14th, 1997 (pp. 164–168). Mahwah, NJ: Lawrence Erlbaum.

Macmillan, C. J. B., & Garrison, J. W. (1988). *A logical theory of teaching. Erotetics and intentionality.* Dordrecht, Netherlands: Kluwer Academic Press.

Murphy, G. L., & Medin, D. L. (1985). The role of theories in conceptual coherence. *Psychological Review, 92,* 289–316.

Muukkonen, H., Hakkarainen, K., & Lakkala M. (1999). Facilitating progressive inquiry through computer-supported collaborative learning. In C. Hoadley (Ed.), *Proceedings of the Third International Conference on Computer Supported Collaborative Learning* (pp. 406–415). Mahwah, NJ: Lawrence Erlbaum.

Nersessian, N. (1989). Conceptual change in science and in science education. *Synthese, 80,* 163–183.

Nersessian, N. (1992). How do scientists think? Capturing the dynamics of conceptual change in science. In R. N. Giere (Ed.), *Cognitive models of science. Minnesota studies in philosophy of science XV* (pp. 3–44). Minneapolis: University of Minnesota Press.

Nurmela, K., Lehtinen, E., & Palonen, T. (1999). Evaluating CSCL log files by social network analysis. In C. Hoadley (Ed.), *Proceedings of the Third International Conference on Computer Supported Collaborative Learning* (pp. 434–442). Mahwah, NJ: Lawrence Erlbaum.

Palonen, T., & Hakkarainen, K. (2000). Patterns of interaction in computer-supported learning: A social network analysis. *Proceedings of the Fourth International Conference on the Learning Sciences* (pp. 334–339), June 14–17, 2000, the University of Michigan, Ann Arbor. Hillsdale, NJ: Erlbaum.

Perkins, D. A., Crismond, D., Simmons, R., & Under, C. (1995). Inside understanding. In D. N. Perkins, J. L. Schwartz, M. M. West, & M. S. Wiske (Eds.), *Software goes to school* (pp. 70–87). Oxford, UK: Oxford University Press.

Piaget, J., & Garcia, R. (1989). *Psychogenesis and the history of science.* New York: Columbia University Press.

Salomon, G. (1997). *Novel constructivist learning environments and novel technologies: Some issues to be concerned with*. Invited key note address presented at the 7th conference of the European Association for Research on Learning and Instruction, Athens, August 1997.

Savery, J. R., & Duffy, T. M. (1996). Problem based learning: An instructional model and its constructivist framework. In B. G. Wilson (Ed.), *Constructivist learning environments. Case studies in instructional design* (pp. 135–148). Englewood Cliffs, NJ: Educational Technology Publications.

Scardamalia, M., & Bereiter, C. (1989). *Schools as knowledge-building communities*. Paper presented at the Workshop on Development and Learning Environments, University of Tel Aviv, Tel Aviv, Israel, October, 1989.

Scardamalia, M., & Bereiter, C. (1991). Higher levels of agency for children in knowledge building: A challenge for the design of new knowledge media. *The Journal of The Learning Sciences, 1*, 37–68.

Scardamalia, M., & Bereiter, C. (1992). Text-based and knowledge-based questioning by children. *Cognition and Instruction, 9*, 177–199.

Scardamalia, M., & Bereiter, C. (1993). Technologies for knowledge-building discourse. *Communications of the ACM, 36*, 37–41.

Scardamalia, M., & Bereiter, C. (1994). Computer support for knowledge-building communities. *The Journal of the Learning Sciences, 3*, 265–283.

Scardamalia, M., & Bereiter, C. (1996). Adaptation and understanding: A case for new cultures of schooling. In S. Vosniadou, E. De Corte, R. Glaser, & H. Mandl (Eds.), *International perspectives on the psychological foundations of technology-based learning environments* (pp. 149–163). Mahwah, NJ: Lawrence Erlbaum.

Scardamalia, M., Bereiter, C., Brett, C., Burtis, P. J., Calhoun, C., & Smith, L. N. (1992). Educational applications of networked communal database. *Interactive Learning Environments, 2*, 45–71.

Sfard, A. (1998). On two metaphors for learning and the dangers of choosing just one. *Educational Researcher, 27*(2), 4–13.

Sintonen, M. (1990). How to put questions to nature. In D. Knowles (Ed.), *Explanation and its limits.* (pp. 267–284). Cambridge: Cambridge University Press.

Thagard, P. (1990). Concepts and conceptual change. *Synthese, 82*, 255–274.

Thagard, P. (1992). *Conceptual revolutions.* Princeton: Princeton University Press.

White, R. T., & Gunstone, R. F. (1989). Metalearning and conceptual change. *International Journal of Science Teaching, 11*, 577–586.

Xiadong, L., Bransford, J. D., Hmelo, C. E., Kantor, R. J., Hickey, D. T., Secules, T., Petrosino, A. J., Goldman, S. R., & The Cognition and Technology Group at Vanderbilt. (1996). Instructional design and development of learning communities: An invitation to a dialogue. In B. G. Wilson (Ed.), *Constructivist learning environments. Case studies in instructional design* (pp. 203–220). Englewood Cliffs, NJ: Educational Technology Publications.

CSCL COMMUNITIES IN POST-SECONDARY EDUCATION AND CROSS-CULTURAL SETTINGS

Earl Woodruff
Ontario Institute for Studies in Education
University of Toronto

Knowledge is not simply another commodity. On the contrary. Knowledge is never used up. It increases by diffusion and grows by dispersion.
—*Boorstin, 1986*

The chapter by de Jong, Voldhuis-Diemanse, and Lutgens (Chapter 3, this volume) and the chapter by Hakkarainen, Lipponen, and Järvelä (Chapter 4, this volume) both make valuable empirical contributions to the ongoing study of computer-supported collaborative learning. More importantly, they make a contribution to our growing understanding of the multicultural use of knowledge building technology. While researchers have been warning us that it is critically important that the classroom culture support a knowledge building approach (Brown & Campione 1996; Scardamalia, Bereiter, & Lamon, 1994) there is little empirical work to directly support this claim or proffer a soundly tested approach. Fortunately, despite their mixed findings, both of the above chapters help us understand what the claim may mean.

FORMING CSCL COMMUNITIES IN POST-SECONDARY EDUCATION

Let us turn our attention to the chapter by de Jong et al. first. The authors report two studies where one examines university educational science undergraduates and the other looks at secondary vocational agricultural students as they participate in a collaborative learning network. Both groups, it is reported, were reluctant to share their knowledge or build on each other's contributions. The authors conclude that simply creating an open-ended environment for discussion is insufficient for collaborative knowledge building to occur. Furthermore, these results are interpreted as suggesting that the teacher needs to have a greater involvement in the knowledge "deepening" phase. Presumably, this would entail working with students' prior knowledge, involving the students' personal wonderments within authentic learning tasks, employing cooperative learning techniques such as jigsaw, and finally, meeting face-to-face each week to generate collaborative solutions.

Although I agree with the above suggestions, and I think it reasonable to assume that the above entailments are involved with the development of the classroom culture, I also believe that it is important to consider the authors' suggestions within the broader context of how communities are created. Given current trends toward thinking about learning and knowing as encompassing social as well as individual activities (Koschmann, 1999; Pea, 1994), and given that acquiring knowledge is understood broadly as a social practice engaged with peers and more knowledgeable others (Brown & Palincsar, 1989; Lave & Wenger, 1991; Wenger, 1998), I believe it may be helpful to consider that a community is held together by four cohesion factors: (1) *function*, (2) *identity*, (3) *discursive participation*, and (4) *shared values* (Woodruff, 1999, 2000). Briefly, function is the goal or purpose of the community; identity is the validation of "self" through membership; discursive participation is the means by which the members' discourse helps to advance the function or goal of the community; and, shared values are the global beliefs held by members that unite them and help to promote an emerging discourse. Theoretically, didactic designs that attend to, and support, these cohesive factors should see better understanding and greater knowledge advances of members within the collaborative learning network—but, how might one create such a community?

Various researchers propose a variety of approaches. Margaret Reil (1996), for example, has been working with online and tele-linked learning communities over the past two decades. She outlines a number of specific design issues we should attend to in creating online communities. In particular, she notes that the unity of purpose needs to be balanced with rich diversity of experiences; the ideal size of the group is related to the function; there needs to be a balance between defined structure and participant creativity; and, we need supports for reflection and evaluation of work. Brown and Campione (1990, 1996), in contrast, propose a general *community of learners* model in which the roles of the student, teacher, and researcher are merged. However, for Lave and Wenger (1991) and Wenger (1998), the paradigm consists of a *community of practice* that is entirely constructed within a relational network of self, practice, and society.

Although the Brown and Campione and the Lave and Wenger approaches share the idea of knowledge dissemination, the change in emphasis is indicative of a particular stance on the sociology of cognition. At the risk of oversimplification, it may still be useful to recognize the oppositional trend that characterizes these two approaches: Categorically, Brown's view is that of communities produced by learners whereas Lave and Wenger concern themselves more with the notion of learners being produced by communities and communities produced by practice (Wenger, 1998). These are not trivial differences for, as Case (1996) has pointed out, the educational implications of these epistemological stances are quite significant and need careful consideration.

Although de Jong et al. describe their work as moving from the "transfer of knowledge" paradigm toward the "learner as thinker" paradigm, it is unclear whether they see the community as produced by the learners or learners being produced by communities. From a teacher's classroom perspective, Brown's vision is more proactive and more easily achieved in the school environment. Hence, de Jong et al.'s instructional advice would suggest they are siding with Brown's approach without directly addressing the sociocognitive implications. Therefore, I believe it is useful to look at the authors' specific suggestions from a community cohering perspective too. So, from the point of view of creating a cohesive learning group, de Jong's suggestions may be underlining the importance for us to:

• *Provide a clear delineation of the group's function.* For example, the function could be to examine and address students' personal wonderments as an authentic learning activity. The teacher, therefore, needs to make the function clearly visible at all times, open up the discussion to periodic review of the group's purpose and goals, and/or collectively develop a mission statement.

• *Promote discursive participation.* One may start by individually examining the student's prior knowledge, but the teacher must continue to encourage students either through encouragements or inducements, public display of participation levels, and/or positive public acknowledgement of one's contributions. Additionally, de Jong's use of cooperative learning techniques such as jigsaw would also guarantee that each student had a defined participatory role.

• *Identify of the group's shared values.* Some possibilities include: making the shared values clearly visible at all times, opening up the discussion to periodic review of the group's shared values, clearly stating the shared values in a mission statement, and, following de Jong et al., meeting face-to-face each week to generate collaborative solutions.

• *Consolidate members' identities as part of the group.* Although de Jong et al. do not provide any specific suggestions, some possibilities include: highly visible or easily accessible members lists, public acknowledgement of an individual's membership, and/or production of membership artifacts.

Supporting de Jong et al.'s conclusion, a small pilot study conducted between Toronto and Vancouver suggested that a CSCL community can form through the open-ended discourse alone by attending to the above principles. In this study, researchers from the two cities (Meyer, Woodruff, Erickson, Yoon, & Haskell, 1998) had a grade 4/5 classroom in Vancouver and a grade 7 class in Toronto investigate the physical science involved in operating a swing. The "swing" unit involved a number of activities where the students were exposed to force and motion concepts, participated in discussion in small working groups, presented their explanations to the whole class, and eventually entered their best explanations of how swings work on the Internet via the same software used in the de Jong studies. Within class and across class interchanges were sustained in the database on an occasional basis for several weeks after the database interchanges began.

Because the Internet exchanges were only a pilot study of the web-communities idea, there were only approximately 140 exchanges over four weeks. However, many of the students central to these exchanges felt strongly connected to their web partners. In response to a questionnaire asking students how they felt about the students at the other school and whether or not they felt like they were classmates, one student wrote:

> After working together on the swing unit I felt like I knew the students very well like if they were one of my best friends.

Another wrote:

> After working together on the swings unit I felt the students were very smart and kind, sometimes I even felt like they were my own classmates.

Equally revealing, others indicated that they knew their feelings were attributable to their level of discourse participation:

> The students at the other school didn't feel like my classmates because I didn't type to them a lot.

Similarly, another noted:

> No, because I hardly worked on the internet or get to really respond to them but once, but I would really want to continue to work with them in the future.

And finally, one student even indicated that more than just the academic discourse is needed to feel connected:

> I did not feel like the students at the other school were classmates of mine because usually you get to know things about the people in your class like what country they come from and what kinds of foods they like. But just talking to kids on the computer about swings does not make me feel like they are my classmates.

Internet communities abound (Turkle, 1995) and, at first blush, sufficient discourse opportunities would appear to be all that is necessary to let "naturally" forming groups come into existence. However, classrooms are not like naturally forming Internet communities. Therefore, I believe de Jong et al. are correct in asserting that the teacher has an important didactic role to play. I would go further, however, and suggest that he or she must attend specifically to the cohesive community-forming factors and pay particular attention to the nature of the discursive participation—a point that will become clearer in the following section.

FORMING CSCL COMMUNITIES IN CROSS-CULTURAL SETTINGS

Let us now turn our attention to the chapter by Kai Hakkarainen, Lasse Lipponen, and Sanna Järvelä as they address the epistemology of inquiry and computer-supported collaborative learning. This work looks at two Canadian grade 5/6 classrooms and one Finnish grade 4 classroom. All students were using a client version of the software used by de Jong, Diemanse, and Lutgens. Hakkarainen et al. are interested in understanding how different practices of computer-supported collaborative learning may influence the epistemological nature of students' inquiry. Aside from its empirical rigor, the value of this investigation can be found in the cross-cultural design and the contribution it makes to our understanding of the classroom culture.

The interesting finding that the chapter is constructed around is that only one of the Canadian classrooms engaged in a large number of explanation-oriented discourse exchanges, while the other Canadian and Finnish classrooms were significantly lower on this dimension. The discourse of the Canadian and Finian classrooms was described as neutral, lacking supportive or critical comments. While the successful class undertook conceptually challenging projects designed to facilitate theoretical understanding, the other classrooms generally sought to develop a factual understanding that did not go beyond general descriptions.

Hakkarainen et al. advance some very plausible explanations for this difference between the classes. For instance, the result could be due, in part, to the fact that the teacher in the successful classroom created a classroom culture that valued deep understanding whereas the other teachers did not. In one case, for example, the Finnish teacher failed to model the inquiry process for the students and, in the other case, the Canadian teacher appeared to value factual information devoid of explanation in favor of examples and details. Hakkarainen et al. emphasize that the implicit epistemological assumptions and cognitive design of the learning tasks carried out by the students can determine the resultant depth of understanding. They suggest the results indicate that teachers need to provide a great deal of pedagogical and epistemological guidance to promote scientific inquiry.

Although I agree entirely with the above conclusion, I think that it understates the depth of the challenge a teacher faces in creating a classroom culture capable of supporting inquiry-driven discourse. To see where I am heading we must change the focus from the students' epistemological license to the forms of discourse expected by their teacher. Studies in the sociocognitive development of knowledge emphasize the importance of student discourse in the constructivist classroom (Woodruff & Meyer, 1997; Roth & Bowen, 1995; Pontecorvo, 1993) such that, under appropriate conditions, evidence of student-generated knowledge can be seen (Meyer & Woodruff, 1997; Scardamalia & Bereiter, 1994). One way, then, to conceptualize the challenge before us is to think of redesigning the classroom discourse. If we think of the classroom in terms of social reproduction, the expected discourse is much what we would see from the two "unsuccessful" classrooms in the Hakkarainen et al. study. That is, the students regurgitate the dominant discourse for the teacher. In most classrooms, this would result in great rewards for the students—indeed, they would be acting exactly as the teacher expected and be so rewarded. In contrast, students in the high explanation-driven classroom understand that they are to create their own explanations and that they will not be rewarded for restating textbook explanations. How is this redesign achieved? Does the dominant discourse wane in favor of the students' self-generated explanations? And, how can a teacher create a classroom culture that suspends the dominant discourse in favor of the students' own understanding?

Consider for a moment what must be accomplished to change the role of the dominant discourse both as embodied in the teacher present in the classroom and as represented in his or her evaluative or corrective statements. First, the students must strive to see themselves as legitimate speakers of the discipline. Second, they must value the contributions of each other as legitimate speakers. And third, they must trust that this is really what the teacher wants them to do.

To demonstrate how difficult this is, I want to look at an instance where a group of students, working collaboratively, failed to advance their knowledge. I believe we need to analyze the details and context of this working group to better understand the conditions that inhibit the discursive generation of knowledge. Students in this group appear to be caught in a tension between the normative teacher-centered discourse and the newly imposed, learner-centered discursive expectations of the experimental classroom. In particular, the example I want to refer to is taken from a group of four female grade 7 students working together in a science class in an inner-city school in Toronto. Detailed procedures and methodologies have been presented previously (Meyer & Woodruff, 1997). Briefly, however, after completing a pre-test on their understanding of the nature of light, groups of students made predictions about what kind of shadow or image they would see when the lights were shone on various objects. The study ran over six sessions of approximately 90 minutes each. Groups were tape-recorded as they documented their observations and jointly constructed explanations of the shadows or images and rated themselves in terms of how well they had done. Finally, students engaged in dialogue oriented toward explaining observed light and shadow phenomena. By design, students work toward an agreeable explanation of certain phenomena of light and then bring this explanation to a larger class presentation for debate (Woodruff & Meyer, 1997). In the final session, an expert was invited to visit the class to discuss student findings and explanations as compared with the "received" scientific explanations.

Interestingly, this particular group of four English speaking 12- to 14-year-old girls was composed of nonwhite individuals from non-Western backgrounds. Their general attendance record at school was low. They described themselves as poor at science and our pre-tests confirmed that they did not have any conventional scientific explanations for the behavior of light. It is informative to examine this group in detail precisely because they do not fit the profile of a successful science student. They are also of interest because they did genuinely appear to be motivated to succeed at the task. In short, then, the group seemed to be one that had tried but failed to generate scientific explanations. The main question is: What went wrong?

Briefly, a summary of our qualitative analysis of the group's transcripts suggest that two sociocognitive factors appeared to be inhibiting the group.

1. The presence of the dominant discourse. The mere presence of the teacher in what has customarily been a teacher-centered classroom could be considered an embodiment of the dominant discourse—defined here as that

known by teachers and students to be the "correct" or "received" view. The normative classroom discourse positions the teacher as the gatekeeper of the knowledge with the correct answers. Nonetheless, the transcript below reveals points where a teacher's presence in the room distracts the students away from their own group's discourse. We pick up the transcript as the teacher comes over and stands beside the group:

T1: ... Your predictions are getting much better, even today. Now we know that it's bigger, different. Good.

G1: I think this is fun, you know. I want to do this kind of thing in science. It's better than what we do in science. We will because we have a lot of core classes today.

T1: I'll give you another minute or so because then we'll come back and see what happened.

G1: T1, how come we do the test after and not before?

T1: You have to do more things than I do. Remember yesterday you moved it around and all that stuff and I didn't do all those tests. It's going to be interesting to see what we see.

G1: You tried it before?

As we can see, merely commenting on the group's progress turns the group away from explanation and toward a conversation with the adult. This does not necessarily need to be the case. Teachers trying to change the normative discourse may do so by repositioning themselves, not as gatekeepers of knowledge, but as co-learners with the students. We see this below, when, at another point in the transcript, one of the other teachers in the room walks over to the group and states:

T2: I'd like you to look at me so that I can confess something to you. One of the things that is really interesting to me is that I don't know any more than you do about light. I've been puzzling right along with you about some of these things and I have lots of confusions myself. Now, there are some things that I know that I don't understand at all. I know what I see. I know what I have seen demonstrated and I know what I see but I don't understand why yet. How many of you are confused in the same way ...

G1: Something that confuses me is when the letter L or whatever the letter is goes upside down and some of the letters don't go upside down. Okay go now.

G2: Something that really, really confuses me is that I don't understand how you can get different shapes out of an L or a T.

This teacher has moved away from the role as gatekeeper of the knowledge and modeled that it is important to talk about what you know and what you don't know. This is one of the types of repositioning that must occur to redesign the discourse of the classroom.

2. The group's low status as legitimate speakers in the dominant discourse. Alongside the predictable conversational moves that the group makes around the presence of the dominant discourse, we see that they do not see themselves as legitimate speakers of the dominant discourse. At points throughout the transcript the group does not pursue consensus about predictions to the same extent as they do about observations and explanations as can be seen by the examples below. In the transcript from the first session we read:

T1: We need to know exactly what we're going to see—your predictions—big, small.

G2: It will be the same size but the cross will be small.

G1: Same size and the cross will be smaller?

G2: Yeah, at least that's what I think.

G1: It was the same size as the other one you said, right? The cross is smaller you said.

G2: Draw a picture.

G1: Or the bulb could be bigger maybe. And the ball might be smaller. The ball might be the same size.

G3: Did you draw a big ball?

G2: Yeah.

G1: Just color it.

G3: ???? and then just a small cross around it. Like this?

G2: I don't care. It doesn't matter. It's not like we're getting marked on it.

G1: It doesn't matter. The picture's not the most interesting part. Do we do the testing now?

Note that the students pose their conjectures in the form of questions to each other, each one indicating a tentative relationship with predictions and therefore with the new scientific classroom discourse. Note, too, that G2 indicates, "It doesn't matter. It's not like we're getting marked on it," which illustrates her desire to view predictions as being somehow outside the dominant discourse, somehow not worthy of her efforts. We see this even on the last day of the transcript; the group is talking about their predictions for what will happen if they shine a light through a piece of cardboard with a number of holes punched out of it in the shape of a circle and we again hear G2 say, "It's only a guess." And a moment later we hear G2 say again, "We're not having a debate M. It's just a guess."

Another way in which the group excludes itself as legitimate speakers in the discourse can be found in their concern about how they evaluate themselves. In the second session, for example, G1 seems inordinately interested in evaluation (6 of her 40 statements in the day's transcript are about self-evaluation). It appears that she uses the topic of evaluation as a conversational move away from convergent discourse about the observations the group has seen and then evaluates the group as a 2.5 or 3 out of 4. G1's retreat from the convergent discourse, and her mediocre evaluation of the group's efforts, suggests that she is hesitant to see herself and the members of the group as legitimate speakers in the discourse.

Although we have only looked at a couple of examples here, the full set of transcripts for this group suggests that the presence of the dominant discourse is embodied in the teachers. As we have seen, the injection of the dominant discourse may prompt students to shift away from consensus building discourse to other topics. But the classroom discourse can change. Encouragingly, as the study progresses, the data suggest that the group adopts or tries out the language of the new discourse that is presented by the classroom teachers (and also is presented by other students who have been evaluated positively for their new style of discourse). Furthermore—only after approximately 6–9 hours of sustained effort and discussion toward understanding—the data suggest that, nearing the end of the transcript, the students appear to change their classroom discourse. Unfortunately, they produce too little, too late, to count the group as a success in deepening their understanding of the nature of light. The positive note, however, is that these are the kind of low-performing science students that should benefit most from our improved understanding of the type of classroom culture a teacher needs to create.

If we can better understand what we need to do to create knowledge-building appropriate classroom cultures and what we need to avoid to ensure that we don't send students mixed messages, then I think we will greatly enhance the role of computer-supported collaborative learning in education. As we have seen, the knowledge-building culture requires subtle and systemic change. The chapter by De Jong, Diemanse, and Lutgens illustrates the need for such change in both European universities and vocational schools. In the same vein, the chapter by Hakkarainen, Lipponen, and Järvelä suggests that, between the Canadian and Finnish classrooms, the normative school culture has a surprisingly uniform effect on students' understanding. Furthermore, their comparison of the two Canadian classrooms suggests that changing the local classroom culture may be the most important factor to consider. I believe we are only beginning to understand the scope of this task, but I would like to suggest that it is critical for the computer-supported collaborative learning community to keep working on the problem.

ACKNOWLEDGMENTS

I am indebted to Melanie Chakravorty and Brian Poser for their research assistance.

REFERENCES

Boorstin, D. J. (1986). Speech to the House Appropriations Subcommittee, quoted in the *New York Times* 23 February, 1986.

Brown, A., & Campione, J. (1990). Communities of learning and thinking, or a context by any other name. *Contributions to Human Development, 21*, 108–126.

Brown, A., & Campione, J. (1996). Psychological theory and the design of innovative learning environments: On procedures, principles, and systems. In L. Schauble & R. Glaser (Eds.), *Innovations in learning: New environments for education.* Mahwah, NJ: Lawrence Erlbaum.

Brown, A. L., & Palincsar, A. S. (1989). Guided, cooperative learning and individual knowledge acquisition. In L. Resnick (Ed.), *Knowing, learning, and instruction: Essays in honor of Robert Glaser* (pp. 393–451). Hillsdale, NJ: Lawrence Erlbaum.

Case, R. (1996). Changing views of knowledge and their impact on educational research and practice. In D. Olson & N. Torrance (Eds.), *The handbook of education and human development* (pp. 75–99) Malden, MA: Blackwell Publishers.

Koschmann, T. (1999). Toward a dialogic theory of learning: Bakhtin's contribution to understanding learning in settings of collaboration. In C. Hoadley & J. Roschelle (Eds.), *Proceedings of the Computer Supported Collaborative Learning (CSCL) 1999: Designing new media for a new millennium: Collaborative technology for learning, education, and training* (pp. 308–313). Mahwah, NJ: Lawrence Erlbaum.

Lave, J., & Wenger, E. (1991). *Situated learning: Legitimate peripheral participation.* New York: Cambridge University Press.

Meyer, K., & Woodruff, E. (1997). Consensually driven explanation in science teaching. *Science Education 80*, 173–192.

Meyer, K., Woodruff, E., Erickson, G., Yoon, S., & Haskell, J. (1998, April). *Intergroup discourse over the web: Students, communities and science.* Paper presented at the annual meeting of the American Educational Research Association, San Diego, CA.

Pea, R. D. (1994). Seeing what we build together: Distributed multimedia learning environments for transformative communications. *Journal of the Learning Sciences, 3*(3), 285–299.

Pontecorvo, C. (1993). Forms of discourse and shared thinking. *Cognition and Instruciton, 11*(3 & 4), 179–196.

Riel, M. (1996, Winter). The Internet: A land to settle rather than an ocean to surf and a new "place" for school reform through community development. *ISTE SIG/Tel Technology in Education Newsletter.*

Roth, W. M., & Bowen, G. (1995). Knowing and interacting: A study of culture, practices, and resources in a grade 8 open-inquiry science classroom guided by a cognitive apprenticeship metaphor. *Cognition and Instruction, 13*(1), 73–128.

Scardamalia, M., & Bereiter, C. (1994). Computer supports for knowledge-building communities. *The Journal of the Learning Sciences, 3*(3), 265–283.

Scardamalia, M., Bereiter, C., & Lamon, M. (1994). The CSILE project: Trying to bring the classroom into World 3. In M. Kate (Ed.), *Classroom lessons: Integrating cognitive theory and classroom practice* (pp. 201–228). Cambridge, MA: MIT Press.

Turkle, S. (1995). *Life on the screen: Identity in the age of the internet.* New York: Simon and Schuster.

Wenger, E. (1998). *Communities of practice: Learning, meaning and identity.* Cambridge, UK: Cambridge University Press.

Woodruff, E. (1999). Concerning the cohesive nature of CSCL communities. In C. Hoadley & J. Roschelle (Eds.), *Proceedings of the Computer Supported Collaborative Learning (CSCL) 1999: Designing new media for a new millennium: Collaborative technology for learning, education, and training* (pp. 675–685). Mahwah, NJ: Lawrence Erlbaum.

Woodruff, E. (2000, April). *Discursive science in the elementary classroom: A sociocognitive view of discourse, progress, and conceptual change.* Paper presented at the annual meeting of the American Educational Research Association, New Orleans, LA.

Woodruff, E., & Meyer, K. (1997). Explanations from intra- and inter-group discourse: Students building knowledge in the science classroom. *Research in Science Education, 27*(1), 25–39.

REDISCOVERING CSCL

Gerry Stahl
University of Colorado at Boulder, USA, and GMD-FIT, Germany

THE AMBIGUITY OF CSCL

In their penultimate sentence, Hakkarainen, Lipponen, and Järvelä (this volume) correctly point out that CSCL researchers have a complex challenge because the educational use of new information/communication technologies is inextricably bound up with new pedagogical and cognitive practices of learning and instruction. The naïve, technology-driven view was that tools such as CSILE would make a significant difference on their own. The subsequent experience has been that the classroom culture bends such tools to its own interests and that this culture must be transformed before new media can mediate learning the way we had hoped they would. So CSCL research has necessarily and properly shifted from the affordances and effects of the technology to concerns with the instructional context. Thus, the central conclusions of Chapters 3 and 4 focus on the teacher's role and say little that pertains to the presence of CSILE.

The two chapters have a similar structure: First they discuss abstract pedagogical issues from the educational or scientific research literature (e.g., the learner-as-thinker or the scientist-as-questioner paradigm). Then they present a statistical analysis of the notes in specific CSILE databases. Finally, they conclude that certain kinds of learning took place.

However, in both cases, one could imagine that the same learning might have taken place in these particular studied classrooms with their particular teacher guidance, *without any computer support and without any collaboration*! While there is no doubt that the concerns expressed and supported in these chapters are of vital importance to CSCL research, one wonders what happened to the CSCL.

The high-level concern of these chapters, which ends up ignoring the role of collaboration and technology, plays itself out at a methodological level. To see this requires reviewing the analysis undertaken in these chapters.

CSCL IN THE UNIVERSITY

The chapter by de Jong, Veldhuis-Diermanse, and Lutgens (this volume) raises three central questions for CSCL environments such as CSILE:

1. Can these environments be integrated into curriculum at the university level?
2. Does their use promote knowledge building?
3. What should the role of the teacher be?

Each of these questions would require a book to answer with any completeness—if we knew the answers. Research today is really just starting to pose these questions. Any answers proposed either supply the writer's intuitive sense of what took place in an experiment or they rely on a methodology whose limitations become obvious in the very process of being applied to these questions. Let us consider each of these questions in turn.

THE CULTURAL, EDUCATIONAL, LEARNING, AND PEDAGOGICAL CONTEXT

Can CSILE (to use this prototypical system as a representative of the class of possible software systems for supporting collaborative knowledge building) be integrated into curriculum? The first issue implicitly posed by raising this question in the chapter was: In what cultural and educational setting? The studies presented here took place in the Netherlands, within the context of a larger European project including Finland, Belgium, Italy, and Greece. Much of the earlier work on CSILE was, of course, conducted in Canada, where the system was developed. There is no evidence presented in the chapter to say that national culture makes any difference in the adoption of CSILE.

A second aspect of context is: At what educational level is CSILE effective? The chapter reports studies at the university level and at a vocational agricultural school at the same age level. The related European studies focused on primary school children 9–11 years old. Systems such as CSILE are most frequently used in primary and middle school classes, although they are increasingly being used in college classes as well. The studies in this chapter are not contrasted with other age groups and there is no reason given to think that educational level makes any significant difference. This is actually a surprising nonresult, because one might assume that collaborative knowledge building requires mature cognitive skills. It may be that, within modern schooling systems, college students have not developed collaborative inquiry skills beyond an elementary school level.

A third aspect has to do with the learning styles of the individual students. This issue is explicitly raised by the methodology of the first (university) study. Here the students were given tests on cognitive processing strategies, regulation strategies, mental models of learning, and learning orientation. Based on these scores, they were classified as having one of four learning styles: application-directed, reproduction-directed, meaning-directed, or undirected. A statistically significant correlation was found between the application-directed learners and the number of notes entered into CSILE. This was the only significant correlation involving learning styles. This may just mean that students who are generally more inclined to engage in tasks were in fact the ones who engaged more in the note creation task of the study—not a very surprising result.

A fourth aspect involves the incorporation of collaboration software into a particular curriculum or classroom culture. As the chapter makes clear, CSILE is not intended for a traditional teacher-centered classroom with delivery of facts through lecture. The use of such a technology as a centerpiece of classroom learning raises the most complex issues of educational transformation. Not only the teacher and student roles but also the curricular goals and the institutional framework have to be rethought. If collaborative knowledge building is really going to become the new aim, what happens to the whole competitive grading system that functions as a certification system integral to industrial society? Is it any wonder that "students are not used to sharing their knowledge"? What will it take to change this?

PROMOTING COLLABORATIVE KNOWLEDGE BUILDING

The chapter's conclusion section cites two arguments for the claim that CSILE resulted in much more collaborative learning by the students. First, it contrasts the study with "past courses in which students were directed through the course by closed tasks." No attempt beyond this half sentence is made to draw out the contrast. Clearly, by definition, a course that has been restructured to centrally include collaborative discussion will at least appear to be more collaborative than its teacher-centered predecessor. But it is then important to go on and consider concretely what took place collaboratively and what specific kinds of knowledge were built collaboratively.

The second evidence for collaborative knowledge building comes from an activity that apparently took place outside of CSILE in a noncollaborative manner: the rewriting of educational policy notes. This seems like precisely the kind of collaborative task that could have pulled the whole course together as a joint project. Students could have collected and shared ideas from their readings with the goal of building an external group memory of ideas that would have been used in collectively rewriting the educational policy. Instead, the individual students had to retain whatever the group learned using CSILE, combine it with individualized learning from readings, and "transfer" this knowledge to the final individual "authentic" task. Thus, the chapter concludes that the use of CSILE "resulted in sufficient transfer of the acquired understanding to work with an authentic problem." There is no evidence of learning or transfer other than a general judgment that the final product was of "high quality."

The remaining evidence for collaborative knowledge building is given by two standard statistical measures of online discussions. The first measure is a graph of the number of notes posted each week of the course by students and by teachers. In the university study, this chart shows a large peak at the beginning and a smaller one at the end—for both students and teachers. There is virtually no addition of new notes for the central half of the course, and only minimal reading of notes occurs then. This is extraordinary, given that the chapter calls this period the "knowledge deepening phase." This is precisely when one would hope to see collaborative knowledge building taking place. As students read, research, and deepen their ideas they should be sharing and interacting. Clearly, they know how to use the technology at this point. If CSILE truly promotes student-directed collaboration, then why is this not taking place? Raising this question is in no way intended to criticize anyone involved in this particular experiment, for this is an all too common finding in CSCL research.

The vocational study also presents a graph of the number of notes posted each week. Here, there are peaks in the middle of the course. But, as the chapter points out, the peaks in student activity directly follow the peaks in teacher activity. This indicates a need for continuing teacher intervention and guidance. The apparently causal relationship between teacher intervention and student activity raises the question of the nature of the student activity. Are students just creating individual notes to please the teacher, or has the teacher stimulated collaborative interactions among the student notes? Because the graph only shows the number of created notes, such a question cannot be addressed.

The second statistical measure for the university study is a table of correlations among several variables of the threaded discussion: notes created, notes that respond to earlier notes, notes linked to other notes, notes revised, and notes read by students. The higher correlations in the table indicate that many notes were responses to other notes and that these were read often. This is taken as evidence for a high level of collaboration taking place in CSILE. A nice sample of such collaboration is given in Fig. 4.2. Here, one student (Elske) has posted a statement of her theory (MT). A discussion ensues, mostly over three days, but with a final contribution nine days later. This collection of 10 linked notes represents a discussion among four people about Elske's theory. It might be informative to look at the content of this discussion to see what form—if any—of knowledge building is taking place.

THE TEACHER'S ROLE

The chapter ends with some important hints about how CSILE classrooms need to be different from lecture-dominated contexts: The use of the collaboration technology must be highly structured with a systematic didactic approach, continuing teacher involvement, and periodic face-to-face meetings to trouble-shoot problems and reflect on the collaborative learning process. These suggestions are not specific to the studies presented; they should only surprise people—if there still are any—who think that putting a computer box in a classroom will promote learning by itself. These are generic recommendations for any form of learner-as-thinker pedagogy, regardless of whether or not there is collaboration or computer support.

The chapter by Hakkarainen et al. comes to a similar conclusion by a somewhat different, though parallel, route. Some of the preceding comments apply to it as well. But it also represents a significant advance at uncovering the quality of the discussion that takes place. In their discussion section the authors are clearly aware of the limitations of their approach, but in their actual analysis they too fail to get at the collaboration or the computer support.

Hakkarainen et al. are interested in the "epistemology of inquiry" in CSCL classrooms. That is, they want to see what kinds of knowledge are being generated by the students in three different classrooms—two in Canada and one in Finland—using CSILE. To analyze the kinds of knowledge, they code the ideas entered into the CSILE database along a number of dimensions. For instance, student knowledge ideas were coded as either (a) scientific information being introduced into the discussion or (b) a student's own view. Ideas of both these kinds were then rated as to their level of explanatory power: (a) statement of isolated facts, (b) partially organized facts, (c) well-organized facts, (d) partial explanation, or (e) explanation.

Statistical analysis of the coded ideas provides strong evidence that the epistemology of inquiry was different in the three classrooms. In particular, one of the Canadian classrooms showed a significantly deeper explanatory understanding of the scientific phenomena under discussion. This was attributed, by the authors, to a difference in the classroom culture established by the teacher, including through the teacher's interactions with students via CSILE. Thus, the approach of coding ideas achieved the authors' goal of showing the importance of the classroom culture to the character of collaborative knowledge building.

THE EPISTEMOLOGY OF SCIENCE

Hakkarainen et al. review certain philosophers of science and characterize the enterprise of science in terms of posing specific kinds of questions and generating specific kinds of statements. This may be a valid conceptualization of scientific inquiry. But, let us consider a different perspective more directly related to collaboration and computer support.

In his reconstruction of the *Origins of the Modern Mind*, Donald (1991) locates the birth of science in the discovery by the ancient Greeks that "by entering ideas, even incomplete ideas, into the public record, they could later be improved and refined" (p. 342). In this view, what drives scientific advance is collaboration that is facilitated by external memory—precisely the promise of CSCL.

Significantly, this framing of scientific knowledge building focuses on the social process and its mediation by technologies of external memory (from written language to networked digital repositories). According to this approach, we should be analyzing not so much the individual questions and statements of scientific discourse as the sequences of their improvement and refinement. Relatedly, we can look at the effects of the affordances of technologies for expressing, communicating, relating, organizing, and retaining these evolving ideas.

Unfortunately, Hakkarainen et al. focus exclusively on the individual statements. They relate their categorization of statements to CSILE in terms of that system's "thinking types," which the CSILE designers selected to scaffold the discourse of a community of learners. However, the thinking type categories that label statements in CSILE were designed precisely to facilitate the interconnection of notes—to indicate to students which notes were responses and which were refinements of other notes.

For purposes of analyzing the use of CSILE in different classrooms, the authors operationalize their view of science. They systematically break down all the notes that students communicated through CSILE into unit "ideas" and categorize these textual ideas according to what kind of question or statement they express. This turns out to be a useful approach for deriving qualitative and quantitative answers to certain questions about the kind of scientific discussions taking place in the classrooms. Indeed, this is a major advance over the analysis in de Jong et al., which cannot differentiate different kinds of notes from each other at all.

However, the reduction of a rich discussion in a database of student notes into counts of how many note fragments ("ideas") fall into each of several categories represents a loss of much vital information. The notes—which were originally subtle speech acts within a complexly structured community of learners—are now reified into a small set of summary facts about the discussion. For all the talk in CSCL circles about moving from fact-centered education to experiential learning, CSCL research (by no means just the chapter under review here, but most of the best in the field) remains predominantly fact-reductive.

Of course, the methodology of coding statements is useful for answering certain kinds of questions—many of which are undeniably important. And the methodology can make claims to scientific objectivity: wherever subjective human interpretations are made they are verified with inter-rater reliability, and wherever claims are made they are defended with statistical measures of reliability.

However, it becomes clear here that the coding process has removed not only all the semantics of the discussion so that we can no longer see what scientific theories have been developed or what critical issues have been raised. It has also removed any signs of collaboration. We do not know what note refined what other note, how long an important train of argument was carried on, or how many students were involved in a particular debate. We cannot even tell if there were interactions among all, some, or none of the students.

To their credit, Hakkarainen et al. recognize that their (and de Jong's) measures capture only a small part of what has taken place in the classrooms. In their chapter they are just trying to make a single focused point about the impact of the teacher-created classroom culture upon the scientific *niveau* of the CSILE-mediated discourse. Furthermore, in their discussion section they note the need for different kinds of analysis to uncover the "online interactions between teacher and students" that form a "progressive discourse," which is central to knowledge building according to Bereiter (2000). For future work they propose a social network analysis, which graphically represents who interacted with whom, revealing groups of collaborators and noncollaborators. Although this would provide another useful measure, note that it too discards both the content and the nature of any knowledge building that may have taken place in the interactions. Methodologically, they still situate knowledge in the heads of individual students and then seek relationships among these ideas, rather than seeking knowledge as an emergent property of the collaboration discourse itself.

WHERE TO REDISCOVER CSCL

Chapters 3 and 4 represent typical studies of CSCL. The first type provides graphs of note distributions and argues that this demonstrates computer-supported collaboration that is more or less intense at different points as represented in the graph. Sometimes, additional analyses of discussion thread lengths provide some indication of processes of refinement, although without knowing what was said and how ideas evolved through interactions during that process, it is impossible to judge the importance of the collaboration. The second type of analysis codes the semantics of the notes to make conclusions about the character of the discussion without really knowing what the discussion was about. It has generally been assumed that the only alternative is to make subjective and/or anecdotal observations from actually observing some of the discussion and understanding its content—and that this would be impractical and unscientific.

A major problem that we have just observed with the prevalent assessment approaches, however, is that they throw out the CSCL with the richness of the phenomenon when they reduce everything to data for statistics.

What we need to do now is to look at examples of CSCL and observe the collaboration taking place. Collaborative knowledge building is a complex and subtle process that cannot adequately be reduced to a simple graph or coding scheme, however much those tools may help to paint specific parts of the picture. One central question that needs to be addressed seriously has to do with our claim that collaboration is important for knowledge building. We need to ask where there is evidence that knowledge emerged from the CSCL-mediated process that would not have emerged from a classroom of students isolated at their desks, quietly hunched over their private pieces of paper. Beyond that, we should be able to trace the various activities of collaborative knowledge building: where one person's comment stimulates another's initial insight or question, one perspective is taken over by another, a terminological confusion leads to clarification, a set of hypotheses congeals into a theory, . . ., and a synergistic understanding emerges thanks to the power of computer-supported collaborative learning.

Before we had systems such as CSILE, collaboration across a classroom was not feasible. How could all the students simultaneously communicate their ideas in a way that others could respond to whenever they had the time and inclination? How could all those ideas be captured for future reflection, refinement, and reorganization? CSCL promises that this is now possible. We have to show that it has become a reality in showcase classrooms—that CSCL systems really do support this and that exciting things really are taking place. Only when our analyses demonstrate this, however, will we have rediscovered CSCL in our analysis of classroom experiments.

MAKING COLLABORATIVE LEARNING VISIBLE

Statistical analysis of outcomes has dominated educational research because it was assumed that learning takes place in people's heads, and since Descartes it has been assumed that we have only indirect access to processes in there. Much work in cognitive sciences, including artificial intelligence, assumes that we can, at best, model the mental representations that are somehow formed or instilled by learning. Whatever we may think of these assumptions, they surely do not apply to collaborative learning. By definition, this is an intersubjective achievement; it takes place in observable interactions among people in the world.

The point is that for two or more people to collaborate on learning, they must display to each other enough that everyone can judge where there are agreements and disagreements, conflicts or misunderstandings, confusions and insights. In collaborating, people typically establish conventional dialogic patterns of proposing, questioning, augmenting, mutually completing, repairing, and confirming each other's expressions of knowledge. Knowledge here is not so much the ownership by individuals of mental representations in their heads as it is the ability to engage in appropriate displays within the social world. Thus, to learn is to become a skilled member of communities of practice (Lave & Wenger, 1991) and to be competent at using their resources (Suchman, 1987), artifacts (Norman, 1993), speech genres (Bakhtin, 1986), and cultural practices (Bourdieu, 1995). The state of evolving knowledge must be continually displayed by the collaborating participants to each other. The stance of each participant to that shared and disputed knowledge must also be displayed.

This opens an important opportunity to researchers of collaborative learning that traditional educational studies lacked: What is visible to the participants may be visible to researchers as well. Assuming that the researchers can understand the participant displays, they can observe the building of knowledge as it takes place. They do not have to rely on statistical analysis of reified outcomes data and after-the-fact reconstructions that are notoriously suspect. Koschmann (1999) pointed out this potential deriving from the nature of dialog as analyzed by Bakhtin and also cited several studies outside of CSCL that adopted a discourse analytic approach to classroom interactions.

According to Bakhtin (1986), a particular spoken or written utterance is meaningful in terms of its references back to preceding utterances and forward to responses of a projected audience. These situated sequences of utterances take advantage of conventional or colloquial "speech genres" that provide forms of expression that are clearly interpretable within a linguistic community. Explicit cross-references and implicit selections of genres mean that sequences of dialogic utterances display adoptions, modifications, and critiques of ideas under discussion, providing an intersubjectively accessible and interpretable record of collaborative knowledge building.

For collaborative learning processes to be visible to researchers, the participant interaction must be available for careful study and the researchers must be capable of interpreting them appropriately. In CSCL contexts, learning may take place within software media that not only transmit utterances but also preserve them; the information preserved for participants may be supplemented with computer logging of user actions for the researchers. If communications are not otherwise captured, as in face-to-face collaboration, they can be videotaped; the tapes can be digitized and manipulated to aid detailed analysis. In either case, it may be possible for researchers to obtain an adequate record of the interaction that includes most of the information that was available to participants. In face-to-face interaction, this generally includes gesture, intonation, hesitation, turn-taking, overlapping, facial expression, bodily stance, as well as textual content. In computer-mediated collaboration, everyone is limited to text, temporal sequence, and other relationships among distinct utterances—but the number of relevant interrelated utterances may be much higher. To avoid being swamped with data that requires enormous amounts of time to analyze, researchers have to set up or focus on key interactions that span only a couple of minutes.

The problem of researchers being capable of appropriately interpreting the interactions of participants is a subtle one, as anthropologists have long recognized (Geertz, 1973). A family of sciences has grown up recently to address this problem; these include conversation analysis (Sacks, 1992), ethnomethodology (Garfinkel, 1967; Heritage, 1984), video analysis (Heath, 1986), interaction analysis (Jordan & Henderson, 1995), and microethnography (Streeck, 1983). These sciences have made explicit many of the strategies that are tacitly used by participants to display their learning to each other. Researchers trained in these disciplines know where to look and how to interpret what is displayed. Researchers should also have an innate understanding of the culture they are observing. They should be competent members of the community or should be working with such members when doing their observation and analysis. For this reason, as well as to avoid idiosyncratic and biased interpretations, an important part of the analysis of interaction is usually conducted collaboratively. At some point, the interpretation may also be discussed with the actual participants to confirm its validity. Collaboration is an intersubjective occurrence and its scientific study requires intersubjective confirmation rather than statistical correlations to assure its acceptability.

OBSERVING COMPUTER-SUPPORTED COLLABORATIVE LEARNING

If collaborative learning is visible, then why haven't more researchers observed and reported it? Perhaps because collaborative knowledge building is so rare today. I have tried to use systems similar to CSILE in several classrooms and have failed to see them used for knowledge building (Stahl, 1999). They may be used by students to express their personal opinions and raise questions but rarely to engage in the kind of ongoing dialog that Donald (1991) saw as the basis for a theoretic culture or to engage in the investigation of "conceptual artifacts" (e.g., theories) that Bereiter (2000) identifies as central to knowledge building. Of the five classrooms reviewed in Chapters 3 and 4, probably only one of the Canadian classrooms advanced significantly beyond the level of chat to more in-depth knowledge building. The exchange of superficial opinions and questions is just the first stage in a complex set of activities that constitute collaborative knowledge building (Stahl, 2000). Even simple statistics on thread lengths in threaded discussion systems (Guzdial & Turns, 2000; Hewitt & Teplovs, 1999) indicate that communication does not usually continue long enough to get much beyond chatting. Hence the reviewed chapters are correct that the classroom culture and pedagogy are critical, but they do not go far enough.

It is probably important for researchers to set up special learning contexts in which students are guided to engage in collaborative knowledge building. Too much of this was left up to the teachers in the studies we have just reviewed despite the fact that teachers in CSILE classrooms are explicitly trained to foster collaborative learning. Student activities must be carefully designed so that learning will require collaboration that will take advantage of computer support. For instance, in the Dutch university case it sounds like the wrong tasks were made the focus of collaboration and computer support. Very few notes were entered into the computer system during the long "deepening knowledge phase" when students were reading. Perhaps through a different definition of tasks, the students would have used the system more while they were building their knowledge by collecting relevant ideas and facts in the computer as a repository for shared information. The final product—the educational policy note—could have been made into the motivating collaborative task that would have made the collection and analysis of all the issues surrounding this meaningful.

A nice success story of a researcher setting up a CSCL situation is related by Roschelle (1996). He designed a series of tasks in physics for pairs of students to work on using a computer simulation of velocity and acceleration vectors. He videotaped their interactions at the computer and in subsequent interviews. Through word-by-word analysis of their interactions, Roschelle was able to observe and interpret their collaboration and to demonstrate the degrees to which they had or had not learned about the physics of motion. He did the equivalent of looking seriously at the actual content of the thread of notes between Elske and her fellow students in the Netherlands. Through his micro-analysis, he made the learning visible.

It is true that Roschelle analyzed face-to-face communication and this is in some ways a richer experience than computer-mediated interaction using software such as CSILE. But communication analysis was originally studied in the context of telephone interactions (Schegloff & Sacks, 1973), so it is possible to interpret interactions where bodily displays are excluded. Computer-mediated collaboration will turn out to look quite different from face-to-face interaction, but we should still be able to observe learning and knowledge building taking place there by working out the ways in which people make and share meaning across the network. By making visible in our analysis what is already visible to the participants, we can rediscover the collaborative learning and the effects of computer support in CSCL contexts.

ACKNOWLEDGMENTS

The view of collaborative learning as visible in interaction is itself a collaborative product that has emerged in interactions of the author with Timothy Koschmann, Curtis LeBaron, Alena Sanusi, and other members of a Fall 2000 seminar in CSCL.

REFERENCES

Bakhtin, M. (1986). *Speech genres and other late essays* (V. McGee, Trans.). Austin, TX: University of Texas Press.
Bereiter, C. (2002). *Education and Mind in the Knowledge Age.* Mahwah, NJ: Lawrence Erlbaum Associates.
Bourdieu, P. (1995). *Outline of a theory of practice* (R. Nice, Trans.). Cambridge, UK: Cambridge University Press. (Original work published 1972)
Donald, M. (1991). *Origins of the modern mind: Three stages in the evolution of culture and cognition.* Cambridge, MA: Harvard University Press.
Garfinkel, H. (1967). *Studies in ethnomethodology.* Englewood Cliffs, NJ: Prentice-Hall.
Geertz, C. (1973). *The interpretation of cultures.* New York: Basic Books.
Guzdial, M., & Turns, J. (2000). Effective discussion through a computer-mediated anchored forum. *Journal of the Learning Sciences, 9,* 437–470.
Heath, C. (1986). Video analysis: Interactional coordination in movement and speech. In Heath, C. *Body movement and speech in medical interaction* (pp. 1–24). Cambridge, UK: Cambridge University Press.

Heritage, J. (1984). *Garfinkel and ethnomethodology.* Cambridge, UK: Polity Press.

Hewitt, J., & Teplovs, C. (1999). An analysis of growth patterns in computer conferencing threads. In C. Hoadley & J. Roschelle (Eds.), *Proceedings of the Third International Conference on Computer Supported Collaborative Learning (CSCL '99), Palo Alto, CA* (pp. 232–241). Mahwah, NJ: Lawrence Erlbaum.

Jordan, B., & Henderson, A. (1995). Interaction analysis: Foundations and practice. *Journal of the Learning Sciences, 4,* 39–103. Retrieved March 8, 2001 from the World Wide Web: http://lrs.ed.uiuc.edu/students/c-merkel/document4.HTM.

Koschmann, T. (1999). Toward a dialogic theory of learning: Bakhtin's contribution to learning in settings of collaboration. In C. Hoadley & J. Roschelle (Eds.), *Proceedings of the Third International Conference on Computer Supported Collaborative Learning (CSCL '99), Palo Alto, CA* (pp. 308–313). Retrieved March 8, 2001 from the World Wide Web: http://kn.cilt.org/cscl99/A38/A38.HTM.

Lave, J., & Wenger, E. (1991). *Situated learning: Legitimate peripheral participation.* Cambridge, UK: Cambridge University Press.

Norman, D. A. (1993). *Things that make us smart.* Reading, MA: Addison-Wesley Publishing Company.

Roschelle, J. (1996). Learning by collaborating: Convergent conceptual change. In T. Koschmann (Ed.), *CSCL: Theory and practice of an emerging paradigm* (pp. 209–248). Hillsdale, NJ: Lawrence Erlbaum Associates.

Sacks, H. (1992). *Lectures on conversation.* Oxford, UK: Blackwell.

Schegloff, E. A., & Sacks, H. (1973). Opening up closings. *Semiotica, 8,* 289–327.

Stahl, G. (2001). WebGuide: Guiding collaborative learning on the Web with perspectives. *Journal of Interactive Media in Education.* Vol. 2001. No. 1. http://www-jime.open.ac.uk/2001/1>http://www-jime.open.ac.uk/2001/1.

Stahl, G. (2000). A model of collaborative knowledge-building. In B. Fishman & S. O'Connor-Divelbiss (Eds.), *Proceedings of Fourth International Conference of the Learning Sciences (ICLS 2000)* (pp. 70–77). Mahwah, NJ: Lawrence Erlbaum. Retrieved March 8, 2001 from the World Wide Web: http://www.cs.colorado.edu/~gerry/publications/conferences/2000/icls/ and http://www.umich.edu/~icls/proceedings/abstracts/ab70.html.

Streeck, J. (1983). *Social order in child communication: A study in microethnography.* Amsterdam: Benjamins.

Suchman, L. (1987). *Plans and situated actions: The problem of human–machine communication.* Cambridge, UK: Cambridge University Press.

II

SECTION II: EMPIRICAL STUDIES OF LEARNING IN COLLABORATIVE SETTINGS

Collaboration and Learning as Contingent Responses to Designed Environments

Rogers Hall

University of California, Berkeley

One of the pleasures (and challenges) of serving as a program chair for the Toronto conference, and now as a co-editor for this volume, is the opportunity to pick broader themes out of a collection of excellent individual studies. In this section of the book, these include papers by David Shaffer, Reed Stevens, Hideyuki Suzuki and Hiroshi Kato, and Victor Kaptelinin and Mike Cole. Each of these invited chapters gives extended attention to how learning environments at a larger scale of analysis could be said to support collaboration or learning. As such, these papers present a serious effort to move beyond any simple sense of technical determinism (i.e., if we build a clever enough widget, they will collaborate together and learn) and to focus, instead, on how to design sociotechnical environments in which productive forms of collaboration and learning can emerge. Each paper in this section includes interesting uses of computing, but the signature term "collaboration" is treated as a contingent and somewhat unpredictable response to the technology, and the consequences of this response for "learning" or development are treated as an open question.

I hope the diversity available in these papers can be used to piece together a framework for studies of CSCL at this broader level of analysis. Specifically, an important question to be addressed is: How are collaboration and learning a contingent response to designed environments? To help with this project, I invited a set of commentaries from scholars who have a particular relation either to the research projects out of which the papers were written or to the traditions of theory and analysis used by the original authors. I decided to ask for comments on pairs of papers, in the hope that the juxtaposition of studies would push toward building a broader analytic framework.

For a pairing of Shaffer's and Stevens' papers, I asked Susan Leigh Star and Ricardo Nemirovsky to write commentaries. Star, working with a variety of colleagues in the social studies of science and technology over the past 15 years, has provided strikingly original concepts for thinking about how people and information technologies (sometimes) work together. These include her analysis of information technologies as "boundary objects" that support coordinated work across scientific communities (Star & Greisemer, 1989) and her recently published book with Geoff Bowker, *Sorting Things Out* (Bowker & Star, 1999), which provides a comparative social history of classification systems ranging from the International Classification of Diseases to skin color categories used to implement policies of apartheid in South Africa. Across these studies, Star directs our attention to how information systems (these would include computer-based learning environments) fit existing work practices, how people adapt aspects of system design to their own local purposes, and how these technologies enable relations across communities.

Ricardo Nemirovsky's work brings an entirely different perspective to bear on the papers by Shaffer and Stevens. Nemirovsky takes a phenomenological stance toward conceptual development and, using this theoretical frame, designs innovative user-configurable modeling environments with real-time computer instrumentation (Nemirovsky, Tierney, & Wright, 1998; see http://www.terc.edu/mathofchange/ for a description of recent technical work). Through an analysis of clinical interview data, Nemirovsky and his colleagues focus closely on the experiences of learners in these environments (Nemirovsky, in press; Nemirovsky & Monk, 2000). Then using findings from these analyses, they work with teachers to reorganize science teaching to include the new technologies in public elementary school classrooms serving ethnically and linguistically diverse communities.

For a pairing of Suzuki and Kato's and Kaptelinin and Cole's papers, I asked Ray McDermott, James Greeno, and Doug MacBeth to write commentaries. McDermott and Greeno have written their commentary together, and I chose them in part because they (along with Mimi Ito) have conducted studies of learners' activities in Cole's 5th Dimension after school clubs over the past several years (McDermott, Greeno, & Goldman, 1996; Ito, 1997). Of course, each also brings a widely influential line of work on children's learning (and failure to be found learning) in classrooms to these commentaries. McDermott's studies of how the interaction order in classrooms gets organized to sort students by achievement has provided us with a basic research program in the ethnography of school literacy (e.g., McDermott, 1993; McDermott, Gospodinoff, & Aron, 1978; Varenne & McDermott, 1998). Greeno, in addition to arguing forcefully for a situative perspective on learning and instruction, has invested considerable energy over the past decade in developing and studying varieties of technology-supported, project-based mathematics instruction at the middle school level (Greeno & MMAP, 1998). As many of these development efforts were undertaken in concert with McDermott, their joined commentary makes particular sense.

Finally, Doug MacBeth brings an ethnomethodological perspective to bear on the second two papers in this section. MacBeth's work, on the one hand, critically appraises prospects for "authenticity" in ongoing calls for educational research that follows a metaphor of cognitive apprenticeship (MacBeth, 1996). Most recently, MacBeth (2000) makes the provocative argument that conceptual change can be seen as an "apparatus" (i.e., a sequentially organized demonstration) developed by researchers in the science education community to displace children's ordinary experience of the world with an idealized version of scientific knowledge (i.e., a version that strips away the historical contingency—and ordinary work—of constructing this very knowledge). On the other hand, he (along with colleague Michael Lynch) have provided detailed studies of the artful achievement of science lessons as demonstrations in their own right (i.e., not as versions of scientific practice), both in school settings (Lynch & MacBeth, 1998) and in the context of children's' television programs produced over the past several decades (MacBeth & Lynch, 1997).

In my view (naturally), this is a remarkable group of scholars (authors and commentators alike), and their contributions to this section provide lively material for understanding collaboratión and learning in CSCL environments. To the extent that their claims, criticisms, and responses can be used to create a collective view of the field, this is a great moment to look forward. In the remainder of this introductory chapter, I will give a description (from my perspective) of the "little logic[1]" driving each of these original papers, including both what is particularly innovative in each analysis and where I think the thinner spots lie. Each provides a "case" (Ragin & Becker, 1992) for thinking about collaboration and learning as a contingent response to design.

Design, Collaboration, and Computation (Shaffer). Shaffer describes an observational study of a design studio in an architecture program at the Massachusetts Institute of Technology; then he uses these observations to propose a model for open-ended learning environments where participants have a high degree of control over their own activity. Central to his model is the idea that unstructured time and slack computational resources become productive for learning when they are supported by relatively well-structured, collaborative forms of conversation. In the architectural design studio, these conversations include "desk crits," "pin ups," and "design reviews." In each, a student seeks criticism and feedback from peers or more experienced instructors for a design-in-progress. Shaffer uses this model to develop mathematics workshops (or programs) for high school and middle school students, each reported as a separate study. His workshops incorporate two widely used software programs (i.e., Adobe's PhotoShop and Kee Curriculum Press's Geometer's SketchPad) to create a hybrid kind of

---

[1]I thank Leigh Star for helping me to think about reading research literatures in this way, paying attention not just to the "findings" but also trying to recover why papers were written, in what historical moment, and for what purpose.

mathematical project in which students explore aspects of graphical design through selected topics in geometry.

Based on a comparison of students' performance on pre/post problem-solving interviews, Shaffer argues that the workshops were successful at teaching selected mathematical concepts (e.g., rotational symmetry). In the study of middle schoolers, Shaffer also looks for processes that contribute to learning through an analysis of individual students' "design histories." These histories consist of recordings of a focal student's interactions with peers and program leaders over the duration of the workshop, along with a history of their project documents. Reporting on one of these case studies, Shaffer observes that "design crits" encouraged a relatively shy student to balance her desire to work alone with her need for feedback from peers and teachers. The skills involved in balancing individual and collaborative activity, Shaffer argues, are particularly important for the modern work place.

By my reading, two of the strongest points in Shaffer's article are (1) his effort to induce and then test a model of the "design studio" as a context for learning and (2) his collection and analysis of students' "design histories." I think the field needs more model building of this sort, and the central component of Shaffer's model (i.e., structured conversations, rich with media, over designs-in-progress) may be quite broadly reusable. In terms of research methods, I also commend his use of longitudinal case studies in an attempt to understand why (or how) participation in some complex environment might lead to changes in students' understandings or performance. There are serious challenges around selecting what to record and then capturing records with adequate technical quality when doing these kinds of longitudinal studies, and Shaffer's third study (of middle schoolers) provides an example of what looks to be a workable method. There are always tradeoffs, and here we get a nicely threaded account of design history but little sense of how talk-in-interaction over design media actually proceed. For a collection of papers illustrating similar tradeoffs in these kinds of studies, see a special issue of *Journal of the Learning Sciences* edited by Sasha Barab and David Kirshner (2001).

There are also, of course, criticisms that can be made of Shaffer's approach. First, all of his studies are carried out in a spectacularly well-endowed cultural setting—the School of Architecture and Media Lab at MIT (Star and Nemirovsky both mention this in their commentaries)—so it is not entirely surprising to read that students, in interviews, express a preference for this setting over their usual mathematics classrooms. Still, innovations in design (including the design of learning environments) need to start somewhere, and Shaffer's studies bring us a nice collection of new (and old, borrowing from Schön's widely influential writing) ideas for thinking about places where people learn. At a theoretical level, Shaffer renders the relation between individual and collective activity as a "balancing skill" that a learner needs to master; then he fast forwards to the "modern workplace" (which he has not studied) as a site where this skill will be essential. As other chapters in this section show quite richly, the relation between individual and collective activity can be theorized in very different terms. This relation, itself, can be seen to develop over time *as* the context for people's work (Stevens' analysis of historically entrenched and emergent divisions of labor). It can be approached as a relation of *mutual constitution* in the codevelopment of individuals and activity systems (Kaptelinin & Cole's analysis of changing patterns of intersubjectivity in a children's after school club). It can also be seen to produce tensions or contradictions in ongoing activity that transform personal identity (Suzuki & Kato's analysis of identity formation in programming activity). These are all theoretical renderings for what people do together in the course of learning, and they index different traditions in the human sciences (i.e., "skill" and information processing, "divisions of labor" and analyses of social worlds of work, intersubjectivity and Activity Theory, identity formation and practice theory).

Using the Division of Labor Concept (Stevens). Stevens' chapter presents a comparative case study of how tool-linked (i.e., paper versus computer) divisions of labor arise in architectural design, based on research conducted in a professional workplace and in a middle school classroom. He analyzes how people, tools, and tasks are coupled or articulated together over the history of design projects, drawing on the concept of "arc of work" originally developed by Anselm Strauss in studies of professional work and training (studies of scientific work by Joan Fujimura and Leigh Star are also cited). In Stevens's comparison of work and school, similar divisions between paper and computer-based design tools appear in both places, but he argues that these reflect very different histories and have quite different consequences for participants.

On the professional side of the comparison, Stevens' followed library remodeling projects in an architectural firm for about a year, observing and making film records of work in this setting. Only junior architects used computer-aided drawing tools (i.e., CAD software), while in sharp contrast, senior architects did what all participants agreed was the "real design" using a paper-based "package" of drawing tools. On the school side of the comparison, Stevens helped implement and then studied a project-based middle school mathematics curriculum. In these projects, students worked as designers for a fictional group of scientists who would "winter over" at a new Antarctic research station. Stevens observed a focal group of students over a 10-week project, making daily film records of their activities and collecting design documents. As with the professional architects, students used both paper and computer-based design tools and, again, a clearly marked division of labor emerged. Two students did the conceptual work of "design" with paper-based tools (base plans, trace, and rulers), while the other two students worked exclusively on mathematical analysis and document preparation at the computer.

In Stevens' comparative analysis, these couplings of people, tool, and task make up the specific practices of divided labor, yet (across cases) they reflect some interesting differences and similarities. There is a prior history to architectural practice that does not exist for middle schoolers. Junior architects are more likely to receive training with CAD tools, whereas senior architects maintain a strong preference for hand and paper-based drawing as a distinct aesthetic and intellectual feature of their work. Because design projects are new in classrooms, students' use of design tools is initially contingent on how assignments are set. Then as pressures mount to complete their work, individuals become accountable to their peers, both for newly developed skills (e.g., rapidly drawing the perimeter of a room on the computer) and for carrying the local history of specific design decisions. The resulting divisions may look similar to adult work, but they have a very different history. In contrast, Stevens finds an interesting similarity across the classroom and workplace in how work is divided at the level of what design tools *afford* their users in multiparty talk. Although extended computer display spaces and file versioning could, in principle, allow a group of designers (children or professionals) shared access to alternatives relevant in a design decision, in practice these layered alternatives are much easier to assemble and use with paper-based tools. Finally, the level at which assessments are made differs substantially across Stevens' cases. In the architectural firm, formal assessments are made in terms of design review, with an explicit focus on the design proposal as a multi-authored product. In the classroom, while design proposals are also assessed as a product of the student design team, more traditional forms of assessment pull individuals out and gauge their capacities on different tasks. What emerges as an effective division of labor in a student design project can be at odds with the intended subject matter curriculum and how it is assessed.

By my reading, Stevens' article makes two important contributions to ongoing studies of computer support for collaborative learning. First, he explicitly studies the kind of workplace that usually appears only as a rhetorical figure in claims about innovative learning environments. For example, Shaffer studies an elite design studio (i.e., in the MIT School of Architecture) to construct an interesting and useful model of learning environments, but he only gestures at the "modern workplace" as a site that would, presumable, be filled with graduate, high school, or middle school alumni of these environments. As Stevens shows, conflicts among generations of participants, the fit of computational media to actual work demands, and the assessment of work products can all look quite different "in the wild." Second, and a product of this same comparative analysis, Stevens helps to identify new, critical dimensions for developing and studying different types of computer support for collaborative learning. These include close attention to history and accountability, to how tools afford learners' participation in activity, and to how different systems of assessment render learning outcomes.

On a more critical note, Stevens' chapter could be read as leaving us awash in site-specific contingencies. How teachers use new curriculum materials, starkly uneven technical infrastructures across schools, and the uneven pace of technical adoption in professional practice are all taken as they are found in his analysis. If CSCL is to be a science of design—a source of innovation for creating new sites for learning—one could argue that Stevens' analysis, and approaches like it, are inherently conservative. Stevens raises this issue himself, noting that similar tensions play out in the CSCW community, and then turns to this fully in his response to the commentaries by Star and Nemirovsky.

Identity Formation/Transformation as a Process of Collaborative Learning (Suzuki & Kato). Suzuki and Kato analyze fragments of conversation recorded between students as they learn to program sumo wrestlers for a classroom competition that uses a LOGO-based system called AlgoArena. Their analysis takes up and seeks to extend Lave and Wenger's (1991) argument that learning should be understood as identity formation that occurs during one's "legitimate peripheral participation" in the practices of a community. In addition, they borrow the idea of "membership categorization devices"—as interactional processes that mutually identify participants and their activities—from seminal work in conversation analysis done by Harvey Sacks (e.g., his analysis of "family" and an assortment of category-bound activities commonly available and made relevant by participants in conversation). This is an interesting combination, because it directs Suzuki and Kato into the details of these students' interactions as they approach the task of programming, imagine and then simulate (on the computer) Sumo wrestling bouts, and then prepare for and participate in a class-wide competition. If identities form (or people learn) in ongoing, mutually accountable activity with others in a "community" (various communities are stipulated in their analysis, but presumably these could be detailed in a longer paper), then fragments of working conversations that are consequential for the overall outcome of the classroom project are good places to look for processes of negotiation and transformation.

This is exactly what Suzuki and Kato's analysis provides. The conversational fragments, which are presented chronologically over the programming project in the classroom for two students (OH and IM), are engaging (even hilarious) in their own right. But the analysis is compelling in the way it threads together mutual changes in both the actions these students take with respect to programming (e.g., coming to see Sumo wrestling or a wrestler's "strength" through the operative terms of program statements) and their stance toward the meaning of engaging in these actions within the wider social organization of the school (i.e., being a "conforming" student or a "brat," in Suzuki & Kato's descriptive terms). A central part of their analysis is a contrast between what are called "everyday" understanding of wrestling, which they attribute to students before the start of the project, and a "programming" orientation toward wrestlers and how they compete with each other that emerges during the unit.

Borrowing also from Activity Theory, Suzuki and Kato want to focus on the "comprehensive environmental arrangement" of the classroom as they analyze learners' conversations and work. To do this, they make conjectures about how "indigenous" cultural categories will interact with those the curriculum seeks to "import" (for a similar distinction between "domestic" and "imported forms" see Hall & Stevens, 1995). In their analysis, an existing opposition between "conforming student/brat" includes category-bound activities that students expect of each other (e.g., doing/refusing to do school tasks), and these conflicts or contradictions influence and are recruited into how students take up (or refuse to take up) programming (also see Mimi Ito's (1997) analysis of students' resistance and accommodation while playing computer games in the kinds of after school clubs studied by Kaptelinin & Cole). They focus on how these category identifications are performed in and through work with a programming environment that makes it possible to quickly build a fighter and then test it out against a cast of progressively tougher "test" wrestlers.

Although not discussed in any detail in their paper, AlgoArena is an interesting example of how a gaming environment could be useful for teaching particular subject matter content. The world to be constructed—of wrestlers, their comparative strengths, and strategies—is initially engaging in the sense that it provides a "figured world" (Holland, Lachicotte, Skinner, & Cain, 1998) for some children. Then, for students who engage around this orientation toward strength and an upcoming tournament, a broader repertoire of programming constructs becomes desirable. My point is that this is a nice combination, presumably by design, of a familiar context, with high interest and engagement for learners, where the intended subject matter (programming) becomes highly relevant, even necessary for learners to pursue their emerging interests. It is possible, of course, to miss entirely the interests or engagements of learners with particular backgrounds or experiences. For example, in the classroom that Suzuki and Kato describe, how do girls engage with and then inhabit what appears to be an overtly masculinized world of sumo wrestling (see Cassell & Jenkins, 1998, for a collection of related articles)?

I also find it interesting that the product of programming (i.e., a potentially strong wrestler) exists in a computer-based world of actions and contests that students, through their programmable surrogates, can enter. It is not just that learners may show interest in programmable wrestling, or even that they come to talk about wrestling using technical terms from the AlgoArena manuals (i.e., Suzuki & Kato use this sort of talk as evidence that learners are "becoming programmers"). This kind of environment may also allow students to *identify with and live through* the computational objects they build during the project. In this broader sense of identification with a self-authored "object world" (Bucciarelli, 1994), are there specific design principles for CSCL environments where learning can be approached as a process of identity formation?

Individual and Collective Activities in Educational Computer Game Playing (Kaptelinin & Cole). Kaptelinin and Cole set out to study how "individual and collective activities interact to create each other" in structured, after school clubs where elementary school children interact with university undergraduates around a "maze" of computer-based games (i.e., the "5th Dimension" as reported in papers by Cole and his colleagues). By design, the "collective" activity that Kaptelinin and Cole study is already a complex practical and theoretical achievement. The children, who come from the local community and participate voluntarily, gain access to resources they would not otherwise have during the school day (e.g., educational computer-based games and one-on-one tutoring with adults). At the same time, the university students complete undergraduate psychology courses with a richer experience of learning and development, since they work with children directly as tutors and field researchers to satisfy course requirements. While this relation between community and university may be self-sustaining to the extent that mutual objectives are met, there is no guarantee that individual participants (children or undergraduates) will be swept along by these shared objectives. This is the theoretical problem that they have set out to study: By what mechanisms or processes do individual participants (children, in this paper) come simultaneously to take up and produce the structure of the 5th Dimension club?

Kaptelinin and Cole use excerpts from undergraduate's field notes to analyze and illustrate what they call a "life cycle" of intersubjectivity as children enter and learn to be participants in the collective structure of a 5th Dimension club. Initially, children come to the club with an interest in the games, but they may not yet understand that they are to form "teams" (dyads) with undergraduates or that their interactions in these teams may be of value to them for gaining access to other club activities. In this initial phase, there is little intersubjective agreement on the structure of collective activity. Later, as the rules of the club are better understood (i.e., they reach intersubjective agreements), children and their undergraduate tutors work together to achieve higher levels of performance on the games. Within undergraduates' field notes, Kaptelinin and Cole find evidence for increased intersubjectivity both in descriptions of highly emotional, joint play (e.g., "Jennifer cheered and I was just as excited") and in a shift toward the use of collective pronouns to describe team play (e.g., "there we did it, moved Jennifer on up"). As children become old-timers in club activities, they enter a third and final phase of learning by independently attending to club rules and even directing the activities of undergraduate tutors to achieve more complex goals. At this "post-intersubjectivity" phase, Kaptelinin and Cole find evidence in undergraduate field notes that children have learned a variety of basic skills and new strategies (e.g., they attend carefully to game instructions and reuse or transfer strategies they had adopted earlier).

While field note excerpts illustrate aspects of individual learning (see Cole, 1996, Chapter 5, for an extended theoretical treatment and analysis of aggregate data), Kaptelinin and Cole's main argument is that progressive phases of intersubjectivity work to reproduce the club's structure (e.g., its rules or methods for adjudicating disputes) by passing it across generations of participants. This is most clearly evident in situations where children who are experienced club participants begin to direct or even to tutor the activities of new undergraduate field observers. In closing their chapter, Kaptelinin and Cole consider design principles for CSCL in terms of this critical link between individual and collective activity. Their recommendations presume a definition of "authentic tasks" as activities where learning depends upon engaging with others around a collective purpose. They argue for learning environments where individuals can enter with diverse interests, can choose which resources would help to pursue these interests, and will have a good chance at initial success to keep their engagement going. There should also be enough time for collaborative teams to form, and it should be clear to learners that effort spent in collaboration can result in meaningful outcomes. In this kind of environment (i.e., one where diverse learning trajectories are possible), conflicts should be expected, and the design challenge is to ensure that their resolution leads to a furtherance of the collective structure.

One issue that Kaptelinin and Cole do not discuss in this paper is how (or whether) there could be mechanisms for building new collective purposes out of the kinds of conflicted trajectories they mention. That is, does the relation of "mutual influence" run from individual to collective levels of organization, and if so, could the 5th Dimension collective structure evolve to have a distinct, site-specific character (i.e., very different community clubs, reflecting very different trajectories of mutual influence)? If not, the 5th Dimension club structure begins to look more conservative, as if it were a generic curriculum developed to address problems of educational inequality, irrespective of local differences across the larger network of sites. Clearly this is not what is intended, and a study by Olga Vasquez is cited to show that club structures can be modified substantially to meet community needs.

Another line of work on this issue came up during an invited "conversation" (Blanton & Cole, 1997) between Mike Cole and Bill Blanton, a research collaborator of Cole's from Appalachia State University, at the CSCL conference in Toronto. They presented a complex case in which the behavior of a child in a 5th Dimension club in San Diego was interpreted as being a "brat" by a UCSD undergraduate (i.e., on the basis of her field experience), and then this comment, made in the context of video-mediated distance learning session, was interpreted as "blaming the victim" by an undergraduate participant in Los Angeles (i.e., a relatively more diverse set of undergraduates doing field work in 5th Dimension clubs as part of coursework at UCLA). Individual activity that undergraduates in San Diego interpreted as being disruptive was reinterpreted in Los Angeles as potentially legitimate resistance to club structure and evidence of racial stereotyping by undergraduate field workers at the other site. The ensuing conversation, mediated very differently by video conference and e-mail, turned to how learning theories might be useful (or not) for undergraduates facing issues of cultural diversity in their field placements.

In this case, intersubjectivity could be said to operate at an entirely different level, since an individual's activity, under distributed interpretation, creates the possibility of changing how club structure(s) are understood across the entire network of 5th Dimension sites. More generally then, differences across sites may provide an interesting and productive way of understanding how club structures, formed out of mutual influence between individual and collective activity, could be said to be the "same" (or very different) at a distance.

REFERENCES

Barab, S., & Kirshner, D. (Eds.). (2001). Rethinking methodology in the learning science. Special issue of *Journal of the Learning Sciences, 10(1, 2)*.

Blanton, W., & Cole, M. (1997, December). An invited conversation with Mike Cole [digitized video]. *Second International Meeting on Computer Support for Collaborative Learning* (CSCL '97), University of Toronto, Ontario, Canada. (Available on T. Koschmann, L. Sadler, M. Lamon, & B. Fishman (Eds.) (2000). *CSCL '97 CD-ROM*. Mahwah, NJ: Lawrence Erlbaum Associates.)

Bowker, G. C., & Star, S. L. (1999). *Sorting things out: Classification and its consequences*. Cambridge, MA: MIT Press.

Bucciarelli, L. L. (1994). *Designing engineers*. Cambridge, MA: MIT Press.

Cassell, J., & Jenkins, H. (1998). *From Barbie to Mortal Kombat: Gender and computer games*. Cambridge, MA: MIT Press.

Cole, M. (1996). *Cultural psychology: A once and future discipline*. Cambridge, MA: Harvard University Press.

Engeström, Y. (1999). Expansive visibilization at work: An activity-theoretical perspective. *Computer Supported Cooperative Work 8*, 63–93.

Fujimura, J. (1987). Constructing 'do-able' problems in cancer research: Articulating alignment. *Social Studies of Science 17*, 257–293.

Greeno, J. G., & MMAP (1998). The situativity of knowing, learning, and research. *American Psychologist 53*(1), 5–26.

Hall, R., & Stevens, R. (1995). Making space: A comparison of mathematical work in school and professional design practices. In S. L. Star (Ed.), *The cultures of computing* (pp. 118–145). London: Basil Blackwell.

Holland, D., Lachicotte, W., Skinner, D., & Cain, C. (1998). *Identity and agency in cultural worlds.* Cambridge, MA: Harvard University Press.

Ito, M. (1997). *Interactive media for play: Kids, computer games, and the productions of everyday life.* Unpublished doctoral dissertation, School of Education, Stanford University.

Lave, J., & Wenger, E. (1991). *Situated learning: Legitimate peripheral participation.* Cambridge, UK: Cambridge University Press.

Lynch, M., & MacBeth, D. (1998). Demonstrating physics lessons. In J. G. Greeno & S. V. Goldman (Eds.), *Thinking practices in mathematics and science learning* (pp. 269–298). Mahwah, NJ: Lawrence Erlbaum Associates.

MacBeth, D. (1996). The discovery of situated worlds: Analytic commitments, or moral orders? *Human Studies, 19*, 267–287.

MacBeth, D. (2000). On an actual apparatus for conceptual change. *Science Education, 84*(2), 228–264.

MacBeth, D., & Lynch, M. (1997, October). *Telewitnessing: Elementary spectacles of science education.* Paper presented in a panel on *Confounding the Boundaries*, S. Newman (Chair), at the annual meetings of the Society for the Social Studies of Science, Tucson, Arizona.

McDermott, R. P. (1993). The acquisition of a child by a learning disability. In S. Chaiklen and J. Lave (Eds.), *Understanding practice: Perspectives on activity and practice* (pp. 269–305). New York: Cambridge University Press.

McDermott, R. P., Gospodinoff, K., & Aron, J. (1978). Criteria for an ethnographically adequate description of activities and their contexts. *Semiotica, 24*, 245–275.

McDermott, R., Greeno, J., & Goldman, S. (1996). Process evaluation report. In M. Cole (Ed.), *Using new information technologies in the creation of sustainable after-school literacy activities: From invention to maximizing the potential.* San Diego: Laboratory of Comparative Human Cognition.

Nemirovsky, R. (in press). How does one experience become part of another? *Journal of the Learning Sciences.*

Nemirovsky, R., & Monk, S. (2000). "If you look at it the other way...": An exploration into the nature of symbolizing. In P. Cobb, E. Yackel, and K. McClain (Eds.), *Symbolizing and communicating in mathematics classrooms: Perspectives on discourse, tools, and instructional design* (pp. 177–221). Mahwah, NJ: Lawrence Erlbaum Associates.

Nemirovsky, R., Tierney, C., & Wright, T. (1998). Body motion and graphing. *Cognition and Instruction, 16*(2), 119–172.

Ragin, C., & Becker, H. (1992). *What is a case? Exploring the foundations of social inquiry.* Cambridge: Cambridge University Press.

Star, S. L., & Griesemer, J. R. (1989). Institutional ecology, 'translations' and boundary objects: Amateurs and professionals in Berkeley's museum of vertebrate zoology, 1907–39. *Social Studies of Science, 19*, 387–420.

Varenne, H., & McDermott, R. (1998). *Successful failure: The school America builds.* Boulder, CO: Westview Press.

5

DESIGN, COLLABORATION, AND COMPUTATION: THE DESIGN STUDIO AS A MODEL FOR COMPUTER-SUPPORTED COLLABORATION IN MATHEMATICS

David Williamson Shaffer
Harvard University
Graduate School of Education

INTRODUCTION

Since the writings of Francis Parker and John Dewey (Dewey, 1915; Parker, 1894/1969), educators have been excited by the possibilities of learning through design activities. The introduction of computational media to education has made this idea only more appealing, as educators see how computers make it possible to explore more areas of human understanding in an open-ended, design-based environment (Kafai & Harel, 1991; Noss & Hoyles, 1996; Papert, 1980, 1993; Resnick & Ocko, 1991; Wilensky, 1995). One important issue in the open-ended approach of learning-by-design is the need to provide students with skills to regulate their learning activities effectively (see Dewey, 1938).

Two of the essential skills in learning are clearly the ability to direct one's own work and the ability to work with others. Dewey wrote in great detail about the role of freedom and social control in students' development, suggesting, in particular, that "freedom" is a necessary (though not sufficient) condition for the development of self-control. By "freedom" Dewey meant not only the physical freedom to move in space but also the more important freedom to make decisions, to "frame purposes," and to exercise judgment (Dewey, 1938). Other theorists similarly emphasize the extent to which learners must control their learning experiences (Gardner, 1993; Papert, 1991; Sizer, 1984). In the same way, many learning theorists have argued that collaboration is a critical part of cognitive development. Vygotsky, for example, argued that the immediate potential for cognitive development could only be fully realized in a collaborative context (Vygotsky, 1978). There is a broad (and growing) consensus that an essential part of learning to think is learning to think with others (see, e.g., Bruner, 1996; Pea, 1993).

Integrating independent activity and activity coordinated with others is thus an essential skill. For students to be successful in relatively autonomous learning (or working) environments, they need to know how to work independently, how to collaborate with their peers and with experts in their learning process, and how to balance these two modes of working and thinking.

This chapter proposes one way of thinking about computers and learning that provides a structure for helping students develop these skills and find this balance. The chapter looks at the architectural design studio as a learning environment that gives students a great deal of autonomy while also providing structures to help them integrate collaborative and independent work.

The design studio can trace its roots back more than a century to the Ecole des Beaux-Arts in France (Chafee, 1977), where young architects learned their craft from a master who acted as the "patron" of an independent studio, or atelier. The impact earlier this century of the Bauhaus (Wingler, 1978) and its focus on specific areas of content knowledge about materials, engineering, and manufacturing added a range of "content" courses to contemporary design education. But the focus of a designer's training is still on work in a studio, under the direction of a master architect. The key features of work in a studio are open-ended projects and a variety of structured, collaborative conversations, including desk crits, pin-ups, and design reviews. In other words, the architectural design studio provides a *structured context for open-ended activities*. This chapter (and the experiments it describes) explores the way in which this structure helps learners integrate self-directed activity with the need to work in collaboration with others.

Taking the design studio as a model for learning in more traditional domains, the chapter explores the possibility of using computers to create a "mathematics studio" where students learn mathematics using the pedagogy of design learning. The focus is on the interplay between autonomy and collaboration in the studio context. Three studies are presented. The first explores how the design studio provides a framework that simultaneously supports both collaborative and independent work—and that gives students a model for integrating these two modes. The second and third studies examine the use of computers to adapt the studio model to mathematics learning.

This linkage of the architectural design studio and the discipline of mathematics was quite deliberate. The "traditional" pedagogy of mathematics—with its emphasis on drill and practice, and on rote acquisition of predetermined algorithms—does a particularly poor job of providing students with opportunities for either control over their own learning or for collaboration (see Boaler, 1996). There is plenty of room to—and reason to—look for an alternative pedagogy. Also, a significant segment of the mathematics education community has endorsed a more open-ended, project-based approach to the teaching and learning of mathematics (see NCTM Commission on Standards for School Mathematics, 1989, 1991). If the "mathematics studio" approach works, it provides a potential model for reform—or at least an alternate pedagogical system that could be adapted for K–12 education. Finally, mathematics was chosen because there exists a wide range of powerful computational tools that make it possible to approach traditional problems in new ways. The studies presented here use only one of these tools (the Geometer's Sketchpad; Jackiw, 1995) to approach geometric thinking from a new perspective. But it is possible to imagine a similar pedagogy used to explore a range of mathematical topics using different but equally transformative tools (see, for example, Harel & Papert, 1991; Kaput & Roschelle, in press; Noss & Hoyles, 1996; Papert, 1996; Resnick, 1994; Resnick, Bruckman, & Martin, 1996; Wilensky, 1995).

The studies discussed here have been presented elsewhere (see Cossentino & Shaffer, 1997; Shaffer, 1996, 1998, in press). These earlier discussions have looked at the "success" of linking mathematics and design, and at the role that new media play in creating such a link. Here the focus is on the pedagogy of the design studio, and in particular on the connections between autonomy and collaboration in design learning. The question is whether the systems of the design studio and the power of new media can help mathematics students take control of their mathematical development and successfully mobilize the social resources they need to understand deep mathematical ideas.

PORTRAIT OF A STUDIO: UNDERSTANDING DESIGN LEARNING

The first study presented here was of a design studio course taught at the Massachusetts Institute of Technology School of Architecture and Planning. The course was a mid-level architecture studio for undergraduate and graduate students, taught by a member of the school's junior faculty. For the study, an observer (this chapter's author) was present for roughly one-quarter of the studio's teaching hours. Observations focused on the work of five students in the studio, with more detailed observations of one student's learning process. Direct observations of the studio were supplemented by interviews with students and teaching staff.

The Lay of the Land

Walking into a design studio is quite unlike walking into a typical classroom. In the MIT studios, 11 students have more space for their own individual drafting areas than most high schools provide for a class of 25–30 students. In addition to this space for individual drafting, the studio uses a meeting space the size of a typical seminar room, as well as a large open space for formal presentations of student work.

The pace of work in the studio is also quite unlike that of a traditional class. Studios at MIT meet from 2–6 pm three days a week. But these are more rough guidelines than a fixed schedule. Students and teaching staff routinely come to studio before or after 2 pm depending on the work they have to do on a particular day. Students and teachers often come in at night or on weekends as project deadlines approach. At any given time during "official" studio hours a class may be meeting around a seminar table discussing projects. Or students may be working at their desks, checking e-mail, stepping out for a cup of coffee, or meeting with faculty.

This informal approach to time in the studio makes it difficult, sometimes, to organize activities. Students may not all be present for a class discussion, and even major events in the semester, such as final reviews, routinely start late and have participants drifting in and out. Problems of time management also come up for students; work is routinely left until the last minute and sometimes suffers as a result. But the large blocks of time allotted to the studio and the flexibility of the routine also make it possible for students to organize collaborative conversations with teaching faculty and with other students as the need for input in the design process demands. And the relative autonomy of students in the studio makes it possible for teaching staff to spend concentrated blocks of time with some students while others are working on their own.

By the standards of a traditional K–12 classroom in the United States, the studio is an extreme example of an "open" learning environment. One might even be tempted to call it "chaotic." But out of the chaos of the studio, directed learning occurs regularly, repeatedly, and widely in studios that may be less well-appointed than those at MIT but nonetheless share its basic structure.

The seeming chaos of the studio is bounded—channeled, if you will—into productive directions by a pedagogical framework: a structure of activities and interactions that do not constrain or remove students' autonomy but rather support it in turning open exploration into understanding. The most significant of these structures (though by no means the only one) is the desk crit, which is discussed in the following section in the context of architectural design, and which is described in some detail in the context of the mathematics studio in the final study presented.

The Crit Cycle

The focus of the architecture studio observed for this project was the design of a new business school for Oxford University in Britain. For purposes of this discussion, though, the specific details of the architectural explorations of the Oxford studio are less important than understanding that the semester of design learning was organized around a series of six assignments on a single project.

A typical assignment was a page or so of written description accompanied by some discussion and clarification from the professor. This would include a summary of the assignment's requirements, explanation of the reason for the particular assignment, description of the professor's expectations, and almost always discussion of examples of work for students to use as models. After this initial introduction, students began working on their response to the assignment. As questions came up, as students ran into problems in their emerging designs, or when students finished some coherent stage of their design process, they would sign up for individual conferences with the professor or with a teaching assistant.

These conferences are known as "desk crits" and are in a sense the heart of the studio process. Crits usually lasted somewhere between 20 and 40 minutes in the Oxford studio. During a crit, a student describes his or her work to the professor, including areas of particular interest or concern in the design. The professor probes the design, asking for clarification where needed, and then isolating potential problem areas. As students present possible solutions, the professor explores the implications of various design choices, suggesting alternative possibilities, or offering ways for the student to proceed in his or her exploration of the problem.

Based on this feedback, the student returns to his or her project, perhaps signing up for a desk crit again before the presentation of the assignment, or perhaps asking for a desk crit with a teaching assistant. Or the student might work out some of the details of the problem in a desk crit with another student.

Pedagogy of the Crit

The pedagogical core of the desk crit is the idea of scaffolding. During a crit, the "critic" works to understand what the student is trying to do with his or her design and then helps the student develop that design idea. This help can take many forms, including offering suggestions, pointing out potential problems, or referring to examples of work by other architects that have addressed similar problems. Often critic and student will "design together," with the critic sketching quickly a series of design possibilities, exploring the consequences of possible design choices. In doing so, the critic both offers design ideas and models design thinking.

Two features of the crit are worth pointing out. One is that the critic works to help the student develop his or her design idea. The student's design idea is central to the process, and the critic's job is to aid the student in realizing that idea. Along the way, the critic offers input and feedback, which the student can adopt, adapt, or ignore. The second point worth making here is again that critics can be professors, teaching fellows, outside experts, other students, and ultimately colleagues and coworkers. The basic format of the crit is the same throughout. The desk crit with the professor thus provides both an opportunity to develop a student's design understanding *and* a model for collaborative work with others.

A Model for Collaboration

The design studio thus provides a provocative model for thinking about collaborative learning. Donald Schön has written at length and with substantial insight about the nature of the desk crit and its importance to learning in the design studio (Schön, 1985). In Schön's analysis, the crit provides a framework for interaction between the professor and student that allows the professor to develop the student's design skills and knowledge through collaborative work on the student's design. Here, though, the key feature of the desk crit is its role as a framework or anchor for learning in the design studio. The crit provides a model for design conversations: When students meet to discuss their work, they talk about "giving" or "getting" a crit from one another.

The design studio thus provides a model for collaboration. The studio also makes it possible for these collaborative conversations to take place during a student's design process. Students have the time and the freedom to ask for a design crit—a structured collaborative conversation—when and where they need it. The studio thus develops not only students' ability to design but also their ability to collaborate and to regulate independent and collaborative work.

A MATHEMATICS STUDIO WORKSHOP

The second project presented in this paper was an attempt to take the basic structure of the design studio and apply it to learning basic concepts in geometry. In particular, in the study described here the goal was to create a computer-supported mathematics learning environment like the design studio: open-ended in space, time, and activity, and using the desk crit as a model for collaborative conversations to help students structure their design activity.

The project brought 12 high school students from public schools in Boston, Massachusetts to the Massachusetts Institute of Technology Media Laboratory for 12 hours during the spring and summer of 1995. In these workshops students used computers to learn about mathematics and art.

About the Workshops

Students spent 12 hours in the project. Workshops were divided into two sections, each lasting approximately six hours. The first section was organized around the concept of mirror symmetry; the second was organized around the concept of rotational symmetry.

Each section of the workshop began with a "warm-up" activity, which lasted approximately one-half hour and presented students with a short mathematical game or puzzle, which was described as an opportunity to "stretch their minds." At the end of each day, there was time for reflection on the day's activities lasting approximately one-half hour. Students wrote in their workshop journals in response to specific questions about the content and structure of the workshop. There was also time to discuss as a group any problems or concerns that came up during the day.

The emphasis throughout the workshop was on creating an open, studio-like atmosphere for learning. Students were encouraged to sit and work where they liked, to use media of their own choosing, to collaborate or work alone as they wished, to eat, take breaks, and go to the bathroom, and to change projects at their own discretion.

The majority of the day was spent on investigations and explorations of the concepts of mirror and rotational symmetry.

Investigations. Investigations lasted approximately one hour, with students working on short problems on their own or in small groups. Students wrote entries in their workshop journals and discussed their observations. In the first day of the workshop, for example, students began their investigation of mirror symmetry by making name tags that read normally when viewed in a mirror. This was followed by a search for words that look the same when viewed in a mirror, and from there to the classification of the letters of the alphabet by their mirror lines. Students worked on each of these problems individually or in small groups at their own discretion, with the whole group discussing the "results" of each problem. Students conducted a similar sequence of investigations involving rotational symmetry using a telidescope in the second section of the workshop.

Explorations. Based on their investigations, students spent two to three hours working on extended projects in design on their own or with a partner. Students worked on one shorter project (approximately one hour) and then

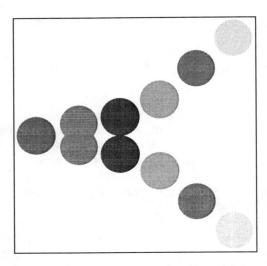

FIG. 5.1. Student work in Escher's World: One student's exploration of mirror symmetry and its effect on the focus of a viewer's attention. The original was in color.

presented their work to the group for discussion, questions, and comments. Following this "peer review," students began a more ambitious project (approximately two hours), integrating ideas about symmetry, principles of design, and feedback from their presentation. In the first day of the workshop, students made a design using mirror symmetry. After discussing their designs, students worked for the remainder of the day creating designs that had mirror symmetry but did not place the focus of the composition in the middle of the design (see Fig. 5.1). In the second section of the workshop, students tried to make designs that used rotational symmetry but presented a lopsided or unbalanced composition.

Space. Workshops took place in a conference room at the Media Lab that had been modified to resemble an art studio. Macintosh computers were provided, with one computer available for every two or three students. The computers were networked to flatbed scanners, color printers, and a large-format color plotter. Computers were equipped with a commercial drawing and image-manipulation program (Adobe Photoshop) and with commercially available dynamic geometry software (the Geometer's Sketchpad). During the investigation portion of the workshops, students were introduced to some of the basic functionality of these programs. Students were able to work on the computers or with traditional materials during their explorations; all of the students chose to use a computer for some portion of their work.

A Compromise. The design of these workshops was, in effect, a compromise between the constraints of space and time and the "ideal" environment of the MIT design studios. Structured "investigations" were used to scaffold students' understanding of the tools being used and of the basic mathematical concepts of mirror and rotational symmetry. The "explorations" that followed were much closer in structure to the open environment of the design studio—and not surprisingly, it was students' experiences exploring mathematical ideas that made these workshops powerful learning environments.

Data Collection. The main source of data for the workshops was structured interviews with each student immediately before and after the workshop and then two to five months after the completion of the workshop. Interviews contained a series of questions about mathematics and art, focusing particularly on attitudes toward these disciplines, as well as a set of traditional mathematics word problems.

RESULTS

Mathematics Learning. The results of the project are presented in more detail in several previous papers (Shaffer, 1997, in press). Briefly, during the workshops, students developed their understanding of the mathematical concept of symmetry. During the workshops all of the students (12/12) were able to make designs using mirror symmetry, and 83% of the students (10/12) were able to make designs using rotational symmetry. Only 1 of 12 students was able to use and explain ideas about symmetry before the workshop, whereas 11 of 12 students were able to do so after completing the workshop. After the workshop students were able to find new examples of symmetry in the world around them: 75% of the students (9/12) reported thinking about symmetry beyond the context of the workshop in post-interviews or follow-up interviews. Students reported seeing symmetry in drawings, chairs, wallpaper, rugs, video games, flowers, and clothing.

Students also began to use visual thinking and began to like mathematics more as a result of the workshop. Before the workshop, only 33% of the students (4/12) used visual representations such as a drawing or diagram to solve word problems in interviews (see Fig. 5.2). After the workshop 75% of the students (9/12) did so. In post-interviews and follow-up interviews, 67% of students (8/12) reported feeling more positive about mathematics as a result of the workshop. This reported change was supported by survey data (collected for 6/12 students), where the overall rating for questions about feelings toward mathematics went up for 67% of students surveyed (4/6).

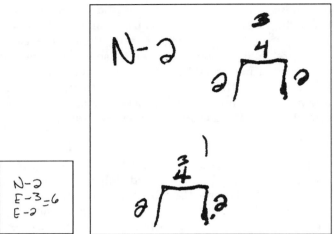

FIG. 5.2. One student's notes while solving a problem during interviews. In the pre-interview (left image) the student did not use a visual representation. While solving a similar problem during her post-interview (right image) the student represented the problem visually and produced a correct solution.

Understanding the Success of the Math Studio.   Students learned about the mathematical idea of symmetry in the mathematics studio workshops, and they learned to apply visual thinking skills to mathematical problem solving. At the same time they discovered they liked mathematics and liked this new kind of learning environment. One student said simply: "If school was like this, attendance would be perfect!"

Previous work has looked in some detail at how the mathematics studio "worked" for students (Shaffer, 1997). This earlier work focused on the importance of students' sense of control over their learning in the studio setting.

Here the focus is on two additional features of the studio model: on the nature of collaboration and on the relationship between collaboration and control. In particular, the next section looks at whether and how the structured collaborations of the desk crits help students learn mathematics. The following section addresses the relationship between social interaction and autonomy in the studio.

The data from the workshops show that collaboration was an important aspect of students' experiences in the workshop. Moreover, the fact that the studio setting gave students control over their collaborative interactions was a key part of the success of the studio.

A look at the relative frequency of student comments in interviews about control and collaboration makes it clear that these were both critical issues in students' experiences of the mathematics studio (see Fig. 5.3). Referring

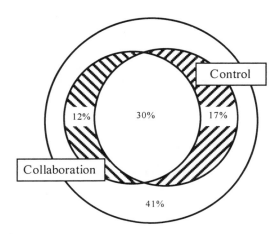

FIG. 5.3. Student Interview responses (proportional to area): Student's references to collaboration and control in mathematics studio workshops show substantial overlap. The area of the regions on the diagram are proportional to the percentage of total student references in each category (Collaboration but not Control = 12%, Collaboration and Control = 30%, Control but not Collaboration = 17%, neither Control not Collaboration = 41%).

to the theoretical work described above in the introduction, excerpts from interviews in the project were coded for control when students referred to freedom of physical as well as intellectual movement or when they talked about making their own choices, judgments, or decisions—in short, when they described in a positive or negative way the effects of their own control (or lack of it) in their learning experience. Similarly, excerpts were coded for collaboration when students referred to ways in which their learning experience was affected by the active participation of others (or lack thereof). This included descriptions of help given to or received from adults or peers, joint work with others, public presentations and feedback on ideas or work, and conversations or other "purely social" interactions—in short, collaboration as it is used here refers to the range of students' relations to other people as it connects to their learning experiences.

By these criteria, more than half of the comments from interviews about the studio as a learning environment (73/123 or 59%) were about either students' feelings of control over their learning experience or students' collaborative interactions with others. Perhaps more interesting, students' comments in these areas show significant overlaps. Students referred to both control and collaboration in 36 excerpts—that is, in almost 75% of the comments about collaboration students referred to the importance of feeling in control of their learning experience. Overall, student comments about collaboration were correlated with comments about control with $r = 0.79$.

There were several ways in which students talked about feeling as if they were in control of their collaborations during the workshops, but the most prevalent comments were about students' control of the timing and extent of their collaborative activity. Students talked about their ability to decide for themselves when to work alone, when to work with a peer, and when to consult with an adult. One student said simply: "[In the workshop] if I don't know something, I just ask you or other friends to sit by me. In class [at school] you can't talk." Similar sentiments were echoed in two-thirds of the comments where students talked about both control and collaboration. In almost all of the comments about working with peers (16/19) and about getting help from adults (16/18), students talked about the fact that in the workshop they were in control of how and when these interactions took place.

It is worth pointing out that all of the student comments described above were made in the context of very general questions about the workshops and students' experiences in them. The interview guidelines asked a series of questions, none of which specifically mentioned control or collaboration. Students were asked: "Did you like the workshop? Was the workshop what you expected? Were there any surprises? How would you describe the workshop to your parent? A teacher? A friend? What (if anything) do you think you learned from the workshop? What in the workshop helped this learning happen? Was workshop like or unlike your classes at school? Did the workshop change your feelings or thoughts about math? Did the workshop change your feelings or thoughts about art? What (if anything) about the workshop helped you change views?" It was in this context that students raised issues of control over their own activities and their ability to control their interactions with others, which suggests two things: that these were significant concerns for these students, and that the changed relationships among control, collaboration, and learning were important aspects of the "success" of the studio as an environment for learning mathematics.

Role of the Medium. This description of the mathematics studio would not be complete without at least mentioning the media used by students and teachers. The idea that different representations are good for approaching different problems (or different aspects of a single problem) is a proposition that is more or less taken for granted in design. An important part of learning to design is learning to chose and use different representations effectively (see Akin, 1986; Mitchell & McCullough, 1991).

Not surprisingly, students' experiences of the workshops reflected both the fact that they had access to computers and the particular software they were using. Most students who used the computers to any great extent during the workshop used the Geometer's Sketchpad program. The Geometer's Sketchpad allows students to create basic geometric figures, such as circles, lines, and arbitrary polygons, and to change the size, orientation, and color of the figures created. More importantly, students can define mathematical relationships between theses objects: ratios, angles, and geometric trans-formations. So, for example, a student could create a line and a polygon and then create the reflection of the polygon in the line.

When objects are moved on the screen in the Geometer's Sketchpad, mathematical relationships are preserved. The display is updated in real time as students "drag" points, lines, and figures on the screen. In this way, students can explore the effects of various mathematical constraints and relations quickly and easily, looking for solutions to mathematical problems that have aesthetic appeal. Sketchpad also preserves a record of a student's actions during a given session with the program. This lets students "undo" their actions; they can step back to and through previous states in their exploration rapidly.

Students commented on the ease with which they could experiment with designs on the computer using the Geometer's Sketchpad. They described the program's ability to hold an image constant, to let them make very pre-cise changes, and to let them explore the consequences of those changes. In other words, students talked about how the computer helped them control their explorations:

> The computer just made everything easy. You didn't have to hold everything right—[the computer] just it did it for you, so . . . you could concentrate on actually what you were seeing instead of just [thinking:] "Well, I think I saw that, let me try that again and see if I see the same thing."

> You drew that dog, and then when you got the mirror on the screen you [moved] it around so that you could get a duplicate of it. . . . When we did it on the computer . . . I could actually move the mirror around the screen, move it in closer, and make like one picture out of the two, and move further apart.

The infinite undo feature of the Geometer's Sketchpad also gave students a sense of control over their exploration. As one student said: "The com-puters helped because it was like easier [than working] on paper [if] you'd have to erase it, or start again. You could just undo it, and then try some-thing differently. That was easier because it was much quicker." Overall six of the seven students who worked extensively with computers com-mented about one or more of these ways in which the computer increased their ability to control their explorations of the mathematical problems of design.

Computers thus helped students develop a sense of autonomy in the mathematics studio. But the control that computers provided was exercised within the structure of the design studio, and in particular within the frame-work of desk crits and other tools of the design pedagogy. Unfortunately, the data collected from these first workshops did not show directly how these structures did—or did not—help students turn this computational control into mathematics learning in the studio environment.

The process through which the collaborative structures of the design studio help students turn computer-based exploration into abstract understanding was thus the subject of a subsequent study—and the next section of this chapter.

A DIGITAL MATHEMATICS STUDIO

Methods

The follow-up study to the workshops described above was a four-week summer program for middle school students in the Boston area. Twelve students (not the same students from the previous workshops) attended the program. Students came from 9 am to 1 pm Monday through Friday for four weeks to one of the graduate design studios at the MIT School of Architecture and Planning. As was the case in the workshops, the activities of the summer program were modeled on the practice of a traditional architectural design studio course, with some additional structures—such as morning and afternoon group meeting, check-in times, and a snack break—provided in the day because of the age of the students.

Generally, working days in the program began with a warm-up activity involving traditional materials: For example, one day began with students cutting out a shape from construction paper and then figuring out a way to make the same shape at one-half size. After the warm-up activity, students were introduced to some piece of the functionality of the software they were using for the program: On the day that began with cutting out shapes at different scales students were shown how to construct dilations in the computational medium. Students spent the rest of the day (approximately two to three hours) on design activities using the concepts introduced.

Design work typically began with the discussion of some "master works" from prominent artists (because of the abstract geometric nature of some of their pieces, examples drew heavily from the work of Kandinsky, Klee, Escher, Lewitt, Mondrian, and Picasso). This discussion of master works was followed by the presentation of a "design challenge." Typically, students were asked to make a design using the mathematical concept introduced in the warm-up activity. Students worked on the design challenge in an initial design phase lasting 45 minutes to an hour, consulting periodically with program leaders or peers for technical help with the software or for more detailed desk crits on their emerging designs. These initial design explorations were followed by a pin-up, where each student presented his or her work-in-progress to the group and got technical, aesthetic, and mathematical comment and feedback from peers and program leaders.

During the pin-up, additional exemplars were shown, and the design challenge was revised to include additional criteria. For example, on the day when students began working with dilations, the original design challenge was to make an interesting composition using multiple dilations of one or more shapes using a single vanishing point. The challenge was later revised to include the idea of balanced composition: Students were asked to make two designs using the same set of dilated objects, one balanced composition and one unbalanced. Students typically worked on the revised challenge for another hour or so, with desk crits continuing throughout. The day usually ended with a pin-up and discussion of students' final products.

Over the course of the program, students were introduced to mathematical ideas such as curvature, parallel and perpendicular lines, translation, rotation, dilation, reflection, and fractal recursion. Students also worked with design principles such as simplest shapes, form, negative space, color, depth, and balance. The mathematical ideas were taken from the basic concepts of transformational geometry and were chosen because of their suitability for exploration with the Geometer's Sketchpad software. The design ideas were taken from Rudolph Arnheim's work on design theory (Arnheim, 1974) and chosen because of their suitability for exploration in conjunction with the mathematical topics of the program.

The summer program used 12 Macintosh computers connected by a an ethernet network to a black-and-white laser printer, an ink-jet color printer, and a large-format (36″ by 70″) color plotter. At the beginning of the program, students often worked in pairs or groups on a single computer, and they often used different computers on different days. As the program progressed, students increasingly worked on their own projects, each using the same machine from day to day. One of the computers functioned as a server, and all student work from each day was archived on the server for later study. Another computer was connected to a 27″ NTSC video monitor for use by students or program leaders during pin-ups or other group discussions. As in the workshops, all of the computers in the project were equipped with the Geometer's Sketchpad (Jackiw, 1995).

Data

As in the workshops, data for the summer program were collected in a series of three interviews: one immediately before the program (pre-interview), one immediately after the program (post-interview), and a final interview three months after the conclusion of the program. In these interviews, students were asked about their experiences and feelings towards art, mathematics, and the program. They also took a short-answer test of 18 geometry questions taken from a variety of geometry text books (see Aichele et al., 1998; Manfre, Moser, Lobato, & Morrow, 1994; Moise & Downs, 1971; Rubenstein et al., 1995a, 1995b; Serra, 1997).

In addition to these interview data, throughout the summer program each of the program leaders wore a "tie-clip" microphone connected to a portable tape recorder in his or her pocket. This allowed the program leaders to move about in the studio and have a record of their various interactions with students. Most of these interactions were, of course, "desk crits" where the program leader and a student discussed the student's design work in some detail. The recorded desk crits provided a means to conduct clinical interviews at key points throughout students' design processes. At the conclusion of the program, transcriptions from these interviews were combined into a single, illustrated design history for each student. Although these design histories were not comprehensive in the sense that they did not represent a continuous recording of students' design work, they do give a detailed account of students' work over an extended period of time.

These design histories were divided into a series of design episodes, identifying a statement of the problem or issue being addressed (an initial condition), a series of design steps (an exploration), and a conclusion to the episode (an insight). Once the design episodes were thus categorized, episodes were coded for the presence (or absence) of mathematical ideas, collaboration with program leaders, collaboration with peers, use of exemplars, and other relevant categories (for more on the coding and analysis of these data see Shaffer, 1998).

Results

The general results of the summer program support the conclusion of the workshops, namely, that students can learn geometry through design activities. In tests of transformational geometry knowledge, students' scores rose significantly between pre-and post-interviews (mean pre $= 9.5$, mean post $= 12.25$; $p < .01$). These gains were stable in final interviews three months later (mean final $= 12.0$), the results of which were significantly different than the pre-interview scores ($p < .05$) but not statistically different from post-interview scores ($p > .49$; see Fig. 5.4).

A more detailed discussion of the data collection, analysis, and results of the summer program described here can be found in other work (Shaffer, 1998). From the perspective of this chapter, it is important to note that the collection and coding of design histories made it possible to construct a logistic regression model of when and how students gained mathematical insights during their design activity. That is, it is possible to create a model that can "predict" the likelihood of whether students will identify abstract mathematical principles or describe general mathematical rules operating

Math Test Scores

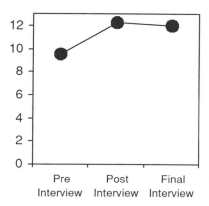

FIG. 5.4. Scores on a test of transformational geometry knowledge rose significantly after the program ($p < .01$) and remained significantly higher three months later ($p < .05$).

in their designs based on what they are doing and who they are (or are not!) working with (see Figure 5.5).

The regression model suggests that collaborative conversations helped students turn their design activity into insights about mathematics. Students were significantly more likely to have mathematical insights if they had a conversation with someone else while making sense of what happened during

Actual (black) vs. predicted (gray) mathematical insights

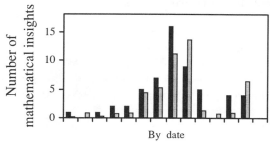

FIG. 5.5. Graph shows for each day the total insights for all participants about mathematics during design episodes (solid bars) as well as mathematical insights predicted by a fixed-effects logistic regression model (gray bars; $p < .001$, $R^2 > .70$).

their design activity. In the logistic model of mathematical insight, nearly 50% of the variability in whether or not students express a mathematical insight is determined by whether or not they collaborate with program leaders or with peers while they are working through the implications of their design activity.

It is true, of course, that the data collection method used in this study—clinical interviews as a part of design desk crits—was likely to over-represent the effects of collaboration on students' work in the studio. Indeed, collaborations with program leaders were involved in 80% of the design episodes where students had mathematical insights. But although the effects of collaboration may be overstated here due to bias in the data collection method, it is clear that collaboration did play a significant role in students' mathematical insights.

Quantitative analysis thus suggests that the desk crit plays an important role in creating collaborations that lead to the development of mathematical understanding. A closer look at one student's experiences in the digital mathematics studio suggests why this is the case.

B—'s Story

The first day of the Escher's World program began with a design challenge: to make a square out of circles. Students looked at several examples of solutions to this design problem (see Fig. 5.6) and were also shown how to construct a circle using the software tool. Later, after a pin-up where students shared their solutions to the original challenge, the problem was revised. Students spent the remainder of the day working on drawing a straight-edged figure of any kind using curved lines (arcs or circles).

B—'s response to these challenges was first to draw the outline of a square "by hand" and "by eye" (see Fig. 5.7), and only after talking with program leaders and seeing the work of her peers did B— begin to use straight lines as

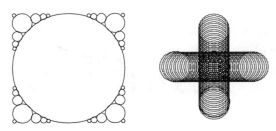

FIG. 5.6. Two examples of drawing a square using circles that students were shown during the summer program.

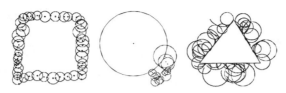

FIG. 5.7. B—'s responses to the challenge of drawing straight edges with curves.

"guides" for her drawing. B—'s work on these first design challenges shows progressively more sophisticated use of the idea of curvature and properties of arcs: In the second image in Fig. 5.7, for example, she uses a single circle with large radius to form one "straight" side of a square; in the final image she uses arcs to "wrap around" the bottom vertices of the triangle. But at this early stage, B— showed little evidence of thinking explicitly about these issues. About the middle image she said only, "I just wanted to use little circles," and when asked why she chose a triangle for the final design, she replied, "It was a simple shape. I'm just fiddling around."

The next day students were asked to make an image of a ball; they were given two rubber balls of different sizes and with different coefficients of restitution (bounciness) to use as models. The challenge was two-fold. First, the images of this round object were to be made using only straight lines. Second, and perhaps more important, the designs were supposed to convey an interpretation of some interesting aspect of the ball: its weight, the texture of its surface, the way it bounces, and so on. In response to this second challenge, we can already begin to see a change in B—'s work. In particular, after making one drawing of a ball "bouncing off of a ceiling" (Fig. 5.8), B— found herself struggling to get the artistic effect she wanted. She called over a program leader and in the course of the desk crit explained, "I want the bottom lighter... not lighter, more open, not really there . . . ." As B— and the critic explored the drawing, they talked about her expressive intent (what

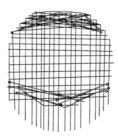

FIG. 5.8. B—'s original image of a ball bouncing off of a ceiling.

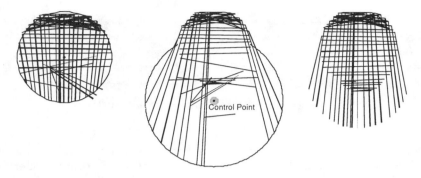

FIG. 5.9. B— and the critic explored the underlying construction of the image, and then B— was able to use the tool to realize her expressive intent in a final design (right). The middle sketch is a reconstruction—the coloring and labeling of the center point were added, and several line segments were removed for clarity.

she wanted from the drawing) and also about the underlying construction of the image.

What they discovered was that by using a circle as a "guide" for the line segments that make up the ball, B— had inadvertently given herself a way to alter the artistic effect of the image. (The circle was "hidden" by the program, but its position was still determining the location of the line segments in the image). By "dragging" the center point of the circle, B— could spread out the segments on the lower edge of the ball. Armed with this discovery, she returned to the design with both a clear intent and a means to manipulate the image. B— spent the remainder of her working time adjusting and reconstructing the design so that, as she said of her final image, "when it goes out, it's sort of . . . motion" representing the movement of the bouncing ball (see Fig. 5.9).

Moving ahead a week or so, B— was working on a design challenge involving rotation and discovered that she could make an "exploding" negative space in the center of the image (see Fig. 5.10; the "vibrating" white space at the center of the rotation is what B— called "explosive"). This idea became the focus of a series of design explorations, a topic that B— returned to consistently in the following days and ultimately the subject of her final project. What in particular about B—'s schooling or upbringing might have made explosions such a compelling theme for her is left to the reader's speculation, but whatever the motive, the problem of making this kind of visually active white space was clearly quite compelling for B—.

B—'s discovery of exploding negative space was accompanied by a realization about the design process. As she put it, "You should start with

FIG. 5.10. B— discovered that it was possible to create an "exploding" negative space (the vibrating white space) at the center of a rotated image.

a few [shapes], play around with them until you find some nice shapes, and then expand [on that]." The question for B— was how to "expand" this design idea. After discussing the problem in desk crits with one of the program leaders, B— began a series of carefully conducted explorations into the workings of "exploding" spaces. She made a set of designs (see Fig. 5.11)—some 10–20 in all—determining the factors that make a rotated shape look explosive: a "nice pointy shape," "enough" points, a dark color, and so on.

At this point, B— found herself stuck. She knew she wanted to make a design that explored the idea of exploding negative space, but she was not sure how to proceed. In a desk crit, a program leader suggested that she think about making "rings of explosions" and perhaps use the same shape in each ring—as if a real object were exploding and sending off shards in all directions. B— liked this idea, but she ran into trouble trying to execute it: She could make an explosion in the inner ring, or in the outer ring, but not in

FIG. 5.11. B—explored the factors that make an exploding negative space from a rotated shape.

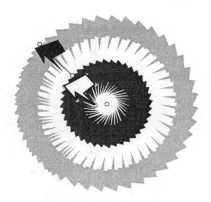

FIG. 5.12. B— and the critic use this image to explore the nature of rotation. B— was frustrated that she could not make the same "explosion" in both rings, until she realized that she needed to rotate by a smaller angle in a large circle to keep the distance between objects the same.

both (see Fig. 5.12). As she had done earlier in designing the bouncing ball, B— called over a program leader when she had trouble getting her design to behave as she expected (and wanted) using the software.

B—'s first explanation for the problem was that there was something wrong with the shape she had chosen. The program leader suggested that they change the color of one of the shapes on each ring of the exploding design (see Fig. 5.12) so they could watch carefully as they changed the shape dynamically. The problem, it turned out, was not with the shape. The problem was that B— had rotated the shape by the same amount in both the inner and outer rings. "Oh," said B—, "you have to rotate the outside one more times—less degrees—[because] they're farther apart.... It's a bigger circle, [and] with a bigger circle you need to rotate it more times to keep it pointy."

With this mathematical insight about the relationships among the size (radius) of a circle, the angle of rotation (subtended angle), and the distance between object and image (an arc or chord length), B— was able to complete her project. The final image (see Fig. 5.13) is of a negative space explosion in the background sending shapes into the foreground flying off in all directions within a rectangular frame.

Patterns Across Design Stories

There are clearly a number of things happening in the course of B—'s design work that lead to her development of mathematical understanding. One of the central issues in the design history above is clearly B—'s use of the

FIG. 5.13. B—'s final image for the museum exhibit showing an explosion in the negative space of the image sending identical shapes off in all directions. The original image was a 26″ × 54″ color poster.

software tool, and particularly the way the Sketchpad program preserves mathematical relationships under dynamic transformation. This issue is discussed in more detail in other analyses of the summer program (see Shaffer, 1998).

In the context of this chapter, there are two important observations to be made about B—'s design activity. The first is that collaborative conversations came about when B— was trying to achieve a particular design effect and was frustrated because of the way she had implemented her design idea in the software. Based on her knowledge of circles, squares, and later of rotation, B— expected that the software (and thus her designs) would act in certain ways. This breakdown of expectations raised questions for B—, and she directed these questions at the software, at her own understanding, and ultimately at her peers and at the program leaders. These questions led to productive discussions, which in turn helped B— think about the abstract mathematical ideas and general design principles in her work.

The other important point is that in B—'s work we can clearly see a movement back and forth between individual activity and collaboration. Just as students in the workshops suggested, the studio format of the summer program made it possible for B— to balance her own interests, abilities, and expressive desires—her own control over her learning experience—and her need for and desire for feedback and help from others.

It is perhaps interesting to note that B— was a painfully shy young woman, barely willing to speak above a whisper. She was planning to move to home-schooling at the beginning of the school year following the program. And yet in her design story, we can see her progressively master the ability to express herself and the ability to mobilize social resources to develop her understanding.

CONCLUSION

These three projects thus show that the design studio, with its combination of loose schedule and structured desk crits, provides a useful model for thinking about collaborative activity in an open learning environment. The design studio provides a framework for collaborative activity that preserves student autonomy in the learning process but also provides a model for collaborative interactions. This work also shows that the design studio model can be used successfully for learning mathematics with the help of computer technology.

More generally, this research suggests that whatever model we take for supporting collaborative activities, students' experiences of collaboration are influenced by their sense of control—or lack of control—over their learning process. Learning to work with others is an essential skill, particularly for the modern workplace. This research suggests that some care is needed in thinking about how to create an environment where both collaboration and personal control of the learning process are given adequate support. The design studio may offer one viable model for creating such environments.

REFERENCES

Aichele, D. B., Hopfensberger, P. W., Leiva, M. A., Mason, M. M., Murphy, S. J., Schell, V. J., & Vheru, M. C. (1998). *Geometry: Explorations and applications* (Teacher's ed.). Evanston, IL: McDougal Littell.

Akin, O. (1986). *Psychology of architectural design. London: Pion.*

Arnheim, R. (1974). *Art and visual perception: A psychology of the creative eye.* Berkeley: University of California Press.

Boaler, J. (1996). Learning to lose in the mathematics classroom: A critique of traditional schooling practices in the UK. *Qualitative Studies in Education, 9* (1), 17–33.

Bruner, J. S. (1996). *The culture of education.* Cambridge, MA: Harvard University Press.

Chafee, R. (1977). The teaching of architecture at the Ecole des Beaux-Arts. In A. Drexler (Ed.), *The architecture of the Ecole des Beaux-Arts.* New York: Museum of Modern Art, pp. 61–110.

Dewey, J. (1915). *The school and society.* Chicago: University of Chicago Press.

Dewey, J. (1938). *Experience and education.* New York: Collier Books.

Gardner, H. (1993). *Multiple intelligences: The theory in practice*. New York: Basic Books.

Harel, I., & Papert, S. (1991). Software design as a learning environment. In I. Harel & S. Papert (Eds.), *Constructionism*. Norwood, NJ: Ablex Publishing, p. 41–84.

Jackiw, N. (1995). *The Geometer's Sketchpad*. Berkeley: Key Curriculum Press.

Kafai, Y., & Harel, I. (1991). Learning through design and teaching: Exploring social and collaborative aspects of constructionism. In I. Harel & S. Papert (Eds.), *Constructionism*. Norwood, NJ: Ablex Publishing, p. 85–110

Kaput, J. J., & Roschelle, J. (in press). The mathematics of change and variation from a millennial perspective: New content, new context. In C. Hoyles & R. Noss (Eds.), *Mathematics for a new millenium*. London: Springer-Verlag, p. 155–170.

Manfre, E., Moser, J. M., Lobato, J. E., & Morrow, L. (1994). *Heath mathematics connections*. Lexington, MA: D. C. Heath and Company.

Mitchell, W. J., & McCullough, M. (1991). *Digital design media: A handbook for architects and design professionals*. New York: Van Nostrand Reinhold.

Moise, E. E., & Downs, F. L. (1971). *Geometry*. Menlo Park, CA: Addison-Wesley Publishing Company.

NCTM Commission on Standards for School Mathematics. (1989). *Curriculum and evaluation standards for school mathematics*. Reston, VA: National Council of Teachers of Mathematics.

NCTM Commission on Standards for School Mathematics. (1991). *Professional standards for teaching mathematics*. Reston, VA: National Council of Teachers of Mathematics.

Noss, R., & Hoyles, C. (1996). *Windows on mathematical meanings: Learning cultures and computers*. Dordrecht: Kluwer Academic Publishers.

Papert, S. (1980). *Mindstorms: Children, computers, and powerful ideas*. New York: Basic Books.

Papert, S. (1991). Situating constructionism. In I. Harel & S. Papert (Eds.), *Constructionism*. Norwood, NJ: Ablex Publishing, 1–12.

Papert, S. (1993). *The children's machine: Rethinking school in the age of the computer*. New York: Basic Books.

Papert, S. (1996). *The connected family: Bridging the digital generation gap*. Atlanta, GA: Longstreet Press.

Parker, F. W. (1894/1969). *Talks on pedagogics*. New York: Arno Press.

Pea, R. (1993). Practices of distributed intelligence and designs for education. In G. Salomon (Ed.), *Distributed cognitions: Psychological and educational considerations*. Cambridge: Cambridge University Press, p. 47–87.

Resnick, M. (1994). *Turtles, termites, and traffic jams: Explorations in massively parallel microworlds*. Cambridge: MIT Press.

Resnick, M., Bruckman, A., & Martin, F. (1996). Pianos not stereos. *Interactions*. Vol. 3, no. 6 (September/October 1996), p. 40–50.

Resnick, M., & Ocko, S. (1991). LEGO/Logo: Learning through and about design. In I. Harel & S. Papert (Eds.), *Constructionism*. Norwood, NJ: Ablex Publishing, p. 141–150.

Rubenstein, R. N., Craine, T. V., Butts, T. R., Cantrell, K., Dritsas, L., Elswick, V. A., Kavanaugh, J., Munshin, S. N., Murphy, S. J., Piccolino, A., Quezada, S., & Walton, J. C. (1995a). *Integrated Mathematics 1* (Teacher's ed.). Evanston, IL: McDougal Littell/Houghton Mifflin.

Rubenstein, R. N., Craine, T. V., Butts, T. R., Cantrell, K., Dritsas, L., Elswick, V. A., Kavanaugh, J., Munshin, S. N., Murphy, S. J., Piccolino, A., Quezada, S., & Walton, J. C. (1995b). *Integrated Mathematics 2* (Student ed.). Evanston, IL: McDougal Littell/Houghton Mifflin.

Schon, D. A. (1985). *The design studio: An exploration of its traditions and potentials*. London: RIBA Publications.

Serra, M. (1997). *Discovering geometry: An inductive approach* (2nd ed.). Berkeley, CA: Key Curriculum Press.

Shaffer, D. W. (1997). Learning mathematics through design: The anatomy of Escher's world. *Journal of Mathematical Behavior, 16*(2), p. 95–112.

Shaffer, D. W. (1998). *Expressive mathematics: Learning by design*. Unpublished doctoral dissertation; Massachusetts Institute of Technology, Cambridge, MA.

Shaffer, D. W. (in press). Escher's world: Learning symmetry through mathematics and art. *Symmetry: Culture and Science*. (no futher info. available at this time)

Sizer, T. R. (1984). *Horace's compromise: The dilemma of the American high school*. Boston: Houghton Mifflin.

Vygotsky, L. S. (1978). *Mind in society*. Cambridge, MA: Harvard University Press.

Wilensky, U. (1995). Paradox, programming, and learning probability: A case study in a connected mathematics framework. *Journal of Mathematical Behavior, 14*, 253–280.

Wingler, H. M. (1978). *The Bauhaus: Weimar, Dessau, Berlin, Chicago*. Cambridge, MA: MIT Press.

THE DESIGN STUDIO: A PROMISING MODEL FOR LEARNING TO COLLABORATE

David Williamson Shaffer
Harvard University Graduate School of Education

It is a great pleasure to engage in the deep discussion that the format of this volume makes possible. One of the strengths of scholarly discourse is the way it takes place over time and distance, providing a chance for reflection and perspective. But the reflective stance of the "Guttenberg Man" (McLuhan, 1962; Donald, 1991) has its disadvantages too, not least of which is a lack of venues for substantive conversation, in depth, in public, about work in progress. So I am delighted to have a trio of distinguished colleagues—Rogers Hall, Susan Leigh Star, and Ricardo Nemirovsky—address issues raised by my paper on the design studio as a model for computer-supported collaboration.

In addition to providing a thoughtful summary of the key points of the paper I originally presented at a Computer-Supported Collaborative Learning (CSCL) conference, Rogers Hall raises several important issues that are present in the paper but not addressed directly.

One is the nature of the Escher's World project as a longitudinal study. In recent years, with the increasingly popularity of and respect for qualitative research, we have seen a number of "micro-genetic" studies of learning. These studies attempt to examine the processes through which learners construct understanding by focusing on a relatively short period of time in great detail. The advantages of this approach are obvious and these studies done a great service in revealing the complex moment-by-moment interactions in episodes of learning (Cobb, 1986; Nemirovsky & Tinker, 1993; Meira, 1995).

The Escher's World study took a different approach, starting from the premise that significant learning may take place across as well as within learning experiences. The methodology looked in less detail at individual learning episodes, but in return was able to capture the evolution of the learning process as specific experiences were accumulated over time. The results complement the microgenetic approach. The emerging picture is still one of a complex set of relationships—and indeed, shows that many of the same issues that appear in each episode (connections between people, tool, and task) are present in the broader frame as well. Perhaps the learning process is fractal in nature, with complexity and structure repeating themselves at each level of analysis.

Hall also raises the issue of the resources that were available to students in the Escher's World project, observing rightly that "it is not entirely surprising to read that students, in interviews, express a preference for this setting over their usual mathematics classrooms." Susan Leigh Star makes a similar point. Star was struck—as I was struck on first encountering the design studio—by the relative openness of the design studio: She describes it aptly as having "substantial slack temporal resources." The question this naturally raises is whether (or how) this model can work in the 50-minute parcels of time that traditional schooling allows.

Star suggests addressing this question in future work. But this is not the only way to look at the issue. It seems to me that there is little about the design studio to suggest that it could function in any reasonable way as a coherent structure within the physical and temporal constraints of the traditional school. Perhaps that means the design studio is not a viable model for other disciplines. Perhaps it means that particular insights from the design studio can be applied in other, more constrained settings. Or perhaps it means that we should explore ways in which the structure of school can be expanded to allow for a wider range of pedagogical approaches.

In any event, I find myself agreeing with Hall that "innovations in design . . . need to start somewhere." We need to understand when and how a model works in order to decide how—or whether—it can and should be adapted to other circumstances.

From her experience as a teacher, Star highlights another fundamental issue in the "design studio model," namely, that students find cooperative work frustrating, and in some sense inherently "unfair." They feel they are being judged on the work of their team members and not solely on their own efforts. As an educator, I have always found this disturbing, because it suggests that our educational system provides young people with a distorted view of the world for which they are supposedly being prepared. In most occupations—perhaps in most situations in life—we are expected to work with others, and our ability to work as part of a team is one of the most important yardsticks by which we become "successful," however one defines that slippery term (Murnane & Levy, 1996; Botkin, 1999).

This is one of the reasons I think the design studio is such a promising model. It provides a venue where students can learn to work together—and learn to work through the discomfort of working with others. The design studio provides an environment where students can learn some of these skills. But it does so by example and practice rather than by didactic training or by blind trial-and-error discovery (Garrett, 1975; Chafee, 1977; Wingler, 1978; Allen, 1980; Ledewitz, 1982; Schon, 1985; Akin, 1986; Anthony, 1987; Rowe, 1987; Frederickson & Anderton, 1990; Coyne, 1993).

Star correctly points out that the "democratic" nature of crits makes them problematic and even potentially dangerous as a pedagogical setting. If it is true that real learning demands real investment in the activity at hand, then when we give relative novices the delicate task of providing constructive criticism, it is possible that feelings can get hurt.

And sometimes feelings do get hurt (Anthony, 1987; Frederickson & Anderton, 1990). The design studio, is, however, not as democratic as it appears on the surface. Although the opinions of all critics are equal, the opinions of some critics are more equal than others. In the design studio setting, I have seen the professor work with a student to blunt harsh comments from peers as well as from outside reviewers—and I have myself intervened with students who needed help understanding how to give feedback constructively and appropriately. The design studio tries to strike a balance between democracy and enlightened despotism, where the goal of the enterprise is to help the students learn to internalize the skills of the professor/teacher as designer, critic, and collaborator (Shaffer, 1998).

Nemirovsky addresses these issues as well, pointing out that collaboration and control are interwoven in issues of power and judgment. He suggests that "students worked on [projects that] were individual, [and] therefore the collaboration that took place was not joint work but interactions between someone who had a request or question and someone else who might have offered a suitable response or suggestion." This, far from being a weakness of the model, is precisely the point. Students in Escher's World were able to balance collaborative work and autonomy in part because their collaborations were a kind of reciprocal teaching around individual projects. Using less jargon, student A was helping student B on student B's project, and vice versa, rather than both students were working together on the same project. The distinction between work as a group and work together on a suite of projects where each student feels ownership of his or her work is a significant feature of the design studio. That feature was fundamental to the experience of students in Escher's World—and was one of our formative design considerations (Shaffer, 1998).

The implicit power dynamics of these different situations are, of course, an interesting question for further study. But it seems to me that the more powerful lesson of the design studio is that the traditional equation of collaborative work and group work may be a disservice to students. It may be that a context in which collaboration is desired, rather than enforced, gives students an opportunity to learn the skills needed to work with others, as well as a chance to see the value of enhancing their own efforts with the insights and expertise of their peers. This was certainly the case with the students in Escher's World.

Nemirovsky raises two other issues about the introduction of design studio methods into the pedagogy of mathematics: the nature of disciplinary boundaries and past history of project-based learning. These points were not addressed in depth in the short commentary, but they were quite deliberately woven into the Escher's World learning environment. So I am grateful to have a chance to touch on them at least briefly here.

The relationship among disciplines is a subject of intense interest to academics and researchers (Martin, Kass et al., 1990; Newmann & Wehlage, 1993; Wiggins, 1993; Kalmbach, 1996; Shaffer & Resnick, in press), but one of the things that the Escher's World experiments showed is that working in an interdisciplinary space comes quite naturally to students. Designing such a space is not a trivial matter, of course. In earlier work (Cossentino & Shaffer, 1999), Jackie Cossentino and I discussed the "mathematics studio" as a "genuine collaboration" between disciplines, where a critical factor was the extent to which the artistic and mathematical perspectives were respected equally. In a sense, we addressed up front, by design (no pun intended), the issue that Stevens (this volume) identified in his study of the design activities "not counting as much," in the end, as traditional mathematical competence.

Nemirovsky's historical concern is that despite the promise of the design studio model as described in this volume and elsewhere, we are a long way from the day when such an environment will be—even could be—the norm for students in a traditional school setting. Nemirovsky suggests an analogy between the failed promises of "activating the immune system to combat cancerous cells" and the history of open-ended, project-based learning environments.

Nemirovsky's analogy was of particular interest to me because I have the distinct pleasure, as part of my current work, to collaborate with physicians and scientists working on innovative approaches to a variety of clinical problems—cancer, coronary disease, stroke, and other ills that still face us despite the tremendous advances of medicine in the past century. One of the things that I am struck by is the way in which these researchers are able to work simultaneously in the lab and in the clinic. They spend hours working on techniques that may be years from helping a patient in even some small way. What motivates this research is a vision of how the future of patient care can and should be. But moments after talking about all of the problems with current treatments—ineffective regimes, harmful side effects, needless suffering because of errors, lack of resources, or inefficiencies—these same men and women walk from their lab into the examination or procedure room, where they do the best they can with the therapies available.

Somehow, these medical researchers are able to find a balance between living for what could be and living with what is. They refuse to let the world as it is blind them to the world as it could be—and they refuse to let the world as it could be blind them to the world as it is.

One of the wonderful things about working as a teacher rather than as a physician is that experience and experimentation can find their way into practice through more subtle and varied routes. The clinician who changes the standard of care is rare, but it is more or less expected that a good teacher will change his or her practice based on experience. There is clearly more that can and should be said about the design studio as a model for education in other fields and more experimental and observational work to be done. But my hope is that even in the short run, the observations made by Stevens, by me in this brief report about a larger body of research, and by the growing body of researchers looking at this approach can help teachers develop new ways of structuring projects and interacting with students, as well as pave the road for larger scale transformations of the educational system as we know it.

In any event, I am grateful to my colleagues for raising these important issues. The dialog has helped advance and clarify my own thinking about the design studio as a model for learning environments—and has given me an opportunity to discuss some of the larger issues raised by the Escher's World project in more depth.

REFERENCES

Akin, O. (1986). *Psychology of Architectural Design*. London: Pion.

Allen, E. (1980). Things learned in lab. *Journal of architectural education*. Winter 1980, pp. 22–25.

Anthony, K. H. (1987). Private reactions to public criticism: Students, faculty, and practicing architects state their views on design juries in architectural education. *Journal of Architectural Education, 40*(3), 2–11.

Botkin, J. (1999). *Smart business: How knowledge communities can revolutionize your company*. New York: Free Press.

Chafee, R. (1977). The teaching of architecture at the Ecole des Beaux-Arts. In A. Drexler (Ed.), *The architecture of the Ecole des Beaux-Arts*. New York: Museum of Modern Art, pp. 61–110.

Cobb, P. (1986). Concrete can be abstract: A case study. *Educational Studies in Mathematics, 17*(1), 37–48.

Cossentino, J., & Shaffer, D. W. (1999). The math studio: Harnassing the power of the arts to teach across disciplines. *Journal of Aesthetic Education*, V. 33, no. 2 (Summer 1999): p. 99–109.

Coyne, R. (1993). Cooperation an individualism in design. *Environment and planning B, 20*(2), 163–174.

Donald, M. (1991). *Origins of the modern mind: Three stages in the evolution of culture and cognition*. Cambridge, MA: Harvard University Press.

Frederickson, M. P., & Anderton, F. (1990). Design juries: A study on lines of communication. *Journal of Architectural Education, 43*(2) (Winter 1990): 22–8.

Garrett, L. (1975). *Visual design: A problem-solving approach.* Huntington, NY: R. E. Krieger.

Kalmbach, J. (1996). From liquid paper to typewriters: Some historical perspectives on technology in the classroom. *Computers and Composition, 13*, 57–68.

Ledewitz, S. (1982). Models of design in studio teaching. *Journal of Architectural Education.*

Martin, B., Kass, H., & Brouwer, W. (1990). Authentic science: A diversity of meanings. *Science Education, 74*, 541–554.

McLuhan, M. (1962). *The Gutenberg galaxy: The making of typographic man.* Toronto: University of Toronto Press.

Meira, L. (1995). The microevolution of mathematical representations in children's activity. *Cognition and Instruction, 13*(2), 269–313.

Murnane, R. J., & Levy, F. (1996). *Teaching the new basic skills: Principles for educating children to thrive in a changing economy.* New York: Free Press.

Nemirovsky, R., & Tinker, R. (1993). Exploring chaos: A case study. *Journal of Computers in Mathematics and Science Teaching, 12*(1).

Newmann, F. M., & Wehlage, G. G. (1993). Five standards of authentic instruction. *Educational Leadership, 50*(7).

Rowe, P. G. (1987). *Design thinking.* Cambridge, MA: MIT Press.

Schon, D. A. (1985). *The design studio: An exploration of its traditions and potentials.* London: RIBA Publications.

Shaffer, D. W. (1998). Expressive mathematics: Learning by design. Unpublished doctoral dissertation in *Media Arts and Sciences.* Cambridge, MA: Massachusetts Institute of Technology.

Shaffer, D. W., & Resnick, M. (1999). Thick authenticity: New media and authentic learning. *Journal of Interactive Learning Research, 10*(2), 195–215.

Wiggins, G. (1993). Assessment, authenticity, context, and validity. *Phi Delta Kappan, 75*(3), November 200–214.

Wingler, H. M. (1978). *The Bauhaus: Weimar, Dessau, Berlin, Chicago.* Cambridge, MA: MIT Press.

6

DIVISIONS OF LABOR IN SCHOOL AND IN THE WORKPLACE: COMPARING COMPUTER- AND PAPER-SUPPORTED ACTIVITIES ACROSS SETTINGS

Reed R. Stevens
University of Washington

INTRODUCTION

> Technology is never purely technological: It is also social. The social is never purely social: It is technological. This is something easy to say but difficult to work with. So much of our language and so many of our practices reflect a determined, culturally ingrained propensity to treat the two as if they were quite separate from one another.
>
> — Law & Bijker, 1992 (pp. 305–306)

The aim of this study is to contribute to a better understanding of how computer use shapes and is shaped by the organization of work and learning in modern institutional life. My approach is broadly comparative and grounded in two case studies from distinct institutional settings, one a classroom and the other a workplace. In both settings, people worked and learned, together and apart. It is the wax and wane of together and apart that this analysis addresses. In so doing, my analysis offers a few grounded concepts for thinking about the forms that collaboration takes, how media support it, and how it takes on meanings for institutional participants in ways that vary with surrounding organizational conditions.

This study argues for the importance of developing relational concepts as a means to accelerate the progress of interdisciplinary research communities such as those of the learning sciences and computer-supported collaborative learning (CSCL). Computer-supported collaborative learning is an emerging perspective that promises to go beyond good old fashioned instructional technology, beyond the interface, and beyond the isolated individual (Koschmann, 1996). The centerpiece of the relational approach that I sketch in this chapter is an extension of the division of labor concept as articulated by Strauss (1985, 1988). My extension explores a three-part relation: how people, tasks, and technologies are divided and coordinated in activity.

Although the division of labor concept will probably strike readers as natural for studying activity in workplaces, it may seem less so for classrooms. I argue here that this concept is equally relevant to understanding classroom life, especially in an era that involves consistent experimentation with new ways of organizing classrooms. Under the traditional social organization of classrooms, each individual student in a particular classroom is assigned the same work and is assessed as an individual; in this situation, there is no apparent division of labor to explore. In contrast, recent experiments in classroom social organization provide students with more discretion to organize their own activities, aside from whatever may be assigned. In addition, these new experiments typically involve having students work in groups. Under the assumption that these conditions—student discretion and group work—are now common in many classrooms, the division of labor concept should be just as important to understanding classrooms as it is to understanding workplaces.

As part of my exploration of the relations among people, tasks, and technologies, this study also addresses sociogenetic questions about how these three-part relations formed in each setting. Answering questions about why a particular technology is being used by someone for some task is one that I believe to be exceedingly complex in almost every case. As this analysis seeks to show, functional explanations are only part of the story. Other considerations include the possibilities that particular technologies are used out of habit, because of contingencies of local history, because they are at hand, or because the proximal authorities insist on them. Recent waves of techno-enthusiasm in education suggest that we take very seriously the question of whether students are using computers because they are "the right tool for the job" (Clarke & Fujimura, 1992) or because they have been given no other options. It is worth noting, in this regard, that it took a very long time for people to seriously question whether textbooks were the right tools for the job of supporting learning. At the other end of the spectrum from techno-enthusiasm, a deep skepticism about computers in classrooms swells (e.g., Cuban, 1986; Healy, 1998). The proposition that this analysis seeks to defend is between the poles: that empirically grounded research on technology in its situations of use can provide well-founded answers to when computers are the right tool for the job and when they are not.

As a study of naturally occurring activities, this comparison takes as its units of analysis *teams* of people doing design *projects*.[1] In following these natural units across time and space in both settings, I realized early on that my study of computers would require an account of media besides computers and that to make sense of computers vis à vis other media, overarching patterns of collective and individual activity needed to be understood. What I also noticed early in my analyses and what spurred this analysis were two comparative facts evident across the settings: (a) Types of media use were asymmetrically distributed with respect to both tasks and people, and (b) the asymmetries were strikingly similar across the settings. Specifically, I found that both settings shared the emergent property that labor was divided between people who did design on paper and people who drafted on the computer (Fig. 6.1). In the case studies that follow, I use these two empirical facts as an analytic starting point for thinking through issues of how specific media support specific collaborative activities or, in other words, what computers are right for and what they may be less right for. Of course, what they may be less right for is not necessarily a permanent condition for the design-abled learning sciences community. In my concluding remarks, I suggest some ways that this comparative analysis can inform further design work.

Turning to the cases, consider first the professional architecture firm, where I did ethnographic and videographic fieldwork for nearly a year. With regard to the distribution of media use, this firm resembled most contemporary firms; despite the promise and increasing ubiquity of computers in architectural firms, the phases of the overall design process that practitioners consider "real design" (architect's phrase) still typically happen on paper. Designs on paper are then translated into digital form using CAD (computer-aided design) programs.[2] During these early conceptual and schematic development design phases, designers work almost exclusively by hand on paper, using a simple but flexible *package* (Fig. 6.2) of base drawings, tracing paper, scale ruler, and corresponding embodied competencies (cf. Stevens & Hall, 1998; Stevens, 1999a).

---

[1]This comparative case study comes from a larger sociocognitive comparison of the classroom and the workplace (Stevens, 1999a) that was part of a still larger comparative research project involving multiple classrooms and workplace settings (see Hall, 1995, for a brief description). From the workplace setting, data collected include approximately 100 hours of field notes and video recordings as well as many documents produced by participants. A similar corpus was collected in the classroom, with fewer hours of videotapes because the duration of the classroom project was shorter.

[2]Beyond the firm where I did my fieldwork, I continued informal inquiries of other architects in the Bay Area region to confirm this attribution of typicality since I have not been able to find any statistical data addressing this issue.

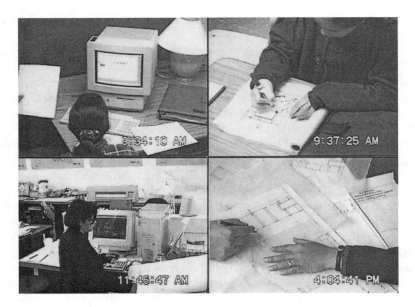

FIG. 6.1. Grid of still images summarizing the comparative findings reported in this study. Counterclockwise from the upper left.: students drafting at the computer (upper left), architects drafting at the computer (lower left), architects designing on paper (lower right), and students designing on paper (upper right).

FIG. 6.2. Detail of the package of tools and media used by architects during the design phase of an architectural project.

This early phase of paper-based designing is high-status work; it is usually done by principal architects (i.e., owners of firms, analogous to partners in law firms) and by architects specially designated as designers. In larger firms, translating hand-inscribed designs into CAD form is usually the work of draftspersons, and the distinction between draftspersons and designer is a common one in the architectural community (Cuff, 1991; Robbins, 1994). In smaller firms, such as the one I studied, the lower status work of drafting paper documents into CAD and working out the necessary details was done by associate and beginning architects because the firm did not employ any designated draftspersons. (These more junior architects are typically younger and at a much earlier stage in their careers than principal architects and are paid a salary rather than participating as owners.) Regardless of the size of the firm, designing and computer drafting are currently regarded as two quite different kinds of activities in architectural practice.

If it is unsurprising that newer computer-based design tools have yet to encroach upon more traditional media in professional designing—because the current generation of principal architects and most associate architects learned exclusively paper and physical model-based design—I present a finding here that is somewhat surprising. In a middle school classroom where a student team was provided with a computer program for designing as well as with paper that was designated for "getting started," a division of labor emerged within the team that mirrored the designers using-paper/draftspersons-translating-paper-into-the-computer division found among professional architects. What makes this occurrence somewhat surprising is that the computer was the intended design tool in the classroom and that as newcomers to architectural design, the students arguably did not yet have any firm investment in paper-based tools.[3] This analysis treats this emergent division of a labor as a puzzle to think through some of the issues of CSCL. My goal is to address this puzzle through a close analysis of how this division emerged and to argue that similarities to the division of labor in the professional setting were more than accidental.

My central argument is that (a) the similarity in the observed divisions of labor across settings can be tied to affordances of different media for collaborative design and that (b) these divisions of labor were productive in both settings from a perspective on the social and material team achievements in each setting but that (c) the division of labor among the students was less productive and more complicated than for the professional team

---

[3]I include the qualifier "arguably" because research in a naturalistic and constructivist mode might show that children have an abundance of prior experience designing on paper in out-of-school practices.

because of differences in the way that individual and collective contributions were understood and assessed.

The remainder of this chapter is organized as follows. I begin by offering some background on the division of labor concept. This is followed by the two case studies in which I describe the local history of media use, collaboration, and divisions of labor in each setting. After these cases, I analyze a key similarity (how forms of media supported collaboration) and a key difference (how the respective systems of assessment supported collaboration) across the settings. These analyses set the stage for a discussion of the educational implications of this work, including methodological implications for future learning-sciences research. I withhold my analysis of implications until the end of the chapter to clearly separate the ethnographic and prescriptive parts of the work. As educational researchers, we routinely face the daunting challenge of speaking both empirically and prescriptively, but to the extent possible, I believe that these ways of speaking should be separated. This gives readers the opportunity to understand the data and analysis first and then, with the author, to take a stance on what these phenomena mean for educational practice and research.

THEORETICAL BACKGROUND

> All of the many ways in which the work of human beings is studied lead back at some point to the obvious, yet infinitely subtle, fact of the division of labor ... The division of labor, in its turn, implies interaction; for it consists not in the sheer difference of one man's [sic] kind of work from that of another, but in the fact that the different tasks and accomplishments are parts of a whole whose product all, in some degree, contribute to.
>
> —Hughes 1971 (p. 304)

The division of labor is, of course, one the most venerable concepts in the social sciences. Economists such as Adam Smith and Karl Marx both recognized that divisions of labor made work processes more efficient but held very different views about the effects of these divisions on the well-being of society and the individual. Emile Durkheim addressed the topic in *The Division of Labor in Society* (published in France in 1893) asking questions about the origins and functions of the division of labor in modern society. For Durkheim, there were two basic types of solidarity to be found across societies. In some societies, solidarity is based on societally enforced similarities between persons, which Durkheim called *mechanical* solidarity. In other, more highly evolved societies, *organic* solidarity is achieved not by enforced similarities but by complementary differences between people within and across various social units (e.g., professions). Unambiguously, Durkheim asserted the moral superiority of societies based in organic solidarity.[4] In making these distinctions, one of Durkheim's central concerns was "the connection between the individual personality and social solidarity" (Durkheim, 1984, p. *xxx*), and he believed that, as societies evolved from mechanical to organic solidarity, increasingly complex and autonomous individual personalities would develop in parallel.

In this century, the issue of the division of labor between people and technology also has absorbed analysts, with some such as Braverman (1974), following Marx in claiming that in capitalist economies, technology "deskills" workers, making them less autonomous (at least in terms of economic self-determination) and, in general, producing deleterious social effects. Contemporary analysts have seen the possibilities of technology, specifically information technologies, more ambivalently, suggesting that computers can both "informate" or "automate," depending on how they are used in a broader organizational context (Zuboff, 1984).

In recent years, Ed Hutchins (1995) and Bruno Latour (1994, 1996) have characterized modern work processes as complex networks of people and technologies acting together and apart (see also Goodwin & Goodwin, 1996; Suchman, 1994, 1995). These analyses have reopened questions about the distribution and redistribution of competencies between people and technologies with new concepts that blur the analytic (and often ontological) line between human and nonhuman actors in sociotechnical networks of activity. Unlike previous theorists, neither Hutchins nor Latour has as yet substantively engaged familiar moral issues about the redistribution of competencies between people and technologies in contemporary work. This research draws upon the analyses of Hutchins and Latour in describing how competencies are distributed between people and technologies but takes a more people-centric perspective by focusing on specific divisions of labor among people because of and around technologies (e.g., computers).

Anselm Strauss, working in the same sociological tradition as his predecessor Everett Hughes, framed his treatment of the division of labor with the observation that little research about this topic actually analyzed concrete cases of working, and in a pair of connected articles (Strauss, 1985, 1988) he provided grounded theoretical concepts for this purpose. Taking

---

[4]Durkheim's moral affirmation of organic solidarity, while unambiguous, was qualified by his assertion that there were many anomic forms it could take that were undesirable and did not foster solidarity. At the time of writing (1893), Durkheim recognized that these anomic forms were the prevalent forms of the division of labor but argued that these were pathological cases produced in a transitional period of social-structural change.

a project as the unit of analysis, Strauss considered the entire collection of persons and tasks[5] comprising a project from inception to completion. "The totality of tasks arrayed both sequentially and simultaneously along the course of [a] . . . project" was what Strauss called an *arc of work* (Strauss, 1985, p. 4). Along this arc, the rights and responsibilities of particular persons with respect to particular tasks vary from loosely to tightly coupled. The characters of specific divisions of labor were regarded by Strauss, as they were by Hughes, as originating in interactional processes of dividing tasks among people and fitting them together across an arc of work. Strauss called this form of ongoing activity *articulation work*.

For analyzing complex sociotechnical systems, one of the gaps in Strauss' scheme is an absence of nonhuman mediators in the relation between persons and tasks. As surely as persons can be coupled to a task, so too can a person be coupled, by right or responsibility, to a specific mediator. Strauss' scheme therefore needs to be expanded to a tripartite scheme (person, task, and mediator) in order to analyze divisions of labor in complex sociotechnical settings. By focusing on an analysis of naturally occurring events involving interaction between people and mediating artifacts, this expansion is consistent with many conceptions of activity theory (Cole & Engestrom, 1993) as well as those of Strauss' intellectual successors (cf. Fujimura, 1987, 1992; Star, 1991; Star & Griesemer, 1989).

In the case study data presented in the following, I focus on early phases of arcs of work in the architecture firm and in the middle school classroom. In each case, two types of tasks are described: designing and drafting. In both cases, particular persons were coupled to designing with hand-inscribed paper media, and other persons were coupled to drafting with computer-assisted design tools. The question I address is how these couplings came to exist, and the answers I provide are different for each setting. These differences reflect the very different sociohistorical trajectories of persons and practices in the classroom and in the architecture firm; however, I also argue that, despite these differences, the basic fact of a parallel division of labor is informative for thinking about how computers support collaboration and learning. In addition, I argue that the implications of the similar division of labor are very different within the distinct organizational environments of a school and of a workplace.

---

[5]Strauss meant tasks in an ecologically valid sense that differs significantly from what has been meant by laboratory psychologists. In Strauss' ethnographic work and here, tasks are discovered in people's naturally occurring activity rather than made to happen, either in the laboratory or in the field. See Cole, Hood, & McDennott (1997) for a brief discussion of different senses of ecologically valid tasks.

CASE I: ARCHITECTURAL DESIGN AT JC

JC Architects is a midsized architectural firm in Berkeley, California. During the duration of my fieldwork, two principal architects, two associates, and an early-career architect worked at JC. At this firm, associates and principals both did "real design," a practice that took place almost exclusively by hand on paper. Although the principal architects used computers frequently (e.g., for writing), they never used and were true novices with the CAD software; one of the principals joked with me that the extent of his capacity with CAD was zooming in and out. In fact, neither principal architect had experience with CAD, and each of them regarded this as a deficiency (that one called "scary") that they wished to rectify. However, both also told me that the amount of other work they were responsible for prevented them from finding the time to learn the technology.

CAD work was done entirely by the three junior architects. Each spent a reasonable proportion of most days at CAD machines, with the youngest among them spending almost all of his time working from red-lined[6] paper documents and lists assembled by principals. Working from red-lines and lists, these juniors updated, revised, and completed drawing sets that were to be used by different groups throughout the design and building process. During early design phases, juniors were responsible for measuring building sites and making to-scale base plans that could then be used by principals, along with tracing paper, to propose and test design ideas through hand-inscription. Later, when the firm prepared to circulate CAD drawing sets to code reviewers or to contractors for building purposes, the juniors were responsible for producing complete drawings that were properly labeled and that followed the appropriate representational conventions for the audience (e.g., the public, the city, or a contractor) that would receive the drawings.

In the project I followed most closely, JC Architects collaborated with a team of consultants to complete a seismic and Americans with Disabilities Act upgrade on two historically preserved libraries in Oakland, California. In this project, many of the major design decisions were made at meetings in which principals and a diverse collection of consultants (e.g., structural and mechanical engineers, historical preservationists, and cost estimators) worked over the surface of work-relevant representations (e.g., plans, sections, elevations, photographs). These collaborative design meetings were temporally unfolding events in which the members of the design team

---

[6]Red-lining is a graphic technique for proposing changes in drawing and communicating these to others. For example, a principal would take a current set of drawings, circle, add marginalia, or redraw certain elements in red pencil and then return the drawings to a junior architect to make the required changes.

used speech, gesture, and inscription in various *coordinations* (Goodwin & Goodwin, 1996; Hutchins, 1995; Stevens, 1999; Stevens & Hall, 1998; cf. diSessa, 1991, for a related sense of *coordination*) to collaboratively make progress with their design problems. Although these resources are in some sense unremarkable, their importance for my argument is that so much of the collaboration seemed to hang on their coordinated use. It was the synchronous coarticulation of these resources, of saying and showing, by which participants made sense, made arguments, and made progress together. In turn, these practices are possible only in a media space that supports these sorts of interactions between people and media, properties lacking in any current version of a computer design environment.

In these meetings at JC, the associates were present but rarely contributed to the decision-making design conversations. Instead, they tracked closely the emerging, agreed-upon decisions made among the other participants and kept lists of tasks to be done or points raised. Following these meetings, the associates would frequently update CAD drawings. As more of the design decisions were made and the direction of the project stabilized, the associates moved into an intense phase of producing CAD drawing sets at 50%, 95%, and 100% completion levels. The final 100% drawing sets are used by building contractors and are documents that the firm is legally responsible for in the building phase.

As the previous paragraphs indicate, doing CAD-related tasks is an essential part of a primary arc of work at JC and falls entirely to the junior architects. Furthermore, facility with CAD has become a precondition for earning an entry-level position in an architecture firm, as it was for the junior architects in this firm. Unfortunately for architects seeking a first job, many (if not most) university architecture programs have only recently begun to provide sufficient CAD instruction, which means that young architects have faced the challenge of either learning CAD themselves or finding other instruction. For example, one associate at JC took an intensive (and expensive) four-weekend course at a local state university to begin learning CAD and then continued to learn, through practical experience, at JC.

Young architects know that they need baseline facility with CAD to secure a position in a firm, and this precondition for employment means that the initial division of labor in architecture is substantively predetermined when junior architects are hired at firms such as JC. Principal architects, because they are fully occupied with tasks for which they are uniquely accountable (e.g., critical early design or client relations), hire junior architects to do CAD that they as principals have neither the time nor the training to do.[7] This of

---

[7]In more static firms, CAD labor—like essential technical work in other fields (cf. Traweek, 1988; Shapin, 1989)—remains the responsibility of some permanent, if interchangeable, draftsperson.

course does not mean that divisions of labor cannot or do not change, especially in firms such as JC that quite clearly had an organizational structure resembling what has been called legitimate peripheral participation (Lave & Wenger, 1991). Here, junior architects are progressively unleashed from their CAD machines as they move toward more principal-like activities and newcomers take on these tasks. However, despite this extended process of organizational change, the division of labor was relatively stable throughout my fieldwork at JC.

Summary: A Stable Division of Labor

As I remarked in the introduction, sociogenetic accounts of the three-part couplings of person, task, and technology are complex. Although the account that follows is tentative, I suggest that it is useful in laying out the heterogeneous, interacting elements that are involved in a sociogenetic story of technology use, and therefore, it represents an alternative to a purely functional account. First, the high status of early-design work and the learning histories of current principals seem like critical considerations. Because current principals learned to design on paper and have done so through their decades-long professional careers, these practices are relatively durable dispositions for practical action.[8] Another critical consideration is functional and relates to how paper practices support collaboration in ways that currently available computer-based systems do not. As I described above, designing involves important collaborative components in which multiple practitioners come together around a table where drawings are lain out. With these representations, participants continuously and fluidly draw, point, and gesture. Consider now how difficult these embodied collaborative practices would be with current versions of computer-based design tools that have relatively small vertical screens and where direct contributions are limited to the person who controls the single mouse or stylus. In other words, whatever benefits computers might have as design tools (see, for example, Mitchell & McCullough, 1995), current software and hardware cannot support one of the fundamental ways that architects currently collaborate with representational media.

As to why drafting, which was a paper-based practice not so long ago, has become predominantly a computer-based one, a number of considerations seem relevant. First, as described to me by a number of architects, engineers initiated the use of CAD, and architects adapted to this to be able to share drawings with them in a uniform medium. Second, drafting, unlike designing,

---

[8]See Bourdieu (1977) for the concept of habitus and my related concept of disciplined perception (Stevens, 1999a; Stevens & Hall, 1998).

has traditionally been regarded as a mechanical production skill rather than a creative or artistic one (Robbins, 1994). This difference suggests that architects do not vest their professional identities in drafting and therefore would not likely resist shifting drafting tasks into a computer environment. Design, being the defining professional activity for architects, remains vested in the tools most closely associated with craft and artistry: paper-based drawing.

This is not to say that there were not tensions about the tools most appropriate for design. This tension was vividly represented for me in a heated discussion between one of the associate architects (age 28, five years out of school) and the newest member of the firm (age 23, six months out of school). Whereas the slightly older, more experienced architect argued at length that people "simply cannot do good design" on the computer (a position also conveyed to me by one of the principals), the younger architect argued that not only could people design this way but that he did.[9] In the mere five years between the schooling of these two architects, computers had come to be thought of and used differently. As such, the tension between these alternative media for design in architecture demonstrates that pure functionality is a limited explanatory resource; the tension makes clear that at issue also is how generations of practitioners identify their craft and how communities displace old-timers with newcomers (Lave & Wenger, 1991).

CASE 2: ARCHITECTURAL DESIGN AT PINE MIDDLE SCHOOL

The second case I consider involves a team of four students in a seventh-grade mathematics class at a middle school in Alameda, California. In this class, the teacher, Ms. Leoni, oversaw eight teams of students doing architectural design projects using MMAP (Middle School Math through Applications) curricular material (MMAP, 1995) under the sponsorship of the University of California, Berkeley, Math@Work project.[10] The main

---

[9]The rate of technological change in architecture, as in many professions, is producing many strata of generational dividing lines, with parallel debates about the appropriate forms of practice. The youngest architect told me a story about an event in architecture school that was informative about this issue. During his last year in school, a fellow student prepared a presentation for a studio course entirely in digital media, and the student's reviewers (e.g., professor and practitioners) were unwilling even to evaluate the work because of the media of presentation. For remarks about similar generational tensions around technology in civil engineering, see Hall and Stevens (1995).

[10]As a participant in this research project, I collected data and, in collaboration with colleague Tony Torralba, helped the teacher Ms. Leoni prepare for and reflect on daily classroom happenings. Rogers Hall and Susan John performed similar activities at a different middle school with a different teacher. The entire Math@Work team (two teachers and four researchers) also met regularly at University of California, Berkeley, to adapt and supplement the MMAP curricular, a facet of which included using the materials I collected at JC Architects to inform our collaborative redesign efforts.

pedagogical premise underlying the development and enactment of the MMAP curriculum, like other prominent educational experiments (see Van Haneghan et al., 1992, and Petraglia, 1998, for a review of related projects), was the establishment of activity structures within which students could learn to use mathematical ideas and tools purposefully and collaboratively.

From the outset, this case presents two analytic challenges distinct from the workplace case. One challenge involves the relative instability of the division of labor in the classroom as compared with that in the architecture firm. As I described in the architectural case, the division of labor in the firm was quite stable over the duration of a year's fieldwork. In the classroom, the individuals who formed the team had no prior experience working together and, thus, changes in their division of labor were frequent initially, though divisions nonetheless stabilized. A second challenge involves the fact that the division of labor that *emerged* among the students competed and coexisted with a different division of labor *assigned* by the teacher (cf. R. Stevens, 2000). The assigned division of labor used in the classroom was developed by Cohen (1994), and it involved having students take on rotating "complex instruction" roles of facilitator, recorder, reporter, and materials manager. Both of these challenges suggest that the classroom case necessitates a more time-compressed, sequential narrative that permits me to focus on how divisions of labor formed initially, how they interacted with the assigned roles, and how they ultimately stabilized.

In the 8- to 10-week curriculum units, collaborative teams of students were asked to play the part of architects designing hypothetical research stations for scientists "wintering over" in Antarctica. Teams of three or four students worked together from initial conception to final presentation. Compared with activities in more traditional classrooms, there was considerable variety in both tasks and media; these included paper- and computer-based design, analysis of mathematical properties of models, explanatory writing, reflective writing, semitraditional worksheets, and poster design. In addition, managing tasks across the arc of project work was challenging for the team because they faced two distinct types of tasks: those that emerged within their team out of their project activity and those that were assigned by the teacher from the curriculum package, usually to focus on a specific mathematical concept. In general, tensions between assigned and emergent modes, both with respect to specific tasks and the divisions of team labor, were ubiquitous (Stevens, 1999, 2000).

The intended sequence of project activity entailed the following: (a) doing research about the conditions in Antarctica and the needs of research station inhabitants, (b) designing an initial structure that satisfied these conditions and needs, (c) analyzing the structure mathematically using specially designed software, (d) revising designs in light of mathematical analysis and other considerations, and (e) presenting work in a final form. The primary intended tool for designing these research stations and for doing subsequent mathematical analysis on costs, efficient uses of space, and insulation was a CAD-like program called ArchiTech. In this Macintosh-based program, students rendered research stations in plan view (i.e., from above) using a tool palette and a mouse. In a separate mode, they used the software to do automatic computations (such as determining building cost, area, and perimeter) and set parameters of the model (such as insulation and temperature). The automatic computations, and the use of the model more generally, served as foundations for many of the mathematical analyses carried out by the teams.

The first question to address in this case involves the origins of the division of labor among the student team that mirrored the division of labor found in the architecture firm. Understanding the local origins of the division of computer and paper in the architecture firm was relatively unproblematic because newcomers were hired to do computer-aided drafting and old-timers did not have this competency. In the classroom case, the members of the team were all newcomers to both the project and to architectural design and, as such, the question of origins is open. This does not imply that individual differences in relevant competencies may not have predated this project and contributed to the emergent division of labor but rather that these differences needed to be discovered, negotiated, and enacted by the team members. Within a week, two students had become the designers, drawing and debating plans for the research station on paper, and the other two students had become the draftspersons, translating the designers' hand-drawn and verbalized ideas into the computer. What set these interactional processes in motion?

The origin of the division of labor can be located initially in a particular class period in which the teacher assigned specific students to specific tasks. The class period in question took place a little more than a week after the class officially began the project. During this class period, the teams were divided into pairs to work on parallel tasks for the first time.[11] Ms. Leoni announced that two team members would begin to design (on paper) and that two members would move to the computer to prepare a formatted list of features that the team had decided would be part of the station's design.

The way that the teacher initially assigned particular students to designing and others to the text-formatting task involved an unintended though clever use of the complex instruction roles. Because the conventions of these roles had already been established and they were textually represented on the wall for each team, Ms. Leoni used them to randomly assign a pair from

---

[11]During the prior week, group activity had taken only two forms; students either completed a single task as a group of four (e.g., discussing what features the station could have prior to designing), or they completed individual versions of the same task in parallel (e.g., each individual writing about their expectations about working in a team).

each team to designing at the table and another pair to a text-formatting task at the computer.[12] The teacher made it clear that she would rotate students through tasks with the use of these role assignments, as she would also use them to assign the actual complex roles. In this particular instance, the reporter and materials manager (Henry and Cathy) were assigned to the computer, and the recorder and facilitator (Ted and Marsha) were assigned to begin designing on a single piece of graph paper.

I recount the details of this mundane classroom event because, in the end, it was Ted and Marsha who became the paper-based designers and Cathy and Henry who became the computer-based draftspersons. This outcome, along with the ethnographic details I have thus far provided, might lead to the inference that the division of labor that formed was simply an accident of the initial random assignment of pairs to particular media and particular tasks, an implication that is neither intellectually interesting nor likely to provide any general insights. However, although I have considered this possible interpretation, the subsequent days' events undermine this simple interpretation. Whereas I argued in the first case that a purely functional explanation of technology use was too simple, here I argue that an explanation based purely on authoritative directive and compliance is likewise too simple. In this case, what emerges is a picture of how divisions of labor emerge from a complex interplay of contingent initial events, personal inclinations, the affordances of particular media, and evolving shared histories among particular students, artifacts, and tasks.

Factors Supporting a Sociogenetic Account

Although the initial pairings probably were relevant to the stable division of labor that emerged, they were not its sole cause. Other important factors that support a more complex sociogenetic account include the following.

Personal Inclinations. Marsha and Ted demonstrated inclinations toward designing that Henry and Cathy did not during discussions that occurred the week before actual work began on the design-on-paper. Ted in particular was very enthusiastic about designing, and when the random assignment of roles chose him to begin with the paper in hand, he was demonstratively pleased. Henry and Cathy also displayed inclinations of their own

---

[12]This may seem like a confusing use of these roles, but from my perspective, it was entirely sensible. I liken it to how preexisting symbolic structures are sometimes used as devices for sorting groups into subgroups, as when people count off numbers one through four in a large group and then all the "ones" collect themselves. Without this device, the teacher would have had to individualize the task assignments for eight teams of four students or would not have been able to organize parallel tasks at all.

toward the computer. Cathy in particular sought out the computer-based tasks, whether they involved drafting or mathematical analyses.

Evolving Couplings. Further evidence that compliance with assigned pairings was not the sole cause of the emergent division in labor can be found in efforts made by team members to reorganize themselves to continue with the types of work they already had underway. By the phrase *evolving couplings*, I am referring to the notion that couplings between each pair in the tripartite relationship of persons, tasks, and tools can develop a history that enhances the likelihood of its continuance (Becker, 1995). The quick evolution of couplings became evident to me when, just a day after the initial pairings had been enjoined, the students resisted Ms. Leoni's attempt to rotate them via another complex role assignment. The resistance took a quiet form, one invisible to the teacher. Because of the bustling environment of the classroom, Ms. Leoni was too busy to monitor whether every assignment she made was followed, and in this case, the students negotiated an alternative among themselves. This sort of negotiation probably takes place very often in classrooms, especially when students want to work with their friends. What was striking about this instance is that students negotiated to continue parts of the project they already felt some commitment to and competence with rather than negotiating to work with the person in the group with whom they were closer friends.

There is more, however, to the character of evolving couplings than students' using discretion to reorganize their assigned tasks and couplings. In my view, there were certain inevitable sociocognitive properties of the evolving couplings that contributed to their stabilization. For example, in the design interactions between Ted and Marsha, the design's history was not entirely represented and available as drawn features on paper. Instead, the design existed in a reflexive relationship between a schematic drawing and an intersubjectively maintained account of the design (Livingston, 1993; Stevens, 1999). What this meant was that becoming part of the design interaction became difficult for the other two group members after just a short time. For instance, while working together, Ted and Marsha drew office spaces where they agreed to put computers for the resident scientists. When Cathy returned to the group table, she showed an interest in the design by attempting to make a design proposal. She suggested that maybe they "should have a computer room," to which Marsha explained that they (she and Ted) already had determined that computers would go in the offices, pointing to what visually for Cathy was just a set of drawn rectangles (i.e., they were not labeled nor bore any identifying icons). When Cathy again proposed a computer room, Marsha asked, "for what?" to which Cathy responded with a tentative "I don't know, a special computer?" and then quickly dropped out of the scene.

A similar point can be made about the evolving coupling between Cathy and the computer-based tools, though for somewhat different reasons. For example, as in all computer-based work, certain iconic and haptic conventions need to be learned to draft structures in the software program Architech (e.g., how to use a bulldozer function to eliminate a wall); once Cathy learned these conventions, she was called upon to do this work while other team members did other tasks to which they had become more closely coupled and accountable. In addition, there were not only sociocognitive properties of these couplings that contributed to the stabilization of the division of labor but also a sort of relational stabilization at work. As members saw others becoming coupled to tasks or persons, they tended to find and seek their own couplings and to hold others accountable to theirs.

Affordances of Media. To this point, I have described how personal inclinations and evolving couplings help explain how particular pairs of persons became coupled to particular tasks. Still to explain is how these person–task couplings came to be coupled to particular media, in this case either computers or paper. Here, an appeal to the properties of the media for particular tasks or, in other words, their affordances (Gaver, 1996; Gibson, 1979) is useful. Recall first that students were asked to "get started" with paper. Once started, however, the designers quickly incorporated some of paper's affordances into their design interactions.

By focusing on the interaction between the designers, I am emphasizing the affordances of paper for collaboration. Despite this focus, it would be an oversight to neglect how paper also afforded the individual designers' expression of ideas during the early, creative problem-solving phase of the overall design process. Students could get their ideas down in a durable form, with resources they appeared to bring to the class: the capacity to draw or trace lines that represented built space from above (i.e., in plan view). In short, paper was a flexible representational resource for designing in a way that the software could not be,[13] and this appeared to be a factor in why, once started, the student designers continued to use paper.

Among paper's affordances for collaboration, portability and availability were two that students exploited in this case. Ted made use of these affordances when he returned to school on the second day of designing with a new sketch of the floor plan. Once he and Marsha began their design discussion, he used his homemade plan to make proposals to Marsha.

---

[13]Current technologies such as Wacom tablets, penlike electronic styluses, and software allow closer approximations to the experience of paper-based drawing. These tools were not used in the classroom design projects nor are they routinely used in professional architectural practice. For a discussion of how technologies can support practices closer to those associated with paper, see A. H. Stevens (2000).

This new sketch differed in some key ways from what he and Marsha had done together on the first day, but it also took many of those features as settled. Because there were now two different versions of the design available in the shared visual space of the group table, the alternative design proposals could be discussed and directly visually compared. Because the computer and software were available only during classtime,[14] Ted would not have been able to produce this alternative proposal had they been designing with the computer. In addition, because the computer-based design interface provided very little screen real estate (13 in.), the designers would not have been able to place two versions in their shared visual field simultaneously.

As the design process between Marsha and Ted progressed, the pair incorporated other affordances of paper into their collaborative design practice. For example, on the basis of demonstrations from their teacher and a visiting architect, Ted and Marsha incorporated "trace" (tracing paper) into their collaborative design interactions in ways that closely mirrored the uses of the professionals. Trace allows for the layering of different alternatives over an existing base drawing. Trace also allows quick tracing of parts of existing structures and redrawing of others, a practice supported by the trace's transparency. In the discussion between Marsha and Ted, trace was used in this way to heatedly debate and draw alternatives to a narrow hallway.

Summary: A Stable Division of Labor

The phenomena that this case study has sought to explicate is how an emergent division of labor, parallel to one found among professional designers, stabilized amidst a field of contingent forces and in opposition to a succession of assigned divisions of labor.[15] Once divisions of labor had stabilized, the designers (Ted and Marsha) used paper to debate and draw possible design features while the draftspersons (Cathy and Henry) translated the design from paper into the computer and undertook other computer-based tasks. This design on paper moved back and forth between the computer

---

[14]Some students had computers at home, but most used a different operating system than the one running in the classroom, and no students had copies of the software at home.

[15]As an interesting aside, it is worth noting that the couplings that stabilized overrode, all else being equal, more likely self-selected couplings, such as those based on gender (Thorne, 1993) and friendship networks. Had either of these preferences prevailed, it would have been the pairs of Ted and Henry on one hand and Marsha and Cathy on the other who organized themselves to work together, and in fact, pairwise socializing sorted out this way. In addition, the coupling of Ted and Marsha as designers also overcame some evident interpersonal repulsion; throughout the unit Marsha displayed evident distaste for Ted but nevertheless continued to work with him and respect his design contributions: a reaffirmation of the maxim that collaboration is not equivalent to cooperation.

draftspersons and the designers, each needing it to pursue their respective tasks of design and drafting. The interaction across the division of labor was efficient; in the end, the team had a complete design in the computer environment, ready for subsequent analyses, which had been forged in a productive paper-based collaborative design process. Finally, and significantly, this emergent division of labor produced an exceptionally successful conclusion to the project for this team. At both times when all eight teams' projects were evaluated by professional architects, this team's project was judged as the most complete and accomplished in the class.[16]

In summary, it is important to highlight the differences in the character of the discussions and activities between the designers and the draftspersons in their respective workspaces. At the table, the designers considered alternatives for the geometry and use of spaces, frequently warranting their proposals with references to normative living practices (e.g., Marsha challenging a proposal by Ted to place a bathroom between a kitchen and living room: "Nobody does that") and arguing in quantitative terms about design issues such as fit, scale, and size (e.g., Ted challenging a proposal of Marsha's: "That hallway's way too big"). In contrast, at the computer, the draftspersons discussed how to use the program to input the designers' work, learning how to manipulate the mouse and tool palette to efficiently place windows, rotate furniture icons, and the like.

Within the team, these differences in types of knowledge across the division were known to the team members, were resources for the organization of their own collective activity, and were treated as ordinary given the many tasks they faced across the arc of the design project. However, because this division of labor emerged in a classroom, the corresponding differences in knowledge were not unproblematic, an issue I turn to in the comparative analysis of the two settings.

COMPARATIVE ANALYSIS

In this section, I offer an example of a strategy for doing comparative analysis that differs from the traditional experimental strategy of staging similarities (e.g., of specific tasks) to achieve comparability. This alternative involves finding first-order similarities in naturally occurring data across cases (i.e., the similar divisions of labor in the two settings) and using these similarities as the basis for subsequent second-order comparisons of similarities and differences. This strategy represents one way to do comparative work while

---

[16]I also observed, less systematically, similar divisions of labor among some of the other teams in which pairs of four student teams favored work at the table and others favored work at the computer.

also observing the criteria of ecological validity (Cole, Hood, & McDermott, 1997; Newman, Griffin, & Cole, 1989).

In this section, I exemplify this across-setting comparative strategy by exploring one similarity and one difference relevant to studies of collaboration, media, and learning. The similarity involves relations between forms of media and the types of collaborative activity they support. The difference involves the ways in which the classroom and the architecture firm were very different environments for the assessment of individuals and collectives.

A Similarity: How Forms of Media Supported Collaboration

In both cases, collaborative design occurred, final designs reflected contributions by multiple participants, and collaborative design interactions happened mostly on and over paper surfaces rather than at computers. Explanations for why paper-based practices claimed priority during critical design phases in the two settings differ significantly, reflecting different site specificities and developmental histories of persons and practices. Nevertheless, in both settings, what appears similar is that, given the specific forms of collaboration observed in each case, the paper-centered practices more easily supported these types of collaboration than could have screen and mouse-based practices.[17]

At JC Architects, design conversations often involved as many as 10 stakeholders seated around a table. In these situations, each participant had spatial access to the table surface where drawings lay, and all had the simple tools (fingers and pencils) for making design proposals visible to themselves and others. Similarly, paper forms could be rearranged on the table so that participants could simultaneously see and compare representations, and these rearrangements could happen quickly, keeping pace with evolving discussions. A ubiquitous roll of trace was always nearby for a participant to unfurl, layer over existing drawings, and quickly sketch a design proposal. Sketches on trace were as easily discarded as saved and, more important, they were saved by different participants for different purposes to develop further.

Although some future version of computer-supported tools may support such embodied collaborative design processes, current versions (such as JC's CAD system, the industry standard) do not. With limited screen estate and with drawing actions being mouse and keyboard controlled, the capacity to simultaneously see multiple representations at an acceptable scale

---

[17]By arguing that paper more easily supported these collaborative practices, I am making a relational point about the media resources available to members in practice, rather than an absolute statement about these particular technological packages.

or to make an inscribed contribution from locations beyond close proximity to (the front of) a small screen is limited. Although their CAD system had layering tools—seemingly digital analogs of tracing paper—creating layers in the machine is not nearly as quick, savable, or discardable as working with trace. In my observations, the layering facility in the CAD environment, unlike trace, was more of a technical distinction than a design-relevant phenomenological resource.

Paper-based practices also prevailed among the student designers, Marsha and Ted, for whom the CAD-like system available was even more limited than the architects' system as a design tool (having even less screen real estate and no layering tools). For example, it was central to the collaboration of the student designers that each member develop a distinct version of the floor plan, and at various moments, each had their respective versions in development simultaneously. This type of simultaneity was one feature of collaboration better supported by available paper resources than by computer-based ones. Although there was plenty of available paper, there was only one computer per group accessible during any one moment. If Marsha and Ted had worked together at the computer, they would have undoubtedly been working on a single version, but for Marsha and Ted, maintaining materially realized, different versions was important. It was important not only because this allowed them to try out design possibilities but because it also made them visible for comparison with the other designer's work. In one instance, simultaneous comparison led to a compromise on the dimensions of a room, and in another, it led to an acknowledgment by Ted that the direction that Marsha was pursuing was "better" than his. Although Ted and Marsha made productive use of simultaneity, they also made use of its opposite—call it temporal independence—in their collaborative design process. Recall that, after the first day of designing, when Marsha retained control of the developing paper version of the floor plan, Ted returned on the second day with a plan of his own. Neither Ted nor Marsha's versions became *the* plan, which instead reflected contributions from both versions. In summary, in both cases, paper-based practices were more finely tuned to the tempo and structure of synchronous collaborative design than computer-based ones could have been.

A Difference: How the Respective Systems of Assessment Supported Collaboration

In both the professional and middle school settings, the division of designing and computer labor led to successful progress through critical phases of projects. Also in both cases, the different experiences of laborers on opposing sides of this divide meant that different, complementary competencies developed. However, the emergence of different competencies has differing implications in the two settings because of the differences in the way the two settings were organized to assess individual and collective units of performance.

In the architecture firm, though it was true that individual members were continuously assessed informally, the relevant assessable social unit in more consequential irreversible assessments (i.e., formal ones) was the team (Stevens, 1999). What this meant was that the different competencies that developed from the division of labor were affirmed by the informal assessment system. Principal architects valued the associate architects for being able to do the CAD work that they could not do but that was critical to longer arcs of work relevant to the success of the firm. Furthermore, because the associates did this CAD work, the principal architects were able to use and further develop their own characteristic competencies in such realms as design, management, and the solicitation of other projects. In turn, as principals brought more architectural jobs to the firm, new people could be hired to do CAD work, and new opportunities were opened up for the associates to participate in and develop these more principal-like activities, thereby moving them along an architectural career trajectory. In short, the division of labor at JC and the commensurate distinct competencies that developed from it were productive and integral to the ongoing success of the firm and to expanding forms of participation for its newcomers (Lave & Wenger, 1991).

In contrast, the division of labor that emerged in the classroom between the designers and the draftspersons was more problematic because the practices of individual and collective assessment were less compatible. From a perspective that treats *the team* of students as the unit of assessment, the division of labor was productive in nearly every way. The team, by dividing labor among its individuals, was able to simultaneously satisfy assignments from their teacher, make progress on a design, and input the design into the software for subsequent mathematical analyses. It also led to a final design and a set of mathematical analyses that were the most highly praised in this class. Finally, it provided these students an opportunity to engage in a collaborative process of inquiry and production that resembled the activities of professional designers. Alternatively, from a perspective that treats the individual team member as the unit of assessment, the division of labor was more problematic. The reason for this was that the division of labor meant that individuals on different sides of the divide (e.g., Ted the designer versus Cathy the draftsperson) developed quite different competencies and understandings[18] that the more formal uniform classroom assessment practices registered differentially.

---

[18]This also was true with regard to other competencies (e.g., mathematical analysis) that resulted from other divisions of labor in this team (see Stevens, 1999; R. Stevens, 2000).

The assessment practices enacted in Ms. Leoni's classroom mixed formal with informal and new with old, but ultimately, the overarching accountabilities faced by the teacher meant that more traditional practices of assessing individuals predominated—in other words, grading of worksheets and tests of mathematical competencies. This meant that the many competencies that emerged in the project did not count. For example, Ted exhibited a significant commitment to the completeness and functional rationale of the design, a commitment that drew his energies away from the activities that were graded. As such, Ted's performance on tests and worksheets involving particular types of mathematics was relatively poor. The irony of this situation was that Ted did display significant mathematical competencies but did so during design interactions, and so these competencies became invisible during the formal and individual assessment events (Stevens, 1999; R. Stevens, 2000).

Classrooms using project-based curricula are somewhat paradoxical ones with regard to the development of diverse student competencies. On the one hand, collaboration in complex, temporally extended projects implies emergent divisions of labor. Because these divisions of labor in turn imply distributions of individual knowledge, the production of consequential individual differences of the types represented in the classroom case study is arguably built into educational initiatives organized around project-based activities. On the other hand, the infrastructure for formal assessment in schools, generally and in this school in particular, is organized for uniformity of educational experiences and of assessment events.[19] Overcoming this infrastructure and putting in its place one that did greater justice to the diversity of competencies that emerge in project-based work would have been a major challenge, one that was surely beyond Ms. Leoni and our research team at the time. As a result, it was unsurprising that Ms. Leoni fell back on traditional assessment practices. In summary, the paradox is that, in hybrid educational settings such as Ms. Leoni's classroom, there are competing organizational forces, some that affirm the development of diverse forms of knowledge and others that penalize this development.

IMPLICATIONS FOR EDUCATIONAL PRACTICE

An overarching goal of this study has been to show that both settings considered here were complex sociotechnical environments, the classroom no less

---

[19]It is worth noting that this uniformity has also been considered a safeguard for many students in a system that often reproduces broader societal prejudices. In other words, uniformity has stood in for equity.

than the architecture firm. In light of this complexity, no magic wrenches are offered for the repair of education as a result of this comparative analysis; however, some implications for research and practice can be drawn.

My analyses of the multiple technologies in use in the classroom have highlighted the unique affordances of paper for the collaboration of student designers and contrasted these to the relative inadequacies of the computer tools. In so suggesting, I hope not to be mistaken as an advocate for a misguided Return to Paper movement; computers in the classroom serve unique and valuable functions.[20] What I do advocate is a genuinely experimental attitude toward the introduction of new technologies into the classroom. By this I mean that researchers and educators should continue to explore how new technologies can support learning in innovative ways but also prepare themselves to acknowledge as many failures or nonevents as they do successes through careful scrutiny of cases. This type of healthy skepticism has been one of the ideals of science for a long time, and it seems particularly appropriate to a cultural moment in which many are swept up in waves of techno-enthusiasm and the prospects of financial gain. To stand on the side of students and learning may be to stand on the side of humble, unplugged, widely available technologies (cf. Stevens & Hall, 1997).

Another implication of this study is that the issue should not be conceived of in "either–or" terms (i.e., either computers or traditional learning technologies). As research in computer-supported cooperative work has shown so vividly over the past decade (cf. Bowker, Star, Turner, & Gasser, 1997), settings are nearly always inhabited by a combination of old and new, digital and analog, standardized and ad hoc. From these combinations, hybrid practices emerge such as those in both of these case studies, in which movement across the digital-and-paper divide became fluid and functional. For educational settings, the implied principle therefore is the maintenance of media diversity. Yrjo Engestrom has argued that a technology (be it a computer or a textbook) always has the potential to be introduced into a setting not as a tool, but as a rule—in other words, "as an administrative demand from above" (Engestrom, 1990, p. 179). The computer could easily become little more than a new rule if users are not given opportunities to use alternative media when they are better suited to the organization of specific tasks. In schools, providing these opportunities is especially crucial for two reasons. First, schools are well known as places where rules predominate. Second, following a constructivist logic, students will perhaps learn most productively if, in an environment of media diversity, they are given opportunities to make choices about what tools are right for what jobs and to learn to "workaround" (Gasser, 1986) the inevitable limitations of specific technologies, rather than simply bending themselves and their tasks to

---

[20]For example, students were able to perform mathematical analyses of relationships between the geometry of floor plans and projected building costs.

these technologies. In the classroom case study described here, this diversity allowed the student team to rediscover a distributed arrangement for doing collaborative design that is an established and productive practice for professionals.[21]

A second implication arises from my analysis of the relationship between emergent practices and traditional assessments in the classroom. By this analysis, the placement of technology in a classroom is only a small part of an educational design endeavor. We also are challenged to implement new assessment practices that recognize and register productive diversities of competence that emerge, because new classrooms are increasingly less amenable to traditional uniform assessment procedures (Hall, Knudsen, & Greeno, 1995/1996). Unless assessment and student activity are better co-ordinated, the sort of conflict I described here between emergent student learning and uniform assessment practices may be resolved in favor of a return to traditional uniform pedagogical practices. In addition, our energies will be well spent thinking about how emergent student learning can become a resource rather than a problem through the design of pedagogical activity structures (e.g., reciprocal teaching and jigsaw) that respect and legitimize what emerges (which, in my analyses, the complex instruction roles did not) while providing opportunities for students to learn from each other (cf. Herrenkohl & Guerra, 1999).[22]

A final educational implication of this comparative study is that professional settings like the architecture firm may provide some valuable guidance for educational design. The notion of design experiments (Brown, 1992; Collins, 1992; cf. Cole, 1996) is now well established in the learning sciences community, but what remains vague are the particular conceptual resources that can serve as the food for our design thoughts. The point is not to make the students into little architects or the classroom into a replica of the firm but to explore how the practices and technologies observed in evolved and evolving adult settings can be selectively borrowed and adapted for use in classrooms.

ISSUES FOR FURTHER RESEARCH

Understanding the Affordances of Technology in Context

In finding a strong similarity across cases in the way that particular forms of media were coupled to particular types of tasks, I have described some of

---

[21]Compare the analysis of diSessa, Hammer, Sherin, and Kolpakowski (1991) of how a group of middle school students reinvented Cartesian graphing in a middle school classroom.

[22]James Greeno (1997) reported that in the Fostering Communities of Learners project (see Brown & Campione, 1994), scripted divisions of labor did not produce significant differences in performance among individuals.

the affordances that can be found in practice. Important to highlight is the fact that many of the affordances I found are quite different from those that might be found in user studies conducted with individuals under laboratory conditions. For example, some of the affordances of the paper observed in both cases were portability, layerability, and availability. Another was shared joint graphical access to paper from different sides of a table for collaborative design. Surely many important affordances can be discovered in laboratory studies, but if these case studies are any measure, there is also a great deal to be learned "in the wild," especially about affordances for collaboration in practice.

Getting a better analytic handle on the affordances of particular technologies for learning in classrooms may help resolve the undergrounded argument between computer advocates and critics. On one hand, critics of computers in classrooms skeptically question the value that computers add to the educational experience as judged in terms of existing educational goals. On the other hand, advocates of computers in classrooms argue that new tools create new and desirable practices or do old jobs better. Under the analysis presented here, the critic and the advocate both articulate a partial truth, but neither perspective is of much heuristic value because a sufficiently grounded corpus from which to make inferences about particular cases does not yet exist.

Understanding Emergent Practices as Features of Educational Settings

A concern with emergence—with what happens alongside and often despite an institution's official story—has animated various lines of interactionist research for some time. Perhaps the perspective has been infrequently extended to educational phenomena because most schools are commonly understood as authoritative disciplinary institutions that leave little room for practices to emerge among students, at least not in classrooms. However, as educators experiment with new participation frameworks in schools that decentralize the teacher's role and provide students with greater discretion about the organization of their activities, this issue deserves further theoretical attention. Schools are particularly complex settings for exploring the issue of emergence because schools, without exception, seek to enact *intended* pedagogical practices. On the basis of the larger study from which this analysis is drawn (Stevens, 1999), the coexistence and frequent collision of the intended and the emergent is routine in project-based classrooms (cf. R. Stevens, 2000). Further case studies of these types of classrooms should be helpful in creating a theoretical language for describing the varieties of ways these two modes coexist, collide, and ultimately hybridize.

CONCLUSION

A century ago, Durkheim forcefully argued that emergent, relatively durable divisions of labor would create a cohesive, diverse, and unrepressive society composed of well-developed individuals. This comparative case study, along with the current interest in distributed cognition and in collaborative, project-based educational initiatives, has provided an occasion for a reinspection of this claim, not at Durkheim's macrosocietal level but rather within and between concrete institutional settings. Perhaps in contrast to Durkheim's overarching theoretical arguments favoring social environments that allow emergent divisions of labor to develop, this comparative case study has made the grounded theoretical argument that such divisions of labor are in themselves neither inherently favorable nor unfavorable for people working and learning across all institutional settings.

My conclusion is a more institution-specific, relational one. The impact of divisions of labor on learners in school depends on the relations among how students, whose labor is divided, come together, how their divided labor is made visible and assessed, and how these divisions enable or constrain changing forms of participation and the development of new competencies. It is from a concern for these relations first that we should consider the role of technologies, however sophisticated or mundane. In this way, we may begin to provide better answers to questions of how particular technologies and learning intersect—or fail to intersect—in context.

ACKNOWLEDGMENTS

This work was supported by NSF Grant ESI 94552771 and a Dissertation Fellowship from the Spencer Foundation.

Thanks are owed to the members of the Math@Work project team (Rogers Hall, Susan John, Donna Luporini, Lisa Lyon, and Tony Torralba) for helpful comments on an earlier draft. I also thank an anonymous reviewer whose sympathetic reading of an earlier draft widened my understanding of relevant sociological resources. My greatest appreciation goes to the designers at JC Architects and Pine Middle School for allowing me to invade their workspaces and learn about their lives.

REFERENCES

Becker, H. (1995). "The Power of Inertia," *Qualitative Sociology, 18*, 301–309.
Bourdieu, P. (1977). *Outline of a theory of practice* (R. Nice, Trans.). New York: Cambridge University Press.

Bowker, G. C., Star, S. L., Turner, W., & Gasser, L. (Eds.). (1997). *Social science, technical systems, and cooperative work: Beyond the great divide.* Mahwah, NJ: Lawrence Erlbaum Associates.

Braverman, H. (1974). *Labor and monopoly capital: The degradation of work in the twentieth century.* New York: Monthly Review Press.

Brown, A. (1992). Design experiments: Theoretical and methodological challenges in creating complex interventions in classroom settings. *The Journal of Learning Sciences, 2,* 141–178.

Brown, A. L., & Campione, J. C. (1994). Guided discovery in a community of learners. In K. McGilly (Ed.), *Classroom lessons: Integrating cognitive theory and classroom practice* (pp. 229–270). Cambridge, MA: MIT Press.

Clarke, A. E., & Fujimura, J. H. (Eds.). (1992). *The right tools for the job. At work in twentieth-century life sciences.* Princeton, NJ: Princeton University Press.

Cohen, E. G. (1994). *Designing groupwork: Strategies for the heterogeneous classroom* (2nd ed.). New York: Teachers College Press.

Cole, M. (1996). Creating model activity systems. *Cultural psychology: A once and future discipline* (pp. 257–285). Cambridge, MA: Belknap.

Cole, M., & Engestrom, Y. (1993). A cultural-historical approach to distributed cognition. In G. Salomon (Ed.), *Distributed cognitions* (pp. 1–46). Cambridge, England: Cambridge University Press.

Cole, M., Hood, L., & McDennott, R. P. (1997). Concepts of ecological validity: Their differing implications for comparative cognitive research. In M. Cole, Y. Engestrom, & O. Vasquez (Eds.), *Mind, culture and activity. Seminal papers from the Laboratory of Comparative Human Cognition* (pp. 49–56). Cambridge, England: Cambridge University Press.

Collins, A. (1992). Toward a design science of education. In E. Scanlon & T. O'Shea (Eds.), *New directions in educational technology* (pp. 15–22). New York: Springer-Verlag.

Cuban, L. (1986). *Teachers and machines: The classroom use of technology since 1920.* New York: Teachers College Press.

Cuff, D. (1991). *Architecture: The story of practice.* Cambridge, MA: MIT Press.

diSessa, A. (1991). Epistemological micromodels: The ease of coordination and quantities. In J. Montagero & A. Tryphon (Eds.), *Psychologie genetique et sciences cognitives.* Geneva: Fondation Archives Jean Piaget.

diSessa, A. A., Hammer, D., Sherin, B., & Kolpakowski, T. (1991). Inventing graphing: Meta-representational expertise in children. *Journal of Mathematical Behavior, 10,* 117–160.

Durkheim, E. (1984/1893). *The division of labor in society.* New York: The Free Press.

Engestrom, Y. (1990). When is a tool? Multiple meanings of artifacts in human activity. *Learning, working, and imagining: Twelve studies in activity theory* (pp. 171–195). Helsinki: Orienta-Konsultit Oy.

Fujimura, J. (1987). Constructing "do-able" problems in cancer research: Articulating alignment. *Social Studies of Science, 17,* 257–293.

Fujimura, J. (1992). Crafting science: Standardized packages, boundary objects, and "translation." In A. Pickering (Ed.), *Science as practice and culture* (pp. 168–211). Chicago: University of Chicago Press.

Gasser, L. (1986). The integration of computing and routine work. *ACM Transactions on Office Information Systems, 4,* 205–225.

Gaver, W. (1996). Situating action II. Affordances for interaction: The social is material for design. *Ecological Psychology, 8*(2), 111–129.

Gibson, J. J. (1979). *The ecological approach to visual perception.* Boston: Houghton Mifflin.

Goodwin, C., & Goodwin, M. (1996). Seeing as a situated activity: Formulating planes. In Y. Engestrom & D. Middleton (Eds.), *Cognition and communication at work* (pp. 61–95). Cambridge, England: Cambridge University Press.

Greeno, J. (1997, September). *Conceptual growth considered as change in discursive practices.* Presented at Cognition and Development Colloquium, University of California, Berkeley.

Hall, R. (1995). Exploring design oriented mathematical practices in school and work settings. *Communications of the ACM, 38*, 62.

Hall, R. P., Knudsen, J., & Greeno, J. G. (1995/1996). A case study of systemic aspects of assessment technologies. *Educational Assessment, 3*, 315–361.

Hall, R., & Stevens, R. (1995). Making space: A comparison of mathematieal work in school and professional design practices. In S. L. Star (Ed.), *The cultures of computing* (pp. 118–145). London: Basil Blackwell.

Healy, J. M. (1998). *Failure to connect: How computers affect our children's minds for better and worse*. New York: Simon & Schuster.

Herrenkohl, L. R., & Guerra, M. R. (1999). Participant structures, scientific discourse, and student engagement in fourth grade. *Cognition and Instruction, 16*, 431–473.

Hughes, E. C. (1971). *The sociological eye: Selected papers*. Chicago: Aldine-Atherton.

Hutchins, E. (1995). *Cognition in the wild*. Cambridge, MA: MIT Press.

Koschmann, T. (Ed.). (1996). *CSCL, Theory and practice of an emerging paradigm*. Mahwah, NJ: Lawrence Erlbaum Associates, Inc.

Latour, B. (1994). Pragmatogonies: A mythical account of how humans and nonhumans swap properties. *American Behavioral Scientist, 37*, 791–808.

Latour, B. (1996). On interobjectivity. *Mind, Culture, and Activity, 3*, 228–245.

Lave, J., & Wenger, E. (1991). *Situated learning: Legitimate peripheral participation*. Cambridge, England: Cambridge University Press.

Law, J., & Bijker, W. E. (1992). Postscript: Technology, stability and social theory. In W. E. Bijker & J. Law (Eds.), *Shaping technology/building society: Studies in sociotechnical change* (pp. 290–308). Cambridge, MA: MIT Press.

Livingston, E. (1993). The disciplinarity of knowledge at the mathematics–physics interface. In E. Messer-Davidow, D. R. Shumway, & D. J. Sylvan (Eds.), *Knowledges: Historical and critical studies in disciplinarity*. Charlottesville: University of Virginia Press.

Mitchell, W. J., & McCullough, M. (1995). *Digital design media* (2nd ed.). New York: Van Nostrand.

MMAP: Middle school mathematics through applications. (1995). *The Antarctica project: A middle-school mathematics unit*. Palo Alto, CA: Institute for Research on Learning, Reinhold.

Newman, D., Griffin, P., & Cole, M. (1989). *The construction zone: Working for cognitive change in school*. New York: Cambridge University Press.

Petraglia, J. (1998). *Reality by design: The rhetoric and technology of authenticity in education*. Mahwah, NJ: Lawrence Erlbaum Associates.

Robbins, E. (1994). *Why architects draw*. Cambridge, MA: MIT Press.

Shapin, S. (1989). The invisible technician. *American Scientist, 77*, 554–563.

Star, S. L. (1991). Power, technology and the phenomenology of conventions: On being allergic to onions. *Sociological Review, 38*, 26–56.

Star, S. L., & Griesemer, J. R. (1989). Institutional ecology, "translations" and boundary objects: Amateurs and professionals in Berkeley's Museum of Vertebrate Zoology, 1907–39. *Social Studies of Science, 19*, 387–420.

Stevens, A. H. (2000). Drawing will never be obsolete: Reflections on the continuities between traditional and digital media. *Column 5*, 14. College of Architecture and Urban Planning, University of Washington.

Stevens, R. (1999). *Disciplined perception: Comparing the development of embodied mathematical practices in school and at work*. Unpublished doctoral dissertation, University of Califomia, Berkeley.

Stevens, R. (2000). Who counts what as math: Emergent and assigned mathematical problems in a project-based classroom. In J. Boaler (Ed.), *Social analysis of mathematics teaching and learning*. New York: Elsevier.

Stevens, R., & Hall, R. (1997). Seeing tornado: How video traces mediate visitor understanding of (natural?) phenomena in a science museum. *Science Education, 81*, 735–748.

Stevens, R., & Hall, R. (1998). Disciplined perception: Learning to see in technoscience. In M. Lampert & M. L. Blunk (Eds.), *Talking mathematics in school: Studies of teaching and learning* (pp. 107–149). New York: Cambridge University Press.

Strauss, A. (1985). Work and the division of labor. *The Sociological Quarterly, 29,* 1–19.

Strauss, A. (1988). The articulation of project work: An organizational process. *Sociological Quarterly, 29,* 163–178.

Suchman, L. (1994). Working relations of technology production and use. *Computer Supported Cooperative Work (CSCW), 2,* 21–39.

Suchman, L. (1995). Making work visible. *Communications of the ACM, 38,* 56–64.

Thorne, B. (1993). *Gender play: Girls and boys in school.* New Brunswick, NJ: Rutgers University Press.

Traweek, S. (1988). *Beamtimes and lifetimes. The world of high energy physicists.* Cambridge, MA: Harvard University Press.

Van Haneghan, J., Barron, L., Young, M., Williams, S., Vye, N., & Bransford, J. (1992). The "Jasper" series: An experiment with new ways to enhance mathematical thinking. In D. F. Halpern (Ed.), *Enhancing thinking skills in the sciences and mathematics* (pp. 15–38). Hillsdale, NJ: Lawrence Erlbaum Associates.

Zuboff, S. (1984). *In the age of the smart machine: The future of work and power.* New York: Basic Books.

DESIGNING DESIGN ACTIVITIES: DILEMMAS BOUND TO OCCUR

Ricardo Nemirovsky
TERC

I have recently read a book about the 20th century history of immunotherapies to cure cancer. Nowadays immunology provides some of the most important conceptual and medicinal means to treat cancer and other diseases, but how it has become so is a complicated twisted story, populated by fads and subsequent disillusions as well as huge financial investments intermingling successes and fiascoes. Drugs that produced stunning cures subsequently emerged as of uncertain therapeutic value, either because of their toxicity, unpredictable effects, or extravagant cost. Remedies that appeared almost magical in laboratory animals did not work with humans. As a result, the field grew cautious. These days it is common that cautionary remarks, caveats, and statements of uncertainty surround the report of a new immunotherapy even if the experimental results were "spectacular." There is an analogy between the history of the idea of activating the immune system to combat cancerous cells and of the idea of learning through open-ended projects chosen and shaped by the learners, the latter entailing the creation of supportive environments in which learners control their own time and activities and knowledgeable teachers focus their energies in helping students to develop their own initiatives. The analogy has two elements: 1. Both ideas are consequential, valuable, and inspiring; and 2. in social practice both ideas are extraordinarily complex, uneven in how individuals react to it, and full of unanticipated secondary complications.

I see Shaffer's chapter as a valuable report of his long-term efforts to create learning environments at a crossroads between art, mathematics,

technology, and open-ended projects, all inspired by his observation of design studios in professional education. Its weakness, in my view, is that he
fails to "problematize" his experience, to disclose the inherent tensions that
students and teachers or studio leaders have to cope with in these learning
environments. One is left with the question, why isn't this happening everywhere? Why aren't these types of approaches, which have been attempted
in many ways by many educators, propagating like wildfire? Is it the blame of
the "system"? Doubtless the educational system tends to perpetuate itself,
but it would be a mistake to lose sight of the intricacy that these innovations entail, which partially account for the strength of the "resistance." The
issue I want to raise is not one of assessing to what extents the learning
environments designed by Shaffer are suitable for regular schools. Yes, he
worked with small groups of students, who volunteered to participate, over
relatively short periods of time, and offered them plenty of technological
resources, but my point is that regardless of how unique or common the circumstances are, there are complexities and tensions that need to be made
explicit if we want to better understand how mathematics learning takes
place through open-ended collaborative projects chosen and shaped by the
learners. I think that Stevens' chapter is a good example of this type of critical examination. To elaborate on the complexities and tensions inherent
in the type of educational experiences reported by Shaffer and Stevens, I
will refer to two dynamics that take place throughout interactions among
students, teachers, and technologies: disciplinary boundaries and collabo-
ration/control.

DISCIPLINARY BOUNDARIES

One of the most significant aspects of Schaffer's work is his exploration of the
overlap between mathematics and art. The main thematic focus he reports
on is "Symmetry," treated in such a way that formal geometric properties
and pictorial compositions are both legitimate subjects of conversation and
work. Although there are content areas that appear to constitute a common
ground between branches of art and mathematics (linear perspective, fractal images, etc.) there are others that appear to dwell in nonoverlapping
territories. There are the works of Escher and Mondrian, but also those of
Pollock and Miro. A few years ago I had the opportunity to see an enthralling
exhibit on number and 20th century painting. The collection included paintings, some of them well known, that in one way or another referred to numbers, number patterns, and so forth. Many of them played with the shape
of numerals, arrays such as the periodic table of elements, and ways to
display sequences. Nevertheless, it is unlikely that one would recognize sophisticated mathematical content—in the form of properties of numbers

and number sequences—in most of these paintings. How should or could a math teacher foster artistic expression in a way that counts as mathematical learning? How would an expressionist painting portraying the infinite as a dark blurred abyss reflect a mathematical understanding of the infinite? It is always possible to frame these activities as "after class" or "extra credit" ones, to avoid potential conflicts on what some would perceive as misuse of time or immaterial tasks. But the issue here is precisely the nature of these potential conflicts: Where do they originate? What do they express? How are they to be addressed?

This issue is not only a matter of painting and mathematics, of course. I had a colleague who taught acoustics at a renowned music college. He is a physicist and a jazz player. He was puzzled by what he saw as students' utter lack of interest in learning about the physics of sound. He thought that acoustics was a legitimate common ground between music and physics but felt perplexed by students' comments suggesting that learning acoustics had nothing to do with becoming a good musician. In a conversation with Jeanne Bamberger about this story, she told me that in her opinion the students were right; in her view the connections between music and physics were not to be found in acoustics, but in relation to "rhythms and patterns." Her description of these conceptual links made me think that not every physicist would recognize physics in them. Disciplinary boundaries get expressed in countless forms, conferring legitimacy to some activities and not to others in the eyes of students, teachers, professionals, administrators, and parents. How appropriateness and relevance are viewed across disciplinary boundaries is particularly critical to the design of open-ended projects chosen and shaped by the students because, among other reasons, students' interests and choices often and naturally trespass those boundaries. There is something complicated in encouraging students to follow the course of their initiatives but censoring ideas when they appear to be beyond the expected thematic foci.

Schaffer does not address these issues except by implying that they are nonissues: Students in his workshops learned mathematics and pictorial art; furthermore, the learning of the mathematics is shown by the test scores. But even if that were the case, there is much to be learned about how these disciplinary boundaries vanish. The chapter describes significant events that point at this fading of boundaries in B—'s story, when she realizes that as a circle gets bigger the elements on it get more separated, or when the geometric transformations implemented in the software are used by B—to create an esthetic portrayal of the motion of a ball bouncing on the floor.

Stevens' description of how CAD became a technology that every architect "must" know, and of how architects cope with this pressure when other demands prevent them from becoming familiar with CAD, illustrates the rapid changes that affect disciplinary boundaries and the consequent production of complex forms of adaptation. Stevens elaborates tangentially on the classroom enactment of disciplinary boundaries between architectural design and school mathematics; in this regard, the key paragraph is this one:

> The assessment practices enacted in Ms. Leoni's classroom mixed formal with informal and new with old, but ultimately, the overarching accountabilities faced by the teacher meant that more traditional practices of assessing individuals predominated—in other words, grading of worksheets and tests of mathematical competencies. *This meant that many competencies that emerged in the project did not count.* For example, Ted exhibited a significant commitment to the completeness and functional rationale of the design, a commitment that drew his energies away from the activities that were graded. As such, Ted's performance on tests and worksheets involving particular types of mathematics was relatively poor. The irony of this situation was that Ted did display significant mathematical competencies but did so during design interactions, and so these competencies became invisible during these formal and individual assessment events. (p. 30, italics added)

Understanding the dynamics posed by disciplinary boundaries is essential to the design of learning environments in which learners can take control on their own learning, collaborate with professionals, and deal with institutionalized expectations. I suggest this as one area of further work that could grow from the rich experiences reported by Shaffer and Stevens.

COLLABORATION/CONTROL

Every teacher is familiar with issues associated with having students work in groups. Sometimes certain group members engage in the work and others seem to procrastinate, sometimes they have difficulties collaborating, the students often express strong preferences for whom they want as their teammates, etc. These are matters that arise in any group work, inside and outside schools. To structure collaboration and control on what they are supposed to accomplish, groups commonly develop a division of labor. Stevens' analysis of division of labor in the context of project-based design work is, I believe, a major contribution. He examines the emergence of division of labor as responding to a large collection of contingent factors and circumstances, which itself is not easily subject to control. Division of labor within a student group gets established along lines that do not necessarily follow teachers' instructions, individual preferences, or consensual agreements. Stevens sees educational technology, such as the CAD software used in the classroom, as participating and forming the ongoing emergent division of labor. He avoids judgments as to whether the technology is good or bad, preferring instead to delineate what the technology becomes part and parcel of. Stevens' notion of division of labor has a great potential to enrich our understanding of group dynamics in the classroom and of associated tensions, such as, for instance, the school expectation of uniform performance embedded in formal assessment procedures that pass over inherent asymmetries generated by divisions of labor.

Shaffer does not examine the dynamics of collaboration and control other than by stating that it worked well and harmonically. This may in part reflect that the projects his students worked on were individual, and therefore the collaboration that took place was not joint work but interactions between someone who had a request or question and someone else who might have offered a suitable response or suggestion. In addition, the students probably did not sense either that they were being assessed or that the results of the assessment were something to worry about. Although Shaffer's ethnography of the design studio in professional education documents multiple forms of collaboration, he does not discuss that some of this collaborative process had an evaluative component, in other words, that some of the more experienced designers who acted as consultants for the students' projects had to decide on whether they passed the course or not. How did this evaluative aspect play out? What counted as valuable work? How did the explicit and implicit judgment norms of the studio influence interpersonal interaction? These types of questions are also relevant to the workshops he designed and conducted. His description seem to portray students who were absorbed in their own projects without taking notice of what others were doing and expecting from them. In all likelihood this was not the case. Probably the students, as they worked on their individual projects, were partially trying to fit tacit criteria of value and quality; to fulfill these norms, it is likely that subtle divisions of labor got established regarding expertise with the technology, easiness with esthetic expressions, and so forth. These questions deserve a deeper exploration, like the one Shaffer offers in relation to B—'s use of Geometer Sketchpad to articulate questions and insights around her evolving project.

Deborah Ball (1993) and Magdalene Lampert (1992) have popularized the view of teaching as coping with emerging dilemmas. I think that the chapters by Stevens and Shaffer suggest the view of designing learning environments as anticipating and dealing with dilemmas. Each one of the dynamics I referred to in this commentary is inhabited by potential dilemmas. Disciplinary boundaries, for example, bring together issues of socio-curricular legitimacy, student initiative and engagement, institutionalized forms of assessment, and professional identities that cannot be all put to rest at once. Also, the dynamics of collaboration/control elicits tensions between individual diversity and expectations of uniform performance, or between the emergence of certain "niches" within group work and the reluctance to occupy them. Even as many of these dilemmas are bound to happen, they are not subject to deterministic treatment. It is up to the participants to recognize their emergence, appreciate their nature, and cope with them in ways that express their ongoing commitments and priorities. Although the designer of learning environments cannot and should not try to take the place of the participants and make on-the-spot decisions for them, he or she can help participants to discern the character of felt tensions and attain a rich grasp of their origins; this is the critical role of case studies. The work of Shaffer and Stevens brings to light the need and significance of case studies in the area intersecting design activities and mathematics learning.

REFERENCES

Ball, D. L. (1993). With an eye on the mathematical horizon: Dilemmas of teaching elementary school mathematics. *Elementary School Journal, 93*, 373–397.
Lampert, M. (1992). Practices and problems in teaching authentic mathematics in school. In F. Oser, A. Dick, & A.-L. Patry (Eds.), *Effective and responsible teaching: The new synthesis* (pp. 295–314). San Francisco: Jossey-Bass.

"Betweeness" in Design Education

Susan Leigh Star
University of California, San Diego

Relational concepts—those that attend to the "betweeness" of relationships—are difficult to write about, difficult to enact, and difficult to teach. These two papers, in addressing a range of issues concerning relational concepts and their pedagogy, tackle these tough questions and add significantly to the educational theory on design as a relational process.

Both articles draw on a rich range of observational data, drawing generals from particulars and moving back again (itself a relational process of sorts). Both speak to the multifaceted nature of design education—visual, manual, collaborative, and increasingly, involving mastery of computers.

DIVISION OF LABOR AND "EVOLVING COUPLINGS"

Stevens takes as his point of departure the sometimes mysterious process of evolving divisions of labor in the design studio and classroom. This in turn becomes "a puzzle to think through some of the issues of computer-supported collaborative learning." Stevens uses the work of sociologists Anselm Strauss and Everett Hughes to discuss the combination of duties, sentiment, skills, and timelines that go into constructing an arc of work. He compares architects at a mid-sized firm with middle school students learning architecture. (This sort of comparison, by the way, would have pleased both Hughes and Strauss, who delighted in comparing things people often segregate, precisely to enrich a conceptual model in the way Stevens

265

has done.) Seeing students as workers and workers as students has both social justice overtones and interesting comparative payoff.

The article adds a dimension often (though not always) missing from the analysis of work and division of labor afforded by Strauss: how responsibilities are distributed across people, technologies, and tasks, within "naturally occurring units" such as projects. The new addition is to take into account how people and technologies are coupled within this multilayered landscape. The distribution is not even, notes Stevens. And which are the right tools for the job? Who uses the tools, for what, and why? What is the meaning of this allocation?

Gregory Bateson's famous example of the "blind man plus stick" as a functioning, indissoluble system has often been invoked as an icon of how we become one with our tools. Stevens' paper both accepts this image and subverts it. Some students gravitate to paper; paper has affordances that some computers, in some spaces, do not. Always, our attention is drawn to the wider web of the tool, context, and history.

In general, in understanding the division of labor in any setting, there are always the sorts of trade-offs discussed here. People come in with what sociologists would call ascribed characteristics—such as race or gender, to which others ascribe many properties. These go beyond the immediate situation and are imported into it. The achieved characteristics of a person within a group mixes up the given and the made, as well as the structural features of their social location with improvisational features local to the setting.

Some unanswered questions for me here concern the role of time, a bit too briefly mentioned in the article. What time horizons do participants have? Some divisions of labor occur over a lifetime, whereas some occur in the space of a bus queue. Are there divisions that collide with each other or prevent each other? Over what time scales, and also over what organizational scales?

LEARNING TO THINK TOGETHER: THE BALANCE OF STRUCTURE AND FREEDOM

Shaffer's article takes up a set of questions closely related to those posed by Stevens. He notes that "There is a broad (and growing) consensus that an essential part of learning to think is learning to think with others." I heartily concur. Yet, as Shaffer notes about computers, learning, and the design studio, achieving the right milieu to support this combination is a challenge. When I have taught undergraduate courses with a group project component, I have usually failed to achieve this combination. Students are nervous about where their grades are coming from. They are angry with lazy team members. They do not understand how to create a division of labor that works, and they find it difficult to get away from the focus on grades.

Of course, this is a result of the educational system in which they are embedded that for decades has rewarded and punished them solely on the basis of grades. I thus read of the MIT design studio setting described by Shaffer with some envy. His analysis does depict a successful "structured context for open-ended activities." It is encouraging to hear about parallel changes in the NCTM Commission on Standards for School Mathematics that might help bring about broader political changes; the news from the public sector here in California on this front is far from optimistic. Empirical studies such as this one provide important demonstrations that more standards, blindly and rigidly imposed, are not the answer.

In this chapter, as well, I am fascinated by the temporal dimensions of design teamwork. The MIT studio students (and faculty) have substantial slack temporal resources—looseness in scheduling, in talking, in performing tasks. I wonder how different the results of this study would be if each session were crammed into rigid 50-minute intervals, with the next group waiting urgently at the door to get in? In future work, Shaffer's model would be greatly enhanced by an investigation into this question, involving comparisons across settings.

The pedagogy of the crit, and the crit cycle, is described as taking place in a democratic, productive, and constructive atmosphere, with crits coming from other students and from professors alike. (I know from teaching writing to students that learning to critique is at least as important to learning to write as is production. It is nice to see this demonstrated in another realm.) It was exciting to read the chapter and to see the design learning emerge iteratively (the diagrams give a very good sense of the development of both the concepts and the skills).

Again calling on a comparative thread, however, I wonder about the celebration of the democratic crit model. I can remember one undergraduate student several years ago, a soft-spoken Asian American young woman, coming into my office in tears after a crit session in her architecture class. On that occasion, the freedom of the crit had become an occasion for tearing down and belittling, and she very nearly left the field of architecture after that semester (I am happy to say she did not, in the end, however). I bring up this example to raise the question of the dynamics of the conversation and the balancing of independence with structured tasks. It seems to me that ground rules and affect are important elements in this mixture as well. These rules are perhaps already well internalized within the design studio described here.

In one of the classic papers to come out of the early feminist movement, Jo Freeman identified what she called "the tyranny of structurelessness." It arose from her observations of women's groups trying to do away with all hierarchy and celebrating the lack of power over each other. Although there were good elements of this lack of hierarchy, of course, it was also common to find tacit exercises of power (all the more powerful because they were tacit and illicit), and as well a kind of "rule by nobody" owing to the lack of structure. The balanced approach taken here by Shaffer helps understand some of these subtle organizational dynamics.

Both papers speak to the organizational side of learning and the importance of attending both to fluidity and fixity in design education.

KEEPING IT COMPLEX IN AN ERA OF BIG EDUCATION

Reed Stevens
University of Washington

I think the open, project-based environments of the sort David Shaffer and I studied productively challenge business as usual in education. Many of the reasons I think so are reflected in this chapter: unexpected but inevitable divisions of labor, the daily collision of emergent and assigned (roles, problems, etc.), and the uncloseable gaps between what people learn and what earns credit. I would add to this list an issue that Nemirovsky's commentary highlights but was underdeveloped in my chapter: the ways that cognition in the wild is often hard to squeeze into singular disciplinary boxes. In both these cases, architecture and mathematics intermingle in ways that were hard to describe, though I have tried to do so elsewhere (Stevens, 1999, 2000).

All of these features—as the commentaries of both Star and Nemirovsky remind us—make these complex places to understand and to design for. For me, this complexity made them interesting, worth studying, and informative for the practices of education and learning. However, in my home state, as across the country, this seems like a somewhat perilous time for those of us who want to "keep it complex"[1] in educational research. This has become an era of intense efforts around standards, accountability, and socially consequential tests for the masses. It has become an era of aspiring technology

---

[1]See Duckworth (1991) for the original use of this evocative phrase and a different but equally important sense of keeping it complex.

millionaires for whom education is an enormous open market. In short, it has become an era of Big Education.

Like Big Science, I expect Big Education to have some positive effects. But bigness has its dangers as well: Primary among these in education is the possibility of a reaction against research that keeps it complex, that reports the dross with the gold about major funded efforts[2], or that asks questions about something other than the improvement of standardized test scores. In light of this possibility, I will devote the thrust of this response to a further explanation of my approach to keeping it complex and suggest how this approach may inform our participation in creating worthwhile learning environments.

One of the reasons I pursued a comparative analysis of the projects in the classroom and the workplace was to set my questions about student uses of learning technologies in a wider context. Schools are too often treated like islands; scholars isolate them analytically and society isolates them practically (Engeström, 1991). Although schools are culturally and historically specific institutions, they are not islands. One element of my response to this balkanization has been to "[s]ee students as workers and workers as students," as Star so nicely puts it. As Star's commentary also indicates, my work has built upon that of Strauss and Hughes, for whom comparison was a fundamental way of seeing. Other scholars who have influenced my comparative perspective include Howard Becker (1986/1972), Lave and Wenger (1991), and those associated with the Laboratory of Comparative Human Cognition (Cole, Engestrom, & Vasquez, 1997). For me, this body of work, along with my own studies, has fundamentally *unsettled* a lot of core issues with respect to business as usual in education, Big or otherwise.

Once these issues *are* unsettled and addressed in sufficiently complex analyses of practice, an obvious question becomes: What next? Can these analyses be translated into effects on the practices of schooling, whether it be to the participant structures of classrooms, the types of discretion accorded students, the roles of teachers, the ways that different subject matters are bounded and assessed, or the way learning technologies are designed and used? For me asking "what next" is critical and I have included some proposed answers in this chapter but in general this is still an open question for me. I can say that the payoff of this type of research is unlikely to show up in next year's test scores. Instead, it has led me to ask: Is this really what we are looking for? If, as I believe, it is not, we need other foundational assumptions to work from. This study suggests two alternative working assumptions: 1. The contingent and emergent organizations of labor, credit, time, assessment, and human relationships on any given day

---

[2]See Brown (1992) and Heath (1999) for good arguments for reporting both the gold with the dross.

in any given classroom are not signs of failed social engineering but constitutive features of educational experience, and 2. when students build their own things—interpretations, tasks, divisions of labor, uses of tools, and social relationships—rather than exclusively accepting what is assigned by the authorities, then we have something both interesting and necessary to work from. This is nothing so new perhaps, but it is easily forgotten in practice.

With respect to how this research might inform thinking about educational technology specifically, I offer the following thoughts. Some have argued recently that we need to focus on designing "learner centered technologies" (Norman & Spohrer, 1996; Soloway & Pryor, 1996) as opposed to borrowing merely user-centered ones designed for other purposes. Learners, it is argued, are a distinctive population with distinctive needs; technologies for learning need to accommodate the fact that peoples' minds and practices are changing over time. These are important points and I take this to be a productive conceptual move toward a collective goal of building a sophisticated approach that is distinctively for learning. However, this new slogan also raises a concern for me about future starting points for studies at the intersection of learning and technology. As this study shows, paper can be a learner-centered technology without having been designed for that purpose. And a computer program specifically designed for that purpose can turn out not to be so centered. It depends, as it depended in these cases, on the practices into which these uses of technology are embedded. What I have argued against therefore is any strong sense of technological determinism—the thing alone rarely makes *the* difference although many differences cannot be made without specific things. In general, if learning often happens in ways that have not been designed for and is sometimes even impeded by having been designed for, then our designing selves need to keep in very close conversation with our empirical selves if we are going to advance the state of the art.

Like Nemirovsky, I want to produce and see from others more careful case studies at the intersection of new technologies and new arrangements for learning. To date, I think the sophistication of our technologies—in the new and hybrid practices they make *possible*—far outpaces the sophistication of our analyses, mine included. The limitations of my analysis are pointed out most clearly by Star's questions about relative timescales in each setting for the observed divisions of labor. Part of the reason for the thinness of this part of my analysis involves the narrow focus I took in the classroom case study, a narrowness that mirrored the current slant of the field. Though I was there nearly every day for an entire school year, I studied only one mathematics classroom. I knew little about what the students I studied did in their other classes. In retrospect, I think I would have had better answers to Star's questions had I looked more broadly at the structure of time *for students across the school day* rather than just at one period in one subject each day.

After all, I did not just observe and record the activities of the architects during "2nd period"; I followed them across their arcs of work into the different spaces and different conversations that made up their days. With the students I only followed them across an arc of work bounded (though not defined) by the curriculum project in a single classroom period. However, from a phenomenological and ethnographic perspective, the students' arcs of work involved much more than architecture projects and math problems in 2nd period; it involved history, science, and English (not to mention recess). The productive discipline-specific focus in cognitive studies in education, of which I count my own work as having, has also perhaps blinded us to this simple fact: Students are shuffled between subject areas during every school day at the ring of a bell. And the cohort of fellow students with whom they work (if they work with others) also shifts from class to class. In short, the organization of school is very different from the organization of a professional workplace and this has consequences for when and among whom collaborative work and learning happen (Hall & Stevens, 1995, Stevens, 1999). In current work, my colleagues and I are trying to stretch our boundaries, looking at student experiences across different subjects (i.e., science and history) to understand issues both about similarities and differences of different subjects for students and about how they experience the fragmented structure of the school day (Stevens, Wineburg, & Herrenkohl, 2001).

Like the best meaning advocates of Big Education, I want to see and am working for an educational system that gets better and includes every student. In my opinion, this is an enormously complex goal that needs to be renewed as a collective project. The approaches that receive the most attention during this era involve top-down directives for standards, testing, and accountability. From above, we also hear simple formulations and promises: a computer for every student like a chicken in every pot. Is there an alternative? I am uncertain about this, but following the results of this study and going back to what Durkheim and Strauss taught us, we might find ways to build a better collective than we have in education. We have inherited divisions of academic labor among assessment, technology, curriculum, and close studies of practice; what we seem to need now is articulation work that draws these pieces together (remaking each in unexpected ways no doubt). I think the need for this articulation work is especially true of designers of educational things and researchers who look very closely (and critically) at what happens when these things are used. And although I have no false optimism about the results (Cuban, 1993), at the end of our day we may at least know that we have taken the complexity of education's phenomena as seriously as those 20th-century immunologists have ended up taking theirs.

REFERENCES

Becker, H. S. (1986/1972). A school is a lousy place to learn anything in. In *Doing things together: selected papers*, pp. 173–190. Evanston, IL: Northwestern University Press.

Brown, A. (1992). Design experiments: Theoretical and methodological challenges in creating complex interventions in classroom settings. *The Journal of Learning Sciences, 2*(2), 141–178.

Cole, M., Engestrom, Y., & Vasquez, O. (Eds.). (1997). *Mind, culture and activity: Seminal papers from the Laboratory of Comparative Human Cognition*. Cambridge, England: Cambridge University Press.

Cuban, L. (1993). *How teachers taught: Constancy and change in American classrooms, 1890–1990* (2nd ed.). New York: Teachers College Press.

Duckworth, E. (1991). Twenty-four, forty-eight, I love you: Keeping it complex. *Harvard Educational Review, 61*(1), 1–24.

Engeström, Y. (1991). "Non scholae sed vitae discimus": Toward overcoming the encapsulation of school learning. *Learning and Instruction, 1*(3), 243–259.

Hall, R., & Stevens, R. (1995). Making space: A comparison of mathematical work in school and professional design practices. In S. L. Star (Ed.), *The cultures of computing* (pp. 118–145). London: Basil Blackwell.

Heath, S. B. (1999). Discipline and disciplines in education research, elusive goals? In E. Lagemann & L. Shulman (Eds.). *Issues in Education Research* (pp. 203–223). San Francisco, CA: Jossey-Bass.

Lave, J., & Wenger, E. (1991). *Situated learning: Legitimate peripheral participation*. Cambridge: Cambridge University Press.

Norman, D. A., & Spohrer, J. C. (1996). Learner centered education. *Communications of the ACM, 39*(4), 24–27.

Soloway, E., & Pryor, A. (1996). The next generation in human–computer interaction. *Communications of the ACM, 39*(3), 16–18.

Stevens, R. (1999). *Disciplined perception: Comparing the development of embodied mathematical processes in school and at work*. Unpublished doctoral dissertation, University of California, Berkeley.

Stevens, R. R. (in preparation). What is a "learning environment"? A Grounded framework for analysis and design.

Stevens, R., Wineburg, S., & Herrenkohl, L. (2001). "Toward a comparative understanding of school subjects." Paper presented at the American Educational Research Association Seattle, WA.

IDENTITY FORMATION/TRANSFORMATION AS A PROCESS OF COLLABORATIVE LEARNING OF PROGRAMMING USING ALGOARENA

Hideyuki Suzuki
Ibaraki University

Hiroshi Kato
National Institute of Multimedia Education

INTRODUCTION

This chapter demonstrates the process of identity formation in the collaborative learning of programming through AlgoArena, educational software for learning programming. In recent years, a number of educational researchers, teachers, and educational system developers have become aware of the potential of collaborative learning (e.g., Koschmann, 1996). Of the various theoretical foundations for collaborative learning, we rely on situated learning theory (Lave & Wenger, 1991; Brown, Collins & Duguid, 1988), which focuses on the social characteristics of human learning. This theory sees learning as the process of change in social relations in which the learner is imperatively situated. In this sense, learning is a social phenomenon, so it is impossible to isolate the "learning of the individual" from the social context in which the individual is embedded. Lave and Wenger articulated this social process of learning by the concept of LPP, Legitimate Peripheral Participation (Lave & Wenger, 1991). In this process, a learner first participates in a community as a peripheral member in the sense that his/her control over the activity of the community and contribution to the activity are limited and partial; at the same time the learner participates as a legitimate member in the sense that he/she supports the authentic activity of the community as an imperative constituent. Then he/she is gradually supposed to expand his/her membership and finally reach the status of a full member of the community. The central emphasis of LPP is that the learning process is considered as the development of one's identity in the community, that is, as one's involvement in the historical development/formation of community practice.

From ethnomethodological viewpoint (Sacks 1972a, 1972b, 1992; Watson, 1997), one's identity in a community is not an internal property of an individual, nor is it defined by external normative structure, but it is an observable feature of social interaction. It is established locally and contingently (but persistently) through interaction with community members in the form of indication, confirmation, and sanction on the basis of historical accumulation of identity formation. Displaying one's identity in a certain occasion intrinsically includes social display of one's understanding about the occasion, for example, displaying an understanding about what is happening, what is viewed as an adequate activity, or who is considered an adequate participant. Therefore, the practice in which the person participates is locally established through the process of identity negotiation. Thus, learning as identity formation in a community can be considered as the process of participation in local and continuous formation of community of practice. In this sense, a community is not a static entity but one that emerges through local interaction. Although we see the persistent nature of a community, this does not mean that the community is an "enduring community" isolated from local interaction. Even if the community appears to endure, there underlies activities of members that locally visualize history or persistency of the community.

This chapters discusses a qualitative study based on participatory observation and close analysis of conversation in an AlgoArena classroom and demonstrates how a learner's identity is formed and transformed in the process of collaborative learning.

ALGOARENA: A TOOL FOR COLLABORATIVE LEARNING OF PROGRAMMING

AlgoArena (Kato & Ide, 1995) is a tool for collaborative learning of programming by novices at the introductory level. The purpose of this software is to foster programming skills through collaborative programming activities in which learners are encouraged to cooperate or compete with others. AlgoArena (see Figs. 7.1 and 7.2) is a simulation of Sumo, the traditional Japanese form of wrestling. Learners are supposed to program the actions of their own wrestlers to defeat other wrestlers using a LOGO-based programming language. The learners then have their wrestlers engage in bouts with opponents programmed by other learners or by the teacher. The process of a bout is graphically presented on a CRT monitor. After the bouts have been fought, learners are supposed to analyze the results and incorporate

FIG. 7.1. A sumo bout on AlgoArena.

solutions into their own programs. The learners then engage in other bouts. The learners' participation in these iterative programming activities is expected to help them develop their programming skills.

AlgoArena has been planned to be the foundation of the community of learners. The bout-game situation provided by AlgoArena encourages learners to have bouts with other learners and to make their wrestlers stronger than others, thus helping them to form a community in which the members share an orientation toward increasing the strength of their respective wrestlers. In the world of AlgoArena, winning and losing are completely based on how the programs are made. Consequently, learners should become highly motivated to improve their programming skills so that they can become winners (i.e., achieve the most admirable status in the community). The orientation given by AlgoArena helps learners form a community for carrying out AlgoArena activities in which collaborative learning can occur.

The shared orientation provides a foundation of interaction through which the learners can talk about their tasks, problems, and interests and sometimes face contradictions. The community of learners and identity in the community are shaped mutually and locally through this interaction. It should also be noted that we do not claim that the application software is the sole catalyst of the formation of the community but that a comprehensive environmental arrangement, including the design of software, a curriculum, class organization, and so forth is needed for this purpose.

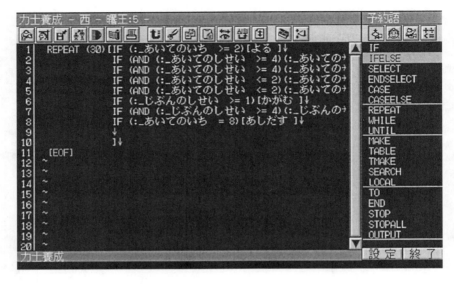

FIG. 7.2. The editor screen of AlgoArena.

PARTICIPATORY OBSERVATION AND VIDEOTAPING IN THE ALGOARENA CLASSROOM

Participatory observation and videotaping were carried out in the AlgoArena classroom. The class was held 12 times during a winter term and 40 ninth-grade students attended the classes. The class activities included instructions on commands for AlgoArena programming and basic algorithms, free programming activities, and a Sumo tournament held during the last class. Two observers working for a computer company participated in the class as assistant instructors to provide technical support and to bring programming culture to the classroom. In the classroom, each pair of students shared one personal computer. A pair of two male students, OH and IM, was chosen for observation; their conversations, actions, and the screen images of their PC were videotaped throughout the classes. Following the teacher's recommendation, we chose to videotape OH because of his fearless demeanor; IM was OH's friend.

Results and Discussion

In this section, we demonstrate how the identities of these learners formed and changed (i.e., how their learning was shaped). Of the various factors that relate to the formation of identity, conversation in the AlgoArena classroom is the focus of this chapter. Focusing on students' in situ conversation should be one of the most effective ways of investigating the process of identity formation, because, as stated above, the process is established through local interaction including conversation.

The transcript notations used in the following fragments are as follows: Underline indicates speaker's emphasis; dash indicates a short pause; hhh indicates aspirations; equal signs indicate no interval between the end of a prior and the beginning of a next piece of speech; empty parentheses indicate unrecovered utterance; words enclosed in double parentheses are notes from the authors; words enclosed in brackets indicate nonlinguistic action.

"It Is Your Strategy, Right?": Introduction of Programming Culture. We will begin by considering how the teacher introduced the observers and what the observers brought to the classroom. Both observers are employees of NEC, a Japanese computer company. On the first day, the teacher introduced them to the students as "software developers (programmers)" and "employees of a computer company" (see Fragment 1).

Fragment 1:
Teacher: . . . They developed the software we will use in this class. They are working for NEC. Mr. SK and Mr. KT from Tokyo, . . . I am sure all of you know NEC. PCs in front of you are all made by NEC, and you may use many NEC products at home. They are developing new software.

After this introduction, the observers started to assist students in programming and using the software. Through the activities the programmers' behavior was introduced to the class. For example, the programmers often consulted a manual for help, browsed through the manual while talking about programs, encouraged students to look at the manual to solve their problems, used computer terms when talking, and presented their way of thinking through conversation. The following fragment shows how KT, one of the observers, showed his way of thinking in a conversation with OH. It is from the fifth day's conversation.

Fragment 2:
[OH and KT are looking at OH's program on a screen]
OH: Well. (2-01)
KT: You intended to wait until the opponent comes near = (2-02)
OH: Uh. (2-03)
KT: = is that right? It is your strategy, right? (2-04)
OH: Well, I don't know why, but I made it as it is. I forgot what I thought. (2-05)
KT: Don't you remember? (2-06)
OH: No. (2-07)

In this conversation, KT asked OH about his intended strategy embedded in the program (2-02, 2-04), but OH was unable to answer the question (2-05). This conversation shows KT's view of programming: The program should be a representation of a strategy, and every description in the program should correspond to the intended strategy explicitly, and thus the programmer is expected to be able to account for the intention under the program. We consider this way of seeing programs as part of the programming culture. OH's failure to answer KT's question shows OH did not see the program as KT did. They had trouble starting up a discussion about the program because they did not share the programmers' viewpoint. This conversation highlights the diversity between KT the "programmer" and OH the "layperson" and presumably contributes to introducing the programmer's way of thinking and talking to OH. The following fragment was from the next day.

Fragment 3:
   [OH called KT for help]
   OH: What I want to do is = (3-01)
   KT: O.K. (3-02)
   OH: = this. [points to a defeat/defeated condition chart in the manual] (3-03)
   KT: [looks at the manual] I see. (3-04)
   OH: That is, I don't want to be pushed out. (3-05)
   KT: I see. You don't want to be pushed out. Well, [points to the chart] when your wrestler is in this status. . . . (3-06)

In this fragment, OH clearly declared what he wanted to do with his program: "he does not want to be pushed out" (3-01, 3-03, 3-05). Therefore, KT was able to advise him (3-06).

It is notable that OH expressed his intention by juxtaposing the verbal expression (3-01, 3-05) and the action, that is, pointing to a defeat/defeated condition chart in the manual (3-03). The chart shows conditions to defeat/be defeated by Push_Out (a Sumo technique). The conditions in this chart were presented as a set of status parameters that can be used in conditional programming. Talking about his intention in reference to the chart displayed OH's understanding that he was going to translate his intention ("to avoid being pushed out") to the program. In short, he was talking about his intention as a matter of programming. This is a kind of programmers' way of talking about their tasks. Interaction with KT allowed the programmers' way of talking and seeing programs to be introduced to OH. In other words, the conversation enabled programming learning because talking like a programmer is an imperative part of being a programmer.

"I'm Going to Make a Strong Wrestler": Orientation to Strength. On the first day, basic instruction on the AlgoArena system, action commands, and simple sequential programming using the commands were provided. The action commands included such commands as move_forward, move_back, push_forward, and throw. A simple program can be formed by sequencing some of these commands. What OH and IM first did was to input the commands and check their functions; then they tried to make their own wrestler. From the beginning, OH and IM were enthusiastic about the bout-situation provided by AlgoArena. Almost all of their conversations centered around the "wrestler's strength"; they discussed how to make their wrestlers stronger, admired the wrestlers' strength, and wanted to beat stronger wrestlers. The following fragment shows their orientation to strength of wrestlers.

Fragment 4:
    OH: I'm going to make a strong wrestler. Move forward. We must grasp the opponent's mawashi (belt). (4-01)
    IM: [inputs grasp_mawashi] Now we've grasped the mawashi, we should throw now. (4-02)

This orientation to the wrestler's strength endured throughout the AlgoArena activity. The orientation provided a continuous shared foundation on which the students talked about their tasks, problems, and interests, and thus on which they shaped their learning (see Fragments 12, 13, 14, 16, and 17). It is notable, as we will show in the following analysis, that their concept of "strength" was transformed through their interaction in which each other's understanding about "strength" was displayed, sanctioned, and sometimes rejected. The process of transformation of their shared concept of "strength" throughout AlgoArena activity is one aspect of their learning.

"He Has a More Powerful Back": Everyday Concepts for the AlgoArena Activity. On the first and second days, the students were utilizing everyday concepts of Sumo or fighting to talk about their tasks. The following fragments demonstrate this tendency well. Fragment 5 is from the first day; Fragment 6 is from the second day.

Fragment 5:
    [OH and IM are talking while looking at the editor screen]
    OH: First, let's crouch. Crouching makes our wrestler take a lower position than the opponent. Taking a lower position may be very advantageous. (5-01)
    IM: [inputs bend_forward] (5-02)

Fragment 6:
 [OH and IM's wrestler was defeated by a sample program]
 IM: This sample wrestler is quite strong. He has a more powerful back
   than Maemukido (name of another sample program). (6-01)
 OH: I missed seeing the bout. Let me have them fight again. (6-02)

In Fragment 5, OH was trying to figure out how he could make his wrestler
stronger. In his analysis, he was making use of everyday knowledge about
fighting, that is, that taking a lower position is sometimes advantageous
(5-01). Following OH's statement, IM input a bend_forward command to
make the wrestler crouch. This action acted as an acknowledgement of OH's
idea and thus showed IM's attunement to his way of seeing the task. In
Fragment 6, IM talked about the strength of the sample wrestler in terms
of the everyday concept of "power" (6-01), although AlgoArena's rules do
not contain any factors corresponding to "power." It seems that IM's way of
talking was sanctioned by the fact that OH continued the talk without any
objection (6-02). These fragments suggest that both OH and IM were seeing
their task not from the viewpoint of programming, but from the viewpoint
of the sport of Sumo.

 "We Are Cool": Voluntary Formation of Shared Activity. At the beginning of the second day, OH and IM were enthusiastic about minimizing the
number of commands in their program.

Fragment 7:
 IM: Let's minimize the number of commands. (7-01)
 OH: Yeah, minimal commands. Then we just need one move_forward
   here. (7-02)
 IM: We, the OH and IM pair, are cool enough to want to try to defeat
   every wrestler by using the least power. We are different from the
   other guys. (7-03)
 OH: Absolutely. (7-04)

In Fragment 7, IM distinguished his team from the others by the words
"the OH and IM pair" (7-03) and "the other guys" (7-03). OH also accepted IM's
display of "team" (7-04): the team working to win using "minimal commands"
(7-01, 7-02). The teacher in the class encouraged the students to make strong
programs, not short ones. Given this, they were engaging in the creation of
a shared and original goal for their activity at the very beginning of the
class.
 One might consider that minimizing the number of commands would be
an activity of programming culture where a short program is thought of as

elegant. However, based on our observation, we do not consider the activity appearing here as an activity of programming culture. The observation shows that they began to eliminate commands in their program when they noticed their wrestler's redundant movement. This implies that they were oriented to reducing redundancy of the wrestler's movement, not to making a short program that is considered elegant.

"No, We Should Do This Stuff": Formation of Divergent Perspectives. An IF command and status parameters were introduced immediately after Fragment 7. The IF command is a logical control command that enables the students to use conditional algorithms such as "if my wrestler is bending back, then make it bend forward." Status parameters are numbers assigned to a wrestler's specific status (e.g., posture, position, and distance from opponents). They are used in conditional programs. Because the parameters are hard to memorize, a status parameter chart that lists all the status parameters was handed out. The following fragment shows the conversation immediately after instruction.

Fragment 8:
> IM: Well, we don't need this one, either. We should delete it, right? (8-01)
> OH: That's enough. Why don't we try this now. [points to status parameter chart] (8-02)

In Fragment 8, their shared goal was frustrated. Since IM's statement (8-01) follows the conversation of Fragment 7, it is apparent that IM intended to continue their existing collaboration. However, OH rejected the goal and proposed a new goal, that is, to program using the IF command and status parameters (8-02). At least at this point, it seems OH accepted the IF command and status parameters as tools for thinking, while IM did not.

It seems that they began to develop different perspectives on their task after Fragment 8. The conversation in Fragment 9 occurred a few minutes after Fragment 8.

Fragment 9:
> [OH and IM are watching a bout]
> OH: Our wrestler gets pushed back when the opponent moves forward. (9-01)
> IM: Yeah, the difference in power is pretty clear. (9-02)
> OH: <u>No.</u> This. We should do this stuff. [points to the status parameter chart] (9-03)
> IM: Why don't you pipe down? (9-04)

They were watching a bout, and their wrestler was pushed back by the opponent. IM attributed this event to the opponent's "power" (9-02). Although this way of talking about events on the CRT screen seems to have been shared on the first day (see Fragment 6), here, OH rejected IM's account of the event and proposed another way of talking about it from the viewpoint of status parameters (9-03). IM rejected sharing this new perspective by exclaiming, "Why don't you pipe down?" (9-04) Here, it is apparent that OH accepted a different perspective from IM's. Thereafter, while OH appeared to be absorbed in programming and showed programming ability, IM kept himself insulated from programming activities.

The observed competence of OH is inseparably related to his use of the IF command and the status parameter chart as a tool for thinking. They are artifacts in which an algorithmic way of thinking and definition of the problem are embedded. Accepting these artifacts as tools for his activity led him to the sphere of programming where a "bout" is defined as a change in status parameters and "making a wrestler win" is defined as an arrangement of these parameters toward a preferable status. As activity theorists have claimed (Engeström, 1986; Bødker, 1991), human ability should be viewed as the performance of a unified activity system composed of human (subject), artifact, and world (object). Utilization of the artifacts led OH (subject) to see his task (object) as a matter of programming; so he solved the problem like a programmer. In this sense, his programming competence is not considered to be the emergence of an internal and individual ability; rather, it becomes observable through the activity system he takes part in. Moreover, by using the terms "IF" and "IFELSE" in his speech, his identity as a programmer (i.e., a person who talks about his tasks in technical terms) is displayed and ready to be tried. As Fragment 16 (16-05) shows, programming-related terms were used as resources for identity formation by OH and IM.

Similarly, IM's lack of competence as a programmer should not be attributed to a lack of internal ability. Instead, his apparent lack of competence resulted from his involvement with a different activity where he presumably established a different type of competence using different artifacts.

"You Are a Total Computer Nerd": Identity Formation With Membership Categories. On the third, fourth, fifth, and sixth days, OH was trying to make a complex program incorporating IF, IFELSE, and REPEAT, while IM was fooling around chatting, watching other bouts, and teasing his friends. The following fragment is from the fifth day.

Fragment 10:
    OH: I've been defeated and defeated! (10-01)
    IM: You can't win? (10-02)
    OH: [starts to browse through the manual] (10-03)
    IM: I, I don't think I can get a computer-related job. It's boring. (10-04)

This fragment demonstrates how they formed their identities by making use of membership categorization devices (Sacks, 1972a, 1972b). According to Sacks, membership categories are classifications or social types that may be used to describe a person, and they are organized, by persons of the society using them, into "membership categorization devices" or "collections of membership categories," which are defined by Sacks (1972a) as "any collection of membership categories containing at least a category, which may be applied to some population containing at least a member, so as to provide, by the use of some rules of application, for the pairing of at least a population member and a categorization device member." A device is then "a collection plus rules of application." For example, categories such as "baby," "father," "mother," etc. belong to the membership category collection "Family." In the same way, "teacher," "doctor," "lawyer" etc. belong to the collection "Occupation." Some collections are made of paired categories, such as "professional/layperson" and "boy/girl." One of the basic rules for application is the consistency rule, which is: "If some population of persons is being categorized, and if a category from some device's collection has been used to categorize a first member of the population, then that category or other categories of the same collection may be used to categorize further members of the population." The point of this rule is the distinction between "correctness" and "relevance" of the categorization. For example, when a person is first categorized as "baby," which belongs to the collection "Family" or "Stage-of-Life," the relevant category applied for further categorization would be either of them. Consequently, applying the categories from different category collections (e.g., "lawyer," "teacher," etc.) will not be relevant even if the categorizations are correct. Another important concept is "category-bound activities" (Sacks 1972a). These are activities in a certain culture that are constitutionally bound to particular membership categories. These activities are expectably and properly done by persons who are the incumbents of particular categories. For example, "crying" is bound to "baby." Sacks notes that categories selected to categorize some member performing a category-bound activity and categories selected to categorize that activity are co-selected. Thus, although it is possibly correct to say of a baby crying that it is a male shedding tears, it is not possibly recognizable as a correct or appropriate description of the scene. Furthermore, Watson (1997) argues that descriptions of activities, through their category-bound characteristics, can substitute for categorization. That is, describing activities of a person may implicitly and sometimes explicitly indicate the category of the person in question.

Let us turn to the fragment. OH started to browse through the manual (10-03). The activity of browsing through a manual may be bound to a category such as "programmer"or "hacker" in this classroom where authentic programmers (i.e., the observers) frequently browsed through a manual.

Consequently, this activity indicates OH's possible incumbency in a computer-related category, which, by the consistency rule, makes computer-related categories relevant in further categorization. Thus IM was able to state "I don't think I can get a computer-related job." (10-04); IM categorized himself as a "person who is not suitable for a computer-related job" (i.e., a "nonprogrammer"). This categorization evokes the category collection "programmer/nonprogrammer", and as a consequence, the connection between the activity "browsing the manual" and the category "programmer." Thus, OH, who browses through the manual, was reflexively categorized as a "programmer." Furthermore, IM, who was categorized as a "nonprogrammer," was not expected to browse through the manual, because the activity "browsing the manual" was bound to "programmer" in the collection "programmer/nonprogrammer." Through this codetermination, a boundary between "programmer (a person who looks in a manual to develop programs)" and "nonprogrammer (a person who does not)" was generated. OH could have protested IM's categorization, but he did not take any action against IM; thus IM's categorization was sanctioned by absence of reaction. Consequently, their identities were mutually and locally constructed through this very conversation. In turn, their activity was organized to be observable as programming activity through utilization of the particular category collection and knowledge about the category-bound activity in this occasion. Work of categorization is no less than formation of shared understanding about what is going on here and now.

The emergence of the category "person who is suitable for computer-related job" (i.e., "programmer") and the connection between the category and the activity "browsing the manual" in this class were presumably made possible by the observers' behavior in the classroom. As we previously discussed the observers brought the programmers' way of behavior to the classroom. Consequently, as shown in the previous analysis, IM and OH were able to define their activity as "programming activity," where the boundary between "programmer" and "nonprogrammer" was relevant.

Fragment 11 shows another example of categorization.

Fragment 11:
   [OH had been talking with SK (observer) about a program technique, and
   SK left]
   OH: Shit. I made this program last night. [shows his program written on
         a small piece of paper to IM] (11-01)
   IM: You are a total computer nerd. (11-02)
   OH: Well, I just had a lot of free time last night. (11-03)
   IM: You don't have to make excuses. (11-04)
   OH: Well, I am not a nerd. (11-05)
   IM: You're changing bit by bit but you don't notice it (11-06)

OH: Really? So I'm in danger, am I? (11-07)

[A few minutes passed while OH was editing his program]

IM: Hey, you showed me the memo because the teacher—the guy left us? (11-08)

OH: <u>Of course</u>. I don't want him to see how I involved I am in this activity. (11-09)

In this fragment, IM categorized OH, who displayed his enthusiasm for programming, as a "computer nerd" (11-02). The category "computer nerd" supposedly overlaps "programmer" in the sense that both categories refer to a "person who engages in computer-related activities," although "computer nerd" has a derogatory implication. OH's response against the categorization was ambivalent: OH first said "Well, I'm not a nerd" (11-05) to protest the categorization, but in his next response it seems he accepted the categorization saying "Really?" (11-07), However, he was also expressing that he had not been a "complete computer nerd" yet by delivering "So I'm in danger, am I?" (11-07). Categorizing OH as "computer nerd" implied IM's lack of incumbency in the category "computer nerd" because of the derogatory implication of this category. Thus, through this conversation, a boundary between "programmer (computer nerd)" and "nonprogrammer (non–computer nerd)" was generated and OH was put on the "programmer" side while IM was put on the other side.

The last exchange in Fragment 11 (11-08, 11-09) demonstrates intricate categorization work in the AlgoArena classroom. "The guy" (11-8) in IM's statement denotes one of the observers. The observer was undoubtedly seen by IM and OH as a "teacher-side person" as IM's rewording, "the teacher—the guy" (11-08), supports. Given this, what IM meant by his statement was: "Did OH intentionally avoid showing the memo to the teacher-side person, the observer?" This question was answered "Of course" (11-09) by OH. In the response, OH expressed aversion to being seen as an enthusiastic programmer by the observer who was a teacher-side person (see 11-09). This exchange suggests the existence of a "brat community" which bids defiance of authorized class activity and regards being a "conforming student" as "not cool." What they established through this exchange was formation of a boundary between "conforming student" and "brat," and they confirmed each other's membership in the "brat community." Why did the identity of "brat" appear here? To answer this question, the characteristics of membership category collections in this classroom should be examined. This fragment shows that there were at least two kinds of membership category collections available in the AlgoArena classroom. One was "programmer/nonprogrammer"; the other was "conforming student/brat." The former collection was introduced into the classroom by AlgoArena activity, but it was not simply imported. When the category collection was brought into the classroom, it was linked to the collection "conforming student/brat," which was presumably indigenous to the classroom. That is, "programmer" was linked to "conforming student," and "nonprogrammer" to "brat." We suppose that this way of linkage was based on the fact that programming activity was introduced by the teacher as one of the class-room activities. Thus, to be an incumbent of the category "programmer" was to be seen as "not brat" and as treachery to the "brat community" in this classroom. This is why OH tried to secure his identity of "brat" when he happened to be seen as enthusiastic about AlgoArena activity (i.e., the activity given by the teacher). "Shit" (11-01) in the first line is also a good example of the identity coordination between "programmer" and "brat." He displayed incumbency in the category "programmer" by showing the product of his moonlight programming, but at the same time, he tried to display his "brat" identity by using a vulgar expression when he happened to be seen as enthu-siastic about AlgoArena activity. It is notable that OH continued to edit his program after he displayed his identity of "brat," which expectably rebels against teacher-controlled activities. What OH tried to do in this fragment was to maintain his identity as "brat" while engaging in AlgoArena activity. In other words, it was, the authors presume, an attempt to redefine Algo-Arena activity from "teacher-controlled activity" to "voluntary activity by the students."

The following fragments suggest the same type of identity coordination.

Fragment 12:
  IM: Isn't this the strong wrestler? (12-01)
  OH: No, it's a new one. His name is Toryushin ((name of the wrestler)).
        Hey, I hate this silly game. (12-02)

Fragment 13:
  IM: IU ((another student)), tell me how to install waza ((Sumo tech-
        nique)). I want Bakabon ((name of his wrestler)) to be the strongest.
        (13-01)
  IU: Bakabon (13-02)
  IM: How silly I am to play this damn game. (13-03)

In both fragments, the students labeled their activity as "silly" (12-02, 13-03). It is interesting that the statements are not consistent with their atti-tude toward AlgoArena activity, that is, OH in Fragment 12 was devising a new wrestler (12-02); IM in Fragment 13 wanted to make his wrestler the strongest (13-01). The identity coordination between "programmer" and "brat" could be a possible answer to the question: Why did they have to talk negatively about AlgoArena activity although they were actually enthusiastic? Display-ing themselves as enthusiastic programmers may have endangered their

```
move_forward
push_forward
move_forward
push_forward
move_forward
move_forward
push_forward
move_forward
move_forward
push_forward
move_forward
move_forward
push_forward
move_forward
move_back
move_forward
push_forward
move_forward
move_forward
push_forward
move_forward
move_forward
move_forward
```

FIG. 7.3. Program made by IM.

identity as "brat," so they had to maintain the identity by labeling their current activity as "silly" when they happened to show their enthusiasm. In other words, they had to reconcile being a "programmer" and being a "brat" to continue AlgoArena activity.

The linkage between the two category collections made identity formation in the classroom complicated. The process inevitably involved coordination between being a "programmer" and being a "brat." The coordination included redefinition of AlgoArena activity from "teacher controlled activity" to "voluntary activity by the students." It would also be true that the coordination made it possible for them to engage in programming activity in the reality of their school life.

"You Should Be the One Who's Ashamed": Two Kinds of Strengths. On the seventh day, IM stated, "I am going to make my own program, so after I do let's have yours and mine have a bout." He then made his own program. Although it was a simple sequential program (see Fig. 7.3), it was strong against OH's program (see Fig. 7.4). OH was unable to defeat IM's wrestler for two days no matter what he did. (It would be fair to say that IM's wrestler was "accidentally" strong.) The following conversation followed after OH's wrestler had been defeated by IM's wrestler several times.

```
REPEAT (30) [move_forward Defense]

TO Defense
IFELSE (:_his_hand = 2)[disturb_hishand][
IFELSE (:_my-posture <= 2) [bend_forward][
IFELSE (:_my-posture =4) [bend_back][
IFELSE (:_my-posture= <=2) [move_forward][Offense]
]
]
]
END

TO Offense
IFELSE (:_his_hand = 2) [disturb_hishand][
IFELSE (:his_posture =4) [slap_down][
IFELSE (:_my-hand =2) [throw][
IFELSE (:distance= 1) [grasp_mawashi][push_foward]
]
]
]
END
```

FIG. 7.4. Program made by OH.

Fragment 14:

    IM: You have to admit my program is pretty good. You should study it very carefully. (14-01)

    OH: You really get the better of me here. [examines IM's program] (14-02)

    IM: This is the program that beat yours all to hell. (14-03)

    OH: But all it has is move_forward and push_forward! (14-04)

    IM: No, it also has a move_back. It uses it to feint. (14-05)

    OH: I'd be ashamed to win with a program like yours. (14-06)

    IM: You should be the one who's ashamed. Who won, anyway? (14-07)

This conversation shows us their divergent perspectives. OH implied that IM should be ashamed of his program (14-06), even though IM's wrestler defeated OH's wrestler time and again. This statement indicates that OH was not seeing the program from the viewpoint of simply winning and losing, but his view of the task would have been "to win by means of an elaborate strategy." OH did not respect IM's wrestler because it was a very simple sequential program. In contrast, IM was seeing his task from the simple viewpoint of winning and losing. From his perspective, OH should have been ashamed because his wrestler could not win (see 14-07). Through this conversation, OH's and IM's identities (i.e., OH as a programmer and IM as a nonprogrammer) became observable again.

"I Am Becoming a Computer Maniac": Relative Characteristics of Identity Formation. On the ninth and tenth days, OH was absent from class. During his absence, IM started to revise his program using IF, IFELSE, and REPEAT commands. During this period, IM spent much time with IU, asking him questions and discussing various points on programming techniques.

IM had changed drastically during these two days. He seemed to have started behaving like OH (i.e., like a "programmer"). He browsed through the manual frequently, trying to use commands and to figure out the reasons for his defeats. What caused the change? One possible answer is that the new human relationship enabled IM to display his competence as "programmer." The newly established IM–IU relationship was apparently different from the old IM–OH relationship. OH was capable of programming; he quickly understood commands and algorithms, and he was one of the most advanced learners in the classroom. Consequently, in the OH–IM relationship, IM may have relatively appeared to be a "nonprogrammer." However, IU was a slightly more advanced learner than IM; he sometimes gave IM information about programming techniques, although sometimes he asked IM questions. Thus, in the IM–IU relationship, IM was able to portray himself as a "programmer." As a result, IM appeared as a colleague programmer. Fragment 15 shows the transformation in IM's identity in the new human relationship.

Fragment 15:

    IM: I'm going to install a lot of fighting strategies into this program. Now, where can I find them? [picks up the manual and starts to browse through it] (15-01)
    IU: ( ) (15-02)
    IM: Hey, I guess I am becoming a computer maniac. (15-03)
    IU: Are you? (15-04)
    IM: I guess so. I am really getting into this silly stuff. (15-05)

This fragment shows an apparent change in IM's identity display from "nonprogrammer" to "programmer." IM categorized himself as a "computer maniac" here. "Computer maniac" supposedly has almost the same meaning as "computer nerd," although "computer maniac" is less derogatory than "computer nerd" is. This would be one reason why the category "computer maniac" was selected by IM to categorize himself. This transformation of identity may be possible in the IM–IU relationship, where IM is a coworker who has almost the same ability as IU. However, IM must not have been able to portray himself as a programmer in the OH–IM relationship, because OH was a much more advanced programmer. It is clear that one's identity is flexible, depending on the social relationship of which the person is a part.

```
REPEAT (22) [Offense]

TO Offense
IFELSE (:_his_posture > 2) [move_forward][move_back]
IF (:_my_posture <= 3) [bend_forward]
IF (:_his_posture = 2) [move_forward]
IF (:_my_posture > 2) [move_forward]
IF (:_my_posture = 4) [push_forward]
IFELSE (:_his_position = 8) [push_forward][grasp_mawashi]
IFELSE (:_his_posture = 4) [throw][grasp_mawashi]
IF (:_my_posture = 1) [bend_back]
IF (:_his_posture = 1) [throw]
IFELSE (:_my_hand = 2) [disturb_hishand][grasp_mawashi]
IFELSE (:_my_leg <= 3) [throw][move_forward]
END
```

FIG. 7.5. IM's new program.

It is interesting that IM was browsing through the manual (15-01) when he categorized himself as a "computer maniac." As we previously discussed, the activity "browsing manual" is bound to the category "programmer." This connection visualized IM's possible incumbency in the category "programmer" and his deviation from "brat community." Because it was noticeable for him, he had to state "Hey, I guess I am becoming a computer maniac" (15-03) to account for/excuse his browsing through the manual to IU as a member of the "brat community." This explains why he labeled AlgoArena as "silly stuff" in his next turn.

"My Forward-and-Push Days": Talking About the History of Learning. On the eleventh day, the students programmed their wrestlers for the Sumo tournament planned for the twelfth day, the last day of the class. OH returned to the class on the twelfth day, and the OH–IM pair was reunited. In the tournament, IM's wrestler, which had been revised using many control commands, had a sequence of victories. Figure 7.5 shows IM's new program. Conversely, OH's wrestler could not win, tying in all his bouts instead.

In the following fragment, IM and OH are talking about the strength of IM's wrestler.

Fragment 16:

IM: Hey, I'm the only one whose wrestler has been winning a lot of bouts in a row. (16-01)

OH: Is that right? (16-02)

IM: Yes, I am running up a string of consecutive victories. (16-03)

OH: Good for you. (16-04)

IM: I changed the content of my program a lot while you were away, using IFELSEs, tons of them, I . . . (16-05)

It is notable that IM attributed the strength of his wrestler to the incorporation of IFELSE commands (16-05). This statement indicates that IM had formed a new viewpoint that explained the strength of a wrestler in terms of how the program was made (i.e., from a programmer's perspective). Through this exchange, IM and OH were able to appear as "programmer" together. The word "IFELSE" was functioning as a shared artifact allowing them to talk about their tasks in a way a programmer would, and through utilizing this artifact in their conversation, they mutually confirmed their programmer identities.

Fragment 17:

[OH and IM are going to have a bout]
OH: I'm definitely going to win this time. hhhh. (17-01)
IM: Don't be too sure. (17-02)
OH: Maybe, you're right (17-03)
IM: But, in my forward-and-push days, I was hhh. (17-04)
OH: hhh, forward-and-push days, yeah. (17-05)
IM: My wrestler has gotten a lot stronger than before, don't you think so? (17-06)
OH: Yeah, it's better than the previous one. (17-07)

In this fragment, IM looked back on his previous programming style by labeling it "forward-and-push days" (17-04). By this statement, IM's simple sequential programming style, bound to the category "layperson," or "nonprogrammer," was transformed into a relic of the past, and IM's present status (i.e., "programmer") was highlighted. Through talking about IM's "forward-and-push days" together (17-04, 17-05), they made sure that both of them were standing in the same position: They are now fellow programmers. In short, their shared identity as "programmer" was formed on the foundation of their learning history; their learning trajectory was shaped by the historical accumulation of the mutual formation of their identities. It should be noted that the "history" was not a stable entity but was formed through this very exchange, and it was utilized as a resource to form their "now." In this fragment, OH's consistent identity as "programmer" becomes apparent. However, the observed sustainability of his identity does not necessarily imply the existence of a "prolonged identity" other than "identity as local establishment." The sustainability of the identity was also a consequence of continuous identity establishment through local interaction. That is, it came about by talking about the historical change of their identities, that is, from "OH as programmer and IM as nonprogrammer" to "OH and IM as fellow programmers."

The last exchange in this fragment (17-06, 17-07) is inconsistent with the fact that OH had never been able to defeat IM's "forward-and-push" wrestler no matter how hard he tried. This exchange shows that they were sharing the same perspective in viewing their activity. That is, both of them were seeing their activity as "producing a strong wrestler through programming techniques" rather than "producing a strong wrestler through any means." From this shared perspective, IM's new program including "tons of IFELSEs" was seen as "stronger" than the previous program that was "accidentally" strong. This shared perspective is their learning achievement at this point in time.

However, this status does not necessarily mean that they had reached a plateau of learning. Although being "fellow programmers" actually implies dissolution of the distinction between "programmer" and "nonprogrammer," the dissolution creates a new difference between OH and IM. The following conversation was subsequent to Fragment 18.

Fragment 18:

  IM: I can't believe that I made this program. I, the man of "push, push, forward." (18-01)
  OH: But you don't put IFELSE in the second brackets. (18-02)
  IU: ( ) difficult. [to IM] (18-03)
  IM: My, my brain will explode. (18-04)
  IU: ( ) hhh, yeah. (18-05)
  IM: hhh, I nearly break down. (18-06)
  IU: Me, too. (18-07)
  OH: Well, so, if you do that, you know. (18-08)
  IM: IFELSE, yeah. (18-09)
  OH: It's like, behavior is more clarified in a bout. (18-10)
  IM: Yeah, it expands the range of action. (18-11)
  OH: Let me see, what should I say? (18-12)
  IM: Well, if in this case, do this, if in another case, do this, if in another case, do this, right? (18-13)
  OH: Yeah. (18-14)
  IM: You can pick from many possible actions. (18-15)
  OH: It increases rules for act. (18-16)
  IM: (   ) (18-17)
  OH: You can take adequate actions, you know. (18-18)

In this fragment, OH pointed out that the IFELSE commands in IM's program were not nested (18-02). Nesting IFELSE commands is an advanced technique of programming and it enables complex strategies to be incorporated into the wrestler's program. A comparison of Fig. 7.4 with Fig. 7.5 shows that OH employed this technique, whereas IM did not. OH's statement indicated IM's relative lack of skill. IM responded: "my brain will explode" (18-04) and then "I nearly break down" (18-06). It seems that IM tried to invalidate OH's statement and to avoid talking about the programming technique by jesting. However, IM started talking about IFELSE nesting (18-09) when OH initiated the topic again (18-08). They talked about the significance of IFELSE nesting and its usefulness in the rest of the conversation (18-10 to 18-18) where both of them appeared as "programmer." IM, who once showed lack of knowledge and reluctance to talk about the advanced technique in the beginning of this fragment, was categorized as "junior programmer," not as "nonprogrammer"; thus OH was reflexively categorized as "senior programmer." This new distinction could be an impetus to the next phase of their collaborative learning.

On the last day, OH and IM were mutually categorizing themselves as "programmer." In their interaction, being a "programmer" did not appear to be a deviation from being a "brat." In other words, the contradiction between "programmer" and "brat" was not relevant in their conversation on this day. Given that the contradiction of programmer versus brat was based on the fact that they saw the AlgoArena activity as a didactic activity given by the teacher; the observed dissolution of the contradiction would at least suggest a change in their conception of the AlgoArena activity, that is, from a compelling educational activity to a student-owned activity in which brats might participate and have fun. The fact that they were engaging in a Sumo tournament on this day, during which they craved for competitions, boasted their own victories, and teased friends who were defeated, would be one explanation for this change. In this situation, to be a "programmer" (i.e., a "person who defeats other wrestlers in bouts") was given a preferable status in the "brat" community, and thus conflict between "programmer" and "brat" seems to have been dissolved.

CONCLUSION

This chapter describes the process of identity formation and transformation in the collaborative learning through AlgoArena. The participatory observation and the close analysis of conversation revealed the following:

1. The membership category collection "programmer/nonprogrammer" appeared in the AlgoArena classroom. The students categorized themselves and others as "programmer" or "nonprogrammer." Through this categorization work, programming activity was mutually visualized; constituted and visualized by the students.
2. The activity "browsing manual" was used as a shared resource for mutual formation of identity as a "programmer."

3. The membership category collection "programmer/nonprogrammer" was linked to the category collection "conforming student/brat" that was indigenous to the classroom, and conflict between "to be a programmer" and "to be a brat" appeared. Thus, identity formation in the classroom inevitably included coordination between "to be a programmer" and "to be a brat." The coordination brought redefinition of AlgoArena activity as "student-owned activity."

4. Identity display was flexible, depending on the social relationship of which the person was a part.

5. Their identity as "programmer" was visualized through historical accumulation of local interaction in which their identity was displayed, confirmed, and sanctioned.

In conclusion, the learning process of OH and IM in the AlgoArena classroom was shaped through their continuous collaborative enterprise in which they mutually and contingently formed and transformed their identities and activities. AlgoArena provided learners with abundant and varied resources for the process.

REFERENCES

Bödker, B. (1991). *Through the interface: A human activity approach to user interface design.* Hillsdale, NJ: Lawrence Erlbaum Associates.

Brown, J. S., Collins, A., & Duguid, P. (1988). *Situated cognition and the culture of learning* (IRL Rep. No. IRL88-0008). [Institute of Research on Learning, CA, USA]

Engeström, Y. (1986). The zone of proximal development as the basic category of educational psychology. *The Quarterly Newsletter of the Laboratory of Comparative Human Cognition, 8*(1), 23–42.

Kato, H., & Ide, A. (1995). Using a game for social setting in a learning environment: AlgoArena—A tool for learning software design. *CSCL'95 Proceedings*, pp. 195–199.

Koschmann, T. (1996). *CSCL: Theory and practice of an emerging paradigm.* Hillsdale, NJ: Lawrence Erlbaum Associates.

Lave, J., & Wenger, E. (1991). *Situated learning: Legitimate peripheral participation.* Cambridge: Cambridge University Press.

Sacks, H. (1972a). On the analyzability of stories by children. In J. J. Gumperz and D. Hymes (Eds.), *Directions in sociolinguistics: The ethnography of communication* (pp. 329–345). New York: Holt, Reinhart and Winston.

Sacks, H. (1972b). An initial investigation of the usability of conversational data for doing sociology. In D. N. Sudnow (Ed.), *Studies in social interaction* (pp. 31–74). New York: Free Press.

Sacks, H. (1992). *Lectures on conversation* (Vol. 1). Oxford: Basil Blackwell.

Watson, D. R. (1997). The presentation of victim and motive in discourse: The case of police interrogations and interviews. In. Travers, M. & Manzo, J. F. (eds.). *Law in Action: Ethnomethodological & Conversation Analytic Approaches to Law* (pp. 77–97). Aldershot, UK: Dartmouth Publishing Co.

GOING BEYOND DESCRIPTION

Hideyuki Suzuki
Ibaraki University

Hiroshi Kato
National Institute of Multimedia Education

We would like to thank the three reviewers, Ray McDermott, James Greeno, and Douglas Macbeth, for giving us their encouraging and inspiring comments. Insights from McDermott and Greeno's review led us to reexamine what we have achieved and still have to achieve in the AlgoArena project. The rethinking helped us to pinpoint future directions in our research and discover what kind of challenges we may yet have to cope with. Macbeth's review, which is critical as well as significant, provided us with an opportunity to reflect on our identity and position when adopting ethnomethodological analysis for researching and designing computer-based learning environments. This reflection further assisted us in confirming our goals.

POLYSEMOUS TOOLS AND SCHOOL REFORM

Conventional computer-based learning systems have aimed at supporting instructors to teach students. Those systems have been designed and operated based on existing concepts of what "learning" and "school" are, and they have contributed to maintaining the present concepts, regardless of the developer's intentions. Some CSCL researchers such as Scardamalia & Bereiter (1996) and ourselves are endeavoring to break the cycle of using this traditional concept, which is a cornerstone in the foundation of such conventional systems. Our goal is to provide alternatives to these concepts. In our project, AlgoArena has acted as an agent for this sought-after change.

Our system aims at reconfiguring the existing relationship between learners, and teachers, learners and learners, as well as learners/teachers and tools. It will strive to create yet another type of learning in schools.

Observation in the AlgoArena classroom clearly showed how AlgoArena contributed to this change in various ways. However, as McDermott and Greeno pointed out, what happened in the AlgoArena classroom was much more complex than we had anticipated. What we observed in the AlgoArena classroom was not a monolithic "alternative activity" brought about by AlgoArena but rather a continuous constitution of different activities (e.g., learning how to program, programming, and playing games) as well as ongoing transitions from one activity to another. More importantly, these were mutually achieved by students through local interaction. Their learning as the process of identity formation/transformation was visualized both for themselves and us as well as observers, through the fact that they participated in the work.

Their learning process was observable through the dynamism of interlocked activities. In the process, AlgoArena appeared as a mediation tool upon which multiple activities were constituted and woven together, and thus, transitions among them were enabled. We believe that the polysemy of AlgoArena was the foundation of this mediation. AlgoArena can be a tool for such activities as gaming practices in which a win–lose situation is of the utmost interest; for programming practices in which the logical composition of commands to represent the algorithm is mainly focused on; and, of course, for school-like practices of programming learning in which achievement in tasks given by teachers and the demonstration of individual competence and improvement are highlighted. This polysemy allows various activities to overlap and conflict with each other in AlgoArena, which provides a common foundation for the activities, and, at the same time, allows students to move from one activity to another passing through AlgoArena.

This observation in the AlgoArena classroom has suggested a strategy to us for reforming school practices through designing educational systems. Our strategy is to constructively produce conflict between existing school activities and others different from the conventional school procedures in terms of shared goals and values. More specifically, our strategy is to produce an expanded field of possibilities upon which artifacts (i.e., tools and shared terms, embedded in school-like activities) would, in the next circumstance, be inserted into different kind of activities such as programming and gaming. These artifacts would be repositioned and given new significance in the different activities, while being exploited as resources for forming the activities recursively. In the opposite direction, in this area, artifacts situated in gaming or programming activity would be brought into school-like activities and be reconstituted in the different relevance systems. Polysemous tools would effectively mediate between these activities, as was the case with AlgoArena. It is expected that traditional school-like activities, in which teachers and students are collaboratively maintaining their roles of the "person who teaches" and the "person who is taught" (see Mehan, 1979), would be relativized in relation to other activities based on the different social relationships and values. In this relativization, the school-like activities, which repeatedly fill the classroom, are deconstructed. It is important that, in this deconstruction work, the school-like activities are not concealed from the students but are visualized for students by juxtaposition with the other activities and thus repositioned.

DURABILITY OF IDENTITIES

According to our definition, identity is visualized for/by members in a community of practice through local interaction in which they indicate and confirm each others' identities. At times, they attack others' identities while defending their own identity against attack. In this way, our concept of identity is compatible with Macbeth's recommendation. However, there may be a subtle but important difference between our two definitions. It has to do with the durable nature of identity: We consider identity to be reproductive. We feel strongly that identity is always mutually constituted/reconstituted through local interactions. However, at the same time, we consider that it appears persistently, repeatedly, and sometimes insistently. We believe that this durability would be established through the exploitation of one's memory about past interactions[1] and artifacts that mark identities (e.g., terms such as "nerd" or "programmer") and certain ways of talking and behaving, all of which serve as resources for constituting a durable nature of identity. Consequently, since durability of identity is also locally achieved, it should be noted that durability of identity is consistent with a locality of identity. In our chapter, we describe identity as an observable feature of local interaction. Moreover, we do not use the description as the wherewithal or practical enactment of "identity formation" as a formal analytic object-process.

---

[1]It should be noted that talking about influence of human memory on interaction does not necessarily lead us to cognitivism. It is incontestable, we believe, that people memorize their past, possibly in their brains, and exploit the memorized information for current interaction. This claim does not simply coincide with the idea that treats memory as substantial or as an internal control structure. We are inspired by Suchman's (1987) notion of plan in treating the problem of human memory brought into local interaction. That is, we consider that memory, no matter whether it is information inside the human brain or inscription, restrains people's actions weakly while it is contingently reconstructed in the very interaction. It is one of the resources for interaction.

RESPONSE TO THE ALTERNATIVE INTERPRETATION

We now reply to the alternative interpretation of our analysis given by Macbeth. Empirical facts do not support his interpretation of OH's statement: "Shit (Aho, in Japanese), I made this program last night." It was uttered before OH typed in the program (the program was written on a small piece of paper. And OH had to type in the program to see the result.), and so he could not know whether his work of the night before had produced good results or had gone for naught. Therefore, "it was uttered as OH discovered that his work of the night before had gone for naught" (from Macbeth's review) is a misunderstanding. We must admit that this was caused by oversight in our demonstration. We should have been very careful in providing ethnographic information in our paper.

Macbeth discusses the strength of the word "shit" as a vituperative expression; however, what is important in the utterance is that this expression was selected and located in a situation where there was no necessity to use it. In this respect, whether it is strong or not does not matter. The utilization of the expression made OH's utterance: "I made this program last night" carry additional connotation rather than simply reporting that he made the program last night. Of course, the meaning of the utterance cannot be fixed by itself. Within the sequence of their conversation, it appeared to observers as well as to the participants that he mentioned his overnight programming in an embarrassed and irritated manner.

ETHNOMETHODOLOGICAL IMAGINATION AND EDUCATIONAL RESEARCH

We question why our delete analysis was considered by Macbeth as anti-ethnomethodology. Perhaps, we should have been more careful to use the term "brat" and "programmer." It is certain that the students were engaged in so-called boundary work and that the resources for the work were given within or through their local interaction. In other words, they mutually visualized a boundary based on linguistic, demonstrative, and inferential resources. They sometimes displayed to each other that they abided in the same ambits and, then, that they were separated by the boundary. This is precisely what our analysis indicated. We utilized the terms "brat" and "programmer" to represent what we observed in the field. The terms were not resources utilized by the students themselves for their local boundary work but were imported by us as researchers to express what they had achieved. The lack of thoroughness of in situ description in our demonstration might have caused the criticism.

We suppose the core of this problem resides in the different stands taken by Macbeth, an ethnomethodologist, and ourselves as educational system designers. In short, Macbeth never commits to educational changes, while we do. He may, as an ethnomethodologist, describe how interaction in school occurs, and how individual achievement or deviation is constituted through local interaction, but he is basically indifferent to drawing implications from the analysis and impinging upon school reform or improvement of educational methods and philosophies. This is exactly what Lynch (1993) calls ethnomethodological indifference. Holding this attitude is an imperative part of Macbeth's qualification as an ethnomethodologist, and it is understandable that he adheres to this attitude in his analysis to preserve the ethnomethodological purity of his research.

In contrast, we commit to the field of education as educational system designers who lean strongly toward school reform. This commitment is an integral part of our professional goals and we cannot abandon it. Our practice necessarily trespasses against the commandment of ethnomethodological indifference. In our project, ethnomethodological analysis is positioned as one of methods in the course of educational reform. It is used to investigate complexity of social relationship in the classroom and how relations among students as well as relations between students and artifacts are changed through local interaction within an computer-based learning environment. For this purpose, we need to describe how members construct the situation. We strive to focus on "their" method to construct their reality and do not have any intention to import extra-situational social structures or norms as an explanation. It would be fair to say that Macbeth and our group share a common ethnomethodological perspective in this stage of our discourse. However, ethnomethodological description is only the halfway point of our research. Our interest goes beyond collecting or accumulating descriptions continuously, although it is certain that ethnomethodological descriptions are somehow instructive. Achievement of a new learning environment with the aid of inspiration by ethnomethodological descriptions is our main professional interest and goal. Designing a new learning environment involves both forming learning activities based on alternative values in classrooms and fostering discourse in which the learning activities are treated as estimable among members of the educational community, which includes teachers, school reformers, educational theorist, and educational system designers. Therefore, our design is a political process, in which we endeavor to influence concrete fields of education. To this end, we need to start to relate what goes on in the AlgoArena classroom to the educational community and, of course, to ourselves. Consequently, in our chapter, vernacular life in the classroom described previously within the situation is to be reconfigured into descriptions that are understandable and meaningful for members of the educational community. In this sense, our research seems to go beyond the ethnomethodological restraint. However, we do not feel we are driven by ambition for theorization. What we are seriously striving to do through our descriptive work where Macbeth found theoretical ambition is to visualize vernacular.

Whereas theorization obscures an agent who theorizes and claims that its outcome is a general fact/truth, visualization provides a description from one particular viewpoint, and thus, correctness or significance of the visualization work depends on its usefulness for a specific purpose, not on consistency with truth.[2] In other words, visualization is based on the viewpoint of people who engage in a certain work; not only does it organize the work; it also gets reconstructed through mutual construction of the work. Visualization work is also embedded in the vernacular. In this sense, reflective consideration from the viewpoint of referential reflexivity (Pollner, 1991) on how we visualize vernacular within the context of our project would be creative. Practically, the reflection would prevent our visualization work from concealing a particular viewpoint and turning into theorization in the course of our design work. Moreover, theoretically, it expands the current notion of the educational system, which is considered as a function system composed of artifacts, learners, and teachers, by adding to it educational researchers who are trying to make the system meaningful within the educational community by analyzing and expressing what goes on in the field.[3]

The viewpoints of both ethnomethodological analysts and that of educational environment designers are compatible in our research. We admit that this is a potential source of theoretical and methodological impurity. However, we believe that our hybridism can be productive in terms of our professional goals.

REFERENCES

Lynch, M. (1993). *Scientific practice and ordinary action: Ethnomethodology and social studies of science.* New York: Cambridge University Press.

Mehan, H. (1979). *Learning lessons: The social organization of classroom instruction.* Cambridge, MA: Harvard University Press.

Pollner, M. (1991). Left of ethnomethodology. *American Sociological Review, 56,* 370–380.

Scardamalia, M., & Bereiter, C. (1996). Computer support for knowledge-building communities. In T. Koschmann (Ed.), *CSCL: Theory and practice of an emerging paradigm* (pp. 249–268). Mahwah, NJ: Lawrence Erlbaum.

Suchman, L. A. (1987). *Plans and situated actions: The problem of human–computer communication.* New York: Cambridge University Press.

---

[2]Strictly speaking, theorization is a type of visualization practice.

[3]We recognize that referential reflexivity leads us to infinite regress. However, infinite regress may be virtually impossible. Since expected outcomes of our project are concrete actions in a concrete field, the regress would be practically resolved because our ideas must be realized within real space and time.

8

INDIVIDUAL AND COLLECTIVE ACTIVITIES IN EDUCATIONAL COMPUTER GAME PLAYING

Victor Kaptelinin
Umeå University

Michael Cole
University of California, San Diego

THE SOCIAL NATURE OF LEARNING: IMPLICATIONS FOR CSCL

There are two distinct (though not mutually exclusive) views on the role of social context in human learning and development. According to the first view, learning is an individual process, which can be facilitated or inhibited depending on how individuals interact with each other. For instance, the need to communicate an understanding of the problem at hand to other participants in a problem-solving session can force people to formulate their ideas more carefully and, thus, improve reflection and planning (cf. Blaye & Light, 1995).

The second view holds that social context cannot be reduced to a set of external "modifiers." It contends that individual learning and social interactions are different aspects of the same phenomenon. This view is often associated with Vygotskian notions of "inter-psychological" functions and the "Zone of Proximal Development" (or ZPD, Vygotsky, 1978), which are becoming more and more popular in the field of CSCL (e.g., Kaptelinin, 1999; Koschmann, 1996; O'Malley, 1995). Vygotsky claimed that there are always two steps in acquiring a new ability: First, the ability emerges as distributed between people (i.e., it exists as an "inter-psychological" function) and, second, it is mastered by individuals (i.e., it becomes an "intra-psychological" function) (Vygotsky, 1983).

Having acquired a new ability, the individual can contribute more to socially distributed processes. Therefore, intra-individual and inter-individual functions mutually constitute each other. In other words, not only does collaboration between the learner and other people change some preexisting individual phenomenon, but it also directs and shapes both the general orientation and specific content of individual development. Participation in a collective activity lays the foundation for the next step in individual development or, according to Vygotsky, creates the Zone of Proximal Development, which is defined as "the distance between the actual development level as determined by independent problem solving and the level of potential development as determined through problem solving under adult guidance or in collaboration with more capable peers" (Vygotsky, 1978).

Undoubtedly, these ideas have profound implications for education, including those related to development and implementation of computer-based environments intended to support collaborative learning. The attempts to apply these ideas in the field of CSCL have revealed, however, the need for a more specific and concrete understanding of the mechanisms underlying learning within the Zone of Proximal Development (e.g., Cole & Engeström, 1993; Kaptelinin, 1999). Vygotsky's original definition of the ZPD allows for different interpretations, which imply different strategies for creating computer-based environments for collaborative learning (see Valsiner & van der Veer, 1991).

In an earlier paper entitled "The Zone of Proximal Development: Where culture and cognition create each other" Cole (1985) discussed the unique role of the Zone of Proximal Development as a mediator between individual and social phenomena. According to this analysis, the notion of ZPD can help to bridge the gap between the individual and the social by introducing a mechanism of their mutual determination. In the present chapter we elaborate on this idea by bringing in concepts from Activity Theory, developed by Vygotsky's disciple Leontiev (1978), as well as empirical data collected within the Fifth Dimension project. From our point of view, these data may indicate some specific ways that individual and social phenomena mutually determine each other.

The rest of the chapter is organized into four sections. The first two sections are brief overviews of, respectively, main concepts used in this paper and of the Fifth Dimension project. The third section introduces the "life cycle" of the individual/social dynamics in the Fifth Dimension and illustrates it with a number of examples. Finally, the fourth section focuses on the implications of the study for computer-supported collaborative learning.

INDIVIDUAL AND COLLECTIVE ACTIVITIES

According to Activity Theory (Leontiev, 1978), the human mind can only be understood within the context of interaction between individuals ("subjects") and the world ("objects"). This interaction takes place at three hierarchical levels: 1. activities, which correspond to human needs and are directed toward objects (i.e., "motives") that can fulfill those needs, 2. goal-oriented actions, which should be carried out to achieve a motive, and 3. situationally determined operations, which should be performed to attain a goal. In human activities, motivation, emotions, goal setting, cognition, and motor processes are integrated into coherent wholes.

Two main ideas underlie Activity Theory. First, the mind does not exist prior to and without activities; rather, it develops as a constituent of human interaction with the world. Activities constitute individuals as subjects by situating them in the objective world. Second, activities are sociocultural in nature. They are determined not by the straightforward logic of biological survival but by various aspects of the sociocultural environment, for instance, norms, routines, expectations, etc., of a specific culture.

There has been a growing interest in Activity Theory in such diverse areas as developmental work research, industrial design, human–computer interaction, and education, including CSCL (see, e.g., Favorin, 1995; Kaptelinin, 1996; Kuutti, 1991; Teasley & Roschelle, 1993).

Originally, Activity Theory was developed as a psychological approach dealing almost exclusively with individual activities (Leontiev, 1978). However, there have been several attempts to extend Activity Theory to cover activities of supra-individual entities, for instance, groups, organizations, and communities. Perhaps, the most well-known new approach to Activity Theory has been proposed by Yrjo Engeström (1987, 1992), who developed the notion of an *activity system* that includes not only individual subjects interacting with objects but communities as well. Therefore, any analysis of a human activity should focus on a three-way interaction among subjects, objects, and communities, mediated by tools, rules, and division of labor (Engeström, 1987). Another approach, proposed by, among others, Arthur Petrovsky (Petrovsky & Petrovsky, 1983) is based on the notion of the *collective subject*. Collective subjects are supra-individual entities (such as groups or organizations) that have their own motives and goals. Therefore, interaction of supra-individual entities with the world can also be interpreted in terms of "subject-object" interactions, and at least some concepts developed within Activity Theory may apply to collective activities.

So far, there has been little overlap between studies of individual and collective activities from the point of view of Activity Theory. Given the basic assumptions of the two above approaches to collective activities, it hardly seems surprising. Both of them, essentially, consider individual activities as component parts of collective ones. According to Engeström, for instance, activities can only be collective. The scope of individual interactions with the world does not transcend the level of actions. In other words, individuals cannot be subjects of full-scale activities; when their actions comprise an activity, we always find a collective activity. The notion of collective subject implies that individual subjects (and their activities) are completely integrated into a higher-level social structure.

Therefore, existing theoretical accounts of collective activities imply that individual activities (or actions) are subordinated to collective ones. From our point of view, it is important that focus on collective activities does not rule out the need and the possibility to study how individual and collective activities interact to create each other. Otherwise one can easily overlook the fact that such interactions do take place in reality, at either individual or supra-individual level. For instance, an information system can fail even if it fits into the general structure of an organization. If people using the system see it as a threat to their own interests, the system will most probably be rejected (see Grudin, 1990). In other words, a collective activity can be disorganized because of a discrepancy between individuals' goals as determined by the structure of the collective activity and the "personal" goals or motives of the individuals. However, differences between individual and collective activities seem to exist within the subjective plane, too. Requirements and demands of a collective activity, which come into conflict with goals and interests of the individual, may cause serious personal problems.

In our view, contradictions between individual and collective activities cannot be considered an exclusively negative factor. Such contradictions and their resolution are an important mechanism underlying learning within the Zone of Proximal Development. As we discuss in this chapter, such contradictions can result in a revision of individual values, goals, and strategies and, consequently, in creating new forms of joint activity.

In summary, our hypothesis about the mechanisms underlying ZPD is based on the assumption that learners are simultaneously involved in two hierarchies of actions. On the one hand, they pursue their individual goals, and, on the other, together with other people they strive to formulate and achieve goals of collective actions. These hierarchies have to overlap, so that some goals belong to both of them; otherwise people would not participate in collective activities at all. This overlapping, however, cannot be complete, and so the learner has two (or more) potentially conflicting perspectives. Such contradictions can be a driving force behind emergence of new individual activities, actions, and operations.[1] This hypothesis is discussed and elaborated on in the following on the basis of empirical data collected within the Fifth Dimension project.

---

[1]These contradictions do not necessarily take the form of a conflict. The learner, for instance, can simply extend his or her repertoire of activities.

THE FIFTH DIMENSION PROJECT: AN OVERVIEW

Objectives

The Fifth Dimension project was initiated in 1986 as an alternative to the technology-centered approach to educational computer use dominant at that time. The focus of the project was not on technological innovations but on the social context of the use of technology that would provide optimal conditions for children's learning and development (Nicolopoulou & Cole, 1993). Sustainability was one of the guiding principles of the project from the outset; an explicit goal was to design a generic social setting that could potentially be incorporated into existing institutions and could survive without special support from researchers. Computer tools—more specifically, educational computer games—were considered as just a component of the target system.

Setting Design

The target setting was designed as a "model culture," with its own rules, norms, artifacts, and mythology. Collaborative computer game playing is the central activity in the setting. This activity is regulated by a set of specially created artifacts, including (a) "task cards," which structure the game playing process and emphasize the educational component of game playing by offering additional game related tasks and stimulating writing and reflection; (b) "the consequence chart," which determines game playing sequences by providing the child with a choice of available games after a certain performance level in a certain game is achieved; and (c) "the Constitution of the Fifth Dimension," which contains the basic rules of the setting. Children are supposed to play together with undergraduate students attending the site. To minimize the power differences between the children and the adults in the Fifth Dimension, a mythical figure of "the Wizard" was introduced into the system. All conflicts between the Fifth Dimension "citizens" can only be resolved by the Wizard who can be contacted via e-mail.

Games

A wide variety of computer games are used in the Fifth Dimension, including knowledge games (e.g., the Carmen San Diego series), simulation/modeling games (e.g., SimSity, Designasaurus), drill-and-practice games (e.g., Word Munchers), logical games (e.g., Pond, Gertrude's Puzzles), and math games (e.g., Shark). Even arcade-style games (e.g., Choplifter) proved to be beneficial when used in an appropriate context. For instance, task cards associated with each game often require that children describe their strategies and write hints to others. Therefore, even a simple, "noneducational" game can stimulate reflection and development of writing skills.

Implementation Strategy

To become sustainable, a Fifth Dimension setting has to obtain necessary resources from external sources on a long-term basis. In other words, it has to meet long-term needs of some institutions. So, the problem was to identify institutions motivated enough to provide necessary support. The specific solution to this problem was establishing a university–community partnership. It was assumed that communities were interested in extending educational opportunities for the children while universities were interested in increasing the quality of undergraduate education. The Fifth Dimension offered a way to meet these needs by combining complementary resources: children, space, and some equipment (community) and undergraduate students to help children learn (university). This strategy proved to be successful. The network of Fifth Dimension sites has been steadily growing and now there are a number of sites in the United States and other countries, including Russia, Sweden, and Finland.

The high ratio of grownups in the Fifth Dimension provides a unique possibility for using the Vygotskian notion of the Zone of Proximal Development in organizing learning processes in the setting.

The Social Setting of the Fifth Dimension in an External Context

Various aspects of learning and development in social context are being studied within the Fifth Dimension project. In this paper we will focus on individual and collective activities, which should be differentiated from other possible levels of analysis, namely the level of the social setting as a whole and the level of "external context."

A comparison of different implementations of the Fifth Dimension model in different institutional environments provides enough evidence for the conclusion that the setting itself is influenced by a higher level context. This context can tentatively be called "external context." In the case of a Fifth Dimension site this external context is usually composed of a research lab, a university department, and a community center. All these institutions provide resources and impose constraints on the setting, while the setting itself provides resources and imposes constraints on collective activities of computer game playing. Also, each of these institutions is primarily interested in one particular aspect of the Fifth Dimension as a whole (e.g., children learning, undergraduates learning, research data). Because specific expectations, criteria, and resources of different institutions are not the same, the specific implementations of the Fifth Dimension are also different.

For example, at the first stage of establishing a Fifth Dimension site in a Mexicano community there was an attempt to use the same Fifth Dimension model that was previously implemented in an Anglo community. This approach was not successful. A number of modifications had to be made (including a different name for the setting) to adapt the generic structure of the social setting to the specific external context (Vasquez, 1993). The same process of adaptation takes place every time a new Fifth Dimension site emerges. The variety of the Fifth Dimension illustrates the ways the external context shapes specific implementation of the same concept.

THREE PHASES OF INTERSUBJECTIVITY

As mentioned previously, we consider interaction between individual and collective activities to be of critical importance for learning and development in social context. In this section we present this idea in more detail and illustrate with empirical data.

Our point of departure is that the same individual can be involved in two or more hierarchies of actions, which can never completely coincide. Therefore, contradictions among interests, values, objectives, and requirements ensuing from different activity structures are practically inevitable. Such contradictions can be resolved either by one activity taking over and the other being discarded (the person abandons collective activity or is forced to take part in it even against his/her will) or by finding a compromise. In the latter case the individual may decide that the collective activity in question matches his/her higher level goals and participating in it would be a reasonable thing to do, even if some aspects of that activity may not seem clear or attractive to the individual. It is important to emphasize that the outcome of such a decision can considerably exceed what has been originally expected by the individual. By actually taking part in a collective activity (even if following its rules and meeting requirements may initially seem an "inevitable sacrifice" people can find out what the activity really is. The underlying logic, implicit meanings and values, and other aspects of an activity, which are difficult to communicate to an outsider, can be readily appropriated by those who have a first-hand experience. In other words, participation in a new activity opens up a possibility for appropriating a new action. Such appropriation, in turn, may have consequences for individual learning, either short-term ones (new action is discarded once the individual has accomplished his/her goal) or long-term ones (new action is added to the repertoire of individual's actions).

In the rest of this section we illustrate interaction between individual and collective activities with empirical data collected within the Fifth Dimension project. More specifically, we give examples of what we call "three phases of intersubjectivity." If the mechanisms outlined above describe learning in social context correctly, then participation in collective activities should go through at least three distinct phases.

At the first phase there is an individual activity and an emerging collective activity. Individuals do not participate in a collective activity yet, but they are involved in establishing a common ground for shared understanding of objectives, procedures, and conditions of their participation. That is why this phase can be defined as "intersubjectivity."

The second phase can be observed when individuals are actually playing computer games in groups. At this phase, which is characterized by established intersubjectivity, both individual and collective activities take place.

The third phase corresponds to situations when collective activities are over but individuals manifest their "residues" in their individual activities or other collective activities. For the lack of a better term, we call this phase "postintersubjectivity." By this we do not imply that intersubjectivity disappears once individuals appropriate collective activities. Undoubtedly, collaboration in long-standing teams can be characterized by both effective appropriation and remarkable intersubjectivity. Rather, "postintersubjectivity" refers to a specific feature of the Fifth Dimension. Namely, collective activities are quite limited in time there. Usually children play different games with different adults when they come to the Fifth Dimension. Therefore, appropriation of a collective activity cannot typically be observed until after the activity is over.

The main source of empirical data about learning and development in the Fifth Dimension are field notes written by undergraduate students after each site visit. A small subset of these field notes are used here to provide examples illustrating the "life cycle" of intersubjectivity.

Phase 1. External Coordination of Individual Activities (Pre-intersubjectivity)

People come to the Fifth Dimension with their individual goals. Children may, for instance, want to play their favorite games, socialize with undergraduate students, or just find out what the Fifth Dimension is about. Undergraduate students may want to learn more about child development, complete course requirements, or have fun playing with children. In the Fifth Dimension people cannot attain their goals alone. The structure of the setting requires that they form teams and get what they want only as a result of coordinated teamwork. In many cases team formation presents no problems, especially when both children and adults are experienced Fifth Dimension citizens:

> I entered the Fifth Dimension at about 3:15 and I was immediately approached by Paul. He did not say anything to me, he just pointed at me and then at the computer. I asked him if he was ready to play and he said yes.
> Tami K., 4/20/95

However, in some cases team formation does present a problem. A child can be interested in a game and wish to follow the rules of the Fifth Dimension but be uncooperative; for instance:

> She was quite confident that she was able to complete the task independently. [. . .] It wasn't like "go away I can do it myself," it appeared to be more of an automatic reaction for her just to do it herself.
> Colleen M., 03/05/94

Even more serious problems emerge if the child does not want to follow the rules of the Fifth Dimension and/or rejects any help.

> When I said 9/4 is the answer he said to me, "you are wrong, that's wrong, that's not the answer." He did not even know that you can divide with fractions and he was not willing to pay attention to me while I told him. I even tried to make a ruler out of paper but he did not want to hear how we could use it to help us.
> Marly Z., 05/17/94

Phase 2. Emerging Group Identity (Intersubjectivity)

When individuals just start acting together, there is usually little indication of intersubjectivity, even when individual activities are relatively well co-ordinated. In problematic cases, described in the previous section, lack of coordination makes intersubjectivity even more difficult to develop. However, eventually most groups enter the phase of true collaborative activity.

> The change that came over Jonathan was remarkable. [. . .] He increased his interaction with me 100%. We joked about the game, and he was constantly filling in any missing background noises, cheering his successes, laughing at or berating the enemy.
> Michael R., 02/05/94

Collaborative game playing at this stage is characterized by efficient coordination of individual efforts, and this is often associated with strong emotions, both positive and negative, shared by members of a team. Also, in such cases undergraduate students often use "we" when they describe joint efforts of a team; for example:

> We were very careful and suddenly with the move of one square, we completed the puzzle. [...] Jennifer cheered and I was just as excited. There we did it, moved Jennifer on up but with the help of Ben and the Wizard of course.
>
> Marly Z., 05/10/94

Note, that in the above example "we" refers to the team, consisting of a child and an adult, which is contrasted to "external persons," who also contributed to the achievement (i.e., a boy from another team, Ben, and the Wizard). The outcome of the team effort was a "promotion" of the child, Jennifer, to the rank of a "Young Wizard Assistant."

Phase 3. Transfer of Group Experience to Individual Activities (Postintersubjectivity)

From children's point of view, the most important features of collective activities in the Fifth Dimension are, probably, the requirement to follow the rules of the setting and the emphasis on educational activities specified in the task cards. In many cases newcomers to the Fifth Dimension consider meeting these requirements an inevitable price they have to pay for the opportunity to have fun, that is, to just play computer games they like. In the previous sections we gave some examples that illustrate the resistance to what children consider as distractions from having fun and how this attitude can be overcome by involvement in a collective activity. Moreover, most children (at least, on some occasions) start paying attention to the specially designed "side" activities and following the rules of the setting without being prompted to do so.

> Henry began to fill out the task card with priority. I was amazed at how much attention he finally decided to give the task card. At every interval when we started playing the game the right way, he'd stop and plot his move and whatever the screen said. One time the screen cleared as soon as he finished a game and he said, "damn I missed it, do you remember the numbers or do we have to play again?"
>
> Marly Z., 05/17/94

Sometimes children even start to take responsibility for the coordination of collective activities.

> Christina did very well in this level. She asked me to write the expressions on her task card as she said them outloud to speed up the process.
>
> Nami K., 05/23/94

Finally, there are numerous documented cases of how participation in collaborative game playing can result in learning outcomes. Children develop basic skills (reading, writing, typing), acquire new facts and problem solving strategies.

> It was great playing this game with Matt because I could tell that he was learning from our interaction. Like I said, eventually he could match the clue to the picture on his own. [. . .] Sometimes in the game, you would run across the same clue or you would end up taking a picture of a robot that you already had a picture of—Matt would remember which pictures he had and he would also remember listening to the clue from before.
>
> Nami K., 05/24/94

CONCLUSIONS

The analyses in this chapter have two broad implications for the field of CSCL. First, successful learning is promoted when it occurs within authentic activities, that is, when learners attain meaningful goals and are intellectually and emotionally engaged in the tasks they carry out. In this chapter we attempted to demonstrate that this idea, which is currently widely accepted within the CSCL community, applies not only to individual activities but to collective activities as well. In other words, educational benefits of collaboration critically depend on the degree to which learners are involved in their collective activity. Putting children and adults together is a necessary but not sufficient condition of genuine collaboration. Therefore, creating environments for computer-supported collaborative learning should include evaluation and support of authentic collective activities.

Second, our study indicates a number of factors that should be taken into consideration when setting up environments for collaborative learning. They include:

Meeting a diversity of interests. People participate in collective activities for a variety of reasons. If collaboration is arranged so that it can accommodate a diversity of individual interests, more people can find it attractive (or the same people can find it more attractive).

Meaningful outcomes of collaboration. If collaboration cannot help people to reach new goals, that is, if by acting alone they can achieve the same (or better) results, children are less inclined to cooperate or can even find cooperation a nuisance. So, collective activities should be arranged so that learners can attain goals that are difficult or impossible to reach alone.

Choice. Genuine collaborative learning rarely takes place when people are forced to collaborate and required to follow prespecified procedures.

Positive outcomes of collaboration are usually observed under conditions that ensure that participants take responsibility for their contribution. Therefore, it is important that CSCL systems provide opportunities for the participants to make choices.

Time. Team identities take time to develop. It is a complex process in which emerging identity, improving performance, and smoother coordination mutually influence each other. Therefore, CSCL settings should allow enough time for development of authentic collective activities.

Initial Success. Our data indicate that initial success can greatly facilitate collaboration, whereas initial failures often result in a lack of interest in the collaborative endeavor.

Shared emotions. As mentioned before, authentic collaboration is often associated with strong emotions shared by the participants. A possibility for learners to share their emotions seems to be an important factor of the development of "collective subjects." Because in the Fifth Dimension collaboration is of the "same place/same time" type, it is easy to express and share emotions there. However, in other types of collaborative environments (e.g., distance learning) limited possibilities for expressing and sharing emotions can be an obstacle to genuine collaboration.[2]

Constructive conflicts. Genuine collaboration does not mean that participants should always agree with each other. Data from the Fifth Dimension document a number of cases where conflicts played a constructive role and resulted in efficient collaborative learning. CSCL environments should not prevent conflicts but rather provide conditions for their constructive resolution.

In this chapter we employed the conceptual system of Activity Theory in an exploration into the nature of learning in the Zone of Proximal Development. We proposed that this learning is determined by an interplay between individual and collective activities. Cultural settings provide resources, affordances, and constraints to involve participants in new collective activities. Although people might enter collective activities for a number of personal reasons, such activities often develop according to their own logic, so that learners have to coordinate two different perspectives—the individual view and the collective view. In the process of such coordination learners can acquire new personal meanings, strategies, and skills.

---

[2]The main problem is not that people do not express their emotions in computer-mediated communication (cf. the phenomenon of "flaming"); it is that such emotions can easily be misunderstood, which negatively influences experiencing shared emotions.

ACKNOWLEDGMENTS

We thank Rogers Hall and an anonymous reviewer for their very helpful comments.

REFERENCES

Blaye, A., & Light, P. (1995). Collaborative problem solving with HyperCard. In The influence of peer interaction on planning and information handling strategies. In C. O'Malley (Ed.), *Computer supported collaborative learning*. Berlin: Springer-Verlag.

Cole, M. (1985). The Zone of Proximal Development: Where culture and cognition create each other. In J. Wertsch (Ed.), *Culture, communication, and cognition: Vygotskian perspectives*. Cambridge, UK: Cambridge University Press.

Cole, M., & Engeström, Y. (1993). A cultural-historical approach to distributed cognition. In G. Salomon (Ed), *Distributed cognitions: Psychological and educational considerations*. Cambridge, UK: Cambridge University Press.

Engeström Y. (1987). Learning by expanding: An activity-theoretical approach to developmental research. Helsinki: Orienta-Konsultit Oy.

Engeström, Y. (1990). *Learning, working, and imagining: Twelve studies in activity theory*. Helsinki: Orienta-Konsultit Oy.

Favorin, M. (1995). Towards computer support for collaborative learning at work: Six requirements. In J. L. Schnasse and E. L. Cunnius (Eds.), *Proceedings of CSCL'95, The First International Conference on Computer Supported Collaborative Learning* (Bloomington, Indiana, USA, October 17–20, 1995). Mahwah, NJ: Lawrence Erlbaum.

Grudin, J. (1990, September). Why CSCW applications fail: Problems in design and evaluation of organizational interfaces. *Proceedings of the CSCW'90 Conference*. Portland, Oregon.

Kaptelinin, V. (1996). Computer-mediated activity: Functional organs in social and developmental contexts. In B. Nardi, (Ed.), *Context and consciousness: Activity theory and human–computer interaction*. Cambridge, MA: MIT Press.

Kaptelinin, V. (1999). Learning together: Educational benefits and prospects for computer support. *The Journal of Learning Sciences*, Vol. 8(3/4). pp. XX–XX.

Koschmann, T. (1996). Paradigm shifts and instructional technology. In T. Koschmann (Ed.), *CSCL: Theory and practice of an emerging paradigm*. Mahwah, NJ: Lawrence Erlbaum.

Kuutti, K. (1991). The concept of activity as a basic unit for CSCW research. *Proceedings Second European Conference on CSCW (ECSCW'91)*. Amsterdam: Kluwer.

Leontiev, A. N. (1978). *Activity. Consciousness. Personality*. Englewood Cliffs, NJ: Prentice Hall.

Nicolopoulou, A., & Cole, M. (1993). Generation and transmission of shared knowledge in the culture of collaborative learning: The Fifth Dimension, its play-world, and its institutional context. In E. A. Forman, N. Minnick, & C. A. Stone (Eds.), *Context for learning: Sociocultural dynamics in children's development*. New York: Oxford University Press.

O'Malley, C. (1995). Designing computer support for collaborative learning. In C. O'Malley (Ed.), *Computer supported collaborative learning*. Berlin: Springer-Verlag. pp. XX–XX.

Petrovsky, A. V., & Petrovsky V. A. (1983). Active personality and Leontiev's ideas. In: V. Zaporozhets, V. P. Zinchenko, O. V. Ovchinnikova (eds.) Leontiev and contemporary psychology. Moscow: MGU Press (in Russian).

Teasley, S. D., Roschelle, J. (1993). Constructing a joint problem space: The computer as a tool for sharing knowledge. In S. P. Lajoie and S. J. Derry (Eds.), *Computers as cognitive tools*. Mahwah, NJ: Lawrence Erlbaum. pp. XX–XX.

Valsiner, J., van der Veer, R. (1991). The encoding of distance: The concept of the "Zone of Proximal Development" and its interpretations. In R. R. Cocking & K. A. Renninger (Eds.), *The development and meaning of psychological distance*. Hillsdale, NJ: Lawrence Erlbaum. pp. XX–XX.

Vasquez, O. (1993). A look at language as a resource: Lessons from La clase Magica. In B. Arias and U. Casanova (Eds.), *Politics, research, and practice*. Chicago National Society for the Study of Education. pp. XX–XX.

Vygotsky, L. (1978). Mind in society: The development of higher psychological functions. Cambridge, MA: Harvard University Press.

Vygotsky, L. (1983). The history of higher mental functions. In *Collected Works* (Vol. 3). Moscow: Pedagogika (in Russian, written in 1931).

THEORIZING THE VERNACULAR

Douglas Macbeth
The Ohio State University

There is a lovely unfairness about writing commentaries on the more considered works of others. There is none of the burden of fashioning a carefully developed and formatted report, and one can read not only for the issues the authors intend but read others into relevance as well. At the same time, the exercise is on condition that we treat the received papers critically but also appreciatively. In the materials at hand, the chapters by Suzuki and Kato, and Kaptelinin and Cole, there is much to appreciate. Both projects take up remarkably similar educational programs on opposite sides of the world and show us something of the new orders of curriculum and instruction that computer-supported learning affords. And they do so with what seem to be very kindred analytic programs, each oriented to the description and analysis of the enacted or "situated" organization of these new kinds of collaborative settings and learning tasks.

One of the attractive features of the task for me, as one whose work affiliates to ethnomethodology and the analysis of conversation, is that Suzuki and Kato also read into relevance these resources. Perhaps even more inviting, Kaptelinin and Cole are Activity Theorists, bringing to bear those substantial resources on their materials. And though I am no close student of the scholarship in Vygotskian studies, I have often wondered whether and how their interests in activity, interaction, and social context would find common ground with the sociological programs I know better. Though welcomed for these reasons, I seem no closer to an answer to that question, or at least no closer to the answer I would prefer. Instead, and precisely because of the continuities I find across the two chapters, their relationships to the analytic programs I know best are more nearly ironic ones. This, of course, is not necessarily grounds for criticism. Ethnomethodology, for example, is hardly the measure of Activity Theory, or the reverse. And there is little point in insisting on a single reading of either program. But still, and hopefully, in bringing one reading to the other, we might be positioned to clarify something about the points of interest they may share. This commentary is then only one half to such a paired discourse, and we can look forward to hearing its other.

With these interests, I want to go directly to the sense of my title. It is intended to convey a critical and ironic reading of both chapters, where the irony I see is this: Whereas the promise of what I will call "local studies"— meaning those programs that set out to reassess the locus of social order, meaning and structure, finding it not in the formal structures of social theory, but rather in the "situated" organizations and practices of everyday life— was one of a radical alternative to theorizing the social world (as in, for examples, Goffman's "interaction order" [Drew & Wootton, 1988], or Blumer's world of relentlessly "distinctive expressions" [1969], or ethnomethodological studies of the constitutive "grammars" of naturally accountable worlds [Garfinkel, 1967; Sacks, 1992]), in these two chapters, local worlds of situated action seem to have become the venue for theorizing order, structure, and the rest, once again.

Put slightly differently, whereas social theory had a historic indifference to everyday life, finding there nothing much of theoretical purchase or interest, but instead the dross of immemorable fiddlings and vernacular experience, the studies of these two chapters are finding formal and/or theorizable contents in the ordinary, everyday activities of computer-mediated simulation games and novice programming. And they do so—and this is the "rub" of the irony—via the very analytic resources and sensibilities that were developed as a thoroughgoing alternative to the taken–for–granted privileges of formal theory and analysis. To make sense of these characterizations, some detail is no doubt in order.

Kaptelinin and Cole examine materials found in one of the several Fifth Dimension programs that are bringing the substantial social, technological, and curricular resources of university–community collaborations to students who would not otherwise know them. The value of these programs is thus tied to issues of social equity and educational opportunity that have their own recommendations, apart from what analytic case studies can tell us about them. There are social issues for which social research may have no particular privilege, and I would expect the authors would agree. Having said that, their study can be no less useful in building a description of the learning they find within these local settings. Fifth Dimension (hereafter 5D) is emblematic of a newly developed kind of learning occasion: computer-supported collaborative learning.

They begin with an introduction to Activity Theory, finding in the social world the constitutive field of individual expression and development (in ways mindful of the social psychology of George Herbert Mead). As they observe,"intra-individual and inter-individual functions" are mutually constitutive. But as they briefly develop different readings of Activity Theory in the literature, they go on to sight a gap in the collected literature that they hope to knit together in the current study. The gap has to do with the question of how indeed "individual and social phenomena mutually determine each other:" "So far, there has been little overlap between studies of individual and collective activities from the point of view of Activity Theory." Turning to Activity Theory's most familiar formulation of the Zone of Proximal Development, they offer the possibility that,"the notion of ZPD can help bridge the gap between the individual and the social by introducing a mechanism of their mutual determination."

The mechanism they develop begins with Leontiev's (1978) structure of "three hierarchical levels" for understanding the context of interaction "between individuals ('subjects') and the world ('objects')." These are:

1) activities, which correspond to human needs and are directed towards objects (i.e., 'motives') which can fulfill those needs, 2) goal-oriented actions, which should be carried out in order to achieve a motive, and 3) situationally determined operations, which should be performed to attain a goal. (p. 2)

And they believe that they may have in the 5D materials some practical demonstrations of how these levels and interdeterminancies actually play out.

The gap, and the proposal to deal with it, thus begins with a binary— the individual and the social—and "individual activities" are central to its formal structure. But at least in a programmatic sense, "individual activities" would seem to run against the grain of other currents of Activity Theory that assign to *social* activity the site and engine of everything from development to meaningful action, whether individual or collective. So too for the notion of "individual goals." Perhaps my reading is defective, but it would seem that Activity Theory itself gives us grounds for pause here; goals would seem, in every case, to own a social genealogy, and it may get more tricky still when we look for them in actual ethnographic settings and observations.

In the vernacular, of course, we can say that on some given occasion, "so-and-so had this goal." But Leontiev is not speaking in the vernacular; his is a formal, theoretical structure. In the particulars of the 5D materials, however, we could then be hard pressed to say just what "goals" (or needs/motives) would lead students to walk into the program, and wonder whether goals are a useful way of describing how they do and what they find, unless, of course, "goals" are preauthorized as our way of speaking of whatever they find and do there. But a language of goal-directed action—using the in-order-to linkages of "motives"—is just the kind of formal analytic modeling that studies of ordinary life, at least, were working to set aside.

Following a discussion of the "higher level context" of the collaborating institutions, and how the model has evolved to meet the needs of the several communities that it works with, the authors proceed to the central analytic formulation of the study: a three-tiered hierarchy of "intersubjectivity." It is the mechanism with which the above gap closing will be worked out: the articulation of individual and social/collective activities. Intersubjectivity is of course a major intersection between more philosophical interests in human social life (as in American philosophical pragmatism and existential philosophies) and social studies of "situated" life and settings.

The hierarchy is straightforward, and the authors find it operating in the practical, interactional tasks of pairs of students and undergraduate volunteers working on the 5D materials:

> At the first phase there is an individual activity and an emerging collective activity. Individuals do not participate in a collective activity yet, they are involved in establishing a common ground... This is why this phase can be defined as 'inter subjectivity.' (p. 5)

The second phase, wherein "individuals are actually playing computer games in groups... is characterized by established intersubjectivity," where "both individual and collective activities take place." And the third phase is a "postintersubjectivity," wherein "collective activities are over but individuals manifest their "residues" in their individual activities or other collective activities."

One can, of course, have these ways of speaking of "intersubjectivity" if one chooses; what intersubjectivity "is" is not going to be settled any time soon. But they also strike me as a difficult moment for theorizing. We may have distinctions with uncertain differences (as between "intersubjectivity" and "established intersubjectivity"). And if these phases are the organizations of intersubjectivity, we can be left to wonder what it is that we observe when colleagues exchange greetings in the hallway, or when classmates engage in chitchat, or strangers coproduce the order of a queue. The phases work to theorize the observations of children and undergraduates who are more and less engaged in computer gaming. But they would be remarkably impoverished formulations if they fail to account for little else of the fullness of social life. It seems that "intersubjectivity" has been measured to just *these* occasions of "collaborative activity." Such a conceptual–theoretical economy—wherein major theoretical terms are tied to singular activities—risks leaving behind an otherwise barren landscape of not-quite intersubjective worlds. And it does: "When individuals just start acting together, there is usually little indication of intersubjectivity, even when individual activities are relatively well coordinated." But this is a remarkable statement. What other basis for acting together—in whatever measure of "coordination"—could there be?

For my tastes, at least, "common understanding" is a far more productive formulation of what the authors could mean for "intersubjectivity," though to use it would specifically deny them the "three-phase" formal structure they have in mind. (See Garfinkel, 1967; Moerman & Sacks, 1984; and Sacks, Schegloff, & Jefferson 1974, *passim* on the practical—and analyzable—achievement of common understanding; see Schegloff, 1992, for an extensive discussion of the achievements of intersubjectivity in the ordered detail of conversational "repair.") Holding aside other literature, the authors' theoretical account of intersubjective phases seems not too far removed from a discourse on task engagement, as a continuum from states of relative diffidence to sustained participation. But again, intersubjectivity would seem to be a good deal more than "agreement to a task."

The risk, and loss, of the treatment is not then only a matter of other scholarship. It extends to how else we could know, describe, and be instructed by the 5D installations. But what that could be—how the practical life of 5D works—is specifically unavailable when we theorize it. Indeed, having established that the 5D programs have a distinctive social–moral order ("The target setting was designed as a 'model culture'; it has its own rules, norms, artifacts, and mythology."), in places the authors speak as though their intent were to enforce it. For example, and notwithstanding that their observations are borrowed from the journal entries of the undergraduate volunteers who work with the children, we are offered the following entry, bracketed by the authors' comments:

> A child can be interested in a game and wishing to follow the rules of the Fifth Dimension, but uncooperative, for instance:
>
>> She was quite confident that she was able to complete the task independently. . . . It wasn't like 'go away I can do it myself', it appeared to be more of an automatic reaction for her just to do it herself. [Colleen M., 3/5/94]
>
> Even more serious problems emerge if the child does not want to follow the rules. . .

Fairly, I think, we can ask: What can be found as "uncooperative" in the above account of a child's confidence to a task? What order of "serious problem" do we have here, and how can it be understood, except as a characterization on behalf of the programmatic aims of the 5D program? None of this critical reading has anything to do with the virtues or recommendations of 5D. Indeed, the summary critique is usefully that we can't *find* the work of such installations in accounts that take interest in them only so far as to render them as evidence on behalf of general theory, on the one hand, or program commitments, on the other. One is left with the impression of formal accounts played out on a docile field of ordinary activities.

These problems, insofar as the reader finds them as "problems" too, are in no way distinctive to Activity Theory. Rather, they seem to follow whenever we set out to theorize the contents of everyday life. In a prior generation of social science, this was the"Procrustean relation" of theory to ethnographic settings: Local sites and actual occasions are stretched and cut to fit the needs of prevailing theory. At least in my reading of the general program of studies of everyday life, they began as a critique of such analytic habits and as a commitment to recovering the local order of ethnographic settings as an order that is practical, and praxiological, and specifically unavailable to our best efforts to theorize them.

A similar impulse, by my reading, can also be found in the chapter by Suzuki and Kato. Though less theoretically driven, their study is no less striking, in part because the authors specifically rely upon the single litera-ture of social science that has been most critical of formal analytic programs and most "articulate" in its indifference to theory (see Lynch, 1999, for an insightful discussion of ethnomethodology's "silence" on theory).

Their chapter looks at a remarkably similar setting in a 9th-grade class-room in Japan. Like 5D, their program brings programmable competitive games into classrooms and professional programmers (including the au-thors themselves) as resources to the children in learning how to use them. The game is a simulation of Sumo wrestling, and the study focuses on two students in particular. They lay out their topic and interest quite directly, viz., to demonstrate "the process of identity formation in the collaborative learning of programming using AlgoArena," a computer simulation game developed by NEC.

"Identity formation" is, of course, an honored topic in social psychology. We can imagine its play in studies of adolescent development, "career com-mitment," newlyweds, and aging seniors. It is a powerful generic, whose power is to be taken seriously: It attaches to something recognizable in our lives and social histories. And indeed, there is something immediately rec-ognizable about it in Suzuki and Kato's materials. Reading their transcripts without benefit of analytic annotations, we can see tensions, conflicts, and transformations in how the pair of students they study take to their tasks of programming the Sumo wrestling simulation game, take seriously the win-ning and losing, and then take seriously their own handiwork in programming both their winnings *and* their losings. Suzuki and Kato speak of a tension be-tween the identity of "classroom brats" and "programmers," and we can see that too; the students are quite expressive in articulating it. Thus, there can be no question that they have found some very nice materials to work with, the kinds of materials whose descriptions could be instructive about other settings and activities across classrooms and cultures.

Nonetheless, I think we want to be careful about how we treat this notion of "identity formation," careful in part because it is among the traditional conceptual "tools" of an older social science program of formulating everyday life as an expression of formal analytic concepts.

What it becomes for the authors is the central interpretive resource for making sense of what the students are doing in their AlgoArena sessions. We are advised to understand the local order of practice and conversation that we observe for how it labors on behalf of their identity formation, e.g.,"the practice in which the person participates is locally established *through* the process of identity negotiation" (emphasis added). Identity negotiation thus becomes the super ordinate process that orders practice and participation, and identity formation is then to be appreciated as practices' goal and achievement.[1] And this is a familiar way of formulating ordinary activities (practices and participation) in social science: We treat what the natives are doing for what they could not know of what they are *really* doing, that is, engaging in their own identity formations. Yet Garfinkel leveraged his ethnomethodological alternative on an exacting critique of just this kind of analytic privileging, whereby ordinary action (and actors) is rendered an "expression" of unseen formal structures. What is so striking here is that the very local order that Garfinkel and his students set out to describe— a praxiological order of "members' methods"—is now being deployed as the wherewithal or practical enactment of "identity formation" as a formal analytic object–process.[2]

How this inversion is organized by Suzuki and Kato is a useful thing to tease out, in part because it substantially turns on their reading of one of the more penetrating formulations of Sacks' analytic program, viz., his discussions of Member Categorization Devices (MCDs) as among the central, order–productive "language games" whereby we produce accountably recognizable worlds. (See Hester and Eglin, 1997; Sacks, 1974, 1992.) We can see how the authors make use of their reading of MCDs in the following

---

[1]And not only practice, but learning: "Participatory observation and close analysis of conversation reveals contingent and local characteristics of identity formation, i.e., learning."

[2]In fairness, the authors qualify the nature of these "identities" as durable things. For example,"... one's identity in a community is not an internal property of an individual... but an observable feature of social interaction." But if by "observable feature" they mean that identities stand to their occasions in a reflexive relationship, then it is difficult to treat the one as though it were operating in the background "through" the other. What is missed in their qualifications is the occasioned character of *whatever* identity might then be observable.

MACBETH

fragments. In the first, we get a sense for their use of the transcribed, conversational materials.

Fragment 3

> [OH (a student) called KT (a programmer) for help]
> OH: What I want to do is =
> KT: OK
> OH: = *this* [points to a defeat/defeated condition chart in the manual]
> KT: [looks at the manual] I see.
> OH: That is, I don't want to be pushed out.
> KT: I see. You don't want to be pushed out. Well, [points to the chart] when your wrestler is in this status. . .

The authors continue:

> Talking about his intention in reference to the chart displayed OH's understanding that he was going to translate his intention ['to avoid being pushed out'] to the program. In short, he was talking about his intention as a matter of programming. This is a kind of programmers' way of talking about their tasks. . . In other words, the conversation enabled programming learning because talking like a programmer is an imperative part of being a programmer. (p. 6)

I want to risk offering an alternative account of the exchange: That in the obliqueness of OH's point to a chart in the manual ["*this*"], and notwithstanding KT's claim of understanding ["I see."], OH proceeds to say what he means and does so in a completely vernacular fashion: "I don't want to be pushed out." In saying again what was on the other end of his indexical point, we can figure that he was speaking that way to be sure that KT does indeed see what he means (perhaps even remarking on the strength of KT's claim of understanding ["I see."] in the bargain). This alternative account is measured to the practical task of speaking to be understood as an ordinary course of action. More simply, we could say that he was speaking as best he could of matters that were still novel to him, that is, how he would make use of the chart to animate his wrestler.

The authors, however, offer a formal account of this work of achieving common understanding. It is probably fair to say that programmers "talk like programmers," at least some of the time. But to transform practical purposes into professionalized intentions ["as a matter of programming"], or to claim that this is a programmer's way of speaking ["I don't want to be pushed out"], strikes me as more than one can reasonably say on behalf of this exchange. The authors' account writes a caption to the scene, but it is difficult to find its analytic grounding. It is difficult to see how an orientation to practical action can deliver such a professionalized, even theorized, account.

The analysis proceeds to focus on a series of exchanges between OH and his student partner, IM, that are indeed very interesting. We see evidence of a schism and disaffection between them, as OH becomes progressively more engaged in the programming task—as different than the "game" task of winning any next round—and IM seems to become alienated, both from the task and his friend. A lovely story then develops, and the authors present it very effectively, as IM goes on to discover his own interests in the practical tasks of programming his wrestler, finds confidence in his efforts to do so, and, in the end, establishes a renewed alignment with his friend. The authors present these materials as the natural history of a conflict of role and expectations for the students between being a "classroom brat," on the one hand, and becoming a "programmer," on the other, and the materials do indeed build a picture of conflict between the students and its resolution. Central to this local history is an exchange in which IM chides OH for becoming a "computer nerd" and OH feels the sting of the accusation.

Fragment 11

> OH: Shit. I made this program last night. [shows his memo to IM]
> IM: You are a total computer nerd.
> OH: Well, I just had a lot of free time last night.
> IM: You don't have to make excuses.
> OH: Well, I am *not* a nerd.
> IM: You're changing bit by bit but you don't notice it.
> OH: Really? So I'm in danger, am I?

This is where Suzuki and Kato directly bring to bear their reading of Sacks' "member categorization devices" to further develop their analysis of identity formation. The question I want to raise is: Just what kinds of "categories" do Suzuki and Kato have in mind, and is this the order of analysis Sacks was pointing to?

This is a delicate but unavoidable question. The delicacy is compounded by the uncertainties of my own reading of Sacks' corpus, but I would venture to speak of it at least this far: What Sacks means by the phrase, and the larger program initiated by Garfinkel and developed in Sacks' natural language studies, was oriented to understanding the praxiologies of naturally accountable worlds, or how durable worlds inhabited by selves, others, truths, facts, and objectivities of unrelieved diversity—*and* order and regularity—are assembled in and as the unremarkable "grammars" of practical action that are the marks of competent members. The point is not to offer a recitation of EM programmatics but to suggest that the "categories" of membership categories, and the reflexive recognizabilities of kinds of persons and courses of action that they achieve, are themselves *occasioned* achievements of order and practice. The "identities" of MCDs are no more—nor less—durably substantial than the practices that bring them into view, for whatever the work of the world is that we are engaged in now (for example, giving an account of a crime scene to one who was not there [Sacks, 1984]).[3]

But instead of this order of "identity practices," Suzuki and Kato seem to be using the occasioned order of interaction to give evidence of something like "real" identities in the world, at least some of which ("programmers") are pedagogical achievements."Identity formation" becomes the formal structure organizing the students' work with AlgoArena, and MCDs become the social technology, and evidence, for achieving it.

A sense for the formalization can be heard in the authors' discussion of the above fragment: "This fragment shows that there were at least two kinds of membership category collections available in the AlgoArena classroom." I want to say that indeed there were, but not because the classroom constituted a normative collection of categories. There were and are indefinite collections available to be found in any next setting, *as* its occasioned, interactional organizations. Settings certainly can have formal roles and identities, as courtrooms have judges, lawyers, and bailiffs, each duly resourced by the setting to show as much. But MCDs are not, in the first instance, a matter of demonstrating a setting's formal features; they are rather the practical grammars whereby accountable descriptions are produced and evidenced locally, as a matter of whatever the practical–interactional work of the parties to the setting may be. But rather than seeing MCDs as an occasioned grammar of accountability, Suzuki and Kato treat the categories "brat" and "programmer" as normative, and they proceed to find further evidence for them in the particulars of the talk. Thus,

> "Shit" in the first line is also a good example of the identity coordination between "programmer" and "brat." He displayed incumbency in the category "programmer" by showing the product of his moonlight programming, but at the same time, he tried to display his "brat" identity by using a vulgar expression. . .

"Shit" thus becomes an emblem of identity. However, as an expression, it is a common one, routinely used by university faculty, hobbyists, and several grandmothers I know. We might better understand it here as a kind of "change of state token" (Heritage, 1984), or an expression that marks a disjuncture or disflunecy in a course of action or state of mind, and also as an instruction to those who overhear it in how they might hear what comes next.

---

[3]The question that Sacks set for himself was not one of 'identities' but how, and by what methods, recongnizable descriptions of ordinary worlds are produced (see Sacks, 1974, p. 218, see also Hester and Eglin, 1997, for a recent collection and extension of studies of membership categorization).

I take it that it was uttered as OH discovered that his work of the night before had gone for naught, and that it was fitted to and marked the discovery of whatever it was that rendered that work now useless. The point is not to insist on this reading of the transcript but rather to suggest how else Suzuki and Kato could take interest in the kinds of materials they are presenting. Nor is it uninteresting to note how OH first treats IM's characterization "You are a total computer nerd" as a remark on how OH had been spending his time ("Well, I just had a lot of free time last night"), that the rejoinder was heard by IM as an excuse, and that that hearing was affirmed in OH's next turn, wherein he returns to the characterization with a direct denial ("Well, I'm not a nerd"). Interesting too is to consider how IM and OH were speaking during the last two turns of the fragment. As Garfinkel (1967) observed some time ago, to know what has been said is to know *how* it has been said, and we can wonder how they were speaking, (e.g., sarcastically, sincerely, as a "real" question, etc.) and what work they were doing in speaking that way. The point, again, is not to impose another reading on their materials but to suggest a very different *kind* of reading, for what we would hope to make of the sequentially ordered, emergent detail of these local affairs.[4]

Reading it as I have suggested, however, still leaves us with the question of whether something like "identity formation" is going on in these materials. My impression is that, yes, something like that *is* going on, if we mean "identity," "conflict," and the like in the vernacular. These are practical, vernacular matters for the participants, who seem to be engaged in the practical tasks of programming their wrestlers as novices might find them (as they might if they were learning to bake, or to build a kite) and negotiating their relationship in its course. That they would be engaged in "becoming programmers" may well be an ambition that others (e.g., parents, teachers, analysts) may have for them, but in ways that are vernacular too.

I want to summarize my critique of both chapters as a question of analytic ambitions. Each chapter is pressing the local life of their respective settings into the service of highly theorized and/or formal analytic programs. This is the business of "theorizing the vernacular," and the irony is, again, that we would take the insights of "activity," "situated action," and the analysis of natural conversation and treat them as articulations of the very program of formal analysis that the ethnomethodologists, especially, were setting aside.

---

[4]As it happens, in one of his most direct discussion of MCDs (Sacks, 1974, p. 222) Sacks takes up a description of a "procedure for praising or degrading members, the operation of which consists of the use of the fact that some activities are category bound." The account is not, however, on behalf of the categories but of the work of doing "praising or degrading" (as we have here). The use of MCDs is not then a "micro" substantiation of prevailing normative orders but a description of how we formulate accountable–observable worlds, worlds that permit doing things such as "praising or degrading."

It is not that the impulse is difficult to understand. However much we might think that "master narrativity" has been discredited and/or deconstructed, these are high times for high theory. Social science cannot easily forswear its theoretical ambitions. "Science without theory" can be as perplexing as "order without rules" (Bogen, 1999). This may be a particular problem for Activity Theory, insofar as its enterprise has something to do with demonstrating the range and power of Vygotsky's genius and that of his students. Such demonstrations are a venerable program in social science. Still, ending where I began, we could imagine a very different tack for honoring and extending Vogotsky's achievements. This would entail an openness to inquires that life and circumstance denied to Vygotsky. It would entail an openness to the possibility that until we had examined the ordered character of the world in the detail of its interactional production, we would not yet know what Activity Theory might have to tell us about the everyday pedagogies of local, situated action. This possibility for honoring Activity Theory, and perhaps extending it, but without fetishizing its theoretical contents, seems specifically closed when we make out ordinary worlds as theory's evidences.

Wittgenstein (1960) wrote a sustained and penetrating critique of philosophy's "craving for generality," and we may be seeing some sense of the phrase here. But if not for theory, then what could the analysis of educational settings and practices in their "lived order" possibly promise? Perhaps only a collection of revealing descriptions of how indeed accountable worlds—including worlds of collaborative learning—are built from the relentless indefiniteness of our talk and action within and about them. But then, description may be instructive too. It may own its own order of pedagogy and may in fact teach us a good many things, even about theory. If so, the task facing those of us who would work with such modest ambitions may be usefully characterized as one of finding a way to be instructed by a world that already owns the order of its affairs. To theorize them, it seems, is to lose them.

No doubt, I have exceeded my mandate in agreeing to write a commentary on these two chapters. An apology may even be in order. But I think the issues raised in these chapters, or at least the issues I see for them, may be of some moment. Very serious issues and understandings hang in the balance, having to do, generally, with what use we can have for the fields of everyday life and action, and how we can manage to be instructed by them.

REFERENCES

Blumer, H. (1969). In (Eds.), *Symbolic interactionism*. Englewood Cliffs, NJ: Prentice-Hall.
Bogen, D. (1999). *Order without rules: Critical theory and the logic of conversation*. Albany, NY: SUNY Press.

Drew, P., & Wootton, A. (1988). *Erving Goffman: Exploring the interaction order.* Cambridge, UK: Polity Press.

Garfinkel, H. (1967). *Studies in ethnomethodology.* Cambridge, UK: Polity Press.

Heritage, J. (1984). A change of state token and aspects of its sequential placement. In J. Atkinson & J. Heritage (Eds.), *Structures of social action* (pp. 299–345). Cambridge, UK: Cambridge University Press.

Hester, S., & Eglin, P. (1997). *Culture in action: Studies in membership categorization analysis.* Lanham, MD: University Press of America.

Lynch, M. (1999). Silence in context: Ethnomethodology and social theory. *Human Studies, 22,* (2/4), 211–33.

Moerman, M., & Sacks, H. (1988). On 'understanding' in the analysis of natural conversation. In M. Moreman (Ed.), *Talking culture.* pp. 180–86. Philadelphia: University of Pennsylvania Press.

Sacks, H. (1974). On the analyzability of stories by children. In R. Turner (Ed.), *Ethnomethodology* (pp. 216–232). Baltimore: Penguin Education.

Sacks, H. (1984). On doing "being ordinary." In J. Atkinson & J. Heritage (Eds.), *Structures of social action* (pp. 413–429). Cambridge, UK: Cambridge University Press.

Sacks, H. (1992). *Lectures on conversation.* Oxford, UK: Blackwell.

Sacks, H., Schegloff, E., & Jefferson, G. (1974). A simplest systematics for the organization of turn taking for conversation. *Language, 5,* 696–735.

Schegloff, E. (1992). Repair after next turn: The last structurally provided defense of intersubjectivity in conversation. *American Journal of Sociology, 97*(5), 1295–1345.

Wittgenstein, L. (1960). *The blue and brown books* (2nd ed.). New York: Harper Torchbooks.

LEARNING TOGETHER, VISIBLY SO, AND AGAINST THE ODDS

Ray McDermott
James G. Greeno
Stanford University

First there is good news, then complex—make that challenging—news, and finally a great deal of work left to do. We can proceed in that order in response to these two excellent papers on reorganizing and rethinking learning.

THE GOOD NEWS

The good news is in four points, three on the learning organized by researchers and a fourth on their theoretical commitments and advances.

A. Both papers report on interesting environments in which children learn how to work with computerized materials.

In the Fifth Dimension, children are invited into a room full of educational computer games, some of which are interesting, most of which are not, but with an interesting twist: The room is also full of adults anxious to engage the children in the pursuit of excellence, not just with the games, but with the construction of a nonschool, community-based institution through which everyone can develop, record, celebrate, and redevelop a mastery. Even children who would not run the same mastery path at school seem to get engaged.

In the classroom with AlgoArena, the children are asked to rely on more traditional classroom social arrangements, on the one hand, but they are

offered a much more interesting simulation world for learning basic programming skills, on the other. The interesting twist lies in the curriculum
materials inviting new, or at least, newly productive social arrangements
that allow for learning to occur even for individuals who show initial reluctance and even alienation.

    B. Both environments were constructed to take advantage of the fact that
       children do not learn just one step at a time inside well-defined tasks.
       Traditionally, tasks well designed by adults are quickly turned into
       tests that assume kids to be equally motivated and, sad to say, dif-
       ferentially skilled, or so unequally motivated that skill level is a moot
       issue. Instead, in our two experimental settings, it is assumed that
       motive, attention, and skill are all subsets to the wider organization of
       tasks in the lives of people doing together things made relevant over
       time.

In the Fifth Dimension, children enter voluntarily and are generally motivated to play the games, many of which seem to be fun (to the extent they
are not too school-like or, more operationally speaking, to the extent they
are not based on what might just as well be random question–answer sets).
What the children find at the Fifth Dimension clubs is not just games but
a small world of persons ready to take their performances seriously. The
computer games define the tasks, on the one hand, but the persons around
the games define their relevance, on the other.

In the classroom with AlgoArena, the children are asked to learn how to
program wrestling matches in a simulated world of Sumo wrestling. Any walk
through a video arcade should convince curious adults that there might not
be a more inherently interesting game for organizing children to the details
of up–down, yes–no, right–left, and if–then rules than a win–lose electronic
wrestling match. Still some children take to the game and others seem to
avoid it—make that avoid it actively. It would seem that the wrestling task is
not just a wrestling task but a wrestling task in the context of other children
orienting to the programming with differential skill and enthusiasm. Those
who avoid the game make it clear they are not just not paying attention;
rather, they are not paying attention in response to, or at least in tune with,
the fact that others are paying attention. AlgoArena is designed to break the
cycle of mutual attention and inattention by requiring and offering the children many ways to cooperate with each other in building the best wrestler.

    C. Both papers point to the changing social worlds of the children as they
       engage the materials together. Children change after all as the world
       allows. Organizing that world is our business; the learning of individual
       children can be our point of interest, but never our point of business;

the learning of individual children can even be our point of concern, but not our unit of analysis. Both papers are lovely in their brief evocation of how the settings gradually acquire their learners.

In the Fifth Dimension, the children can be shown to pass through three stages. First they find someone to work with, even if they had no such intention upon initial entrance. Then they find a rich vocabulary to talk about gaining mastery over the games and sharing it with various sorts of adults: the college students wanting to learn how to work with children and keeping elaborate notes on their progress; parents or other community representatives happy to see kids focused and learning for a few hours; and researchers examining the process with questions about the relation between their practice and the community of learners they are trying to create. In a third stage, the children start to contribute to the life of the club by sharing their mastery, teaching others, contributing to a maintenance of the rules that guide behavior, and participating all the other jobs entailed in being a member of a community. Most importantly, the kids (and the adults) work out a learning space with enough sharing of perspectives to mediate the division of labor between teachers/learners, experts/novices, and individuals/the collective.

In the classroom with AlgoArena, one pair of boys was studied carefully. Initially while one boy was trying to understand the programming behind the wrestling the other boy seemingly had trouble paying attention, and vigilantly so. The first boy seemed to understand immediately that learning to program a game is the issue before the pair, and not the wrestling. The other boy tunes in, if at all, to the wrestling, and chides the first boy for his being a computer nerd. Over the next two weeks, with the help of others, the second boy is gradually absorbed and develops a different identity in relation to both his partner and the task. Most importantly, the kids (and the software) work out a learning space with enough sharing of perspectives to mediate the division of labor between computer nerd/regular student, programming/wrestling, showing off/achievement, and, perhaps most of all, cooperation/competition.

D. The authors of both papers have put together conceptual materials both to follow the learning of various children and to theorize how learning is organized and can be encouraged.

Kaptelinin and Cole built a social environment, attended to activity from the perspectives of both individuals and collaborative groups, and explained it with concepts taken from the sociohistorical tradition of Vygotsky and subsequent Activity Theorists. Suzuki and Kato built their own computerized game world with which children can learn programming, attended to ways that individuals' local identities changed in their interactions with each other, and explained it with concepts from recent efforts to articulate a situated theory of learning.

Suzuki and Kato's paper gives an example of a kind of conceptually integrated analysis we hope will become more prevalent. "Identity" is a notoriously polysemous term, and its introduction in a discussion of group interaction can be seriously problematic. Suzuki and Kato consider identity as an aspect of an individual's participation in an activity system, which has been called *positional identity* by Holland et al. (1998). Following Lave and Wenger (1991; also see Wenger, 1998) they consider an individual's identity as a *trajectory of participation*, a view that focuses on continuities and changes in a person's patterns of participation within a group or as he or she participates with different people or in different activity settings. Rather than conceptualizing identity in opposition to participation, this idea treats identity relationally, as an aspect of participation, and can show ways in which aspects of identity are transformed in interaction. This relational view of identity also illustrates an important constraint on theoretical analyses of identity. Individuals' identities are not simply characteristics that they have acquired; instead, identities can be understood only in relation to the participation structures of communities and the functions of activity that are important in the communities in which the individual participates.

This is good news, indeed. Not long ago, some of us wrote articles about social interaction in classrooms, and others of us wrote articles about individual learning, but we lacked conceptual resources to support consideration of these perspectives in close enough relation to each other to justify discussing both levels simultaneously. That the papers under review address questions about both individual change and interaction is a signal of and a contribution toward an integration between theories of individual and group activity that we celebrate gratefully.

THE COMPLEX AND CHALLENGING NEWS

To the good news, we can add the complex and challenging, both for the design and organization of learning environments and for the advancement of scientific understanding of learning.

  A. Regarding the design of learning environments, we can start with a question: Why have the authors had to work so hard to organize a little bit of learning?

For at least one million years, children entering human cultures have learned pretty much whatever was asked of them—languages, arts, technologies, religions, relationships, and each of these on multiple levels in turn well articulated with each other, sometimes even duplicitely so.If nothing else, the species—Homo sapiens—indeed can learn. And, and this is important enough to start a sentence with two "ands," and (OK, three), they can do all this learning without developing elaborate theories of learning. So really, what is the news? Kids working in a Fifth Dimension club or in a classroom with AlgoArena seem to learn what is put in front of them. So did the Tale children of traditional Africa in the classic account of agricultural learning by Meyer Fortes (1936). So did the Hanunóo children in the Philippines learn hundreds of plant names and uses and hundreds poems and love songs in a script ill designed to fit their language (Conklin, 1960). So have most children in most cultures. Some learn a little more quickly, or others a little more efficiently, but they all can eventually, and, if not disrupted by others, usually do. Why do we in third millennium nation states with huge financial investments in school systems have to make so much of individual differences that we must constantly remind each other that all children can learn?

There are wider environments than after-school clubs and classrooms. Call them whole cultures or political economies (where the use of the term whole should not allow us to forget that they all leak terribly, always did, and will continue to do so even more so in today's global economy).[1] These environments seem to have their way with learning, not just because they demand and pay off certain kinds of learning, but because they have so restricted the theories of learning that dominate the worlds of school, after school, and/or any other institution set for learning, including even educational computer games. These whole systems seem to isolate only certain kinds of activity as learning, or perhaps better phrased, they recognize quite regular kinds of activity as learning only at certain well-marked times; and worse, they seem to be hell bent on measuring it and making it count—as measured and often without regards for its use—as a stepping stone to institutional enhancement. By the workings of this system, many problems, deeply political and economic problems, are treated as if they were only problems of motivation and learning. They are, of course, rarely learning problems, but always problems of institutional arrangement and rearrangement. We do not have learning problems as much as we have terribly problematic theories of learning. We have learning problems to the extent learning theories have been institutionalized as a handmaiden to

---

[1]Talk of "whole cultures" is happily out of style. Leakage rules. We use "whole" only to draw attention to the orders of organization far greater than the after-school programs and classroom. Relations among various orders are complex and outstrip simplifying explanatory devices such as cause and effect or part and whole. We cannot resist citing James Boon's latest play with the word culture as "multi-spatio-ethno-fragmented-scapes/scopes-as-processually-practiced-and-agentively-reinvented-contestatorially" (1999, p. 2).

the divisions of the wider culture and political economy (Varenne & McDermott, 1998).

Before the Fifth Dimension, who made learning such an onerous task that children and adults have to work so hard to rediscover that it can be fun? And before AlgoArena, who made programming such an identity sore point that some take to it and show it off and others reject it while keeping an eye to working on the task under a softer social stare? And even in both of these nurturing contexts, who continually makes learning something people have to avoid, show off, rediscover, reinvent, and work hard to display as theoretical, interesting, and fundable? The answer is: No one in particular, of course. The treatment of learning as a commodity is ubiquitous. Like all commodities it is produced and consumed, of course, but it is also distributed unequally and cleverly, attractively, and often invidiously represented (DuGay, 1997, by way of Marx). All this takes a great deal of work to maintain and even more work to resist and reorganize. It even sits in the very language we use to talk about the world. It even sits in the very language we use to talk about learning.

The two programs under review are important not because they made learning happen but because they made learning happen visibly. They made learning happen visibly and against the odds. It would be so easy for children to enter the Fifth Dimension, recognize the smell of commodified learning, and leave. Many do. And in the same way, it would be so easy for the young student teachers to degrade the children for not coming or not learning well when they stay. And it would be so easy for the inattentive boy to continue being cool and avoid the learning that could be done with AlgoArena. The two programs are working against the odds. Everything is in place to document what the children cannot do in any situation recognized as formal education. Because the adults work hard to counter what is already in place, against the odds, the children eventually focus and learn what there is to be learned. Eventually, the hard work the adults have put into Fifth Dimension and AlgoArena pays off in a community practice of learning together (Greeno et al., 1999).

Among the tools available for children and adults to make learning difficult are some of the dichotomies that the children had to overcome in the Fifth Dimension and the AlgoArena classroom: the dichotomies between individual/collective, teacher/learner, expert/novice, computer nerd/regular student, showing off/achievement, and, perhaps most of all, cooperation/competition. These dichotomies are less choice points than symptom displays. There is no intrinsic reason for any of these divisions of labor; in each case, we might just as well be Lilliputians fighting with bloodletting intensity over which end of the egg should be opened. The achievement of the work reported in the two papers is that they have developed contexts in which the dichotomies that disrupt much educational activity were momentarily overcome and transformed. The problem is not that the dichotomies do not make sense. The problem is that they make sense too easily and too thoroughly; once defined as opposites, the terms erase the complexities that divide them and overdetermine the arguments that follow in their wake.[2]

There are three ways to handle such dichotomies:

1. The usual and antagonistic stand is to pick one (or the other) and argue as best you can—go, for example, with individual over collective, teacher over students, or computer nerd over regular kid interested in wrestling. The result, either way, yaw rehtie, should be exactly what we already have.

2. The second and polite stand is to pick both and argue for some interaction—go, for example, with individual but urge cooperation, make curriculum and teacher goals more important than student learning, or celebrate those who "stand out" but help the others to "catch up."

3. The third is to confront the situation that pitted the contrasting terms and to build new settings in which more constructive issues might be addressed—create, for example, social contexts in which it is possible and necessary for people with mixed competencies to help each other get done jobs more important than their individual institutional biographies, allow teachers to learn from the students and about the students as part of their job, and build materials that encourage participation without, well, at least for the moment, competition. This requires one to always look for a new angle.

---

[2]In *Democracy and Education*, Dewey (1916) cumulatively lists 37 dualisms that must be confronted if progressive learning institutions are to survive. A current list of annoyances is in the accompanying chart:

Conceptual dichotomies disrupting learning		
theory/practice	individual/social	quantitative/qualitative
objective/subjective	abstract/concrete	context bound/context free
art/reality	middle class/poor	majority/minority
scientific/constructivist	particular/generalizable	stimulus/response
smart/dumb	nature/nurture	laboratory/natural

These dichotomies gloss important divisions in our experience. They are essential to daily discourse and sometimes essential to organizing people in response to inequalities. *But we cannot afford to trust them as analytic tools.* They offer simplifications, both convenient and misleading, because they come to us without a description of the perspective or level at which they are designed to be meaningful.

B. Theoretically, we can ask:Why has it taken so long to address questions about individuals and questions about groups in the same discussion? Or, perhaps more constructively, we can ask: What makes it so hard to achieve a coherent account of activity that doesn't make one or the other of these levels invisible?

We find some clues about this in the concepts the authors present in explaining their findings. Toward the goal of an explanatory account in which concepts about individuals and concepts about groups function coherently, these papers have made the glass closer to being full, but it is not completely full as yet.

For example, Kaptelinin and Cole conceptualize individual activities and collective activities as distinct entities that are present to varying degrees at different phases of a pair's learning to interact with each other. They hypothesize that individuals participating in a group "are simultaneously involved in two hierarchies of actions. On the one hand, they pursue their individual goals, and on the other, together with other people they strive to formulate and achieve goals of collective actions." Of course, these two hypothesized activity systems are not unrelated; we need "to study how individual and collective activities interact to create each other." But they are considered—in Kaptelinin and Cole's discussion, as in many others—as conceptually distinct, and the distinction is important in their explanation of changes in patterns of interaction that they reported.

This framing creates an ontological dichotomy between groups and individuals, which may be as problematic for the theoretical enterprise as we believe it is for the design of learning environments. The alternative, for theory, is to locate the distinction in theoretical perspectives—make it an epistemological distinction rather than ontological. We can construct explanatory concepts that refer to properties of activity at the level of a pair or group, and we can construct explanatory concepts that refer to properties of activity at the level of individual participants.[3] Any activity we consider can be characterized from both of these perspectives. This view implies that we need to work on understanding how any activity is organized, both from the perspective of whatever group of people is conducting the activity *and* from the perspectives of the individuals who are participating in the group. The activity of the group is a system, and the activities of its individual participants are systems that interact, and if we understand what is happening, we should be able to give coherent analyses at both levels and to give a coherent account of how the two analyses are related.

---

[3]One theorist who takes this view is Rogoff (e.g., 1995), who identifies *intrapersonal* and *interpersonal* planes of activity as two of the perspectives that are available for theoretical analysis.

According to this view, we would look for analyses of progress in activities, say collaborative game playing, that explain changes either at the individual or group level, and preferably at both. But the analysis we would prefer would recognize that individuals and groups are present and significant throughout the development sequence, rather than having one of the levels come into play and disappear. In this perspective, getting to a point where the members of a group are coordinated in joint activity is an achievement that they have accomplished collectively, as well as an achievement to which they have contributed individually. If a group did not reach such a point—that is, if their activity did not become coordinated in a way that looked like they had a shared collective goal—that would be something the group accomplished also and would be an outcome that the individuals contributed to as well. Kaptelinin and Cole's analysis of the phases of intersubjectivity is insightful—the activities of these adults and children did become better coordinated as they interacted around games, which provided a shared resource for their development of the coordination that they achieved. What seems problematic to us, theoretically, is their interpretation that collective activity was absent at the beginning and somehow came into being where it had been absent. Instead, we suppose, as does Cole more consistently in other accounts (Cole, 1996), that the adult–child pairs were functioning collectively from the beginning, and one of the things they accomplished involved learning how to be coordinated better as a pair.

As we have written earlier, we believe that Suzuki and Kato's analysis of identities in participation provide important and encouraging progress toward understanding individuals' participation and community in a more integrated way. But this highlights further challenges as well. The students came to their work on AlgoArena from participating in other settings and had participated with each other before this activity began, and therefore they were ready to participate in different ways in the AlgoArena activities. And the social arrangements in the classroom created affordances for some kinds of participation more than others. We will need to broaden our analyses to understand the next layer of the collective/individual interaction.

And then there is, of course, much more to do. Both papers are a source of insight and inspiration. These studies have made learning happen and to happen visibly. Tomorrow they will have to do it again. The end result will not come and remain in steady state. They are working against the odds. So are we all, and it is good to have model examples and a conceptual toolkit to help make our way.

ACKNOWLEDGEMENTS

We appreciate Mizuko Ito's corrections to the text. We have relied on Cole (1996) and Ito (1998) for further accounts of Fifth Dimension clubs

REFERENCES

Boon, J. (1999). *The cross-cultural kiss: Edwardian and earlier, postmodern and beyond.* The David Skomp Distinguished Lectures in Anthropology, Indiana University.

Cole, M. (1996). *Cultural psychology.* Cambridge, MA: Harvard University Press.

Conklin, H. C. (1960). Maling: A Hanunóo girl. In J. Casagrande (Ed.), *In the company of man.* Urbana: University of Illinois Press

Dewey, J. (1916). *Democracy and education.* London: Macmillan.

DuGay, P. (1997). *Doing cultural studies: The story of the SONY Walkman.* Beverly Hills, CA: Sage.

Fortes, M. (1936). Learning in Taleland. Africa.

Greeno, J. G., McDermott, R., Cole, K. A., Engle, R. A., Goldman, S., Knudsen, J., Lauman, B., & Linde, C. (1999). Research, reform, and the aims of education. In E. Lagemann & L. S. Shulman (Eds.), *Issues in education research.* San Francisco: Jossey-Bass.

Holland et al. (1998). *Identity and agency in cultural worlds.* Cambridge, MA: Harvard University Press.

Ito, M. (1998). *Interactive media for play: Kids, computer games, and the production of everyday life.* Unpublished docttoral dissertation, Stanford University.

Lave, J., & Wenger, E. (1991). *Situated learning.* New York: Cambridge University Press.

Rogoff, B. (1995). Observing sociocultural activity on three planes: Participatory appropriation, guided participation, and apprenticeship. In J. V. Wertsch, P. del Rio, & A. Alvarez (Eds.), *Sociocultural studies of mind* (pp. 139–164). Cambridge, UK: Cambridge University Press.

Varenne, H., & McDermott, R. (1998). *Successful failure.* Boulder, CO: Westview Press.

Wenger, E. (1998). *Communities of practice.* New York: Cambridge University Press.

ENDING THE CONVERSATION JUST BEGUN

Victor Kaptelinin
Umeå University

Michael Cole
University of California, San Diego

There is an unlovely unfairness in getting so deep, exciting, and thought-provoking feedback and a feeling that a "real" discussion is about to begin at the moment when the discussion is in fact over. It is too late to rewrite the chapter completely and it is impossible to deal in this short response with all the fascinating questions raised in the commentaries. After some agonizing on what we should and should not reply to, we decided to single out the following handful of issues.

Life Versus Theory.   Macbeth makes a general point about potential dangers of theoretical generalizations. He points out that theories, essentially, prevent us from understanding the "lived order" of a setting. Also he suggests that descriptions of "how indeed accountable worlds are built from the relentless indefiniteness of our talk and action within and about them" should be used instead of theoretical generalizations. We totally agree that life is infinitely richer than any theoretical accounts, and we feel that in a way we "murdered to dissect" the interaction between a child and an adult who try to negotiate a joint object, when we cut a complex socio-cognitive-emotional process into three stages. Nonetheless, a complete immersion into the everyday life of a setting is associated with certain drawbacks, as well. One of the authors of the paper (Victor Kaptelinin) was involved in the Fifth Dimension for only a few months. However, he discovered very soon that it was almost impossible to explain what the Fifth Dimension is to people "from the outside." Detailed descriptions could get you only that far, and communication and reflection create a need for generalization, despite the fact that the latter is always an oversimplification.

A danger of an immersion into a setting can also be illustrated with a comment of Macbeth's. He rightly points out that the fact that a child wants to complete a task independently does not present a problem from the point of view of our theoretical account. The reason why the chapter qualifies it as a "problem" is an unreflected transfer of experiences of a person involved in everyday activities of the Fifth Dimension, where kids working independently were considered as a "problem" because of local norms and attitudes at the setting.

In our view, the contradiction between the indefinitely rich everyday life and theoretical constructions is a fundamental, unavoidable, dialectical one. Even though we agree with Macbeth on the limitations of conceptual constructs (in general), it is hardly possible to be limited to "instructive descriptions," no matter how rich and insightful they are. There is a real and present need to make theoretical generalizations if one does not limit himself or herself to observations, interpretations, and understanding only, but one has to act, as well. The "lived order" of the world in which the Fifth Dimension has been invented and is being implemented, evolved, localized, etc. requires theoretical generalizations as a tool of action.

Intersubjectivity. Perhaps, the choice of "intersubjectivity" for the purpose of differentiating among three stages in the life cycle of collective activities is not perfect. As Macbeth points out, "intersubjectivity" has a very broad meaning, and one can claim that phenomena that can be called intersubjective take place as soon as people are engaged in any type of communication, even at the stage that we call "pre-intersubjective." It is true that "intersubjectivity" can mean different things. According to Webster, "intersubjective" can be defined as "1. Connecting or interrelating two consciousnesses or subjectivities. 2. Existing between, accessible to, or capable of being established for two or more subjects" (*Webster's Third New International Dictionary.* Merriam-Webster, 1993, p. 1883). Therefore, it can have a variety of meanings: (a) subjective phenomena that exist between two or more "consciousnesses or subjectivities," (b) anything that somehow relates two or more subjects, or (c) objective phenomena that several subjects agree upon. We use this word in the first of the above meanings and, accordingly, do not equate coordination of individual activities with intersubjectivity. If each of individuals is following his or her familiar routine but there is no subjective phenomena that exist between the individuals, then there is no intersubjectivity in the meaning in which we use this word. Once again, this usage can be criticized, but at the moment it is difficult for us to find a better alternative. "Common understanding," "task engagement," and the other alternatives we considered and eventually discarded seem to be limited in the sense that they do not take into account collective action or only deal with certain aspects of individual activities. However, the fact that we do not see a better option now does not mean it does not exist! Perhaps, it does but we just have not succeeded in finding it so far.

Individual Versus Social Activities. The criticism that we separate "individual and social activities" appears to be a misunderstanding. We differentiate between individual and collective activities, both of which are social in nature.

Emerging Collective Activities. McDermott and Greeno find problematic our interpretation " . . . that collective activity was absent at the beginning and somehow came into being where it had been absent. Instead they believe that the adult–child pair were functioning collectively from the beginning, and one of the things they accomplish involved learning how to be coordinated better as a pair." From our point of view, there is no disagreement between the chapter and the commentators in that collective activity is a developing entity and in the Fifth Dimension collective activities have life cycles. For each collective activity it is possible to identify a point of time in the past when this activity had not yet existed. It is much more difficult to indicate the exact point where a collective activity begins (e.g., when a child and an adult introduce themselves to each other?, when they decide what they are going to do next?, when they start a game?). So, when one says that a pair starts functioning collectively "from the beginning," it might be a little problematic to define what "the beginning" is. Therefore, in our view the comment does not indicate a theoretical disagreement between their view and the one presented in the chapter, but rather it emphasizes the importance of establishing operational criteria for various phases of collective activities. We agree that development of such criteria should have a high priority in applications of Activity Theory in the area of CSCL.

Unfortunately, space limitations do not allow for a discussion of many important ideas formulated in the commentaries by Macbeth and by McDermott and Greeno. Some of them, for instance the strategy for an analysis of individual and collective activities, outlined by McDermott and Greeno, deserve a special discussion.

III

SECTION III: TECHNOLOGIES FOR COLLABORATION AND LEARNING

Becoming More Articulate About the Theories That Motivate Our Work

Timothy Koschmann
Southern Illinois University

In the closing panel at CSCL '97 Roy Pea (2000) called upon us to make explicit in our work "the relation between theory, research, methodology, conclusions, [and] implications." This is good advice, if not always put into practice, for all researchers. It is of special importance, however, for those of us who work in the still developing field of CSCL. It is critical that we strive to be more articulate about the theories that underlie and motivate the designs of our technological artifacts, pedagogical activities, and assessment methods. For this reason, we examine four projects in this section, focusing on the theories underlying the design and evaluation work described. In keeping with the conversational theme of the book, commentaries were solicited for each chapter from a range of researchers with different areas of specialization. Though each of these chapters raises multiple issues for consideration, I focus only on a single issue for each.

Continuity and Interaction in Participatory Simulations. Vanessa Colella begins her chapter by posing the question, "What should count as a worthwhile educational experience?" To begin to formulate an answer, she turns to the American pragmatist philosopher John Dewey. Dewey (1939/1991) wrote, "Continuity and interaction in their active union with each other provide the measure of the description of the educative significance and value of an experience" (p. 26). To understand Dewey's approach to evaluating an educational experience, therefore, we need to appreciate his paired principles of continuity and interaction.

Describing the principle of continuity, Dewey (1939/1991) observed "every experience both takes up something from those that have gone before and modifies in some way the quality of those which come after" (p. 19). Garrison and Scheckler in their commentary on Colella's chapter point out that continuity arises from habits. They write, "Beliefs, for Dewey, are habits and habits are embodied dispositions to act evincing emotions." Colella proposes that consideration be given to two aspects of continuity when evaluating educational experiences, namely "appropriateness, based upon an understanding of the person entering the experience, and educative value, based upon the directions that it propels that person." Educative value, in turn, must be judged on the basis of the potential for growth on the part of the learner. Garrison and Scheckler write, "Growth means living a life of expanding capacity, meaning, and value."

As described by Dewey (1939/1991), the principle of interaction "assigns equal rights to both factors in experience—objective and internal conditions. Any normal experience is an interplay of these two sets of conditions. Taken together, or in their interaction, they form what we call a *situation*" (p. 24). The term *situation* is used in a special sense here. For Dewey, situations "are instances or episodes (or 'fields') or disequilibrium, instability, imbalance, disintegration, disturbance, dysfunction, breakdown, etc. "that occur" in the ongoing activities of some given organisim/environment system" (Burke, 1994, p. 22). The notion of *inquiry*, so central to Dewey's later writing, is closely bound to situations defined in this way. In fact, Dewey (1941/1991) defined inquiry as "the set of operations by which the situation is resolved (settled, or rendered determinate)" (p. 181). Colella writes, "In order for an experience to have educative value, it must be initially problematic in some way, spurring learners on to disambiguate their situation through inquiry." As discussed by Hall (1996), the principles of continuity and interaction are not independent but rather should be viewed metaphorically as paired coordinates of an experience.

Colella's chapter presents a particular form of educational experience to be evaluated using these Deweyan criteria. Colella, once a high school science teacher herself, designed an instructional activity she terms "Participatory Simulations" to engage students in a form of scientific inquiry. A crucial part of the simulation is a bit of technology known as "Thinking Tags"; these are programmable badges used to simulate the spread of disease within a population. Each participant is issued one such badge. One or more badges contain a "virus" at the beginning of the simulation that is communicable from badge to badge when participants "meet." The object for participants is to collaboratively develop a method for analytically determining the origins of the disease and how it was spread.

The task that Colella set for herself, that of applying Dewey's criteria to this particular educational activity, is a daunting one. What would count as compelling evidence that the badge simulation (or any other educational intervention) was appropriately matched to the participants' prior beliefs and habits? How could we judge whether the experience was growth producing in the sense described earlier? And most critically, how do we determine whether or not the participants authentically experience the situation as problematic? Clearly no simple pre-test/post-test evaluation will provide the answers. Garrison, whose work is primarily in educational philosophy (e.g., Garrison, 1995), and Scheckler raise an important issue with respect to design: Can true Deweyan inquiry be produced through "rule-constrained role-playing activities"? David Hammer, an educational psychologist with interests in classroom discourse (e.g., Hammer, 1995), raises a different issue pertaining to method: How do we begin to describe the discursive practices of teachers that lead to the social construction that Dewey labeled as inquiry? While no definitive answers are provided here, this chapter and its associated commentaries provide us with a lovely set of questions to ponder and pursue.

Reflexive Awareness in Video-Mediated Collaboration. The second chapter in this section, by Hiroshi Kato and coauthors, describes an experiment using the AlgoBlock system. AlgoBlocks (Suzuki & Kato, 1995) are a set of manipulatives that enable groups of programmers to collaboratively construct computer code. Each block corresponds to an instruction in the Algol programming language. In the experiment described here, a remotely located instructor guides a group of university students through a programming task. The authors trained two cameras on the instructor, one on his face, the other capturing the movement of his hands. The study involved placing monitors displaying the instructor's face and hands in different locations in the room and analyzing how these arrangements were used differentially by the students while performing their task. Our reflexive awareness of others' gaze and bodily orientations is the fundamental focus of study here, but one that raises critical questions of a methodological sort. Specifically, how do we go about conducting rigorous analyses of participants' awareness in observed situations? As noted by the authors, awareness is closely related to notions of intersubjectivity as discussed by ethnomethodologists (e.g., Heritage, 1984) and mutual orientation as studied by conversation analysts (Goodwin, 1986). The authors of the chapter, therefore, turn to these fields for methodological guidance.

Randy Smith, in the first commentary on this chapter, notes that "an assessment of another's visual field happens with such speed and ease that it has the invisibility of the taken for granted." Smith has done considerable research of his own with regard to mutual awareness among interactants (e.g., Smith, O'Shea, O'Malley, Scanlon, & Taylor, 1991) and he reminds us here of some of the complexities involved in studying such matters. The second commentary was provided by Curt LeBaron, whose expertise is in research on language and social interaction, specializing in gesture and how people employ their bodies in communication (cf., LeBaron & Streek, 2000). He calls here for a general reassessment of the underlying models of communication employed by CSCL researchers. The third and final commentary was written by Charles Crook, author of what is considered by many to be a classic treatise on CSCL (Crook, 1994). He cautions us that in studying mutual understanding we not rely too heavily on what can be observed in the moment (i.e., talk, gesture, gaze). Crook writes, "If it is hard for us to take account of the reflexive nature of communication as manifested in the visual detection of gesture and posture . . . then it is surely hard for us to take account of the more subtle reflexive forms that arise from shared histories." All would agree, therefore, with his closing observation that the authors of this chapter have provided us with a "generous arena" for further exploration.

Procedural Facilitation of Scientific Argumentation. Procedural facilitation has been a central topic of research and theorizing in CSCL since the early days. Scardamalia, Bereiter, McLean, Swallow, and Woodruff (1989) described it in these terms:

> [Procedural facilitation] is a theory based approach to providing learners with temporary supports while they are trying to adopt more complex strategies. These supports include turning normally covert processes into overt procedures; reducing potentially infinite sets of choices to limited, developmentally appropriate sets; providing aids to memory; and structuring procedures so as to make it easier to escape from habitual patterns. A cardinal principle is that these supports should be designed so that when they are withdrawn the learner is carrying out the mature process independently. Thus it is essential that design of procedural facilitations be based on adequate models of the mature process, and that it also be informed by models of the immature process. (p. 54)

Philip Bell's chapter applies this notion to the development of skills for scientific argumentation.

He describes the rationale behind the development of a particular piece of software, the SenseMaker argumentation tool. Unlike what Bell describes as "discussion-based tools," such as CSILE, that impose a structure on group exchanges, SenseMaker is designed to "support a more rhetorical construction of arguments by individuals." The SenseMaker interface uses *evidence dots* and *claim frames* as the primitives from which students are expected to construct personalized perspectives on science-related issues. Evidence dots can be dragged into claim frames and can be color coded to reflect students' assessments of the contributions of particular pieces of evidence to particular claims. Claim frames can be hierarchically nested to construct larger arguments. An external software component enables learners to elaborate on their arguments and provide explanations.

Bell's work rests on a theory of scientific inquiry attributed to Koslowski (1996) whereby scientific inquiry is viewed as a process of coordinating emerging evidence with an existing set of theories. Past research (Kuhn, 1991) has shown that children and even many adults find this difficult to do. The purpose of SenseMaker, in Bell's terms, is to make "thinking visible," that is, to make the normally covert process of argument construction into an overt procedure. This raises a host of questions, however. Are these the right sort of developmentally appropriate supports for the desired forms of argumentation? Do students actually employ them as useful tools in constructing their arguments? And finally, but perhaps most importantly, do students develop new habits for thinking as a result of their experiences using the SenseMaker tool; that is, are they more likely to be skillful at coordinating evidence and theory in the future? Settings in which learners are called upon to collaboratively produce arguments are valuable sites for exploring these basic and applied questions. Bell seeks evidence of procedural facilitation, for example, in the transcripts of the presentations made by students at the conclusion of their unit of study.

Richard Duschl, a researcher in science education (cf., Duschl & Hamilton, 1998; Gitomer & Duschl, 1998), takes issue with two aspects of the design of the SenseMaker tool. He argues, first, that the program depends too heavily on web-based resources for student argument construction and, in so doing, neglects other possible resources such as the past understandings the students bring to the situation. Second, scientific reasoning seems to entail more than simply coordinating theory and evidence. According to Duschl, it involves prediction of new findings from theory, constructing connections among theories, and the development of new ways of representing and communicating scientific models. Though he applauds the contributions made by Bell and colleagues, he sees need for additional work in this area.

A second commentary was provided by Mark Felton and Deanna Kuhn, who do research on the development of argumentation skills (cf. Kuhn, 1991). They acknowledge the value of tools such as SenseMaker in facilitating comparison of student-generated arguments and speculate that such forms of facilitation may contribute to the development of skills for "alternatives-based" argumentation (Kuhn, Shaw, & Felton, 1997). They warn, however, that participation in a single experience, such as the project described by Bell, may not be adequate for developing those skills. Bell provides a response to both commentaries.

Establishing a Frame of Analysis for Studying Mobile Computing. The final chapter by Geraldine Gay, Robert Rieger, and Tammy Bennington examines the education implications of an emerging technology. The technology is mobile computing made possible by the advent of self-powered, palm-sized computers and low-cost, high-bandwidth wireless communications. These miniaturized computers, sometimes referred to as Personal Digital Assistants (PDAs), extend the possibilities of "any time, any place" computing in new and unexplored ways. The Gay et al. chapter explores what happens when educational field experiences and instructional technology are brought together using mobile computing.

The question the authors wished to address was how is learning changed when students have access to hand-held computers in the field? Traditional pre-test/post-test methods only speak to one aspect of this question (i.e., was something acquired from the experience?), while remaining silent with respect to *how* the nature of the learning was changed. A frame of analysis that focuses on individual learners was unlikely to reveal what they needed to investigate. They decided, therefore, to apply an analytic lens borrowed from Activity Theory to take a broader view of the learning process. Rather than focusing on changes in performance as a function of experience, Activity Theory attends to object-directed, practical activity with a particular interest in the ways in which such activity is mediated through the use of tools. There is a rich tradition of applying Activity Theory in CSCL research (e.g., Crook, 1994; Kaptelinin & Cole, this volume; Newman, Griffin, & Cole, 1989). With regard to the mobile computing project, Activity Theory provides a useful analytic lens for examining how the activity was transformed through the introduction of PDAs as mediational resources.

Bonnie Nardi, who has written extensively about the application of Activity Theory to human–computer interaction research (cf. Nardi, 1996), provides a commentary on the Gay et al. chapter. She praises the chapter for its careful evaluation work and extended frame of analysis. She suggests, however, that the chapter authors have not yet fully explored all of the insights that could be obtained from applying an activity theoretic lens to their data. In particular, she notes that the notion of conflicting objectives, an important feature of analyses based on Activity Theory, might be helpful in understanding the students' mixed responses to the technology.

The second commentary for this chapter was provided by Sasha Barab. Barab's interests are in Ecological Psychology and its application to educational research (Barab et al., 1999). Like Activity Theory, Ecological Psychology attends in a critical way to the means by which features of the materials environment can mediate learning. Barab is encouraged by the potential of mobile computing, as described by Gay et al., to dissolve some of the barriers between classrooms and the outside world and believes such efforts are in keeping with the ecological view of how technologies can contribute to the advancement of learning.

Becoming More Articulate About Our Theories.   For each chapter, I have focused on a single theoretic issue either alluded to within or raised by the chapter. These issues are not specific to individual chapters, however, but instead have implications that cut across all of the chapters and, indeed, all research in CSCL.

The issue of choosing a frame of analysis appropriate to the research question, for example, came up in the discussion of the Gay et al. chapter but has bearing for all four chapters. To be useful, any research report, no matter how it is positioned theoretically, must provide an adequate description of the context of the study. An exhaustive description is never possible, of course, because what counts as context is endlessly expansible. The key is to define a "minimally meaningful context" (Barab, this volume), but it is difficult to provide guidance as to how to do this in the general case. In CSCL research, it is particularly important that the reader be able to reconstruct in detail what the participants were actually doing when engaged in the activities of the study. One aspect of being more articulate about our theories, therefore, is being more explicit about our analytic frames and our reasons for choosing them.

Procedural facilitation was visible in all of the projects described in this section. It is most evident in the Kato et al. and Gay et al. chapters, in which the AlgoBlocks manipulatives and the programs installed on the PDAs provided for the students in the field are each designed to scaffold the development of certain skills. It is less evident in the Participatory Simulations described by Colella in which the Thinking Tags were not necessarily designed to directly support the development of scientific reasoning skills on the part of the students. Here the scaffolding is more subtle and falls to the teacher and the activity facilitator, a point developed by David Hammer in his commentary, rather that to the technology. As an aside, there is a chicken-and-egg sort of paradox to artifactual forms of procedural facilitation such as Bell's SenseMaker software. As Bell observed, the tool is ostensibly designed to introduce students to the distinction between evidence and theory, but at the same time seems to assume "that students would have to develop this type of meta-knowledge *before* they could use the knowledge representation productively as an inscriptional system" (italics added). How students actually accomplish this is an important and researchable question.

Questions of this sort fall into a line of inquiry that might be described as studies of "thinking practices," borrowing a term from Goldman and Greeno (1998). There are a host of practices that are relevant to collaboration and learning. Reflexive awareness, as discussed in the Kato et al. chapter, is just one example. Others might include how inscription is employed within joint activity (cf. Stevens, this volume), how aspects of the visual field are made salient to newcomers (Goodwin, in press), how objects (Streeck, 1996) and gestures are imbued with meaning (LeBaron & Streeck, 2000), and how joint reference is accomplished (Hanks, 1990). There are methodological issues still to be worked out, but there can be no question about the importance of elucidating these practices for future research in CSCL.

Colella's introduction of Dewey's writings into this discussion is much appreciated. Lagemann (1989) has recounted how in the last century Dewey's influence on educational research has been eclipsed by that of E. L. Thorndike. Dewey, however, has much to offer for researchers interested in studying collaboration and learning. His call for more "trans-actional" forms of inquiry in the social sciences (Dewey & Bentley, 1949/1991), for example, speaks to the problem of defining appropriate frames of analysis taken up earlier. Even more importantly, Dewey's conceptualization of learning as a process of meaning construction[1] makes visible its inherently social nature, an aspect of learning obscured within the Thorndikean tradition. Dewey's conceptualization, therefore, would appear to be the more useful one upon which to construct a practice-based science of learning in settings of joint activity.

If CSCL is to grow and prosper as a field, we must all make an effort to become more articulate about the theories that underlie our work. This is necessary not only to define a place for CSCL in the wider world of research on instructional technology but also to help us define directions for our own future work. The authors of these chapters and commentaries have done an exemplary job of raising some important issues for our consideration. Now it is up to us to carry forward the conversation.

REFERENCES

Barab, S., Cherkes-Julkowski, M., Swenson, R., Garrett, S., Shaw, R., & Young, M. (1999). Principles of self-organization: Learning as participation in autocatkinetic systems. *Journal of the Learning Sciences, 8*, 349–390.

Burke, T. (1994). *Dewey's new logic: A reply to Russell*. Chicago: University of Chicago Press.

Crook, C. (1994). *Computers and the collaborative experience of learning*. London: Routledge.

Dewey, J. (1991). Logic: The theory of inquiry. In J. A. Boydston (Ed.), *John Dewey: The later works, 1925–1953, Vol. 12*. Carbondale, IL: SIU Press. (Originally published in 1938)

Dewey, J. (1991). Experience and education. In J. A. Boydston (Ed.), *John Dewey: The later works, 1938–1939, Vol. 13* (pp. 1–62). Carbondale, IL: SIU Press. (Originally published in 1939)

Dewey, J. (1991/1941). Propositions, warranted assertability, and truth. In J. A. Boydston (Ed.), *John Dewey: The later works, 1939–1941, Vol. 14* (pp. 168–188). Carbondale, IL: SIU Press. (Originally published in 1941)

Dewey, J., & Bentley, A. (1991). Knowing and the known. In J. A. Boydston (Ed.), *John Dewey: The later works, 1949–1952, Vol. 16*. Carbondale, IL: SIU Press. (Originally published in 1949)

Duschl, R., & Hamilton, R. (1998). Conceptual change in science and in the learning of science. In B. Fraser & K. Tobin (Eds.), *International handbook of science education* (pp. 1047–1065). London: Kluwer Academic Publisher.

Garrison, J. (1995). Deweyan pragmatism and the epistemology of contemporary social constructivism. *American Educational Research Journal, 32*, 716–740.

Gitomer, D., & Duschl, R. (1998). Emerging issues and practices in science assessment. In B. Fraser & K. Tobin (Eds.), *International handbook of science education* (pp. 791–810). London: Kluwer Academic Publishers.

Goldman, S., & Greeno, J. (1998). Thinking practices: Images of thinking and learning in education. In J. Greeno & S. Goldman (Eds.), *Thinking practices in mathematics and science learning* (pp. 1–14). Mahwah, NJ: Lawrence Erlbaum.

---

[1]For example, Dewey (1938/1991 wrote: "the meaning which a conventional symbol has is not itself conventional. For the meaning is established by agreements of different persons in existensial activities having reference to existensial consequences" (p. 53). He went on, "words mean what they mean in connection with conjoint activities that effect a common, or mutually participated in, consequence" (p. 59).

Goodwin, C. (1986). Gestures as a resource for the organization of mutual orientation. *Semiotica, 62*, 29–49.

Goodwin, C. (in press). Practices of seeing, visual analysis: An ethnomethodological approach. In C. Jewitt & T. van Leeuwen (Eds.), *Handbook of visual analysis*. London: Sage.

Hall, R. (1996). Representation as shared activity: Situated cognition and Dewey's cartography of experience. *Journal of the Learning Sciences, 5*, 209–238.

Hammer, D. (1995). Student inquiry in a physics class discussion. *Cognition and Instruction, 13*, 401–430.

Hanks, W. (1990). *Referential practice*. Chicago: University of Chicago Press.

Heritage, J. (1984). *Garfinkel and ethnomethodology*. Cambridge, UK: Polity Press.

Koslowski, B. (1996). *Theory and evidence: The development of scientific reasoning*. Cambridge, MA: MIT Press.

Kuhn, D. (1991). *The skills of argument*. New York: Cambridge University Press.

Kuhn, D., Shaw, V., & Felton, M. (1997). Effects of dyadic interaction on argumentive reasoning. *Cognition and Instruction, 15*, 287–315.

Lagemann, E. C. (1989). The plural worlds of educational research. *History of Education Quarterly, 29*, 185–214.

LeBaron, C., & Streeck, J. (2000). Gesture, knowledge, and the world. In D. McNeill (Ed.), *Review of language and gesture: Window into thought and action*. New York: Cambridge University Press.

Nardi, B. (1996). Activity theory and human–computer interaction. In B. Nardi (Ed.), *Context and consciousness: Activity theory and human–computer interaction* (pp. 7–16). Cambridge, MA: MIT Press.

Newman, D., Griffin, P., & Cole, M. (1989). *The construction zone: Working for cognitive change in school*. New York: Cambridge University Press.

Pea, R. (2000). Closing panel: Where do we go from here? In T. Koschmann, L. Sadler, M. Lamon, M., & B. Fishman (Eds.), *CSCL '97 CD-ROM*. Distributed in R. Hall, N. Miyake, & N. Enyedy (Eds.), *Proceedings of CSCL '97*. Mahwah, NJ: Lawrence Erlbaum.

Scardamalia, M., Bereiter, C., McLean, R., Swallow, J., & Woodruff, E. (1989). Computer-supported intentional learning environments. *Journal of Educational Computing Research, 5*, 51–68.

Smith, R., O'Shea, T., O'Malley, C., Scanlon, E., & Taylor, J. (1991). Preliminary experiments with a distributed, multimedia, problem solving environment. In J. Bowers & S. Benford (Eds.), *Studies in computer-supported cooperative work: Theory, practice, and design* (pp. 31–48). Amsterdam: Elsevier.

Streeck, J. (1996). How to do things with things: *Objects trouves* and symbolization. *Human Studies, 19*, 696–735.

Suzuki, H., & Kato, H. (1995, October). Interaction-level support for collaborative learning: AlgoBlock, an open programming language. In J. Schnase & E. Cunnius (Eds.), *CSCL 95: Computer support for collaborative learning* (pp. 349–355). Rahwah, NJ: Lawrence Erlbaum Associates. Retrieved November 2, 2000 from the World Wide Web: http://www_cscl95.indiana.edu/cscl95/suzuki.html

Participatory Simulations: Building Collaborative Understanding Through Immersive Dynamic Modeling

Vanessa Colella

MIT Media Laboratory

The students in a science classroom are chattering away as they play with the latest computer simulation. A virus is about to wipe out a small community. Will the inhabitants discover a way to survive? A small group of students in one corner stare intently at a computer, waiting for the results. As they wait, the virus mysteriously infects a few players on the other side of the classroom. Shrieks echo through the room as each new set of red lights indicates that another player has succumbed to the disease. Each player struggles to evade the spreading disease. Without warning, red lights emblazon the whole population. The disease has run its course.

Think for a moment about the image that story conjures up for you. If you pictured this game unfolding, you might have pictured groups of students huddled around a desktop computer playing the latest simulation game—a sort of "SimVirus" or new virtual reality "Outbreak." Perhaps a few students sat close to the monitor while others jumped around behind them as their "players" fell ill. Perhaps a few fought for control of the mouse as they tried in vain to save their "player." Children playing such a game would observe the results on screen and then decide how to use that information to better understand the simulation model.

Much of our imagination about how computers can be used to enable new kinds of learning in the sciences is constrained by the box and monitor motif of the computer in the late 1990s. However, the game described above is not played on a computer, at least not a traditional computer. This chapter explores Participatory Simulations, in which students become players in unique, "life-sized" games that are supported by small, wearable computers. In keeping with the calls for inquiry-based science, developing skills for systems thinking, and fostering collaborative learning in science classes (National Committee on Science Education Standards and Assessment, 1996; Project 2061, 1993), this project explores how learning takes place in the environment created by a Participatory Simulation.

Participatory Simulations take the simulation off of the computer screen and bring it into the experiential world of the child. The students above are not just watching the simulation; in a very real sense they *are* the simulation. By wearing small computers called Thinking Tags, the students each become agents in the simulation. The students do not need to struggle to keep track of which player is sick, for the flashing red lights belong to their classmates. The questions that follow—Who got them sick?, When?, How?, Why?—are not merely part of examining a computer model, they are part of discovering the underlying mysteries of their very own viral epidemic.

This chapter presents a new kind of experiential learning environment called Participatory Simulations. After a brief survey of Dewey's principles of experience, we compare Participatory Simulations to an established, computer-supported learning environment—microworlds. Then, we explore the activities of a Participatory Simulation in a high school biology classroom and report on the results of this pilot study. We discuss students' immersion in a Participatory Simulation and their inquiry process as they attempt to solve the problems that are embedded in the simulation. The chapter closes with a discussion of design criteria for Participatory Simulations and a look toward expanding their use in classrooms.

DEWEY'S PRINCIPLES OF EXPERIENCE

There is a long history of theoretical claims that children construct their own knowledge through experience (Dewey, 1916, 1988; Montessori, 1912; Papert, 1980; Tanner, 1997). In *Experience and Education*, Dewey posited an "organic connection between education and personal experience" (Dewey, 1988, p. 11). Dewey believed that by engaging in activities that held meaning for them, children would build lasting understanding. "When children are engaged in an activity of interest to them that poses difficulties, they look for a method of coping with the difficulties and thus acquire new skills" (Tanner, 1997, p. 44). His theory of education centered on learners' experiences and how they learn from those experiences through inquiry.

But Dewey was not advocating a haphazard adoption of learning through projects and activities. He articulated two principles of experience—continuity and interaction—that enable educators to discriminate among and evaluate experiences. The learning potential of an experience is determined by the extent to which it respects both of these principles.[1] "Continuity and interaction in their active union with each other provide the measure of the educative significance and value of an experience" (Dewey, 1988, p. 26). A brief description of these principles will serve as a framework for evaluating educational experiences in general and Participatory Simulations in particular.

Imagine a lifetime of your experiences arranged on a time line. As you travel along the time line, you move from one experience into the next, bringing the habits and knowledge acquired from past experiences into those of the present and carrying the effects of present experiences into the future. Expressed in this way, the principle of continuity speaks to the connected nature of all of your experiences. The principle of continuity instructs that educative experiences should be evaluated on two counts: appropriateness, based upon an understanding of the person entering the experience, and educative value, based upon the direction that it propels that person. How, then, does continuity help to differentiate educationally sound experiences from those that are "mis-educative"? According to Dewey, though every experience is by necessity lodged in a continuum, only experiences that lead to growth should be considered educative (Dewey, 1988).

If the principle of continuity can be represented on a time line, then the principle of interaction can be envisioned as an expanded view of a particular point on that time line. Each point is a situation, or interaction of the internal character of the learner and the external or objective conditions of the experience.

> An experience is always what it is because of a transaction taking place between an individual and what, at the time, constitutes his environment, whether the latter consists of persons with whom he is talking about some topic or event . . . the toys with which he is playing; the book he is reading . . . or the materials of an experiment he is performing. (Dewey, 1988, p. 25)

Creating educational experiences requires considering the interplay, or interaction, between the individual and the external conditions or surroundings that facilitate the experience. The value of an experience is dependent on the type of interaction it facilitates and the type of response it evokes.

Good educative experiences facilitate positive interactions between the learner and the experience, and those interactions, in turn, evoke responses that "lead to growth." But how are we to evaluate growth? Dewey theorized that experiences "develop children's habits of thinking" by presenting "difficulties that suggest the need to find an effective way of dealing with them"

---

[1]Inspiration for this argument comes from Hall (1996) and personal communication with Timothy Koschmann.

(Tanner, 1997, p. 142). The difficulties or ambiguities embedded in an activity or experience stimulate the need for reflective inquiry. Good experiences must be adapted to the learner; prepare the learner for the social responsibilities of adulthood; and exert the "maximum influence in forming habits of acute observation and of consecutive inference" (Dewey, 1910/1997, p. 44).

For an experience to have educative value, it must be initially problematic in some way, spurring learners on to disambiguate their situation through inquiry. An inquirer first turns the indiscriminate aspects of the situation into "problems" that can be solved and subsequently undertakes a process of investigation that leads to problem resolution (Dewey, 1938/1998b). Rather than existing only in the mind, inquiry is an active process that, in the ideal case, allows inquirers to discover the validity or invalidity of their hypotheses by observing the outcomes of their actions in the world.

> It is a commonplace that in any troubled state of affairs *things* will come out differently according to what is done. The farmer won't get any grain unless he plants and tills; the general will win or lose the battle according to the way he conducts it. Neither the grain nor the tilling, neither the battle nor the outcome of it, are "mental" events . . . Resolution of the indeterminate situation is active and operational. (Dewey, 1938/1998b, p. 172)

Or, as Schön (1992) put it, "inquiry combines mental reasoning and action in the world" (p. 121).

It is inquiry that moves a learner from a state of confusion in a problematic situation to a state of understanding. During the process of inquiry, the learners generate suggestions or ideas that they feel might disambiguate their problematic experience. These propositions are tested and evaluated based upon the results they produce in the world. The iterative testing of many propositions culminates in a judgment, which is grounded in the initial, indeterminate situation and informed by evidence that hypotheses suggested and, upon experimental action, generated (Dewey, 1938/1998a, p. 200). The process of generating ideas, testing them, and reevaluating the original problem based on new evidence is an active and engaged process. "The inquirer does not stand outside of a problematic situation like a spectator; he is *in* it and *in transaction with* it" (Schön, 1992, p. 122, emphasis in original).

Dewey insisted that teachers should not wait for children to stumble into educative experiences. Instead, he argued that educators are responsible for creating and facilitating experiences for students. Because a student comes to a new situation bearing his or her own "internal conditions" and past experiences, educators are primarily responsible for shaping the objective (external) conditions. Educators should select aspects of the surroundings that "are conducive to having experiences that lead to growth. Above all, they should know how to utilize the surroundings, physical and social, that exist so as to extract from them all that they have to contribute to building up experiences that are worthwhile" (Dewey, 1988, p. 22). Creating educational experiences is a complex task, requiring that educators "productively manage both what learners bring to the situation (e.g., their attitudes, habits, interests, and material artifacts) and the manner in which their interaction with the situation will generate productive activities (e.g., engaging in inquiry that leads further into valued aspects of subject-matter practice)" (Hall, 1996, p. 213).

Although a learner's experience is critical to the learning process, experience alone is often not enough. Some experiences provide greater learning opportunities than others do, and even the best learning experience can fail to positively impact a child. Without adequate support, children might fail to sufficiently pursue a project, missing opportunities to gain deep insights. Or they might focus on only one aspect of a problem, missing the potential for creating connections with other concepts or experiences. One of a teacher's responsibilities, in addition to creating the setting for the experience, is to support children's inquiry and help ensure that learning opportunities are not squandered.

Dewey's Laboratory School provides one example of students and teachers pursuing educationally valuable experiences. There, skillful teachers surveyed their environment, in and out of school, to better enable children's learning experiences (Tanner, 1997). Yet, activity was not undertaken for its own sake. Activities were constructed with Dewey's principles in mind, ensuring that experiences were adapted to accommodate individual students' needs and lead to students' continuing growth. The children's activities had close ties to the school curriculum. Their "handwork was a way of learning facts and concepts—of working out processes and developing appreciations" (Tanner, 1997, p. 73). Children built and sewed and cooked and tended, all in the context of educative experiences. The teachers were charged "to select those things within the range of existing experiences that [had] the promise and potential of presenting new problems which by stimulating new ways of observation and judgment [would] expand the area of further experience" (Dewey, 1988, p. 50). The children employed the method of organized cooperative inquiry, derived from the success of the scientific enterprise, "as they sought answers to problems that had significance to the embryonic community" (Tanner, 1997, p. 14).

DESIGNING EXPERIENCES

Like the teachers in Dewey's Laboratory School, many educators, both before and after Dewey, have taken up the task of designing educative experiences. Not surprisingly, these educators have often focused on selecting or creating particular materials to enable an experience. When developing his concept of kindergarten, Friedrich Froebel pioneered the idea that particular objects, which he called "gifts," could be given to children to stimulate certain kinds of exploration. He argued that these gifts would provide experiences for children that would likely lead to certain kinds of cognitive development (Brosterman, 1997).[2] Much of his notion of kindergarten focused on how the orderly delivery of the gifts would enable children to build knowledge in a coherent fashion. Years later, Vygotsky wrote extensively on the notion that tools (like Froebel's gifts) could enrich and broaden both the scope of activity and the scope of thinking of the child (Vygotsky, 1978). Other researchers have even speculated about the ways in which the objects present in the environment could actually induce development (Fischer, 1980).[3]

Not surprisingly, computers fit right into this lineage. Even before the prevalence of personal computers, Seymour Papert envisioned a future in which computer-based tools would provide children with a whole range of transformative developmental experiences (Papert, 1980). He imagined that constructions within these powerful computing engines would become fodder for children's imaginative and intellectual ruminations, much like gears (his own childhood tool) had become for him. The fact that computers could take on so many different roles, potentially a role per child, was especially exciting.

Much effort has been expended to build computational tools that provide opportunities for children to engage in computer-based experiences, many of which would not be accessible to children without those tools (Resnick et al., 1998). Virtual communities offer places for children to construct alternate realities (Bruckman, 1998); computer-based modeling environments enable the design and construction of complex paper sculptures (Eisenberg & Eisenberg, 1998); microcomputer-based labs facilitate children's collection of scientific data (Tinker, 1996); and Newtonian-based environments allow exploration of the laws of physics (White, 1993). Each of these computerized tools supports exploration, investigation, or creation—activities central to an educative experience. The next section compares one class of computer-based tools, microworlds, with a new class of experiences called Participatory Simulations.

A Computational "Sandbox"

Microworlds were originally conceived to give children a sort of computational sandbox—a small world in which they could manipulate "objects" on

---

[2]See also Lillard (1972) for related work.
[3]For another perspective on the importance of tools in the development of understanding see Norman (1993).

the computer screen. In a real sandbox, children use buckets, shovels, and sand to create miniature castles. While creating these sandcastles, children often grapple with concepts like shape and scale. What base supports the tallest sandcastle? How big should two pebbles be if they are meant to represent a prince and a princess? A computerized sandbox offers more than just a sandbox on a screen. In a microworld—as in the real world—a child can take actions that have discernible effects on the world. But in a microworld, the child also has some access to the formal rules that govern his actions. Microworlds offer a nonformal entry into a world based on formal logical constructs.

Picture a girl playing with a toy horse in her room. She can move the horse around and even have it "talk" to other animals in the barnyard. The horse might "gallop" and "trot" as she alters the speed with which she flies the horse around her play space. In a microworld, her horse could still move around in space, talking to other animals, but she might begin to investigate the mathematical relationship between the horse's two speeds. Depending on the microworld, the computer might even show her an equation that relates those speeds. Or she could make the galloping speed dependent on the trotting speed. Certainly, she could perform similar mental operations in the real world, but the microworld can provide a seamless transition from the nonformal, naïve operations in the real world to the formal descriptions and investigations of those operations in the microworld. In fact, research has suggested that microworlds whose formal descriptions closely mirror children's experience with patterns and activities can be better learning environments (diSessa, 1988).

Most often, a microworld focuses on a limited set of formal rules, constraining the types of actions a child can take but providing an opportunity to learn more about the rules governing those actions. Roschelle (1996) describes one such learning activity, during which two girls build up an understanding of the Envisioning Machine, a microworld that facilitates exploration of velocity and acceleration. Like many microworlds, the Envisioning Machine provides "an intermediate level of abstraction from the literal features of the physical world" (p. 241). The computer becomes a bridge linking the patterns and activities in the microworld (in this case, motion of a ball or particle) with the formal expression of those patterns and activities (arrows representing velocity and acceleration), by connecting pattern and activity to representations of the underlying processes. This bridge enables children to interact with both the processes and patterns they observe and the formal systems that govern those patterns and processes. Much as Froebel's gifts facilitated specific activities and, in so doing, helped children develop new understandings, microworlds can broaden the range of activities and thoughts in which children can engage.

Benefits of Microworlds

Teaching often involves creating and organizing special experiences to help children learn certain ideas. Whether those experiences are focused on how and why bean seeds grow toward the light or what might be contaminating the local stream, they are created and organized to help children learn. The flexibility of microworld environments opens up the range of possible experiences that can be created. Some researchers have claimed that "the computer is ... more flexible and precise in crafting experiences that can lead to essential insights" (diSessa, 1986, p. 224).

Teachers and researchers have constructed microworlds that make possible countless experiences, from exploring geometric relationships to building river ecosystems. For example, different microworlds enable children to focus an exploration on particular aspects of physics (the Envisioning Machine), mathematics (Logo), or politics (SimCity). One class of microworlds, which enable focused exploration of complex, dynamic systems, has gained mainstream popularity in the past few years. Game software such as SimCity (Maxis, 1993) and SimLife (Maxis, 1992) helped generate popular interest in complex systems. Programs such as Model-It (Jackson, Stratford, Krajcik, & Soloway, 1994), Stella (Roberts, Anderson, Deal, Garet, & Shaffer, 1983), StarLogo (Resnick, 1994), and Sugarscape (Epstein & Axtell, 1996) enable users to experiment with complex systems and develop better intuitions about the mechanisms that govern dynamic interactions.

These microworlds let children experiment with real concepts in play space, or as Pufall (1988) said, they create "a context within which children can think about discrete space as *real* and not about discrete space as *an abstraction* from the analogue worlds of sensory-motor experience" (p. 29, emphasis in original). With microworlds, learning experiences are no longer constrained by what the real world has to offer. We can both limit and augment the real world, sometimes creating simplified spaces for exploring complex topics, other times creating wholly new experiences on-screen. Pufall (1988) further speculated that the new interactions microworlds enable might "alter children's patterns of development, by allowing [them] to interact in ways [they] cannot interact with the 'real' world."

Costs of On-screen Learning

In spite of the many benefits of learning within a microworld, there is a price to be paid for moving on-screen. Without trying to exhaustively cover the benefits of learning in the real world—which has, after all, sustained human existence for thousands of years—it is worth mentioning that there are human ties to real space that are lost in cyber-learning. Though some users become enamored of the machine (Turkle, 1984), others feel distanced from the patterns and processes they observe on a computer screen. For some people, this distance leads to a general distaste for the "cold," unemotional world of computing (Turkle & Papert, 1992). Others are inclined to believe everything they see on a computer, not questioning the validity or appropriateness of simulation results. Sociologist Paul Starr (1994) witnessed one user's lack of intellectual curiosity about the underpinnings of SimCity and another group's disinterest in rigorously questioning the assumptions underlying a computer model designed to forecast future health care costs. In SimCity, the underpinnings of the model are hidden from the user, perhaps stifling curiosity. But the assumptions in the health care model were readily accessible, suggesting that developing a full understanding of a computer model is a formidable task.

As much research on microworlds has shown, these challenges are not insurmountable. Many microworld environments engage students in deep reasoning and sophisticated analysis (e.g., Eylon, Ronen, & Ganiel, 1996; Goldman, 1996; Papert, 1980; Roschelle & Teasley, 1995; Rothberg, Sandberg, & Awerbuch, 1994; Schoenfeld, 1990; Tabak & Reiser, 1997; White, 1993). Microworlds enable a diverse set of experiences, encouraging children to broaden the scope of their intellectual investigations. Effective microworlds do not turn learners' "experience[s] into abstractions. [Instead, they turn] abstractions, like the laws of physics, into experience" (diSessa, 1986, p. 212). By actualizing these experiences, microworlds enable learners to directly experience simulations. Or, more precisely, they enable users to enjoy experiences with those simulations that are as direct as we can make them (diSessa, 1986).

In the past, direct interaction with a simulated environment meant manipulating agents or parameters in a microworld or controlling an avatar in a virtual world. New technology allows us recast the notion of "directly" interacting with a computationally simulated experience. We can now deploy simulations in the real world, facilitating a more direct experience for learners. Our goal is that, just as microworlds have greatly enhanced the learning experiences available to students, Participatory Simulations will provide another range of learning experiences, upon which students and teachers can draw.

Participatory Activities

The Participatory Simulations Project investigates how direct, personal participation in a simulation leads to a rich learning experience that enables students to explore the underlying structure of the simulation. The idea to use direct, personal participation to help children (or learners) gain a new perspective or build a better understanding is not a new one. Dewey emphasized the value of personal participation in educative experiences throughout the curriculum. In the social sciences, perspective-taking activities are quite common (Seidner, 1975). Students might be asked to take on the role of community activists or politicians and simulate a debate on the future of the logging industry. This debate gives the participants a way to represent the characters and think about how the various characters might feel about an issue.

Activities like these are less common in the sciences, where the mechanisms to be studied are not human feelings and behavior but concepts such as planetary motion or molecular interactions. Nonetheless, students sometimes take on those kinds of roles as well, perhaps pretending to be planets in orbit, in an effort to illustrate those phenomena. However, these activities are very different from their social science counterparts. Whereas the social science activities might help the students to think about how a politician, for instance, would feel and behave under certain circumstances, the science activities do not necessarily help students to think about the underlying mechanisms of processes such as planetary motion. Role-playing activities attempt to create links between personal experience and a deeper understanding of why that experience happened, yet the science-based activities often end up being little more than large-scale illustrations.

Researchers have attempted to connect personal and physical interactions to underlying (nonhuman) mechanisms in a variety of ways. Papert (1980) tried to forge links between human action and the rules of Turtle Geometry by asking children to pretend they were the turtle and then translate that understanding into a symbolic representation of the instructions for the turtle's movement. Resnick and Wilensky (1998) expanded upon this idea, involving large groups of people in activities to help them gain a richer understanding of the rules governing emergent systems. Recently, Wilensky and Stroup (1999) developed a network architecture that gives students control over individual agents in a simulation environment. Researchers in systems dynamics also use group activities to help learners develop systems thinking capabilities (Booth Sweeney & Meadows, 1995, 1996; Meadows, 1986; Senge, Roberts, Ross, Smith, & Kleiner, 1994). Participatory Simulations build on these group activities, adding computational tools to create an explicit link between personal experience in real space and the underlying rules that mediate those experiences (Colella, 1998; Colella, Borovoy, & Resnick, 1998).

Another Way to Learn From Experience

Participatory Simulations facilitate another way for learners to collaboratively investigate the relationship between patterns and processes in the world and the rules that give rise to those patterns and processes. Participatory Simulations combine the notion of a microworld, in which models can be executed, with the affordances of real-world experience, enabling learners to become the participants in computer-supported simulations of dynamic systems in real space. Small, distributed computers create a life-sized microworld by deploying consistent, computational rules in real space. Learners can experience and influence this simulation directly. This interaction, though still mediated by technology, is qualitatively different from other technology controlled role-playing games that facilitate interaction through avatars or with the components of a microworld. Direct participation reduces the separation (to use Dewey's terminology) between the internal state of individuals engaged in the activity and the external (objective) conditions that support the experience. Participants' personal connections to the educational situation enable them to bring their previous experiences to bear during the activity, establish strong connections to the activity and the other participants, and, we hope, draw upon their experience in the future.

THE PARTICIPATORY SIMULATIONS PROJECT

The Participatory Simulations Project looks specifically at how a new kind of learning environment can facilitate data analysis, collaborative theory building, and experimental design and can lead to a richer understanding of scientific phenomena. By involving a large number of students (typically between 15 and 30) in a physical experience, the project brings a microworld off of the computer screen and into a child's world. The next section will briefly introduce the activities of Participation Simulations and the way in which those activities are technologically and pedagogically supported.

The Participatory Simulations Project is an extended research endeavor, studying the use of personal exploration of computer-supported environments in science learning. Close to 2,000 people have participated in various activities at schools, in workshops, and at conferences. This chapter reports on a three-week-long pilot project at a local high school.

Participants

This Participatory Simulations Study took place in a public high school classroom. All of the students volunteered for the project and were told that they would be participating in a project to learn about dynamic systems in science. Class time for five days over a three-week period was devoted to activities associated with the Participatory Simulations Study. The chosen Biology class consisted mainly of tenth grade students.

Sixteen students participated in the study. The teacher also participated in the activities, and on day four a student teacher observed the class and participated in the activities. The researcher (author) was the facilitator of the classes. In addition, two students videotaped the activities.[4]

Technological Support

We use small, wearable computers to enable direct participation in the simulation. Previous work in augmented reality and wearable computing has explored augmenting a person's interactions with the world (Feiner, MacIntyre, Hollerer, & Webster, 1997; Feiner, MacIntyre, & Seligmann, 1993; Starner et al., 1997) and providing users with real-time, contextual information (Rhodes & Starner, 1996). This project borrows some ideas from personal or wearable computing by outfitting each participant with their own Thinking Tag. Participants wear the Thinking Tag throughout the simulation. Like other wearable computers, the Tags collect information for the participants (like how many other players they have met) and help them to interpret the state of other players (for example, whether someone is "sick" or "healthy").

Unlike the traditional notion of wearable computing, which focuses on connecting users to an external network such as the Web, the Tags connect all of the participants in their own network, which facilitates inter-user connectivity and provides the computational support for the simulation. Rather than just transforming the experience of an individual, Participatory Simulations transform the interactions among people by linking them through a personalized network of communicating computers. Participants become players in a computationally mediated system comprised of people and their small, personal computers.

Participatory Simulations are supported by a variation of the Thinking Tag technology developed at the Media Lab (Borovoy, McDonald, Martin, & Resnick, 1996). The Tags are used to transform each participant into an "agent" in a simulation of a dynamic system. In these decentralized simulations, no one Tag acts as a server and no large (traditional) computer is necessary to run, experiment with, or analyze the system. We developed a new version of the Thinking Tags[5] to facilitate collaborative analysis of many iterations of the simulation. As in the original Thinking Tag design, we took care to ensure that the enhanced information display would not interfere with participants' social interactions (Borovoy, Martin, Resnick, &

---

[4]One student was a member of the Biology class who preferred to not be filmed for religious reasons and the other was a classmate from a different Biology class.

[5]Special thanks are owed to Kwin Kramer for designing and building this version of the Thinking Tags.

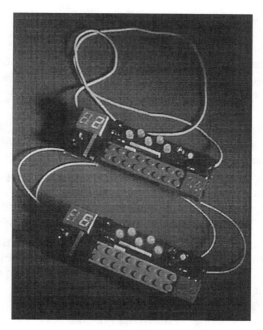

FIG. 9.1. Two virus Tags. The top Tag has met two people and is not sick. The bottom Tag has met six people and is "sick" as indicated by the five flashing LEDs.

Silverman, 1998; Borovoy et al., 1996; Ishii, Kobayashi, & Arita, 1994; Ishii & Ullmer, 1997).

Like the original Thinking Tags, the Tags built for Participatory Simulations are complete, albeit miniature, computers with input and output devices and displays for the user. Each Tag possesses an infrared transmitter and receiver, allowing it to dynamically exchange information with all other Tags in the simulation. As the simulation is running, the Tags are constantly exchanging information via infrared, though this exchange is invisible to the participants. The Tags have two display devices, a double-digit number pad and five bicolor LEDs (see Fig. 9.1). During the simulation the information displayed on the Tags changes, and participants watch the Tags to discover information about themselves and about other players. A resistive sensor port acts as an input device, allowing users to attach small tools to their Tags and enabling them to "dial-in" information or change the program their Tag is running. This carefully chosen set of inputs and outputs provides a rich set of user interactions, both during the simulation and during the subsequent analysis.

The Initial Disease Simulation

Aside from a very brief introduction to the researcher and the Media Lab, the students' first experience in the Participatory Simulations Study was playing a disease simulation game. Each student was handed a Tag and the basic features of the technology were explained, namely that:

- the Tags communicate with one another by infrared, "like a television remote control," so that directionality is important when interacting with another player,
- the number pad displays the number of different people each participant has interacted with, and
- the five LEDs flash red when the Tag is sick.

In addition, the students were given one other guideline for the simulation—they were told that they were free to stop playing anytime they wanted and could do so simply by turning their Tag around to face their stomachs (or turning it off) and sitting down.

The context was set for the first simulation by giving the students a challenge: Meet as many people as they could (kept track of on the number pad) without getting sick. They were told that one of the Tags contained a virus. As indicated above, the students were told nothing about how the virus moved from one Tag to another, nor were they told anything about the degree of contagiousness, the possibility for latency, or any other underlying rule that could affect the spread of the disease, leaving them in an ambiguous situation. None of the students' questions about the behavior of the virus were answered. Instead, they were given the opportunity to experience and explore the disease simulation for themselves.

Activities

In the Participatory Simulations Study, students participated for 45 to 55 minutes on each of four days and 90 minutes on the last day. The project was divided into three distinct phases. On the first day (phase 1) students were introduced to the researcher and a few other examples of technology that operate on the same general principles as the Tags (Resnick et al., 1998). On days two, three, and four (phase 2) students participated in disease simulations, or "games," and analyses of those simulations. This phase had three distinct components: the initial disease simulation, the discussion of that simulation, and the development and execution of experiments to test hypotheses about that simulation. The students completed six disease games over the course of the three days, with the discoveries from one simulation leading to the design of the next. Finally, on day five (phase 3) students reflected on their experiences in the Participatory Simulations Study and asked to participate in one final simulation game.

Data Collection

Bringing new computational tools into a classroom can fundamentally alter the structure of the class's interactions. The unit of analysis in the Participatory Simulations Study was not the individual child nor the individual child plus the tool, but the whole cognitive system in the classroom (Newman, 1990; Salomon, 1993). Newman defines the cognitive system as follows:

> The teacher creates a social system in the classroom that supports certain kinds of discourse and activities; students collaborate within the system, contributing observations, answers, and concrete products such as texts, projects, and data. The cognitive system includes the externalized tools, texts, data, and discourse, all of which is produced by and for the activities. (p. 187)

During the Participatory Simulations Study, attention was paid to how all aspects of the learning environment (the group of students, their conversations, and the tools they employed) contribute to building scientific understanding.

This study analyzed conversations and explicit collaborative discussions during the activities. The main source of data for the Participatory Simulations Study was a complete videotape log of the sessions that, in particular, aimed to capture all of the whole-group conversations. In addition, audiotape backups were made of every session and facilitator logs were kept throughout the project. Students were occasionally asked to write down their ideas about the simulation dynamics, and all of those student responses were kept. Video records were logged and transcribed. Forty episodes were chosen as key events, based upon their identification as dense interactional segments. Each of the episodes was coded to identify the presence of four activities: immersion in the simulation, identification and analysis of evidence, experimental design and prediction, and negotiation about scientific vocabulary. The episodes were also coded by a second person in a blind test with an inter-rater reliability of .945.

RESULTS

Immersion in the Simulation

One of the key components of the Participatory Simulation is its ability to give the students a real experience that is mediated by a set of underlying formal rules. One measure of success of the Participatory Simulations, then, is the extent to which students feel as though they *actually* experienced the simulation—or in Dewey's terms, the extent to which the simulation experience fulfilled the principles of continuity and interaction. In this case, we can judge the experiential quality of the simulation by investigating the extent to which students really felt like they were in the midst of an epidemic striking members of their small community.

The following episode depicts some of the excitement and tension that permeates the learning environment:

Episode 1

Doug:	I got it from her.
Student:	You all got the <u>vi~rus</u>!
Stacy:	I'm dead.
Doug:	(to Tony) Oh, you got the virus now.
Tony:	(looking at Tag) You got it started.
Rick:	(singing) I ain't got the <u>vir~us</u>.
Student:	I'm healthy.
Meredith:	(holding Tag up) I don't have the virus.
Researcher:	Who in this room met the most people?
Chorus of students:	I have 14, I got 16, I got 13 with no virus, me too, I got 14 with no virus.
Student:	I need some medicine.

Students display a robust and persistent willingness to suspend their disbelief and behave as though the simulation activity is real. When Stacy exclaims that she is "dead," she is not talking about an external agent or avatar—she is talking about herself in the simulation. Similar references occur throughout the study, as when a student declares that he needs medicine.

It is important to note that it is not surprising that the students refer to "the virus," as they were told before the game that one of the Tags had a virus. Instead, the claim is that the learning environment promotes a strong connection between the students and the simulation. These students actually speak and interact as though they are sick, even though they are merely wearing Tags that show a number and "red lights" or "no red lights." They clearly know on one level that this is just a game, but they are engaged in the activity in a profound manner.

Returning briefly to the principles of experience, we can ask whether or not this Participatory Simulation satisfies continuity and interaction. As the students play the first virus game, they articulate connections between their internal state and external conditions of the disease simulation. They are engaged with and immersed in the experience. The Participatory Simulation allows the inclusion of the prior knowledge, attitudes, habits, and interests that the students bring to the experience. The activity "arouses curiosity, strengthens initiative, and sets up desires and purposes" (Dewey, 1988, p. 20) in the students, propelling them to develop an understanding of the simulation environment.

This level of engagement permeates the next four days of the research project. As each game unfolds, the students once again have a "real-life" experience of an epidemic invading their small community. They do not need to imagine what it would be like for all of them to be struck by some mysterious disease, for in the context of the Participatory Simulation, many of them have been struck by that disease. Their task is not to mentally construct the dynamics of an epidemic from a written description or a set of equations. Instead, they need to figure out what is happening in their community. This compelling, immersive experience is one of the key components of the Participatory Simulation and sets the stage for the learning activities that follow.

Though engagement in the immersive experience is an integral and important component of Participatory Simulations, the immersive component per se does not determine the activity's educative value. The experience's potential for leading to growth rests on its ability to allow the students to problematize their indeterminate situation (and later to inquire into its underlying structure). In this case, considerable learning occurs as students are able to step back from their immediate experience and analyze the situation. Ackermann (1996) has described this process as "diving-in" and "stepping-out," as students move back and forth between full immersion *in* a problem and thinking *about* a problem. Similarly, Sterman (1994) distinguishes between the features of learning *in* and *about* dynamic systems.[6] Many scientific problems offer the chance to step outside of the problem and think clearly about it. Few problems that are appropriate for study at a high school level offer the chance to step so convincingly *into* a problem. Participatory Simulations create a unique opportunity for students to enjoy both of these important perspectives during the processes of defining and solving problems.

The notion of stepping *into* a scientific problem in order to better understand it has not always been highly valued by researchers. The scientific community has traditionally valued detached, objective modes of experimentation, at the expense of more "connected" methods; however, some examples from scientific practice indicate that a revaluation of connected science may be in order.[7]

Participatory Simulations can bring connected science to the classroom without forcing students to abandon the exploration of scientifically important problems. Earlier, evidence revealed that the students in this

---

[6]See also diSessa (1986).

[7]See Keller (1983) for an example of how "diving-in" to a problem can yield innovative and previously unimagined solutions to scientific questions and Wilensky (1993) and Wilensky and Reisman (1998) for discussions of connected mathematics and science.

study are intimately connected to their disease simulation. Many feel as though they have become sick or cry out that they have "died." As students collect data and design experiments, they remain in touch with the problem at hand. A nontrivial characteristic of the Participatory Simulations environment makes this connection possible—the students are collecting data about and experimenting on themselves.

The students in a Participatory Simulation generally step back from the activity and stop playing the game when a small majority of their Tags becomes sick. As they finish, students sit down, assess their own states, and begin to ascertain what happened to their classmates. After everyone is done playing, the facilitator reconvenes the entire group, and they begin to examine what happened. First, they establish who gained the highest number of points without getting sick. Then, they begin a collaborative exploration to discover why the game unfolded as it did.

Problem Definition and Hypothesis Construction

At the close of the first simulation, there is no clearly defined problem for the students to explore, but they are certainly in a problematic situation. Almost all of the students in the class are sick—a surprising outcome for many of the participants who thought that they had avoided the virus. The facilitator asks if there is anyone in the class who managed not to get sick. The students begin "comparing notes" in an attempt to explain the outcome of the simulation.

First the students accumulate data, and then they begin to make assertions based on the available information. Some of the students' initial assertions are hypotheses about *why* something happened, some are suggestions about *how* they could prove or disprove a particular hypothesis, and others are ideas about *what* problem they should be investigating in the first place. Students offer supporting evidence for or contradictory evidence against many of these assertions. As the available evidence accumulates and ideas proliferate, the potential for constructing testable hypotheses about the viral behavior grows.

In the following episode, students are presenting their pieces of data from the simulation. Notice that data in a Participatory Simulation are really observations about a student's behavior or state during or after the game.

Episode 2

Rick: We should all meet each other.
Joan: I met Doug like two minutes before he gave the virus to other people and I didn't get sick.
Allison: How do you clear these?
Student: I need a medicine, I need an antibiotic.

Researcher:	Is there anyone who started with the virus other than this guy in the front?
Rick:	Doug. (Supplying the name of the guy in front.)
Allison:	That's just 'cause Doug's dirty.
Joan:	Doug didn't start off with the virus.
Researcher:	Who started out with the virus?
Allison:	'Cause I met him, I met him.
Joan:	'Cause I met Doug and I didn't get the virus.
Allison:	Doug was the second person I met.
Doug:	I . . . I met her and then, I just, the virus was just like pop.
Allison:	I didn't get the virus until I got it from somebody else.

Here data are presented (some before this episode begins) that culminate in the notion that Doug has infected a lot of people. But the students' suggestions are not especially focused on running experiments or testing hypotheses. When the researcher restates the question, "Who started out with the virus?" the students continue offering suggestions and ideas but do not respond directly to the question.

It is still apparent that the students are still highly engaged in the disease metaphor, even though they are no longer playing the game and are now evaluating its outcome. The students are busy contributing evidence about whether or not Doug started out with the virus when Allison says, "that's just 'cause Doug's dirty." Clearly, Doug's personal behavior has nothing to do with this particular simulation (and her characterization may not even be accurate), but for Allison it feeds into the connection between the external conditions of the experience and her own internal feelings (in this case, about Doug). Yet, this interaction between the students and the experience does not prevent them from participating in the more objective problem-solving endeavor. Just moments later, Allison is fully involved in gathering evidence about Doug's state. The ability of the students to keep both of these perspectives in mind shows that the immersive experience students have with the disease game can remain influential, even while they are puzzling over the dynamics of the simulation. Students are able to "dive-in" to and "step-out" of the problem throughout the Participatory Simulation, solidifying their connection to the problem *and* facilitating their scientific discoveries throughout the investigation process.

A later episode reveals the students' more structured attempts to test the validity of the proposition that a person could be infected by the last person he or she met:

Episode 3

Liz:	All right, I'm all set; I'm not meeting nobody else.
Liz:	I'm sick.

Rick: Oh, I just boot beeped[8] her.
Stacy: Liz's the first one. Liz's the first one to get sick!
Stacy: Who'd you share with?[9] Do you remember?
Allison: (While writing on the board) Wait, who was the last one you
           shared with?
Liz: Rick.
Allison: Wait, you gotta go in order.
Stacy: OK, look at, Doug, Rick was the last person she shared with.
Liz: It's Rick's fault, it's all Rick's fault.
Stacy: No 'cause I shared with Rick.
Liz: I shared with Rick too.

As students describe their observations, for example, "Rick was the last person she shared with," others respond, either with data from their own experience or with hypotheses that might provide an interpretive frame for the previous data. For instance, Liz hypothesizes that "it's all Rick's fault" after a number of observations that sick people had recently shared with Rick. This interpretive frame turns out to be inadequate to explain everyone's experience. Two students quickly rebut Liz's hypothesis with observations that they had each met Rick and were not yet sick.

At this point, students have converged on a few problematic issues in their situation that they would like to solve, including discovering the identity of Patient Zero (the person who started out with the virus) and describing the way that the virus moves from one person to another. Their ill-structured presentation of fragments of evidence seen earlier has given way to collecting evidence that might suggest which hypotheses warrant further investigation. This pattern of inquiry is consistent with the notion that ideas lead to more directed observation, which in turn brings new facts to light and suggests fruitful directions to pursue (Dewey, 1938/1998b).

Experimental Design

During a Participatory Simulation, the rules of the simulation are fixed. Students explore the simulation by altering their own behaviors and observing the effects of those alterations on the dynamics and outcome of the simulation. In this study, as the students develop a sense of the kinds of outcomes they can produce, they begin to propose more specific actions that they feel

---

[8]Because the Tags make a tiny "beep" each time they interact with another Tag, some students began describing a meeting as "beeping" or "boot beeping." This language was laced with innuendo about the type of interaction that students felt the Tags were simulating.

[9]"Sharing with" is another way that students talk about meeting one another.

will shed some light on the disease dynamics. Their "observation of facts and suggested meanings or ideas arise and develop in correspondence with each other. The more facts of the case [that] come to light in consequence of being subjected to observation, the clearer and more pertinent become the conceptions of the way the problem constituted by these facts is to be dealt with" (Dewey, 1938/1998b, p. 173). Their suggestions become ideas that, when examined in reference to the situation, engender the capacity to predict and test solutions to their problematic situation.

In this section, we will explore their experimental design and execution. Just as their descriptions of the experimental state during the data collection phase were about *their own* state, their experimental design involves varying *their own* behavioral dynamics to elucidate the viral dynamics. Students offer ideas about how they could use variations in their own behavior to discover patterns in the viral behavior. As the experimenting proceeds and hypotheses are refined, the students improve their ability to predict the viral outcome based on a certain set of (experimentally configured) behaviors. Through experimenting and collecting additional data about the relationship between their own behavior and the behavior of the virus (by conducting additional simulations), they are eventually able to state the rules that govern the viral behavior. This process is a form of scientific experimentation, in which a system is probed under various conditions to reveal the underlying processes that govern the system's behavior.

In Episode 2 the first example of experimental design was uttered. Rick proposed a method to figure out why some people didn't get sick when he exclaimed, "We should all meet each other." At that time, his proposal was ignored by most of his classmates, as there was no community agreement on what aspect of the problematic situation was under investigation. In contrast, we now see students' propositions for a variety of experiments to reveal the underlying dynamics of viral transmission.

Episode 4

Researcher:	Do you have a strategy to avoid that [the virus]?
Allison:	Stay away from people.
Student:	But you don't know who.
Allison:	That's what makes it confusing.
Rick:	I know how we could get it, everyone turn on them badges and just turn 'em around and then whoever has the uh, whoever's thing lights up first.
Doug:	How 'bout all the people, each one [has a] partner, and then only meet with one person and whoever gets sick.
Rick:	Everyone turn their badge around so no one can communicate with them and whoever's thing turns red first.

Doug: But can't the host not get sick, like the person who has
        the virus his buttons won't get red but he could give it to
        someone else?
        Yeah, we could pick groups, like um, they communicate with
        each other, they communicate with two people and if they
        get sick then these are the people who have the virus.
Stacy: Go around the room again like we did before and then as
        soon as your thing turns color, like, yell, out, you know what
        I'm saying, when it turns color, try to see who was the first
        person.
        And then we could record, like, who we shared with.

In this episode, a number of students describe possible experimental protocols. Rick wants everyone to avoid meeting other people in order to determine whose Tag shows viral symptoms ("lights up") first. He feels his plan
will help determine the identity of Patient Zero (the initial host). Doug is concerned that Rick's plan does not control for the possibility that Patient Zero
may just be a carrier and never display the symptoms of the virus. Stacy
wants to run an unconstrained simulation and watch for the first appearance of viral symptoms. Over time, many students propose experiments,
and the group decides which ones they want to conduct, often based on a
comparison between the data the experiment is expected to produce and
the currently available facts. Because there is a high level of iterativity and
flexibility in Participatory Simulations, it is easy to accommodate as many
experiments as the students want to run.

The students in the study exhibit a remarkable level of pride and ownership about their proposed experiments. All students possess the ability to
articulate experiments, which, after all, are really prescriptions for altering
their own behavior in a way that they feel will illuminate the rules of the virus.
Any student can offer an experimental suggestion or direct the group to take
a particular action and observe the results. It is up to the group to determine
whose suggestion makes the most sense given the problem at hand.

Episode 5

Allison: I think we should just turn ours on and wait and see whoever
          gets sick first.
Rick: (Leaping out of his chair) THAT WAS MY PLAN!
          You got that on tape right, I said it first!
... conducting the experiment ...
Rick: We're supposed to chill.
Student: Allison you wanna exchange?
Allison: No, we're not supposed to have anybody.
          Everybody's supposed to have zero.

Stacy:	Is everybody supposed to have zero?
Researcher:	That's what I thought.
Rick:	This is my experiment!
Tom:	Oh, I get it. We're trying to see if anybody turns up red.
Student:	One minute.
Allison:	I think we should give it ten minutes.

The students conceive the experiments and retain complete control over the experimental runs, though the facilitator can aid students during those runs. This student control is possible because of a unique attribute of Participatory Simulations—there is no simulation unless all of the student-agents create one. If any class member becomes marginalized, either because he or she is confused as to the nature of the experiment or because he or she is trying to subvert the experimental process, the group pulls him or her back in.[10] Re-running a simulation or conducting an experiment in this environment necessitates the participation of every student. Otherwise, it is as if the simulation is only partially running, and that situation yields unusable results.

Episode 6

Stacy:	Oh look, it's red.
Allison:	Just only beep her once and that's the only person you meet with is Stacy.
Rick:	Why? Then we're all gonna end up with it!
Allison:	No, 'cause we have to see who's immune.
Doug:	I'm not going to beep her.
Rick:	I don't want to beep her.
Allison:	You have to or else the experiment won't work.

In both Episodes 5 and 6 there is community negotiation about the design and execution of the experiment. Students continue to offer ideas for new experiments and ask for explanations about why certain propositions are expected to yield particular pieces of information from the simulation. But, once the group has begun to collect data, students exert pressure on one another to comply with the stated protocols. The nature of the Participatory Simulation ensures that all of the class members work together. In this way, Participatory Simulations differ from collaborative environments where the facilitator must keep all of the students together. As Allison explains to her classmate, Rick, "you have to [participate with us] or else the experiment won't work."

---

[10]See Granott (1998) for a discussion on defining the size of, and subsequently analyzing, the unit of collaboration.

So far, we have explored qualitative data in support of three claims: 1. The students are immersed in the simulation; 2. They help each other gather evidence, define the problem, and build theories about the dynamics of the system; and 3. They design and execute experiments to test hypotheses about the rules of their simulation environment. In the next section, we will step back to see how the students' experimental design evolved over the course of a number of simulations.

Progression of Experimental Design and Inquiry

The students in this pilot study were challenged to meet a lot of people without catching the virus. They were then able to work together as they figured out what was happening in the simulation. As in a traditional microworld, the students needed to understand the underlying rules of the simulation in order to fully comprehend its dynamics and the final outcome. In this case, understanding was defined as the ability to articulate the underlying viral dynamics. This task was manageable because students could test their hypotheses about the underlying rules by collecting data about and running experiments on themselves. The students learned about these rules not by mastering a specific symbolic representation of them but by continuing to modify their own behavior and observe the resulting viral dynamics until they could reliably predict an experimental outcome. For instance, at the end of the study, they could predict who would or would not get sick after meeting Patient Zero and how long it would take for an infected person to show symptoms of the virus.

During this study, the students played a total of six virus "games." Each simulation game took only a few minutes to play; however, students typically spent more time—up to 25 or 30 minutes—discussing each game and planning their strategy for the next one. In the first few games, students were not inquiring into a well-defined problem. Instead, their focus was on general observation and data collection. As they gained further experience in the simulation environment, they agreed on a few specific problems that they wanted to solve. In the later games, they were more systematic as they designed experiments and collected data to confirm or deny their hypotheses.

An analysis of the episodes from the first Participatory Simulation game reveals that instances of data collection and preliminary data analysis are more frequent than instances of experimental design. As the students tried to make sense of the first game, there was much discussion about each individual's experience in the simulation. There was almost no focus on designing experiments to elucidate the dynamics of the system. As a result of their lack of experimental planning, Game Two followed a very similar pattern of behavior and appeared to yield little new information about the dynamics of the system. In spite of this aimless appearance, Games One and Two were not a waste of the students' time. The evidence that the students gathered and the experiences that they accrued became the foundation for their more systematic approach to problem definition and experimental design in Game Three.

Game Three took place on the second day of participatory activities.[11] During this game, the students agreed on a problem: figuring out how the virus spread from student to student. Then, they worked together to analyze the data that they had collected. In addition, more focused experimental design emerged during this game. The concurrent pursuit of gathering new facts and designing and running new experiments continued through the next three games, increasing in the number of occurrences per game, until the group could articulate the underlying rules of the simulation.

This pattern of activity is consistent with Dewey's pattern of inquiry. As summarized by Hall (1996), "inquiry proceeds by a reflective interplay between selecting conditions in a situation that frame a problem and conceiving of related activities that will bring about a solution" (p. 211). In the Participatory Simulations environment, students framed multiple problems and executed experimental actions to discover the solutions to those problems. They "directed and controlled the transformation of their indeterminate situation into a determinately unified one" (Dewey, 1938/1998b, p. 178). Although this pilot study does not allow us to conclude that the Participatory Simulation alone caused students to engage in inquiry, it does allow us to observe that this environment enabled students to define a problem, engage in progressive inquiry, and solve the problem. Our hope is that this experience will be one of many in which the students build and practice the skills of inquiry.

Revealing the Rules

After four days of collaborative work and increasingly sophisticated experimental design, the students in this study articulated the underlying rules of the disease simulation,[12] namely:

- The virus is latent (invisible) for approximately three minutes.
- Patient Zero gets sick after approximately three minutes.
- Any person whose Tag has the virus, even if it is not visible, can infect another person's Tag.

---

[11]Our experience in this and other Participatory Simulations has shown that allowing time for independent reflection results in more proficient problem definition and experimental design.

[12]Because the Tags are fully programmable, these rules can be modified or completely changed for a different Participatory Simulation.

- The probability for infection when meeting an infected Tag is 100%.
- People with Tags numbered 1 or 2 in the ones position (1, 2, 11, 12, 21, etc.) are immune to the virus.
- Immune Tags are not carriers of the disease.

DESIGN CRITERIA FOR CREATING IMMERSIVE LEARNING ENVIRONMENTS

This section describes some of the classroom level decisions that were implemented during the Participatory Simulations Study and looks at how those decisions supported and shaped the students' experiences.

Create a Compelling, Direct Experience

Participatory Simulations bring students into direct contact with an experience. Like many other experiences that teachers create for their students, Participatory Simulations create a personally compelling learning environment that connects the internal and external conditions of the situation. Because the simulation occurs in real space with students as agents, there is no gulf between participants' immediate experience and the simulation—they *are* the population that is being affected. Participants' internal conditions or responses to the simulation are not treated as separate from their inquiry into the simulation. Though the Participatory Simulation is an intentionally contrived environment, the students are immersed in the experience, often exclaiming that they have "gotten sick" or "caught HIV."

Far from preventing inquiry or impeding the study of important scientific material, participants' personal experience in the simulation reduces the barrier to entry for the design and execution of scientific experiments. Any participant can collect data (by reporting on their own experience or that of a peer) or propose an experiment (by suggesting a new pattern of human behavior). The virus simulation analyzed here supported a rich set of experiential and experimental outcomes in a socially meaningful context.

Facilitating Similar but Nonidentical Experiences

The activities in a Participatory Simulation are designed so that every student has a similar and meaningful experience. Similar experiences of the activity ensure that the students share a common base, from which they explore the simulation. When a participant describes his or her experience of the activity, his or her classmates can understand and relate to that description, in part based on their own experiences. Later, when students collect data and propose experiments, they are all equally prepared to take part in these activities. Meaningful experiences ensure that every participant's experience is important with respect to understanding the behavior of the whole simulation. Because a Participatory Simulation is a completely distributed system, no single Tag is "running" the whole simulation. No one student's Tag is more or less important than any other student's Tag,[13] and similarly, no student's experience is any more or less important than any other student's experience. In fact, all of the students must contribute their experiences to the group discussion in order to make it possible to understand the dynamics of the system. The activities themselves enable a "social organization in which all individuals have an opportunity to contribute something" and "to which all feel a responsibility" (Dewey, 1988, pp. 34–35).

However, not every experience is designed to be identical. Students whose Tags are immune to the virus have experiences that differ consistently from those of their classmates. Students who elect to behave in a particular manner—perhaps meeting a lot of people or perhaps interacting with no one at all—also have incongruous experiences. The asymmetry of experience is created not by the differing talents of the students but by their differing experiences of the activity. To decipher the underlying mechanisms of the whole virus simulation, students must first develop an understanding of what happened to them and then listen to what happened to other people. As their descriptions build one by one, the students begin to develop an understanding of the system as a whole. The experiences that differ from the mainstream can then be identified as outliers, and alternative hypotheses can be proposed for those data points.

Participatory Simulations enable a kind of collaborative learning in which every child's experience builds toward an understanding of the whole. However, Participatory Simulations set up a different structure for collaboration than many other forms of collaborative learning do (Aronson, Blaney, Stephan, Sikes, & Snapp, 1978; Collins, Brown, & Newman, 1989; Slavin, 1996), because only a collaborative effort that engages all of the participants will enable the group to construct a model of the whole simulation. Every student needs to share his or her experience of the simulation and every student must participate in the experimental runs of the simulation. The process involved in building a collective understanding of the whole system pushes students to make their thinking overt (Brown & Campione, 1990) as they explain their ideas and predictions to their classmates. This environment is particularly rich for looking at the process of collaboration because the technology supports and mediates a problem context that involves the whole group, allows face-to-face collaboration, and provides a computational substrate for experimental design and execution.

---

[13]With the possible exception of Patient Zero who begins the infection; however, that designation is chosen randomly at the beginning of each game, meaning that (in this case) Patient Zero might be Doug the first game, Rick the second, and Liz the third, etc.

Keep the Technology Unobtrusive

As in earlier work with Thinking Tag technology, care was taken to preserve natural social interactions, using the Tags to augment, not take over, communication and collaboration. In the Participatory Simulations Study this design choice accomplished two important goals. First, the Tags do not get in the way of the natural communication between students. Second, though the technology is quite unobtrusive, the students become deeply engaged in the disease experience.

There are many well-documented and varied examples of computer-supported collaborative learning (e.g., Koschmann, 1996). Participatory Simulations provide another example of a computer-based collaborative environment that fully supports natural communication among students. Participants use voice, gesture, and expression to communicate with one another, rather than sharing information through text and images on-screen. Students' interactions with each other and the simulation are not constrained by large monitors or awkward technology configurations.[14] Moreover, the minimal technology display seems to encourage students to use their own imagination and prior experience during the activities. The students are able to use social cues and knowledge about each other to enhance their engagement in the game. Picture Rick's pride when he exclaimed that he wasn't sick: "I'm the man . . . that's right, I'm a clean head again . . . You all want to be like me." Or the initial suspicion that Tom was the first carrier: "Who started out with it? I think Tom did. Why? Because . . . look at him. (laughter) Sometimes you can tell like that." Or the notion that Doug started out with the virus because he was "dirty." On the last day of the project, two students recall their experiences:

Episode 7

Tony: You don't feel good when you have the virus unless there's something not working up there. . . . Yeah, 'cause I didn't like it, I got it [the virus] when I wasn't even in the room and that was just upsetting to me. It's a hard thing to deal with.

Episode 8

Doug: Say you have HIV or something, a virus, and it don't show up in your system right away, you could give it to someone else without knowing.

---

[14]See Stewart, Bederson, and Druin (1999) and Stewart, Raybourn, Bederson, and Druin (1998) for a different approach to enabling multiple students to interact with a single computer.

The students who participate in Participatory Simulations use the framework of the simulation, their own imagination, prior knowledge, and past experience as they become immersed in the simulation. They feel as though they are really sick even though there is very little explicit visual support for the metaphor of the game.

The Tags' minimal display does not impair the students' ability or willingness to become immersed in the simulation, and the unobtrusive nature of the Tag technology supports rich interactions among a large group of students. This result may have implications for designing engaging educational technology, the budget for which rarely rivals that of pricey virtual reality games where fancy graphics and head-mounted displays provide all of the context for a "virtually real" experience.

Add Coherent, Consistent Rules to the Experiential World

For many years role-playing games have entertained children and adults. These games, such as Dungeons and Dragons, enable participants to adopt certain personas and, in so doing, require that the participants behave like their characters would in any given situation. Computers, and in particular the Internet, have expanded the range and popularity of these games (Turkle, 1995). The Thinking Tags create a new kind of role-playing game, which combines the immediacy of real-life adventure with the consistent rules of mediated games. Without constraining the communication or the behavior of the students, the Tags provide a tremendous amount of structure in the environment. The Tags carry the underlying rules of the simulation (viral rules in this study) into the students' world. In some sense, the Tags transform the students into agents in a microworld, even as they allow the students to retain their own personalities.

Bringing a microworld into the realm of students' experience enables them to explore the underlying formal structure of that world without abandoning their own perspective. They make use of the consistent behavior of the Tags as they design experimental protocols to reveal the rules that govern viral behavior. Each of these components of the Participatory Simulation arises because the Tags create an environment that is initially mysterious but upon further reflection and action becomes transparent. The use of the Tags allows the students to reach transparency through a new path that draws upon the students' own personal experiences and their own systematic explanations of those experiences.

When designing this Participatory Simulation, we constructed a simulation that explores a few important concepts, rather than creating a simulation that closely mirrors a real life situation. In this example, we focus on the concepts of latency and immunity. Though many students compare this Participatory Simulation to HIV, we do not model any of the complexities of HIV transmission (and the infection rate of 100% is quite different from that of HIV). We purposely include the artifact of only being able to meet another person once in this simulation because it makes the model tractable, not because it increases fidelity to a real world disease. Roughgarden (Roughgarden, Bergman, Shafir, & Taylor, 1996) called this type of model, which seeks to capture the most fundamental parts of the system and illustrate a general principle, an "idea model." Participatory Simulations allow us to create a rich learning environment that is based upon a "small cluster" of essential ideas (diSessa, 1986), in this case latency and immunity. It may be that more complex systems models are better explored through other media, including microworlds and traditional simulation environments.

Enabling Students to Create Their Own Solutions

In the pilot Participatory Simulations study, students were not given a specific vocabulary to use when discussing the rules of the simulation, nor were they given an alternative written representation to describe the data they collected or the hypotheses they proposed. This lack of predefined structure for meaning-making activities appears to be both promising and problematic.

Throughout the activities, but especially after the third game, the students endeavor to clearly express their ideas so that others can follow the points they are making. In time, they begin to agree on ways to talk about the activity that everyone can understand. Here, they use the Tag numbers to express the concept of immunity.

> Episode 9
>
> Tony: It was a pattern like that 20 21 thing. The numbers.
> Meredith: It was 1 2 11 21.
> Tony: I ~said~ the 21 thing.
> Meredith: It wasn't specific.
> Tony: It was specific—you knew what I was talking about. It was specific enough.

When Tony mentions the "20 21 thing," he is referencing the fact that he thinks a certain set of Tags are immune to the virus. When Meredith corrects him by indicating *exactly* which Tags are immune, he protests, pointing out that even if his comment was not precise, it was sufficient for her to understand what he meant.

This type of discourse is consistent with that of many other Participatory Simulations we have run, in which participants digress from data collection or experimental design to settle on a precise meaning for "immunity" or "carrier." (In the case of immunity, students typically discuss whether or not immune people can infect others even if they never show symptoms of the virus. In the case of a carrier, participants usually debate whether or not a carrier can ever show symptoms of the disease.)

In its current implementation, facilitators of a simulation do not provide correct definitions for these or other debated terms, even if the definition that the students ultimately agree on is not precisely correct. This process allows the students to arrive at their own vocabulary for articulating the rules of the simulation. Although we have not yet undertaken extensive research in this area, the consistency with which various student groups work to define specific meanings for their descriptions of the simulation suggests that more research into this activity may be warranted.

Similarly, the facilitator in this study did not suggest any kind of alternative representation for the data or the rules of the simulation. Some groups of students try to design charts, diagrams, or other graphical depictions to aid in their analyses of the problem. The group in this pilot study drew a chart on the board of the last person that each student had met (during Episode 3). Unfortunately, unlike creating representations for systemwide behaviors and outcomes, it is quite difficult to represent individual behaviors and outcomes in agent-based simulations (like this Participatory Simulation) in a manner that illuminates the key interactions (e.g., Feigenbaum, Kannan, Vardi, & Viswanathan, 1999). Other researchers have explored the cognitive gains that people make when creating their own representations (Bamberger, 1998; diSessa, Hammer, Sherin, & Kolpakowski, 1991; Greeno & Hall, 1997; Hall, 1996; Nemirovsky, 1994), and we hope to find a way to include such activities in future Participatory Simulations.

REFLECTIONS

As Salomon (1995), Newman (1990), and others have noted, it is difficult to isolate a set of variables that, when altered in a classroom, change the nature of the learning that takes place. This difficulty is certainly illustrated in this study, where the technology mediates a new activity, changes the relationships among the students, and extends the standard notion of scientific exploration. Nonetheless, this pilot study suggests an opportunity to reevaluate the role that experience can play in understanding the mechanisms that govern patterns and processes in the world. Participatory Simulations are designed educational experiences that fulfill Dewey's principles of continuity and interaction and enable students to make inquiries into meaningful problems. Much work remains to be done to determine the best ways to utilize Participatory Simulations and other similar activities in the context of classroom learning goals.

ACKNOWLEDGMENTS

Portions of this chapter appeared as an article in the *Journal of the Learning Sciences*, published by Lawrence Erlbaum Associates and are reprinted here with permission (Colella, 2000). Special thanks are owed to my advisor, Mitchel Resnick, for his support and valuable insight throughout the project, to Timothy Koschmann for his helpful comments and many enlightening conversations about Dewey, to Brian Smith for his candid feedback and assistance, and to Mark Guzdial for his encouragement. I would also like to thank Jeremy Roschelle and an anonymous reviewer for their contributions to the chapter. Thanks are also extended to the members of the Epistemology and Learning Group at the MIT Media Laboratory, especially Richard Borovoy and Kwin Kramer. I am indebted to the many students and teachers who have participated in this project. This research has been generously supported by the LEGO Group, the National Science Foundation (Grants 9358519-RED and CDA-9616444), and the MIT Media Laboratory's Things That Think and Digital Life consortia.

REFERENCES

Ackermann, E. (1996). Perspective-taking and object construction: Two keys to learning. In Y. Kafai & M. Resnick (Eds.), *Constructionism in practice: Designing, thinking, and learning in a digital world* (pp. 25–35). Mahwah, NJ: Lawrence Erlbaum.

Aronson, E., Blaney, N., Stephan, C., Sikes, J., & Snapp, M. (1978). *The jigsaw classroom.* Beverly Hills, CA: Sage.

Bamberger, J. (1998). Action knowledge and symbolic knowledge: The computer as mediator. In D. Schön, B. Sanyal, & W. Mitchell (Eds.), *High technology in low-income communities* (pp. 235–261). Cambridge, MA: MIT Press.

Booth Sweeney, L., & Meadows, D. (1995, 1996). *The systems thinking playbook: Exercises to stretch and build learning and systems thinking capabilities.* Contact L. Fowler (603) 862–2244.

Borovoy, R., Martin, F., Resnick, M., & Silverman, B. (1998). *GroupWear: Nametags that tell about relationships.* Paper presented at CHI '98, Los Angeles, CA.

Borovoy, R., McDonald, M., Martin, F., & Resnick, M. (1996). Things that blink: Computationally augmented name tags. *IBM Systems Journal, 35,* 488–495.

Brosterman, N. (1997). *Inventing Kindergarten.* New York: Harry N. Abrams, Inc.

Brown, A., & Campione, J. (1990). Interactive learning environments and the teaching of science and mathematics. In M. Gardner, J. Greeno, F. Reif, A. Schoenfeld, A. diSessa, & E. Stage (Eds.), *Toward a scientific practice of science education* (pp. 111–140). Hillsdale, NJ: Lawrence Erlbaum.

Bruckman, A. (1998). Community support for constructionist learning. *Computer Supported Collaborative Work: The Journal of Collaborative Computing, 7,* 47–86.

Colella, V. (1998). *Participatory simulations: Building collaborative understanding through immersive dynamic modeling.* Unpublished master's thesis, MIT Media Laboratory, Cambridge, MA.

Colella, V. (2000). Participatory simulations: Building collaborative understanding through immersive dynamic modeling. *Journal of the Learning Sciences, 9*(4), 471–500.

Colella, V., Borovoy, R., & Resnick, M. (1998). *Participatory simulations: Using computational objects to learn about dynamic systems.* Paper presented at CHI '98, Los Angeles, CA.

Collins, A., Brown, J. S., & Newman, S. E. (1989). Cognitive apprenticeship: Teaching the craft of reading, writing, and mathematics. In L. B. Resnick (Ed.), *Knowing, learning, and instruction.* Hillsdale, NJ: Lawrence Erlbaum.

Dewey, J. (1910/1997). *How we think.* Mineola, NY: Dover Publications.

Dewey, J. (1916). *Democracy and education.* New York: The Free Press.

Dewey, J. (1938/1998a). General theory of propositions. In L. Hickman & T. Alexander (Eds.), *The essential Dewey: Volume 2: Ethics, logic, psychology* (pp. 197–200). Bloomington: Indiana University Press.

Dewey, J. (1938/1998b). The pattern of inquiry. In L. Hickman & T. Alexander (Eds.), *The essential Dewey: Volume 2: Ethics, logic, psychology* (pp. 169–179). Bloomington: Indiana University Press.

Dewey, J. (1988). Experience and education. In J. Boydston (Ed.), *John Dewey: The later works, 1925–1953* (Vol. 13, pp. 1–62). Carbondale, IL: Southern Illinois University Press.

diSessa, A. (1986). Artificial worlds and real experience. *Instructional Science, 14,* 207–227.

diSessa, A. (1988). Knowledge in pieces. In G. Forman & P. Pufall (Eds.), *Constructivism in the computer age* (pp. 49–70). Hillsdale, NJ: Lawrence Erlbaum.

diSessa, A., Hammer, D., Sherin, B., & Kolpakowski, T. (1991). Inventing graphing: Meta-representational expertise in children. *The Journal of Mathematical Behavior, 10*(2), 117–160.

Eisenberg, M., & Eisenberg, A. N. (1998). Shop class for the next millennium: Education through computer-enriched handicrafts. *Journal of Interactive Media in Education, 98*(8).

Epstein, J., & Axtell, R. (1996). *Growing artificial societies: Social science from the bottom up.* Washington DC: Brookings Institution Press.

Eylon, B., Ronen, M., & Ganiel, U. (1996). Computer simulations as tools for teaching and learning: Using a simulation environment in optics. *Journal of Science Education and Technology, 5*(2), 93–110.

Feigenbaum, J., Kannan, S., Vardi, M., & Viswanathan, M. (1999). Complexity of graph problems represented by OBDDs. *Chicago Journal of Theoretical Computer Science, 1999*(5), 1–27.

Feiner, S., MacIntyre, B., Hollerer, T., & Webster, T. (1997). *A touring machine: Prototyping 3D mobile augmented reality systems for exploring the urban environment.* Paper presented at the ISWC, Cambridge, MA.

Feiner, S., MacIntyre, B., & Seligmann, D. (1993). Knowledge-based augmented reality. *Communications of the ACM, 36*(7), 52–62.

Fischer, K. (1980). A theory of cognitive development: The control and construction of hierarchies of skills. *Psychological Review, 87,* 477–531.

Goldman, S. (1996). Mediating microworlds: Collaboration on high school science activities. In T. Koschmann (Ed.), *CSCL: Theory and practice of an emerging paradigm* (pp. 45–82). Mahwah, NJ: Lawrence Erlbaum.

Granott, N. (1998). Unit of analysis in transit: From the individual's knowledge to the ensemble process. *Mind, Culture, and Activity, 5,* 42–66.

Greeno, J., & Hall, R. (1997). Practicing representation: Learning with and about representational forms. *Phi Delta Kappan.*

Hall, R. (1996). Representation as shared activity: Situated cognition and Dewey's cartography of experience. *The Journal of the Learning Sciences, 5*(3), 209–238.

Ishii, H., Kobayashi, M., & Arita, K. (1994). Iterative design of seamless collaboration media. *Communications of the ACM, 37*(8), 83–97.

Ishii, H., & Ullmer, B. (1997). *Tangible bits: Towards seamless interfaces between people, bits, and atoms.* Paper presented at CHI '97, Atlanta, GA.

Jackson, S., Stratford, S., Krajcik, J., & Soloway, E. (1994). Making dynamic modeling accessible to pre-college science students. *Interactive Learning Environments, 4,* 233–257.

Keller, E. F. (1983). *A feeling for the organism: The life and work of Barbara McClintock.* San Francisco, CA: W. H. Freeman.

Koschmann, T. (Ed.). (1996). *CSCL: Theory and practice of an emerging paradigm.* Hillsdale, NJ: Lawrence Erlbaum.

Lillard, P. (1972). *Montessori: A modern approach.* New York: Schocken Books.

Maxis. (1992). SimLife [computer software]. Orinda, CA.

Maxis. (1993). SimCity [computer software]. Orinda, CA.

Meadows, D. (1986). *FishBanks, LTD* (http://www.unh.edu/ipssr/index.html/ipssr/lab/ fishbank.html). Durham, NH: Institute for Policy and Social Science Research.

Montessori, M. (1912). *The Montessori method.* New York: Frederick Stokes Co.

National Committee on Science Education Standards and Assessment, N. R. C. (1996). *National Science Education Standards.* Washington, DC: National Academy Press.

Nemirovsky, R. (1994). On ways of symbolizing: The case of Laura and velocity sign. *The Journal of Mathematical Behavior, 3,* 389–422.

Newman, D. (1990). Using social context for science teaching. In M. Gardner, J. Greeno, F. Reif, A. Schoenfeld, A. diSessa, & E. Stage (Eds.), *Toward a scientific practice of science education* (pp. 187–202). Hillsdale, NJ: Lawrence Erlbaum.

Norman, D. (1993). *Things that make us smart: Defending human attributes in the age of the machine.* Reading, MA: Addison-Wesley Publishing Company.

Papert, S. (1980). *Mindstorms: Children, computers, and powerful ideas.* New York: Basic Books, Inc.

Project 2061. (1993). *Benchmarks for scientific literacy.* Oxford: Oxford University Press.

Pufall, P. (1988). Function in Piaget's system: Some notes for constructors of microworlds. In G. Forman & P. Pufall (Eds.), *Constructivism in the computer age* (pp. 15–35). Hillsdale, NJ: Lawrence Erlbaum.

Resnick, M. (1994). *Turtles, termites, and traffic jams: Explorations in massively parallel Microworlds.* Cambridge, MA: MIT Press.

Resnick, M., Martin, F., Berg, R., Borovoy, R., Colella, V., Kramer, K., & Silverman, B. (1998). *Digital manipulatives: New toys to think with.* Paper presented at CHI '98, Los Angeles, CA.

Resnick, M., & Wilensky, U. (1998). Diving into complexity: Developing probabilistic decentralized thinking through role-playing activities. *The Journal of the Learning Sciences, 7,* 153–172.

Rhodes, B., & Starner, T. (1996). *Remembrance agent: A continuously running automated information retrieval system.* Paper presented at the First International Conference on the Practical Application of Intelligent Agents and Multi Agent Technology.

Roberts, N., Anderson, D., Deal, R., Garet, M., & Shaffer, W. (1983). *Introduction to computer simulation: A system dynamics modeling approach.* Reading, MA: Addison-Wesley.

Roschelle, J. (1996). Learning by collaborating: Convergent conceptual change. In T. Koschmann (Ed.), *CSCL: Theory and practice of an emerging paradigm* (pp. 209–248). Mahwah, NJ: Lawrence Erlbaum.

Roschelle, J., & Teasley, S. (1995). The construction of shared knowledge in collaborative problem solving. In C. O'Malley (Ed.), *Computer-supported collaborative learning* (pp. 69–97). New York: Springer-Verlag.

Rothberg, M., Sandberg, S., & Awerbuch, T. (1994). Educational software for simulation risk of HIV. *Journal of Science Education and Technology, 3*(1), 65–70.

Roughgarden, J., Bergman, A., Shafir, S., & Taylor, C. (1996). Adaptive computation in ecology and evolution: A guide for future research. In R. Belew & M. Mitchell (Eds.), *Adaptive individuals in evolving populations: Models and algorithms* (Proceedings Volume XXVI Santa Fe Institute Studies in the Science of Complexity, pp. 25–30). Reading, MA: Addison-Wesley.

Salomon, G. (1993). On the nature of pedagogic tools: The case of the writing partner. In S. Lajoie & S. Derry (Eds.), *Computers as cognitive tools* (pp. 179–196). Hillsdale, NJ: Lawrence Erlbaum.

Salomon, G. (1995). *What does the design of effective CSCL require and how do we study its effects?* Paper presented at the Computer Supported Collaborative Learning (CSCL) Conference, Indiana.

Schoenfeld, A. (1990). GRAPHER: A case study of educational technology, research, and development. In M. Gardner, J. Greeno, F. Reif, A. Schoenfeld, A. diSessa, & E. Stage (Eds.), *Toward a scientific practice of science education* (pp. 281–300). Hillsdale, NJ: Lawrence Erlbaum.

Schön, D. (1992). The theory of inquiry: Dewey's legacy to education. *Curriculum Inquiry, 22*, 119–139.

Seidner, C. (1975). Teaching with simulations and games. In R. Dukes & C. Seidner (Eds.), *Learning with simulations and games* (pp. 11–45). Beverly Hills, CA: Sage.

Senge, P., Roberts, C., Ross, R., Smith, B., & Kleiner, A. (1994). *The fifth discipline fieldbook: Strategies and tools for building a learning organization.* New York: Currency Doubleday.

Slavin, R. (1996). Research on cooperative learning and achievement: What we know, what we need to know. *Contemporary Educational Psychology, 21*(4), 43–69.

Starner, T., Mann, S., Rhodes, B., Levine, J., Healey, J., Kirsch, D., Picard, R., & Pentland, A. (1997). Augmented reality through wearable computing. *Presence, 6*, 386–398.

Starr, P. (1994). Seductions of Sim: Policy as a simulation game. *The American Prospect, 17*(Spring), 19–29.

Sterman, J. (1994). Learning in and about complex systems. *System Dynamics Review, 10*(2–3), 291–330.

Stewart, J., Bederson, B., & Druin, A. (1999). *Single display groupware: A model for co-present collaboration.* Paper presented at CHI '99, Phildelphia, PA.

Stewart, J., Raybourn, E., Bederson, B., & Druin, A. (1998). *When two hands are better than one: Enhancing collaboration using single display groupware.* Paper presented at CHI '98, Los Angeles, CA.

Tabak, I., & Reiser, B. (1997). *Complementary roles of software-based scaffolding and teacher-student interactions in inquiry learning.* Paper presented at the Computer Support for Collaborative Learning (CSCL) Conference, Toronto, Canada.

Tanner, L. (1997). *Dewey's laboratory school: Lessons for today.* New York: Teachers College Press.

Tinker, R. (Ed.). (1996). *Microcomputer based labs: Educational research and standards.* Berlin: Springer-Verlag.

Turkle, S. (1984). *The second self: Computers and the human spirit.* New York: Simon & Schuster.

Turkle, S. (1995). *Life on the screen.* New York: Simon and Schuster.

Turkle, S., & Papert, S. (1992). Epistemological pluralism and the revaluation of the concrete. *Journal of Mathematical Behavior, 11*, 3–33.

Vygotsky, L. S. (Ed.). (1978). *Mind in society: The development of higher psychological processes.* Cambridge, MA: Harvard University.

White, B. (1993). ThinkerTools: Causal models, conceptual change, and science education. *Cognition and Instruction, 10*(1), 1–100.

Wilensky, U. (1993). *Connected mathematics: Building concrete relationships with mathematical knowledge.* Unpublished doctoral dissertation, MIT Media Laboratory, Cambridge, MA.

Wilensky, U., & Reisman, K. (1998). *ConnectedScience: Learning biology through constructing and testing computational theories—An embodied modeling approach.* Paper presented at the Second International Conference on Complex Systems, Nashua, NH.

Wilensky, U., & Stroup, W. (1999). *Learning through participatory simulations: Network-based design for systems learning in classrooms.* Paper presented at the American Educational Research Association (AERA) annual meeting, Montreal, Canada.

PARTICIPATORY SIMULATION: PROSPECTS AND POSSIBILITIES

Jim Garrison
Teaching and Learning
Virginia Tech

Rebecca K. Scheckler
Center for Research on Learning and Teaching
Indiana University

Our response assesses the prospects and possibilities of Participatory Simulations from the perspective of an expanded understanding of the two Deweyan principles used to evaluate any educational experience. Vanessa Colella cites from Chapter 3 of John Dewey's (1938/1988) *Experience and Education*: "Continuity and interaction in their active union with each other provide the measure of the educative significance and value of an experience" (p. 26). Our response largely confines itself to Chapter 3 and 4 of that work.

Dewey (1938/1988) proclaims that "this principle [of continuity] rests upon the fact of habit, when habit is interpreted biologically" (p. 18). Beliefs, for Dewey, are habits and habits are embodied dispositions to act evincing emotions. This allows him to overcome mind versus body dualism. Embodied continuity means every experience modifies our habits, thereby affecting the quality of subsequent experiences. The embodied character of continuity is something with which most versions of computer-mediated instruction cannot readily cope. Participatory Simulations such as that designed by Colella are a very good start.

Habits provide the biological basis for growth. As Dewey notes, "Growth, or growing as developing, not only physically but intellectually and morally, is one exemplification of the principle of continuity" (p. 19). Growth as organic, developmental continuity moves *into* subsequent phases; it is rarely linear: "Every experience is a moving force. Its value can be judged only on the ground of what it moves toward and into" (p. 21). Growth means living a life of expanding capacity, meaning, and value.

Dewey observes that "all human experience is ultimately social . . . it involves contact and communication. The mature person, to put it in moral terms, has no right to withhold from the young on given occasions whatever capacity for sympathetic understanding his own experience has given him" (p. 21). When designing instructional technologies, we must not forget that education is a moral (and aesthetic) interaction before it is a cognitive interaction. Dewey (1925/1981) reminds us that experience involves "things had before they are things cognized" (p. 25). Dewey condemned "intellectualism," by which he meant, "the theory that all experiencing is a mode of knowing," reducible to the refined objects of science (p. 25). Relying too much on cognitive psychology can lead designers of instructional psychology into intellectualism. We note that Timothy Koschmann (1996) views computer-supported collaborative learning (CSCL), of which Participatory Simulation is an application, as distinguished from other work in educational technology in its reliance on "socially oriented theories of learning" (p. 16). This approach puts Participatory Simulation much closer to a Deweyan concept of education than other forms of instructional technology.

Interaction, according to Dewey (1938/1988), "assigns equal rights to both factors in experience—objective and internal conditions. . . . Taken together, or in their interaction, they form what we call a *situation*" (p. 24). He uses the unified notion of situation to overcome knower versus known and subject versus object dualisms. Dewey insists:

> The conceptions of *situation* and of *interaction* are inseparable from each other. An experience is always what it is because of a transaction taking place between an individual and what, at the time, constitutes his environment. . . . The environment . . . is whatever conditions interact with personal needs, desires, purposes, and capacities to create the experience. . . . (p. 25)

Later Dewey (1931/1985) replaced "situation" with "context." Cognitive psychology finds it difficult to acknowledge that all knowing, feeling, and acting are contextual. Koschmann (1996) discusses how theories of situated cognition have influenced CSCL. We note, though, that much more than the cognition of the student (e.g., bodies, feelings, and desires) is situated in the educational experience. Currently, Participatory Simulation recognizes the presence of the student's body, but it could go farther in developing its active role in constructing meaning in interaction with other bodies.

Chapter 4 of *Experience and Nature* discusses "social control." Dewey (1938/1988) concludes that "control of individual actions is effected by the whole situation in which individuals are involved, in which they share and of which they are cooperative or interacting parts" (p. 33). We acquire our habits from our habitat, and the most influential habitat is formed by the customs of the social institutions wherein we interact. For example, people play games and "games involve rules, and these rules order their conduct" (p. 32).

Finally, teachers teach subject matter to students. To do so, teachers must know their students' needs, desires, and state of cognitive development and not just subject matter. The image is of a triangle composed of student, teacher, and subject matter enclosing a pedagogical space. The ideal is that the "teacher loses the position of external boss or dictator but takes on that of leader of group activities" (see p. 37).

Clearly, Participatory Simulation with its emphasis on social participation in "life-sized," rule-constrained, role-playing activities accentuating communication and community is a giant step beyond the detached spectator stance offered by traditional mouse-manipulated, screen-focused versions of virtual reality. It is equally clear that it goes far down the path of Deweyan pedagogy. Participatory Simulation not only talks about "continuity," "interaction," "situation," habits," "collaborative learning," and "rules governing action," it enacts them in the classroom. We heartily endorse all these accomplishments. Below we seek to blaze the trail further in the hope that Participatory Simulation will follow Dewey to the end. We believe this is a promising research program, which is likely to prosper. What follows are some suggestions for further articulating the program.

Participatory Simulations, as Colella indicates, "provide another range of learning experiences." We applaud these possibilities. Our concern is that, as Colella mentions, her study involves "a traditional microworld" wherein "the students need to understand the underlying rules." This in effect creates a bi-level system. We appreciate the fact that the simulation is oriented toward students participating in a genuine community of inquiry rather than their being involved in memorizing predetermined facts and theories. This is immensely important, in part, because it is excellent preparation for participating in the kind of communicative democracy Dewey envisioned. Collela's simulation emphasizes the important relationship between social control expressed by democratic social relations and good science as knowledge claims verifiable by the community. However good our intentions, though, there is always the danger of unintended consequences. The notion that unchanging, indubitable rules lie below a "student's behavioral dynamics" could lead students who participate in such simulations to tacitly learn a foundationalist epistemology and a version of convergent metaphysical realism that Dewey rejects. Varying the programming of the badges does provide a more dynamic simulation, but it might still reinforce foundationalism.

A bi-level conception could bolster, albeit unintentionally, the knower versus known and subject versus object dualisms Dewey decried. It might also reinforce the widely rejected theory of knowledge as correspondence to, or representational copy of, underlying reality. The temptation is to assume a "God's eye" view wherein we may step outside ourselves, and outside existence, to see things as a god would. This temptation is especially strong in those cases where the system designer does, in fact, create the rules governing the context. Perhaps this sense of control leads some designers of instructional systems to assume a naive epistemology and metaphysics. Our sense is that Colella is not naïve, but we must all remain wary.

The cognitive emphasis in Participatory Simulation may show itself somewhat in the bi-level construction where the underlying level not only controls a student's conduct but also provides the only telos for the experience. Again, it is obvious that this is not the educational intention; still, unintentional consequences are, perhaps, present. We are concerned with the reduction of the student's body to little more than a computer holder, the lack of an opportunity for the student to affect the rules of the computer simulation, and, at least at one level, the removal of the student from the basis of the simulation. We note Papert's opinion that, ideally, "the learner in effect 'teaches' the computer" (cited in Koschmann, 1996, p. 9) and wonder how the learners in Colella's microworld will teach their "computer tags." It seems rather that the tags are training the students and even disciplining them for their wrong guesses at the rules of the simulation. We regret that students can only experiment with the rules derived by the creator of the simulation and not at all with the world that gives rise to the simulation. Addressing this concern in future work will advance this valuable research program. Despite our reservations, we acknowledge that there is a place for prestructured simulations as long as their limitations are acknowledged and compensated for elsewhere in the curriculum. We also acknowledge that what we are asking for is difficult to do and Colella has done a good deal already; we are only pointing out possibilities for further research. It appears that Participatory Simulations push the traditional notion of microworlds to its limits. The next stage of inquiry may need to go beyond those limits.

Dewey called such conceptions as those we have discussed "the spectator view of knowledge." Dewey (1929/1984) wrote *The Quest for Certainty* to refute the notion that inquiry could ever arrive at unchangeable, eternal, and immutable knowledge of fixed reality. Instead, Dewey thought: "If we see that knowing is not the act of an outside spectator but of a participator inside the natural and social scene, then the true object of knowledge resides in the consequences of directed action" (p. 157). For Dewey the neo-Darwinian, all existence evolves, including the laws of evolution themselves. Furthermore, for him, human nature is a part of nature, which means our continuous interactions with the rest of existence are transformational and creative:

> The doctrine that nature is inherently rational was a costly one. It entailed
> the idea that reason in man is an outside spectator of a rationality already

complete in itself. It deprived reason in man of an active and creative office; its business was simply to copy, to re-present symbolically, to view a given rational structure. (p. 169)

For Dewey, humankind is an intimate participant in an unfinished and unfinishable universe wherein our creative actions alter the course of events and not a spectator of an inherently rational, rule-driven completed cosmos.

At least three responses are available to the advocates of Participatory Simulations. First, one might choose to simply reject Dewey's theory of knowledge and metaphysics. Those devoted to Enlightenment ideals of rationality will find this alternative attractive. Second, one might begin to construct simulations that resemble Dewey's trans-actional, trans-formative realism wherein embodied and impassioned students actually alter the world they study. For example, consider simple actions such as how collecting flowering plants results in the transportation of seeds to a new site and thus the introduction of a species into a new habitat. We urge the exploration of such possibilities further. Finally, one may just point out that we should not confuse simulation with reality.

Surprisingly, the last alternative is not an option for a Deweyan. Colella repeatedly distinguishes "reality" from "virtual reality" and "simulations," but all experience is experience of reality; what else could it be? We may, nonetheless, make false inferences from experience, but that is a *logical* not a metaphysical, mistake. For instance, in Zöller's "illusion" the lines appear to converge although they are "truly" parallel. The "illusion" is, nonetheless, "real," even if we make a flawed inference. Likewise, virtual reality is "real," even if we should mistakenly infer we are not in a flight simulator. It is a question of determining the correct context.

At the very least, if simulations are simulating "reality," then designers of simulations must engage fundamental metaphysical and epistemological questions if for no other reason than that their simulations will dramatically influence the answers the students themselves tacitly learn. It is vitally important that the simulations we design disclose their construction and open themselves to critique.

Participatory Simulations go a long way toward closing the gap between computerized instructional technology and Deweyan pedagogy. We applaud this progress and challenge Colella and others to go even further. Clearly, improvement in computerized instructional technology is occurring, and equally clearly, there is more work to do.

REFERENCES

Dewey, J. (1925/1981). Experience and nature. In J. A. Boydston (Ed.), *John Dewey: The later works* (Vol. 1). Carbondale, IL: Southern Illinois University Press.

Dewey, J. (1929/1984). The quest for certainty. In J. A. Boydston (Ed.), *John Dewey: The later works* (Vol. 4). Carbondale, IL: Southern Illinois University Press.

Dewey, J. (1931/1985). Context and thought. In J. A. Boydston (Ed.), *John Dewey: The later works* (Vol. 6, pp. 3–21). Carbondale, IL: Southern Illinois University Press.

Dewey, J. (1938/1988). Experience and education. In J. A. Boydston (Ed.), *John Dewey: The later works* (Vol. 13, pp. 1–62). Carbondale, IL: Southern Illinois University Press.

Koschmann, T. (1996). Paradigm shifts and instructional technology: An introduction. In T. Koschmann (Ed.), *CSCL: Theory and practice* (pp. 1–23). Mahwah, NJ: Lawrence Erlbaum Associates.

POWERFUL TECHNOLOGY AND POWERFUL INSTRUCTION

David Hammer
University of Maryland at College Park

POWERFUL TECHNOLOGY

I first learned about simulating an epidemic several years ago from biology teachers on LabNet.[1] In one version (Averill, 1993), each student is given a small cup of clear liquid, and they are told that someone in the room has "AIDS": That student's cup is "contaminated" with sodium hydroxide (a base). The students then "exchange fluids" in pairs, combining the fluids in their cups and splitting the mixture. After several rounds, they each test their fluids with litmus paper. Some of the tests are positive for "AIDS" (the litmus paper turns blue, indicating a basic solution); others are negative, and the class tries to determine who was the original carrier.

Another version of the activity uses live bacteria (Powel, 1993): The students each get a small dish with a piece of candy sitting in liquid, which they use to wet their hands; the liquid in one dish is a culture of bacteria.[2] This time, the students shake hands with each other, to provide the contact, and they test for infection by trying to grow bacteria from their hands on agar plates, which they incubate overnight.

---

[1]LabNet was an electronic community of science teachers, defunct as of February, 1998. See Ruopp, Gal, Drayton, & Pfister (1993).

[2]The particular bacteria chosen do not present a health risk to the students as used in the activity.

I do not remember the details of our conversations, but I do remember the teachers' enthusiasm about the activity. Still, I am sure they would have been delighted to have Thinking Tags, instead of or in addition to their solutions and cultures. There are many advantages, as Colella describes: The Tags allow for the onset and detection of "disease" during the simulation rather than afterward; the detection is straightforward and automatic; the Tags are much easier for the teacher to prepare; the "rules of the game" are programmable, making the simulation easy to customize (e.g., to make the probability of infection on contact 70% rather than 100%); and so on. Here is a compelling example of how well-designed technology can enhance classroom activity.

Reading the chapter, I was struck that Colella did not discuss this connection to instructional practices among biology teachers,[3] perhaps because she did not expect it to be of interest to her audience. For whatever reason, it reflects a gap in communication between teaching and research in educational technology. At the same time, Colella's work illustrates how filling that gap could benefit developers as well as teachers. What other ideas are there in the teaching community that could be so naturally and effectively enhanced with technology?

POWERFUL INSTRUCTION

It would be a mistake, moreover, to attribute the success of this activity solely to the technology. That this was a rich and productive learning experience for the students is clear, and it is clear the Tags helped that experience happen.

Still, students could become similarly immersed in the older versions of the activity. Given time and skilled guidance, they would be able to pose and explore questions such as "What is the probability of transmission in a single interaction, and what affects that probability?," "What is the delay, if any, between getting infected and being contagious?," and "What are the probabilities of false positives or false negatives in the tests?" I am sure that this happens in some classes, with teachers who feel at liberty to devote this depth of attention and have the expertise to facilitate it.

I am also sure that the Tags would often be used as a demonstration: The class would run the simulation once, discuss what it shows about the spread of disease, and move on. Whether it is because they are pressed for time, in a constant rush to cover a standardized, mandated curriculum,[4]

---

[3]I do not know the origins of these activities; I found Averill (1993) and Powel (1993) in a search for something to cite for this commentary. Powel (1993) describes her version as an adaptation of an activity in a laboratory manual (Mangino, 1975).

[4]The constraint of time is reflected in Averill's (1993) and Powel's (1993) plans for the activities as one-shot, teacher-directed demonstrations.

or because they are not prepared to think about learning and instruction in this way, most teachers would not use the Tags in the manner Colella describes.

That is to say, what happened in these classes depended substantially on the ways in which the teacher (or teachers) facilitated, encouraged, and guided the students' engagement and participation in a classroom version of scientific inquiry. This was not only powerful technology; it was also powerful instruction, and the two are not twinned.

As Colella writes, "one of a teacher's responsibilities...is to support children's inquiry and help ensure that learning opportunities are not squandered." But she does not discuss how she or the students' regular teacher took on that responsibility in her account of the activity. We know that "the teacher participated in the activities," but there is no mention of how. Colella notes that she was the "facilitator," but she says little about her influence in that role. In fact, she attributes far more "facilitation" to the Tags than to herself; in several places she implies that her role was minimal.

Nevertheless, there are clues of teaching contributions throughout. First, there is little doubt that the regular teacher of the class, as a participant, was *teaching* by any meaningful definition of the term. It is implausible to suppose he did not have a substantial influence, at least to "creat[ing] a social system in the classroom that supports certain kinds of discourse and activities" (Newman, 1990, quoted in the introduction).

The evident teaching was by Colella. "Conversations and explicit collaborative discussions" are not only for research; they are part of effective instruction, and largely for the same reason: They provide information about the students' understanding. That information allows the teacher to assess the students' progress, diagnose their strengths and needs, and make judgments regarding whether and how to intervene (Hammer, 1997).

It is clear Colella was making these judgments and acting on them. In Episode 1, she asks "Who in this room met the most people?," prompting a "chorus" of response. In Episode 2 she asks "Is there anyone who started with the virus other than [Doug]?" and then "Who started out with the virus?" to help focus students' attention on the task, and to promote the idea that Doug was not Patient Zero. Episode 4 begins with Colella's question, "Do you have a strategy to avoid [the virus]?" again, guiding the students toward a productive line of thinking. In Episode 5, she affirms "That's what I thought," lending her authority to Allison's understanding of an experiment.

There is more we can infer that the teachers accomplished, such as helping the students contend with the "ambiguous situation" of knowing so little, when "none of [their] questions about the behavior of the virus was answered." It is difficult to imagine students entering smoothly into this novel mode of classroom activity; certainly many of them would be uncomfortable. How did Colella and the teacher help them?

To understand what happened in this activity, we would need to understand how the teachers interpreted and navigated moments of instruction such as these. More generally, to understand the contributions of technology to classroom instruction, we need to understand the interactions between the tools and the teaching. We need to consider not just how technology can help students learn but how it can help teachers help students learn. This is more reason for greater and more substantive contact between developers and teachers.

HOW CAN TECHNOLOGY HELP TEACHERS TEACH?

That question sounds "teacher-centered" ("bad") rather than "student-centered" ("good"), but with respect to the development of educational technology this is a false dichotomy. Colella is working within a community that has a long history of developing wonderful technological tools, working toward the sort of engagement, participation, and learning evident in this chapter. But students do not generally engage, participate, and learn in these ways—and they did not here—without facilitation, support, and guidance by talented teachers.

This is not at all to disparage technology; it is to frame its role with teachers in mind. Ultimately, teachers must carry out student-centered instruction. To help them do that, developers of educational technology need to engage in some "teacher-centered" thought: How can their tools support teachers in attending, diagnosing, and responding to their students' abilities and needs?

This chapter is an example of powerful tools supporting and supported by powerful instruction. It highlights the need for greater attention to how that can happen and for substantive collaboration with teachers in the development and assessment of educational technology.[5]

REFERENCES

Averill, E. (1993). *The spread of AIDS* [On-line]. Available:
   http://www.accessexcellence.org/AE/AEPC/WWC/1993/the_spread.html (1999, June 10).
Hammer, D. (1997). Discovery learning and discovery teaching. *Cognition and Instruction, 15*(4), 485–529.

---

[5]The BGuiLE Project (Reiser, Tabak, Sandoval, Smith, Steinmuller, & Leone, 2001) is an example of this sort of collaboration, drawing on teachers' expertise to aid the development of educational software and studying the affordances of the software for learning and instruction in classroom contexts.

Mangino, R. A. (1975). *A laboratory manual for microbiology*. Portland, ME: J. Weston Walch.

Newman, D. (1990). Using social context for science teaching. In M. Gardner, J. Greeno, F. Reif, A. Schoenfeld, A. diSessa, & E. Stage (Eds.), *Toward a scientific practice of science education* (pp. 187–202). Hillsdale, NJ: Lawrence Erlbaum.

Powel, M. B. (1993). *Demonstrating an Epidemic* [On-line]. Available: http://www.accessexcellence.org/AE/AEC/CC/epidemic.html (1999, June 10).

Reiser, B. J., Tabak, I., Sandoval, W. A., Smith, B., Steinmuller, F., & Leone, T. J. (2001). S. M. Carver & D. Klahr (Eds.). *Cognition and Instruction: Twenty five years of progress*. Mahvah, NJ: Lawrence Erlbaum.

Ruopp, R., Gal, S., Drayton, B., & Pfister, M. (1993). *LabNet: Toward a community of practice*. Hillsdale, NJ: Lawrence Erlbaum.

DEFINING AND EXPLORING ROLES IN PARTICIPATORY SIMULATIONS

Vanessa Colella
MIT Media Laboratory

Let me begin by thanking the authors of both commentaries. I welcome the new perspectives that Hammer, Garrison, and Scheckler bring to my work on Participatory Simulations, as their insights have caused me to reflect on and refine my own perspectives. I hope that my response will clarify some areas of uncertainty and open the way for future dialogue on the ways that direct experience can augment learning.

Garrison and Scheckler raise some crucial questions about the relationship between the students and the rules that comprise the simulation. In particular, they worry that, in a Participatory Simulation, students are simply "spectators of an inherently rational, rule-driven" enviornment. I fear that my explanation may have overemphasized the viral rules, which are programmed into the Tags, relative to the students' behavioral decision rules, which they continually create and modify. I highlighted the viral rules because the Tags are a novel aspect of this learning enviornment. However, their importance should not overshadow the influence of the students' strategies, or behavioral decision rules, on the course of the simulation. It is the combination of the viral rules and the students' decision rules that give rise to the patterns of disease that students observe. Unlike a traditional computer simulation, but much like the natural scenarios that they simulate, the Tags will not run a simulation on their own (you can turn them on, but in the absence of people interacting the patterns of infection are trivial). Without the simultaneous execution of both sets of rules there is no simulation.

By modifying their strategies (deciding who to meet and when to meet them), students are able to exert a high degree of influence over the ongoing dynamics of the simulation. In the reported simulation, the more interactions that students have with one another, the more likely they are to pass the disease around their community. Alternatively, the fewer the total number of sick individuals at any given time, the smaller is the probability of interacting with a sick person. For instance, imagine that a group of students decides that during a simulation they will "pair up" and meet only with their partners. This behavior dramatically reduces the number of interactions in the group, decreasing the likelihood that any individual student will get sick and also decreasing the prevalence of disease in the community.[1]

This example is simplified, as it does not include other important characteristics of the reported simulation, such as latency and immunity. But I hope that, even without taking all of the complexity of the simulation into account, it does demonstrate how the students' decisions can change the course of action in the simulation. In a Participatory Simulation, students do "alter the world that they study."

Seen in this light, it is clear that the students in a Participatory Simulation are not mere "computer holders," as Garrison and Scheckler contend. Furthermore, the Tags do not "control students' conduct," nor do they "discipline the students for wrong guesses." Instead, it is precisely by modifying their own behavior that students produce the altered patterns of infection, which in turn enable them to uncover the characteristics of the virus.

Of course, the viral rules that are programmed into the badges can also be changed. One might run a variety of simulations with a group of students, with each simulation based on a different set of badge parameters. Students could explore the behavior of a latent disease, a disease with delayed recovery, the influence of random or conferred immunity, and so on. It is this variability that sets Participatory Simulations apart from their noncomputational counterparts. Although I do not disagree with Hammer that students and teachers become highly engaged and immersed in "older versions of the activity," I maintain that the technology does add an important component to the activity—namely, the opportunity for students to experience and explore a wide variety of scenarios, each based on different assumptions and parameters. In the original activities cited by Hammer, students could speculate about the effects of probabilistic transmission and pose hypothetical questions, which they cannot explore. In a Participatory Simulation, students can experience that scenario and explore their questions. And, more complex rules can easily be constructed. Immunity might degrade over time or be bolstered by long periods of health; the disease could mutate into a more infective strain; the infectious period

---

[1]See Anderson and May (1992) for a classic treatment of disease dynamics.

might not begin immediately after infection; or a short bout of disease could be followed by recovery. Modifications like these, and the ability to directly explore them, can add to the richness of the learning environment and enhance the classroom utility of activities such as Participatory Simulations.

Garrison and Scheckler point out that another way to enrich the learning experience and also help students to see the malleability of the underlying viral rules is to engage students in building their own simulations. While this kind of constructionism is the foundation for much of our work (Papert, 1980), our initial focus in the Participatory Simulations project is on enabling students to design and implement the experiments that illuminate both the viral rules and the impact of their own behavior on the simulation dynamics. In other work, we have focused on enabling students to design and create their own simulations (Colella, Klopfer, & Resnick, 1999; Colella, Klopfer, & Resnick, 2001; Resnick, 1994). Here we challenge students to investigate and articulate observable patterns in the simulation. We feel that both approaches are important and valid, and we hope that they will both be encouraged.

As Hammer reminds us, the success of all of these activities, from experiencing and exploring a Participatory Simulation to constructing a computer model, depends in a large part on the teacher. Though the Thinking Tag technology enables new learning activities, I agree that the instructor's contribution is critical. In the design and development of the Participatory Simulations project, I drew heavily on my own teaching experience and the advice and input of participating teachers and students. The study reported was conducted after many preliminary studies helped shape the activity. Although those iterations were not reported here, perhaps they will reassure readers that such activity is a part of this research. Hammer correctly points out the lack of research into the role of the facilitator. Such research would be a welcome addition to this growing field. I hope that this project will be one of many that reduces the gap between research and practice, in particular by creating artifacts and activities that address classroom needs.

REFERENCES

Anderson, R., & May, R. (1992). *Infectious diseases of humans: Dynamics and control*. Oxford: Oxford University Press.

Colella, V., Klopfer, E., & Resnick, M. (1999). StarLogo community of learners workshop. *Logo Exchange, Journal of the ISTE Special Interest Group for Logo-Using Educators, 17*(2), 20–22.

Colella, V., Klopfer, E., & Resnick, M. (2001). *Adventures in modeling: Exploring complex, dynamic systems with StarLogo*. New York: Teachers College Press.

Papert, S. (1980). *Mindstorms: Children, computers, and powerful ideas*. New York: Basic Books.

Resnick, M. (1994). *Turtles, termites, and traffic jams: Explorations in massively parallel microworlds*. Cambridge, MA: MIT Press.

10

Designing a Video-Mediated Collaboration System Based on a Body Metaphor

Hiroshi Kato
National Institute of Multimedia Education

Keiichi Yamazaki
Saitama University

Hideyuki Suzuki
Ibaraki University

Hideaki Kuzuoka
University of Tsukuba

Hiroyuki Miki
Oki Electric Industry Co., Ltd.

Akiko Yamazaki
Future University Hakodate

INTRODUCTION

Most of the distance education systems in use today have been built on the basis of a bidirectional video-mediated teleconference systems, that is, views of a lecturer's face and/or learning material are transmitted to the learners' sites, and vice versa. In such a system, however, it has been pointed out that gaze, gesture, and other body movements are generally not as accessible as in normal face-to-face communication. Heath and Luff (1991, 1992) found asymmetries in interpersonal communication through video-mediated presence systems. Resources, such as gestures and gazes, that a speaker might ordinarily use to shape the way in which a recipient should participate were found to be unreliable. Thus, the prevailing systems are not sufficient particularly for conducting collaborative learning where nonverbal interaction is crucial, such as in a scientific experiment or in a physical exercise, although they may be acceptable for an educational situation such as a lecture in which the maintenance of social interaction is less critical.

Research in computer-supported cooperative work (CSCW) has studied this problem mainly in regard to the transmission of hand gestures and the question of eye contact. Some CSCW systems, such as VideoDraw (Tang & Minneman, 1990) and ClearBoard (Ishii & Kobayashi, 1992), provided solutions in this respect. However, such flat work-support systems show clear limitations if one uses them for remote support for collaborative work involving the manipulation of physical objects (i.e., remote out-of-the-box collaboration), because such work requires that objects be allowed to spread out in a three-dimensional space and that participants be allowed to move around. Thus, an essentially flat work-support system cannot be turned into one that supports spatial activities; and it is physically impossible to accomplish perfect eye contact if participants are allowed to move around. Consequently, it is necessary to devise a system for supporting remote collaboration among many participants in different positions and in different environments (Kuzuoka, 1992; Kuzuoka, Kosuge, & Tanaka, 1994; Kuzuoka, Ishimoda, Nishimura, Suzuki, & Kondo, 1995).

The purpose of this research is not simply to point out the physical limitations of these CSCW systems but to try to clearly delineate the intrinsic limitations. We refer to the concept underlying in the distance education systems in use today as the "face-to-face metaphor." The ultimate aim is to create an environment in which distant people talk as if in close face-to-face conversation (Fig. 10.1). However, it remains unclear how the face view is used in collaboration, why it is helpful, and what is the unsolved or newly produced problem, if any.

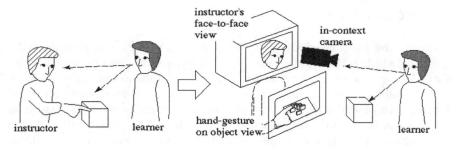

FIG. 10.1. The face-to-face metaphor concept.

To examine the face-to-face metaphor's validity, our pilot investigation included remote collaboration experiments deploying cameras and monitors in different spatial arrangements. Regarding the use of several cameras and monitors, we were influenced by the work of Gaver and Heath on Multiple Target Video (MTV) (Gaver, Sellen, Heath, & Luff, 1993; Heath, Luff, & Sellen, 1995), who analyzed which pictures were important and what kind of image received attention. We, rather, were more interested in the ways of resource arrangements in the shared workspace. As a result, our pilot investigation suggested that the face-to-face metaphor might be problematic; for example, when an instructor faced students through a monitor, she had difficulty in pointing at a specific object for them because she was not sure whether or not they were orienting themselves to her pointing. In addition, our initial study revealed that too many communication resources could cause confusion for the users. Consequently, how to utilize limited communication resources to constitute a shared workspace has become our concern. We, therefore, concentrate on the question of how monitors displaying various body parts (e.g., a face, hands) should be arranged in the workspace to support smoother collaboration. The question also involves how people use body images distributed in the shared workspace as resources for reciprocal actions. Accordingly, we need to establish the validity of redistributing the body images and bodies themselves in a way based on a body metaphor concept, which will be introduced in the next section.

BODY METAPHOR CONCEPT

As a part of the pilot investigations, we analyzed the instruction in an ordinary face-to-face situation to see how an instructor and learners positioned themselves during instruction. We found the following to be important. When an instructor points out an object to the learners, (1) the learners should be able to see the instructor's pointer; (2) the instructor should be able to see that the learners are orienting themselves toward the object as well as the pointer while they are watching his/her pointing; (3) the instructor should be able to reassure the learners by actions or words that the instructor is aware of the learners' orientation and when the learners intend to draw the instructor's attention to initiate a conversation with him/her (4) the learners should be able to see the face of the instructor and (5) the instructor should be able to notice the learners' orientation toward himself/herself. It should be noted that this reflexive awareness was accomplished mainly by the bodily actions and positioning rather than by utterance. These findings are supported by ethnomethodological studies on cooperative work by Heath (1986), Goodwin (1981), Nishizaka (1991), Yamazaki (1994), and Yamazaki & Yamazaki (1996). Therefore, our claim is that enabling the

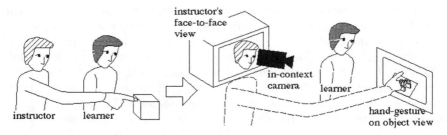

FIG. 10.2. The body metaphor concept.

instructor to see how the learners are looking at what the instructor is pointing out and enabling the learners to be aware of the instructor's observation
of their activities is important. Conditions (1) through (5) were naturally
achieved in the face-to-face situation, where the instructor's pointing was
seen by the learners and the instructor simultaneously, and where the instructor took the position from which he/she could see the learners and
their workspace together in the context (Fig. 10.2). In this situation, it was
crucial that the instructor's face was sufficiently apart from his/her hands,
so that he/she could discern the learner's glancing at his/her face.

To build a remote shared workspace where natural ways of instruction are
fulfilled, we propose a "body metaphor" concept (Fig. 10.2) as a design principle of a video-mediated collaboration system. Modeling the ordinary body
positioning of an instructor and learners in everyday instruction scenes, it
provides guidelines for placement of communication resources, such as cameras, face view and hand-gesture monitors, and objects to be manipulated.

EXPERIMENTS

Task

We used AlgoBlock (Suzuki & Kato, 1995) as the subject matter for the remote
collaboration experiments. AlgoBlock is a tangible programming language
with elements shaped like a block (Fig. 10.3). Each command corresponds to
a kind of blocks; learners can construct a program by connecting those
blocks to each other by hand. Learners are supposed to make a simple program that guides a submarine to its destination appearing on a CRT screen.

AlgoBlock was devised as a tool to bring the originally individual work of
writing a program into the sphere of collaboration. By giving the commands
of the programming language usually hidden inside the computer a tangible
form such as a block, the tacit work of programming is turned into one
with overt actions involving visible body movements. Since the movements

FIG. 10.3. An example of the AlgoBlock session (left) and the screen image (right).

can be observed by other participants, such an observation can then be reciprocally used as a resource in cooperative work. By transforming mental work into physical actions, AlgoBlock can enrich the resources for collaboration.

There are two reasons why we have employed AlgoBlock for this study. First, because of the reasons above, AlgoBlock makes it easy for observers to analyze how the collaboration proceeds. The resources used by the learners for collaboration become visible to an outside observer as well as to the learners themselves. Second, tasks performed using AlgoBlock can be a good model of collaborative work involving physical movements, such as in a scientific experiment or a physical training session.

Workspace Setting

In the experiment, communication resources, such as video monitors, video cameras, and AlgoBlocks, in the workspace of both the instructor's and the learners' sites were arranged as follows.

The learners' site had three cameras (two in front of the learners and one on the ceiling) and three monitors. One of the front cameras was able to pan, tilt, and zoom according to remote control by the instructor. The other, referred to as the in-context camera, was fixed in such a way as to simultaneously capture the table used for assembling AlgoBlocks, the monitors in the back of the room, and all the learners. The ceiling camera captured all the learners and the whole workspace. The three monitors showed the instructor's face, his/her hand gestures, and the AlgoBlock screen. The in-context camera and the remote-controlled camera were set near the face-to-face view monitor. The monitor, referred to as the hand-gesture view, showed the image from the hand-gesture camera at the instructor's site, in which the instructor's hand-gesture appeared. The instructor's voice was reproduced from the speaker in the face-to-face view monitor.

The instructor's site had two cameras: one, referred to as the hand-gesture camera, for capturing the instructor's hand gestures on the hand-gesture monitor and the other, referred to as the face-to-face camera, for the face view of the instructor. Three monitors were placed in front of the instructor. On the left, from the instructor's point of view, was a personal computer display for remote control of the camera mentioned earlier, with the view taken by that camera. The monitor in the middle, near which the face-to-face camera was set, showed the view of the in-context camera. The monitor to the right, referred to as the hand-gesture monitor, could be switched among the in-context camera, the remote-controlled camera, the ceiling camera, and the AlgoBlock screen. Because this monitor was viewable in the hand-gesture camera, learners could observe the instructor's pointing gesture on something shown on the hand-gesture monitor.

We tried the following arrangements of monitors;

- Pattern 1 (Fig. 10.4): This setting was modeled on the teleconference-based distance education systems (i.e., based on the face-to-face metaphor). The front of the room had the face-to-face view (right) and the hand-gesture view (left). The AlgoBlock screen was placed at the back of the room. In short, all of the devices for communicating with the instructor were gathered on one side of the room.
- Pattern 2 (Fig. 10.5): This setting was based on the body metaphor. Only the face-to-face view was in front, and the hand-gesture view and the AlgoBlock screen were placed at the back.

In pattern 2, we paid special attention to the following points:

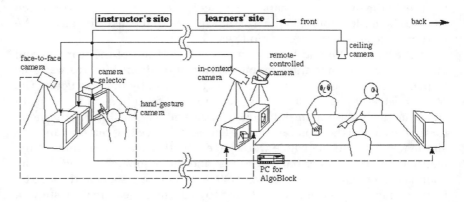

FIG. 10.4. Experimental setting of pattern 1 (face-to-face metaphor).

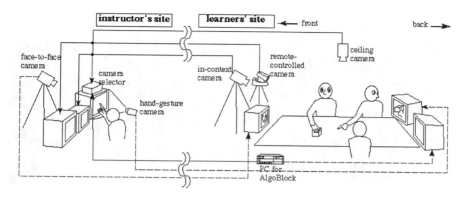

FIG. 10.5. Experimental setting of pattern 2 (body metaphor).

1. At the learners' site, the hand-gesture view was positioned opposite to the instructor's face-to-face view.
2. The in-context camera was positioned to capture the hand-gesture view in the context of the learner's site.

The only difference between these two settings was the location of the hand-gesture view in the learner's site. This difference addresses the issues of whether the instructor could see his/her own hand gestures in the context of the learner's site and whether the instructor could clearly determine which of the views the learner was looking at. Pattern 2 allows the instructor to check whether the learners were looking at his/her hand gesture and how they were responding to the instruction.

Other Experimental Conditions

The experiment was conducted with four groups with each group consisting of one instructor and two learners. All subjects were university students. Before the experiment, experimenters taught the students who played the role of instructors how to use AlgoBlock. An experimental session for each group took one hour, during which both patterns were tried.

OBSERVATIONS

The following was observed by taking a close look at how the monitors transmitting body images were mutually used as resources for collaboration and communication.

personal computer display   hand-gesture monitor   hand-gesture view   AlgoBlock screen
in-context view

Instructor's site   Learner's site

FIG. 10.6. Scenes from the experiment using pattern-2 setting (left: instructor's site, right: learners' site shown in the in-context view). Face-to-face view is next to the camera, and hand-gesture view and AlgoBlock screen are facing the camera.

Observability of Learner's Orientation

When giving directions in pattern 2, the instructors used their in-context view to check how learners watched the hand-gesture view (Fig. 10.6). When the instructor gave particularly detailed directions, she alternately viewed the hand-gesture monitor and the in-context view so as to make sure that the learners were watching her pointer in the hand-gesture view (Table 10.1; the context of this segment is shown in the Appendix).

In this transcript, time proceeds from left to right. Here we had two learners L2 and L3 in the learners' site, and an instructor I1 in the instructor's site. The horizontal rows beginning with the subject symbols give utterances in Japanese, and the English translations appear in parentheses below. The

TABLE 10.1
Transcript From Pattern-2 Setting Experiment

	P – – – – – –	P – – – – – – – – – – – –	
I₁ {	HM – – – – – – – – – – –C – – – HM – – – – –C – – – – – HM – – – – – – – – – – – – – C		
	tunagerutokiwa kono block o konodengen o kitte kirankya ikenain remain desuyone		
	(When you connect these blocks, this switch, you have to switch off the power.)		

I_1:
P – – – – – –   P – – – – – – – – – – – –
HM – – – – – – – – – – –C – – – HM – – – – –C – – – – – HM – – – – – – – – – – – – – C
tunagerutokiwa kono block o   konodengen o kitte kirankya ikenain remain desuyone
(When you connect these blocks, this switch, you have to switch off the power.)

L_2:
AL – – – – – – – – – – – – – H –
hai
(yes)

L_3:
H –

direction of gaze is recorded above the dialog, where "----" indicates continuation. AL and H stand for the AlgoBlock screen and the hand-gesture view in the learners' site, respectively. HM and C stand for the hand-gesture monitor and the in-context view in the instructor's site, respectively, and P indicates that the instructor was pointing at the hand-gesture monitor.

The instructor ascertained, before giving directions, whether or not the learners were taking a position for watching the hand-gesture view. When she saw that they did not take up a watching position, she used the indexical word "kono" (these) so that the learners were led to watch the hand-gesture view. The instructor even withheld instruction briefly when she noticed that the learners were not watching the hand-gesture view.

The learners' posture of watching the hand-gesture view suggests "recipiency" (Goodwin, 1981; Heath, 1986), that is, through gaze and other nonverbal cues the listener is displaying attentiveness to the speaker. We found that the in-context view in pattern 2 was frequently used for the instructor to monitor learners' recipiency. This is enabled by the mutual monitoring attained in pattern 2.

In pattern 1 (Fig. 10.7), by comparison, monitoring recipiency was not easy. As shown in Table 10.2, the instructor (I4) asked, "Can you see my hand?," and even after the learner (L5) affirmed, "Yes, I can," such reconfirmations as "Here you can see a submarine, can't you?" and "Does my hand show?" were asked repeatedly. In addition, the instructors often exaggerated their pointing actions on the hand-gesture monitor by moving their hands vigorously. One of the causes of this difficulty was that the instructor was

personal computer display / in-context view   hand-gesture monitor

not used (hand-gesture view was located in the other side) AlgoBlock screen

Instructor's site   Learner's site

FIG. 10.7. Scenes from the experiment using the pattern 1 setting (left: instructor's site, right: learners' site shown in the in-context view). Face-to-face view and hand-gesture view are next to the camera, and AlgoBlock screen is facing the camera.

TABLE 10.2
Transcript From Pattern-1 Setting Experiment

I4:	\<watching in-context view and hand-gesture monitor alternatively\>
	Mazu: (3.0) Temiete masu? (At first, can you see my hand?)
	\<looking at in-context view\>
L5:	A: mietemasu. (Ah: Yes, I can.)
I4:	A: mietemasuka. (Ah, you can.)
I4:	Kono burokku wa: tatenimo yokonimo tsunagerun desune.
	(These blocks can be connected both in rows and in columns.)
L5:	Hai. (Yes.)
I4:	hh Sorede: hhh Nante yobundarou. Kono sensuikan wo:
	(And, what can I say, this submarine.)
L5:	Sensuikan (Submarine)
I4:	Kokoni ariasume, sensuikan. (Here you can see a submarine, can't you?
L5:	Hai. (Yes.)
I4:	Korewo, mauz: kokoni. korega go:ru de:.
	(This, in the first place. This is a goal)
L5:	Ah: Yes (Ah, Yes.)
I4:	Korega go: ru de: A: te: utsutte masuka?
	(This is a goal. Well, does my hand show?)
L5:	A: utsuttemasu. (Yes, it does.)
I4:	Go: ru de:. (The goal)

not able to know whether or not learners were showing recipiency. Because the hand-gesture view was located beside the in-context camera and near the face-to-face view, the instructor could not monitor how learners were watching their pointing. Thus, in pattern 1, communicative asymmetry (Heath & Luff, 1991, 1992) emerges more clearly.

Awareness of an Instructor

In pattern 2, hand-gesture view was utilized as a resource for reciprocal actions. In the transcript of Table 10.1, immediately after the learner (L2) looked at the hand-gesture view and said "hai" (yes), the instructor (I1) removed her finger from an object on the screen. This action could show her acknowledgment, but it was not certain what she had acknowledged at this moment. The next action clarified it. She moved her pointing finger on the screen to another object. Consequently, her action turned out to be about the object pointed to first. This action can be understood as her acknowledgment to the learner's (L2) acknowledgment ("yes"). In addition, it also displayed that her attention had moved to the next object. Thus, the end of a series of instructions about the object pointed to at first was collaboratively achieved, and then the instruction about the next object became relevant.

In this way, the instructor's finger movement was utilized as a resource to show the instructor's understanding about the learner's action. This, coupled with the instructor's face-to-face views and the instructor's oral response, constitutes a valuable resource for learners to know that the instructor is watching their actions. In other words, it can enhance the learner's awareness of the instructor. This is accomplished by the in-context view in pattern 2, which enables the instructor to monitor how learners are watching the hand-gesture view.

In contrast, in pattern 1, the instructor sometimes removed his/her finger from the monitor before the learners displayed their understanding of what the instructor was pointing at or kept it on the screen for an unnecessarily long time. This was because the instructor could not know how carefully the learners were watching his/her finger. Moreover, since the instructor did not know which of the views, hand-gesture or face-to-face, and what in the view the learners were looking at, the instructor sometimes failed to catch what the learners were currently paying attention to.

Surrogate for an Instructor

When, in pattern 2, learners tried to begin a question, or when the AlgoBlock operation had been successfully completed, they often looked at the face-to-face view to get the instructor's reaction or acknowledgment. In this sense, the action of facing toward the face view, rather than face view itself, was given a certain meaning through their interaction.

Table 10.3 shows a transcript from pattern 2. This is the scene when a learners (L6 and another) succeeded in reaching a goal. As shown in the transcript, the instructor (I7) was looking at either the hand-gesture monitor (HM) or the in-context view (C), (which view he was watching is uncertain from the videotape) and one of the learners (L6) was looking at the AlgoBlock screen (AL) to see the execution process of their program. As soon as he knew that the trial was successful (when the sound effect representing the submarine's successful arrival to the goal (Snd) started), he said "yo:shi"

TABLE 10.3
Transcript From Pattern-2 Setting Experiment

```
                   Snd - -- - -- - -- - -- - -- - --
    ⎧ AL — – – – – – – – – – –FV – – – – – – – – – AL – – – – – – – – – – – – – – – –
L6 ⎨   Yo :: shi < snap >                              Muzukasii desu.
    ⎩   (Good.)                                        (It was difficult.)

    ⎧ HMorC — – – – – – – – – – – – – – – – – – – – – – – – – – – – – – – – – – – – – – – –
I7 ⎨             Omedetou gozaimasu.
    ⎩             (Congratulations!)
```

(good) and snapped his fingers on both hands. Then, he turned his face to the face-to-face view (FV). At that moment, the instructor said "Congratulations!"

There can be several moments when the instructor's congratulations become relevant: at the moment when the submarine arrives at the goal after the snapping, after the learner's remark, and after the sound effect. The observations show that the learner's action of turning his face to the instructor's face view could also provoke the instructor's reaction. By those interactive actions, the learner marked a boundary of an activity followed by the instructor's verbal acknowledgment, which is also considered as an instructor's evaluative remark about the result. In this way, the end of a session was achieved successfully through collaboration. This happened because in pattern 2 the face-to-face view was far enough apart from the other resources. That is, when a learner orients to the face-to-face view, his/her face overtly turns toward it, so the instructor can easily catch the action. As the result, turning to the face-to-face view is like looking into the instructor's face to draw his/her attention in an ordinary face-to-face situation. In this sense, the instructor's face view in the learner's site of pattern 2 played the role of the instructor's representative or surrogate.

In pattern 1, by contrast, the instructor, not knowing the learner's orientation to himself/herself, often failed to coordinate a proper moment to reply, react, and acknowledge the learners.

By comparing pattern 1 with pattern 2, the merit of the body metaphor design in a remote collaborative learning system has become clear.

Remaining Problems

There remain some problems common to both patterns. One of the problems was that learners could not know which views the instructor was oriented to. There was an asymmetry in communication resources between the learners and the instructor, that is, learners could not observe the instructor's in-context view, while the instructor could. Therefore, it sometimes happened that learners began to talk regardless of the instructor's state of attention, although the trouble was restored easily by conversation. Learners tended to anticipate that the instructor was watching their actions at any time, even though this was not always the case.

This asymmetry in system design arises from the difference in the roles between an instructor and a learner, since we presupposed an educational situation rather than equally collaborative work. Introducing a new in-context view at the learner's site just like the one at the instructor's site may solve this problem. However, adding more monitors may possibly not be as effective as we suppose, as utilization of communication resources can be confusing. Instructors sometimes pointed outside the hand-gesture camera's capture range on the hand-gesture monitor or even pointed at a monitor that learners could not see, and the same kind of confusion may possibly also happen at the learner's site. This occurred because it was not always clear what information was transferred to the other site, although it was possible for the instructor to know, if he/she carefully watched the in-context view. However, it could be troublesome for the instructor to have to watch another monitor to see how his/her own fingertip appeared on the hand-gesture view in the learner's site.

One possibility is that there were too many resources to use or that the relationship among various communication resources was too complicated to understand. Therefore, a closer examination to validate the necessity of individual resources and/or a more sophisticated integration of those resources needs to be investigated in our future work.

CONCLUSIONS

It is well known that in everyday communication, speakers' positions, both with respect to each other and to shared artifacts, plays an important role (Goodwin, 1981, 1995). Because communication takes place using the bodies of individuals, it depends strongly on the deployment of those bodies. If one wants collaboration through a video-mediated communication system to occur in a natural way, the spatial arrangement of functional resources originating from body part functions becomes a fundamental issue. Consequently, we have proposed the concept of a body metaphor in configuring a video-mediated communication system.

By deploying three communication resources (objects for manipulation, face view, and hand-gesture view) based on the body metaphor, it became clear which one of them learners were orienting to. Specifically, the instructor could see learners looking at the instructor's pointing. Hence, the instructor could recognize the learner's recipiency, and the learners were aware of the instructor's observation. In addition, it turned out that the learner could use the face view as a surrogate of the instructor to get the instructor's attention and to mark a boundary of an activity interactively.

We have been doing field studies in classrooms and elsewhere for several years. Taking such findings into account in addition to the findings discussed here, we hope to refine the body-metaphor concept by figuring out a better balance between the understandability and the richness of communication resources, so that we can develop more practical systems for remote collaboration and learning.

ACKNOWLEDGMENTS

The authors would like to thank Dr. Tammo Reisewitz and Mr. Ron Korenaga for their contributions to this work. We would also like to thank Dr. Graham

Button for his insightful comments on this paper. This research was supported by grants from Grant-in-Aid for Scientific Research (A) 07309018 (Head researcher: Keiichi Yamazaki), 1996 CASIO Science Promotion Foundation, and the 1996 Telecommunication Advancement Foundation (TAF).

APPENDIX

Transcription Before and After Table I

(Instructor (I1) is explaining to the learners (L2 and L3) how to operate the AlgoBlock system.)

L2:   Maa, yattemimasho:. (Anyway, let's make a try.)
I1:   Hhhh (laugh)
L3:   Hai. (Yes.)
L2:   Hai, jaa, jaa yattemimasu. (Yes, then, then, We will try.)
I1:   Soreto:, a, sumimasen, sono;, tunagerutokiha: kono burokkuo,
      (And, ah, excuse me but, you know, when you connect these blocks,)
L2:   Hai. (Yes.)
I1:   Kono: dengen'o, kitte, kiranakya ikenaindesuyone.
      (this switch, you have to switch off the power.)
I1:   Kokoni, yokoni, kokoni, arimasuyone.
      (Here, on this side, here it is, isn't it?)
L2:   Ah, korene. Hai, hai. (Oh, it is. Yeah, Yeah.)
I1:   A, kokono wakini aru. (Ah, it is on this side.)

REFERENCES

Gaver, W., Sellen, A., Heath, C., & Luff, P. (1993). One is not enough: Multiple views in a media space. *Proceedings of INTERCHI'93*, 335–341.
Goodwin, C. (1981). *Conversational organization: Interaction between speakers and hearers.* New York: Academic Press.
Goodwin, C. (1995). Seeing in depth. *Social Studies of Science 25*, 237–274.
Heath, C. (1986). *Body movement and speech in medical interaction.* Cambridge, UK: Cambridge University Press.
Heath, C., & Luff, P. (1991). Disembodied conduct: Communication through video in a multi-media environment. *Proceedings of CHI'91*, 99–103.
Heath, C., & Luff, P. (1992). Media space and communicative asymmetries: Preliminary observation of video-mediated interaction. *Human Computer Interaction, 7*, 315–346.
Heath, C., Luff, P., & Sellen, A. (1995). Reconsidering the virtual workplace: Flexible support for collaborative activity. *Proceedings of ECSCW'95*, (pp. 83–99).
Ishii, H., & Kobayashi, M. (1992). ClearBoard: A seamless medium for shared drawing and conversation with eye contact. *Proceedings of CHI'92*, (pp. 525–532) ACM.

Kuzuoka, H. (1992). Spatial workspace collaboration: SharedView video supported system for remote collaboration capability. *Proceedings of CHI'92*, (pp. 33–42) ACM.

Kuzuoka, H., Ishimoda, G., Nishimura, Y., Suzuki, R., & Kondo, K. (1995). Can the GestureCam be a surrogate? *Proceedings of ECSCW'95*, 181–196.

Kuzuoka, H., Kosuge, T., & Tanaka, M. (1994). GestureCam: A video communication system for sympathetic remote collaboration. *Proceedings of CSCW'94*, (pp. 35–43) Mahwah, NJ: Lawrence Erlbaum Associates.

Nishizaka, A. (1991). *The social order of therapy II*. Mejigakuin Ronsou, 475, Bulletin of Meijigakuin University. (In Japanese)

Suzuki, H., & Kato, H. (1995). Interaction-level support for collaborative learning: AlgoBlock—An open programming language. *Proceedings of CSCL'95*, (pp. 349–355) Mahwah, NJ: Lawrence Erlbaum Associates.

Tang, J., & Minneman, S. (1990). VideoDraw: A video interface for collaborative drawing. *Proceedings of CHI'90*, 313–320.

Yamazaki, K. (1994). *The pitfalls of a beautiful face—Ethnomethodological studies on sexuality.* Tokyo: Harvest-sha. (In Japanese)

Yamazaki, K., & Yamazaki, A. (1996). *Ethnomethodology of discrimination—Organization of category and organization of situation.* In Series: *Contemporary Sociology 15.* Tokyo: Iwanami-shoten. (In Japanese)

Awareness in Video-Mediated Communication

Randall Smith
Sun Microsystems

I enjoyed this study and think it addresses a crucial issue in distance learning, in particular, but for all of synchronous collaborative technology in general: how to provide for awareness of participants actions and perceptions. The future availability of high-bandwidth communications will allow possibly several video streams to link two remote sites. Thus what may appear to be a somewhat unusual configuration of cameras and monitors used in this work may in fact become commonplace. Figuring out how to configure a transparently useful technology in this kind of context is therefore interesting.

The authors compare a "pattern 1" setting, in which the instructor has difficulty interpreting students' gaze, with a "pattern 2" arrangement in which the instructor can not only more easily interpret student gaze but also see one of the monitors that the students can see. The authors name the two patterns the "face-to-face metaphor" (pattern 1) and the "body metaphor" (pattern 2). However, I would like to see them named the "scrambled body metaphor" and the "not a metaphor" systems. I do not at all intend to be negative, for what I find interesting is that by nearly abandoning the physical metaphor in pattern 2, the authors have improved the awareness within the group.

In the pattern 1 setting, the instructor might call out to get the attention of students, only to see them suddenly turn to stare at some off-screen point. As they gaze at the monitor showing the instructor's face, the instructor sees the tops of the heads of the students, all staring at . . . something. As anyone who has lived with this kind of system knows, it is difficult to know exactly when someone is gazing at your image or at some other nearby object. There is no sense of eye contact, and if there is any metaphor operating at all, it is perhaps as though remote collaborators are looking at your feet.

Understandably, while the students see the hand-gesture monitor near the instructor's facial image, it is difficult for the instructor to know which they are watching. Perhaps my left foot is my face, and perhaps my right foot is my hands. The body gets scrambled.

In pattern 2, the hand-gesture monitor is across the student's table from the face-gesture monitor and can be seen even by the instructor. Thus it becomes clear what the students are looking at. And in order to see her own actions, it may not even be necessary for the instructor to see her own hands in the physical world, as she can watch them in the context of the student group on the monitor at the remote site.

This is so unlike any real-world experience that I would say it is not particularly useful to consider it a metaphor at all. It is just a combination of technologies assembled to address a particular problem. Thus pattern 2 might be called the "no metaphor" system.

So my only large concern with this work is that it might seem to suggest that a "face-to-face" metaphor is problematic when compared with a "body metaphor." Perhaps this is unfairly generalizing the claims, and the authors simply intend to compare two particular configurations without a great desire to generalize: If so, then what I say here may be taken as suggesting a generalization, rather than an attempt to correct one. I hope to explain why this work is particularly interesting in that it can be seen as addressing very deep issues with synchronous collaboration technologies.

I see the authors as trying to provide their remote collaborators with a key property we enjoy in the real world: Sometimes this property is called "reflexive awareness," "mutual awareness," "workspace awareness," (Gutwin & Greenburg, 1996), or "WYSIWITYS" (What You See Is What I Think You See) (Smith, 1992), but whatever the name, the notion is pretty much the same. I will indulge in a brief elaboration on this topic, as I think exactly what is meant by WYSIWITYS or "reflexive awareness" or whatever it gets called is not as widely appreciated as it should be. I will simply use the term "awareness," though my intent is to imply awareness of something very specific, namely, awareness of other participants' actions and perceptions.

I would rather that the authors have framed their work as studying how to provide for a certain kind of awareness as I think this deeper property will give them what they wish to achieve. For example, in the section on the Body Metaphor Concept, each of the five important features listed (and many other similar benefits) would fall out naturally if they had a system that fully supported awareness. The authors correctly point out that the physical world is a system that does support this kind of awareness, and they refer to the real-world face-to-face setting as an example.

The pattern 1 (more problematic) setting has problems precisely because of it fails to provide awareness, and not really because it attempts to be in some sense face-to-face. As I describe below, face-to-face metaphors that are more accurate than pattern 1 have provided for quite problem-free awareness for tasks that are somewhat similar to the AlgoBlocks scenario.

I believe that failure to properly provide for awareness is a widespread problem in collaborative technology. Users fall into confusion about what can be seen by remote collaborators and must "go meta" or "breakdown to process" to ask about what is visible to other participants. Because the authors show how lack of awareness can be a problem, and how it can be constructively addressed, this chapter's contribution is of broader interest.

AWARENESS

When you and I meet in physical reality, you are able to construct a fairly accurate model of what I can see and vice versa. This is *not* to say that we see the same thing. On the contrary, we may be facing each other in discussion and see very little in common. Yet I can tell from your direction of gaze that my gestures are visible to you or that perhaps I need to bring my hand out from behind some obstacle to make my gesture visible. In human conversation, the assessment of another's visual field happens with such speed and ease that it has the invisibility of the taken for granted.

As designers, we are used to focusing on making the functioning of the technology clear to users. But in synchronous collaboration, we need to clearly present something quite different: the state of perception of the other users. For example, the problem is *not* that you need to see my hand but that I need to know that you see my hand. Some arbitrary combination of communication technologies is not at all likely to deliver on this. In fact, it is somewhat remarkable that the physical world does so well here: For vision and sound, it arises from the physics of our world. (Consider two objects A and B that are emitting or scattering light or sound: If light or sound travels from A to B, then it will also travel from B to A. This is *not* true for light from objects A and B if they are connected by video cameras and monitors. Reality has a fundamental physics supporting reflexive awareness, but a video link does not.)

Video links are notorious violators of mutual awareness. As has been noted, gaze awareness is rendered nearly useless when the camera is off-axis from the monitor. In the 1980s at Xerox PARC and at Rank-Xerox EuroPARC (Now Rank Xerox Research Centre Cambridge) where a number of studies of awareness breakdowns were done, we explored a method of putting the camera at the exact center of the monitor (Smith, O'Shea, O'Malley, Scanlon,

& Taylor, 1991). A half-silvered mirror rests in front of the monitor but is inclined at 45 degrees. This mirror deflects much of the light headed toward the monitor off to the side where it is captured by the video camera. Thus, as a user gazes into the center of the monitor, the camera depicts their face as gazing directly into the camera. (This technique is similar to that employed by "teleprompters": A teleprompter enables one to look into the camera while reading the text of a speech. We essentially replace the text with a view of the remote collaborator.)

The result provides an extremely natural sense of eye contact, and we were pleased to observe that first-time users were completely unaware of eye contact as an issue when using the system. When given a shared screen application with which to operate alongside these specially equipped video links (not overlapping with the video link, as with the later ClearBoard work), users can easily interpret the gaze of their collaborator: looking directly at them for conversation or turning to the side to glance at the computer screen for work in the shared space. Thus a face-to-face metaphor that properly provides for gaze awareness for two users can work very smoothly. It is easy to tell when a remote user is watching gestures "out of the box" as the authors call it, once gaze interpretation is restored.

The authors' AlgoBlocks work is admittedly a new setting, one in which students are free to walk about. Nevertheless, perhaps there could be similar benefit for attending to awareness at the video link level even in this setting. For instance, the instructors would benefit from direct eye contact with any student, and they could tell when a student was looking at them, versus looking at an off-camera object such as the hand-view monitor. (However, there are fundamental limitations to such video link awareness, as I discuss later.)

The author's solution for the case of the instructors own hand gestures has a kind of elegant cleverness, and they find it to be effective: showing the student's view of the instructors hands to the instructor through the instructors "in-context" view. This enables the instructor to see if and when the students attend to his or her hands. The authors' comparison of this solution with the less carefully designed pattern 1 in which the instructor does not see the hand view illustrates the advantages and subtlety of designing for awareness.

The authors show how communication problems still exist and list several. Each of these can be seen as arising from inadequate provision for awareness. Perhaps the authors could proceed to find solutions to each of these problems, by further repositioning monitors and cameras, or by adding yet more video channels. However, as they speculate, "a possibility is that there were too many resources to use or that the relationship between the various communication resources was too complicated to understand." This is a natural concern when one starts to stretch a metaphor a bit too far (or to ignore metaphors completely).

But this is a major reason why I find this work interesting. Many attempts to provide awareness do so by trying to adhere to a real-world metaphor. Because the real world provides awareness, our analogous technology should inherit that property as well. For example, in a three-dimensional (3D) shared virtual reality, my "avatar's" direction of gaze reveals to you what I can see. However, the authors take a rather different approach: They realize the need to provide (for at least certain types of) awareness but do not feel particularly constrained by metaphors. For example, instructors can see their hands in front of them in the real world but also, when they look at the remote site monitor screen, they can see a miniature "hand-gesture view" monitor screen behind the participants at the remote site. That is, they have their hands in front of them and their hands in a monitor behind remote students. (Of course, in this monitor is yet another monitor, the overhead camera view at which the instructor gestures!)

Perhaps a lesson here is that without tight adherence to a metaphor, providing awareness may be quite burdensome. I will indulge in two final examples to reinforce a point: Providing for awareness can be difficult even with a metaphor. The first refers to our own work with video links and half-silvered mirrors; the second addresses shared 3D virtual reality.

It may seem that we had found a way to provide awareness using the half-silvered mirror trick. But our primary testing scenario had the participants seated at the computer screens alongside the video–mirror–camera apparatus. When users get up to walk around in the space, we found that they can simply walk off-camera while watching the screen the entire time. The monitor is viewable (through the half-silvered mirror) from a wide range of positions, yet the video camera only shows a narrow slice of the room. This leads to a violation of awareness, in that users could not tell if their actions were perceived by remote collaborators, who may or may not be watching while off-camera. Hence we put the monitor into a box, whose four walls limited the angle of view of the screen. The idea is that a user must be on-camera in order to look into the screen. The resulting system came to be called a "video tunnel." Though this was much better in supporting awareness, we found it was difficult to find the perfect balance between depth of the monitor box and angle of view of the camera. Actually, it can be shown through a rather careful geometrical analysis that for anything less than a 180-degree, "fisheye" viewing camera, any spaces linked through a camera–monitor pair, regardless of mirrors and barriers, will always violate awareness! There will be portions of the space visible to the camera, yet from which the monitor cannot be seen, or there will be portions from which the monitor can be seen that are invisible to the camera, or both. So even trying to adhere to a simple "tunnel metaphor" can never be perfect.

As a second example of metaphor-based awareness, consider shared 3D virtual reality in which an avatar represents each user. One may expect the depiction of one's direction of gaze through the avatar to provide awareness. This is approximately true in many situations, and yet careful study shows that there can still be problems (Hindmarsh, Fraser, Heath, Benford, & Greenhalgh, 1998). The avatar's face suggests a nearly 180-degree field of view, comparable to that which we enjoy in reality. However, the users typically have a much smaller field of view in the shared world. Perhaps depicting the avatar with an appropriate face mask or "blinders" would help; yet the field of view is so small that the probability of a nearby avatar being visible at all is somewhat low. These two examples show how difficult it can be to achieve full awareness, even when adhering to a physical metaphor. Widening the field of view would clearly help, but it may make using the 3D interface more difficult.

A final general question for future study lies perhaps beyond the scope of the current work: At what point is learning harmed by breakdowns in awareness? Our recent study at Sun Laboratories indicates that even collaborative learning can be quite robust in the face of a video link technology that does not really support gaze awareness (Sipusic et al., 1999).[1] And we found that there were several users who preferred *not* to use our video tunnel, suffering through the awareness problems in return for having the monitor viewed from nearly any point in their office.

The authors' experience provides further evidence that awareness can be provided for certain applications, though it appears to be difficult to achieve perfectly. In particular, exploring ways to configure communication technologies for awareness without adherence to a metaphor is an interesting line of research. We need to address the challenge of providing more naturally functioning social technologies that the future will bring us, no doubt surprisingly soon.

REFERENCES

Gutwin, C., & Greenburg, S. (1996). Workspace awareness for groupware. *Companion Proceedings of the CHI '96 Conference on Human Factors in Computing Systems* (pp. 208–209). New York: ACM Press.

Hindmarsh, J., Fraser, M., Heath, C., Benford, S., & Greenhalgh, C. (1998). Fragmented Interaction: Establishing mutual orientation in virtual environments. In S. Greenburg & C. Neuwirth (Eds.), *Proceedings of 1998 ACM Conference on Computer Supported Work* (pp. 217–235). New York: ACM Press.

Sipusic, M. J., Pannoni, R. L., Smith, R. B., Dutra, J., Gibbons, J. F., & Sutherland, W. R. (1999). *Virtual collaborative learning: A comparison between face-to-face tutored video instruction (TVI) and distributed tutored video instruction (DTVI)* (Tech. Rep.). Available at http://www.sun.com/research/techrep/1999/abstract-72.html

---

[1]Also see Smith, Sipusic, and Pannoni (1999).

Smith, R. B. (1992). What you see is what I think you see. *ACM SIGCUE Outlook (Bulletin of the Special Interest Group for Computer Uses in Education), 21*(3), 18–23.

Smith, R. B., O'Shea, T., O'Malley, C. Scanlon, E., & Taylor, J. (1991). Preliminary experiments with a distributed, multimedia problem solving environment. In J. Bowers & S. Benford (Eds.), *Studies in computer supported cooperative work: Theory, practice and design* (pp. 31–48). Amsterdam: Elsevier.

Smith, R. B., Sipusic, M. J., & Pannoni, R. L. (1999). Experiments comparing face-to-face with virtual collaborative learning. In C. Hoadley (Ed.), *Computer support for collaborative learning* (pp. 558–566). Mahwah, NJ: Lawrence Erlbaum.

TECHNOLOGY DOES NOT EXIST INDEPENDENT OF ITS USE

Curtis D. LeBaron

Brigham Young University, Marriott School of Management

During the 20th century, there were two communication revolutions. The first was a revolution in communication technologies, including the telephone, the radio, the television, and the Internet. Each advance introduced radical changes in epistemology, social organization, political power, and more. The second communication revolution was less dramatic but also consequential: Through research on language and social interaction, we advanced our understanding of social life, which exists only as we perform it through everyday communication. Naturalistic studies of human interaction have revealed how human knowledge, social organizations, political power, and more are accomplished through vocal and visible forms of communication, as people create shared meanings, achieve common understandings, and coordinate social action.

Neither of these revolutions occurred in isolation from the other. On one hand, naturalistic studies of human interaction have been heavily influenced by new technologies. Field notes, transcripts, photographs, audio tapes, films, videotapes, and multimedia have not only facilitated research—they affected research findings. Gregory Bateson and Margaret Mead (1942) reported using photographs in their anthropological work because photographs could capture and present behavioral events better than verbal descriptions. Harvey Sacks founded the field of conversation analysis after discovering recordings of telephone conversations, which "provided the proximate source for the focused attention to talk itself—perhaps the most critical step toward the development of conversation analysis" (Schegloff, 1992, p. xvi). Adam Kendon studied talk until 1963, when he "discovered"

433

film and began to analyze embodied interaction: "It became apparent at once that there were complex patterns and regularities of behavior, and that the interactants were guiding their behavior, each in relation to the other" (Kendon, 1990, p. 4). Using multimedia technology, LeBaron (1998) digitized and then micro-analyzed video recordings and found patterns of hand gestures that were identifiable because the computer provided a nonlinear environment within which to work, making it possible to analyze multiple videotaped images simultaneously, juxtaposing them on the screen.

On the other hand, knowledge of human interaction has been an impetus for technological invention and advance. For instance, Alexander Graham Bell began his career as a speech teacher working with deaf children. For years, he had carefully and closely studied combinations of signing, spelling, reading, and lip reading. Although he was a relative newcomer to electronics and telegraphy, he won a head-to-head inventors' race against Thomas Edison and Elisha Gray, who were both at the height of their productivity. Bell acknowledged that his knowledge of everyday forms of communication had informed his invention of the telephone (Hopper, 1992). With rigor, Kato et al. (this volume) demonstrate how understanding of face-to-face interaction may inform technological design. Citing a few ethnomethodological studies (e.g., Heath, 1986; Goodwin, 1981), the authors employed a "body metaphor" concept. That is, they analyzed instruction in "an ordinary face-to-face situation to see how an instructor and learners positioned themselves during interaction," and they designed a video-mediated collaboration system that incorporated "natural ways of instruction" within a long-distance classroom. My purpose in this commentary is to applaud the trajectory of this research and to suggest the following points as guides for future work of this sort.

Point One: The "Sender–Receiver" Model of Communication Is Misleading and Obsolete. During the telecommunications boom associated with World War II, Shannon and Weaver (1949) proposed a basic model of how humans communicate. According to their model, communication begins with a source or sender, who encodes thoughts or feelings into a message that is then transmitted across a channel to a receiver, who in turn decodes the message and thereby understands the information transmitted. Although this model was widely accepted and continues to be taken for granted by most researchers and laypersons, it has been repudiated by three decades of research on language and social interaction. The sender–receiver model fails because it describes how machines may work—not how humans interact. During everyday communication, interaction is largely constitutive of the component parts that the sender–receiver model presupposes. That is to say, it is through communication that participants perform and realize their relative roles, interactively negotiating the meanings of so-called messages, orienting toward some symbol systems as relevant and recognizable, in many ways constituting their communicative context—temporal, spatial, material, social.

A growing body of research offers a constitutive view of communication and human interaction (e.g., Atkinson & Heritage, 1984; Kendon, 1990; Drew & Heritage, 1992; Sacks, 1992 (1964–1972); Ten Have & Psathas, 1995; Ochs, Schegloff, & Thompson, 1996; Duranti, 1997; Glenn, LeBaron, & Mandelbaum, in press). Only a handful of studies are mentioned here. Heritage (1984) observed that messages are not inherently meaningful because communicative behaviors are subject to inference and open to negotiation: "Utterances accomplish particular actions by virtue of their placement and participation within sequences of action" (p. 245). Furthermore, physical objects and things—not just spoken or gestured messages—may become (situated) symbols through their appropriation and use by interactants (Streeck, 1996). Among the things that messages may accomplish is the instantiation of social roles (Schegloff, 1992)—everything from sender–receiver to mother–daughter. Button (1992) identified question-and-answer structures of speech whereby people may perform the roles of interviewer and interviewee. In the face of multiple categorization possibilities for any person (an interviewer may be a father as well, for instance), the warrantable use of a categorization by a researcher resides in the participants' orientation to and constitution of their activities (Button, 1992, p. 230). Similarly, Koschmann and LeBaron (in preparation) examined hand gestures performed by medical students who interacted with a teacher or "coach"; among other things, it was argued that the sequential and spatial organization of participants' gestures were a means by which teacher–student roles were continually performed. Even built spaces made of mortar and steel are given shape and significance through social interaction (Goffman, 1961; Scheflen, 1976). LeBaron and Streeck (1997) examined a police interrogation during which the room itself was a constraint and a resource for interaction: Participants moved their bodies and spoke in ways that appropriated the built space and interpreted its significance, making possible certain arguments that eventually moved the suspect toward confession.

Point Two: Communication Is More Than the Sum of Behaving Body Parts. Human interaction is an embodied process. In an effort to understand communication, researchers have routinely dissected the process according to bodily features (e.g., eyes and mouth), forms (e.g., "closed" and "open"), and functions (e.g., "looking" and "pointing"). Such discursive distinctions may have some heuristic value for researchers, but they are arguably arbitrary and should not be taken too seriously by those who attempt to study human interaction or design new technologies. During naturally occurring communication, a host of "verbal" and "nonverbal" behaviors necessarily occur together, providing for their mutual performance and interpretation, making suspect any isolated examination or treatment of one (Moerman, 1990; Streeck & Knapp, 1992; Streeck, in press). Every communicative behavior occurs imbued with the significance of co-occurring others, altogether orchestrated.

Several researchers have documented people's orchestrated use of what is too often regarded as separate "channels" of behavior. For example, Goodwin (1980) explicated subtle forms of coordination between utterance-initial restarts and shifts in participants' eye gaze (hence attention) toward the speaker. Heath (1986) studied the organization of speech and body movement (especially shifts in posture and eye gaze) during medical consultations, whereby patients may direct their doctor's attention toward parts of their body that need medical attention. Streeck (1993) showed how hand gestures may be "exposed" (i.e., made an object of attention during moments of interaction) through their coordination with indexical forms of speech (e.g., words such as "this") and eye gaze (which may perform "pointing" functions). After analyzing videotapes of face-to-face interaction, Jarmon (1996)[1] proposed an amendment to the turn-taking model published by Sacks, Schegloff, and Jefferson (1974), which was based upon their analysis of audio recordings. Jarmon concluded that "embodied actions" (such as facial expressions) are in some ways similar to grammatical units and may alter the projectability of turn boundaries or even function as a complete turn. Similarly, Goodwin (1996) examined grammar as interactionally situated—not limited to phenomena within the stream of speech but encompassing structures and organization associated with "the endogenous activity systems within which strips of talk are embedded" (p. 370). (See also Atkinson, 1984; Bavelas, 1994; Goodwin, 1986; Goodwin & Goodwin, 1986; Kendon, 1972, 1980, 1987; LeBaron & Streeck, 2000; and Schegloff, 1984.)

In sum, recent research on language and social interaction has taken up a constitutive and holistic view of human interaction. This revolution within the field of communication will undoubtedly influence technological invention and advance. Kato et al. (this volume) illustrate how a study of naturally occurring interaction may inform technological design. However, their research also shows a tendency to assume a sender–receiver model of communication and to dissect embodied communication along discursive lines. The roles of teacher and student (hence sender–receiver) were presupposed and literally built into the technological design: "The learners' site had three cameras . . . the instructor's site had two." Furthermore, cameras were used to dissect the participants' communicating bodies along the discursive lines, separating the "hands" from the "face."

---

[1]Frustrated by the constraints of transcripts and printed pages, Jarmon (1996) published the first CD-ROM dissertation in the United States. Multimedia technology enabled her to present her data and analysis without privileging vocal and written forms of communication.

Point Three: Technology Does Not Exist Independent of Its Use. This concluding point follows from the previous two. According to a constitutive view of communication and human interaction, technology is what people use it to do. Too often, researchers regard technology as another component of the sender–receiver model, as something that impinges upon human interaction. What needs to be more fully acknowledged is that human interaction impinges upon technology, shaping what it *is* through the ways that it is used. Moreover, what technology *is* may change over the course of human interaction. With the invention of the telephone, users had to accomplish leave-taking without the sorts of visible cues associated with face-to-face interaction. (See Kendon, 1990, for a description of subtle body behaviors whereby face-to-face conversations may be brought to a close.) Nevertheless, telephone users evidently contrived vocal devices whereby leave-taking may be cued and telephone conversations may be jointly terminated (Schegloff & Sacks, 1973). Through interaction, people eventually orchestrated their interaction to compensate for technological limitations. Kato et al. (this volume) seem to succumb to the object-constancy myth. That is, they seem to presuppose that their technology is what they have designed it to be, that their users' communication is largely an effect or consequence of their design, and that their technology and its use would not change over the course of extended and less-controlled interaction. Perhaps the object-constancy myth is a symptom of their experimental method, which seems somewhat at odds with the naturalistic research they cite and celebrate. Technology does not exist independent of its use, which causes problems for researchers who want to conduct controlled experiments upon it.

REFERENCES

Atkinson, J. (1984). *Our masters' voices.* London: Methuen.

Atkinson, J., & Heritage, J. (Eds.). (1984). *Structures of social action.* New York: Cambridge University Press.

Bateson, G., & Mead, M. (1942). *Balinese character. A photographic analysis.* New York: New York Academy of Sciences.

Bavelas, J. (1994). Gestures as part of speech: Methodological implications. *Research on Language and Social Interaction, 27(3),* 201–221.

Button, G. (1992). Answers as interactional products: Two sequential practices used in job interviews. In P. Drew & J. Heritage (Eds.), *Talk at work* (pp. 101–34). Cambridge: Cambridge University Press.

Drew, P., & Heritage, J. (Eds.). (1992). *Talk at work.* Cambridge: Cambridge University Press.

Duranti, A. (1997). *Linguistic anthropology.* Cambridge: Cambridge University Press.

Glenn, P., LeBaron, C., & Mandelbaum, J. (Eds.) (in press). *Studies in language and social interaction* Mahwah, NJ: Lawrence Erlbaum.

Goffman, E. (1961). *Asylums.* New York: The Free Press.

Goodwin, C. (1980). Restarts, pauses, and the achievement of a state of mutual gaze at turn-beginning. *Sociological Inquiry, 50,* 277–302.

Goodwin, C. (1981). *Conversational organization: Interaction between speakers and hearers.* New York: Academic Press.

Goodwin, C. (1986). Gestures as a resource for the organization of mutual orientation. *Semiotica, 62*(1/2), 29–49.

Goodwin, C. (1996). Transparent vision. In E. Ochs, E. Schegloff, & S. Thompson (Eds.), *Interaction and grammar* (pp. 370–404). Cambridge: Cambridge University Press.

Goodwin, C., & Goodwin, M. (1986). Gesture and coparticipation in the activity of searching for a word. *Semiotica, 62*(1/2), p. 51–75.

Heath, C. (1986). *Body movement and speech in medical interaction.* Cambridge: Cambridge University Press.

Heritage, J. (1984). *Garfinkel and ethnomethodology.* Cambridge, UK: Polity Press.

Hopper, R. (1992). *Telephone conversation.* Bloomington: Indiana University Press.

Jarmon, L. (1996). *An ecology of embodied interaction: Turn-taking and interactional syntax in face-to-face encounters.* Doctoral dissertation, published on CD-ROM, University of Texas at Austin.

Kendon, A. (1972). Some relationships between body motion and speech. In A. W. Seigman & B. Pope (Eds.), *Studies in Dyadic Communication* (pp. 177–210). Elmsford, NY: Pergamon Press.

Kendon, A. (1980). Gesticulation and speech: Two aspects of the process of utterance. In M. Key (Ed.), *The relationship of verbal and nonverbal communication* (pp. 207–228). The Hague: Mouton.

Kendon, A. (1987). On gesture: Its complementary relationship with speech. In A. Siegman & S. Feldstein (Eds.), *Nonverbal behavior and communication* (pp. 65–97). Hillsdale, NJ: Lawrence Erlbaum.

Kendon, A. (1990). *Conducting interaction: Patterns of behavior in focused encounters.* Cambridge: Cambridge University Press.

Koschmann, T., & LeBaron, C. (in preparation). *Learner articulation as interactional achievement: Studying the conversation of gesture.*

LeBaron, C. (1998). *Building communication: Architectural gestures and the embodiment of new ideas.* Unpublished doctoral dissertation, University of Texas at Austin, UMI, AAT 98-38026.

LeBaron, C., & Streeck, J. (1997). Built space and the interactional framing of experience during a murder interrogation. *Human Studies, 20*, 1–25.

LeBaron, C., & Streeck, J. (2000). Gestures, knowledge, and the world. In D. McNeill (Ed.), *Language and gesture.* Cambridge: Cambridge University Press.

Moerman, M. (1990). Exploring talk and interaction. *Research on Language and Social Interaction, 24*, 173–187.

Ochs, E., Schegloff, E., & Thompson, S. (Eds.). (1996). *Interaction and grammar.* Cambridge: Cambridge University Press.

Sacks, H. (1992 (1964–1972)). *Lectures on conversation,* Jefferson, G. (Ed.). Cambridge: Blackwell.

Sacks, H., Schegloff, E., & Jefferson, G. (1974). A simplest systematics for the organization of turn-taking for conversation. *Language, 50*, 696–735.

Scheflen, A. (1976). *Human territories: How we behave in time and space.* Englewood Cliffs, NJ: Prentice-Hall.

Schegloff, E. (1984). On some gestures' relation to talk. In J. Atkinson & J. Heritage (Eds.), *Structures of social action* (pp. 266–296). Cambridge: University Press.

Schegloff, E. (1992a). Introduction. In G. Jefferson (Ed.), *Lectures on conversation* (pp. ix–lxii). Oxford: Basil Blackwell.

Schegloff, E. (1992b). On talk and its institutional occasions. In P. Drew & J. Heritage (Eds.), *Talk at work* (pp. 101–34). Cambridge: University Press.

Schegloff, E., & H. Sacks (1973). Opening up closings. *Semiotica, VIII, 4*, 289–327.

Shannon, C., & Weaver, W. (1949). *The mathematical theory of communication*. Urbana: University of Illinois Press.

Streeck, J. (1993). Gesture as communication I: Its coordination with gaze and speech. *Communication Monographs, 60*, 275–299.

Streeck, J. (1996). How to do things with things. *Human Studies, 19*(4), 365–384.

Streeck, J. (in press). The body taken for granted: Lingering dualism in research on social interaction. In P. Glenn, C. LeBaron, & J. Mandelbaum (Eds.), *Studies in language and social interaction*. Mahwah, NJ: Lawrence Erlbaum.

Streeck, J., & Knapp, M. (1992). The interaction of visual and verbal features in human communication. In F. Poyatos (Ed.), *Advances in nonverbal communication*, 3–24. Amsterdam: Benjamins B. V.

Ten Have, P. & Psathas, G. (Eds.) (1995). *Situated order: Studies in social organization of talk and embodied activities*. Lanham, Maryland: University Press of America.

MANAGING INTERSUBJECTIVITY IN VIDEO-MEDIATED COLLABORATION

Charles Crook
Loughborough University

Much is expected of video-mediated communication. Many people who need to instruct, negotiate, or otherwise coordinate human action are finding this technology powerfully seductive. Yet, in practice, this apparently most vivid medium of communication has not lived up to users' expectations. This chapter by Kato and colleagues reminds us of why the task of mediating communication with video is so daunting: It reminds us of the complexity inherent in routine conversation. Indeed it is sobering to reflect on our limited intuitions about the conduct of such interpersonal exchange—so limited that we come to expect unproblematic reproduction of the experience with face-on-face recording technologies.

The heart of the problem is the behavioral management of intersubjective understandings. Intersubjectivity involves mutual knowledge of psychological states (Rommetveit, 1979). That is, I know things; you know I know things; I know you know this; and so forth. We have learned from various traditions of social psychological research that this mutuality is significantly derived from the perception and interpretation of highly subtle features in human social action (Garfinkel, 1967; Potter & Edwards, 1992). To be sure it is quite possible to orchestrate an instructional exchange in the fashion of talking heads, and sometimes we may do so quite successfully. But this really does require an effort of orchestration, stretching all the narrative resources of the "literate mind" to sustain coherence and engagement. More usually and more naturally, we handle the intersubjectivity of instruction by relying on the free play of cues arising from our bodily interplays within shared space. The present research nicely illustrates how disoriented we may become when the interpretative potential of shared space is denied—when we must instruct over a distance. The technical ingenuity of these researchers created some improvement in the quality of exchange (although I look forward to closer analyses of the communicative flow that underlies this difference). This is a significant observation. Evidently it invites further work to be done on exploring the parameters of organizing "views" and I hope we can look forward to reading more of that enterprise.

One motive for encouraging this general program of research is the promise of video technology for enriching distance instruction. In relation to such ambitions, it is important to note that Kato and colleagues have addressed the challenge of intersubjectivity through a particularly accessible task context. They examine the guidance of learners in their manipulation of concrete objects within a circumscribed space. This is a situation in which participants derive states of intersubjectivity from the mutual interpretation of cues arising from visual attention and manual action. One might say that this is the most tractable of interpretative problems to resource: The salient events can be readily captured on video and—with some ingenuity (as illustrated here)—they can be communicated over distances. However, the intersubjectivity that lies at the heart of instructional practice is constructed from a richer array of knowledge than that to be captured by cameras tracking movements and glances in the here-and-now. It is also derived from histories of interaction: from mutual understandings constructed over longer periods of time and enriched by joint participation in more elaborate forms of corporate organization. If it is hard for us to take account of the reflexive nature of communication as manifest in the visual detection of gesture and posture (as this chapter suggests), then it is surely hard for us to take account of the more subtle reflexive forms that arise from shared histories. Yet I suggest that the awareness of this common knowledge and common experience is a crucial resource for learners at both the motivational and cognitive levels. One hopes that visionary researchers of computer-mediated distance education will embrace this broader sense in which intersubjectivity has to be achieved as well as address parameters associated with the immediate environment of social exchange. In any event, the arena is a generous one—with ample room for researchers at a variety of disciplinary boundaries.

REFERENCES

Garfinkel, H. (1967). *Studies in ethnomethodology*. Englewood Cliffs, NJ: Prentice-Hall.
Potter, J., & Edwards, D. (1992). *Discursive psychology*. London: Sage.
Rommetveit, R. (1979). On the architecture of intersubjectivity. In R. Rommetveit & R. Blakar (Eds.), *Studies of language, thought and verbal communication* (pp. 93–107) London: Academic Press.

ON AWARENESS OF SHARED ORIENTATION, AND OTHER MATTERS

Hiroshi Kato
National Institute of Multimedia Education

Keiichi Yamazaki
Saitama University

Hideyuki Suzuki
Ibaraki University

Hideaki Kuzuoka
University of Tsukuba

Hiroyuki Miki
Oki Electric Industry Co., Ltd.

Akiko Yamazaki
Future University Hakodate

We would like to begin by thanking the three reviewers for their insightful critiques, which helped to open up new aspects of our research to consideration and discussion. The research project described in the paper was carried out by a diverse team of researchers working in the fields of educational technology, cognitive science, ethnomethodology, human–computer interaction, and computer-supported cooperative work (CSCW). The members of the team shared common interests in learning and human interaction and in the design of technology supporting those activities. However, it was not our intention to create a unified discipline that would transcend the differences in our respective fields and backgrounds. Rather, we sought to make the most of that diversity. By allowing each of the members to base their contributions on their own individual field, such as system development, experiment design, and interaction analysis, we were able to work together despite our disciplinary differences. But we are convinced that it was that multidisciplinary approach that made our work both more fruitful and more exciting. Moreover, it was through that approach that we were able to illustrate concretely the relevance of the ethnomethodological point of view in the field of information technology.

CONCERNING THE USE OF METAPHORS

What we intended to represent by the term "face-to-face metaphor" was simply the naive concept that underlies much of the design of distance education systems: that high-definition view of facial expressions and the maintenance of eye contact make it possible to provide a good environment for collaboration based on a simplistic model of real-world interactions. We do not mean to deny the value of facial expressions and gaze, only to suggest that shared orientation (specifically, making participant's orienting actions and the objects to which they are oriented mutually observable) is more essential. The experimental setting was designed in such a way that the instructor could observe each learner's orientation, and the learners could see the view provided to the instructor along with the instructor's hand gesture on the view screen. This approach to awareness should be distinguished from the eye-contact approach, in which it may be possible for a line of sight to be mutually perceived while the object being viewed remains out of sight to one or more participants. (Admittedly, neither approach is inconsistent, and the final outcome in each may be the same.) Therefore, as Smith correctly observed, the problem does not reside in the face-to-face bodily formation of the participants.

Smith also commented that the "body metaphor" might better be described as "no metaphor," which is correct from the user's point of view. The concept of a "body metaphor" (which perhaps should be rephrased as "distributed body metaphor") is a design rationale for designers, rather than a metaphor employed by the participants in the experiment. Along similar lines, we are currently working on research into the concept of "embodied space," in which an instructor can point directly to objects in the learners' real workspace by using a remotely controlled laser pointer (Yamazaki et al., 1999).

REGARDING AWARENESS

Ethnomethodological studies have revealed that our everyday interaction is achieved collaboratively by monitoring the relevancy of each other's action. In his analysis of how conversation is organized, Goodwin (1981) demonstrated that a speaker monitors whether or not a hearer is paying attention (orientation to the speaker) and, at the same time, that the hearer displays his/her readiness to hear the speech (recipiency) by gaze or body movement. Likewise, when a speaker points at a physical object by hand gesture, it is necessary that he/she be aware from the hearer's posture, gesture, or words that the hearer is in a position where he/she can look at the object as well as the pointing action itself (Goodwin, 1996, 1998). That is, to achieve the pointing socially, the hearer should be aware of the speaker's orientation, and vice versa.

Although the term "awareness" usually involves a broad set of concepts, what we wanted to verify in our experiment was a particular type of awareness: specifically, shared orientation. This should be distinguished from other forms of awareness such as those supported by eye contact, because as stated previously, shared orientation does not necessarily require eye contact. Hence, we used the term "awareness" with some trepidation, knowing that if taken in the general sense, the essential difference between the two approaches might not be sufficiently distinct.

ON THE ASYMMETRY OF SETTING

Taken at any given moment, an electronic communication channel is necessarily one way. Because of this limitation, each communication channel must have discrete sender and receiver terminals. As Smith indicated, that is the fundamental difference between electronic and real-world communications. Therefore, from a technical standpoint, to emulate real-world communications in an electronic environment it is necessary to share time or combine at least two one-way communications channels.

However, as LeBaron stated, social roles such as those of instructor and learner are not fixed but are contingent upon the local social interactions between the participants. This reality may have contributed to a certain conceptual confusion. That is, although the communications channels have fixed roles such as sender or receiver, the social roles are contingent. For a sender (communications channel) to be a sender (social role) in such a system, it is necessary, but never sufficient, for the participant to be on the sender terminal of a channel.

In the chapter, we referred to participants as "instructor" or "learner" and described scenes in which one participant (the instructor) taught the others (learners). However, this is not because we perceived their social roles to be determined *a priori*. We did not view these membership categories as canonical when performing interaction analysis but only used the terms as markers for convenience of reference.

The room setting in the experiment was admittedly asymmetrical, but this is not so unnatural given the spread of remote lecturing over the Internet or communication satellite links. The experiment was designed asymmetrically for practical reasons, as the result of asymmetries in the experimental conditions (e.g., one set of participants was experienced in the use of AlgoBlocks, while the other was not; only one set of AlgoBlocks was available at the time of the experiment.) However, we have been working on a new symmetrical form of distance collaboration equipment named "Agora" (Yamashita et al., 1999), which supports face-to-face collaboration over a shared DigitalDesk-like table in which people can collaborate as if they were playing a game of contract bridge. In the future, we hope to investigate the differences in emergent roles in symmetrical and asymmetrical settings.

THE ISSUE OF COMMUNICATIONS ALONG DISCURSIVE LINES

We have dealt with the issue of how the functions of face and hands emerge in social interactions and how distributed body resources are reorganized by participants in telecommunications. Our experiments revealed that, even if a body part's actual spatial disposition is not maintained in the positioning of communications devices, participants were able to establish nonverbal, holistic communications. As shown in Table 10.3, the action of a learner turning to view the instructor's face monitor succeeded in drawing the instructor's attention, just as if the learner had turned to face an instructor in the same room. This is in spite of the fact that the actual action displayed on the instructor's monitor was the learner looking back. This suggests that people can correlate body parts scrambled by communications devices and invent a contingent communications system and that such a system is not deliberately designed, but emergent.

SHARED KNOWLEDGE AND HISTORY

It is very difficult to analyze "internal" knowledge or memory without resorting to uncertain conjecture, so for the sake of methodological rigor we have tried to deal with knowledge and history as social artifacts that are made observable through people's interactions. But in no sense do we mean to deny the significance of knowledge and history as resources. In the future, we intend to conduct an experiment with the goal of improving instructional resources by carrying out long-term observation of how the historical accumulation of social interactions gives rise to new forms of communication. In particular, we are interested in analysing set of actions and their accompanying articulation and the ways in which they organize an instructional scene.

REFERENCES

Goodwin, C. (1981). *Conversational organization: Interaction between speakers and hearers.* New York: Academic Press.

Goodwin, C. (1996). Professional vision. *American Anthropologist, 96*, 606–633.

Goodwin, C. (1998). *Pointing as situated practice.* Paper presented at the Max Planck Workshop on Pointing Gestures.

Yamashita, J., Kuzuoka, H., Yamazaki, K., Yamazaki, A., Miki, H., Kato, H., & Suzuki, H. (1999). Agora: Supporting multi-participant tele-collaboration. *Human–Computer Interaction, 2*, 543–547.

Yamazaki, K., Yamazaki, A., Kuzuoka, H., Oyama, S., Kato, H., Suzuki, H., & Miki, H. (1999). GestureLaser and GestureLaser Car: Development of an embodied space to support remote instruction. *Proceedings of ECSCW99* (pp. 239–258). Dordrecht: Kluwer Academic Publishers.

USING ARGUMENT MAP REPRESENTATIONS TO MAKE THINKING VISIBLE FOR INDIVIDUALS AND GROUPS

Philip Bell
University of Washington

INTRODUCTION: DESIGNING FOR KNOWLEDGE INTEGRATION IN THE CLASSROOM

Through the design, enactment and study of educational innovations we can advance our understanding of individual and social mechanisms associated with learning and development (diSessa, 1991; Mendelson, 1996). As designers of instruction, curriculum, and technology, we need to find productive mechanisms for making our theoretical influences and commitments as well as the hypotheses embedded in our designs clear to each other. Our theoretical approaches and influences should be foregrounded and refined as they inform our design efforts. The overall goal of the research presented in this chapter is to inform the development of a knowledge base of pragmatic design principles that can shape educational innovations that make use of educational technology and orchestrate the use of the innovations in science classrooms with the goal of promoting knowledge integration (Linn, 1995; Linn, Bell, & Hsi, 1998). With our innovations, we seek to help students develop a principled understanding of scientific topics, make appropriate connections between these scientific ideas, and apply this integrated knowledge to real-world and classroom experiences. Knowledge integration, which can be taken as a particular view of conceptual change, is an individual learning outcome focused on domain-specific conceptual understanding although it is often powerfully influenced by social learning mechanisms. This chapter explores how to orchestrate collaborations around abstract argument representations in the classroom to promote individual learning.

THE SENSEMAKER ARGUMENT EDITOR

SenseMaker is one software component of the Knowledge Integration Environment (KIE). Overall, KIE represents an integrated set of software learning tools coupled with a project-based framework for middle and high school science curriculum focused around Web resources (Bell, Davis, & Linn, 1995; Linn, Bell, & Hsi, 1998). In KIE, students engage with Web resources as pieces of scientific evidence to be interpreted, explored, and applied in their science projects. KIE seeks to promote a more integrated student understanding of complex science concepts and processes. The KIE framework includes a project-based curriculum structure to scaffold students' science inquiry along with appropriate software tools used as part of those activities. Custom KIE software includes a Web-based discussion tool called SpeakEasy, an online guidance system called Mildred, and the SenseMaker argumentation software highlighted in this study. Students move among the various software components that make up the learning environment as appropriate for their activities during the designed curriculum activities.

Our approach is to provide students with learning opportunities and tools that will help them express and reflect on their conceptual ideas about natural phenomena, explore and compare their ideas to those of others, and make sound discriminations among the set of ideas under consideration. Over the course of seven classroom trials, we have improved our understanding of how to scaffold students as they use the SenseMaker argumentation tool as part of a knowledge integration process. In this chapter I report on the lessons learned from the first four of these trials. They serve to characterize important aspects of the continuous refinement process involved with evolving the instructional materials and approach. Specifically, this research explores the relationships among students' use of the software to develop scientific arguments and engage in debate, individual dimensions of their learning, and their collaboration that occurred in the classroom.

SenseMaker Rationale

Information technologies such as the Web continue to become more ubiquitous in our culture and our schools. Yet, the educational implications and possibilities of these vast and diverse ecologies of information have yet to be fully explored. Many metaphors have been used to better understand the Web's role in education, including thinking of it as an encyclopedia, a library or as an online textbook. Indeed, these metaphors may be appropriate for subsets of Web resources. However, the approach taken by this research is to view select science-related resources on the Web as *evidence* that students can actively interpret, critique, and employ in arguments. Over the past four years, the KIE project has followed this approach and built a framework for Internet-based curriculum and custom software tools. The design of KIE has been continually shaped by sociocognitive research performed within classroom settings.

How can students best be supported when engaging in the construction of arguments using scientific evidence from the Web? What do students learn from engaging in such activities? A number of software development efforts—including CSILE (Scardamalia & Bereiter, 1991), the Multimedia Forum Kiosk and SpeakEasy (Hsi & Hoadley, 1997), Belvedere (Suthers, Toth, & Weiner, 1997)—have explored how technology can support group argumentation and knowledge construction. Research has revealed how groups can productively collaborate using these tools; however, there is not yet an accepted approach for supporting students with scientific criteria as they engage in group exploration of a topic. This chapter describes research on these issues surrounding our design of an argument-building tool called SenseMaker that attempts to combine scientific criteria for argumentation and knowledge representations into the learning process. Students were using SenseMaker as part of a classroom debate project focused on the nature of light. The use of the tool in the debate project has strong individual and collaborative components. By studying these individual and collaborative uses of the tool in an instructional context, the goal is to study the use of Sense-Maker as a knowledge integration tool and to infer design principles for software tools that support argumentation during classroom debate activities.

As cognitive research has provided important insights into learning and development, there has been an increased desire by educational researchers to develop a *design science* for instruction that is theoretically principled yet grounded in research taking place within naturalistic learning settings—often classrooms (Brown, 1992; Collins, 1992; diSessa, 1991; Glaser, Ferguson, & Vosniadou, 1996; Linn, 1990; Salomon, 1990). The strong design orientation of this approach is important. When coupled with a focus on theory development and an empirical analytical process, design provides the means by which we can explore new possibilities associated with ever-changing technologies at the same time as we refine our theories of learning and collaboration. Through iterative cycles of design, enactment, and research, we can develop and hone innovations that catalyze new forms of learning, and our understanding of learning and development can be advanced in the process.

SenseMaker Design and Functionality

A number of software environments have been developed with a similar goal of supporting students' argument construction; these include CSILE

(Scardamalia & Bereiter, 1991), SpeakEasy (Hsi & Hoadley, 1997), Belvedere (Cavalli-Sforza, Weiner, & Lesgold, 1994; Suthers, Toth & Weiner, 1997), Convince-Me (Ranney & Schank, 1998), and Euclid (Smolensky, Fox, King, & Lewis, 1988). This genre of argumentation software is composed of two relatively distinct subgenres: (a) discussion-based tools that support a more dialogical form of argumentation by a group (e.g., CSILE or SpeakEasy) and (b) knowledge representation tools that support a more rhetorical construction of arguments by individuals (e.g., Euclid or SenseMaker). It is important to note that each type of software can involve *both* individual and collaborative uses. In the discussion-based tools, individuals typically compose personal explanations that are contributed to a structured group space. In knowledge-representation tools, individuals construct structured, personal arguments that can then be contributed to a group space that may or may not have a particular argumentative structure. Given this rough characterization, we see that to some degree the difference in the subgenres resides with where students receive scaffolding for argumentation in their process.

SenseMaker provides a spatial and categorical representation for a collection of Web-based resources (or evidence items in this case) (see Fig. 11.1).

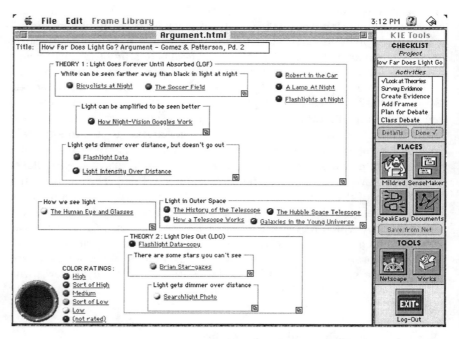

FIG. 11.1. SenseMaker argument jointly constructed by a student pair for use in a classroom debate about the properties of light (along with the KIE tool palette).

This chapter describes students engaging in a debate project about the properties of light. Using SenseMaker, students group evidence items into conceptually-framed categories and create scientific arguments based on their understanding of the topic. The SenseMaker software allows small groups of students to organize and annotate a collection of evidence associated with a project that can then be shared and compared with others. Within the software students work with *evidence dots* representing individual pieces of evidence on the Web and *claim frames* corresponding to conceptual categories (or groupings) for the evidence. Claim frames that are conceptually connected can be interrelated by hierarchically nesting one inside of another. For example, in Fig. 11.1 the claim "Light gets dimmer over distance, but doesn't go out" is a conceptual claim these students are using to support the "Theory 1: Light Goes Forever Until Absorbed" claim in which it is nested. This larger claim frame represents one of the main theories under debate in that particular classroom project, which will be described in detail later in this chapter.

For a given KIE project, students are presented with a collection of salient evidence items to explore. As students explore and interpret the evidence, they drag the evidence dots into the claim frame they believe it supports.[1] Evidence items can be duplicated so that they can be categorized under multiple claim frames. This is important because it is possible for competing theories to be able to account for the same evidence. Also, the knowledge integration view of conceptual change acknowledges that students may simultaneously hold multiple views of a given phenomena or scientific concept at a given time (Linn, diSessa, Pea, & Songer, 1994). This functionality is beneficial in that it allows students with fragmented or uncertain knowledge of the topic to more fully express their range of ideas in their argument. The claim frames are used and created by students to represent their understanding of how the evidence items fit into the theoretical context of the debate.

The design of the SenseMaker software was influenced by trade-offs among the instructional goals for the software, psychological research on student argumentation, and philosophy of argumentation in science. The software is designed to enable student construction of arguments that are rooted in their own conceptual understanding while also being constrained such that they conform to central features of scientific argumentation (e.g., the use of empirical evidence to support scientific claims or conjectures, the expression and exploration of a range of perspectives or hypotheses on an

---

[1]In the most recent Java version of SenseMaker, we have allowed students to define the relationship between an evidence item and a claim as either *supporting* or *contradicting* (represented by dots and crosses, respectively). Although it was possible to express such relationships in the Macintosh version of SenseMaker, the change has proven to be a valuable shortcut for students and in keeping with philosophical perspectives on scientific argumentation.

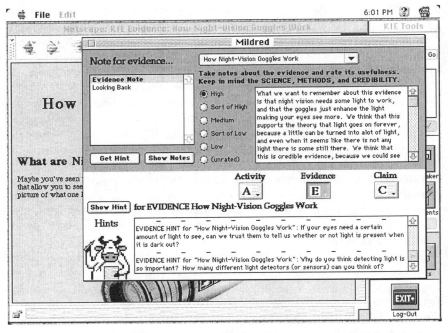

FIG. 11.2. Mildred, the guide, and note-taking software component in KIE.

issue, and the application of scientific criteria to evidence). Driver, Leach, Millar, and Scott (1996) provide a summary of relevant epistemological commitments associated with scientific reasoning and argumentation.

During KIE projects, students are typically asked to take notes on the evidence and claims associated with a project (as shown in Fig. 11.2). As they do this, KIE also includes a way for students to rate the evidence and claims along specific dimensions (e.g., low to high usefulness in the debate). When students change the rating for a piece of evidence, its dot color in the SenseMaker representation correspondingly changes (shown as different shades of gray in Fig. 11.1). Students elaborate on their specific scientific ideas in the Guide component of the KIE software and use SenseMaker to develop broad conceptual categories in which to group the evidence. Taken together, these tools allow student groups to develop personalized, structured arguments for their theoretical position in the debate.

Theoretical Background for SenseMaker

Significant research in cognitive and developmental psychology has focused on understanding how students engage in scientific argumentation. It has been argued that the ability to engage in argumentation is strongly dependent on the individual development of epistemological knowledge about argumentation and evidence (Kuhn, 1993). Kuhn (1991) has also documented that middle school students rarely call upon salient evidence to evaluate claims or fail to differentiate between evidence and hypotheses. The approach explored by the present research is that students may be able to construct more normative scientific arguments if provided with specific forms of scaffolding during instruction. With KIE, we are focused less on students' spontaneous argumentation and more on the specific learning effects associated with supporting students' argumentation in terms of their conceptual and epistemological understanding. I take the view that argumentation in science involves both generalized meta knowledge about argumentation (e.g., being able to coordinate empirical evidence with theoretical ideas) as well as domain-focused meta knowledge (e.g., specific scientific criteria for evaluating experimental results).

But, how can we tell when a student argument is scientific or not? As described by Koslowski (1996), the view of scientific inquiry espoused in a line of research influences its depiction of scientific argumentation. Similar to the approach of Koslowski, the perspective taken here is that an adequate depiction of scientific inquiry and argumentation would ask students to regularly coordinate new evidence with their personal theoretical ideas about the phenomena. By actively encouraging students to build upon their prior knowledge, students are encouraged to call upon and refine (or "bootstrap" in Koslowski's terminology) their scientific ideas through a knowledge integration process. More scientific arguments would then consist of evidence and theory coordinations that involves students' prior knowledge of science or theorized conjectures.

As students engage in argumentation, it has been found that many tend to: (a) focus on evidence that directly demonstrates intuitive ideas in a naive realist manner, (b) preferentially focus on a single piece of evidence rather than a set, and (c) equate theories with potential "truths" (Driver et al., 1996). These can be taken to be specific features of students' epistemological metaknowledge of science. Students may only tacitly understand such knowledge, but it is likely to influence heavily how students build arguments to support their theoretical positions. Indeed, early classroom trials of the KIE software corroborated the prevalence of these epistemological inclinations. It was thought that perhaps an appropriate knowledge representation tool along with new associated practices might be able to facilitate students' construction of more scientific arguments, especially in the context of a classroom environment aimed at encouraging students to develop a more sophisticated understanding of the nature of science.

Students' epistemological metaknowledge is also related to their understanding of the nature of science. One might easily hypothesize that students with different epistemological beliefs about the scientific process, for example, might construct qualitatively different types of arguments. Given the embodiment of important epistemological constraints on scientific argumentation in SenseMaker, one might also hypothesize that students working with the software would develop an understanding of specific epistemological metaknowledge (e.g., how scientific claims can be supported or contradicted with evidence or how different scientific claims may or may not be related to each other). Both of these aspects are transparent in the SenseMaker interface. In fact, we might expect that students would have to develop this type of metaknowledge before they could use the knowledge representation productively as an inscriptional system (Pea, 1993). Research on SenseMaker has indeed supported this conjecture (described in Bell, 1998).

How should argumentation be presented to students? Toulmin (1958) proposed a microstructure for the analysis of scientific arguments involving data, warrants, backings, rebuttals, and conclusions. This philosophical taxonomy influenced the design of an early version of the Belvedere software (Cavalli-Sforza et al., 1994). Should such philosophical categories serve as scaffolds for students as they construct arguments? SenseMaker follows a different approach. Rather than presenting students with a comprehensive tool for constructing scientific arguments that are philosophically sound (e.g., in a Toulminian sense), SenseMaker provides an intermediate, proto-form representation involving a coordination of evidence, claims, and explanations. SenseMaker representations are readily approachable to a broad range of students and yet capable of supporting their intellectual work in the classroom. Indeed, students using early versions of the Belvedere system found the philosophical categories difficult to use in their argumentation, and the interface was subsequently simplified (Suthers, Toth, & Weiner, 1997). Of course, the decision to use an intermediate argument representation in SenseMaker was an interface decision and does not preclude the philosophical categories from being used in the analysis of the arguments that students construct with SenseMaker. In fact, we have elsewhere described analyses of students' SenseMaker arguments from the perspective of Toulmin's micro-argument structure (Bell, 1998; Bell & Linn, 2000).

Making Thinking Visible

The design of KIE and SenseMaker has been guided by an instructional framework called *scaffolded knowledge integration* that has been derived from detailed studies of designed innovations going into classrooms (Linn, 1995; Linn, Bell, & Hsi, 1998). The framework is predicated on a repertoire-of-models view to describe student cognition during science learning. Rather than expecting learners to have highly coherent mental models or elaborated theories that drive their opinions, the repertoire view acknowledges that students often have relevant pieces of knowledge and intuitions about a topic that may not initially be well connected (diSessa, 1996; Linn, diSessa, Pea, & Songer, 1995). Given the repertoire perspective and a goal to promote knowledge integration, the scaffolded knowledge integration framework provides instructional design principles about such things as the appropriate conceptual level for content and how to provide social supports for learning. One tenet of the framework involves *making thinking visible* for the students. SenseMaker accomplishes this particular goal by serving as a tool that students can use to construct explicit knowledge representations that are understood by the teacher and other students. The cognitive apprenticeship framework (Collins, Brown, & Holum, 1991) called for making the thinking of experts visible to students. We have extended this idea to include three distinct forms:

1. **Modeling Expert Thinking**—SenseMaker can be used to model the scientific arguments of expert or historical scientists. For example, we often introduce the SenseMaker tool to students by presenting them with competing historical arguments from Isaac Newton and Johannes Kepler about the nature of the relationship between light and perceived color. The context of this historical debate provides an opportunity to bring up salient aspects of metaknowledge of explanation and argumentation. In addition to those ideas already discussed, this activity also demonstrates how individuals with differing theoretical ideas about a topic might explain the same set of evidence items quite differently from one another and construct distinct SenseMaker representations. It also highlights productive aspects of comparing knowledge representations of different individuals in order to understand their thinking.

2. **Providing a Process to Support Individual Reflection**—A more common use of SenseMaker is to engage a small group of students (or individuals) in the construction of their own argument about a particular topic. As they elaborate their argument, they make their individual understanding of the evidence and the debate visible in their argument representation through a process of theorizing, reflection, and articulation. A central design goal is for the argument representation to promote conceptual reflection in individual students as they engage in this sense-making process. Through this reflection and articulation mechanism, students visibly express their current understanding in their argument representation.

3. **Promoting the Collaborative Exchange and Discrimination of Ideas**—The organization and structure provided by the SenseMaker representation becomes an easy way for a group to communicate and compare their differing perspectives about a topic. In other words, the joint

construction of a SenseMaker argument by a small group can then be shared and compared with arguments from other small groups. In the process, particular conceptual and epistemological ideas of groups are made visible and can more easily become productive topics of conversation. We encourage classes of students to identify differences and unpack the underlying conceptual or epistemological reason for the difference. It can also be important to highlight points of concordance across arguments. Since SenseMaker arguments are Web objects, students can share their representations with other individuals electronically and arguments can be "Web-casted" throughout a classroom for simultaneous group viewing and analysis.

For these different forms of making thinking visible, it is important to realize that students' knowledge of a particular debate topic may not be fully depicted in their argument representation. The SenseMaker representation can only be taken as a vague shadow of their actual understanding of the topic. This distinction is not always made by researchers who methodologically use knowledge representations constructed by subjects (e.g., concept maps) to better understand the thinking of individuals. For the students, however, the representational artifact and the associated argumentation process can support and shape their reasoning. Students working on the joint construction of a SenseMaker argument often engage in productive discussions focused on knowledge integration issues (e.g., when students in a small group have differing interpretations for a piece of evidence).

With SenseMaker we hope to present students with an opportunity to integrate their knowledge through both individual and group learning mechanisms. That is, we encourage students to apply their prior knowledge about a particular topic, make their thinking visible in their SenseMaker argument, collaborate with others by comparing their arguments or exchanging perspectives on the evidence, and forge new connections between their scientific ideas and natural phenomena. For the present research, I explore which students engage in these various learning events associated with making thinking visible and which of the events lead to knowledge integration. Classroom studies involving SenseMaker have explored potential relationships among students' SenseMaker arguments, their epistemological ideas, and their changes in conceptual understanding.

RESEARCH CONTEXT AND DATA SOURCES

A middle school physical science class participating in the KIE research project based at the University of California, Berkeley uses the Sense-Maker tool. Approximately 180 students distributed over six class periods participate each semester. Over 1,000 students have used the SenseMaker software in their classroom projects. This chapter analyzes the first four classroom trials of SenseMaker. In this classroom, students complete six weeks of hands-on, laboratory experiments on the topic of light involving the collection and analysis of real-time data. Topics covered in the portion of the curriculum on light include: light sources, vision, reflection, absorption, energy conversion, diffuse reflection (or scattering), and light intensity over distance. Students also conduct the introductory debate project involving Newton and Kepler that focuses on the relationship between light and color.

After the light lab sequence and the Light & Color Project, students engage in a debate project called "How Far Does Light Go?" during which they contrast two theoretical positions about the propagation of light. Their inquiry on the debate topic involves the interpretation and critique of a shared corpus of Web-based, multimedia evidence derived from both scientific and everyday sources. The first theoretical position in the debate is the scientifically normative view that "light goes forever until it is absorbed," whereas the second position is more of the naive realist view that "light dies out as you move further from a light source." During the activity, it is quite common for students to make statements such as "if you can't see light, then it can't be there" (see Linn, Bell, & Hsi, 1998, for details). Many students initially align themselves with the "light dies out" perspective—although they do so for a variety of underlying reasons. The SenseMaker software guides students' organization of the evidence in the project into an argument and makes their underlying justifications available for productive individual and group reflection.

Students begin the project by stating their personal position on how far light goes. Pairs of students collaborate throughout the project on a computer station. After stating their initial opinion, student pairs begin exploring and developing an understanding of the evidence. Students also identify some of their own evidence based on their life experiences and continue to refine an argument for one theory or the other using SenseMaker. During a classroom debate, student teams present these final arguments as part of a classroom discussion and respond to questions from the other students and the teacher. Students conclude by reflecting upon issues that came up during the project and once again state their opinion about how far light goes.

Data sources used for this research include: (a) a written assessment of conceptual understanding administered at the beginning and end of the semester, (b) a written assessment of students' epistemological ideas about science administered at the beginning of the semester, (c) the SenseMaker arguments and evidence notes produced by student pairs during the debate project serving as an artifact of their inquiry, (d) a self-report completed by students after the debate project on how they made use of the SenseMaker software, and (e) videotape and field notes of students throughout the two-week debate project.

RESULTS

This section summarizes empirical research on students' learning during the How Far Does Light Go? debate and the SenseMaker arguments they construct. This includes an investigation of the individual and collaborative uses of SenseMaker as they influenced student learning.

Do Students Make Individual Conceptual Progress?

Students develop a more principled understanding of science by engaging in KIE projects. Through our design-based research methods, we investigate both individual and social mechanisms for learning. As we are interested in how to promote knowledge integration and are concerned with the learning of science by *all* students (NRC, 1996; AAAS, 1989), we routinely assess the learning of science by individual students. At the beginning and end of the semester, students complete a written assessment of their understanding of the topics covered by the curriculum. One question asks students to reason about an everyday situation where the driver of a car is approaching a distant bicyclist at night. Students are asked to describe the distance the light travels away from the headlights of the car and why. This question assesses the principal scientific idea of the How Far Does Light Go? project. Student explanations written in response to the test questions were coded into categories representing a full scientific conceptual model for light, a partial scientific model, some other causal model, or a descriptive or vague response. Figure 11.3 presents student responses on the pre-test and post-test to the car and bicycle question (see Bell & Linn, 2000 for details). Looking at the change in post-test response levels compared to pre-test responses, we see that almost half the students in the class are moving into the full model category by the end of the class. Students' learning about this particular topic has been connected to their engagement in the How Far Does Light Go? project in particular (Bell, 1998). Similar conceptual changes have been documented for different cohorts of students across multiple classroom trials; this is even though additional metaknowledge learning focused on specific aspects of scientific argumentation and debate has been incorporated into the project over that time frame (Bell, 1998). In other words, even though students were being asked to critique evidence along specific criteria, to elaborate their arguments with more conceptual detail in the claim frames, and to learn how to compare their argument to those of others, students were still learning about light propagation to the same degree.

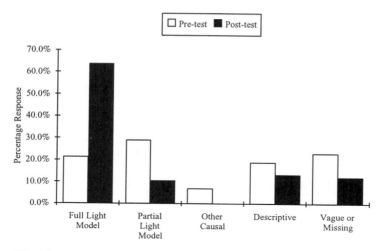

FIG. 11.3. Students' overall progress on the light debate topic from the beginning to the end of the class ($N = 172$).

Can Middle School Students Construct Arguments That Are Scientific?

As the SenseMaker software and the How Far Does Light Go? debate project have been improved, there have been corresponding improvements in student arguments. Arguments have continued to become increasingly elaborated and individually customized. From early classroom trials with SenseMaker, it proved to be quite difficult to get students to frame out their SenseMaker arguments with conceptual categories for the evidence. Instead, students often built categorical or logistical frames. Conceptual frame building has been increasingly accomplished by students as specific scaffolding has been incorporated into the surrounding software, project materials, and classroom instruction (Bell, 1998).

A completed SenseMaker argument is an artifact of the inquiry process each group engaged in as they explored the evidence. Compare the argument displayed in Fig. 11.4 to the one shown in Fig. 11.1. If these two groups were participating in the same classroom debate and had been asked to compare their final arguments, they might start out by discussing why they categorized the Searchlight Photo evidence or Brian Star Gazes evidence as supporting different theories in the debate. Or, they may discuss their underlying reasons for creating different, custom frames for the evidence. As we shall see later, these simple differences in claim frames and evidence categorization in the SenseMaker representation can lead to substantial discussions about differing conceptual or epistemological ideas held by students.

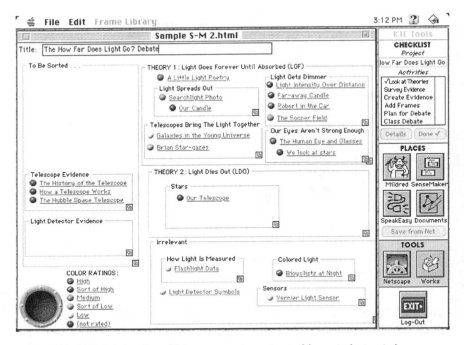

FIG. 11.4. Another SenseMaker argument constructed by a student pair for use in the same classroom debate about light as represented in Fig. 11.1.

The developmental psychology literature has documented that students in early adolescence often fail to spontaneously coordinate theoretical ideas with instances of evidence in their arguments (Kuhn, 1991). However, when scaffolded with an argumentation process involving a knowledge representation tool attuned to important epistemological criteria for arguments, students did not have difficulty conjecturing about how evidence may be related to the theoretical debate at hand. When students' evidence explanations were analyzed in detail I found that they used causal warrants (i.e., theoretical conjectures about the evidence) 70% of the time to connect evidence items to the debate in Classroom Trial 3 and 80% of the time in Classroom Trial 4 (Bell, 1998). This is in contrast to students offering simple phenomenological descriptions of the evidence, which occurred only 16% of the time in their arguments. This finding corroborates the finding of Reiner, Pea, and Shulman (1995) who found that when students were engaged in a more authentic scientific inquiry process with light phenomena, their explanations shifted from being descriptive to including more causal conjectures. It should also be noted that students were not superficially engaging with the evidence items. On average, SenseMaker arguments contained 10 evidence explanations with each explanation consisting of 65 words in length. In sum, most student groups were producing elaborate SenseMaker arguments focused on the conceptual issues in the debate.

Can a Frame Library Help Students Build Arguments?

As mentioned in the previous section, it was clear that students needed scaffolding as they created new conceptually focused frames for their evidence (Bell, 1998). In Classroom Trial 4, a Frame Library feature was included in the SenseMaker software consisting of a menu of possible frames students could use (see Fig. 11.5). The library was designed to model for students possible frames and good criteria for new conceptual categories. It included a full range of conceptually focused frames students had created in previous classroom trials—not just scientifically normative ideas. The goal was to support students in expressing their personal ideas about the debate.

In Classroom Trial 4, the use of the SenseMaker software was modeled for students by engaging them with hypothetical arguments from Newton and

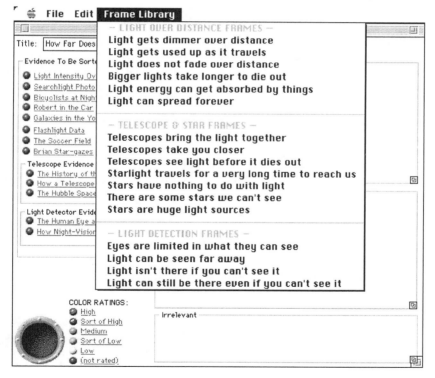

FIG. 11.5. The Frame Library in SenseMaker used to scaffolding students' frame-building during the Light Debate Project.

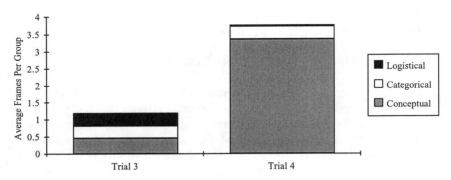

FIG. 11.6. Average number of different types of frames created by student groups in Classroom Trials 3 and 4 in their SenseMaker arguments.

Kepler about the relationship between light and color. These hypothetical arguments demonstrated to the students how different SenseMaker arguments can be constructed about the same evidence based on one's individual ideas. This introduction to some of the practices associated with argument representations along with the scaffolding provided by the Frame Library allowed students to create more conceptual frames in their arguments focused on the scientific issues of the debate than in any previous trial. On average, student groups in Classroom Trial 4 each added four frames to their argument and 85% of all the frames added were conceptually focused. This is in strong contrast to previous trials in which less specific scaffolding was provided and students created fewer frames, many of which were not conceptually focused (as indicated in Fig. 11.6).

But, did some groups make more use of the Frame Library than others? In Classroom Trial 4, 60% of the groups came up with more custom conceptual frames of their own than they borrowed from the library, 14% created equal numbers of custom conceptual and library frames, and only 25% of the groups borrowed more conceptual frames from the Frame Library than they created on their own. Only 13 groups out of 88 relied solely on the Frame Library for their frames. When students were asked after the project about their use of the Frame Library, 70% of the them reported finding it useful. It seems that for most groups the Frame Library played a facilitating role in their frame building.

But how were they using it? even though the Frame Library was presented to students in the same manner, there is evidence that different groups were using the library for different purposes. There were several different types of uses that were detectable from students' self-reports about the Frame Library functionality. Some found it useful for finding words to suit their specific ideas. Here is one student's reactions to the Frame Library:

> Because if something is on the tip of your tongue, or you have a good idea but the words can't come out, you can get help from the library [to] form some things you might want or need.

Sometimes the library was just a starting point for students before they created their own new frames. For example, one student from a group that created four custom frames of their own and no library frames reported:

> [The Frame Library] gave me ideas, but I couldn't always use the ideas and even if I found one I could use, I usually had to change it to fit my arguments. Not all the frames I agreed with, and I couldn't be sure how correct the frames were. Usually it was easier just to make my own frame, but it was useful for getting ideas.

In a more strategic use of the library, there were groups that looked to the library for different perspectives on the debate so as to better understand how other students would be thinking about the topic. Here is the reaction of a student from a group that created five custom conceptual frames of their own and did not add any frames from the library:

> You could see what people had previously thought of and what people in our class may think that is different from our opinion. It showed us some ideas for getting started on making our own frames.

The Frame Library helped students elaborate and customize their own SenseMaker arguments with conceptual frames that made their thinking visible. Once the arguments were more fully articulated, there were also secondary effects of the library during the debate discussions when the argument representations became a focus for group evaluation and comparison.

Are Student Arguments Related to Their Epistemological Ideas About the Nature of Science?

Songer and Linn (1992) found that students with a dynamic view of the nature of science were more likely to integrate their own knowledge during a science class than were those with a static view. That is, students who believe that science consists of an evolving body of knowledge proceed to develop a more integrated understanding during science class. The present research further investigates this finding by exploring potential relationships between students' epistemological beliefs and the arguments they create while working on the How Far Does Light Go? debate. In other words, if student beliefs about the nature of science influence their knowledge integration, we may detect this influence in the scientific arguments they create.

An epistemology assessment was administered three months prior to students' construction of the SenseMaker arguments during the How Far Does Light Go? project. Student responses were coded along several epistemological dimensions, one of which was an assessment of students' understanding of the process of science as being either dynamic or static (see Davis, 1998, for details). Each category was created from an amalgam of multiple choice responses to similarly focused questions.

Given this particular assessment, students' beliefs about the nature of science were found to be moderately connected to the SenseMaker arguments they constructed. Students with a more dynamic view of the scientific process created arguments that included more multiple warrants (or scientific conjectures) in their evidence explanations ($r = .16$, $n = 172$, $p < .04$) and used more frames from the Frame Library to categorize the evidence ($r = .18$, $n = 172$, $p < .02$). Since the observed correlations are relatively small (although statistically significant), it would appear that only select students are guided to participate in this aspect of science class by their epistemological beliefs about the nature of science (see Bell & Linn, 2000, for more details). Current analyses are exploring more detailed profiling of students' epistemological beliefs as they may relate to their participation in classroom activities and how they might be influenced by such activities.

A competing interpretation of this data might focus on the nature of student epistemologies or the means of measurement. That is, the identified correlations over three month's time might indicate that epistemologies are stable for only a subset of students, or that student epistemologies are diverse and the instrument and coding scheme was only partially successful in capturing the dynamic view of science. Subsequent analyses derived from a detailed study of student's free responses indicated epistemological sophistication as a result of the debate project and use of SenseMaker (reported in Bell & Linn, 2001).

How Do Groups of Students Benefit From Argument Representations?

SenseMaker arguments can also be used to foster meaningful collaboration between students as a means of making an individual's thinking visible to his or her peers. This collaboration occurs in two distinct forms during the debate project: as a student pair is jointly constructing their argument and during the classroom debate when groups are sharing and comparing their arguments.

Using Argument Representations to Make Thinking Visible for Individuals. As students work together to jointly construct a SenseMaker argument, learning opportunities regularly present themselves. For example, the SenseMaker interface makes student thinking visible to the students as they categorize evidence into frames and rate the evidence items. On numerous occasions, the act of making these visible decisions within the software led to productive discussions among the students within a small group. The simple decision in the interface design to have students drag an evidence item into one conceptual frame or another regularly leads to productive conceptual discussions *even though* they have already discussed the evidence item itself, perhaps received hints about it from the Guide software component, and composed an explanation connecting the evidence to the debate. The simple act of ultimately categorizing an evidence item as supporting one of the theory frames (or perhaps more than one) often leads to further productive peer discussion about their interpretation of the evidence item and the meaning of the theories involved in the debate. The simple interface design choice of categorizing evidence into claim frames serves as an epistemological force that productively shapes the interaction between the student pair.

Using Argument Representations to Make Thinking Visible for Groups.
A second set of collaborative uses for the argument representations revolves around the classroom debate at the end of the project. As student groups presented the details of their arguments, their SenseMaker argument was electronically Web-casted to the computer screens distributed throughout the classroom. Because all of the groups also had a hardcopy version of their own SenseMaker argument, the Web-casting allowed students in the audience to visually compare their argument to the SenseMaker representation of the presenting group. Given that SenseMaker had largely become an accepted representation in these classes for depicting knowledge claims along with evidentiary support, students could ask specific questions about the argument of the presenting group to see how they were thinking differently about the debate.

What follows is a series of transcript segments that details a single group's presentation during the classroom debate—the capstone activity of the How Far Does Light Go? project. As I am concerned here with the collaborative use of the SenseMaker representations to support learning, commentary is provided to highlight use of the representations and to follow the conceptual and epistemological issues involved with the debate sequence. Project debates are typically conducted over a two sequential 50-minute periods. The transcript segments that follow make up a complete presentation sequence from the debates; this sequence is typical of presentations made on the second day of debating. On the first day of debates, the teacher and researcher typically are more directly involved as they describe and model the analytical use of the Web-casted SenseMaker arguments during the question–answer period for each group presentation. In this transcript, KIE evidence items that are referenced are shown in italicized text and references to claim frames in SenseMaker are displayed in bold text.

Transcript Segment 1	Commentary
[Presenter]	
Ok. My name is [Presenter] and my partner is [Absent-Presenter], but he's not here right now. And we supported the theory that **Light Goes Forever**. And some of the evidence that supported our theory that we thought the best—was the best—was the *Hubble Space Telescope* and *How Night Vision Goggles Work*. And I picked the *Hubble Space Telescope* because even though you were—even though . . . you couldn't see the stars with your eyes, the telescope could see light—stars and light millions of miles away. And so that like supported it so that it would . . . so you could see it. And then the other piece of evidence that I picked is *How Night Vision Goggles Work*. And I picked that because that the night vision goggles have to pick up light and they like magnify it so that you can see it. And so even though there isn't a lot of light there you can—it's being—there's enough to be able to see with night vision goggles. And then I think the light—when you see it goes and it spreads out a lot and then it can also change into other forms of energy—but it's still there. Then my third piece of evidence that I picked was the *Time Exposure Photo*, and it's from something that I wrote. And I think that when you take a time exposure picture then if you leave the shutter open for a long time it may . . . be . . . you can probably see stars that you couldn't normally see because just enough light is reaching the film so that you will be able to see it. And on the back of my paper I drew this thing because I didn't have enough time to write it on my SenseMaker. And so my most important frame that I created was **"light can be magnified to see."** And I— in that box I put *How Night Vision Goggles Work* and the *Hubble Space Telescope* and my piece of evidence that I wrote which was *Time Exposure Photo*. [Audience-Member-1]? (calling on someone to ask a question who has their hand raised)	Student begins describing the argument her group constructed.

As suggested by the teacher, she highlights the evidence they found most compelling in the debate.

WARRANT: Telescopes can detect light from distant stars that human eyes cannot.

WARRANT: Eyes are limited detectors of light; for faint light to be visible, it often needs to be magnified to be detected.

MULTIPLE WARRANTS: Light spreads out as it travels; light can be converted to other forms of energy.

Student cites custom evidence created by her group.

WARRANT: When a camera shutter is left open, the film is able to detect light that human eyes cannot.

CITES CUSTOM FRAME: Light can be magnified to be seen. |

Students in this particular school have not engaged in a formalized class-room debate before this particular project. The teacher provides them with an initial structure for their presentation as they are not familiar with making an evidence-based, oral argument of this sort. On this particular day, one of the students in the group presenting was absent, so the presentation was made by the remaining individual. The presentation begins with a formal description of the group's position in the debate:

The group presentation serves as the culminating event for students after having investigated the topic for six or seven days. Figure 11.7 shows the presenter explaining the frame they thought was most important and the evidence they categorized inside of it. Students index the argument representations in this manner throughout the debates.

After a group has finished making its formal presentation, the floor is opened for questions from other students in the audience and the teacher and researcher.

In this segment, Audience-Member-1 brings up a piece of evidence not yet mentioned in this particular presentation. As we had hoped, students were

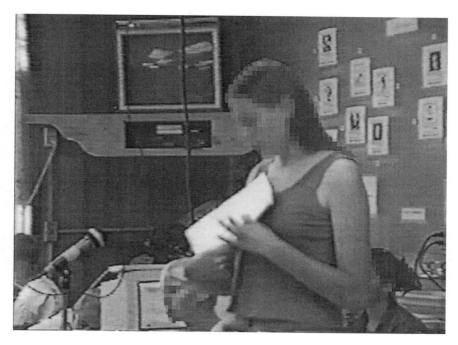

FIG. 11.7. Student presenting during the classroom debate, pointing to her SenseMaker argument and explaining her reasoning about one of her evidence categorizations.

Transcript Segment 2	Commentary
[Audience-Member-1] Why do you have *Brian Star Gazes* in the **LGF** (**Light Goes Forever** frame)? Isn't it irrelevant cause it doesn't have much information?	TOOL MOTIVATED CLARIFICATION QUESTION: Audience member asks about the placement of an evidence item not yet mentioned in the presentation. EPISTEMOLOGICAL ISSUE RAISED: Student implicitly describes criteria for 'relevant' evidence—it must have significant information.
[Presenter] I'm not really sure why I put it there, but let me checkö . . . **[Teacher]** Do you remember that piece of evidence? **[Presenter]** No. **[Teacher]** That's the one where Brian looks up and can't see some stars and uses a telescope he can. **[Presenter]** Oh yeah. I put it in **Light Goes Forever** because with this—with a telescope he can see stars that he can't see without—he can see stars that he can't—with a telescope that he can't see with his eye because the light is reaching the telescope but—so it's still there. Ok, [Audience-Member-2]?	EVIDENCE RECONSTRUCTION CONCEPTUAL UNPACKING WARRANT: Light must be reaching telescope if you can see stars with the instrument.

Transcript Segment 3	Commentary
[Audience-Member-2] Why did you put *Robert in the Car* in the **Light Dies Out** frame because it shows he could still see the light from real far?	TOOL MOTIVATED CLARIFICATION QUESTION / DIFFERENT PERSPECTIVE: Audience member presents different interpretation of a piece of evidence not yet mentioned in the presentation.
[Presenter] Well, yeah but if you go further away you can't see it just with your eye so I put it in **Light Dies Out**. [Audience-Member-3]?	Presenter extends the context of evidence item to highlight their perspective.

cued to ask their question by comparing their SenseMaker argument to that of the presenting group, which led the presenter to conceptually unpack their reasoning. The epistemological issue raised implicitly by Audience-Member-1 is not addressed. The particular epistemological issue is common: Some students believe that short evidence items have less import on the debate than many substantial evidence items.

In this segment, we see a new piece of evidence introduced into the discussion, again motivated by an analysis of the SenseMaker argument. The audience member here is offering a different perspective on the evidence item, taking its categorization in the presenter's argument as indication of

Transcript Segment 4	*Commentary*
[Audience-Member-3] Why did you put *The Soccer Field* in **Irrelevant**?	TOOL MOTIVATED CLARIFICATION QUESTION: Motivation is left unstated.
[Presenter] I put *The Soccer Field* in **Irrelevant** because . . . oh yeah—because it was the one with the flashlight and they held the light back and then the light from the car—like headlights they—it went further so it didn't—I don't think it really made a difference. Or I don't think it really supported either theory because it did go a long ways, but the light intensity wasn't as strong.	EVIDENCE RECONSTRUCTION CONCEPTUAL UNPACKING: Presenter offers a weak rejoinder as to why they consider the evidence to be irrelevant.
[Teacher] About one or two more questions and then we're going to bring closure to this.	
[Presenter] [Audience-Member-4]?	
[Audience-Member-4] For *The Soccer Field*, doesn't that kind of prove how far light keeps going if it keeps showing as its—as [the guy] keeps moving back and the light—light gets stopped like a reflection or would it stop that light because <UNCLEAR>.	DIFFERENT PERSPECTIVE, extending the previous exchange. WARRANT: Light is being stopped at different distances like a reflection.
[Presenter] Well, I don't think it really supports either theory because I know that the light is still there and it's being absorbed and it's spreading out so much that you can't see it, but the light energy is still there. [Audience-Member-5]?	CONCEPTUAL UNPACKING MULTIPLE WARRANTS: Light energy is still present at a distance; it gets absorbed and spreads as it travels. YIELD (implicit): Presenter is talking as if the evidence supports Light Goes Forever position and is no longer irrelevant.

a different interpretation than their own. We see the presenter employ a strategy very common to these debates: She extends the context of an evidence item to highlight her personal perspective. Students and the teacher often move beyond the original evidentiary description and employ such thought experiments to make their point. These moves are most successful when the person can call upon common knowledge of the group to support their elaboration—especially shared everyday or classroom experiences (see Bell, 1996, for a further description of such strategies).

Again we see a new piece of evidence brought into play from a difference in argument representations. The SenseMaker arguments are being used to hold students accountable to the breadth of their argument, not just the pieces they chose to present during their formal presentation. In classroom runs prior to the use of SenseMaker and in particular prior to the Web-casting of presenters' argument, the practice of exploring the breadth of an argument was extremely rare. Without the public viewing of the argument representations, students in the audience had little to go on for postulating how the presenting group was thinking about any of the evidence except those explicitly mentioned during their formal presentation. The SenseMaker presentation provides sufficient information as to how the presenting group is thinking about the whole evidence collection to motivate a pointed question. It does so without being overwhelming given the limited amount of time students have to explore each other's argument during a debate presentation (approximately 2 or 3 minutes). The argument maps provide sufficient representational infrastructure to productively shift the discourse of the debate.

In the transcript segment, the presenting group had categorized a piece of evidence as "Irrelevant" that other students in the class had incorporated into their own arguments. After one student brings up the issue, a second audience member calls the presenter on her first attempt to describe away

Transcript Segment 5	Commentary
[Audience-Member-5] How come you put *Flashlight Data* in **Light Dies Out** if you actually never saw it die out?	TOOL MOTIVATED CLARIFICATION QUESTION/DIFFERENT PERSPECTIVE (implicit in question) EPISTEMOLOGICAL ISSUE RAISED (implicit): Good evidence demonstrates the theory it supports.
[Presenter] What? **[Audience-Member-5]** You put the *Flashlight Data* in	Audience member restates question. *(Cont.)*

Transcript Segment 5	Commentary

Light Dies Out, but did you act—do you like know—how do you know it died out? **[Presenter]** I don't know that it died out, I just kind of guessed. Ok. [Audience-Member-6]?

YIELD (implicit): Acknowledgement of different evidentiary criteria—'guessing' is not sufficient cause.

[Audience-Member-6] Alright. For *Light Intensity Over Distance* do you—so you think that the light's dying out or it keeps on going but it's spreading out but it's still there?

TOOL MOTIVATED CLARIFICATION QUESTION/COMPETING PERSPECTIVES: Audience member asks presenter to select between two perspectives.
MULTIPLE WARRANTS: Light dies out; light spreads out but is still there.

[Presenter] When I did that piece of evidence I put it in **Light Dies Out** because I thought that it died out, but now I realize that it just like—it spreads out—and I didn't have time to change it.

ACKNOWLEDGEMENT OF OPINION CHANGE: Presenter states changed perspective since they created their SenseMaker argument.

WARRANT: Light spreads out over distance.

[Audience-Member-6] Yeah. **[Teacher]** Ok. Thank you. Good job. <audience members and teacher clap>

why the evidence was irrelevant. Ultimately, she implicitly yields to the perspective that the evidence is relevant by providing an explanation in keeping with the Light Goes Forever theory position.

In the final segment, we still see more attention paid to this notion that light continues to spread forever and weaken in intensity and that this warrant can account for evidence the presenter categorized as supporting the Light Dies Out position.

In this final segment of the presentation, an audience member pulls in yet another new piece of evidence into consideration identified from the SenseMaker of the presenting group. When asked to confirm if they ever actually saw the "light dying out" in the evidence item, the presenter relents that she "just kind of guessed" when they categorized that evidence item. An immediate, follow-up question builds on the same issue and poses two competing perspectives to the presenter on yet another evidence item. The presenter explains away why they had categorized this final piece under the Light Dies Out theory by producing a scientific warrant typical of the Light Goes Forever position. She acknowledges how she would now change her argument representation to match her current understanding. It is interesting to note that she expressed this warrant in her initial, formal presentation and so the genesis of the idea did not come from the question–answer period itself. However, over the course of her presentation, members of the class were calling her original Light Dies Out categorizations of evidence into question. The presenter successfully responded to their questions by putting forth a more coherent perspective from the Light Goes Forever position.

Stepping back from the specific details, we can observe some other features of the preceding transcript segments. First, it was apparent that students were comfortable working with the SenseMaker argument representations in this manner. Aspects of the presenting group's argument were referenced frequently. In this particular presentation, all of the questions asked were motivated by an analysis of the SenseMaker representation of the presenting group. (This was not always the case, of course, although it was quite common in Classroom Trial 4 when Web-casting was used during the presentations.) Second, the collaboration that occurred around the argument representations led students to articulate a range of scientific warrants related to the debate and ultimately led to a differentiation between alternate perspectives by the presenter. This is an example of argument representations making group thinking visible. Different perspectives held by students were voiced and discussed in the public forum. Third, argument criteria were highlighted that would make student arguments more scientific. In particular, argument breadth and coherence were highlighted in this presentation. Over the course of this presentation, students were grappling with a broad range of evidence items involved in the project and the presenter even pulled evidence of her own into consideration. This is an encouraging move away from the tendency to preferentially focus on individual evidence items. The SenseMaker representation contributed to their epistemological awareness of argument breadth by always providing a view of the entire evidence corpus. In terms of argument coherence, the presenter was being encouraged to reconsider her categorization of evidence into the Light Dies Out frame, and she admitted ultimately to wanting to make changes to the argument to make it more coherent with the Light Goes Forever perspective. Students also demonstrated a facile coordination of pieces of evidence with theoretical ideas: specific warrants of their own as well as the theoretical positions in the debate. Finally, it is striking that the debates seem to be driven primarily by student discourse; the teacher's participation is subdued and mostly takes the form of facilitation. As mentioned previously, the teacher and researcher are typically more involved in the first day of the debates in order to set the tone and model appropriate interaction strategies for the students. The teacher and researcher typically only account for 10% of the turns of talk during the debates overall (Bell, 1996). The classroom debates are a time for students to present their arguments, pursue thought experiments, and make progress on the topic collectively. It is important to note that students come to the debate after having primed the collaboration by putting significant individual effort into their own SenseMaker argument. Students overwhelmingly come ready to defend their position, conceptually unpack their argument, and make progress on differentiating various perspectives. In these transcript segments, we see students engage in such activities; the argument representations are supporting students by serving as the mediating artifact of much of the discussion and in the process they highlight salient, scientific criteria for the endeavor.

A direction for further study is how to provide an explicit mechanism for raising and resolving epistemological issues related to argumentation during the debates. Student arguments were elaborated enough to productively discuss conceptual details of the debate topic and apply some scientific criteria to their arguments (e.g., coordinate evidence with theoretical ideas, pursue argument breadth and coherence). But, epistemological metaknowledge was left at an implicit level in these segments. Although the teacher at other times explicitly brings up the issues, making such conversations more explicit and student controlled might help to promote their understanding of those issues.

The argument representations were particularly useful in making group thinking visible because (a) they made unique aspects of the perspectives of the student teams visible in the representation and because (b) they contained common, core elements that cut across all student arguments and that facilitated easy comparison of arguments. This tension between flexibility and uniformity needs to be balanced during the design of a knowledge representation tool as used here. Such representations need to provide ample flexibility for students to make salient aspects of their own thinking visible and yet constrain the representational elements to a shared collection of objects so that the group can productively compare, analyze, and discuss them.

How Do Students Value the Individual and Collaborative Uses of SenseMaker?

As detailed in the previous sections, SenseMaker can involve both individual and collaborative uses during KIE projects. After the most recent classroom trial, students were asked if argument construction before the classroom debate (a more individual-focused use) or argument comparison during the classroom debates (a more collaboration-focused use) constituted more of a learning experience for them personally. Student responses provide us with a window on some of their epistemological ideas about argumentation and debate.

TABLE 11.1
Collaboration-Focused Uses for SenseMaker Students Reported as Helping
Them Learn the Most During the Debate Project*

Collaboration-Focused Response Category	Student Example	Percent ($N = 176$)
Social Expansion of Repertoire (accretion only)	"I think you learn more from other people because you already know what you have in your idea, but you may learn new things from other people, like what they thought about other things. Maybe the other people have a better idea which makes you think for a while."	18.8
Social Discrimination of Repertoire	"I already know what I believe and what I support so I do not need to see what I believe as much as seeing someone else's ideas. By seeing other people's ideas you can see why they think things and the reason they think that. It could change your opinions."	15.3
Provides Window onto Thinking of Others	"I think this because it shows how each person think, which evidence supports what, how each different person feels and views each piece of evidence."	8.0
Collective Strategy	"Because there are many more people involved and thereby you can learn something from everyone."	2.8
Prefers Passive Watching	"I learn more by listening and hearing things rather than reading them."	1.1

*Categories are listed from most to least frequent ($N = 176$).

Students' open-ended replies to the question were coded into categories of like responses and the results are shown in Tables 11.1 and 11.2 along with prototypical examples for each category. Looking across all response categories, students were almost evenly split in terms of how they viewed SenseMaker as supporting their collaborative- and individual-focused learning, 46% versus 40%, respectively. (Unique student statements that occurred only once accounted for 9.7% of the responses and were not included in the tables.)

Collaborative Uses. Within our theoretical view of learning, students are each marshalling, communicating, and restructuring a repertoire of conceptual models as they engage in classroom activities. This learning process is viewed as including both individual and social mechanisms. Table 11.1 shows student responses involving collaboration-focused uses for SenseMaker. The top response category describes how students are

TABLE 11.2
Individual-Focused Uses for SenseMaker Students Reported as Helping Them
Learn the Most During the Debate Project*

Individual-Focused Response Category	Student Example	Percent ($N = 176$)
Promotes Individual Thinking (general)	"You don't really learn what other people tell you. You mostly learn what you have figured out for yourself."	13.1
Promotes Individual Learning (specific)	'I feel creating our own SenseMaker argument w/the evidence & frames helped me learn more 'cause w/out it, I would learn anything from the presentations. I need to first know my opinion before being swayed by other people.'	10.8
Promotes Individual Expression (no explicit learning reference)	"This let my evidence be organized. It helped us to support our theory by using our ideas with evidence to support these sub-ideas."	10.2
Prefers Self-Understanding	"I learn more from creating arguments myself because I know exactly what I'm thinking and sometimes it's hard to understand what people are trying to say. However, if someone explains something very thoroughly and coherently then I might learn more from them, so it varies."	3.4
Prefers Active Creation	"Because you learn more in the process of doing than by looking at something that's already done."	2.3

*Categories are listed from most to least frequent.

aware of the expansion of their repertoire of ideas during collaboration. One student wrote:

[SenseMaker] shows me different ideas of people and lets me think about what other people think. It kind of widens my horizon.

However, beyond just expansion in the number of ideas under consideration, it is also desirable for students to discriminate among these ideas. As indicated by the second most prevalent student response, discussing different SenseMaker arguments in a group setting also provided a means of comparing and discriminating among different ideas. In the words of another student:

You can't learn anything from your own work. You must see what other people think to compare ideas and learn more.

Beyond having the collaborative uses of SenseMaker actively influence how they are thinking about the topic, 8% of the students also reported that it simply "provides a window onto the thinking of others." This category represents a more passive collaborative use of the representations. A few students described a collective strategy for making progress on the debate topic as a group. The transcript segments from the previous section jibe with self-reported, collaborative uses for SenseMaker students identified after the debate.

Individual Uses. Many students reported that SenseMaker promoted individual-focused learning in the project time leading up to the classroom debate. As shown in Table 11.2, the most frequently cited individual-focused response describes how SenseMaker promoted more thinking about the topic in general terms. One student described it this way:

> Making your own [SenseMaker] is a hands-on experience and gives you a chance to really think about your opinion.

Beyond the generalities of SenseMaker supporting deeper thought, 11% of the students described in specific terms how they learned from constructing their SenseMaker argument. One student reflected on the process of categorizing evidence into frames:

> You put a lot of thought into what fits in what category, and you need to analyze the evidence yourself before you create frames. So, I find that I learn more because I see all how one piece of evidence may fit in w/ two or more categories.

The final, most prominent response category that was individual-focused described how SenseMaker allows individuals to express their own ideas:

> I felt that I learned more creating my own because I put my past experience and knowledge into it. I know the author was a creditable [sic] source.

Note the pointed difference between this last perspective, which stresses building off of one's prior knowledge, compared to the student who talked about not being able to "learn anything from your own work." It is clear that students have very different (at least professed) approaches for their own learning; it is likely that they actually benefit from very different uses of SenseMaker. The project affords both individual and collaborative uses of the argumentation tool through the design. Students' perceived uses for SenseMaker are encouraging; these self-reports need to be further corroborated with attributed, actual uses of the software during the project.

Still, students' self-reports reflect many of the original design goals for the software.

CONCLUSIONS AND IMPLICATIONS

As this chapter has documented, middle school students are capable of creating arguments with the SenseMaker software that are complex, personally focused, and scientific. These arguments can become the productive focus of collaborative debate and lead to knowledge integration. This chapter has described how argument representations can make student thinking visible for individuals and groups. This section discusses broader conclusions and implications of this work.

Design and Study the Package

Supporting the individual and collaborative uses of argument representations involved developing not only the necessary software tools but also activity structures and instruction focused on the development of students' metaknowledge about argumentation and evidence. The activity structures promoted the desired forms of inquiry with the tools during argument-construction and debate activities. The metaknowledge instruction (e.g., introducing SenseMaker with arguments from Newton and Kepler) helped students refine more scientific criteria for the use of the knowledge representation tool for argumentation, debate, and learning. Taken together, the innovation described in this chapter involves the coordinated design and use of a number of different components including software, activity structures, multiple project contexts, Web resources to serve as evidence, assessment instruments, student handouts, and specific instructional approaches for use during the project (see Bell, 1998, for details).

The range of components associated with the innovation highlights the package-like nature of successful, educational innovations, especially those that make use of technology (Salomon, 1996). This orientation brings with it increased attention to the systemic interaction of these components and aspects of individual and group cognition. It also calls for the study of how cognitive activities are being distributed and coordinated around the designed package (Pea, 1993). In this study for example, the coordination of the Webcasting of SenseMaker arguments along with the debate presentations from the student groups qualitatively changed the conversations taking place after each presentation. Important aspects of the presenting groups' thinking had been represented in their argument, which was subsequently broadcast to each of the groups in the audience. This distribution of their intellectual work throughout the setting fed into the lines of audience questioning in a way that expanded on the coherence and breadth represented in the original argument.

Attend to Individual and Collaborative Mechanisms of Learning

Individual and collaborative dimensions of learning are sometimes presented as if they are mutually exclusive theoretical perspectives. Indeed, there are synergies to be had with attention to both dimensions. Specific individual and collaborative uses of the SenseMaker argument representation are afforded by its design. At an individual level, simple features of the interface (e.g., coordination of evidence with claim frames, the elaboration of nested subframes, etc.) allow for student self-expression of ideas and can promote individual reflection on prior knowledge and theorizing. Student arguments are also moderately connected to individual epistemological beliefs about the nature of science. As has been described, students developed an individual, integrated understanding of the debate topic by participating in various aspects of the project. Students reported benefiting from both individual and collaborative learning mechanisms.

At a collaborative level, SenseMaker representations can make student thinking visible during collaboration with peers and teachers. After the argument representations are successfully introduced to the community as an inscriptional system, it was common for students to accept them as an account of how other groups were thinking about the debate topic and evidence. Collaborative work around the argument representations can help students expand their repertoire of models and help them express and discriminate among these different perspectives on an unsettled or controversial topic.[2]

There is a balance to be struck between supporting individual- and collaboration-focused learning opportunities with software and curriculum. There were almost equal numbers of students who preferred using Sense-Maker individually and collaboratively to support their learning. This finding may well relate to underlying differences in student epistemologies and calls for designing learning environments and curricula that can be flexibly used by students with different inclinations. Given our attention to individual and collaborative dimensions of learning, the KIE research group has found it productive to design for both aspects as we develop new innovations. Indeed, there is evidence that the collaboration during the debate definitely benefited from the individual refinement of arguments earlier in the project.

---

[2] We have also started to investigate the use of argument maps as a means of collaboration and communication for scientists and other stakeholders involved in a current controversy in science. Information about this new work can be found online at http://scope.educ.washington.edu/.

Arrange Epistemological Forces During Individual and Group Activity

An undercurrent of this chapter has been the "epistemological forces" associated with the design of learning experiences and knowledge representation tools for individual and group engagement. DiSessa (1995) has called for a focus on epistemological forces associated with the development of exploratory learning environments. It is an applicable frame of reference to apply to the design of learning environments more broadly, including the technological and nontechnological components of an innovation. Applied epistemology remains a neglected focus in the design of innovative learning environments although efforts have been made to bring its relevance to the foreground (diSessa, 1995; Duffy & Jonassen, 1992). In the development of educational technologies, it is far too easy for technological forces to solely shape the design and research of those innovations. Attention to technological forces is necessary, but not sufficient, for creating innovative learning technologies.

A more crucial focus might be to adopt a research and design perspective that focuses on understanding, arranging, and following epistemological forces associated with these innovations within the settings in which they are used. What forms of knowledge are catalyzed by the design of a particular innovation? How are they catalyzed? How do communities develop relevant epistemological metaknowledge about intellectual approaches that are new to them? How can we leverage off of existing epistemological forces in our educational designs?

There is extensive, detailed research yet to be done on how to engage in the *nuanced* design of technology-intensive innovations that support specific forms of learning and development. Technological forces need to be attended to in order to inform some aspects of that work, but attention to the arrangement of epistemological forces will help keep the work focused on how to promote learning through designed learning environments.

Develop and Refine Design Principles

An overarching objective for this work has been to formulate and refine design principles for argumentation software and debate curricula to promote knowledge integration. Such design principles serve to articulate the scaffolded knowledge integration framework (Linn, 1995; Linn, Bell, & Hsi, 1998). A detailed formulation of these principles are presented elsewhere for this research (Bell, 1998; Bell & Linn, 2000); however, examining one principle related to the present work might serve to highlight the nature of these principles.

As evidenced by the uses of the SenseMaker representations to support knowledge integration, an important design principle involves *presenting student groups with an initial knowledge representation that includes many shared elements that can be flexibly arranged and customized by individual student groups in a way that highlights their personal understanding of the topic.* In this research of the How Far Does Light Go? project, the shared elements involved the set of evidence items, the claim frames representing the theories, and the "Irrelevant" frame. Students expressed their understanding of the debate through their placement of the evidence and creation of additional claim frames. A collection of such representations then became a productive focus for group inquiry and comparison. By expressing their own understanding around these shared elements, students were reflecting about the conceptual issues of the debate and putting intellectual equity into their representations in such a way that it could be "cashed in" during classroom discussions. The liquidation of the individual, intellectual equity was largely mediated through a focus on the elements that were held in common across arguments, however differently arranged (e.g., "why did you put Brian Star Gazes under Light Dies Out?"). Elsewhere, I have attempted to describe appropriate features for cognitive design principles that might actually be useful for subsequent designs or other designers (Bell, 1998; Bell & Linn, 2000). A representation of the design principle emerging here is beyond the scope of this chapter. The main thrust of it might attempt to capture the individual and collaborative benefits of being able to flexibly interrelate knowledge objects in a knowledge representation that are held in common across a set of these representations. Such a principle would likely be applicable to similar design situations involving individual and group learning events associated with knowledge representations.

We could consider such design principles part of a larger endeavor to focus research in the field on the sharing and refining of sets of such principles as a means of making progress on developing a design science for educational innovations. This approach is sympathetic with other calls for focusing on design as a central feature in the scientific endeavor of doing research in the learning sciences (Brown, 1992; Collins, 1996; diSessa, 1991; Linn, 1990; Salomon, 1996). A goal should be to formulate pragmatic design principles that do actual design work in support of the cognitive outcomes of interest. Principles should provide details about when they apply to certain situation and when they do not, and they should be sensitive to the particular qualities of cognition and learning associated with an innovation (diSessa, 1991). Principles that are described as being generally applicable in all or most educational design situations are of limited usefulness. That is, general guiding principles are only of moderate use until detailed design principles are established. Given the package-like nature of these innovations, design principles may also be contingent on each other to be effective. We will need to describe how specific principles are interconnected.

As I have described in this chapter, engaging students in argumentation using evidence from the Web can be a knowledge integration activity. Learning can result from individual as well as collaborative mechanisms of making thinking visible around and through knowledge representations. If we better understand how these mechanisms can be facilitated in complex classroom settings through the design of software tools such as SenseMaker, technology will then be able to be used more powerfully as a learning partner in today's classrooms.

ACKNOWLEDGMENTS

The author would like to acknowledge the rest of the KIE Research Group for their collaboration and insight: Marcia C. Linn, Doug Clark, Alex Cuthbert, Elizabeth A. Davis, Brian Foley, Christopher Hoadley, Sherry Hsi, Doug Kirkpatrick, Linda Shear, Jim Slotta, and Judy Stern. In particular, Elizabeth A. Davis provided feedback on different drafts of this manuscript as well as analyses involving students' epistemological ideas about science from her research. This material is based on research supported by the National Science Foundation under Grant No. RED-9453861. Any opinions, findings, and conclusions or recommendations expressed in this publication are those of the author and do not necessarily reflect the view of the NSF.

REFERENCES

American Association for Advancement of Science (AAAS) (1989). *Science for all Americans: A Project 2061 report on literacy goals in science, mathematics, and technology.* Washington DC: AAAS.

Bell, P. (1996). *Debate as an instructional form in science education.* Unpublished master's thesis, University of California, Berkeley.

Bell, P. (1998). *Designing for students' science learning using argumentation and classroom debate.* Unpublished dissertation, University of California, Berkeley.

Bell, P., Davis, E. A., & Linn, M. C. (1995). The knowledge integration environment: Theory and design. In *Proceedings of the Computer Supported Collaborative Learning Conference '95* (pp. 14–21). Mahwah, NJ: Lawrence Erlbaum.

Bell, P., & Linn, M. C. (2000). Scientific arguments as learning artifacts: Designing for learning on the Web in KIE. *International Journal of Science Education, 22*(8), 797–817.

Brown, A. L. (1992). Design experiments: Theoretical and methodological challenges in creating complex interventions in classroom settings. *The Journal of the Learning Sciences, 2*(2), 141–178.

Cavalli-Sforza, V., Weiner, A., & Lesgold, A. (1994). Software support for students engaging in scientific activity and scientific controversy. *Science Education, 78*(6), 577–599.

Collins, A. (1992). Toward a design science of education. In E. Scanlon & T. O'Shea (Eds.), *New directions in educational technology.* New York: Springer-Verlag.

Collins, A., Brown, J. S., & Holum, A. (1991). Cognitive apprenticeship: Making thinking visible. *American Educator, 6*(11), 38–46.

Davis, E. A. (1998). *Scaffolding students' reflection for science learning.* Unpublished dissertation, University of California, Berkeley.

diSessa, A. A. (1991). Local sciences: Viewing the design of human–computer systems as cognitive science. In J. M. Carroll (Ed.), *Designing interaction: Psychology at the human–computer Interface* (pp. 162–202). Cambridge, England: Cambridge University Press.

diSessa, A. A. (1995). Epistemology and systems design. In A. A. diSessa, C. Hoyles, R. Noss, & L. Edwards (Eds.), *Computers and exploratory learning.* Berlin: Springer-Verlag.

diSessa, A. A. (1996). What do "just plain folk" know about physics? In D. R. Olson (Ed.), *Handbook of education and human development: New models of learning, teaching, and schooling.* Cambridge, MA: Blackwell Publishers.

Driver, R., Leach, J., Millar, R., & Scott, P. (1996). *Young people's images of science.* Philadephia: Open University Press.

Duffy, T., & Jonassen, D. H. (1992). *Constructivism and the technology of instruction: A conversation.* Hillsdale, NJ: Lawrence Erlbaum.

Glaser, R., Ferguson, E. L., & Vosniadou, S. (1996). Introduction: Cognition and the design of environments for learning. In S. Vosniadou, E. D. Corte, R. Glaser, & H. Mandl (Eds.), *International perspectives on the design of technology-supported learning environments* (pp. 363–377). Mahwah, NJ: Lawrence Erlbaum.

Hsi, S., & Hoadley, C. M. (1997). Productive discussion in science: Gender equity through electronic discourse. *Journal of Science Education and Technology, 6*(1), 23–36.

Koslowski, B. (1996). *Theory and evidence: The development of scientific reasoning.* Cambridge, MA: MIT Press.

Kuhn, D. (1991). *The skills of argument.* Cambridge, UK: Cambridge University Press.

Kuhn, D. (1993). Connecting scientific and informal reasoning. *Merrill-Palmer Quarterly, 39*(1), 74–103.

Linn, M. C. (1990). Establishing a science and engineering base for science education. In M. Gardner, J. G. Greeno, F. Reif, A. H. Schoenfeld, A. diSessa, & E. Stage (Eds.), *Toward a scientific practice of science education* (pp. 323–341). Hillsdale, NJ: Lawrence Erlbaum.

Linn, M. C. (1995). Designing computer learning environments for engineering and computer science: The scaffolded knowledge integration framework. *Journal of Science Education and Technology, 4*(2), 103–126.

Linn, M. C., Bell, P., & Hsi, S. (1998). Using the internet to enhance student learning in science: The knowledge integration environment. *Interactive Learning Environments, 6*(1–2), 4–38.

Linn, M. C., diSessa, A., Pea, R. D., & Songer, N. B. (1994). Can research on science learning and instruction inform standards for science education? *Journal of Science Education and Technology, 3*(1), 7–15.

Mendelsohn, P. (1996). Mapping models of cognitive development to design principles of learning environments. In S. Vosniadou, E. D. Corte, R. Glaser, & H. Mandl (Eds.), *International perspectives on the design of technology-supported learning environments* (pp. 323–344). Mahwah, NJ: Lawrence Erlbaum.

National Research Council (NRC) (1996). *National Science Education Standards.* Washington, DC: National Academy Press.

Pea, R. D. (1993). Practices of distributed intelligence and designs for education. In G. Salomon (Ed.), *Distributed cognitions: Psychological and educational considerations* (pp. 47–87). Cambridge: Cambridge University Press.

Ranney, M., & Schank, P. (1998). Toward an integration of the social and the scientific: Observing, modeling, and promoting the explanatory coherence of reasoning. In S. Read and L. Miller (Eds.). *Connectionist of Social Reasoning and social behavior.* Mahwah, NJ: Lawrence Erlbaum.

Reiner, M., Pea, R. D., & Shulman, D. J. (1995). Impact of simulator-based instruction on diagramming in geometrical optics by introductory physics students. *Journal of Science Education and Technology, 4*(3), 199–226.

Salomon, G. (1990). Studying the flute and the orchestra: Controlled experimentation vs. whole classroom research on computers. *International Journal of Educational Research, 14,* 37–47.

Salomon, G. (1996). Studying novel learning environments as patterns of change. In S. Vosniadou, E. D. Corte, R. Glaser, & H. Mandl (Eds.), *International perspectives on the design of technology-supported learning environments* (pp. 363–377). Mahwah, NJ: Lawrence Erlbaum.

Scardamalia, M., & Bereiter, C. (1991). Higher levels of agency for children in knowledge building: A challenge for the design of new knowledge media. *The Journal of the Learning Sciences, 1,* 37–68.

Smolensky, P., Fox, B., King, R., & Lewis, C. (1988). Computer-aided reasoned discourse or, how to argue with a computer. In R. Guindon (Ed.), *Cognitive engineering in the design of human–computer interaction and expert systems* (pp. 109–162). Amsterdam: Elsevier.

Songer, N. B., & Linn, M. C. (1992). How do students' views of science influence knowledge integration? In M. K. Pearsall (Ed.), *Scope, sequence and coordination of secondary school science, Vol. II: Relevant research* (pp. 197–219). Washington, DC: National Science Teacher's Association.

Suthers, D. D., Toth, E. E., & Weiner, A. (1997). An integrated approach to implementing collaborative inquiry in the classroom. In R. Hall, N. Miyake, & N. Enyedy (Eds.), *Proceedings of CSCL '97: The Second International Conference on Computer Support for Collaborative Learning* (pp. 272–279). Toronto: University of Toronto Press.

Toulmin, S. (1958). *The uses of argument.* Cambridge: Cambridge University Press.

MAKING SCIENTIFIC THINKING VISIBLE: THE ROLE OF EVIDENCE DIVERSITY AND THEORY ARTICULATION

Richard A. Duschl
King's College London

INTRODUCTION

A generally agreed upon strategy for the reform of science education is that of making students' thinking more visible. Curriculum, instruction, and assessments models are being reconsidered and redesigned to promote and facilitate (1) students' capacities to reason and reflect on their reasoning and (2) teachers' abilities to monitor, assess, and coordinate such reasoning and reflection. SenseMaker, a component of the Knowledge Integration Environment (KIE) Internet-based learning suite developed at the University of California, Berkeley, is a tool designed to make thinking visible and, in turn, make possible assessments of students' knowledge construction and scientific beliefs.

A very obvious question to ask is, What thinking do we wish to make visible? Within the studies reported by Philip Bell the focus seems to me to be thinking about concepts and about the evidence that supports belief in such concepts. The context is one that supports students' construction of arguments for one of two theories of light propagation (i.e., light goes on forever or light dies out). The issue that I want to raise in this brief response concerns the constraints that are embedded in the KIE task environment framework. I will focus my comments and suggestions for modifying Sense Maker and KIE around two domains that I feel are constrained by the present design and implementation of Sense Maker and KIE: *evidence diversity* and *theory articulation*. I will argue that each domain, when properly construed,

487

is critically important for developing in learners an ability to do science and to understand the nature of doing science.

EVIDENCE DIVERSITY

KIE principally relies upon Web resources to provide students with scientific evidence. Within the context of theories of light propagation in a debate project called "How Far Does Light Go?" students are presented with the knowledge claims and evidence they can use to support one of two arguments: Light goes forever until absorbed versus light dies out. The arguments students generate are the results of an inquiry process students completed in groups as they explored the evidence and claim frames located on the Internet.

While I applaud the decision of KIE designers to engage students in the evaluation of competing explanations, I must take issue with the lack of diversity that exists with the evidence presented to the students. Specifically, I do not understand why students' personal experiences and experiments are not part of the inquiry process. Presently, all evidence is obtained from the computer task environment. I wonder, for example, what effect a consideration of black holes would have on students' commitments to either of the two theories. Surely, some of the students are aware of these astronomical bodies.

Science is a way of knowing that places strong value on linking knowledge claims (e.g., models, theories, explanations) to evidence. The comprehensive and thorough research reported by Bell clearly demonstrates how effective SenseMaker and KIE can be at supporting students evaluation of competing explanations. What about the evaluation of the evidence? Missing from the KIE Internet Web resources are the inclusion of sources of data that would facilitate argumentation about the selection of evidence itself. Consequently, missing from the students argumentation is any discourse on "what counts" as good/reliable sources of evidence or good/reliable patterns of evidence. In turn, then, opportunities to engage students in argumentation and conversations about the criteria for determining what constitutes good/reliable data are lost as well.

Such a situation, I suggest, seriously constrains the attainment of epistemological metaknowledge. With respect to the stated goals of developing students' conceptual and epistemological understanding, the instruction design principles, which are based on Scaffolded Knowledge Integration, appear to favor the conceptual over the epistemological. Exclusion of personal experiences and experiments as sources of information constrains the inquiry process, and argumentation process, in very artificial ways. In turn, this exclusion influences the development of epistemological metaknowledge concerning the role of evidence in constructing and evaluating explanations. In fact, I would venture to argue that the constraints on evidence end up serving as constraints on the students' epistemological metaknowledge—an important goal of the KIE research program. Bell is sensitive to such issues when he writes in the last section of the paper about the balance between technological and epistemological forces that influence the design of learning environments.

Thus, while I support the strategies used to make thinking visible (e.g., modeling expert thinking, providing a process to support individual reflection, and promoting the collaborative exchange and discrimination of ideas) I am critical of what it is students are being asked to work with. If instruction is organized such that evidence diversity is constrained for purposes of achieving "central" aspects of scientific knowledge, then I want to ask how the inquiry approach reported here by Bell, and elsewhere by KIE colleagues, avoids falling into the trap Schwab (1960) warned us about long age, namely the teaching of science as a rhetoric of conclusions.

THEORY ARTICULATION

I tend to agree with Bell in his comments about giving attention to both the technological and epistemological forces that inform the design of learning environments. In particular, he is correct to caution us about the design of learning environments that avoid epistemological forces. He writes, "[a] more crucial focus might be to adopt a research and design perspective that focuses on understanding, arranging, and following epistemological forces associated with these (technological and nontechnological) innovations within the settings in which they are used." With regard to the set of questions Bell then poses concerning future research efforts incorporating epistemological forces, let me offer the following comments inspired by Stellan Ohlsson's 1992 article "The cognitive skill of theory articulation: A neglected aspect of science education?"

Ohlsson argues that scientific literacy involves knowing how to apply scientific theories. Knowing the content of a theory is differentiated from the procedures used to apply a theory. The latter he refers to as the skill of theory articulation, a skill he maintains must be explicitly taught. Driver, Leach, Millar, and Scott (1996) also advocate explicitly addressing the epistemological basis for making scientific knowledge claims. "Our aim in including this aspect is to increase students' awareness of the methods by which scientific knowledge claims are made and to promote an appreciation of both their power and limitations. We see three strands to this curriculum emphasis: Evaluation of evidence, Nature of explanation, Evaluation of theory, and Predictions from theory" (Driver et al., 1996, pp. 144–145).

We can expand the realm of possible epistemological forces by considering the various and sundry ways philosophers, historians, and sociologists of science have adopted to describe and analyze the structure and restructuring of theories. Here are some examples: (a) the prediction from theory of novel facts; the reduction of one theory to another; (b) the shift in observation from sense perception observations to theory-driven observations; (c) the review and evaluation of observations to distinguish among fact, artifact, and irrelevant and anomalous data; and (d) the representation and communication of scientific models. The last of these formed the epistemological basis for the Project SEPIA unit "Acids & Bases." Through a carefully structured, assessment-rich instructional sequence in which conceptual, epistemological, and discourse goals are addressed (see Duschl & Gitomer, 1997), students are engaged in iterative processes of empirical investigations and model building. With each new set of empirical data, students are requested to develop, evaluate, and revise models of acid and base molecules and of the process of neutralization. Research (Erduran, 1999) on the implementation of the unit showed that students are capable of engaging in discourse that incorporates elementary notions of sophisticated features of chemical models, for example, the compositionality of chemical models.

SUMMARY

My position is that by selecting epistemological forces and goals mined from the scholarly field of science studies and incorporating them into the design of curricula and the design of learning environments, both a pedagogical framework that supports teachers' abilities to engage in formative assessments and a science discourse learning environment for students rooted in argumentation are created that promote the explicit development of theory articulation. Our experience in Project SEPIA is that it takes three or four years to begin to sort out the ways to explicitly promote epistemological goals. Bell's program of research suggests the same. I look forward to subsequent reports by Bell and KIE colleagues that lay out the detailed design principles informed by epistemological forces that serve to support students learning science, learning to do science, and learning about the nature of science.

REFERENCES

Driver, R., Leach, J. Millar, R., & Scott, P. (1996). *Young people's images of science.* Philadelphia: Open University Press.

Duschl, R., & Gitomer, D. (1997). Strategies and challenges to changing the focus of assessment and instruction in science classrooms. *Educational Assessment, 4*(1), 37–73.

Erduran, S. (1999). *Merging curriculum design with chemical epistemology: A case of teaching and learning chemistry through modelling.* Unpublished doctoral dissertation, Vanderbilt University, Nashville, TN.

Ohlsson, S. (1992). The cognitive skill of theory articulation: A neglected aspect of science education? *Science & Education, 1,* 181–192.

Schwab, J. (1960). The teaching of science as enquiry. In J. J. Schwab & P. F. Brandwein (Eds.), *The Teaching of Science.* Cambridge, MA: Harvard University Press.

SCIENCE AS ARGUMENT

Mark Felton
San Jose State University

Deanna Kuhn
Columbia University

We have been especially interested in Bell's work because of its alignment with our own in its linking of science and argument. Characterizing science as argument (Kuhn, 1993) both depicts it in a way that is compatible with the modern philosophy of science and lays important groundwork for conceptualizing what it is that might be important for science education to accomplish. We want students to develop a way of thinking in and about science, whether or not they go on to acquire extensive scientific knowledge. Exactly what this way of thinking is, however, needs better articulation than it has had.

Perhaps the major contribution our own work can make in this respect is the recognition that both the weaknesses and the strengths that students display in scientific reasoning extend well beyond the domains of science. Underpinning the weaknesses, we believe, is a lack of metacognitive reflection on one's own thought. Adolescents (and even many adults) commonly fail to critically examine their own theories and the evidence bearing on them, in both their informal thinking about everyday topics and their thinking within formal academic studies. As a result, they may not contemplate alternative theories, distinguish conclusive from inconclusive arguments, or distinguish theories from evidence (Klahr, Fay, & Dunbar 1993; Kuhn, 1989, 1991, 1999). When asked to support a claim with evidence, they are likely to offer details or examples to elaborate the theory, rather than evidence bearing on its correctness. In so doing, adolescents demonstrate a fundamental misunderstanding of the nature of evidence and its relation to theory.

Yet adolescents improve in these respects under supportive conditions, and it is possible to identify developmental paths along which such improvement occurs. One effective means of support involves externalizing adolescents' thinking and having them reflect on it, ideally in a social context of peers. It is exactly this idea of "making thinking visible" that lies at the heart of Bell's approach. The computer environment of SenseMaker supports the construction of "representational artifacts" that students are then able to reflect on. Students are asked to externalize their thinking by identifying a theory and supporting evidence. This connection of claim and evidence is referred to as an "argument frame." The advantages of this feature are many. First, argument frames encourage the distinction between theory and evidence. Students must fill one part of the frame with the theory they wish to support and another with the evidence that provides that support. This visually represented division of theory and evidence scaffolds the distinction between the two.

In addition to scaffolding the distinction between theory and evidence, the argument frames in SenseMaker help students compare the arguments they construct. The Web environment from which they draw provides an array of evidence and counterevidence bearing on theories. Students must identify evidence to support a theory and construct argument frames that they must later defend. Thus, not only are they exposed to alternative forms of evidence, they are exposed to alternative ways of supporting a position. They can then compare these and construct the best argument in their favor. Externalizing such arguments as computer-based artifacts facilitates the often difficult process of weighing their relative strength.

The other critical component of Bell's approach, as we see it, is peer discourse. In argumentive discourse, adolescents have been shown to co-construct advanced arguments that weigh theories against alternatives, counterarguments, and even counterevidence (Pontecorvo & Girardet, 1996; Resnick, Salmon, Zeitz, Wathen, & Halowchak, 1996). In our own research, we have found that extended engagement in argumentive discourse enhances subsequent use of alternatives-based arguments (Kuhn, Shaw, & Felton, 1997). The mechanisms, we believe, involve the "explicitation" of one's own thinking (in the course of communicating it to peers), as well as exposure to the ideas of peers.

Bell builds this social support into the KIE curriculum. As he notes, in constructing their argument frames students have put "intellectual equity" into their understandings, setting the stage for debate (of these understandings). Whereas the SenseMaker activity provides insight into the structure of arguments, the classroom debate provides an opportunity to compare, contrast, and critique arguments with one's peers. While working in the computer environment, students draw from the same pool of evidence to support their arguments. This finite pool provides students a common field of evidence to draw on in supporting or discounting theories. This common ground promotes substantive discussion, as do the software-guided KIE activities more directly. Ultimately, the process of critiquing argument frames introduces precisely the kind of argumentive discourse that we have found advances students' argumentive reasoning (Felton & Kuhn, in press; Kuhn, Shaw & Felton, 1997). A single debate episode, in our experience, however, is insufficient to produce much change. There is neither the time for students to gain experience in argumentive discourse nor the structure that will help them gain insight into that process.

Extended argumentive discourse provides adolescents the opportunity to test the integrity of their arguments. In Bell's project, students must defend their argument frames against the critiques and counterclaims of their peers. If their reasoning cannot withstand critical scrutiny, they must either strengthen their argument or abandon their position. We have found that this process of engaging in close scrutiny of arguments about a topic helps students to refine their thinking about the topic (Kuhn, Shaw & Felton, 1997). However, the effects of argumentive discourse may not be limited to students' thinking on a particular topic. How should we conceptualize what more it might provide?

When students engage in extended argumentive discourse, they gain two important experiences. First, they gain experience in critiquing their opponents' arguments, and second, they gain experience in defending their own arguments. Clearly, these experiences enable adolescents to refine their thinking about the topic. But such experiences, we believe, also may influence their cognitive skills more broadly. In our research on the development of argumentive discourse skills (Felton & Kuhn, in press; Felton, 1999), we have found that over time and with practice, adolescents develop identifiable argumentive discourse skills that transcend a specific topic.

Dialogue is not merely a means to the end of producing a better argument; it comprises an important set of skills in its own right. Extended dyadic discourse, accompanied by scaffolded reflection on this discourse, we have found, promotes the development and transfer of broad-based skills of argument (Felton, 1999). These center on probing the strength of an argument through critical questioning. Such skills may eventually be internalized and practiced by adolescents to evaluate the strength of their own arguments. If this is the case, then extended experience in argumentive discourse, when adequately scaffolded, may be the key to at least one crucial dimension of argumentive reasoning development.

Here it is more difficult to know how successful Bell's approach has been. The empirical data Bell offers regarding the effects of the SenseMaker experience are largely those documenting increased topic understanding. To be fair, this is his stated goal. Bell foremost seeks to promote deeper understanding of scientific phenomena (the physics of light energy, in the example he discusses). But to what extent have students also developed the "metaknowledge" Bell refers to, in affirming diSessa's (1995) call for attention to the "epistemological forces" underlying learning tools? Metaknowledge about argument, in our view, is real and identifiable, teachable (though not easily), and of critical importance.

To achieve the broader goal of fostering such knowledge, a third piece of the scaffolding we might provide (in addition to representational artifacts and peer discourse), in our view, should be designed to promote students' reflection on their own argumentive discourse. Our research suggests that discourse, in the absence of scaffolded reflection, promotes only limited advances that do not transfer to a new content domain, whereas the addition of scaffolded reflection produces metastrategic and strategic knowledge of argumentive discourse strategies that transfers to new topics (Felton, 1999). The scaffolding enlists adolescents in observing and explicitly evaluating one another's debates.

Some of the metaknowledge we refer to is explicity epistemological. Bell quotes a wonderful moment in a classroom debate when a student asks, "Why did you use Brian Star Gazes in [the argument frame]. Isn't it irrelevant cause it doesn't have much information?" Bell demonstrates that such moments do happen in his work. The critical questions are these: What epistemological understanding is being communicated, why do such exchanges occur, and how can we help make them occur consistently? Although Bell's current data show only minimal relations between epistemological understanding and complexity of arguments, we urge him not to abandon this line of inquiry. Ample evidence now exists to show that epistemological understanding develops along a predictable course (see Hofer & Pintrich, 1997, for a review). Differences among students in epistemological thinking are more than just "variable" and dichotomously classified, for example, as "social" versus "individual." They are best understood in a developmental framework. The effort to understand them should not be abandoned because adequate epistemological understanding is essential for mature scientific thinking (Kuhn, 1999). Students must see the point of science if they are to engage seriously in it.

Finally, we were glad to see Bell's sensitive discussion of the cognition/ technology interface. We agree with him that much research remains to be done on "how to engage in the *nuanced* design of technology-intensive innovations that support specific forms of learning and development." Both sides of this relationship need attention. We need to know more about the cognitive development that is occurring, as well as the potential forms that technology can take in supporting it. Ultimately, the strength of Bell's innovative work lies in the rich opportunities it offers adolescents to develop skills entailed in scientific thinking. His efforts stand to be enriched and advanced by furthering our understanding of what is developing cognitively and how.

REFERENCES

diSessa, A. (1995). Epistemology and systems design. In A. diSessa, C. Hoyles, R. Noss, & L. Edwards (Eds.), *Computers and exploratory learning.* Berlin: Springer-Verlag.

Felton, M. (1999). *Metacognitive reflection and strategy development in argumentive discourse.* Unpublished doctoral dissertation, Columbia University.

Felton, M., & Kuhn, D. (in press). The development of argumentative discourse. *Discourse Processes.*

Hofer, B., & Pintrich, P. (1997). The development of epistemological theories: Beliefs about knowledge and knowing and their relation to learning. *Review of Educational Research, 67,* 88–140.

Klahr, D., Fay, A. L., & Dunbar, K. (1993). Heuristics for scientific experimentation: A developmental study. *Cognitive Psychology, 25,* 111–146.

Kuhn, D. (1989). Children and adults as intuitive scientists. *Psychological Review, 96*(4), 674–689.

Kuhn, D. (1991). *The skills of argument.* New York: Cambridge University Press.

Kuhn, D. (1993). Connecting scientific and informal reasoning. *Merrill-Palmer Quarterly, 39*(1), 74–103.

Kuhn, D. (1999). Metacognitive development. In L. Balter & C. T. Le-Monda (Eds.), *Child psychology: A handbook of contemporary issues.* (pp. 259–286) Philadelphia: Psychology Press/Taylor & Franci.

Kuhn, D., Shaw, V., & Felton, M. (1997). Effects of dyadic interaction on argumentive reasoning. *Cognition and Instruction, 15,* 287–315.

Pontecorvo, C., & Girardet, H. (1993). Arguing and reasoning in understanding historical topics. *Cognition and Instruction, 11,* 365–395.

Resnick, L. B., Salmon, M., Zeitz, C. M., Wathen, S. H., & Holowchak M. (1993). Reasoning in conversation. *Cognition and Instruction, 11,* 347–364.

SCIENCE *IS* ARGUMENT: TOWARD SOCIOCOGNITIVE SUPPORTS FOR DISCIPLINARY ARGUMENTATION

Philip Bell
University of Washington

In this response, I attempt to provide additional, relevant details about the context of the research study presented in my chapter, and I also describe directions for future research that I perceive based on my work as well as the thoughtful commentaries from Duschl and from Felton and Kuhn. Specifically, I will present a brief argument that we still have much to learn about how to support students in developing a sophisticated understanding of disciplinary forms of argumentation.

THE KNOWLEDGE INTEGRATION LEARNING CONTEXT

There is additional information about the context of my study that I believe sheds light on issues raised by the commentary authors. In particular, Duschl argues that students should be supported in theory articulation and a critical evaluation of a sufficiently diverse set of evidence that includes experimentation and personal experiences. With regard to supporting students in applying scientific theories, I believe Duschl is highlighting an important tension in science education: supporting students in a knowledge construction process (to avoid the development of a "rhetoric of conclusions") while also ensuring that students are making progress toward normative scientific knowledge. I agree that one manner in which to productively work within this tension is to follow and carefully arrange epistemological forces through instruction (although the specific details might well differ).

In our curriculum sequence, we relied upon iterative cycles of computer-assisted experimentation activities and evidence-focused Internet projects focused on (in the order in which they occurred) argument and evidence critique, argument construction and debate, and evidence-informed design. This eighth-grade sequence covering thermodynamics and light topics is the result of research and development efforts of the KIE project and those of an affiliated project called Computers and Learning Partner (CLP) (Linn & Hsi, 2000). Student's application of theoretical knowledge to specific contexts is supported in our curriculum sequence through explicit support for their theorizing and development of principled scientific understanding in each activity in accordance with underlying, target conceptual models about thermodynamics and light (see Linn, Bell & Hsi, 1999; Linn & Muilenburg, 1996, for details about the intermediate conceptual models found in the curriculum).

Felton and Kuhn raise a concern that a single instructional episode is perhaps not sufficient for learning how to engage in argumentative discourse. The instructional project that was the focus of my chapter took place approximately midway through the 15-week curriculum sequence. Serving as an umbrella for all of the curriculum activities was an instructional focus in that classroom on learning through careful attention to scientific evidence and explanation. That is, there was a concerted effort to foster a knowledge integration community within the classroom such that students regularly critiqued evidence and claims using specific scientific criteria (Davis, 1998), produced and tested explanatory conjectures about natural phenomena (Bell, 1998; Foley, 1999; Hoadley, 1999), and reflected upon how their personal life experiences were related to their scientific ideas (Linn & Songer, 1991; Linn & Hsi, 2000). Indeed, students' inquiry and interactions during the light debate project were being leveraged off of the classroom norms and epistemic practices that had been fostered prior to that point focused on scientific evidence, explanation, and argumentation. With specific regard to argumentative interaction during the culminating classroom debates, the nature of the student discourse was relatively sophisticated given the brevity of the project (as described in my chapter). This highlights the possibility that students may have relevant epistemological knowledge that can surface for such purposes (see Hammer & Elby, in press, for a detailed discussion of this possibility).[1]

Argumentative discourse might well have been a more sustained focus of instruction in this classroom, but educational innovation can be characterized as a "zero-sum game" at a curricular level. To focus on argumentative discourse to a greater degree would have necessitated sacrificing some

---

[1]Indeed as a specific example, the teacher involved in this study often introduced the classroom debate activity by making a courtroom debate analogy that served to highlight notions of supporting, contradictory, and irrelevant evidence being coordinated with claims being made.

other part of the existing curriculum sequence that also included laboratory experimentation, working with computer simulations, and scientific design. Given the performances demonstrated in the light debate project, I would argue that most of the students in these classes were still able to engage in important epistemic practices associated with scientific argumentation and debate with the scaffolding provided (see Bell, 1998; Bell & Linn, 2000, for details). This allowed me to explore the specific focus of this study: the connection between argumentation and conceptual learning.

EVIDENCE DIVERSITY

With regard to the issue of evidence diversity raised by Duschl, I believe we are in relatively close agreement. The approach we have been following with KIE (and with our subsequent SCOPE and WISE projects[2]) has indeed engaged students with a diverse set of evidence where many of these pieces were designed to be personally relevant to the students. For example, during the light debate project students worked with a variety of evidentiary forms as part of the shared corpus designed into the project (represented in the argument maps found in my chapter). This collection included evidence that depicted:

- *laboratory experiments* conducted by the students prior to the light debate project,
- *everyday life experiences* that would be common to all (or most) of the students (e.g., seeing cars from afar on the highway, viewing searchlights in the night sky, using a telescope to view stellar phenomena, observing people in light and dark clothes at night), and
- *relevant knowledge artifacts from expert scientific practice* (e.g., a *Hubble* telescope image of a distant galaxy; information about light detection devices including telescopes, probes, and human eyes).

After students explored this pool of evidence, they were also encouraged to identify and include two additional pieces of evidence in their arguments based upon their own life experiences that they believed were relevant to the debate. Having students explore a common corpus of evidence was a strategy for establishing common ground during the classroom debate discussions, but we were also supporting students in connecting the topic (and the associated scientific ideas) to their own life experiences involving light

---

[2]See http://scope.educ.washington.edu/ and http://wise.berkeley.edu/ for details on these projects.

by having them author the additional evidence. It was a means of increasing the personal relevance of the project and increasing the opportunities for knowledge integration.

SUPPORTING THE EPISTEMIC PRACTICES OF ARGUMENTATION

A primary focus of my research with the light debate project was exploring the possible connection between students' argumentation—viewed as an important epistemic practice of science—and their conceptual learning about the topic. I have been concerned with the possible interrelationship of these two dimensions. To accomplish this, it was necessary to develop design knowledge for supporting the epistemic practices associated with scientific argumentation and debate. This approach stands in contrast to some developmental approaches that have not historically explored the use of instructional scaffolds as a means of exploring cognition and learning. I embarked upon this endeavor assuming that students might be able to engage in such practices with the appropriate supports in place. Understanding students' specific epistemological moves and how they develop over time into established individual and group practices is an important area for further research. This will help us understand to what degree students are constructing novel epistemologies of science versus leveraging off of other familiar life experiences to aid them in the endeavor.

I am in agreement with the two commentaries that epistemological sophistication is an important benefit of argumentation-focused instruction. In fact, we have subsequently documented changes in students' understanding of the role of debate in science as one specific example of such epistemological learning (Bell & Linn, 2001). Through a current research effort called "Science Controversies On-Line: Partnerships in Education" (SCOPE), derived from the light-debate work with KIE, we continue to explore how students can learn about the dynamic and controversial nature of science by exploring project-based curriculum sequences that depict current scientific controversies. We also continue to refine our sociocognitive supports for argumentation and debate.

SURFACING THE DISCIPLINARY CHARACTER OF SCIENCE

It is also worth mentioning that without specific forms of support in the instruction, it is highly unlikely that students will spontaneously construct arguments that attend to the subtle disciplinary characteristics of science (e.g., attempting to make sense of a collection of empirical evidence

according to specific scientific criteria). In an increasing array of documented studies, various forms of sociocognitive scaffolding have enabled
sophisticated forms of thinking with children and adolescents (see Metz,
1995, for a discussion). For the range of specific forms of support embodied in the KIE approach and in the practice of the teacher involved in this
study, I have identified a set of localized, interconnected design principles
that describe how to support scientific argumentation, causal explanation,
and collaborative debate (Bell, 1998). Sandoval (1999) has explored similar
issues in a different instructional system and context and within a different
field of natural science.

Given the possible variation in forms of sociocognitive scaffolding and the
subtleties of argumentation in various fields of science (as well as other disciplines), additional design experimentation work is necessary to establish
these connections between designed classroom experiences and the corresponding understanding of disciplinary forms of argumentation by students.

Felton and Kuhn have argued (in their commentary and elsewhere) that
they have found it productive to view *science as argument.* Indeed, at one
level it is possible to view a variety of disciplines as argument—mathematics,
history, literary criticism, among many others. For cognitive, rhetorical, and
social purposes, a domain-general characterization of argumentation can
be conceptualized as spanning across disciplines. Accordingly, the research
program conducted by Kuhn and colleagues (and others) has made significant progress on understanding the development of argumentation as a
domain-general form of thinking involving the complex coordination of cognitive and metacognitive skills.

With more attention paid to domain-specific cognition, I am currently exploring ways in which the nature and role of argumentation might also vary
by discipline (or subdisciplines), especially in ways that could be instruc-
tionally important for students as they develop various images of these
disciplines. With the SCOPE project, we are exploring comparative forms
of argumentation across subdisciplines within the natural sciences. In another project,[3] colleagues and I are exploring differences in argumentation
between natural science and history for instructional purposes.

An example might help make the case for disciplinary forms of argumentation at least at a course level. In some fields of the natural sciences evidence
is plentiful because it can be easily generated (in the sense that results are

---

[3] This research project currently underway uses a comparative psychology frame to explore
the disciplinary differences and similarities between science and history argumentation as it can
occur in fifth-grade classrooms. One goal of this effort is to bring increased coherence to the
school day for students and teachers as they encounter forms of argumentation in these two
subject matters that may be both similar and different in subtle, but important, ways (Wineburg,
Stevens, Herrenkohl, & Bell, 1999). See http://www.pathsproject.org/ for details.

experimentally replicable). Correspondingly, this makes knowledge claims more readily testable and refinable in those fields, and it thereby impacts the nature of the arguments constructed. This is in stark contrast with historical arguments where evidence can be scarce and fundamentally not replicable through experimentation or other means. What would we want students to understand about this epistemological difference as they learn to construct, critique, and interpret arguments in these two disciplines?

This disciplinary research direction hinges upon there being substantive differences in the cognition and epistemic practices surrounding argumentation in various disciplines. I would argue that this assumption largely remains an open research question, contingent upon details of possibly localized cognitive and social activity still not well understood. The educational entailments become: What version of these epistemic practices should be brought to students and how?

Although there may be domain-general cognitive features of argumentation that could be considered as being "shared" by both disciplines (e.g., evidence getting coordinated with conjectures in a search for cause), the subtle disciplinary variation in criteria and practices that account for *quality* arguments in those differing areas of inquiry might also be considered relevant educational outcomes. In other words, it would be desirable for students to be able to critique disciplinary arguments accordingly, engage in inquiry appropriate for the construction of disciplinary arguments, and otherwise learn through engagement with disciplinary arguments in ways modulated by these disciplinary characteristics. This brings us to a issues of educational design: How might we go about introducing students to these nuanced, and somewhat distinct, forms of argumentation? How can students be scaffolded to create disciplinary arguments? If we are successful in systematically answering these questions, the distinctive nature of each discipline will become available to students for their inquiry and learning.

I have become increasingly convinced that argumentation and debate represent important instructional contexts for science learning. We still need to better understand how students benefit from making connections between important forms of disciplinary argumentation and their epistemological understanding of these endeavors. We are only now beginning to understand how to design learning environments to support students in these disciplinary practices and specifically how knowledge representations can foster reflection, collaboration, and learning during this process.

REFERENCES

Bell, P. (1998). *Designing for students' science learning using argumentation and classroom debate.* Unpublished doctoral dissertation, University of California, Berkeley.

Bell, P., & Linn, M. C. (2001). Beliefs about science: How does science instruction contribute? In B. K. Hofer & P. R. Pintrich (Eds.), *Personal epistemology: The psychology of beliefs about knowledge and knowing.* Mahwah, NJ: Lawrence Erlbaum.

Davis, E. A. (1998). *Scaffolding students' reflection for science learning.* Unpublished doctoral dissertation, University of California, Berkeley.

Foley, B. (1999). *Learning with computer visualization tools: Models, representations and knowledge integration.* Unpublished doctoral dissertation, University of California, Berkeley.

Hammer, D., & Elby, A. (2001). Challenges to some assumptions about student epistemologies. In B. K. Hofer & P. R. Pintrich (Eds.), *Personal epistemology: The psychology of beliefs about knowledge and knowing.* Mahwah, NJ: Lawrence Erlbaum.

Hoadley, C. M. (1999). *Scaffolding scientific discussion using socially relevant representations in networked multimedia.* Unpublished doctoral dissertation, University of California, Berkeley.

Linn, M., Bell, P., & Hsi, S. (1999). Using the Internet to enhance student understanding of science: The Knowledge Integration Environment. *Interactive Learning Environments, 6*(1–2), 4–38.

Linn, M. C., & Muilenburg, L. (1996). Creating lifelong science learners: What models form a firm foundation? *Educational Researcher, 25*(5), 18–24.

Linn, M. C., & Songer, N. B. (1991). Teaching thermodynamics to middle school students: What are appropriate cognitive demands? *Journal of Research in Science Teaching, 28*(10), 885–918.

Metz, K. E. (1995). Reassessment of developmental constraints on children's science instruction. *Review of Educational Research, 65*(2), 93–127.

Sandoval, W. (1999). *Inquire to explain: Structuring inquiry around explanation construction in a technology-supported biology curriculum.* Unpublished doctoral dissertation, Northwestern University.

Wineburg, S., Stevens, R., Herrenkohl, L. & Bell, P. (1999). *A comparative psychology of school subjects: Promoting epistemological sophistication in elementary science learning through the study of history.* National Science Foundation Research Proposal, Research in Educational Policy and Practice program.

12

USING MOBILE COMPUTING TO ENHANCE FIELD STUDY

Geri Gay
Robert Rieger
Tammy Bennington
Human-Computer Interaction Laboratory
Cornell University

INTRODUCTION

As information technologies transform classrooms and other learning environments, students and educators have become more comfortable with accessing and sharing electronic information. Whereas many educators rely on desktop technologies, textbooks, libraries, and lectures as principal curricular resources, teachers in the natural and biological sciences have included important "outdoor" or "field" investigations in their repertoire of learning, teaching, and research activities. Their students usually find this hands-on experiential learning critical to understanding the subject matter and to developing the practical skills required for engaging in related research. Students of plant biology are frequently attracted to the discipline because of the opportunities it offers to leave the lecture hall to explore and learn in field environments, and the skills developed in the field are a critical component and indicator of professional expertise.

Although learning from the field cannot be adequately replicated using multimedia technologies, and it is questionable that such replication is even desirable, the computer's strength at information organization and retrieval can support learning and research in the field. Rather than replacing the field experience, new technologies can enhance fieldwork by making it pedagogically more rewarding. Mobile computers can provide immediate access to comparative collections and relevant classificatory information and can facilitate data entry and organization in the field. Many different technologies are converging to make such uses of mobile computing possible and feasible, namely wireless networking, pen-based computing, voice recognition, positioning systems, and camera and vision systems. These technologies provide the ability to move away from the desktop, allow interaction with numerous devices, and make information available through a wireless connection to a remote server.

Hand-held computers are approximately one-fourth the size of a laptop computer. Some of these models receive user input from a scaled-down keyboard, whereas others rely on an electronic pen and incorporate handwriting or speech recognition. Some are equipped with bar code readers or offer plug-in capabilities for special scientific probes and other customized features. For years the misfit younger sibling of the hardware and software community, hand-held computers (sometimes called personal digital assistants) have functionally come of age (Kleinrock, 1997).

Our research raises numerous questions regarding the pedagogical, technical, and evaluative implications of the use of a new generation of mobile computers for teaching and learning in the natural sciences. Cornell University's Human-Computer Interaction Laboratory (HCI) has undertaken a number of small experiments to evaluate the use of computing systems for delivering curricular content and enabling communication around the field experience. We are currently developing prototypes for data retrieval and input. We hypothesize that students will flourish in situations that provide an opportunity to test skills and theories in the "just-in-time" and "nomadic" field context, an opportunity enabled by mobile computing. We want to explore how highly portable computing systems can transform learning and teaching experiences in the field setting. This chapter sets the background for the mobile computing research projects we have initiated and describes the effectiveness of various applications ranging from accessing content to using mobile systems for interaction and collaboration. The projects include the provision of mobile computers to visitors to the Cornell University gardens and greenhouses and the use of mobile computers to facilitate learning and teaching in field settings.

LITERATURE

These experiments have been informed by the emerging concerns of Activity Theory, an approach to the design and evaluation of technology that attempts to redress the shortcomings of cognitivist, or information-processing, approaches to human–computer interaction (Kuutti, 1996). As outlined by Nardi (1996), Kuutti (1996), and others (Kaptelinin, 1996; Kaptelinin & Cole, 1997), Activity Theory focuses attention on action, doing, and practice, but within the "activity" as the unit and context of analysis. Activity Theory is exerting an increasing influence over studies of learning and human–computer interaction and serves as a useful "mediating device" that enables understanding of the potential role of mobile computers in learning activities.

Activity Theory has been inspired by the work of the Russian semiotician and psychologist L. S. Vygotsky, who posited the unity of perception, speech, and action and the centrality of mediating devices in the development of mind and thought. In its contemporary multidisciplinary incarnation, heavily influenced by the works of Leont'ev, Activity Theory provides a coherent framework and discursive resources with which to talk about and understand human activities, conceived as multilevel, multidimensional, dynamic, collective, context-sensitive, and mediated by cultural artifacts. The explanatory potential of Activity Theory lies in its attention to multiple dimensions of human engagement with the world and the framework it provides for configuring those dimensions into a coherent whole around "activity." Nardi (1996, p. 73), citing Leont'ev, defines an "activity" as entailing a subject, object, actions, and operations. The subject, as individual or collective agent, is motivated to pursue an object or goal and thereby undertakes actions in pursuit of that goal. Actions are *intentional*, in a phenomenological sense, and are carried out through variously routinized operations. Critical to understanding these processes of engagement is appreciating the significance of the mediating role of cultural artifacts in human activities, social-historical context, and the transformative power of mediating devices.

Cultural artifacts (i.e., language, symbols, instruments, mobile computers) play a central formative role in the development of human consciousness as agents engage with the world through artifacts. Activity Theory, as it has been applied to human–computer interaction or, perhaps more appropriately, *computer-mediated activity* (Kaptelinin, 1996), draws attention to the dialectical process by which consciousness, learning, and development simultaneously shape and are shaped by technology. Hence, sustained, longitudinal research on the introduction of computer technology into learning settings and activities is an important pursuit.

Understanding computer-mediated activities via an Activity Theory approach further requires an understanding of social-historical context, that is, how activities and mediating devices emerge from particular cultures and practices, from the particularities of situated actions including agents' needs and goals, and from the activity itself (Nardi, 1996, p. 76). This rich and complex notion of context, which can flexibly accommodate "contexts" of more or less restricted scope, enables Activity Theory to incorporate and thereby enrich itself from the contributions of situated action approaches (e.g., Suchman, 1987, 1–12), situated learning (e.g., Lave and Wenger, 1991), and other sociocultural approaches such as ethnomethodology and symbolic interactionism.

Directly implicated by the contextualized and mediated nature of human activity is the formative and transformative potential of cultural artifacts. Computer technologies, as mediating devices, can enable and transform activities through enabling and transforming actions, goals, social relationships, and individual agents themselves. Such transformative power requires that the introduction of an artifact be accompanied by serious consideration of the potential transformations it could effect and by documentation of the transformations it actually induces. Because of the complexity of factors, both internal and external, that comprise any activity, transformations remain contingent and necessitate continued study to understand their historical emergence.

Our research portends that the introduction of mobile computers into the field experience can potentially transform the activities of learning and researching in and from the field. The experiments described below were designed to elicit initial feedback regarding the usefulness, usability, and desirability of mobile computers in field settings and activities. Clearly, their introduction into situated learning/teaching settings and activities will transform those settings, activities, and even agents. Likewise, mobile computers themselves will be transformed through their implementation and continued use. Activity Theory provides a theoretical and methodological framework to enable the systematic exploration of these transformations.

MOBILE COMPUTING

Learning and teaching activities can be greatly enhanced by mobile and wireless computers and appropriate communication tools that foster collaboration. A shared database can potentially overcome the fragmentation of knowledge into myriad specializations. As students work on projects supported by multimedia resources in the field or at the point of learning, they can bring different disciplines to bear on problems (though whether they in fact do is a matter for investigation). Likewise, multimedia enables the expression and representation of knowledge in different forms (e.g., graphics, film clips, video, spoken and written text). Hence it can augment the acquisition of tacit knowledge that is part and parcel of socialization into a community of practice (i.e., a profession) and provide students with an opportunity to learn in diverse contexts. The introduction of computing and computing resources at the point of learning, here the field, seems to be particularly appropriate for developing and maintaining, although simultaneously transforming, communities of practice.

In the 1980s, a group of researchers at Xerox PARC, led by Mark Weiser, initiated a research program with the goal of moving human–computer interactions away from the desktop into our everyday lives. This work represented the beginning of research into the area of ubiquitous computing (Weiser, 1991). The intention is to create a computing infrastructure that permeates the environment so much that we do not notice the computer anymore—it becomes ubiquitous and invisible. While palmtop computers are at the periphery of Weiser's vision, these devices represent an evolutionary step toward supporting the user in diverse locations and activities. The defining characteristic of ubiquitous computing is the attempt to break away from the traditional desktop and move computational power to the site of the activity in which the user is engaged. Weiser refers to making computing "an integral, invisible part of people's lives" where hundreds of objects in our environment have computational capabilities and are invisibly networked, helping us, or mediating our activities, without our awareness of their critical role.

Although a wealth of literature describes technology's potential for supporting science education, little has been written from an education or communication perspective about the value of mobile computing in learning- and teaching-related activities. The "Science Learning in Context" project at the Concord Consortium, funded by the National Science Foundation, plans over the next few years "to develop hardware, software, and curriculum material that use portable, networked, hand-held computers in student field projects" (Concord Consortium, 1997). The Center for Innovative Learning Technologies (http://cilt.org) includes a "Low Cost Ubiquitous Computing" theme team that is currently "(a) scanning these technological horizons, anticipate implications for learning, and provide feedback to the marketplace [sic], and (b) developing prototypes that exemplify the potential payoff of alternative strategies" (Tinker & Brodersen, 1998). These projects will undoubtedly yield useful information, including valid and reliable methods for assessing effectiveness.

Several related projects have concentrated alternatively on technical concerns. Researchers at Auburn University (Foster, 1995) teamed with BellSouth Laboratories to investigate patrons' accessing library information using mobile computers. This "Library without a Roof" project showed that it was feasible to gather information from library public access catalogs, databases, and the Internet using wireless equipment. The StudySpace Project (Schnase, 1995) at Washington University's School of Medicine seeks to research and understand information retrieval in "nomadic computing environments." Their work looks at the convergence of geographic information systems and hypermedia technologies to help learners gain access "anytime/anyplace." Like the research at Auburn, StudySpace avoids considering the value of mobile computing in learning contexts. Carnegie Mellon's "Wireless Andrew" (Bartel & Bennington, 1997) involved building an experimental campus-wide high-speed wireless network. The "Nomad Project" (Grace-Martin & Gay, in press) demonstrated how e-mail, the Web, and library databases could be delivered through wireless portables.

In a similar vein, several researchers have examined applications of "just-in-time" instructional delivery, in which information and training are provided to learners at the appropriate moment and within a relevant context. Schorr (1995) presents promising results from an experiment "to bridge the technology learning gap between college and the workplace" that relies heavily on "just-in-time" computer application. Goodyear (1995), with support from the European community, examines computer-mediated communication with a "just-in-time" perspective. He describes the advantages of distributed access to information made possible by technology. Kribs and Mark (1995) surveyed trainers in industry, military, and higher education and suggest that awareness of the benefits of enabling "just-in-time" learning is high in the first two sectors but that higher education lags behind in the "just-in-time" trend. We believe that our work with mobile computers can contribute to reducing that lag through providing applications that make information immediately available in field-situated learning.

THE MOBILITY HIERARCHY: OBJECTIVES MOTIVATING THE USE OF MOBILE COMPUTING APPLICATIONS IN EDUCATION

One challenge we face as researchers interested in the transformative potential of various computer technologies is to find useful ways of organizing the work that has been accomplished so as to reveal the role and relevance of emerging hardware, software, and pedagogy. Our inquiry has been guided by a "mobility hierarchy" (Table 12.1) involving four different kinds of objectives motivating the use of mobile computers in educational settings. The simplest applications provide tools to achieve the objectives of Level 1, Productivity, whereas the most complex applications provide tools to achieve multiple objectives, so that an application that enables collaborative work will also provide features for collecting and analyzing data. Various users pursue objectives employing these applications in diverse settings; the contextual features of these settings can be seen as falling along a series of descriptive, sometimes measurable, continua, such as synchronicity, individual or group use, information storage versus construction, and content versus communication intensity.

Level One (Productivity) applications are mostly content-intensive, whereas Level Four (Collaboration & Communication) applications are mostly communication-intensive. Level One audiences are generally single users; Level Four audiences generally involve multiple users. Level One

TABLE 12.1
Levels of Objectives: Mobile Computer in Education

Level 1	Level 2	Level 3	Level 4
Productivity	Flexible Physical Access	Capturing & Integrating Data	Communication & Collaboration

Sample Applications			
• Calendars • Schedule • Contact • Grading	• Local database • Interactive prompting • Just-in-time instruction	• Network database • Data collection • Data synthesis • Mobile library	• Real-time chat • Annotations • Data sharing • Wireless e-mail

Content-intensive Users: Individual Mostly asynchronous Information storage Hardware-centered Isolation	Communication-intensive Users: Group Mostly synchronous Knowledge construction Network-centered Interconnection

focuses on isolated activity; Level Four is aimed at interconnectivity. Levels Two and Three represent middle-range applications, such as personal tour guides, computer-aided instruction, database activity, mobile libraries, and electronic mail. These applications demonstrate a mix of the contextual characteristics. For example, a Level Three application such as a mobile library is neither focused solely on information storage nor knowledge construction. How these various characteristics and operations play out in particular activities and settings can be illuminated through further research informed by Activity Theory. However, the hierarchy provides a useful heuristic device for identifying possible objectives of computer-mediated activities and integrating them with the contextual and operational features represented by the continua.

RESEARCH QUESTIONS

Based on the extant literature and discussions with university and high school faculty and nonformal educators, the research team prepared the following questions:

- How can the use of mobile computing technology enhance field laboratory experiences for formal and nonformal learners?

- In what ways, if any, does the mobile computing environment encourage or motivate students to collaboratively contribute to learning activities?
- How can mobile computers enhance learning and teaching about the scientific investigation process, such as data gathering and analysis?
- In what ways might student users take advantage of and benefit from the many tools afforded by the technology?
- What changes to curricula, if any, will this new instructional delivery system or mediating device require?
- What features and capabilities should the mobile computing systems provide for different learning and teaching activities?
- How do students at various levels of experience use the resources? Are students able to build on skills in this environment?
- Are traditional evaluation methods appropriate for mobile computing instructional delivery systems?

MOBILE COMPUTING PILOT STUDIES

Our long-term research objective is to develop, refine, and evaluate various uses of mobile computing in formal and nonformal educational settings. As we work toward this goal, pilot mobile computing curricula and applications are being developed for undergraduate courses at our primary research site, the Cornell Plantations. The Plantations contains an arboretum, botanical garden, greenhouses, and natural areas surrounding the Cornell campus. The site offers excellent field environments that are already widely used by faculty for teaching and research. These pilots studies (four of which are described below) include applications that allow easy search and retrieval of technical data and enable access to digitized images (i.e., seasonal photos, cross sections, pathogens, etc.). With faculty collaborators, we are conjointly designing teaching activities that rely on mobile computing hardware and software. A primary objective is to allow more rigorous presentation of concepts and theories as part of the field exercises.

In studying each of the applications we explore three broad areas that we feel are unique to mobile computing technologies:

- customizing applications based on physical context and the needs of diverse users;
- capturing and integrating data into learning communities (i.e., social context) and;
- mapping levels of interaction and annotation.

We are currently developing various evaluation protocols to assess the use of mobile computers in formal and nonformal learning activities, including electronic, online tracking systems to record student use and progress. We are also seeking to distribute tools for working with mobile computers such as guidelines, examples for use, and evaluation methods, both quantitative and qualitative.

The project is a natural extension of the Human-Computer Interaction Laboratory's previous research and development of tools and computing environments for undergraduate education (Gay, 1995; Gay & Lentini, 1995). The HCI team examined the use of multimedia databases in a networked design environment to learn how students access database resources and shape messages throughout the design process. This work involved studying how engineering design is currently taught, creating database resources and collection tools, and researching how these resources were used. The research team constructed prototype interfaces, the "Netbook," to help students access and organize information from large databases. The Netbook was used by students for assembling materials from multimedia databases, constructing their own understandings of the material, and communicating that understanding to others. Mobile computers now extend the Netbook tool, allowing data collection and interpretation to occur in nomadic environments.

The four pilot applications described here all enable use of the material in both desktop and mobile computing environments. Table 12.2 summarizes the audience or users, content, and learning activities for each pilot.

Customizing Applications Based on Physical Context and Needs: *Plantations Pathfinder* and *Ladybug*

The first two applications, *Plantations Pathfinder* and *Ladybug*, are designed to supply information and provide a collaborative space for visitors and students as they move about the gardens and greenhouses. The program serves as an electronic tour guide, or interactive docent, enabling visitors to customize their visits and access information about plant uses, history, economics, etc. (see Figs. 12.1–12.4).

The Plantations is a "living museum" and as such is continually changing. An electronic guide can be kept up to date more readily than printed materials. It can keep a record of the interests of an individual visitor or group of visitors, enabling them to collect information or compile a "journal" that they can later print out at the visitor center and take home. As a collaboration tool, the system enables users to input information that can then be uploaded to an electronic discussion forum. Much like the visitor feedback books found at museums and other tourist sites, users of the application can view the reactions and advice of others.

TABLE 12.2
Summary of Pilot Applications

Application	Users	System Content	Learning Activities
"Plantations Pathfinder"	Non formal learners (casual visitors)	Historic garden information (demonstration of plants and their role in modern and ancient history)	Plan tour; retrieve and record information; use electronic reference guide; access field notes of other learners
"Ladybug"	Non formal learners	Greenhouse plant database	Scan plant barcode tags; retrieve and record database information; take guided tours; view featured exhibits
"Cornucopia"	Formal learners (students enrolled in plant genetics course)	Corn genetics test plot	Access genotype and phenotype database; use electronic field instruments to measure data; record field measurements using computer input form; use desktop visualization tools; immediately compare class data; use desktop applications for group collaboration exercises
"Soil Texture by Feel"	Formal learners	Horticulture laboratory exercise	Follow step-by-step procedures with branching; make annotations to lab findings; upload data and procedures to desktop and discuss

User Scenario. Prior to visiting the facilities, users log on from a desktop to the Plantations or greenhouse Web site where they can access the interactive tours and databases they will be using on a handheld computer when they visit the site. At the Web site, users receive more information about each garden, including a multimedia database that highlights the thousands of plant varieties cared for the by the Plantations staff. In the Ladybug Project, plants have a barcode that allows users to receive up-to-date information via wireless systems. Once at the actual Plantations, for example, visitors may want to learn more about historic varieties of squash. They can borrow the hand-held personal computer from the visitors center, consult the application, add entries to a personal journal, and make notes that can be saved while touring the squash garden. They can also review and search the comments of previous visitors.

Evaluation. Our research team collected user responses to these two systems via (1) feedback sessions conducted with prospective visitors and students and (2) a printed survey administered to volunteer educators at

FIG. 12.1. Plantations Pathfinder opening screen.

the Plantations who work directly with the targeted user audience. Many of these respondents expressed enthusiasm for the prototype, although some noted that it would not be suitable for every visitor. The respondents suggested that the application could provide more in-depth information than the existing labeling system and more timely information than printed resources. They saw value in handheld computer presentations of plant locations, images, taxonomies, historical and care information, and sources for purchasing plants. Other visitors were less enthusiastic and expressed

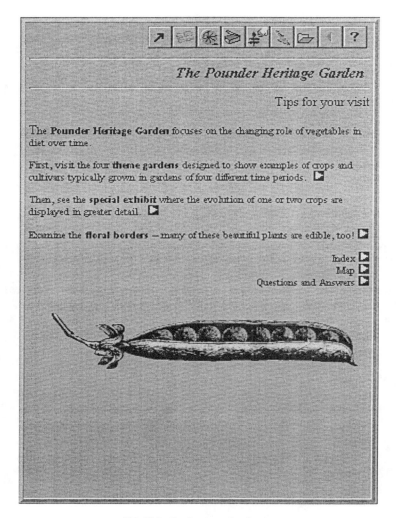

FIG. 12.2. Garden tour tip sheet.

concern about how the presence of the computers would negatively affect the experiential dimensions of their tour, saying "It could spoil the joys of wandering in a garden," and "I wouldn't want it to get in the way of us and the garden." Greenhouse staff and affiliated faculty were encouraged by Ladybug's ability to automate mundane tasks, improve the visitor, experience, and facilitate collection management. It was evident that respondents' evaluations of the technology were shaped by the objectives motivating their involvement with the garden.

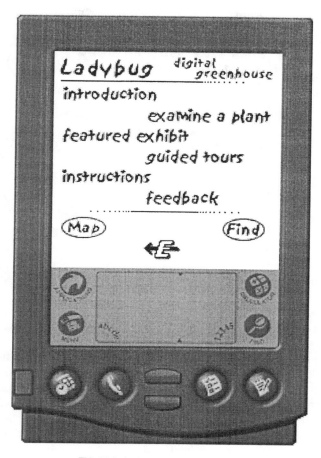

FIG. 12.3. Ladybug opening screen.

Capturing and Integrating Data Within Particular Social Settings: *Cornucopia*

The third application, *Cornucopia*, is designed for use by undergraduate genetics students during laboratory exercises conducted in a corn test plot adjacent to the Cornell campus. The application provides users with a searchable interface (see Figs. 12.5 and 12.6) to access corn genotype, phenotype, historical, geographical, and other information. The application demonstrates fundamental concepts in plant genetics and evaluation through making digital images of variety traits, genetic models, cross sections, and simulations of selection processes available in the field. The structure of the application is easily modified to accommodate

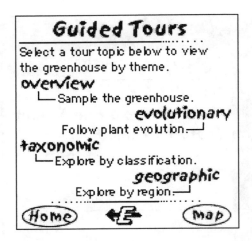

FIG. 12.4. Plantations Pathfinder opening screen.

the content of field-sited learning in other disciplines such as zoology or biology.

User Scenario. One week before the first outdoor field study, the instructor explains the exercise to the genetics class and demonstrates the mobile computing hardware they will be using. She refers students to a URL that displays the same interface they will be using on the mobile computers. On the day of the field study, the students meet at the Test Plot and each team is provided with a mobile computer, a data collection instrument, and a memory card, which inserts into the mobile computer and holds the lab data entry form and genotype/phenotype database. The teams are responsible for reviewing the database and collecting data— such as plant height, soil pH, temperature, humidity, and growth stage—for 10 varieties of corn. They enter their data directly into the mobile computer, which performs rudimentary analysis and displays results. Their flash cards are then given to the instructor who loads data from each of the teams onto a laptop computer for more sophisticated analysis and visualization. After the field study, the teams' files are uploaded to the class Web site for further review and as subject matter for online discussions.

Evaluation. As part of an iterative and participatory development process, our initial evaluations of Cornucopia have included feedback sessions with prospective student users and interviews with faculty and developers. In addition to specific interface suggestions, students and faculty have expressed interest in and enthusiasm for the devices

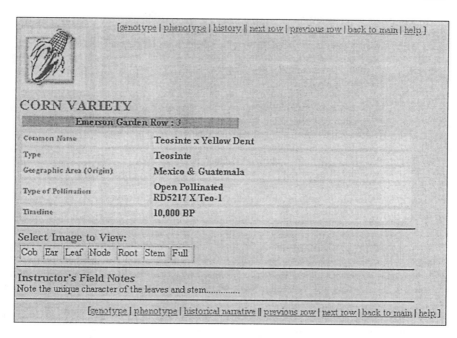

FIG. 12.5. Cornucopia database interface.

and applications. They have also suggested other approaches, such as transferring the desktop applications they currently use to the mobile environment. Several expressed interest in accessing Web sites from the field, for example, the database MaizeDB, which is available on the Web (http://teosinte.agron.missouri.edu/query.html). Respondents also suggested that simulations be provided, for example, a simulation that demonstrates how plants respond to variable growing conditions.

In this and other prototypes, mobile interfaces have presented unique and complex design challenges. Cornucopia developers have offered design and programming suggestions based on their experiences with mobile computing technology (summarized in Table 12.3). These suggestions confirm the necessity of understanding in detail the objectives of the field activities and of carefully considering how the technology contributes to the realization of those objectives.

Levels of Interaction and Annotation: *Soil Texture by Feel*

The purpose of the fourth prototype, *Soil Texture by Feel*, was to continue to test the effectiveness of handheld devices for data collection, annotation, and analysis in field settings (see Figs. 12.7 and 12.8). Researchers prepared

TABLE 12.3
Design and Planning Suggestions for Mobile Computing Applications

Screen	• Use limited/small graphics
	• Avoid HTML-based tables (currently)
	• Avoid color
	• Maximize contrast between text and background for visibility
	• Minimize repeated menu items on each screen (i.e., create navigator or pull down menus rather than take up valuable screen real estate)
	• Use large/simple fonts
Portability	• Create context-free information (modular)
	• Minimize the amount of back and forth shifting that the user needs to do between screens by making each screen self-contained
	• Create a docking environment with a desktop application
Content	• Keep content specific to the field environment
Planning	• Avoid making the mobile computer into a mini-desktop
	• Use it as a dedicated tool to optimize its strengths and minimize its limitations
	• Focus on tutorials, data collection, or diagnostics
Other	• There is a lack of integration between forms and HTML use of other development languages (i.e., Visual Basic or Visual C++ or other for creating a more natural feel to the application)

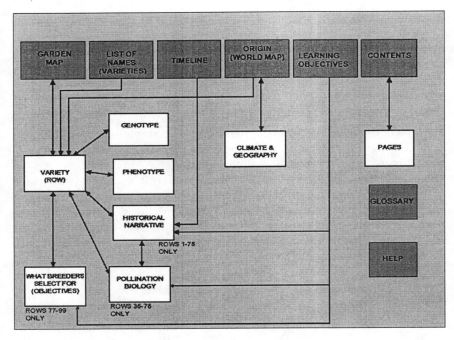

FIG. 12.6. Cornucopia content model.

HORT 491: Plant Establishment Soil
Texture By Feel

The mineral particles found in soil range
enormously in size from microscopic clay
particles to large boulders. The most abundant
particles, however, are sand, silt, and clay. They
are the focus of an examination of soil texture,
or the composite sizes of particles in a soil
sample. While there are other ways of
measuring soil texture, we will be using the soil
texture by feel method for this experiment.

Start with step 1

FIG. 12.7. Soil Texture by Feel opening screen.

a mobile computer program to assist horticulture students in learning about soils and soil types.

User Scenario. After being provided with an overview of the purpose of the test and instructions on the use of the handheld devices, students proceed in pairs to a test field known to contain a variety of soil types. They open the *Soil Texture by Feel* application, which provides step-by-step instructions comparable to a traditional lab manual. The application has hierarchical branching so as to customize responses based on observations entered by the students. For example, if users indicate that the soil manifests

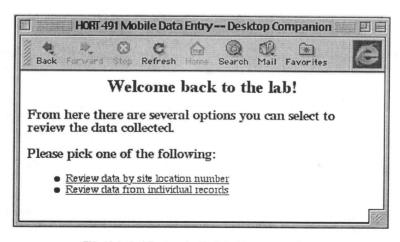

FIG. 12.8. Soil Texture by Feel desktop companion.

claylike properties, they would be linked to the "clay" branch from which they would continue the description and identification process in a continually narrowing sequence. Throughout the activity, they are able to enter notes and receive contextual help. By the end of the exercise, the pairs of students have identified the various soils and are then prompted to upload the data to a central site where their classmates can access all of the collected data, analyze group findings, and make comments and annotations.

Evaluation. The 20 students (10 male and 10 female) who participated in the initial testing of the application were randomly chosen from an upper-level horticulture class. The majority were landscape architecture students; the others included horticulture, floriculture, and plant science majors. Group One conducted a "texture by feel" experiment in pairs using the traditional pencil and paper method. Group Two conducted the same experiment using the mobile computer prototype. Each pair in Group Two was given a short orientation on how to use the device. Upon completion of the exercise, the data were uploaded to a central Web site. Students were then able to view the aggregated data. The evaluation survey focused on their perceptions of ease of use, the degree to which the application aided their understanding, its general helpfulness in performing different tasks, and the trust they placed in the technology.

There was no significant difference between the two groups' evaluations of the ease of use of the two different technologies. However, Group Two rated the variable "aided in understanding" slightly higher than did Group One. Despite relatively high rankings, comments made by Group Two testers seemed to reflect poorly on the systems overall purpose and function:

- "It helped but the paper sheet we received was just as good."
- "It made it easy not to think for yourself; just press the buttons."
- ". . . if anything, more hands-on [work] such as writing and act of counting, would be conducive to learning."

These comments clearly highlight the importance of focusing our attention on how the technology meets particular user needs and how it affects the process of learning. In the continuing iterative design of this application, we need to clarify the sequence of cognitive processes involved in learning to identify soil types through the use of traditional paper and pencil. The above comments draw attention to the possibility that this mobile computer application eliminated or enabled students to pass over steps within this learning process. Regarding the degree of trust they had in the technology, students rated trust in both technologies highly but expressed concerns applicable to computer technology in general: "I am familiar enough with computers to never trust completely," "They are probably as reliable as people", and "My writing on paper won't disappear."

The evaluations of the *Soil Texture by Feel* prototype seem to suggest enthusiasm for the overall concept and the potential uses of such applications but tepid support for this particular prototype as a substitute for paper-based systems. Learners have fairly clear ideas about the promise of the hardware for various learning activities. Trust seems high for the devices; however, this may be specifically directed to the particular application which is localized, technologically simple, and limited in scope and content. Once wireless connectivity, complex applications, and actual graded coursework are introduced, trust may diminish. Moreover, trust in the technology cannot be evaluated independently of the social relations sustaining its use.

As we proceed with our iterative design and development process, it is imperative that we collect detailed observational data on the contexts and practices of use and conduct in-depth interviewing to elicit richer insights into the diverse objectives that motivate users' interest in and use of mobile computing applications. Only by further understanding these objectives and the social relationships through which they emerge and are pursued can we develop applications customized to particular activities and the contextual features of those activities.

CONCLUSION

The purpose of developing mobile computing applications is to provide resources and communication abilities where they are needed as well as to help prepare students for applied scientific practice. Mobile computing can potentially enable students to share information, coordinate their tasks and, more generally, function effectively in collaborative activities. Such skills will prepare students to make the transition to a working world that increasingly stresses interdisciplinary teamwork. Carefully constructed mobile computing applications can support, or mediate, the socialization of students into various communities of practice through a combination of online help, expert advice, resources, peer collaboration, and the opportunity to learn. Hence, it conduces to the development and realization of authentic learning experiences.

A powerful insight that has emerged from the testing of the prototypes, confirming the potentially transformative power of mediating tools posited by Activity Theory, was the transformation that the new technology effected in the teacher–student relationship in the field setting. The teacher is no longer the "expert," in the sense of the single authoritative figure who confirms students' findings. Students are able to consult multiple authorities in the form of comparative collections as well as elicit rapid feedback from peers. Teaching activities, and perhaps teachers themselves, will need (or be compelled) to change to meet the new social and organizational dynamics of the transformed learning and teaching activities. Assignments need to be designed and communicated differently, for example, to encourage peer communication and collaboration. Teachers might more appropriately conceive their roles less as "experts" and more as "facilitators." Future research, for moral as well as academic reasons, should focus on understanding the interactions of the tasks and social relationships that comprise activities in field settings in order to anticipate the diverse social implications of these newly introduced tools. Because tools play a fundamental mediating role within a systemic model that includes subjects, objects, and community (Kuutti 1996), their introduction and use have extensive moral ramifications in that designers of technology are equally engaged in the design of subjectivity and community.

It is important to remember that we introduce these tools into existing social situations with their own cultures, norms of interaction, and routinized practices. New tools, then, will be interpreted and used accordingly, but they also can potentially transform those cultures and practices. In our exploratory studies, we found that students used the mobile computers proficiently, but we also found that some beliefs held by many of the users strongly shaped the use of program features in unexpected ways that could frustrate designers' expectations for change.

We are continuing to explore questions such as how the use of mobile computers in field settings transforms thinking, learning, teaching, the teacher–student relationship, student–student relationships, the collection/recording/storing/manipulation of information, assessment and desirability of various skills, the field "experience," and mobile computers themselves. Mobile computers have the potential to support authentic learning experiences in the field through facilitating the collection, organization, retrieval, and analysis of information "just-in-time." Further, such support can enhance collaboration and communication among participants in the field setting and those distant from it, during the field experience and after it. The mediation of mobile computing applications thereby challenges traditional distinctions between "the field" and "the classroom," creating new learning and teaching activities and possibilities.

REFERENCES

Bennington, B. J., Bartel, C. R. (1997). Wireless Andrew: Experience building a high speed, campus-wide wireless data network. In *Proceedings of the third annual ACM/IEEE international conference on Mobile computing and networking*. New York: ACM. 55–65.

Bransford, J. D., Sherwood, R., Hasselbring, T., Kinzer, C., & Williams, S. (1990). Anchored instruction: Why we need it and how technology can help. In D. Nix and R. Spiro (Eds.), *Cognition, education and multimedia*. Hillsdale, NJ: Lawrence Erlbaum.

Bransford, J. D., & Stein, B. S. (1993). *The ideal problem solver* (2nd ed.). New York: Freeman.

Brown, J., Collins, A., & Duguid, P. (1989). Situated cognition and the culture of learning. *Educational Researcher, 18*(1), 32–42.

Bruner, J. (1985). Vygotsky: A historical and conceptual perspective. In J. V. Wertsch (Ed.), *Culture, communication and cognition: Vygotskian perspectives*. Cambridge: Cambridge University Press.

Collins, A., Brown, J. S., & Newman, S. E. (1988). Cognitive apprenticeship: Teaching the craft of reading, writing, and mathematics. In L. B. Resnick (Ed.), *Cognition and instruction: Issues and agenda*. Hillsdale, NJ: Lawrence Erlbaum.

Concord Consortium (1997). Science learning in context [HTML document]. Available from http://hub.concord.org/slic/

Fischer, G. (1995a). Conceptual frameworks and computational environments in support of learning on demand. In A. DiSessa, C. Hoyles, & R. Noss (Eds.), *The design of computational media to support explanatory learning* (pp. 463–480). Heidelberg: Springer-Verlag.

Fischer, G. (1995b). *Mastering high-functionality computer systems by supporting learning on demand* (Project report, National Science Foundation). Available from http://www.cs.colorado.edu/homes/hcc/public html/

Forman, E. A., & Cazden, B. C. (1985). Exploring Vygotskian perspectives in education: The cognitive value of peer interaction. In J. V. Wertsch (Ed.), *Culture, communication and cognition: Vygotskian perspectives*. Cambridge: Cambridge University Press.

Foster, C. (1995). PDA's and the library without a roof. *Journal of Computing in Higher Education, 7*(1), 85–93.

Gay, G. (1995). Issues in accessing and constructing multimedia documents. In E. Barrett & M. Redmon (Eds.), *Contextual media: Multimedia and interpretation*. Cambridge, MA: MIT Press.

Gay, G., & Lentini, M. (1995). Use of communication resources in a networked collaborative design environment. *Journal of Computer-Mediated Communication, 1*(1) [HTML document]. Available from http://cwis.usc.edu/dept/annenberg/vol1/issue1/contents.html

Gay, G., Mazur, J., & Lentini, M. (1994). The use of hypermedia to enhance design. *Computer Graphics, 28*(1), 34–37.

Gay, G., & Mazur, J. (1993). The utility of computer tracking tools for user-centered design. *Educational Technology, 34*(3), 45–59.

Goodyear, P. (1995). Situated action and distributed knowledge: A JITOL perspective on EPSS. *Innovations in Education and Training International, 32*(1), 45–55.

Grace-Martin, M., & Gay, G. (in press). Web browsing, mobile computing and academic performance. *Special issue on curriculum, instruction, learning and the internet*. IEEE and International Forum of Educational Technology & Society.

Holland, D. C., & Valsiner, J. (1988). Cognition, symbols, and Vygotsky's developmental psychology. *Ethos, 16*(3), 247–272.

Kaptelinin, V. (1996). Activity theory: Implications for human–computer interaction. In B. Nardi (Ed.) *Context and consciousness: Activity theory and human computer interaction* (pp. 103–116). Cambridge, MA and London: MIT Press.

Kaptelinin, V. & Cole, M. (1997). Individual and collective activities in educational computer game playing. In *Proceedings of the international CSCL'97 conference on computer support for collaborative learning*. Hillsdale, NJ: Earlbaum. Online at lchc.ucsd.edu/people/mcole/activities.html

Kleinrock, L. (1997). *Nomadicity: Anytime, anywhere in a disconnected world* [HTML document]. Available from http://www.tticom.com. Los Angeles, CA: Technology Transfer Institute.

Kribs, D., & Mark, L. (1995). The impacts of interactive electronic technical manuals: Issues, lessons learned, and trends in training and education. *Journal of Instruction Delivery Systems, 9*(4), 17–23.

Kuutti, K. (1996). Activity theory as a potential framework for human–computer interaction research. In B. Nardi (Ed.), *Context and consciousness: Activity theory and human computer interaction* (pp. 17–44). Cambridge, MA and London: MIT Press.

Lave, J. (1988). *Cognition in practice: Mind, mathematics, and culture in everyday life.* Cambridge: Cambridge University Press.

Lave, J., & Wenger, E. (1991). *Situated learning: Legitimate peripheral participation.* Cambridge: Cambridge University Press.

Mead, J., & Gay, G. (1995). Concept mapping: An innovative approach to digital library design and evaluation. In *Proceedings of the 37th Allerton, Institute,* University of Illinois at Urbana-Champaign [HTML document]. Available from http://edfu.lis.uiuc.edu/allerton/95/index.html

Nardi, B. (1996). Studying context: A comparison of activity theory, situated action models, and distributed cognition. In B. Nardi (Ed.), *Context and consciousness: Activity theory and human computer interaction* (pp. 69–102). Cambridge, MA and London: MIT Press.

Newman, D., Griffin, P., & Cole, M. (1989). *The construction zone: Working for cognitive change in school.* Cambridge, England: Cambridge University Press.

Petraglia, J. (1998). *Reality by design: The rhetoric and technology of authenticity in education.* Mahwah, NJ: Lawrence Erlbaum.

Resnick, L. (1987). Learning in school and out. *Educational Researcher, 16*(9), 13–20.

Rogoff, B., & Lave, J. (Eds.). (1984). *Everyday cognition: Its development in social context.* Cambridge, MA: Harvard University Press.

Rorty, R. (1979). *Philosophy and the mirror of nature.* Princeton: Princeton University Press.

Schnase, J., Cunnius, E., & Dowton, S. (1995). The StudySpace Project: Collaborative hypermedia in nomadic computing environments. *Communications of the ACM. 38*(August), 72–83.

Schorr, A. (1995). The quick response center: An interactive business learning environment. *Interpersonal Computing and Technology, 3*(4), 57–65.

Soloway, E., Sherwood, R., Hasselbring, T., Kinzer, C., & Williams, S. (1996). Technological support for teachers transitioning to project-based science practices. In T. Koschmann (Ed.), *CSCL: Theory and practice of an emerging paradigm* (pp. 269–307). New York: Lawrence Erlbaum Associates.

Spiro, R. J., Poulson, R. L., Feltovich, P. J., & Anderson, D. K. (1988). Cognitive flexibility theory: Advanced knowledge acquisition in ill-structured domains. In *Proceedings of the Tenth Annual Conference of the Cognitive Science Society* (pp. 375–383). Hillsdale, NJ: Lawrence Erlbaum.

Suchman, L. A. (1987). *Plans and situated actions: The problem of human-machine communication.* New York: Cambridge University Press.

Tinker, R., & Brodersen, B. (1998). *Learning with ubiquitous, low-cost computing* [HTML document]. Available from http://cilt.org/themeteam/ubiq.htm

Vygotsky, L. (1962). *Thought and language.* Cambridge, MA: MIT Press.

Weiser, M. (1991). The computer for the 21st century. *Scientific American, 265*(3), 66–75.

Wertsch, J. V. (Ed.). (1985). *Culture, communication and cognition: Vygotskian perspectives.* New York: Cambridge University Press.

Wertsch, J. (1998). *Mind as Action.* New York and Oxford: Oxford University Press.

ACTIVITY THEORY AND DESIGN

Bonnie A. Nardi

Agilent Technologies

Since the publication of *Context and Consciousness: Perspectives on Activity Theory and Human–Computer Interaction* (Nardi, 1996a) in 1996, people have often asked me, as the editor of the volume, what impact Activity Theory is having on the world of technology design. Gay, Rieger, and Bennington's paper is a happy answer to this question. Their fruitful use of Activity Theory to study mobile computing devices shows the specific ways Activity Theory can inform design. Following an Activity Theory approach, the authors opt for "sustained, longitudinal research on the introduction of computer technology." They pay careful attention to the sociohistorical context of technology use and the mediation of human activity by cultural artifacts. Taking a cue from the emphasis on human development in Activity Theory, the authors ask, "What features and capabilities should the mobile computing systems provide for different teaching and learning activities?" The authors assess users' motivations and understand that there will be a diversity of motives, not a one-size-fits-all world.

Going about technology design from this set of perspectives is far from standard in human–computer interaction research. Often design proceeds from a gadget-centric viewpoint divorced from a context of use. While this approach has yielded much new technology, often it is technology that fails to meet human needs. Such an approach rarely considers how technology aids learning, or how the technology itself can grow and develop as users learn with it and from it.

Although most design is engineering-driven (with some input from survey-based market research), there are continuing efforts within the human–computer interaction community to apply sound theory to design. In moving beyond a cognitive science focus, Activity Theory and the distributed cognition paradigm have been called into service to inform human–computer interaction design. Distributed cognition shares much with Activity Theory in considering a system of people and technology as they operate together. Distributed cognition differs from Activity Theory in seeing people and technologies as symmetrical nodes in a system (Hutchins, 1995). So a distributed cognition analysis considers how information propagates across people and technologies regardless of whether the information is received and used by a human or a machine. Distributed cognition has as its goal a theory that does not have to change when it "crosses the skin" (Hutchins, 1995). By contrast, the principle of the asymmetry of people and things is central to Activity Theory (Kaptelinin, 1996). Technology is said to *mediate human activity*, rather than humans and machines being ontologically equivalent (Nardi, 1996b).

The principle of asymmetry has far-reaching implications for design. Only people develop and have motivations they seek to satisfy through work as they transform objects. Only people have conflicts because of opposing motives. In a system where people and technology are the same there will be little attention to human development, motivation, and conflict. It seems to me that Gay, Rieger, and Bennington have gotten the most leverage from Activity Theory in precisely those areas where Activity Theory differs from the distributed cognition approach. They have put to good use Activity Theory's emphasis on human development, human motivations, and the diversity that varying human motivations bring to the use of technology. The authors speak of "the diverse objectives that motivate users' interest in and use of mobile computing applications" (see Nardi & O'Day, 1999, for more on diversity). They have designed with this diversity of objectives in mind.

Another strength of Gay, Rieger, and Bennington's work is their careful evaluation. At the professional conferences I attend, such as the CHI conference (Computer–Human Interaction, the major HCI conference, sponsored by the 80,000 member Association for Computing Machinery), the papers typically offer rosy reports of end-user response to the prototype systems described. But we know that with sustained use in everyday settings there are going to be varying reactions to technologies and that users will discover many shortcoming and limitations. A commitment to sustained research encourages us to come to grips with the limits of our designs. So, in Gay, Rieger, and Bennington's research, the greenhouse staff liked the automation of routine tasks offered by the Ladybug technology, but visitors to the garden voiced some negative opinions. The technology did not meet their needs in terms of "objectives motivating their involvement with the garden." Here Activity Theory set the course in three ways for it enables us: (1) to look at the reactions of a *variety of users* in actual use within the context of the activity system as a whole with its diverse participants, (2) to consider the varying *motivations* of different users, and (3) to observe technology use *over time*.

DIGGING A LITTLE DEEPER

I would have liked for the authors to dig deeper as they considered the Activity Theory notion of the transformation of culture and practice through the introduction of new technology. In particular, it would have been useful for the authors to adopt a more questioning attitude to the notion of ubiquitous computing. A closer examination of what study participants told them could have encouraged the authors to more critically examine ubiquitous computing, an assumption of the research. Study participants said things such as "[The technology] could spoil the joys of wandering in a garden" and "[The computing technology] helped but the paper sheet we received was just as good." Another study participant noted that "[The technology] made it easy not to think for yourself; just press the buttons." Another observed, "... if anything, more hands-on [work] such as writing and ... counting would be conducive to learning." "My writing on paper won't disappear," declared one study participant.

Again, I applaud the authors for taking these statements seriously and reporting them in their work. But I would urge more analysis of what these statements mean. To me they suggest a movement away from the idea of ubiquitous computing, These statements make clear that some people do not want computers between them and the rest of the world in all settings, nor do they want to yield the work of the hands to invisible computers. Applying an anthropological sensibility to Activity Theory research is generally a good idea, in my opinion, and could have been utilized here to orient more fully to the meanings of study participants' statements. Anthropology insists that we look not just for behavioral patterns or quantitative analysis of survey data but that we try to understand meaning in human life. This is of course consistent with Vygotsky's "cultural-historical" approach, but with the methodological rigor that anthropology has developed in studying meaning.

Gay, Rieger, and Bennington's paper provides inspiration for those interested in using theory to inform design. Its appreciation of the diversity of users' needs, honest reporting of negative user feedback, and commitment to evolving technology in concert with users' experiences over time exemplify the frutiful use of theory in design.

REFERENCES

Hutchins, Edwin (1995). *Cognition in the wild*. Cambridge, MA: MIT Press.

Kaptelinin,V. (1996). Computer-mediated activity: Functional organs in social and developmental contexts. In B. Nardi (Ed.), *Context and consciousness: Activity theory and human–computer interaction*. Cambridge, MA: MIT Press.

Nardi, B. (Ed.). (1996a). *Context and consciousness: Activity theory and human–computer interaction*. Cambridge, MA: MIT Press.

Nardi, B. (1996b). Concepts of cognition and consciousness: Four voices. Invited paper, *Australian Journal of Information Systems, 4*(1), 64–79. Reprinted in *ACM Journal of Computer Documentation*, February, 1998.

Nardi, B., & O'Day, V. (1999). *Information ecologies: Using technology with heart*. Cambridge, MA: MIT Press.

HUMAN–FIELD INTERACTION AS MEDIATED BY MOBILE COMPUTERS

Sasha A. Barab

Indiana University at Bloomington

In this chapter, Gay, Rieger, and Bennington are concerned with developing an account of the role mobile computers will have in transforming the *activities* of learning and conducting research in the field. It is their perspective, "that students will flourish in situations that provide an opportunity to test skills and theories in the 'just-in-time' and 'nomadic' field context, an opportunity enabled by mobile computing." In addressing these potential transformations they suggest Activity Theory as providing a useful theoretical and methodological framework from which to begin the systematic examination of the potential of mobile computers. In this commentary, I will highlight and expand upon three potential transformations derived from the theoretical base of Activity Theory and the research discussed in this chapter: (1) a shift from a focus on human–computer interaction to a focus on computer-mediated activity or, said another way, to human–field interaction as mediated by technology; (2) a shift in the goal of instruction, from moving the field into the classroom to moving the classroom into the field; and (3) a shift from an emphasis on teacher as "expert" to the mediating role of "learning facilitator."

In adopting the theoretical and methodological lens that Activity Theory (AT) offers, the authors are adhering to a particular theoretical perspective with respect to human–computer interaction or, from an Activity Theory perspective, subject–object as mediated by computer interaction (Leont'ev, 1974, 1989; Nardi, 1996). Thus, from an AT perspective, the "minimal meaningful context" for understanding human activity moves beyond the human mind or even the human–computer interaction and must include the human actor (subject), the object (tangible or intangible) that is acted upon (transformed), and the dynamic constraints (tools, rules, divisions of labor, community) that mediate these relations (see Barab, Barnett, Yamagata-Lynch, Squire, & Keating, in press; Engeström, 1987, 1988). There are many different transformations that a subject can have on an object, and in addition to the constraints listed above, the subject's goals and intentions can provide boundary conditions, constraining which particular affordances (opportunities for action) of the object the activity will transform (Young & Barab, 1999).

With respect to technology (i.e., mobile computers), AT is concerned with how tools mediate the relationship between subject and object, both enabling and limiting that relationship. Therefore, it is not simply the human–computer (subject–tool) interaction (HCI) that is fundamental to understand but the more complete subject–object interactions as mediated by the computer that become crucial. This perspective expands the unit of analysis from the mind of the individual (as in traditional cognitive research) or from the human–computer interaction (as in traditional HCI research; Carroll, 1987, 1991) to the entire activity system (context). For AT, the context is not simply a container nor a situationally created experiential space; it refers to an entire activity system, integrating the subject, the object, the tools (and even communities) into a unified whole (Engeström, 1988).

The central learning and research issue related to mobile computers, from an AT perspective, is how these tools constrain subject–object relations and allow for novel transformations and outcomes. The central question then becomes, "how information technology may enable an activity to have an object that would otherwise have been impossible to grasp" (Kuutti, 1996, p. 35). In conceiving the transformative potential of mobile computers, the authors initially find it useful to think of this potential along a "mobility hierarchy ... [which] provides a useful heuristic device for identifying possible objectives of computer-mediated activities." The simplest applications allow for increased productivity and involve individual work, while the more complex activities involve communication and knowledge construction and involve collaborative work.

As an ecological psychologist by training and a commune child of the 1960s by birth, I was initially resistant to the notion of the computer infiltrating and possibly distancing the learner from direct experience in the field. Throughout much of one's life, and especially in schools, individuals spend inordinate amounts of time experiencing preprocessed information (Reed, 1996a). Although there is nothing inherently wrong with processed information, there is something wrong with a culture that invests so much in second-hand information, "yet does little or nothing to help us *explore the world for ourselves*" (Reed, 1996b, p. 3). Gay et al. wrote, "While learning from the field cannot be adequately replicated using multimedia technologies, and it is questionable that such replication is even desirable, the computer's strength at information organization and retrieval can support learning and research in the field." By this we might conclude that the authors were not "technopolists," to borrow Postman's (1992) loaded term; instead they offer a balanced, even tentative, vision of the role of technology in field studies.

Rather than subverting "direct experience" and communion with the field, mobile computers have the potential to move the learning experience from the artificial confines of the classroom and out to more naturalistic field settings. This is in sharp contrast with traditional schooling practices in which what is being taught is abstracted from its naturalistic (ecological) space where it has real function with the world and, instead, is told to learners in a classroom context, "where school-assigned meanings become the goal— complex problems are solved to get a good grade, completed for the purpose of satisfying a teacher or parent, not for the functional purposes for which these practices initially emerged as important" (Barab et al., 1999, p. 382). All too often, schools set up a content-culture incongruity in which learners are expected to learn content implicitly framed in the culture of schools but whose use and value is explicitly attributed to those and cultures outside of schools (Barab & Landa, 1997). The data reported in this chapter suggest that mobile computers have the potential to support a shift in the opposite direction, suggesting that technology can "provide the ability to move away from the desktop."

Using mobile technologies, students are able to become knowledgeably skillful with respect to various content *in situ*, and learning is driven by their current (not pedagogical) needs. For example, students participating in the *Soil Texture by Feel* project begin the learning process by "digging in the dirt," and then receiving contextual support using the a branching software to identify soils. At these "teachable" moments, the technology is responsive to individual needs, providing students with "just-in-time" information that supports their scientific inquiry as well as extended collaboration and networking with peers. This potential of technology to provide contextualized information as needed by the learner, also, potentially, reconfigures the role of teacher.

Some educational theorists (Barab & Duffy, 2000; Duffy & Jonassen, 1992) are now advocating a view of the teacher as a mediating element between subject and object, in much the same way that certain HCI researchers (Kuutti, 1996; Kaptelinin, 1996; Nardi, 1996), influenced by AT, conceptualize the computer as a mediating device. This is consistent with an ecological perspective in which it is suggested that instruction implies mediating key elements of the larger context so as to facilitate the merging of learner and environment into a single system (Barab et al., 1999). The role of the learning facilitator is no longer to play "teacher expert" or "didactic caretaker" of information. Rather, it is his or her responsibility to establish and support an environment that affords goals from which the individual develops intentions whose realization requires the appropriation of specific practices that bring about functional object transformations.

> The facilitator must enter, support, and become part of the learner's and the community's ecosystem, where he has the responsibility to provide constraints (scaffolding) as initial conditions that work to promote naturally emerging dynamics. However, over time, as the learner becomes "coupled" with an intention and resonates with the boundary conditions, it is the responsibility of the facilitator to gracefully remove himself from the interaction, allowing the learner to establish direct effectivity/affordance relations with the community. (Barab et al., 1999, p. 354)

In closing, Gay et al. suggested that mobile computers in field settings have the potential to transform thinking, learning, teaching, student–student relationships, the teacher–student relationship, and relationships among subjects and objects more generally. In this commentary, I have used principles central to Activity Theory and ecological psychology to highlight three potential transformations as they relate to the impact of mobile computers in mediating subject–object relations. Future research must explore how technology can support (and not limit) collaborative opportunities for learning in naturalistic field settings. It is essential that educators and designers continue to explore means of engaging students in direct experience with the natural world, and not simply with abstracted content introduced in classrooms. This will involve researching issues of trust, authenticity, goals and intentions, community, and what types of scaffolding the computer can have in mediating relations between subject and object. A grounded understanding of these issues will allow us to actualize the potential of mobile computing applications to challenge traditional distinctions between "the field" and "the classroom," extending learning and teaching possibilities.

REFERENCES

Barab, S. A., & Landa, A. (1997). Designing effective interdisciplinary anchors. *Educational Leadership, 54*, 52–55.

Barab, S. A. (1999). Ecologizing instruction through integrated Units. *Middle School Journal, 30*, 21–28.

Barab, S., Barnett, M., Yamagata-Lynch, L., Squire, K., & Keating, T. (in press). Using activity theory to understand the contradictions characterizing a technology-rich introductory astronomy course. To appear in *Mind, Culture, and Activity*.

Barab, S. A., Cherkes-Julkowski, M., Swenson, R., Garrett. S., Shaw, R. E., & Young, M. (1999). Principles of self-organization: Ecologizing the learner-facilitator system. *The Journal of The Learning Sciences, 8*(3&4), 349–390.

Barab, S. A., & Duffy, T. (2000). From practice fields to communities of practice. In D. Jonassen, & S. M. Land. (Eds.). *Theoretical Foundations of Learning Environments* (pp. 25–56). Mahwah, NJ: Lawrence Erlbaum Associates.

Carroll, J. M. (1987). *Interfacing thought: Cognitive aspects of human–computer interaction.* Cambridge, MA: MIT Press.

Carroll, J. M. (1991). *Designing interaction: Psychology at the human–computer interface.* Cambridge, MA: Cambridge University Press.

Duffy, T. M. , & Jonassen, D. H. (Eds.). (1992). *Constructivism and the technology of instruction.* Hillsdale, NJ: Lawrence Erlbaum.

Engeström, Y. (1987). *Learning by expanding.* Helsinki: Orienta-konsultit.

Engeström, Y. (1988). Developmental studies of work as a testbench of activity theory: The case of primary care medical practice. In S. Chaiklin & J. Lave (Eds.), *Understanding practice: Perspectives on activity and context* (pp. 64–103). Cambridge, MA: Cambridge University Press.

Kaptelinin, V. (1996). Activity theory: Implications for human–computer interaction. In B. Nardi (Ed.), *Context and consciousness: Activity theory and human–computer interaction.* Cambridge, MA: The MIT Press.

Kuutti, K. (1996). Activity Theory as a potential framework for human–computer interaction research. In B. Nardi (Ed.), *Context and consciousness: Activity theory and human–computer interaction.* Cambridge, MA: The MIT Press.

Leont'ev, A. (1974). The problem of activity in psychology. *Soviet Psychology, 13*(2), 4–33.

Leont'ev, A. (1981). *Problems of the development of mind.* Moscow: Progress.

Leont'ev, A. (1989). The problem of activity in the history of Soviet psychology. *Soviet Psychology, 27*(1), 22–39.

Nardi, B. (Ed.). (1996). *Context and consciousness: Activity theory and human–computer interaction.* Cambridge, MA: The MIT Press.

Postman, N. (1992). *Technopoly: The surrender of culture to technology.* New York: Alfred A. Knopf.

Reed, R. S. (1996a). *Encountering the world: Toward an ecological psychology.* New York: Oxford University Press.

Reed, R. S. (1996b). *The necessity of experience.* New Haven, CT: Yale University Press.

Young, M. F., & Barab, S. (1999). Perception of the raison d'etre in anchored instruction: An ecological psychology perspective. *Journal of Educational Computing Research, 20*(2), 113–135.

DIGGING DEEPER INTO MOBILE COMPUTING: UNCOVERING THE COMPLEXITIES OF ACTIVITY THEORY

Tammy Bennington
Geraldine Gay
Robert Rieger
Cornell University

We have been encouraged by Nardi's and Barab's appreciative comments regarding our research on mobile computing. As Nardi notes, we initiated this research with a prejudicial desire to improve field-located learning experiences through the introduction of the hand-held devices, a predisposition that clearly influenced the direction of the project. We are grateful that Barab considers us non-"technophilists," but we tend toward that end of the technological continuum and need occasional reminders of our technophilic proclivities.

After reflecting on our initial foray into mobility, and prodded by Nardi's recommendation that we "dig deeper," we have assumed a more "questioning attitude" and are currently continuing to explore mobile computing from a perspective that integrates a central concern with meaning as well as phenomenological experience into our Activity Theory framework. Since we presented this paper, Cornell's Human–Computer Interaction Group (formerly the Interactive Media Group) has initiated a more comprehensive project involving the introduction of wireless mobile computers into two undergraduate courses, one in computer science and one in communication. As we explore how mobility transforms learning, teaching, communication, and collaboration in these two contexts, we are closely attending to the diversity of ways the participants construe both the activities in which they are involved and the tools that are mediating those activities.

We are readdressing the issues raised in our hand-held research that, as Barab points out, are implicative for instructional settings and practices, that is, (1) how mobile computing can facilitate the deconstruction of boundaries among classroom, field, library and noneducational sites and (2) how access to information from the field in a just-in-time fashion potentially transforms the teacher–student relationship into one of collaborative negotiation, facilitation, and knowledge creation. Understanding both issues has informed our attempts to foster experiential learning and communities of practice.

We continue to find Activity Theory—particularly the notions of activity, mediation, contextual learning, and goal orientation—a generative framework for such research. However, the conceptual and methodological challenges posed by our research has made us aware of the need to further explore and develop, both theoretically and in the context of mobile computing, each of these notions.

Activity: In our work with the hand-held and laptop computers, we realize that several coconstitutive activities are integrated to form any particular "learning activity," for example, communication, collaboration, facilitation, information seeking, to name only the most obvious. Within a classroom in which students are working on laptop-mediated collaborative projects or within a field situation in which they are accessing information through hand-helds, these various activities imperceptibly merge into and facilitate one another. Yet each entails different actions and operations, different computer applications, different conceptual and representational tools, and sometimes different forms of communication and group dynamics. We have been challenged in constructing a model that can accommodate such complexity and integration. However, we find Engeström and Miettinen's (1999, pp. 9–10) notion of an "activity system," similar to Barab's ecological notion of system above, useful in our attempts to conceive of and model the "systemic structure of activity" (Engeström, 1999, p. 24).

Mediation: We have also been intrigued by the implications of Barab's metaphorical characterization of the teacher as "mediating element" and his reference to an ecological notion of mediation as entailing or facilitating the merging of elements into a system. These metaphors are provocative and point toward likely synergy between ecological theory and Activity Theory. However, we do maintain a strict theoretical and moral distinction between human and nonhuman "elements" in any conceptualization of such systems—the asymmetrical relation to which Nardi refers. But we believe, like Engeström (1999), that the concept of mediation in Activity Theory is undertheorized. It tends to be used (and we have used it) to gloss over complexity and diversity of phenomena. It subsumes diverse and interactive relationships such as enabling, synthesizing, transforming, orienting, and facilitating. We need to tease out in detail the textured relationships among artifacts and other elements of the activity system and develop more nuanced understandings of "mediation" that can encompass the contextual functioning of artifactual and human mediators.

Contextual Learning: Reflecting further on our research results, we also perceive the significance of attending more carefully to the social contexts of situated learning activities. Not only are the relationship between teacher and student, and the transformed role of teacher as facilitator, of interest but so are the relationships among all participants as a community of practice. Group dynamics and communicative practices create different individual and group learning experiences as well as different emotional experiences and senses of community, all of which in turn mediate the learning activity. In our current work with laptop computers, we are observing very different learning contexts mediated by different pedagogical styles, disciplinary cultures, group dynamics, and degrees of cooperation and trust among participants. Again, to adequately understand and represent the complexity of learning activities we are turning to a systemic model that can accommodate greater complexity within each element of the Activity Theory model.

Goal Orientation and Motivation: The objectives, needs, and desires that motivate an activity significantly shape the tool-using experience. As was clear in some of the comments from users of the Pathfinder tool, the technology sometimes interfered with the desired and expected direct engagement with the gardens; however, other users who explicitly wished a more formal learning-oriented experience, perceived the tool as enhancing their experience. These examples indicate the significance of subject's objectives, motivations, desires, and expectations in constituting an activity and its meanings. They further draw our attention to the relevance of phenomenological descriptions and explications of subjects' embodied engagement in activities and with artifacts, for example, "digging in the dirt" or toting around a laptop computer on one's shoulder. Because a focus of our research has been mobility, entailing a concern with subjects' embodied engagement with time and space and how it is transformed by mobile computing, we are keenly aware of the significance of incorporating the embodied, sensory, and aesthetic experiences of artifact use into the understanding of activity.

Reflecting on and learning from our research and from the constructive feedback we have received from Nardi, Barab, and other colleagues has deepened our interest in and commitment to "activity" as both theoretical framework and unit of analysis. We offer the preceding observations out of a wish to carry forward the current conversation regarding the potential of Activity Theory to enhance our understanding of computer-mediated activities. Participation in the conversation has generated for us numerous rich opportunities for applying the theory, and now we are endeavoring to flesh out undertheorized elements. We are confident that the exploration of ubiquitous and mobile computing will contribute to that process.

REFERENCES

Engeström, Y. (1999). Activity Theory and individual and social transformation. In Y. Engeström, R. Miettinen, & R. Punamaki (Eds.), *Perspectives on activity theory*. Cambridge: Cambridge University Press.

Engeström, Y., & Miettinene, R. (1999). Introduction. In Y. Engeström, R. Miettinen, & R. Punamaki (Eds.), *Perspectives on activity theory*. Cambridge: Cambridge University Press.

Author Index

SUBJECT INDEX

A

Accomodation, learner, 192
Activity system, 299
Activity Theory, 189, 192
  and CSILE program. *See* CSILE program
  and Distributed Cognition, 530
  and division of labor, 230
  and Fifth Dimension Project, 327
  and knowledge building, 65–68
  and mobile computing, 513, 525, 540
  and use of artifacts, 284
  applied to collective activities, 299
  components of, 59–62, 509
  computers in. *See* Computer-mediated
    activity
  conflicting perspectives of learners in, 300
  consciousness in, 509
  constructive program for, 322
  cultural artifacts in. *See* Cultural artifacts
  explanatory potential of, 509
  frame of analysis in, 352, 508, 533–534
  in CSCL research, 352
  in human-computer interaction, 352, 508–9
  intentionality in, 509
  Leont'ev's contributions to, 509
  levels of interaction in, 298–299, 313

  mediation of artifacts in, 530, 534, 535,
    540–541
  motivation in, 531, 541
  principles of asymmetry in, 530, 540
  social-historical aspects of, 509
  study of meaning in, 531
  subject-object interaction in, 534
  the role of contradiction in, 300f, 303,
    509
  theory of mind in, 299
  transformation of culture in, 531
  Vygotsky's influence on, 509
Actor-Network theory, 229
After school clubs, 192, 193–195
Agora, 446
AlgoArena, 191
  as polysemous tool, 336
  changes in classroom brought about by,
    336
  class activities in, 278
  design principles of, 325–326
  divergent perspectives in, 283
  identity formation in, 275, 278–279,
    284–295, 316, 327, 333
  joint activity in, 282–283
  learning programming in, 276–277
  programming competence in, 284